Alsace Lorraine Champagne

F. Jalain/EXPLORER

... A quiet, quaint and ancient town
Among the green Alsatian hills,
A place of valleys, streams and mills,
Where Barbarossa's castle, brown
With rust of centuries still looks down
On the broad, drowsy land below ...

Henry Wadsworth Longfellow

R. Mattes

The northeastern corner of France is at once the intimate cradle of French culture and the public stage of European development. Figures of legend such as Clovis, the first Christian king, Joan of Arc, defender of the crown, or statesman Charles de Gaulle; literary lions including fabulist Jean de La Fontaine and poet Paul Verlaine, are integral to the Gallic national identity. Gothic architecture, which represents a defining moment in French art, reached its apogee in cathedrals at Reims and Strasbourg. From the medieval trade fairs of Champagne, through the strife of terrible wars and finally the establishment of the European parliament, the region has long been a continental focal point, whether in conflict or in peace. The influence extends well beyond the open plain of Champagne and the blue line of the Vosges: it was in Strasbourg that Gutenberg first developed his concept for a printing press, which would revolutionise communication; about 50 years later, geographers in St-Dié baptised the distant continent of "America". Travellers today are seduced by the wonderful mountain landscapes and glacier lakes, popular with ramblers and cross-country skiers; half-timbered villages set amid thick forests or lush vineyards. Traditional Christmas markets and St-Nicholas festivities brighten the year-end holiday season with fragrant baked goods, toys and games for children. The charms of fine cuisine, based on fresh local products, seasonal fish and game, and venerable recipes appeal to both refined palates and hearty appetites. Sauerkraut, Quiche Lorraine, savoury cured ham, wild boar from the Ardennes Forest, Munster cheese with a dash of cumin... their enjoyment is enhanced by peerless Alsatian wines. And when it's time for gingerbread cakes, sugar tarts, or ice cream made from the delectable golden plum mirabelle, pop the cork on the world's favourite sparkling nectar: Champagne tastes better than ever here in the land that gave it birth!

2

Contents

Key ——————————————— 4

Using this guide ——————————— 5

Map of principal sights ——————— 6

Map of touring programmes ————— 10

Map of places to stay ——————— 11

Introduction ——————————— 17

Landscapes ——————————— 18

Economy ———————————— 25

Historical table and notes ————— 27

Architecture and art ——————— 35

Traditions and folklore —————— 53

Language and Literature ————— 56

Regional cuisine ———————— 59

Wine and Champagne —————— 61

Sights ————————————— 64

Practical information —————— 346

Planning your trip ——————— 348

Getting there ————————— 351

Motoring in France ——————— 352

General information —————— 353

Accommodation ———————— 355

Regional specialities and wines ——— 358

Shopping ——————————— 361

Active tours —————————— 362

Sports and recreation —————— 366

Spas and hydrotherapy ————— 367

Discovering the region —————— 370

Calendar of events ——————— 375

Admission times and charges ——— 379

Useful French words and phrases —— 379

Index ———————————— 380

Key

	Sight	Seaside Resort	Winter Sports Resort	Spa
Worth a journey	★★★	≅≅≅	✳✳✳	⚜⚜⚜
Worth a detour	★★	≅≅	✳✳	⚜⚜
Interesting	★	≅	✳	⚜

Tourism

⊘	Admission Times and Charges listed at the end of the guide	►►	Visit if time permits
◉⇒	Sightseeing route with departure point indicated	AZ **B**	Map co-ordinates locating sights
⛪ ⛪	Ecclesiastical building	🛈	Tourist information
✡ ☪	Synagogue – Mosque	⚰ ⁙	Historic house, castle – Ruins
▣	Building (with main entrance)	∪ ☼	Dam – Factory or power station
■	Statue, small building	☆ ⋒	Fort – Cave
†	Wayside cross	⚲	Prehistoric site
◎	Fountain	▼ Ѱ	Viewing table – View
•—•—■•	Fortified walls – Tower – Gate	▲	Miscellaneous sight

Recreation

🏇	Racecourse	🏃	Waymarked footpath
⛸	Skating rink	◆	Outdoor leisure park/centre
≋ ▨	Outdoor, indoor swimming pool	🎢	Theme/Amusement park
⛵	Marina, moorings	🐂	Wildlife/Safari park, zoo
⌂	Mountain refuge hut	⊛	Gardens, park, arboretum
▫▪▫▪▫	Overhead cable-car	◉	Aviary, bird sanctuary
🚂	Tourist or steam railway		

Additional symbols

══ ══	Motorway (unclassified)	✉ ◉	Post office – Telephone centre
❶ ➊	Junction: complete, limited	▱	Covered market
⊏⊐ ▬	Pedestrian street	⁙✕⁙	Barracks
⌶═══⌶	Unsuitable for traffic, street subject to restrictions	△	Swing bridge
⊞⊞⊞ ----	Steps – Footpath	∪ ✗	Quarry – Mine
🚃 🚐	Railway – Coach station	**B** **F**	Ferry (river and lake crossings)
▫++++▫	Funicular – Rack-railway	⛴	Ferry services: Passengers and cars
•—• ◉	Tram – Metro, Underground	⛴	Foot passengers only
Bert (R.)...	Main shopping street	③	Access route number common to MICHELIN maps and town plans

Abbreviations and special symbols

A	Agricultural office (Chambre d'agriculture)	**P**	Local authority offices (Préfecture, sous-préfecture)
C	Chamber of commerce (Chambre de commerce)	**POL.**	Police station (Police)
H	Town hall (Hôtel de ville)	🛡	Police station (Gendarmerie)
J	Law courts (Palais de justice)	**T**	Theatre (Théâtre)
M	Museum (Musée)	**U**	University (Université)
		❸	Hotel

Using this guide

Your Michelin green guide is full of information of different kinds:

● **Thematic maps**: the main Sights, Touring programmes (must-sees for those on a tight schedule), Places to stay (choosing your day's destination point with regard to availability of hotels and the surroundings). The map on the bottom of this page shows which Michelin maps cover the area of this guide.

● **Introduction**: learn more about the region before you go, or as you tour; read about the landscape, history, customs, cuisine, art and contemporary development.

● **Towns and sights**: presented in alphabetical order for easy reference. Smaller villages are listed as excursions from the bigger places to visit.

Sections on major cities (Colmar, Metz, Mulhouse, Nancy, Reims, Strasbourg, Troyes) include a selection of travelling tips in blue boxes, with suggestions on where to eat or have a drink and how to get the most out of your trip. Consult the **Michelin Red Guide France** for a complete selection of hotels and restaurants throughout the region.

● **Practical information**: useful addresses for planning your trip, looking for lodgings, outdoor activities and more; opening hours and admission charges for monuments, museums and other tourist attractions (as indicated by blue clocks in the text); festival dates; suggestions for thematic tours on scenic railways, through vineyards etc.

● **Index**: list of attractions, famous people and events, and other subjects covered in the guide.

Let us hear from you! We are interested in your reaction to our guide, in any ideas you have to offer or good addresses you would like to share. Send your comments to Michelin Tourism Department, 38 Clarendon Road, Watford, Herts WD1 1SX, England, or www.michelin-travel.com

Bon voyage!

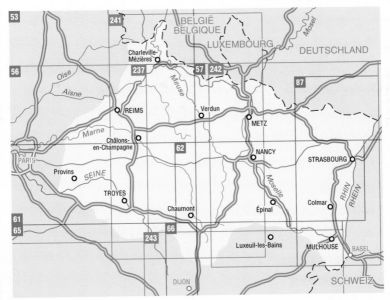

Principal sights

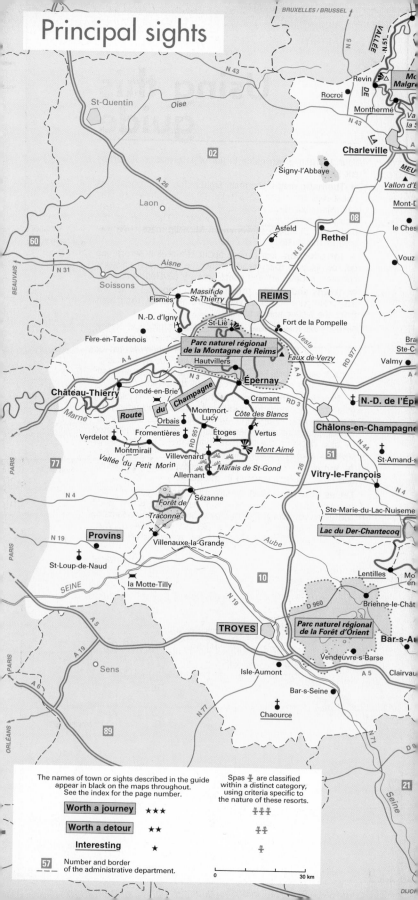

BRUXELLES / BRUSSEL

VALLÉE N. N.51

Mo
Malgr

Revin

Rocroi

Monthermé

MEU

Charleville

Signy-l'Abbaye

Vallon d'E

Mont-D

le Ches

Asfeld

Rethel

Vouz

St-Quentin

Oise

02

Laon

A 26

Soissons

Aisne

60

N 31

BEAUVAIS

N 43

08

N 51

Fismes

Massif de
St-Thierry

REIMS

N.-D. d'Igny

St-Lié

Fort de la Pompelle

Fère-en-Tardenois

**Parc naturel régional
de la Montagne de Reims**

Faux de Verzy

Bra
Ste-C

Valmy

Hautvillers

Épernay

N 3

Château-Thierry

Condé-en-Brie

Cramant

RD 3

N.-D. de l'Ép

Route *du* **Champagne**

Côte des Blancs

Châlons-en-Champagne

Orbais

Montmort-
Lucy

Marne

Verdelot

Fromentières

Étoges

Vertus

RD 951

Montmirail

Villevenard

Mont Aimé

St-Amand-

77

Vallée du Petit Morin

Allemant

Marais de St-Gond

Vitry-le-François

A 26

N 4

PARIS

Sézanne

N 4

Forêt de
Traconne

51

Ste-Marie-du-Lac-Nuiseme

N 19

Provins

Villenauxe-la-Grande

Aube

Lac du Der-Chantecoq

PARIS

St-Loup-de-Naud

10

Lentilles

Mo
en

D 960

Brienne-le-Chât

la Motte-Tilly

SEINE

N 19

A 5

A 19

PARIS

TROYES

*Parc naturel régional
de la Forêt d'Orient*

Bar-s-A

A 6

Sens

Isle-Aumont

Vendeuvre-s-Barse

Clairvau

A 5

89

ORLÉANS

N 77

Bar-s-Seine

Chaource

21

Seine

N 71

D 9

DIJON

The names of town or sights described in the guide
appear in black on the maps throughout.
See the index for the page number.

Worth a journey	★★★
Worth a detour	★★
Interesting	★

Spas ⚕ are classified
within a distinct category,
using criteria specific to
the nature of these resorts.

⚕⚕⚕

⚕⚕

⚕

57 Number and border
of the administrative department.

0   30 km

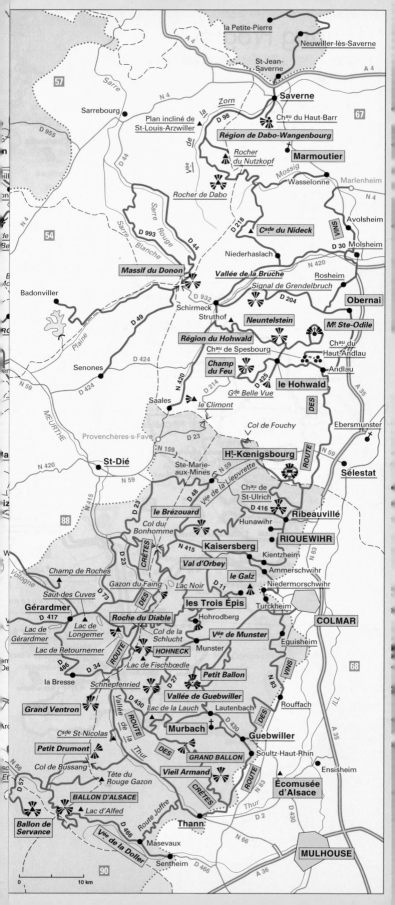

1 St-Thierry-Massif and Brie: 250 km / 155 mi (2 days)

2 Ardennes and Argonne : 450 km / 280 mi (3 days)

3 Champagne: 400 km / 248 mi (5 days including one day to visit Reims)

4 The Othe and Perthois regions: 550 km / 342 mi (6 days including one day to visit Troyes)

5 Northern Lorraine, along the Meuse: 550 km / 342 mi (4 days)

6 Southern Lorraine, Spa towns, Moselle: 450 km / 280 mi (3 days)

7 Northern Vosges: 350 km / 217 mi (2 days)

8 Southern Vosges, Alsace wine route: 700 km / 435 mi (5 days)

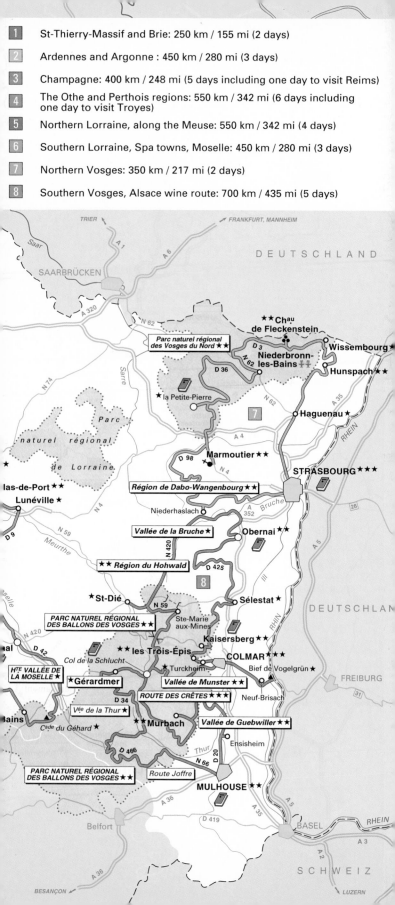

Featured in this guide ...

REGIONAL NATURE PARKS

 1967, the French government created the *Parcs naturels régionaux* in order to
 eserve inhabited rural zones and protect their natural and cultural heritage. A
 arter is drawn up with the local residents to define the park's limits and programme
 activities. The objectives also include economic development, as well as welcoming
 urists interested in learning more about nature and regional traditions. In Alsace,
 rraine and Champagne-Ardenne, travellers can explore five nature parks:

arc naturel régional de Lorraine – Created in 1974, with headquarters at Pont-à-
 ousson. There are several *Maisons du Parc*, which serve as mini-museums: rural
 aditions and crafts in Lucey and Hannonville-sous-les-Côtes; salt marshes and salt
 llection at Marsal; art and history at Vic-sur-Seille. Lake Madine offers a chance to
 ol off and relax. *See page 167.*

arc naturel régional des Vosges du Nord – Inaugurated in 1976, this woodland
 ark is home to 75 000 people. Ancient castles, Maginot Line fortifications and more
 an a dozen museums testify to the historical heritage of the area. Visitors can find
 ut more at the *Maison du Parc* in La Petite Pierre. *See page 333.*

arc naturel régional des Ballons des Vosges – This is one of the largest nature
 arks in France, created in 1989 and encompassing 200 towns and villages. Stop at
 e *Maison du parc* in Munster to find out more about the flora, fauna and traditional
 estyles in the mountains. *See page 72.*

arc naturel régional de la Montagne de Reims – The park, designated in 1976, is
 oaked in vineyards and crowned with wooded groves. The main headquarters is in
 ourcy, and there are other information and nature centres along the way, including
 e Escargot museum at Olizy. *See page 183.*

arc naturel régional de la Forêt d'Orient and Lac du Der-Chantecoq – Travellers
 ho are looking to unwind will have ample opportunity to swim, water-ski, tour on
 ke or horseback or perhaps just sit back and watch the majestic cranes as they rest
 n their way from Scandinavia to Spain and back again on their annual migration ...
 ee pages 115 and 130.*

SOMETHING DIFFERENT

 or travellers who enjoy the out-of-the-ordinary or the out-of-the-way, here are a few
 uggestions for discovering the region.

Hidden valley – The Meuse River starts in Langres and snakes all the way to the
 orth Sea, crossing through Belgium. Neither the river nor the Ardennes Forest pay
 uch heed to national borders, and visitors have every reason to do the same. From
 harleville-Mézières (France) to Namur (Belgium), the landscapes are spectacular and
 e welcome always warm. Cruises on the river leave from Charleville-Mézières,
 Monthermé and Revin. *See page 176.*

Enough wine? Try beer! – Kronenbourg, well-advertised as "the beer from Alsace"
 pens its doors to tourists at breweries in Champigneulles and Strasbourg. In the
 egion, try *bière de mars* ("March" beer) in the spring, *bière de Noël* at Christmas, or
 ière blanche* ("white" beer), made from malted wheat. *See page 372.*

Industrial arts – Mulhouse is reputed for its seven museums which recount the
 xceptional industrial development of this independent-minded town, and demonstrate
 he democratisation of decorative arts: the textile museum, the railway museum, the
 utomobile museum, the wallpaper museum, the printed fabrics museum, the historical
 useum, the museum of electric energy. *See page 198.*

Medieval merriment – The town of Provins is proud of its red roses, 12C ramparts,
 nd spectacular hilltop setting. From June to the end of October, visitors are treated to
 estivities and events inspired by history, including sound and light shows, falconry
 emonstrations, and displays of medieval warfare. *See page 232.*

Timeless tradition – See craftworkers, tour the village in an ox cart, watch a
 istorical play, put the children on a merry-go-round then settle on a shady terrace for
 a country meal in the *Écomusée d'Alsace*, between Mulhouse and Guebwiller. The
 open-air museum is great for a family outing. *See page 119.*

Choosing where to stay

The maps here and on the previous pages show a number of "overnight stops" – good-sized towns which deserve a visit and which offer many opportunities for accommodation. Besides the hotels and camp sites listed in the **Michelin Red Guide France**, these places offer other forms of accommodation (furnished rooms, country cottages, board and lodging); look in the **Practical information** section at the back of this book for the names and numbers of organisations and tourist offices which can provide the details.

Accommodation

The **Michelin Red Guide** of hotels and restaurants and the **Michelin Guide Camping Caravaning France** are annual publications which give a detailed selection of hotels, restaurants and camp sites.

The final listing is based on regular on-the-spot enquiries and visits. Both the hotels and restaurants are classified according to the standard of comfort of their amenities. Establishments which are notable for their setting, decor, quiet and secluded location or especially warm welcome are indicated by special symbols.

The Michelin Red Guide France also gives the addresses and telephone numbers of the local tourist offices.

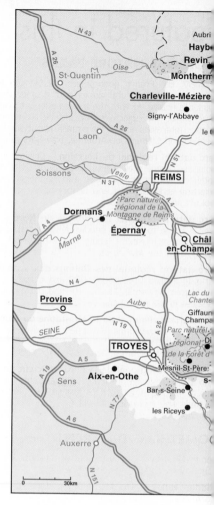

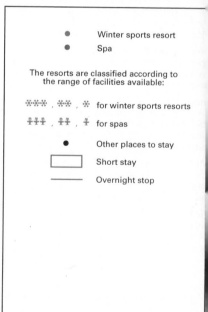

- ● Winter sports resort
- ● Spa

The resorts are classified according to the range of facilities available:

❄❄❄ , ❄❄ , ❄ for winter sports resorts

‡‡‡ , ‡‡ , ‡ for spas

- ● Other places to stay
- ☐ Short stay
- ─ Overnight stop

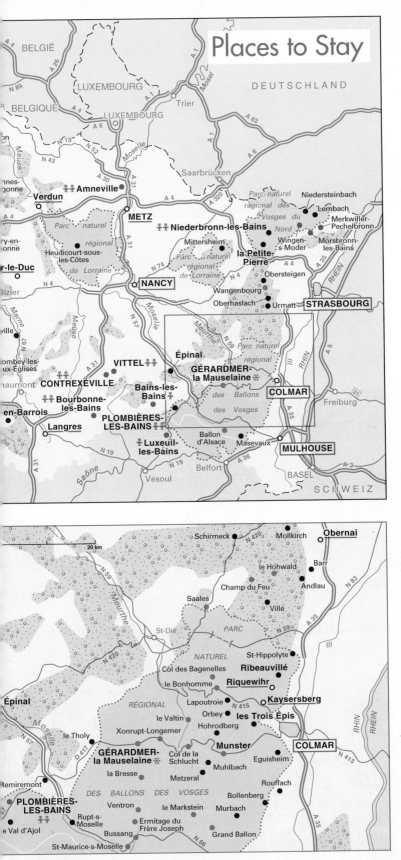

Places to Stay

BELGIË
BELGIQUE
LUXEMBOURG
DEUTSCHLAND
Trier
Saarbrücken

Amneville
Verdun
Parc naturel
METZ
Niederbronn-les-Bains
Mittersheim
régional
Parc naturel régional de Lorraine
la Petite-Pierre
Heudicourt-sous-les-Côtes
de Lorraine
NANCY
Obersteigen
Wangenbourg
Oberhaslach
Urmatt
STRASBOURG

Parc naturel régional des Vosges du Nord
Niedersteinbach
Lembach
Merkwiller-Pechelbronn
Wingen-s-Moder
Mörsbronn-les-Bains
RHEIN

VITTEL
Épinal
GÉRARDMER-la Mauselaine
COLMAR
Freiburg

CONTREXÉVILLE
Bains-les-Bains
Parc naturel régional des Ballons des Vosges
Bourbonne-les-Bains
PLOMBIÈRES-LES-BAINS
Langres
Luxeuil-les-Bains
Ballon d'Alsace
Masevaux
MULHOUSE

Saône
Belfort
BASEL
Vesoul
SCHWEIZ

20 km

Schirmeck
Mollkirch
Obernai
le Hohwald
Barr
Champ du Feu
Andlau
Saales
Villé
St-Dié
PARC
St-Hippolyte
Ribeauvillé
NATUREL
Col des Bagenelles
Riquewihr
le Bonhomme
Kaysersberg
Épinal
RÉGIONAL
Lapoutroie
les Trois Épis
le Valtin
Orbey
Xonrupt-Longemer
Hohrodberg
le Tholy
GÉRARDMER-la Mauselaine
Munster
Col de la Schlucht
Eguisheim
COLMAR
Muhlbach
la Bresse
Metzeral
Remiremont
Rouffach
DES BALLONS DES VOSGES
PLOMBIÈRES-LES-BAINS
Ventron
le Markstein
Bollenberg
Murbach
le Val d'Ajol
Rupt-s-Moselle
Ermitage du Frère Joseph
Grand Ballon
Bussang
St-Maurice-s-Moselle

15

Hunawihr

Introduction

Landscapes

ADMINISTRATION

This guide covers three of France's 22 *régions* (the largest type of administrati▮ district): Alsace, Lorraine, and Champagne-Ardenne. Each region is made up of *dépa▮ tements* (numbered 01 to 96 alphabetically, which numbers are used as identificatio▮ on automobile license plates and in postal codes). Thus, Alsace includes Bas-Rhin (6▮ and Haut-Rhin (68); Lorraine contains Meurthe-et-Moselle (54), Meuse (55), Mosel▮ (67) and Vosges (88); in Champagne-Ardenne are the *départements* of Ardennes (08▮ Aube (10), Marne (51) and Haute-Marne (52). The French *départements* were create▮ in 1790 and generally given the name of the main river within their territory. Th▮ country is further divided into *arrondissements*, which are split into *cantons* and final▮ *communes* which are managed by an elected mayor. There are 36 556 mayoralties ▮ France.

REGIONS

The easternmost portion of the area covered in this guide is the **Alsatian plain**. Bare▮ 30km/19mi in width, it stretches, north to south, over 170km/106mi. The borde▮ with Germany is traced by the Rhine, which forms an alluvial basin with the Ill; ▮ porous, friable blanket of marl and loam deposits, consisting predominantly of si▮ (known as *loess*). At the southern end, the pebbly soil of the **Sundgau** region links it t▮ the Jura range.

Like a wall at the other edge of the narrow plain, the **Vosges** mountains rise abruptl▮ running parallel to the Rhine for the whole length of Alsace. This ancient range forme▮ by folding movements of the earth 300 million years ago is made of crystalline roc▮ (granites, porphyries) and ancient sedimentary rock, mostly sandstone. At the souther▮ end, the mountain tops have distinctive, rounded shapes locally known as *ballons*. Th▮ glaciers of the quaternary period left behind high mountain lakes. To the north, th▮ lower altitude has resulted in a thicker sedimentary crust, and a forest cover.

The western slope of the range is more gradual than the Alsatian side. The geological history of the **Ardennes** uplands is a complex one, the result of intense folding, faulting, uplifts and denudations, with some of the older strata of rock thrust above the younger. The highest point of the plateau in France is the Croix de Scalle (502m/1 647ft), on the border with Belgium. The Meuse flows through deeply entrenched meanders between the tip of the French Ardennes, Givet, and Charleville-Mézières. The rugged **Argonne** Forest is drained by the River Aisne.

The region of **Champagne** is part of the Paris Basin, a vast bowl-like formation contained by the Ardennes and the Vosges (north and east) and the Morvan and Massif Armoricain (south and west). The landscape has been shaped by a series of concentric layers, one on top of the other in diminishing size, like a stack of saucers, with the oldest and smallest on top. The plateau of **Lorraine** marks the eastern rim of the basin.

HOW THE LAND WAS FORMED

The Vosges and Alsace

Primary (Paleozoic) Era – About 560 million years ago, France was covered in water. The earth's crust underwent a great upheaval and the so-called "Hercynian folds" pushed up the bedrock of the Vosges and what is now the Black Forest, constituting a crystalline massif dominated by granite.

18

Secondary (Mesozoic) Era – This era began about 200 million years ago. The Vosges, planed down by erosion, were surrounded by the sea which filled the Paris Basin at different periods. At the end of the Secondary Era, the range was covered in water; sedimentary soils (sandstone, limestone, marl, clay, chalk) piled up on top of the primitive bedrock.

Tertiary Era – About 65 million years ago, a tremendous folding of the crust of the earth brought out the Alps. In reaction to this movement, the old Hercynian hills slowly lifted up. In the first phase, the Vosges and the Black Forest reached an altitude of nearly 3 000m/9 843ft. In the second phase, the central zone, unbalanced by the upheaval, collapsed inward. This sunken area was to become the Alsatian plain, separating the Vosges from the Black Forest, and explaining the symmetry of the structure and relief found between the two areas.

Quaternary (Glacial) Era – The earth underwent a global cooling period some two million years ago. Glaciers covered the southern Vosges. Descending slowly, they widened the valleys and steepened the slopes, gouged the rock and left hollows which were later filled with water (Lac Noir, Lac Blanc). When the climate warmed, the accumulated earth and stones carried by the glaciers were finally deposited in formations known as *moraines*, some of which created natural dams and lakes (lac de Gérardmer). Since the glaciers retreated, rainwater, rivers and streams have further eroded the Vosges. The old stone peaks have been laid bare in the south, whereas the northern end of the range, preserved from the harshest glacier aggression, has retained a thick sandstone mantle.

Ardennes: Hercynian history

At the end of the Paleozoic Era, the European continent was subject to a period of mountain-building resulting from the collision between Africa and a North American-North European continent. The Hercynian belt extends in western Europe for more than 3 000km/1 860mi from Portugal, Ireland and England in the west through Spain, France (Brittany, Massif Central, Vosges and Corsica), and Germany (Black Forest, Harz) to the Czech Republic in the Bohemian Massif. Analyses of the rocks and

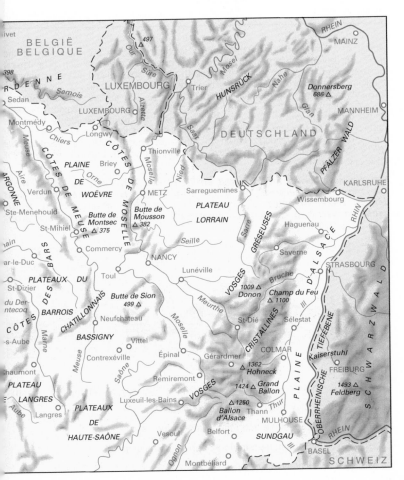

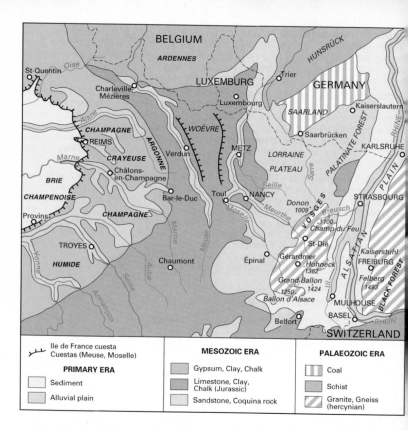

	MESOZOIC ERA	PALAEOZOIC ERA

Cuestas legend:
- Ile de France cuesta
- Cuestas (Meuse, Moselle)

PRIMARY ERA
- Sediment
- Alluvial plain

MESOZOIC ERA
- Gypsum, Clay, Chalk
- Limestone, Clay, Chalk (Jurassic)
- Sandstone, Coquina rock

PALAEOZOIC ERA
- Coal
- Schist
- Granite, Gneiss (hercynian)

geological structures found in these zones indicate that they are the result of the seabed spreading, subduction of the oceanic crust and plate collision. The lateral compression of the upper layers of the earth pushed accumulated sediment upward, bringing ridges of hard, old rocks together like the jaws of a clamp.

Thus, the Ardennes uplands emerged around 550 to 220 million years BC. Spreading over the countries of France, Germany and Belgium, the region has been eroded over time until it now appears as a mostly flat plain. The Meuse River has marked a course through the very hard stone, revealed in the dramatic canyon-like walls of dark rock through which it winds (described under Meanders of the MEUSE). Near Givet, the river valleys widen as the water passes over bands of shale and limestone.

The Jurassic period affected the entire planet, but takes its name from the mountains because of the marine deposits first described and defined there, evidence of the shallow seas which covered many continental areas when the global climate was warmer and there were probably no polar ice caps.

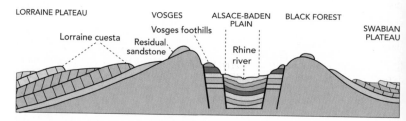

LORRAINE PLATEAU — VOSGES — Vosges foothills — ALSACE-BADEN PLAIN — BLACK FOREST — SWABIAN PLATEAU

Lorraine cuesta — Residual sandstone — Rhine river

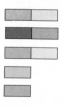

- Sedimentary deposits from the Tertiary era (1st and 2nd phase)
- Clay and chalk from the Cretaceous
- Limestone and marl from the Jurassic
- Sandstone (strongly bonded grains of sand)
- Primitive bedrock

20

orraine and Champagne

These two regions form the eastern part of the **Paris Basin**. At the end of the Primary era, and into the early Tertiary Era, this vast depression was a sea. A great variety of edimentary deposits – sandstone, limestone, marl, clay, chalk – piled up 2 000m/6 562ft deep. By the middle of the Tertiary Era, the water began to drain from this wide "saucer", whereas the rim, in particular to the east and southeast, rose nder the effects of Alpine folding. Erosion worked to flatten out the land, creating he **Lorraine plateau**, where geology served to create a homogeneous landscape; greater diversity of soil composition created the more diversified landscapes of the **Pays des ôtes**.

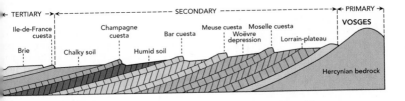

The illustration of the eastern part of the Paris Basin shows the formation of cuestas (côtes). The characteristic of this type of escarpment is a steep cliff on one side and a gentler dip or back slope on the other. This landform occurs in areas of inclined strata and is caused by the manner in which different types of soil and rock react to weathering and erosion. Here, the resistant layers (limestone) surmount softer layers (clay, marl). Running water digs a channel in the hard layer until it reaches the more porous zones below. The softer areas are washed away and leave a depression, which is hemmed in by the abrupt rise of the hard rock (the front de côte or steep face); the softer surface slopes back at a gentle angle. This back slope, protected from wind, is characterised by loose, fertile soil whose chalky layers below the surface help the soil warm up quickly in the spring. These areas are ideal for cultivating vineyards.

The Champagne region is made up of many small pays, areas with distinct climates and soils. **Champagne crayeuse** refers to the chalky soil which gave the region its name (etymological descendent of "calcareous plain"). This zone forms a circle with a circumference of about 80km/50mi, with Paris near the centre. The **Brie and Tardenois plateau** is crossed by a few rivers (the Marne, the two Morins and the Seine); impenetrable marl holds in humidity, whereas siliceous limestone forms the upper layer. The **Barrois** is another plateau, crossed by the valleys of the Saulx and the Ornanin, home to the towns of Bar-le-Duc and Ligny-en-Barrois. It extends into the **Côte de Bars**, where the vineyards of the Aube *département* grow.

Between the Champagne and Bars cuestas, lies the region known as **Champagne humide**, a verdant and well-watered area of woodlands, pastures, and orchards. The creation of the lake-reservoirs in the **Der-Chantecoq** and **Orient** forests have further transformed the lay of the land, where the heavy, clay-rich soil is more suited to grazing than growing.

FORESTS AND WILDLIFE

Alsace and the Vosges

The Vosges mountains are particularly lovely for the forest cover, which changes subtly according to altitude, orientation and the composition of the soil. The southern part of the range is known as *Vosges cristallines*, in reference to the granite content of the high mountains. The *ballons* and other summits are rounded, with moderate slopes on the western face. Facing the Alsatian plain, however, the rocky faces appear sharper and steeper. The Bruche River marks the separation with the *Vosges gréseuses* – the "sandy" northern end. The range diminishes in altitude and the red sandstone so prevalent in the construction of castles and churches has also sculpted the landscape. The forest blanketing the whole hilly area is sometimes a harmonious mixture of species, and sometimes dominated by a single species, creating a variety of colours and distinctive woodland environments.

Facing the region of **Lorraine**, the lower hills of the north are exposed to the wet western winds, and dominated by beech trees. Firs grow at an altitude of 400m/1 312ft altitude. In the higher southern peaks, Scotch pine grow above 700m/2 297ft. Beyond 1 000m/3 280ft, conifers yield to deciduous varieties, including

21

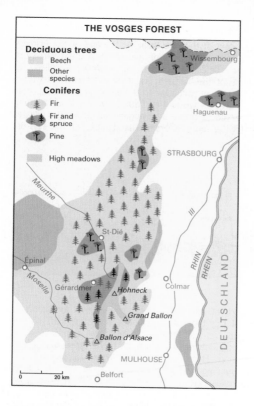

THE VOSGES FOREST

Deciduous trees
- Beech
- Other species

Conifers
- Fir
- Fir and spruce
- Pine

High meadows

Wissembourg
Haguenau
STRASBOURG
Meurthe
St-Dié
Épinal
Moselle
Gérardmer
Hohneck
Colmar
Grand Ballon
Ballon d'Alsace
MULHOUSE
Belfort
RHIN RHEIN
Ill
DEUTSCHLAND

0   20 km

beech, maple, mountain ash. On the highest ridge tops, there are no trees at all, just low brush and bilberry bushes. On the warmer slope facing the **Alsatian plain**, firs begin to grow at 600m/1 968ft. Just above the vineyards, groves of chestnut trees can be found; in the past their wood was used to stake out the grape vines. The warm, dry climate is congenial to spruce. A large population of oak flourishes in the Harth Forest, east of Mulhouse.

Storks – No discussion of the wildlife in Alsace would be complete without the mention of storks. These stately, long-necked creatures from the Ciconiidae family are symbolic of the region, where they are believed to bring good luck.

Each spring, their return is awaited anxiously. After years of decline (due to hunting in their winter habitat in Africa and accidents involving high voltage electric lines), the population seems to be stabilising and the gracious animals are once again a common sight. The European continent is home to 40 50 000 couples, 80 of which were living in Alsace in 1990. The storks come to roost, typically atop chimneys, in the month of March. Storks are voiceless, or nearly so, but announce their presence by clattering their bills loudly. The male arrives first, and begins work on a large platform of twigs and vines. The circular nest is refurbished yearly, and may weigh up to 500kg/1 100lb for 2m/6.5ft in diameter. Most nests are under 1m/3ft high, but exceptionally they may reach double that height.

When the chosen mate has arrived, the couple produce three to six eggs in a season, which hatch after 36 days of incubation by both parents. Generously nourished with insects, larva, lizards, newts, mice, moles and snakes, baby storks grow quickly; they begin testing their wings at about four weeks and are flying one month later.

Vosges Lakes – On each side of the crest of the Vosges, many lakes add to the pleasure of an excursion to the mountains. The largest is Gérardmer (115ha/284 acres), on the Lorraine side; one of the region's most popular winter resorts is located along its banks. The deepest lake is Lac Blanc (71m/233ft), on the Alsatian side.

The lakes were created by the glaciers which once covered the range, hundreds of centuries ago. Most are found at high altitudes, in bowl-like formations with steep waterfront terrain (Lac de Corbeaux, Lac Noir, Lac Blanc etc). Many of them are now used as reservoirs, particularly useful for meeting the needs of textile plants when water is in short supply.

Other lakes, in the valleys, were formed by glacier deposits, moraines, which retain or deviate waters. Gérardmer and Longemer are such lakes.

Stork nest

Lac Blanc

Ardenne

The French Region of Ardenne is the southwest margin of the larger Ardennes highlands and the adjacent lowlands in the Meuse and Aisne valleys. The thick, apparently impenetrable forest has been the scene of battles since the French Revolution. In addition to the sandstone, limestone and quartzite found in neighbouring regions, the Ardenne region is famous for the blue slate quarried there. The oldest sections of the forest are majestic with hardwoods such as oak, beech and yellow birch; younger growth includes European white birch and willows. The variety of soil quality has a strong influence on the height of trees: on the plateau a mature oak may yield only a dozen logs for the fire; an ash further south in the Signy-l'Abbaye area may climb more than 30m/110ft.

Game is abundant in the Ardenne forest, where hunting is popular. The region's emblematic animal is the wild boar, *sanglier*. The wild population has returned from the brink of extinction thanks to better management. There is also a limited hunting season (two to six weeks, depending on the district) on the plains, for pheasant, partridge and hare. Each hunting permit is delivered with tags which the hunter must affix to the animals captured. Deer are now found only in animal parks; few escaped the devastation of the Second World War, and the population has been restored thanks to the Belval animal reserve. Things have changed considerably since the days of Charlemagne: on 8 December 799, the Emperor and his party bagged two bison, two aurochs, 46 boar, 28 stags and a wolf, using spears, bows and arrows.

Argonne

The southernmost part of the French Ardenne is wooded and hilly, more temperate in every way than the highlands. The massif is a natural barrier between Champagne and Lorraine, about 65km/40mi long and 15km/10mi wide, rarely exceeding 200m/650ft in altitude. The Aire and Aisne river systems cut deep valleys through this region which has been of great strategic importance. Beech groves are common on the slopes, and it is not unusual to see regal chestnuts atop the crests. Shrubs, berry bushes and reeds provide shelter for birds and other creatures; bluebells, lungwort and daffodils grow wild on the forest floor. Some species have migrated to the area from other regions of France, including heather from Brittany; specialists may look out for a non-indigenous blue lily from England, a souvenir from soldiers of the First World War.

Recognise common species by looking for distinctive features of bark, leaves, and shape:

Beech trees can be recognised by their limbs which divide into flexible twigs; the long, pointed buds grow alternately. The leaves are well-shaped ovals, fringed

Beech

23

with cilia when young; light green in spring and summer, they turn a familiar copper-colour in fall. The bark is smooth, light grey, and often marked by white patches of lichen.

Spruce have twisted needles which grow two-by-two and are blue-green. The pale bark comes off in thin strips from young shoots; as the tree ages, the bark turns grey-brown, thickens and develops deep cracks.

Fir bear horizontal branches with light green needles; these are flat and disposed in a regular pattern like the teeth of a comb. The underside is clearly marked with two silvery lines. The crown of older trees is rounded. The grey bark is dotted with resin bubbles. The cones sit upright on the branches and fall apart when they reach maturity – this is why cones of the fir tree are not found scattered on the ground.

Scotch pine trees have pointed crowns and the branches dip downwards, hanging in a thick fringe said to resemble the tail of a spaniel. The dark green needles are sharp, growing in a circle around the branch. The cones hang down from the ends of twigs. At maturity, the seeds fall out and the cone remains on the tree intact for several months. The reddish bark forms scales which are more distinct in older trees.

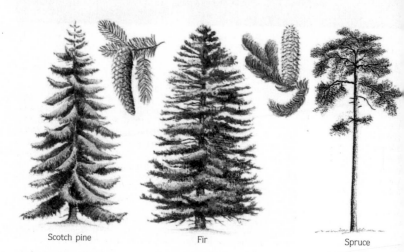

Scotch pine   Fir   Spruce

Oak trees are a genus of the beech family, and there are about 450 known species. Recognise oak by the alternate simple leaves, usually lobed or toothed. The most familiar feature of oaks is the acorn, which varies slightly in appearance (arrangement of scales on the cup, fused scales, hairy-lined shells) from one subgenus to another.

Chestnuts are tall trees with furrowed bark and lance-shaped leaves. In spring, the male flowers stand upright like candles on the end of branches; the female flowers are arranged at the base of these catkins. The spiky fruit contains two or three edible nuts (used as feed for livestock or milled into flour); the table variety, *marrons*, come from choice trees bred to produce one large nut in the bur.

Bird sanctuaries and other animal reserves are found around many of the region's lakes and nature parks. There are numerous "discovery trails" and nature centres where visitors can learn more about the environment, the flora and fauna of the region. For more detailed information, look in *Practical information* at the end of this guide.

Big Bad Wolf

The Ardennes Forest extends over the present-day borders of Belgium and Luxembourg; for many local inhabitants, being an *Ardennais* is more significant than being French or Belgian. At the end of the 19C, the thick forest was the perfect environment for smuggling cheap coffee and tobacco into France. Dogs were trained to make runs at night, and "Little Red Riding Hoods" carried innocent baskets for "Grandmother" while they stuffed their underclothes with contraband. Notorious customs officers, known as *noirs* because of their black uniforms, developed the habit of thoroughly searching any young lady found alone in the forest, and were generally despised as predators by the native country folk.

Economy

Alsace has become a symbol of the transnational European economy. For the past 30 years, regional development has centred around this theme. Strasbourg, seat of the Council of Europe, was one of the first "Eurocities" on the continent. Mulhouse has expanded its commercial activities through close ties with the cities of Basel and Fribourg across the Rhine. Because of its history, language and traditions, Alsace is able to develop privileged trading partnerships with the bordering nations of Germany and Switzerland. The Rhine river valley, long a significant communications corridor, has contributed to regional prosperity. As early as the 8C-9C, boats left Strasbourg for the North Sea, where they sold wine to the English, Danish and Swedish. Steam ships made their appearance in 1826. But it was the construction of the Canal d'Alsace, begun in 1920, which modernised navigation on the Rhine, at the same time harnessing the considerable energy resources provided by the river between Basel and Strasbourg. A strong local policy for encouraging investment has made Alsace the second most dynamic region in France for capital growth. Of 160 regions in the European Union, Alsace is ranked 13th for prosperity.

While the fertile plain of Alsace could be used for growing many different crops, the long strip at the foot of the Vosges is used almost exclusively for the cultivation of grapes: 14 566ha/36 212 acres. All of the wines are bottled in the region of production (almost 150 million bottles), and represent more than 18% of total French still white wine production. This activity involves 7 000 winegrowers. Grapes make up more than half of overall crop production in the region (40% of total agricultural output). On the domestic market, one-third of still white AOC wines consumed in France are from Alsace. The export market takes up 25% of the yearly production (about 40 million bottles).

Lorraine's reputation as an industrial leader has been tarnished since its most brilliant period in the late 19C. First the textile crisis, then the decline of the steel industry and the closure of coal mines pushed the area into a deep economic slump. Local policy-makers have had to work overtime to find innovative solutions for recovery. These include the creation of "technopoles" in Metz and Nancy, districts zoned for the development of high-tech industries. Subsidies have been allotted to areas around the Meuse Valley, Longwy and Thionville for similar development projects. Diversification is slowly making inroads where heavy industry once dominated: manufacture of synthetic fabrics for tyre manufacture, paper products, service industries and tourism are expanding. Lorraine is also involved in joint development projects with its neighbours in Germany and Luxembourg.

Recently, 2 000 new jobs were created in Hambach for the manufacture of the Innovate Smart Car, the "mini car for the year 2000". A collaborative effort, the mixed diesel/electric or petrol automobile has design by Swatch and quality by Mercedes. Farms in Lorraine are France's leading producers of rape seed, used for making cooking and salad oil; the flowering plants make bright yellow fields. The region actively promotes "quality labelling" of agricultural products, including beef, cheese and eggs. Wood and wood processing operations (parquet flooring, panelling, furniture etc) also account for a significant share of French production.

Champagne – Clearly the most important export (20% of total) for this region is its namesake sparkling wine. But it should be noted that in recent years, an accumulation of stock and subsequent lowering of prices have pushed leading traders to rethink their marketing philosophy. Related economic activities include bottling and processing plants and farm machine manufacture. The "Packaging Valley" association brings together 250 businesses specialising in packaging products and processes. Agriculture, shored up by government subsidies, has also made steps towards increased profitability through diversification. Milk products have taken on an important role; the region produces 25% of all the ice cream in France (mostly in Haute-Marne). Research is underway on the chemical components of natural substances, used in non-food products: biological fuels from rape seed, alcohol and ethanol from sugar beets, paper products and adhesives from wheat starch. Research is carried out in a European institute, the *Agropôle*, in Reims.

The textile industry offers employment to a significant number of people in Champagne-Ardenne, especially in Troyes and the Aube *département*. Among the world famous manufactures of knitted goods: Absorba, Petit Bateau, Lacoste (the alligator shirts were created in Saint-Dizier and Troyes), Dior, Benetton. 35% of all French socks and 58% of infant layettes are made here.

Ardenne – Foundry and metalworks are leading sources of employment, and many automobile and appliance makers place orders with local plants (Citroën, Ford, Électrolux, General Motors, BMW, Porsche). Various industries related to automobile equipment have also set up shop (automotive textiles, safety parts, machine tools), as well as plants producing parts for high-tech projects such as Ariane rockets, TGV trains, Airbus, Rafale fighter jets and the Channel Tunnel. More recently plastics have taken off, in some instances replacing metal parts and devices, and also in the packaging field.

Most of the businesses in Ardenne are small and medium-sized firms engaged i subcontracting. The network of companies is supported by the CRITT (Regional Centr for Technology Transfer) in Charleville-Mézières, which works in research and deve opment of new and rare materials, microanalysis, non-destructive controls, thermi and themionic treatments and other highly specialised testing. In an immense effort t revitalise the region after the damage of the War and the decline of heavy industry the government offers significant fiscal advantages to companies choosing to locate i Ardenne. Their employees benefit from the exceptionally clean and quiet natura environment and the transport network which puts them no more than a few hour away from major European capitals.

Tourism has become an important economic factor in all of the regions covered in thi guide. Local authorities have sought to enhance and promote the value of the man historical towns and sites, natural resources and the recreational opportunities the provide. Improvements in the **transportation network** have helped this effort. Interna tional airports in Strasbourg and Basel-Mulhouse provide connections to Europea capitals. A high-speed train (TGV) is scheduled to begin serving eastern France i 2000. The network of *autoroutes* is dense and practical, making it easy to reach th area by car, from the north or south. The waterways have adapted to tourism as well and there are many possibilities for short trips and longer cruises through th countryside. Major investments around the region have stimulated the development o golf courses, marinas and water sports recreation areas, trails for walking, riding an cycling, and various mountain sports resorts. Many tourists also enjoy a stay at one o the spas – especially after enjoying the fine wines and hearty cuisine of the region *(se Practical information at the end of the guide for details)*.

Historical table and notes

Prehistoric inhabitants

Human settlements in Champagne and the Ardennes had developed into small villages by the Neolithic Era (4500-2000 BC). By the Bronze Age (1800-750 BC), the region had already established what would become a long tradition of metal working. Different tribes gave their names to future cities: Lingones (Langres), Remi (Reims), Catalauni (Châlons), Tricasses (Troyes). In Alsace and Lorraine, Celtic and Germanic tribes occupied the land at the time of the Roman invasion.

BC

58-52	Roman conquest. In Champagne and Ardennes, the people lent their support to Ceasar's troops. In Alsace, the Germanic tribes were forced to retreat to the east of the Rhine.
27	Under Emperor Augustus (27BC-14AD), Champagne was part of the province of Belgium. A sophisticated civilisation developed under the *Pax Romana*; villas were built, trading centres grew and roads improved communication. The area's thermal springs were appreciated for their curative powers.

Christianity and monarchy take root

AD

69-70	Following the death of Nero, the Roman Empire weakened. Assembly held in Reims.
3-5C	Missionaries travelled the region; Germanic invasions: Alemanni, Vandals and Huns successively carried out raids.
486	The regions of the Meuse and Moselle came under the control of the Merovingian king Clovis, establishing a Frankish kingdom. While the Franks were not numerous, they became the ruling class of the territories conquered.
498	St Remi persuaded Clovis to convert on Christmas day.
511	Death of Clovis. Champagne was divided into incoherent parcels, constituting several small kingdoms.
683	The duke of Étichon, father of St Odile, ruled Alsace. After his reign, the land was divided into "Nordgau" and "Sundgau", each ruled by a count.
774	Charles Martel seized some church property for the secular state. At the same time, the region was organised into parishes, and the power and authority of the church grew stronger; a balance of powers developed.
800	The title of emperor was revived and conferred upon Charlemagne. The Holy Roman Empire was a complex of lands in western and central Europe ruled by Frankish then German kings for 10 centuries (until renunciation of the imperial title in 1806). The empire and the papacy were the two most important institutions of western Europe through the Middle Ages.
816	Louis I, (known as "The Pious" and also "The Debonair"), son of Charlemagne and Hildegarde the Swabian, was crowned emperor in Reims by Pope Stephen IV; a forceful French monarchy began to take shape.
817	Louis I, in accordance with his father's will, divided Charlemagne's realm among three sons from his first marriage: Bavaria to Louis the German, Aquitaine to Pepin, and Lothair he named co-emperor and heir.
829	Louis' second marriage to Judith of Bavaria had produced a son (Charles the Bald), to whom he granted the realm then known as Alemannia. From this time on, the sons formed and dissolved alliances, overthrew their father twice, and territories were passed back and forth or seized outright by the brothers who continued fighting for decades after their father's death.
839	Pepin dead, another attempt at partition divided the empire between Lothair and Charles, with Bavaria left in the hands of Louis the German. The following year, Louis I died.
843	Under the Treaty of Verdun, Lothair received *Francia Media* (today, parts of Belgium, the Netherlands, western Germany, eastern France, Switzerland and much of Italy); Louis the German received *Francia Orientalis* (land east of the Rhine); Charles received *Francia Occidentalis* (the remainder of present-day France). This treaty marked the dissolution of Charlemagne's empire, and foreshadowed the formation of the modern countries of western Europe.

870	Lothair left the land of Lotharingia (Greater Lorraine) to a son who di without a legitimate heir. By the Treaty of Meersen, Charles receive western Lorraine and Louis the German an extremely large expansion his territories west of the Rhine. The region today known as Alsa remained separate from the rest of the French kingdom for the ne seven centuries.
911	Louis IV died, the last of the east Frankish Carolingians. The ma dukes controlling the feudal states in the region elected Conrad, duke Franconia, as successor; he was followed by Henry (918) and th began more than a century of Saxon rule in the region.
959	Lotharingia was divided into two parts: Upper Lorraine (Ardenne Moselle Valley, Upper Meuse Valley) and Lower Lorraine (northern pa of the realm, including parts of modern Belgium and the Netherlands)
late 9C and 10C	Raids by Northmen destabilised Charles' reign; power struggles conti ued as rival dynasties emerged and the feudal system took hold of th people. In France, the Carolingian dynasty waned.

The Middle Ages

987	Hugues Capet crowned, the first of 13 French kings in the Capetia dynasty, which lasted until 1328.
11C	The domains of Tardenois, Château-Thierry, Provins, Reims, Châlor and Troyes, through marriage agreements, came under the authori of the counts of Blois (the king's immediate vassals, but also his mo dangerous rivals).
1098	Robert de Molesme founded the abbey at Cîteaux.
25 June 1115	Claivaux abbey founded by St Bernard.
1125-1152	Thibaud II, count of Blois, strengthened the economy by creatin sound currency and cashing in on trade between Italy and the Nether lands. Communication routes improved, many trade fairs (Lagny, Pro vins, Sézanne, Troyes, Bar-sur-Aube) were the meeting place for Nor dic and Mediterranean merchants.
1015	On the site of a temple to Hercules, a Romanesque cathedral wa begun in Strasbourg. St Bernard said Mass there in 1145, before was destroyed by fire.
1152	French King Louis VII repudiated Eleanor of Aquitaine, who late married Henry Plantagenet, bringing western France under the Englis crown. For three centuries, the French and English remained "hered itary enemies".
1176	The new cathedral at Strasbourg was begun, inspired by the Gothi style.
1179-1223	Philippe Auguste reigned as the "king of France" rather than the "kin of the Franks".
1210	Construction started on the cathedral at Reims.
1284	The brilliant court and unified counties of Champagne joined th French crown with the marriage of Jeanne, Countess of Champagn and Navarre, to Philippe le Bel.
1337	Beginning of the Hundred Years War.
14C	In Alsace, 10 cities formed the "Decapole", to resist against th excesses of the feudal system; gradually these cities (Strasbourg, Col mar, Haguenau, and others) freed themselves from their overlords.
1429	Joan of Arc, aged 17, led the French armies to victory over th English at Orléans, thus opening the way for the coronation of Charle VII at Reims.
1434	Gutenberg settled in Strasbourg and formed a partnership with thre local men for the development of a secret invention. Their associatio ended acrimoniously in a court of law; in 1448, in Mainz, his printin press saw the light of day.
1480	The Upper Duchy of Lorraine (Lower Lorraine was no longer a unifie duchy) united with Bar and Vaudémont, and became known simply a Lorraine.

The Renaissance

Late 15C	After a century of strife in Champagne, trade flourished anew under the reign of Louis XI.
1507	In St-Dié, the *Cosmographiae Introductio*, a work by several scholars, first gave the name "America" to the continent discovered by Chris- topher Columbus, in honour of the navigator Amerigo Vespucci.
1515-59	Uprisings against the house of Austria in Mézières, Ste-Menehould, St-Dizier and Vitry.

| 1525 | The revolt of peasants *(Rustauds)* ended with their massacre in the town of Saverne. |
| 1562 | The massacre at Wassy signalled the beginning of the Wars of Religion in Champagne, which devastated the region for the following century. |

The unification of Lorraine and Alsace with France

1552-53	Henri II occupied Metz, Toul and Verdun, defeating Charles Quint.
1572	The St Bartholomew's Day massacre undermined the power of Protestants in the regions of Champagne and Ardennes.
1635-37	An outbreak of plague in Lorraine killed half of the population; the Thirty Years War, plague and famine ravaged the entire region.
1648-53	The period was marked by serious unrest caused by the far-reaching peasant revolt known as *la Fronde*, and persistent Spanish offensives in Champagne.
1678	The Nijmegen peace agreement confirmed the unification of Alsace and France.
1681	Louis XIV revoked the independence of Strasbourg.
1738	Stanislas Leszcynski, former king of Poland, father-in-law of Louis XV, named duke of Lorraine.
1766	After the death of Stanislas, Lorraine was definitively annexed by France.

Héloïse and Abélard

The story of these two lovers is one of the world's best-known tragic tales. **Pierre Abélard** (1079-1142) son of a Breton knight, sacrificed his inheritance to devote himself to the study of philosophy and logic, attracting students from around Europe. Around 1118, Fulbert, a prominent clergyman at the Notre-Dame cathedral, entrusted the education of his brilliant niece **Héloïse** (1101-1164) to the scholar. They fell in love. Héloïse bore a son, Astralabe, and the couple married in secret, to protect the philosopher's career. Her family's outrage caused the young woman to seek refuge in a convent. As for Abélard, the bride's relatives wreaked their vengeance by cutting off "the parts of his body with which he committed the offence". He became a monk at the abbey of St-Denis. Ever a controversial character, he was finally able to obtain authorisation to retreat to a lonely site near Nogent-sur-Seine (in the Aube *département* of Champagne-Ardenne), le **Paraclet** *(page 218)*. The convent Héloïse had entered at Argenteuil was dispersed in 1129. Abélard received permission to create and endow the Community of the Paraclet for his beloved and her sister nuns. The two met again after 10 years of separation. Moved by the words he had written in his famous *Historium calamitatum* ("History of My Troubles"), Héloïse also wrote of her passionate love for him: *The lovers' tenderness we shared together was so sweet to me, that I could no more condemn it than could I erase its memory without pain.* Yet chaste love was to be their lot for the rest of their days. Abélard was continually criticised for his views, by figures as influential as Bernard de Clairvaux. After a reproof from Pope Innocent II, he retired to the monastery of Cluny in Burgundy. There abbot Peter the Venerable helped him make peace with his faith and his fellows before he died in 1142. His body was first sent to the Paraclet; it now lies alongside Héloïse in one of the most visited tombs in the Père-Lachaise cemetery, in Paris. *(For information on books about Abélard and Héloïse, turn to Suggested reading, page 37.)*

Riches and power are but gifts of blind fate, whereas goodness is the result of one's own merits.

Letter, Héloïse to Abélard

Revolution and Wars

1791	Louis XVI and his family were arrested in Varennes-en-Argonne.
1792	Rouget de Lisle sang the *Marseillaise*, the future French national hymn in Strasbourg.
1794	Near Saverne, Chappe's telegraph began operation.
1785	Napoleon Bonaparte became an officer of the French army.
1789	The French Revolution toppled the king, proclaimed the rights of man and destroyed the ancien régime.
1798	Mulhouse, the last independent town in Alsace, united with France.
1799	Napoleon instituted a military dictatorship and named himself First Consul.
1804-15	Napoleon had himself crowned emperor after victories in Austria and Russia, and successfully consolidated most of Europe as his empire until about 1810. The revived Allied coalition and his defeat at Waterloo led to his final exile.
1815-71	France was ruled by a limited monarchy, with the exception of a brief republican period (1848-52).
1870-71	At the outcome of the Franco-Prussian War, Alsace and part of Lorraine were in German hands.
1885	Pasteur administered the first rabies vaccine to a young Alsatian shepherd.
1906	Captain Dreyfus, a native of Mulhouse, was reinstated and decorated with the Legion of Honour, the conclusion of the scandalous "affair" of 1894.
1914-18	The violent conflicts of the First World War lasted four years; at the end, Alsace and Lorraine were once again in French territory.
1928	Construction of the Grand Canal of Alsace.
1930-40	Construction of the Maginot Line.
1940-44	Germany invaded France; Alsace and Lorraine occupied.
Late 1944	Lorraine liberated by French and Allied armies.
1949	The Council of Europe established headquarters in Strasbourg.
1952	Dr Albert Schweitzer, native of Kaysersberg, awarded the Nobel Peace Prize.
1963	Canalisation of the Moselle River.
1974	Works completed on the Rhine in Alsace, with the inauguration of the hydroelectric plant at Gambsheim.
1976	Paris-Metz-Strasbourg motorway opened.
1977	The Palais de l'Europe (European Economic Community) buildings inaugurated in Strasbourg.
1964-84	Mines and metalworks suffer inexorable decline.
1993	Strasbourg confirmed as the seat of the European Parliament with elected membership.

The Franco-Prussian War

From July 1870 to May 1871, the war also known as the Franco-German War came to mark the end of French hegemony on the continent and formed the basis for the Prussian Empire.

Napoleon III's ambitious plans appeared to Prussian chancellor Otto von Bismark as an opportunity to unite northern and southern German states in a confederation against the French. Within four weeks, French troops had been effectively bottled up in the fortress at Metz. The rest of the army, under Marshal Mac-Mahon and accompanied by Napoleon, was surrounded and trapped at Sedan on 31 August. By 2 September, they had surrendered.

French resistance fought the desperate odds under a new government of national defence, which had assumed power and deposed the emperor on 4 September 1970, establishing the Third Republic. With Paris under siege, negotiations were stalled while Bismark demanded Alsace and Lorraine. Léon Gambetta, a provisional government leader, organised new armies after escaping from Paris in a balloon. Despite their valiant efforts, and the Paris insurrection which declared the independence of the *Commune de Paris*, capitulation was at hand. The Treaty of Frankfurt was signed on 10 May: Germany annexed all of Alsace and most of Lorraine, with Metz; France had to pay a heavy indemnity. Thus French influence on German states came to a halt and the Prussian domination of Germany was ensured. For the next 40 years, until the First World War, an uneasy peace held sway as further consequences were felt: the papacy lost power and Italian troops entered Rome; the Russian government repudiated the Treaty of Paris and began an aggressive campaign in Eastern Europe.

he First World War (1914-1918)

fter the Franco-Russian defensive accord of 1892, the Germans responded with the
o-called **Schlieffen plan** (named after Marshal von Schlieffen). The plan counted on the
ow mobilisation of Russian troops, and called for a six-week campaign to conquer
rance by way of an invasion of Belgium and a northern attack, bypassing France's
olidly defended eastern flank. Once victory in France had been achieved, the plan
alled for transporting German troops to the Russian front, where the northern giant
ould be beaten in a few short months.

ugust-September 1914 – French troops crossed the border on 7 August and
ntered Mulhouse the following day, but had to withdraw to Belfort under the enemy's
ounter-attack. On 19 August, after grim combat, Mulhouse was captured anew and
he Germans retreated towards the Rhine. Preparing an offensive, the French took
ontrol of mountain passes in the Vosges. Meanwhile, on 14 August, the First and
econd French Armies had penetrated occupied Lorraine. An assault launched on 20
ugust was met with such a violence of firepower that the French troops were
ecimated, and forced to pull back to the Meurthe. The defensive line between
adonviller and Nancy formed a funnel shape, with the town of Charmes at the small
nd. The Germans took advantage of this position to attack Charmes, but met with
esistance. From 26 August to 9 September they brought their force to bear on the
astern front, the line of the Vosges towards upper Meurthe and on to Nancy.
et German commander **Moltke** spread his infantry too thin, and hesitation cost him
he **Battle of the Marne** (5-10 September 1914) along with his military command.
Marshal **Von Kluck** pushed the German troops towards the Seine. For the French, **Joffre**
nd **Gallieni** attempted a bold attack on the German's right flank. Four thousand

31

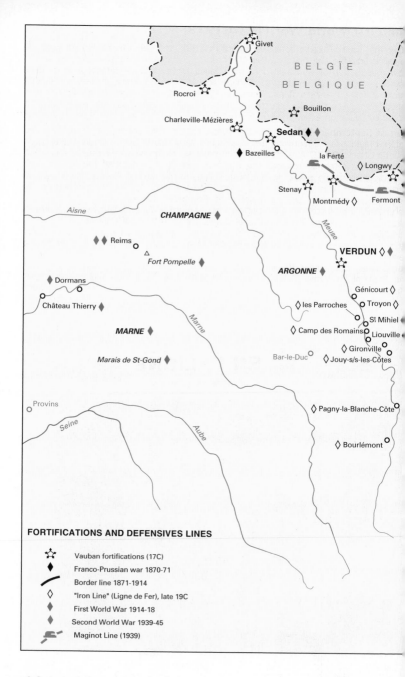

FORTIFICATIONS AND DEFENSIVES LINES

✧ Vauban fortifications (17C)

◆ Franco-Prussian war 1870-71

— Border line 1871-1914

◇ "Iron Line" (Ligne de Fer), late 19C

◆ First World War 1914-18

◆ Second World War 1939-45

⬗ Maginot Line (1939)

reinforcement troops were carried to the front in the famous **Marne taxis**. British soldiers were able to drive into the opening thus created in the German line, forcing a retreat as far as the Aisne Valley.

A terrible war of attrition settled in along the front from the Jura mountains to the North Sea, through the heart of Alsace and Lorraine.

Trench warfare (1915-1918) – After the Battle of the Marne the German position stabilised along the pre-war border in Lorraine, the Vosges and Alsace. Fierce localised combat pitted the armies against each other as they strove to take and hold strategic positions (les Éparges, Ailly woods, le Linge, le Vieil-Armand). In February 1916, the Germans concentrated their efforts on Verdun; the stakes were high as the site became a giant battlefield which was to determine the outcome of the war.

The **Second Battle of the Marne** began with a German incursion in June 1918; Foch led the French forces in powerful resistance. Under pressure from all sides, the Germans fell back to the so-called Hindenburg line. On 26 September of the same year, Marshal **Foch** launched a general offensive which finally brought about German defeat and the Armistice of 11 November 1918, executed at Rethondes.

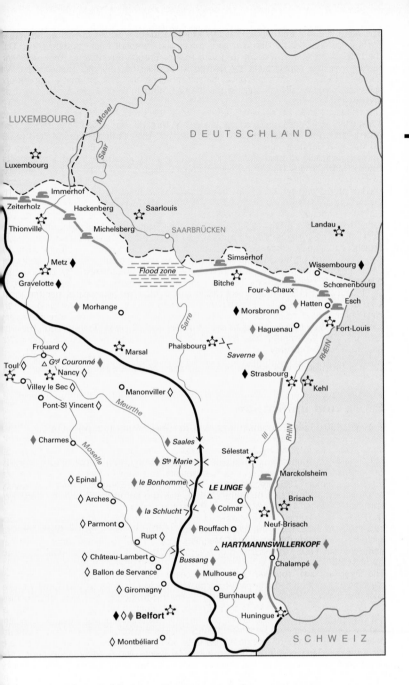

The Second World War (1939-1945)

Virtually every part of the world was involved in this conflict: the Axis powers (Germany, Italy and Japan) and the Allies (France, Great Britain, the United States, the Soviet Union and, to a lesser extent, China) were, of course the main players. The war was in some ways a continuation of the disputes left unresolved at the end of the First World War. France expected that if another war occurred, it would resemble the last one, and so built up a continuous defensive front, the Maginot Line, which also responded to the very low demographics of the eastern regions of France after the first war. This siege mentality, coupled with the old guard's refusal to modernise offensive and defensive weapons or to develop new strategies, proved poor preparation for the onslaught to come.

The period of 1939-41 is often sardonically referred to as the *Sitzkrieg* or **Phony War** – the French expression is the sheepish *drôle de guerre*. A combination of French procrastination, German *Blitzkrieg* ("lightening war") tactics and Russian perfidy led to the fall of Poland, and eventually to Soviet occupation of Latvia, Lithuania and Estonia.

The Allies still dithered while Finland suffered a massive Soviet offensive; Norwegia[n]
ports were occupied by German naval forces and Denmark taken by Blitzkrieg. Th[us]
the belligerents staked a claim to a vast area of Europe. Perhaps the first significar[t]
riposte was the appointment by George VI of Winston Churchill to head the Wa[r]
Cabinet. The great and energetic statesman made the first of many inspiration[al]
speeches, prophetically announcing that he had "nothing to offer but blood, toil, tear[s]
and sweat."

On 10 May 1940, a German offensive drove the Dutch to surrender within day[s].
Meanwhile, armoured units made their way through the supposedly impenetrab[le]
Ardennes Forest – simply bypassing the Maginot Line, France's illusory defence. B[y]
20 May, the Germans had reached the coast. Not until D-Day, 6 June 1944 was th[e]
Norman peninsula wrested from German occupation by American, British and Canadia[n]
troops. More troops landed in Provence on 15 August. The Allied armies then race[d]
westwards and northwards to liberate France. Paris was liberated on 25 Augus[t].
Verdun at the end of the month. Nancy and Épinal followed in mid September. Th[e]
fierce German defence did not yield in Metz until 22 November.

Fighting continued in Alsace as German hopes of recovering the region for its ow[n]
refused to die. But French offensive forces took Belfort and Mulhouse, and encircle[d]
German troops in the Battle of Haute-Alsace. To the north, General **Leclerc** launched h[is]
Strasbourg campaign from Saverne, taking the city on 23 November. Controlling th[e]
two extremities of the Alsatian plain, the Allies then crossed the Vosges and cam[e]
down into the vineyards, where more brutal fighting awaited them. By 19 Decembe[r]
one pocket of resistance remained, around Colmar, protected by the flooded River I[ll.]
On 1 January 1945, the Germans rallied and re-occupied Strasbourg, but the insist[-]
ence of General de Gaulle (Eisenhower wished to retreat to the mountains) and th[e]
hard-fighting local resistance recovered the city for the French. **De Lattre de Tassigny**
meanwhile, was busy squeezing the "Colmar pocket" with French and America[n]
divisions. The Wehrmacht was forced over the last bridge still under its control, a[t]
Chalampé, on 9 February.

German capitulation was marked by the signature of the Armistice at Reims on 7 Ma[y]
1945.

Peace and unification

9 May 1950: Robert Schuman proposed the idea of the European Coal and Stee[l]
Community (ECSC), later established by the Treaty of Paris (April 1951). Schuman'[s]
declaration was inspired by Jean Monnet's idea of "building Europe" step by step. Si[x]
States laid the foundations: Belgium, France, Germany, Italy, Luxembourg and Th[e]
Netherlands. The ECSC was given a "parliamentary assembly", which met for the firs[t]
time in September 1952 in Strasbourg. By 1979, the European Economic Communit[y]
as provided by the Treaty of Rome (1957), saw the European Parliament elected b[y]
universal suffrage: 410 Members from 9 Member States.

By 1993, the Member States numbered 12, and the Treaty on European Union cam[e]
into force. In June 1994 the fourth European Parliament elections by direct universa[l]
suffrage were held: the number of Members rose to 567 to take account of Germa[n]
unification. In 1995, the accession of Austria, Finland and Sweden increased Member[-]
ship to 626.

The **European Union**, founded to promote peace and economic stability, freedom o[f]
movement, and a unified approach to problems of security, defence, and social welfare[,]
operates through the Parliament, which meets in Strasbourg, but also other bodies[:]
the Commission makes proposals for European legislation and action; the Council c[f]
the European Union is made up of one minister for each Member State governmen[t]
and for each subject; the European Council decides broad policy lines for Communit[y]
policy and for matters of foreign and security policy and justice; the Court of Justice i[s]
the supreme court of the European Union (15 judges and 9 advocates-general); th[e]
Court of Auditors monitors the management of Community finance. Advisory bodie[s]
include: the Economic and Social Committee consisting of 222 representatives o[f]
various economic and social groups; the Committee of the Regions consisting of 22[2]
representatives of local and regional authorities, who bring a regional and loca[l]
dimension to the Union.

Among the main aims of the Union, the goal of a single European currency i[s]
becoming a reality in many countries. The euro is now the currency used by bankin[g]
and financial institutions in many EU nations, and will replace French francs, alon[g]
with the currencies of other participating nations, in the year 2002.

Art

ABC OF ARCHITECTURE

Religious architecture

I. Ground plan of a church

Axial chapel: in churches which are not dedicated to the Virgin this chapel, in the main axis of the building, is often consecrated to the Virgin (Lady Chapel)

Ambulatory: in pilgrimage churches the aisles were extended round the chancel, forming the ambulatory, to allow the faithful to file past the relics

Chancel, nearly always facing east towards Jerusalem

Arm of the transept, often extending outward

Bay: transverse section of the nave between two pillars

Chevet

Radiating or apsidal chapel

Sanctuary

Transept chapel

Transept crossing

Side chapel

Nave

Side aisles

Narthex

Porch

II. Cross-section of a church

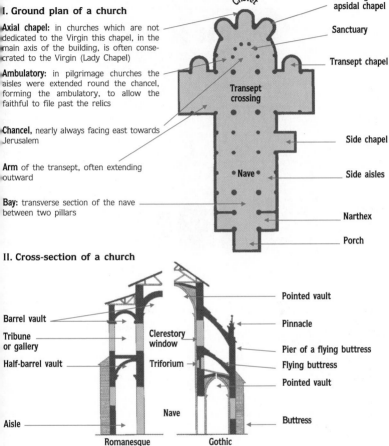

Barrel vault

Tribune or gallery

Half-barrel vault

Aisle

Clerestory window

Triforium

Nave

Romanesque

Pointed vault

Pinnacle

Pier of a flying buttress

Flying buttress

Pointed vault

Buttress

Gothic

III. MÉZIÈRES – Notre-Dame-de-l'Espérance Basilica (15 C)

Keystone pendentive: characteristic of late or Flamboyant Gothic period, embellishments, added in the Renaissance

Lierne: a short, intermediate rib

Tierceron: an intermediate rib between the main ribs

Diagonal rib

Transverse arch: reinforcing arch under a vault

Transverse rib

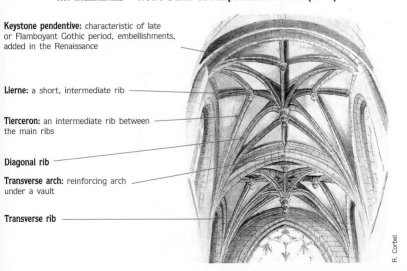

IV. MARMOUTIER – Romanesque façade of St-Étienne (c1140)

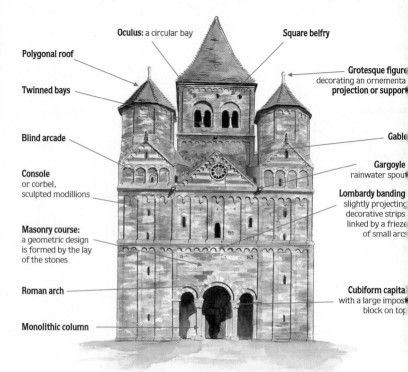

Oculus: a circular bay

Square belfry

Polygonal roof

Grotesque figure decorating an ornamental **projection or support**

Twinned bays

Gable

Blind arcade

Gargoyle rainwater spout

Console or corbel, sculpted modillions

Lombardy banding slightly projecting decorative strips linked by a frieze of small arcs

Masonry course: a geometric design is formed by the lay of the stones

Cubiform capital with a large impost block on top

Roman arch

Monolithic column

V. REIMS – Chevet of the cathedral (1211-1260)

The cathedral in Reims can be compared to Chartres. Both are great works of Gothic architecture, which reached an apogee in Champagne and the Ile-de-France region between the late 12C and mid-13C.

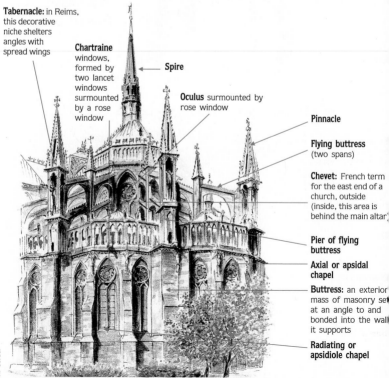

Tabernacle: in Reims, this decorative niche shelters angles with spread wings

Chartraine windows, formed by two lancet windows surmounted by a rose window

Spire

Oculus surmounted by rose window

Pinnacle

Flying buttress (two spans)

Chevet: French term for the east end of a church, outside (inside, this area is behind the main altar)

Pier of flying buttress

Axial or apsidal chapel

Buttress: an exterior mass of masonry set at an angle to and bonded into the wall it supports

Radiating or apsidiole chapel

R. Corbel

VI. Strasbourg – Central façade of Notre-Dame cathedral (12-15C)

'he abundant detail of Flamboyant Gothic is evident in the central doorway, richly sculpted and crowned with ›penwork gables.

Great rose window, made up of sixteen geminated (split) petals
Pinnacle
;able: decorative, vertical triangle ıbove certain doorways, here ıcorporating openwork
Sculpted **rose** cornerpieces
Embrasure embellished with statues
Jamb shaft: vertical member forming part of the jamb of a door
Arch: a curved construction which spans an opening; a series of arches forms the **archivolt**
Tympanum made of four historiated bands
Archivolt: the series of arches
Bronze door leaf
Band sculpted ornamental strip
Upright post or bearing shaft of a portal, generally a statue is bonded to it
R. Corbel

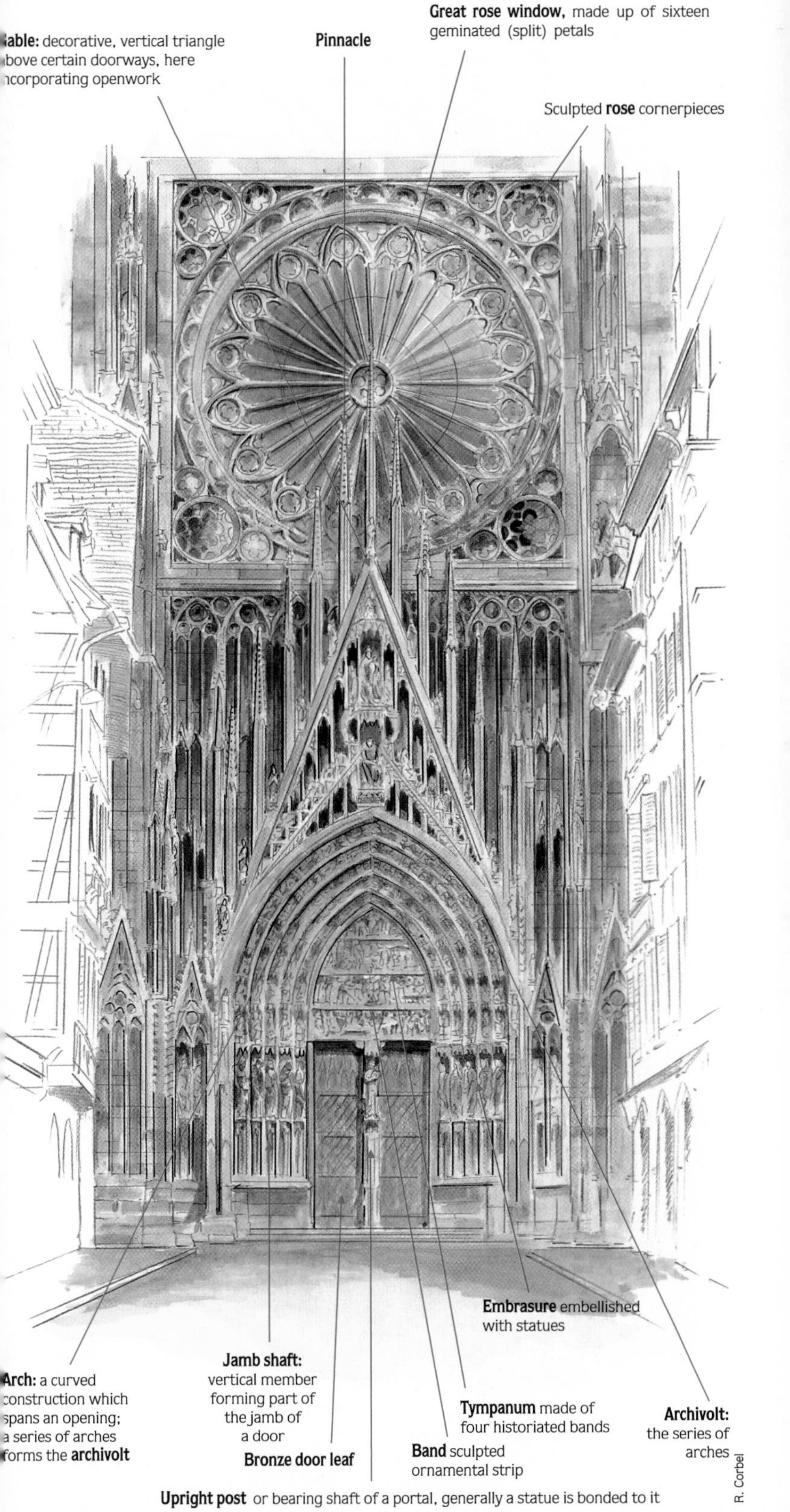

VII. MOUZON – Interior of the Abbey church (1195-c1240)

The elevation of the nave embraces four storeys (arcades, gallery, Triforium, clerestory windows), typica of primitive Gothic art (second half of the 12C).

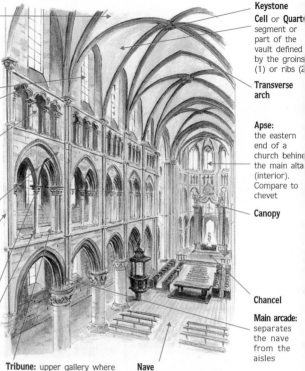

Sexpartite vault, ribbed vault whose lateral triangles are bisected by an intermediate transverse rib producing six triangles within a bay

Clerestory window

Trefoil arch

Blind Triforium: series of simulated openings between the large arcades and the clerestory windows

Corner piece: between the arch and its frame

Engaged column, partly embedded in or bonded to the wall

Crocket capital

Shaft of a column: between the base and the capital

Tribune: upper gallery where small groups can convene

Nave

Keystone

Cell or **Quart** segment or part of the vault defined by the groins (1) or ribs (2

Transverse arch

Apse: the eastern end of a church behin the main alta (interior). Compare to chevet

Canopy

Chancel

Main arcade: separates the nave from the aisles

VIII. THANN – Choir stalls in St-Thiébaut (14C-early 16C)

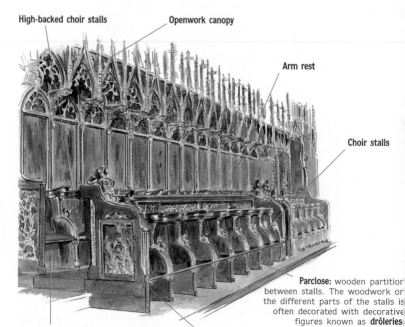

High-backed choir stalls

Openwork canopy

Arm rest

Choir stalls

Parclose: wooden partition between stalls. The woodwork or the different parts of the stalls is often decorated with decorative figures known as **drôleries**

Misericord (or **Miserere):** a bracket on the underside of a hinged choir stall which can be turned up to support a person standing during long services (from the Latin for "compassion")

Cheek: the vertical uprights at the end of a row of stalls

R. Corbel

38

Civil architecture

IX. SAVERNE – Katz House (1605-1668), no 76, Grand'Rue

Half-timbered houses, numerous in Alsace, illustrate the skill of local carpenters, especially between the 17-19C.

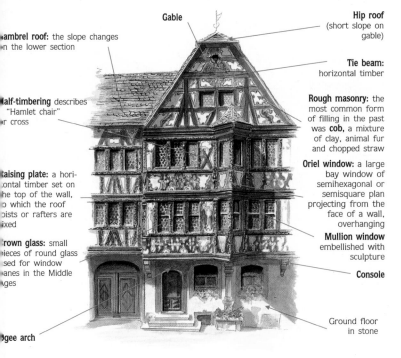

Gable

Hip roof (short slope on gable)

Mambrel roof: the slope changes on the lower section

Tie beam: horizontal timber

Half-timbering describes "Hamlet chair" or cross

Rough masonry: the most common form of filling in the past was **cob**, a mixture of clay, animal fur and chopped straw

Raising plate: a horizontal timber set on the top of the wall, to which the roof joists or rafters are fixed

Oriel window: a large bay window of semihexagonal or semisquare plan projecting from the face of a wall, overhanging

Crown glass: small pieces of round glass used for window panes in the Middle Ages

Mullion window embellished with sculpture

Console

Ogee arch

Ground floor in stone

X. LUNÉVILLE – Château (18C)

Also known as "Petit-Versailles", this château was designed by the architect Germain Boffrand.

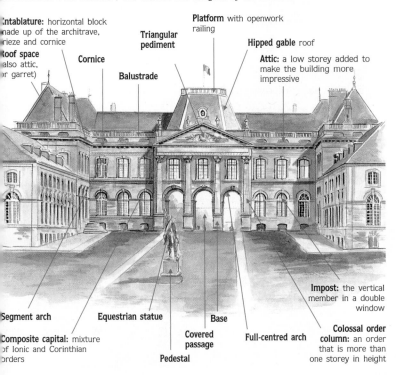

Entablature: horizontal block made up of the architrave, frieze and cornice

Platform with openwork railing

Triangular pediment

Hipped gable roof

Roof space (also attic, or garret)

Cornice

Attic: a low storey added to make the building more impressive

Balustrade

Impost: the vertical member in a double window

Segment arch

Equestrian statue

Base

Composite capital: mixture of Ionic and Corinthian orders

Covered passage

Full-centred arch

Colossal order column: an order that is more than one storey in height

Pedestal

XI. CONTREXÉVILLE – Thermal springs gallery and pavilion

The design expresses the architectural eclecticism typical of spa town; neo-Byzantine style predominates

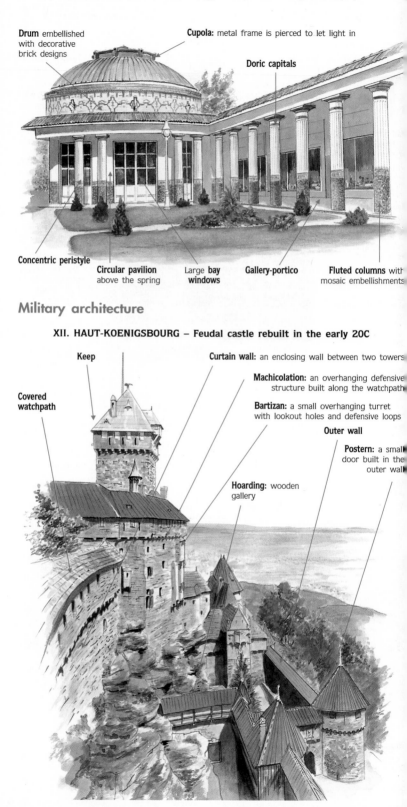

Drum embellished with decorative brick designs

Cupola: metal frame is pierced to let light in

Doric capitals

Concentric peristyle

Circular pavilion above the spring

Large **bay windows**

Gallery-portico

Fluted columns with mosaic embellishments

Military architecture

XII. HAUT-KOENIGSBOURG – Feudal castle rebuilt in the early 20C

Keep

Covered watchpath

Curtain wall: an enclosing wall between two towers

Machicolation: an overhanging defensive structure built along the watchpath

Bartizan: a small overhanging turret with lookout holes and defensive loops

Outer wall

Postern: a small door built in the outer wall

Hoarding: wooden gallery

XIII. NEUF-BRISACH – Stronghold (1698-1703)

The polygonal stronghold was developed in the early 16C, as firearms became more common in warfare: the cannon mounted on one structure covered the "blind spot" of the neighbouring position. This stronghold was built by Vauban, opposite the formidable Breisach, handed back to the Hapsburgs under the Treaty of Ryswick (1697).

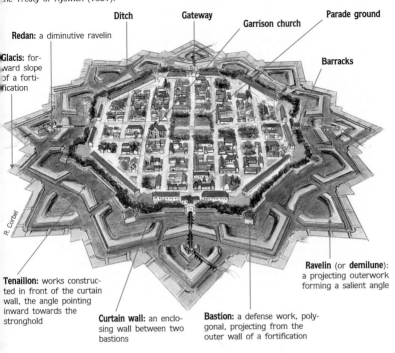

Ditch

Gateway

Garrison church

Parade ground

Redan: a diminutive ravelin

Glacis: forward slope of a fortification

Barracks

R. Corbel

Ravelin (or **demilune**): a projecting outerwork forming a salient angle

Tenaillon: works constructed in front of the curtain wall, the angle pointing inward towards the stronghold

Curtain wall: an enclosing wall between two bastions

Bastion: a defense work, polygonal, projecting from the outer wall of a fortification

Other architectural terms used in this guide

Ashlar	Hewn masonry or squared stones lain in regular courses, as distinguished from rubble work.
Bailey	Space enclosed by the outer walls of a castle (also: *ward*).
Barbican	Outwork of a medieval castle, often with a tower, defending a gate or bridge.
Bartizan	An overhanging battlemented corner turret, corbelled out; sometimes as grandiose as an overhanging gallery (illustration XII).
Battlements	Parapet of medieval fortifications, with a walkway for archers, protected by merlons, with embrasures between them.
Buttress	Vertical mass of masonry built against a wall, so strengthening it and resisting the pressure of a vaulted roof (illustration II).
Clerestory	Upper stage of an elevation, consisting of a range of tall windows (illustration VII).
Crenellation	The low segment of the alternating high and low segments of a battlement.
Donjon	French term for the castle *keep* (illustration XII).
Glacis	A bank sloping down from a castle which acts as a defence against invaders; broad, sloping naked rock or earth on which the attackers are completely exposed (illustration XIII).
Machicolation	In medieval castles, a row of openings below the projecting parapet though which missiles could be rained down upon the enemy.
Merlon	The high segment of the alternating high and low segments of a battlement.
Portcullis	A heavy timber or metal grill that protected the castle entrance and could be raised or lowered from within to block passage or to trap attackers.
Postern Gate	A side or less important gate into a castle; usually for peacetime use by pedestrians (illustration XII).
Rustication	Worked ashlar stone with beveled edges defining conspicuous joints.
Wicket	Person-sized door set into the main gate door.

ARCHITECTURE IN ALSACE

Religious architecture

Romanesque churches – In Alsace, Carolingian influences persisted longer tha
elsewhere in France; the flowering of Romanesque art took place in the 12C, lagging
century behind the rest of the country.
Yet this lag did produce some happy consequences: Alsace, at the crossroads of France
Germany and Italy, was able to assimilate the most diverse trends and add a regiona
touch to create a very original style.

Exterior – Most of the churches in Alsace are small or modest, and laid out in the form o
a Latin cross with short lateral arms. The 11C church at Ottmarsheim still shows th
Carolingian polygonal ground plan, inspired by the Palatine chapel in Aix-la-Chapell
(Aachen).
Among the distinctive local features, **tours lanternes** ("lantern towers") are found abov
the transept crossing (Ste-Foy in Sélestat is a good example). **Belfries**, both square an
round, often rise from the angle made by the main body of the church (chancel an
nave) and the transept crossing. The western façade, with or without a porch, i
flanked by belfries several storeys high.
The east end culminates in a semicircular apse; flattened chevets (Murbach) are th
exception. The side walls, gables, apse and façade are embellished with Lombard
banding, slightly projecting decorative strips linked by a frieze of small arcs.
Under the influence of artisans in Basel, arched doorways rest on slender columns
historiated tympana were frequent adornments in the 12C *(see the photograph of th
doorway of the cathedral at Verdun page 44).*

Interior – The architecture is ascetic; arcading and bays without decorative moulding are
surmounted by a wall, with one or two windows which flare open wider on the inside
The chancel is not ringed by an ambulatory. Vaulting was not used until late in the 12C
The main supports are Roman arches which shape the ribbed vault. They rest on thick
rectangular pillars flanked on four sides by engaged columns. The side aisles are
covered with groined vaulting formed by the intersection of the long vault of the side
aisle and the transverse vaults.

Decoration – The spare decoration is mostly found on doorways, in plain geometric
patterns; only the church at Andlau has any interesting sculptures.
The **capitals**, the wide upper portion of columns supporting arches, are an important
part of the architectural style. Ribs from more than one vault can rest on a single
pillar. In Alsace, the Romanesque churches usually have very simple, cubic capitals, with
little variety of sculpted forms – a few rare figures and some foliage. Some churches
have tried to palliate the plain and sober decoration with paintings, such as those in
Ottmarsheim.

Gothic churches – After some searching, Gothic art in Alsace reached a rare degree
of perfection: the cathedral in **Strasbourg** is proof enough. Many Gothic buildings, civil
and religious, went up between the 13C and the 14C: in **Colmar**, the Unterlinden
cloisters, St-Martin church, the "Koifhus" (Customs House); in Wissembourg, St-
Pierre-St-Paul; St-George in Sélestat, to name a few.
At the end of the 15C, Flamboyant Gothic appeared on the scene in **Thann** (St-
Thiébaut) and Strasbourg (St-Laurent doorway on the cathedral).
During the 16C, while the Renaissance was influencing civil architecture, religious
buildings remained true to the Gothic spirit. The churches in **Ammerschwihr** (16C) and
Molsheim (16C-17C) well reflect this.
Traces of the **Renaissance** are more evident in charming private residences and admi-
rable public buildings.

Classical style – In the 17C, a long period of trials and warfare halted nearly all
construction of new civil and religious buildings. Under French authority, Alsace rebuilt
and embellished monasteries. Yet there are a few churches dating from this time,
including St-Pierre in **Colmar** (Regency style), and Notre-Dame in **Guebwiller**, built by the
abbots of Murbach on a strict Classical design.
Baroque influences are apparent in the abbey church at **Ebersmunster**, lavishly decorated
with sculptures, mouldings and frescoes.

Civil architecture

Town halls – As early as the Middle Ages, Alsatian towns sought a degree of
independence. Town halls were built to serve the municipal authorities, a symbol of
power and an illustration of architectural preferences of the times.
The lovely town halls in **Ensisheim, Mulhouse** (the covered porch was inspired by Swiss
buildings), **Obernai, Rouffach, Kaysersberg, Molsheim** and **Guebwiller** as well as the old town
hall of Strasbourg (today the Chamber of Commerce), testify to the intensity of local
politics.

Bourgeois and princely manors – In most of the towns in Alsace, visitors will see
neighbourhoods or street corners which recall the prosperity of bygone days.

icturesque places like **Riquewhir, Kaysersberg**, the "Petite France" district of **Strasbourg** nd "Petite Venise" in **Colmar** have a rich architectural heritage of traditional 6C-17C private residences. Overhanging elements mark the façade, and the upper toreys culminate in sharp points; both stone and wood are used as building mate- ials.

uring the Renaissance, many amusing details were added: fancy gables, wooden alleries around towers, wrought-iron work, sculpted or painted wooden panelling n the façade. The two most distinctive features of Alsatian manors built in the 5C and during the Renaissance are the gables and the oriel windows.

ables perch ornately atop buildings. In Strasbourg, the Maison de l'Œuvre Notre-)ame is topped with gable mounting squarely upwards like a set of stairs; in :olmar, curling scrolls adorn the sloping sides of the gable on the Maison des êtes.

riel windows — These arge bay windows of emihexagonal or semi- quare plan project from he façade, creating an overhang, as on the Mai- on des Têtes *(photo- graph)*. The oriel window provides a break in the uniformity of a façade and creates a lively play of light and shadow. For a building located on a narrow street, it can be a precious source of ight, and a good vantage point for watching the comings and goings of the town. Prestigious res- idences built for the pow- erful lords, prelates and financiers in the 17C — once the devastating Thirty Years War was past and Alsace was in the hands of Louis XIV — and the 18C are distin- guished by the increase in French influence on the banks of the Rhine. While 18C residences do not have the imaginative style of Renaissance houses, they are admirable for their graceful balconies,

Colmar – Maison des Têtes

R. Mazin/DIAF

delicate corbels and elegant bay windows, as well as the fine quality of stone. The luxurious palaces of the Rohan family, in **Strasbourg** and **Saverne**, are splendid examples of Classical architecture.

Wells and fountains — Especially popular during the Renaissance, fountains went up on many town squares, red sandstone columns supporting a statue of the patron saint, a figure from history or legend or a heraldic emblem.

Military architecture

All along the Vosges hillsides, rising above the plain of Alsace, the vestiges of ancient fortresses and feudal keeps mark the horizon. More recent vestiges also interest the visitor: magnificent ramparts built and renovated by Vauban, German defences put up between 1870 and 1914, concrete pillboxes and armoured towers from the above and below-ground works that made up the **Maginot Line** *(see page 47)*, and numerous forts and blockhouses left from the Second World War.

Defensive castles — Sentinels in times of war, all of these castles have kept their proud allure, even those which are little more than an isolated keep or a lone wall crumbling under moss. The reconstitution of the Haut-Koenigsbourg castle, by the order of Kaiser Wilhelm II, was controversial from the outset. Still today, some prefer the romantic reverie of ruins to the academic demonstration of a pristine reconstruction.

Verdun – Porte Chausée

Medieval walled cities
In the Middle Ages, town and cities built fortifications to defend themselve from both feudal lords an enemies from abroad. A city would build a ring c protective walls, with stra tegically located tower and just a few gateway which could be closed u and protected. These gate ways still stand in man towns ("Porte Haute") towers ("Tour du Diable" "Tour des Sorcières" mark the line of the ol fortified wall.

ARCHITECTURE IN LORRAINE

Religious architecture

Romanesque churches – In the 10C and early 11C German prelates held juris diction in Metz, Toul an Verdun, bringing the architectural influences of the Rhineland; an example is the western chancel of the Verdun cathedral. But by the end of the 11C, influences from Champagne and Burgundy had grown stronger.

The churches in Lorraine are mostly basilicas, often simplified to the extreme. The smaller churches have only a nave, a chancel and an apse. The doors are crowned with a semi-circular tympanum, the façades are sparsely decorated. Ribbed vaulting is common in Romanesque building; it was introduced in Lorraine in the last third of the 12C. Towers are generally square, and placed atop the square shaped by the transept. Among the most characteristic churches of this period, one is in **Mont-Devant-Sassay**; part of **Notre-Dame de Verdun** is also a good illustration of the style.

Gothic churches – Like all regions which were long under German influence, Lorraine was slow moving from Romanesque to Gothic architecture.

In **Toul** and **Metz**, the cathedrals bear the marks of French influence. Indeed, they were designed by masters who had already worked in Champagne and Ile-de-France, the cradle of the French Gothic style.

Verdun Cathedral – arched doorway and historiated tympanum

The links between Lorraine and France were numerous at that time, and French predominance was felt in many fields: students from Lorraine travelled to the University of Paris; the famous trade fairs in Lorraine made it an economic centre; the dukes of Lorraine were well aware of the ambitious plans of the Capetian kings next door.

Other Gothic edifices worth citing: **Avioth**, where the great ambulatory of the church was frequented by pilgrims, St-Étienne in **St-Mihiel** and the **St-Nicolas-de-Port** basilica, whose magnificent façade was completed in the 16C.

Renaissance – The most significant works from this period are the Chapelle des Évêques in the cathedral at **Toul** and the church at **St-Gengoult**.

Civil architecture

Renaissance – The monumental doorway of the old ducal palace at Nancy *(see page 210)*, so finely wrought, dates from the 16C. Few châteaux from the period are still standing, but visitors can admire those at **Louppy-sur-Loison**, **Cons-la-Grandville** and **Fléville**.

Classical architecture – The 18C was the heyday of this style. Although there was a pronounced taste for French styles, the traditional Italian influence remained present. Robert de Cotte designed the château de la Grange and the Verdun bishopric in this style.
Germain Boffrand, a student of Jules Hardouin-Mansart, superintendent of buildings for the French king, drew the plans for the Lunéville château, the "Versailles of Lorraine", for the benefit of Duke Leopold. For Marc de Beauvau, *Grand écuyer de Lorraine*, the Duke's Riding Master, he built the lovely château d'Haroué. But the most impressive examples of Classical architecture are found together in the city of **Nancy**. When he was granted the duchy of Lorraine in 1737, former Polish king Stanislas Leszczynski undertook a plan to beautify his new capital. In particular, he called on Boffrand's disciple, **Emmanuel Héré**, and a metalwork craftsman from Nancy, **Jean Lamour**. Their work still shines on the Place Stanislas (on the UNESCO World Heritage List), Arc de Triomphe, Place de la Carrière, and the ensemble constitutes one of the masterpieces of European urban architecture.

Military architecture

Many defensive castles were erected in the Middle Ages. Today most have been reduced to ruin, or mere vestiges remain: Prény, Sierk, Tour aux Puces (Thionville), Châtel-sur-Moselle.
Few of the former fortified towns have kept all of their walls, exceptions being **Montmédy** and **Neuf-Brisach**. Often, it is the gateways which have remained standing: Porte de France in Longwy, Porte des Allemands in Metz, Portes Chaussée and Châtel in Verdun, Porte de la Craffe in Nancy, Porte de France in Vaucouleurs, Portes de France and d'Allemagne in Phalsbourg.

ARCHITECTURE IN CHAMPAGNE-ARDENNE

Religious architecture

Romanesque churches – As in Lorraine, most of the works dating from the Carolingian period have disappeared. Of the many sanctuaries built in the 9C, only the chancel of the abbey at Isle-Aumont remains.

Architecture in the year 1000 – A period of reconstruction followed the Norman and Hungarian invasions. The East Frankish Ottonian Empire (962-1002) had a strong influence on contemporary artistic style at the time.
Churches from the early 11C often look like big basilicas, with sturdy framework allowing for many openings to provide light; there are towers outside, galleries and sometimes an ambulatory inside. The interior decoration is usually very simple, based on geometric patterns.
Three churches in Champagne illustrate this style: Notre-Dame in **Montier-en-Der** (rebuilt in 1940), St-Étienne in **Vignory** and St-Remi in **Reims**. St-Étienne is one of the most remarkable monuments in the region because it has changed so little over time. St-Remi, on the other hand, has been renovated many times, and yet the Romanesque elements are easily recognisable, in particular the sculpted capitals adorned with foliage and figures.

End of the 11C and 12C – The traditions of the year 1000 continued to grow through the 11C, while at the same time, Gothic influences from the neighbouring Ile-de-France were making inroads. Romanesque architecture from this period is mainly represented by a few buildings around Reims and in Ardenne. Covered porches are common, and because of this are often referred to as *porches champenois*. The Carolingian influence is apparent in the plain decorative effects: capitals and cornices are embellished with rows of geometric designs, palmettos, and notched patterns.

Romanesque traces in vestigal monastic buildings hint at what great beauty must have been there: the cloisters of Notre-Dame-en-Vaux at **Châlons-en-Champagne**, the doorway of St-Ayoul in **Provins**, the chapter house in St-Remi in **Reims**.

The birth of Gothic – Gothic art originated in Ile-de-France in the 12C and quickly spread to Champagne, where manpower and financing made construction possible. The primitive Gothic style has echoes of the Romanesque: the use of embellished decoration was restrained and structures remained simple. Experimentation was taking place, too, with the edification of the abbey church at **Mouzon**, Notre-Dame-en-Vaux in **Châlons-en-Champagne**, St-Quiriace in **Provins**, the abbey church at **Orbais**, where the architect Jean Orbais designed a remarkable chancel which served as a model for Reims cathedral. The chancels of Notre-Dame in **Montier-en-Der** and St-Remi in **Reims**, which date from the origins of Gothic art, have a distinctive feature: columns stand in the ambulatory at the entrance to the side chapels, and support ribs of both chapel and ambulatory vaults, forming an elegant and airy colonnade.

The apogee of Gothic art – The golden age of the great cathedrals was the **13C-14C**; brilliantly lit by vast bays and vivid rose windows, they are covered in delicately carved sculptures.

When the cathedral at **Reims** was built, architects were already seeking to lighten the walls and interiors with immense bays: St-Amand-sur-Fion, the cathedrals at **Châlons** and **Troyes** and in particular St-Urbain show the accomplished fruits of their labours.

R. Mazin/DIAF

Reims cathedral – Smiling Angel

Decline – Gothic architecture then moved into its Flamboyant period **(15C-16C)**, just before it began to wane. The overabundance of decorative elements tended to mask the essential lines of the buildings. In Champagne, the basilica of Notre-Dame de l'Épine is the best example.

The Renaissance (16C) – Most of the architectural achievements of the Renaissance concern civil construction, but a few churches which were enlarged or renovated are worth mentioning: St-André-les-Verges, Pont-Ste-Marie, les Riceys, Auxon, Bérulle. Many beautiful windows and statues were produced in Troyes during this period.

Civil architecture

Gallo-Roman vestiges – Although not many major monuments are still intact, there are some very interesting vestiges. In **Reims**, remains of the ancient urban settlement include a triumphant arch, the Porte Mars (decorated with farming scenes celebrating the prosperity of the Roman Empire), and a crypotoporticus; in **Langres**, a gateway stands. In **Andilly-en-Bassigny**, archeological research has uncovered a villa complete with its thermal bath. Museums in Troyes, Reims, Nogent-sur-Seine and Langres have extensive collections including pottery, glass, statuary and domestic objects.

Outside of the cities, the hubs of civilisation, the countryside was dotted with estates known as *villae*. At the centre of a farming operation, each villa was a luxurious and well-equipped residence. The main house was not only very comfortable, but also richly decorated with paintings, mosaics, marble floors and wall panels and statues. Nearby, stood buildings for servants and craftsmen, and farther off the farm buildings. These settlements thus were home to a fair number of people, engaged in various activities. The villa-centred organisation of country life went into decline in the 3C as threats of invasion made it necessary to build protective walls.

Indeed, successive waves of invasions destroyed Gallo-Roman civilization in the 5C. Cities locked their gates, monuments were destroyed or abandoned. In the Middle Ages, the final remains were mostly broken apart for other uses.

The Renaissance – Italian influence brought about a major change in style notable for a renewed interest in forms from ancient civilization: columns and superimposed galleries lend grandeur to monuments of the period. Niches, statues and medallions are set into the façades; pilasters frame the bays (**Joinville** château and Renaissance manors in **Troyes** and **Reims**).

Classical architecture – In the Ardennes region this style is best represented by the masterpiece in the Henri IV-Louis XIII style, the Place Ducale in **Charleville**. There are many similarities with the famous Place des Vosges in Paris.

In the 18C, the construction of large urban squares on the Classical model was popular in France. In Paris, the Place Louis-XV (now Place de la Concorde) inspired similar works in **Reims** (Place Royale) and **Châlons-en-Champagne**, where the town hall is further evidence of the Parisian influence.

Military architecture

Located on the French border, Ardennes still boasts a few fortifications, including the impressive château of Sedan, the largest in Europe, which was built between the 15C and the 18C. There are fortified churches in the "Thiérache" region of *Champagne humide (see page 21)* dating from the 16C and 17C; a few traditional fortifications erected by Vauban; the **Villy-la-Ferté** fort was part of the Maginot Line.

Most **fortified churches** were built up at the end of the 16C and early 17C to serve as refuges. The region, neighbouring both the Netherlands under Spanish rule and the Prussian Empire was rocked by incessant warfare.

Vauban – **Sébastien le Prestre de Vauban** (1633-1707) took inspiration from his predecessors, and in particular from **Jean Errard** (1554-1610) of Bar-le-Duc, who published a treatise on fortifications in 1600. Able to learn his lessons from the many wars of siege which occurred in his century, Vauban promoted fortifications in the countryside. His opinion was that they should rise up around a stronghold and be organised according to the principle of the fortified camp. The defensive perimeter was stretched as far as possible in order to force the enemy to use more men to hold the siege; thus the number of men available to keep watch was reduced and the enemy became more vulnerable to a surprise attack from rescuers of the besieged.

Vauban's system is characterised by bastions which function with advanced ravelins – projecting, arrow-shaped outworks – all surrounded by deep ditches. One of the best examples of his work is in **Rocroi**. Taking advantage of natural obstacles, using materials found nearby, he also sought to bring some beauty to his fortifications, by bestowing monumental stone entrances upon them.

On the northern front in the Ardennes Forest, he set up a system known as the *Pré carré*. This consisted of two lines of strongholds located near enough to one another to prevent enemy passage, and to offer help in the case of attack. Although most of these fortified places are in today's Flanders and Hainaut regions, Ardennes was defended by the **Charlemont** fort on the front lines, and by Rocroi, **Mézières** and **Sedan** on the rear lines.

The Maginot Line – Devised by War Minister Paul Painlevé and his successor, **André Maginot** (1877-1932), this line of defensive fortifications was under study by 1925. It includes a series of concrete works placed at the top of a hill or on the hillside all along the northeastern border from the Ardennes Forest to the Rhine. The fort of **Villy-la-Ferté** is a good example of the defensive architecture of the line. Unfortunately for the French, this stronghold was without troops at the crucial moment, which meant that the resistance of May-June 1940 was pathetically vain.

Having observed that some of the more modern fortresses had held out against the German offensives of the First World War, Maginot, who was crippled for life as a combatant at the outbreak of that war, was inspired to build what he thought would be a permanent defence against German attack. He diverged from the circular defensive designs of past ages, to adopt the linear form.

Soldiers found it to be an immense improvement for their comfort: there were air-conditioned areas, recreation zones, living quarters, supply storehouses, and rail lines connecting various segments. The concrete used in construction was thicker than any known before, and the guns the heaviest ever used.

While today it is known as a military blunder, this sturdy network did what it was designed to do. Its shortcomings are due to the lack of ability of its planners to anticipate how much warfare would change in two decades. In addition, neither time nor budget permitted the French to protect all of their borders with the ingenious bunkers and fortresses. Not only were there gaps, but the line ended, for all intents and purposes, just north of the city of Sedan. French generals confidently supposed that Belgium itself was sufficient defence, in view of their defensive alliance and the supposedly impenetrable nature of the Ardennes forest. The generals, however, were thinking of foot soldiers, and when the Germans arrived, they were riding in tanks. In May 1940, they entered and occupied Belgium; they crossed the River Somme and struck at Sedan. Once this breakthrough accomplished, they had only to go around the rear of the line, rendering it useless.

Although it failed to foil the German invasion, the Maginot Line itself was never taken. The ouvrages remained intact, and not a single piece of artillery was put out of commission.

Besides the famous series of fortifications, the Maginot Line today also has a series of museums and tourists facilities; a tour is both easy to undertake and educational. Turn to page 161 for full details on visiting this historic site.

Sculpture and stained glass

Alsace

The finest examples of **sculpture** in Alsace are found in the embellishment of churches: statues, low reliefs and funerary monuments. The most famous sculptor to come from Alsace was **Auguste Bartholdi**, from Colmar, who made the Belfort Lion (a copy can be found in Paris, Place Denfert-Rochereau) and what may be the world's best-known statue, the Statue of Liberty which stands in New York Harbour.

Some of the most remarkable **religious sculptures** in the region are found in **Andlau** on the church porch. In the 13C, Gothic artists had a field day on the **Strasbourg** cathedra (low relief of the Death of the Virgin, the Angels' Pillar); the 4C statuary shows a more fluid style (Virtues and Vices, Wise and Foolish Virgins).

The doorway of St-Thiébaut in **Thann** and St-Laurent's doorway on the Strasbourg cathedral illustrate the opulent art of the Flamboyant period (15C). **Hans Hammer** sculpted the pulpit in Strasbourg cathedral, which is often referred to as lace tattoed from stone.

The best examples of **funerary sculpture** are also found in **Strasbourg**, in St-Thomas church: the tomb of Bishop Adeloch (12C), in the form of a sarcophagus, and the tomb of Marshal Maurice de Saxe.

The proudest piece of **sculpture in wood** is no doubt the Issenheim altar in the Unterlinden Museum in **Colmar**. The paintings are by Grünewald, but some of the glory must go to **Nicolas de Haguenau**, who carved the gilded statues of saints Anthony, Augustine and Jerome; Sébastien Beychel crafted the lower section which shows Christ in the midst of his Apostles.

Beautiful carved screens and altars are also on view in **Kaysersberg, Dambach** and **Soultzbach-les-Bains**. Elsewhere, there is a profusion of pulpits, organ lofts, and choir stalls **(Marmoutier, Thann)**, which demonstrates the skill and artistry of local artisans.

Lorraine

Romanesque decoration of churches was often rather awkward. The doorway of Mont-Devant-Sassey, dedicated to the Virgin, is in fact an inferior reproduction of statuary in Reims. A better example is Notre-Dame in **Verdun** where the Lion's Door (photograph page 44) is carved with a Christ in Majesty surrounded by symbols of the Apostles; though some find it lacks elegance, it does have its own original beauty.

In the 16C, **Ligier Richer**, working in **St-Mihiel**, brought new life to the art of sculpture, and his influence is felt throughout Lorraine.

Many mausoleums were embellished with **funerary art** between the 16C and the 18C. Perhaps the most remarkable example of Richer's work is in St-Étienne **(Bar-le-Duc)**; known as the Tormented Soul (le Transi, see p 78), the skeletal figure with one arm raised high adorns the tomb of René de Châlon. Licher also sculpted the tomb of Philippa de Gueldre in the Église des Cordeliers in **Nancy**; the tomb of René II in the same church is by Mansuy Gauvain. In Notre-Dame-de-Bon-Secours, the tomb of Stanislas and the mausoleum of his wife Catherine Opalinska are the work of Vassé and the Adam brothers, respectively.

St-Étienne cathedral in **Metz** was built between the 13C and the 16C. The church has been called "God's lantern" because of the many stained-glass windows. The oldest date from the 13C, and the most recent are contemporary, including some designed by painter Marc Chagall.

Champagne-Ardenne

Gothic **sculptures** on buildings are made in fine-grained limestone which is easy to carve, and are both ornamental and figurative. The **Ateliers de Reims** workshops were especially productive in the 13C, and the masterpieces produced there are visible on the Reims cathedral. The smiling angel (page 16) is a good illustration of the delicate mastery of sculptors from the Reims school. During the **14C-15C**, while the Hundred Years War raged, artists favoured funerary art such as gisants (recumbent figures) and monumental sepulchres showing scenes from the Passion of Christ.

The first half of the 16C was an exceptionally creative time for sculptors in **Troyes**, as styles segued from Gothic to Renaissance. The treatment of draped fabric and folds in clothing, of embroideries and jewels shows extraordinary attention to detail. Facial expressions suggest a range of emotion, and in particular give an impression of sweetness, sadness or timidity. The great master of this type of sculpture created the statue of St Martha in Ste-Madeleleine church **(Troyes)**, the Pietà in **Bayel** and the Entombment in **Chaource**. The Flamboyant altar screen in Ste-Madeleleine is from the same period.

The emergence of the Italian style is also evident in St-Urbain, where a statue of the Virgin holding grapes has graceful posture and a gentle expression, marking a departure from Gothic Realism. As of 1540, such maneristic, refined representations had completely invested the Troyes School of Sculpture, and put an end to its distinctive appearance. Churches installed many works by **Dominique Florentin**, an Italian artist who married a native of Troyes and settled there, training students in his workshops.

ome works in **stained glass** have survived the wars, pollution and the 18C practice of
eplacing coloured windows with milky-white ones (to make it easier to read the
:urgy).
he windows in the **Strasbourg** cathedral date from the 12C, 13C and 14C, and
though they have been damaged over time, they are remarkable in number.
he **13C** saw the creation of the windows in the chancel of the **Troyes** cathedral as well
s those in Notre-Dame de **Reims** (apse and rose on the façade), a few in St-Étienne in
nâlons-en-Champagne and finally the great windows of **St-Urbain** in **Troyes**, which are
ost typical of the era. Very colourful, they portray solitary characters (bishops) in the
igh panels, whereas the lower panels, more easily studied by visitors, illustrate the
ves of the saints or episodes from the life of Christ. The compositions are enlivened
y complex backgrounds and the expressive attitudes of the figures; some panels tell
s something about the daily life of the time.

Window in Ste-Madeleine de Troyes – The Creation
(1500)

1 the **16C**, painting on glass
ecame popular and many pieces
'ere ordered for donations to
iurches (the donor's name or like-
ess often appearing thereon). Car-
)ons (basic drawing patterns)
iade it possible to reproduce the
ime image over and over, which
xplains the wealth of windows in
ie small churches of the Aube
egion. Some of the artists' names
re known to us today: Jehan Sou-
ain, Jean Verrat, Lievin Varin.
arly in the 16C, colours exploded
n the scene, as seen in the spec-
icular upper windows in the **Troyes**
athedral, which were installed be-
ween 1498 and 1501. In these
rindows the contours of the draw-
igs are clearly defined and the
echnical prowess is evident in
ngraving, pearling, brushed gri-
aille which creates a three-dimen-
ional illusion, and inlays of differ-
nt coloured glass as used in the
tars.

he most common themes are the
assion, the life of the Virgin, the
ree of Jesse, Genesis, the Sacrifice
f Abraham. Divided into panels,
ie windows should be "read" up-
vards from the bottom. The first rows often represent the donors and their patron
aints.
s of 1530, polychrome effects were abandoned by the masters in favour of grisaille –
ones of a single colour – on white glass with golden yellow and blood-red highlights.
:alian influence is found in the evolution of the drawings. The architectural back-
rounds were inspired by the Fontainebleau School.
1 the 17C, the tradition of stained-glass craft continued in Troyes with **Linard Gontier**,
vho brought back polychrome windows with a new technique of enamelling on white
lass, which produced bright hues. He is considered the master of monumental
ompositions, with works such as the "Mystical Winepress", in the Troyes cathedral.
le was also an exceptional miniaturist and portraitist, working in grisaille.
1odern stained-glass windows of interest can be found in the church at **St-Dié**. In
accarat, St-Rémy church has windows made of crystal.

Tourists should refrain from visiting churches during services.

Decorative arts and painting

Merovingian treasures

The Merovingian period refers to the first dynasty of Frankish kings founded by Clov
and reigning in France and Germany from about 500 to 751. Recently, art historian
have become more interested in works from this often neglected time. In the Cham
pagne-Ardenne region, a trove of funerary objects has been uncovered in the man
necropolises that once served local communities. In the archeological museum in Troye
the tomb of Pouan, a prince, reveals much to us about the artistic temper of the time
Gold and silver work was highly prized. The decorative items on view in the museum
include **fibulae** (clasps resembling safety pins), belt buckles, parts of shields, swor
handles, among other things. The eastern influence is obvious in the designs, i
particular the fantastic animal turning its head to look back. Styles and technique
were also adapted by Germanic invaders. The rarity of precious metals led to
preference for gold and silver beaten into fine sheets or pulled into threads; othe
metals were also substituted for a precious effect, including copper, tin and bronze.
Arms made during the Merovingian period are another illustration of the prowess o
metalwork masters. Various metals, always high quality, were juxtaposed in th
forging process. They were welded together and hammered. The layered structur
thus created was both resistant and elastic. The most common arms: long double
edged swords, axes and the *scramasax*, a sort of sabre with one cutting edge.
In addition to metalwork, a speciality of Germanic regions, some sculptural works hav
also survived. In Isle-Aumont, a set of sarcophagi show the evolution of style betwee
the 5C and the 8C.

Alsace

In the 15C, great **painting** began to appear in Alsace, with the arrival in Colmar o
Gaspard Idenmann, creator of a Passion inspired by the Flemish style, now on view in
the Unterlinden Museum. Another Colmar resident, **Martin Schongauer**, painted th
magnificent *Virgin in the Rose Bower (in the Église des Dominicains, see page 106)*
Students under his direction painted a series of Passion works (also in the Unterlin
den), and created other remarkable works, such as the Buhl altar screen. The grea
German artist **Mathias Grünewald** painted the high altar of the Antonite church in
Issenheim. This screen *(photograph page 102)* sets a Crucifixion of fearful realism
against exquisite figures of the Annunciation and a Heavenly Choir. Some excellen
portraitists (Jean-Jacques Henner) were Alsatian, as were a number of draftsmen
engravers and lithographers, including **Gustave Doré**, who was from Strasbourg.

In the realm of **decorative arts**, Alsatian craftsmen excelled in woodwork, ironwork, tin-
smithing and working precious metals. They have a reputation as skilled watch and clock
makers, as the astronomical clock in Strasbourg cathedral proves.
Ceramics made the **Hannong** family, creators of the "old Strasbourg" style, eminent for
generations; their production is on view in the Strasbourg museum. In the second half
of the 19C, Théodore Deck of Gueb-
willer brought new ideas to ceramic
arts and refined techniques.

Schongauer's masterpiece

Lorraine

The region, with its wealth and as a
cosmopolitan crossroads, produced
many painters, miniaturists and
engravers over the centuries. Some
achieved fame beyond the local area.
Arts in the 17C were imprinted with
the influence of **Georges Lallemand**, a
native of Nancy who established
himself in Paris in 1601; **Jacques Bellange**, master of Mannerism; **Claude
Deruet**, official court painter *par
excellence;* **Georges de la Tour**, known
for his remarkable candlelit and torchlight effects incorporating deep
black "nights"; **Claude Gellée**, a landscape painter; **Jacques Callot**, a great
draftsman and engraver (most of his
works are together in the museum
of the history of Lorraine in Nancy).
In the 19C, **Isabey** was the leading
painter of miniature portraits, and
one of the favourite painters of Imperial society, alongside **François
Dumont**, from Lunéville.

Prouvé-Martin:
La Parure leather box

Gallé:
Ceramic dog in costume

Vallin: Masson dining room

Gallé:
Fourcaud
glass vase

École de Nancy

Daum:
"Figuier de
Barbarie"
(prickly pear)
glass lamp

Gruber: water lilies and colocynth, stained glass

Mention must be made of **Épinal**. In the 18C-19C, this town specialised in th
production of pretty coloured prints, which were sold around France by street ve
dors. The pictures became so well-known that it is common nowadays to use th
expression *image d'Épinal* to refer to any simplistic or naive representation of life.

Ceramic production in Lorraine was mostly centred around **Lunéville** and **Sarreguemine**
enamellers settled around **Longwy**.

Crystal – Lorraine has several famous crystal manufacturers, including those in **Bacc**
rat, Daum and **Saint Louis**. This activity was able to develop, especially in the 16C, than
to the abundance of wood (to stoke the fires), water and sand in the region. Today,
addition to traditional glassware, as appreciated by the royal and imperial courts
Persia, Russia, Germany and Italy, these venerable companies produce objects design
in contemporary styles by Salavador Dali and Philippe Starck, among others.

Art Nouveau and the 20C

At the end of the 19C, a movement to rehabilitate decorative arts and architectur
known as **Art Nouveau**, came to the fore. It is easily recognisable by its use of lon
sinuous lines, often expressed in the shapes of vines and tendrils, flower stalk
butterfly wings and other curvaceous natural forms. Some of the artists who made th
style famous were Mucha (Czechoslovakian designer immortalised in poster format
Hector Guimard (designed the Art Nouveau entrances to Paris Metro stations), Ame
ican glassmaker Louis Tiffany (stained-glass lamps), and Spanish architect Anton
Gaudi (works in and around Barcelona), who took the style to the outer limits.

In France, the first works to appear were in Nancy, made by **Émile Gallé**; he produce
glassware inspired by the patterns and forms of nature. His work was hailed at th
Universal Exhibitions of 1884, 1889 and 1900 in Paris. Soon a group of artist
working in various media (glass, wood, ceramic, engraving and sculpture) had gath
ered around him. Some of their names were **Daum, Majorelle, Vallin, Prouvé**; together the
formed the **École de Nancy**.

Between 1900 and 1910, the influence of the Nancy School became apparent in loc
architecture (about 10 years behind decorative arts); Nancy is now, with Brussel
Vienna and Paris, one of the great centres of Art Nouveau architecture in Europe.

The second half of the 20C saw some **architectural achievements** in the larger towns: th
Tour de l'Europe in Mulhouse (1966); the Tour Altea in Nancy (1974); the Palais d
l'Europe (1977) and the Palais des Droits de l'Homme (1995) in Strasbourg.

The most famous artist of the 20C to come from the region was **Jean (or Hans) A**
(1887-1966). He was born in Strasbourg when it was spelled Strassburg and part o
Germany, and trained there as well as in Weimar and Paris. A leader of the avant
garde, he produced sculptures, paintings and poetry. In Paris, he was acquainted wit
Modigliani, Picasso and Robert Delaunay as well as writer Max Jacob. He sough
refuge in Zurich, Switzerland during the First World War, and while there became on
of the founders of the Dada movement along with Tristan Tzara. After 1922, he too
the same path to Surrealism as other Dadaists. Yet their early attitudes of nihilism an
attacks on social and artistic conventions as well as their fascination with the bizarre
the irrational and the fantastic made an indelible mark on the century, and stand at th
root of Abstract Expressionism and Conceptual art.

Arp fled to Zurich during the Second World War; his wife, artist Sophie Taeuber die
there. After the war he returned to their home in Meudon, just outside Paris. A fin
collection of Arp's works and other modern and contemporary art works are assem
bled in the Musée d'Art Moderne et Contemporain in Strasbourg *(page 291)*.

Traditions and folklore

ALSACE

Both the mountains and the plain are rich in local colour, and legends abound in Alsace. Of course, visitors today are not likely to see women wearing distinctive, bow-shaped black headresses, unless there is a local heritage *fête* in progress. But the preservation of so much architectural patrimony – a miracle considering the strife and wars that long plagued the region – provides a setting which vividly evokes the past.

Some local traditions do persist, in particular those associated with saints' feast days. Each village celebrates the feast day of its patron saint, la **fête patronale**, also known as *messti* (Bas-Rhin), and *kilwe* or *kilbe* (Haut-Rhin) in local dialect. Folk dancing and traditional costumes enliven the festivities. Ribeauvillé has held its especially popular fair in early September for centuries.

Anne Gaël

Many seasonal traditions would seem very familiar to a visitor from the United Kingdom or North America: brightly lit and sparkling trees, red and green ribbons, gingerbread men, and markets full of "stocking stuffers" in December; carnival celebrated with doughnuts; Easter which brings a rabbit who hides coloured eggs in the garden.

Legends often surround lakes, rivers, and the romantic ruins of castles. There are religious legends as well, often remembered in traditional ceremonies like the one held in Thann every 30 June, when three pines are set afire. While the realm of legend sometimes reflects aspects of reality and history, the advantage here is that good always conquers and evil is inevitably punished. The characters in these legends are knights and ladies, monks and beggars, saints and demons, gnomes and giants.

The most famous legend in Alsace may be the story of **Mont Ste-Odile**. The patron saint of Alsace (Odilia, Ottilia and other variations are found) was the daughter of Duke Adalric; she founded a nunnery on a mountain around the year 700 and was its first abbess. From these historical facts, a legend has grown, which recounts the birth of a blind Odile, rejected by her father, and spirited away to safety by her mother. By this account, Odile, now a beautiful young woman, was baptised by St Erhard, her uncle, and miraculously recovered her sight. Her father decided to marry her off, despite the girl's religious vocation, and he pursued her through the forest as she ran from the

---

The Legend of the Lac du Ballon

Long ago, a green meadow lay like an emerald in the blue velvet folds of the Vosges Forest, below the majestic Grand Ballon. The field belonged to a man who earned his living making charcoal, a *charbonnier*. A covetous bourgeois from the Guebwiller Valley tried to buy the field, and when the collier refused, he bribed a local judge into forcing the forfeit of the land.

The proud new owner arrived with a fancy golden wagon to cut the fragrant hay, and he passed by the collier's simple dwelling with a smug, victorious grin. The wronged man shook his fist, and called on Providence to render the justice which the courts of law had denied him.

Suddenly, a menacing gloom came upon the sky and a violent storm erupted in the high mountains, followed by a downpour so heavy it cut off all sight like a thick dark curtain. When the light returned, a round lake appeared in the place of the field, its deep waters covering the bourgeois, his wagon and horses.

As you gaze on the lake, remember the French proverb: *Charbonnier est maître chez soi* ("even a charcoal-burner is master in his own house"). Every man's home is his castle.

53

fate he had devised for her. Suddenly, a rock opened up and enfolded her, protectin
Odile from the duke. From that rock, a sacred spring came forth. Adalric got th
message and built her a convent instead.

Many pilgrims came to visit the holy woman. It is said that, upon encountering a sic
man dying of thirst, Odile struck the ground with her cane and brought forth a spring
He drank and was cured; many people came to pray at the site and wash their eye
with the curative water. Her intercession is still sought after by those with diseases c
the eye.

LORRAINE

The traditional emblem of Lorraine is the **Croix de Lorraine**, a cross with two horizonta
arms, the shorter one above the longer. It appeared on coins minted by the dukes o
Lorraine, made famous by General de Gaulle who took it for his personal standard
and is found on everything from biscuit tins to postage stamps. Its origins can b
traced to the kingdom of Hungary, which used such a cross as its coat of arms. Whe
the Árpád dynasty expired, a series of Angevin kings came to power, beginning with
Robert of Anjou (1308-42). Ultimately, René II inherited the title from the dukes o
Anjou and brought the emblem to his duchy of Lorraine. In 1477, the cross blazed on
banners rallying the people to the Battle of Nancy, and from that time on it has been
known as the Lorraine Cross. In an amusing reminder of days long past, when the
Metz football club faced off against Slovakian adversaries, both teams' uniforms bore
the emblem!

St Nicholas has also held a special place in the hearts of the people of Lorraine since
the days of the Holy Roman Empire. With his bishop's mitre and back pack full o
toys, he travels Lorraine on the night of 5-6 December. The patron saint of the regior
is celebrated in all the towns and villages with festive lights and parades. The beautifu
Flamboyant church of St-Nicolas-de-Port was the site of many pilgrimages; the town
was once one of the liveliest in Lorraine.

The countryside around Remiremont is reported to be populated by a variety of **fairies**
Some of the local place names give a good indication of this (the French word for fairy
is *fée*): Château-des-Fées on the Fays plateau; Pont-des-Fées (or "Fairies' Bridge") –
there is one in Saint-Étienne-les-Remiremont and another across the Vologne (a
tributary of the Moselle which comes down the mountains from Retournemer Lake);
Grottes-des-Fées ("Fairies' Cave"); numerous other names of caves, streams and rocks
refer to legends of the diminutive beings with magic powers.

There are fairy bakers and pastry chefs, who make delicious treats in their lairs and
send the sweet aroma out to lonely shepherds or field workers. Some have even
reported finding lovely cakes laid out on a white cloth, which they enjoyed without any
ill effects. Other fairies have a mean streak, such as the laundress fairy, **Fée Herqueuche**,
a scaggle-tooth hag, with her bald head under a straw hat and rags on her skinny
body. She washes witches' clothes at night, and tramples the clean work of honest
washerwomen with her dirty feet.

CHAMPAGNE-ARDENNE

In this region, as elsewhere in France, recent years have seen a renewed interest in
ancestral traditions, including religious and pagan festivities and activities related to
daily life in the countryside (harvest, crafts, family celebrations etc).

Carnival costume parades are coming back in style in many towns and villages where
the custom had nearly died out. Around the textile centre of Sedan, costumes were
commonly made from canvas sacks used to hold spools of yarn; five or six people
would climb into one and forwardly march along broadside. Near Mézières, carnival-
goers stick their heads through the rungs of a horizontal ladder draped with white
cloth and pop out one or several burlesque faces at a time. Popular games are
blindfold races, horseshoe throwing, wheelbarrow races, with the loser buying a round
at the nearest café.

At nightfall, the crowd gathers round for the bonfire. A procession through the streets
bears a sort of scarecrow who, from village to village, may be named Nicolas,
Christophe, Joseph or Pansard, and may be dressed as a ragged beggar or a bri-
degroom. As the carnival figure burns and sparks fly up, dancing and singing mark the
end of the festive day. In some places, the ashes from the fire are believed to have
special powers, or bring good luck, especially to young couples.

Although Mardi Gras is associated with the Christian rite, the carnival has well-
documented pagan origins and is clearly associated with chasing out winter and
preparing for spring.

A funny tradition still observed in villages is the May Day *charivari*. Young rascals band
together on the eve of 1 May and spend the dark night going from house to house,
where they quietly make off with anything that isn't nailed down or locked up:
ladders, barrows, benches, rakes … The whole lot is then piled up on the main square,
where everyone gathers the next morning, to laugh or complain according to temper,
and to recover the goods.

LIFE IN THE COUNTRYSIDE

Villages – Most of the people living outside main urban centres live fairly close to their neighbours in villages. This has been the custom since the first settlers arrived. Rather than a response to a perceived need for protection, this pattern is more likely a result of communal farming and forestry techniques.

In **Alsace**, the houses in a village are generally detached from one another, and may even be facing in different directions. Some villages are little more than a group of farmhouses around a belfry. Traces of a more glorious past may remain: a ruined castle rising above the roof line, a lovely church in an otherwise unremarkable place. In any case, one of the most conspicuous features of the Alsatian village is the care the inhabitants take to keep their doorways swept, windows sparkling, and geraniums in bloom.

In **Lorraine**, the houses in the village are generally attached, and stand along both sides of the street in an orderly row. Often, there is an entranceway wide enough to accommodate a tractor or wagon, and a smaller doorway into the building itself. The large entrance opens onto the farmyard, and often the farm extends far back beyond the main house, with the usual collection of buildings and equipment scattered about. Nowadays, most inhabitants reserve the small front yard for a flower garden.

On the dry plain of **Champagne**, sizeable villages grew up around fresh water springs, often quite far from one another. While the streets are narrow and confined, through an open gate you may glimpse a spacious courtyard with neatly kept buildings holding presses and other equipment needed to maintain and harvest grapes. In the southern part of the region, around Bar-sur-Aube, Bar-sur-Seine, Langres and the Blaise Valley, villages can be seen from afar as the buildings are predominantly made of bright white limestone. In the Argonne Forest, the linear look of houses lined up along the road is reminiscent of neighbouring Lorraine.

Houses and farms – While houses and farms in rural **Alsace** have many things in common, there are also many subtle differences from one area to another. Gables, the colour, shape and disposition of timbers, the materials, patterns and embellishments used to fill in the frame vary from north to south. In the **vineyard** region, the ground floor, in stone, is used for pressing grapes and storing wine. An outside stair leads to the living areas above. The Ecomusée *(page 119)* is a good place to see various building techniques.

In a typical **Lorraine** village, the older buildings have gently sloping roofs covered with a kind of hollow tile. The traditional farmhouse held the living area, barn and stables under one roof. The limestone walls are coated to preserve the mortar joints.

The **Champagne** region is home to many winegrowers. Their houses are typically low, made of millstone, local chalk-stone or brick. In **"dry" Champagne**, the farmyards are generally bordered by the living area (facing the street), the barn (facing the fields) and other buildings for animals. In the southeast, half-timbering appears, filled in with blocks of chalk-stone or tuffy-stone covered with plaster. In the greener or **"wet" Champagne**, timbers are cut from pine and poplar, held with cross beams and daub, or earthen bricks.

Chavanges – Half-timbered house in Champagne

De Laubier/PIX

Around **Troyes**, brick is commonly used in decorative patterns between the timbers. A traditional dwelling in the **Argonne** Forest has a dark brick façade on the ground floor and a roughcast plaster storey above. The flat tiles of the roof extend out over the sides of the house.

The region of **Ardenne** is rich in schist and quartzite stone, often used for building; the blue slate quarried here is of excellent quality. These materials make the houses rather gloomy looking. To defeat the rigours of winter, all of the farm buildings are close together, making for a single, long building, in contrast to the rectangular courtyard with outbuildings seen in more clement neighbouring areas.

Language and literature

ALSATIAN DIALECT

"His tongue is German, but his sword is French." Thus did Napoleon Bonaparte describe General Jean-François Kléber, a native of Strasbourg who held a prominent position in Bonaparte's Egyptian campaign. In fact, Alsatians do not speak German, but rather an Alemannic dialect which evolved from High German, as did the modern German language spoken in Germany, Austria and parts of Switzerland today. Of course, the influence of the French language has been felt over time, distancing the dialect even further from its origins.

Over time, as the region was controlled by French or German authority, one or the other language was imposed as the official language used in schools and by the administration. As in other corners of the world, distinct regional dialects were not recognised until recently, and years of neglect (and outright repression) have taken their toll. Interest in local history in all of France's regions was renewed as the events of 1968 shook up conventional cultural values. Since that time, the Alsatian dialect has received official recognition and is no longer forbidden in the schoolyard; volumes of poetry and books of popular songs and tales are displayed in bookstores.

LITERATURE IN ALSACE-LORRAINE

In this border region, literary tradition has three expressions: French, German and dialect. German works represent the oldest, most prestigious tradition. The **Renaissance Humanism** and the **Reform** marked the golden age of Alsatian literature. Gutenberg worked on developing his printing press in Strasbourg before getting it up and running in Mainz. The wonderful collection of the Humanist library in Sélestat is testimony to the regional attachment to the written word. The German author Goethe lived in Strasbourg in 1770-71, a memorable time because it marked the beginning of the so-called *Sturm und Drang* ("storm and stress") movement. This style of literature exalted nature, feelings and human individualism, and was strongly influenced by the ideas of French author Jean-Jacques Rousseau, and by the works of Shakespeare which had just been translated.

The **20C** was marked by the upheavals of war. German literature was still most prevalent, but by the end of the First World War, numerous works had been published in dialect, certainly in response to the need to express cultural identity in a region caught in the middle of a terrible power struggle. Between the wars, the French language got a foothold and today it is the language most commonly heard and used.

CHAMPAGNE: CRADLE OF FRENCH LITERATURE

In the **12C**, Champagne was home to many authors writing in the emerging French language. Bertrand de Bar-sur-Aube is reputed to have composed *Aimeri de Narbonne*, the best-known chapter of the ballad of William of Orange (later to inspire Victor Hugo). Chrestien de Troyes (c 1135-c 1183) wrote tales of chivalry based on the legends of Brittany, including the characters Lancelot and Perceval. The search for the Holy Grail and the Crusades inspired Geoffroy de Villehardouin (1150-1213), who wrote about his adventures in *History of the Conquest of Constantinople*. Another medieval bard, Jean, Sire de Joinville, described travelling to Egypt with St Louis (1309). The Count of Champagne, Thibaud IV, crowned king of Navarre in 1234, preferred to pen poetry, whereas his countryman Ruteboeuf entertained with biting satires of the church, the university and tradesmen.

In the **17C**, **Paul de Gondi cardinal de Retz** (1613-1679), took time out from politics (as a leader of the rebellion known as the *Fronde*) to note down his favourite maxims. After his retirement, he wrote his *Mémoires*, considered a classic of 17C French literature.

Another major figure from the century was **Jean de la Fontaine**, celebrated for his *Fables*. Born in a bourgeois family in Château-Thierry, he married a local heiress in 1647, but separated from her 11 years later. An outstanding feature of his character was his life-long ability to attract wealthy patrons, thus freeing himself from the pedestrian worries of earning a living so he could devote his time to writing 12 books of fables and other works. The first collection of six books is based on the Aesopic tradition, whereas the second takes its inspiration from East Asian stories. His use of animal characters is a light-hearted ploy for expressing the everyday moral experience of humankind; his poetic technique has been called the exquisite quintessence of the preceding century of French literature. La Fontaine's *Fables* continue to form part of the culture of every French schoolchild, and his reputation has lost none of its glow.

The **18C** brought bold thinkers to the fore. In 1713, the philosopher, **Denis Diderot**, was born in Langres. His early life was a time of financial and religious crisis. He studied law, aspired to be an actor, wrote sermons for missionaries for a miserable wage and considered an ecclesiastical career. Over time, he progressed from his Roman Catholic faith to deism and finally atheism and philosophical materialism. In 1745 he was

Fables of La Fontaine

The Cicada and the Ant

The Cobbler and the Financier

The Two Friends

The Heron

The Frog Who Would be
as Big as an Ox

The Bear
and the Lover of Gardening

engaged to translate the *Cylopaedia*, authored by Ephraim Chambers, but he soo made radical changes in the work. Working with a team of authors including scholar scientists and priests, he created the *Encyclopédie*, a "rational dictionary" which co ered the basic premises and contemporary applications of all arts and sciences. Hi unconventional views landed him in prison, but neither incarceration nor censorshi prevented him from carrying on with the work, although the later volumes wer published in secret. When the *Encyclopédie* was completed in 1772, Diderot was lef without an income. The patronage of Catherine the Great of Russia provided for hir in his old age. As his friends and contemporaries left this life, he retired into his famil circle. His last words were: "The first step towards philosophy is incredulity."

Diderot was well-acquainted with another 18C luminary, **Voltaire** (pseudonym of Fran çois-Marie Arouet). Although his classical tragedies for the stage were popularl acclaimed, when Voltaire turned his talents to satire (of the Regency and establishe religion), he met the same fate as Diderot, imprisonment. After his release, a quarre with a nobleman resulted in a two-year exile to England, where he mastered the language and enjoyed the company of Alexander Pope, Jonathan Swift, William Con greve and even Queen Caroline. Upon his return to France, Voltaire found refuge i Champagne in the château of Mme du Châtelet in Cirey-sur-Blaise. They lived a lif both studious and passionate, translating Newton, conducting experiments in thei laboratory, travelling and frequenting high society. She died in childbirth in 1749 ending their complex relationship of 15 years, and leaving her lover bereft.

Voltaire's most famous work is probably *Candide* (1758), a satirical masterpiece o philosophical optimism. His long life spanned the waning of classicism and the dawn o revolution; his ideas and actions had a significant influence on the evolution o European civilization. In particular, his letters stand as a testimony to his defence o clear thinking in a world where complications seek to defeat us at every turn.

The **19C** and **20C** produced two figures whose memory has been perpetuated by modern-day songwriters and film directors: **Paul Verlaine** and **Arthur Rimbaud**.

Verlaine was born in Metz in 1844, Rimbaud 10 years later in Charleville. The older poet was from a comfortable background, the well-educated son of an army officer; the younger was raised in poverty by his mother and yet distinguished himself as a gifted student. After graduating with honours from the Lycée Bonaparte, Verlaine became a clerk in an insurance company, then a civil servant. His early work was published in respectable literary reviews; he married and had a son. During the Franco-Prussian War, he was the press officer for the Paris insurgents of the *Commune*. Meanwhile, Rimbaud, a restless and despondent soul, lived on the streets of the capital in squalor, reading everything he could get his hands on — including the "immoral" poetry of Baudelaire and works on the occult — and shaping his own poetic philosophy.

In 1871 the two met, moved to London and carried on a scandalous affair. While Verlaine vacillated between decadent thrills and anguished repentance, Rimbaud was seen as his friend's evil helmsman on their *Drunken Boat*. In 1873, a violent quarrel in Brussels ended with Rimbaud shot in the wrist and Verlaine in prison for 18 months. Rimbaud, both distraught and exhilarated, feverishly completed *A Season in Hell: ... As for me, I am intact, and I don't care.*

By his 20th birthday, Rimbaud had given up writing and turned to gunrunning in Africa. In 1891, his right leg was amputated, and he died the same year. He has been cited as an inspiration by many, in particular the Beat poets, Jim Morrison, Bob Dylan and Patti Smith.

Verlaine, released from prison, became a devout Catholic and moved to England where he taught French. In 1877, he returned to France and began writing the series of poems to be published as *Sagesse* ("Wisdom" — or perhaps, simply "wising up"). Further heartbreak (the deaths of a favourite student and the poet's mother) and a failure to reconcile with his wife drove Verlaine back to drink, but sympathetic friends encouraged him to continue writing and publishing, and supported him financially. His significant body of work marks a transition between the Romantic poets and the Symbolists.

The Quotable Voltaire

In this best of all possible worlds ... all is for the best. — Dr Pangloss in Candide

The secret of being a bore is to tell everything.

Love truth, but pardon error.

History is no more than a portrayal of crimes and misfortunes.

Thought depends absolutely on the stomach, but in spite of that, those who have the best stomachs are not the best thinkers.

I disapprove of what you say, but I will defend to the death your right to say it.

Regional cuisine

ALSACE-LORRAINE

Charcuteries – Ham and Strasbourg sausages are featured in the classic *assiette Alsacienne*, an array of pork meats; but *foies gras* (fattened livers) hold pride of place. This delicacy has been appreciated since the Roman era; in 1778 a young local chef, Jean-Pierre Clause, created the prototype goose liver *pâté en croûte* (wrapped in a crust). Today there are over 40 variations on his theme on sale in local delicatessens. In Lorraine, traditional dishes are loaded with butter, bacon and cream. **Potée** is a pot roast made with salt pork and sausages, white cabbage and other vegetables. Of course, **Quiche Lorraine** is famous fare: a creamy pie made with beaten eggs, thick cream and bacon bits. Pâté from Lorraine is made from veal and pork.

Choucroute – Strasbourg is the capital of this cabbage-based speciality made with white Alsatian wine. The savoury white cabbage is heaped with sausages, pork chops, bacon, ham; occasionally a bit of partridge, a few crayfish or a truffle find their way in. It is best enjoyed with a big glass of beer or a good regional wine.

Fish and fowl – Chicken dishes are popular in Alsace, and menus often list *coq* and *poularde* (pullet hen), served with mushroom and cream sauce; local *coq au vin* is made with Riesling wine. Fresh trout from mountain streams is a delicious treat, in cream or Riesling sauce. Other local fish recipes are eels stewed in wine sauce (*matelote*), fried carp, pike and salmon.

Choucroute

H. Amiard/TOP

Les marcaireries – Dairy farmers and cheese makers in the Vosges are known as *marcaires*. Traditionally, they take their herds up to the high pasturelands (*chaumes*) on 25 May (the old feast day of St Urbain), and bring them down again on 29 September. Nowadays, farms which serve country fare to travellers may be called by the more usual French name of *ferme-auberge*, but the local traditions remain the same.

Munster and Géromé – The perfect way to polish off an Alsatian meal is with one of these two cheeses which are only made in the Vosges. Munster is an unpasteurised, soft fermented cheese, which many enjoy with a dash of cumin. It was first made in these mountains in the 15C, and is a significant source of income for mountain-dwellers.
On the Lorraine side, Géromé – a word in dialect which means "from Gérardmer" – also has a long-standing reputation. It is made with unheated whole milk to which rennet (for solidifying) is added immediately. The cheese is aged for four months in a cool cellar until the crust turns russet and the interior is creamy. Cumin, aniseed or fennel seeds may be served with a portion.

Pastries – There are as many different tarts in Alsace as there are fruits to make them with. Any chef is proud to pull a perfect **Kugelhopf** out of the oven, a delightful puff of flour, butter, eggs, sweetened milk, raisins and almonds. Other special desserts are *macarons de Boulay* (dainty biscuits of egg whites and almonds), *madeleines de Commercy* (soft, buttery cakes), *bergamotes de Nancy* (hard sweets flavoured with citrus rind).
Waffles *(gaufres)* were traditionally made at carnival time in irons forged with unique designs, both religious and profane. Hot waffles sprinkled with sugar or dripping with chocolate are still a popular treat, but the old-fashioned irons are now rare collector's items. **Meringues** were first served in France at the table of Duke Stanislas, in Nancy.

Beer – Breweries abound in Alsace (Schiltigheim, Strasbourg, Hochfelden, Obernai, Saverne) – *(for information on tours see Practical information, page 372)*; Stenay is home to the Beer Museum; the Brewery Museum is in St-Nicolas-de-Port. Beer has always been made from the same elements: pure water, barley, hops and yeast. Barley transforms into malt, giving colour and flavour; hops provide the bitterness. Each brewery cultivates its own yeast, which gives each brand its distinctive taste.
Beer has been enjoyed since Antiquity: Egyptians called it "liquid bread"; Hippocrates defended its use as a therapeutic medicine. Today, beer production starts with the reduction of malt to flour, the addition of water, and heating at a low temperature.

While the mixture is stirred, the starch contained in the grain turns to sugar. I another tank, non-malted grain such as corn is prepared in the same way. The tw tanks are mixed into a **mash**, which is filtered to become the **stock** or **wort**. The hop are added to the **wort kettle** where the mixture is heated, then filtered again. Fer mentation takes place at temperatures between 5-10°C/40-50°F. Pasteurisation make the final product more stable, and industrial chilling enables year-round production Beer leaves the brew house and has yeast added to it, which turns the sugar int alcohol over two weeks, in large tanks kept at low temperatures. The yeast i removed after maturation: a final filtration and it's ready for the bottle.

CHAMPAGNE-ARDENNE

Champagne – Savoury sauces, rich meats and fresh produce are the ingredients o fine cuisine in the region. Sauces made with Champagne garnish many recipes fo chicken, pullet, thrush, kidneys, stuffed trout, grilled pike, crayfish and snails. Smokec ham and sausage are used in *potée champenoise*, a popular dish at grape harvest time served with mounds of fresh cabbage, a vegetable which is at its prime in the fall Brenne-le-Château has its own recipe for choucroute, Troyes is celebrated for it *andouillettes* sausage and Ste-Menehould is famous for dishing out pigs feet anc mashed potatoes.
In the *pays d'Othe* region, sometimes called "little Normandy", apple orchards, though less numerous today than in the past, still produce fruit for making sparkling cider although nowadays it is more of a hobby than an industry.

Ardenne – The isolation of this region has contributed to the conservation of loca traditions. The cuisine is hearty and fortifying, based on natural products found in the wooded hills. Game and fish are prominent on the menu: young boar, venison, rabbit with *sauce chasseur*; woodcock and thrush roasted in sage leaves or served *en terrine* with juniper berries; rich pâtés of marinated veal and pork meats.
Smoked ham cured over juniper or broomwood and boudin sausages are on display in local *charcuteries*.
Salads made with fresh wild greens are flavoured with *crétons* or *fritons*, local terms for crunchy bacon bits. A menu offering plain country fare may feature *baïenne*, a satisfying dish of potatoes, onions and garlic.

Cheese from Champagne

Cheese – South of Troyes, the region has specialised in the production of creamy cheeses such as Chaource, which are only slightly aged. This cheese has been served at the best tables since the 12C. It can be enjoyed within five days after it is set out *(frais)* or may be left to firm up for about 20 days *(fait)*. Firmer cheese may be covered with a thin film of white mould. Some other regional cheeses are varieties of **Cendré**, with a powdery dusting of grey ash (Châlons-en-Cham-pagne, les Riceys and the Marne Valley). **Maroille** is a fragrant cheese from Thié-rache which is usually enjoyed at harvest time. **Mostafait** is a white cream cheese blended with butter and tarragon. **Rocroi** is from the town of the same name; **Igny** shares its name with the Trappist monastery that produces it; **Troyen** is a regional cheese that resembles Camembert.

Pastries – At carnival time, doughnuts are a festive treat, variously known as *frivoles* or *fiverolles* or *crottes d'âne* ("donkey turds"!). At Easter, little tarts *(dariolles)* are filled with a flan mixture made from milk and eggs. Gingerbread is still made with a reliable recipe from the 13C.
In Reims, many varities of delicate biscuits are served with Champagne: *massepains, croquignols, bouchons*.
In the Ardenne region, crêpes are called *vautes* or *tantimolles*; hard sugar biscuits are served with coffee; soft cakes served at wedding banquets were sometimes baked with a silver ring inside, for luck. Blueberry pie is delicious in the summer, and at Christmas time there are many sorts of seasonal sweets, including little red candy animals.

Wine and Champagne

VINS D'ALSACE

The vineyards of Alsace stretch from Thann to Wissembourg, over about 100km/60mi, but the main area to explore starts just south of Marlenheim, where travellers join the famous **Route des Vins** *(see the chapter in Sights for touring advice)*. The route meanders through a sea of grape vines and many winegrowing villages; all devoted to the production of wine. The most exciting time to visit is certainly the fall, when the harvest is in full swing and the leaves are vivid red. The eastern foothills of the Vosges are well exposed, and the climate is sunny and mild.

Varieties – The wines of Alsace are identified, not by geographical area, but by grape variety. **Riesling** is a bright star in the constellation of white grape varieties. Most of the wine produced in the valley of the Rhine River valley is made from these grapes, which create a sophisticated, subtle bouquet.

Gewürztraminer is a heady, fragrant wine with an intense bouquet.

The wine to choose if you wish to quench a thirst is **Sylvaner**, dry and light, with a fruity note.

Pinot blanc wines are generally considered well-balanced, with a fresh and supple character.

Pinot gris, called **Tokay Pinot gris**, is a distinguished grape which produces opulent, full-bodied wine.

The flavour of fresh grapes has a strong presence in **Muscat d'Alsace**.

The only red variety is **Pinot noir**. These grapes have grown in popularity in recent years, and go into fruity rosé or red wines marked by a cherry aroma and taste. The red wines are firmer and more complex than the rosés.

Edelzwicker is the name given to the only wine made from a blend of varieties, including the less noble Chasselas.

Vin d'Alsace is an *Appellation d'Origine Contrôlée*, and is always bottled in the region of production. It is generally served in a round glass with a thin green stem. Most Alsace wines are best when fairly young (one to five years after harvest), and should be chilled.

Before a meal, a sparkling Crémant or sweet Muscat is a good apéritif; Sylvaner goes well with assorted cold cuts served as a starter. Riesling or Pinot accompany fish, fowl, meats and, of course, choucroute. Flavourful cheeses and desserts do well with the rich aroma of Gewürztraminer.

Eaux-de-vie – Cherries, mirabelles and raspberries are used to make sweet liqueurs: kirsche in the Vosges, quetsch and mirabelle in Lorraine. Clear raspberry liqueur is served in a snifter to increase the pleasure of the aroma. The **musée des Eaux-de-vie** in Lapoutroie shows how such liqueurs were traditionally made.

CHAMPAGNE

A long and prestigious past – When Roman soldiers arrived in Champagne, grapes were already cultivated on the slopes. The first bishops of Reims encouraged this activity; vineyards flourished around monasteries and the many travellers attending trade fares or coming to the royal court boosted sales. Even the popes favoured Champagne, starting with Urbain II, a native of the region. During the Renaissance, Pope Leon X had his own vineyard to keep him supplied. St Bernard, in Clairvaux, introduced the Arbanne stock, which created the basis for Côte des Bars vintages.

Champagne has been called the "nectar of the gods" and the "wine of kings". Henri IV, impatient with the Spanish ambassador's recitation of his master's aristocratic titles, interrupted him by saying, "Tell His Majesty the King of Spain, Castille and Aragon that Henri, lord of Ay and Gonesse, is master of the greatest vineyards in the world ..."

At that time, Champagne was a still wine with only a hint of sparkle. That sparkle caught the eye of **Dom Pérignon**, who carefully studied the wine's characteristics and developed blending. The popularity of Champagne grew throughout the centuries, admired and imbibed by kings and their courts and figures of romance such as Mme de Pompadour and Casanova.

Political revolutions came and went, but Champagne remained. Napoleon was a faithful client, and Tallyrand plied the participants at the Congress of Vienna with Champagne in hopes of gaining a better settlement. The Prince of Wales, the future Edward VII, speaking of the Most Honourable Order of the Bath, is reputed to have said, "I'd rather have a bath of Champagne."

The vineyards – The vineyards cover about 30 000ha/74 130 acres, in the *départements* of Marne, Aube and Aisne. The most famous areas of production are the Côte des Blancs, the Marne Valley and the Montagne de Reims, where the great vintages originate. The grapes grow half-way up the limestone slopes, above the chalky bedrock and in the sandy clay soil of the Côte de l'Île de France. The only varieties allowed are Pinot noir, Pinot Meunier and Chardonnay; the vines are planted close together and pruned low.

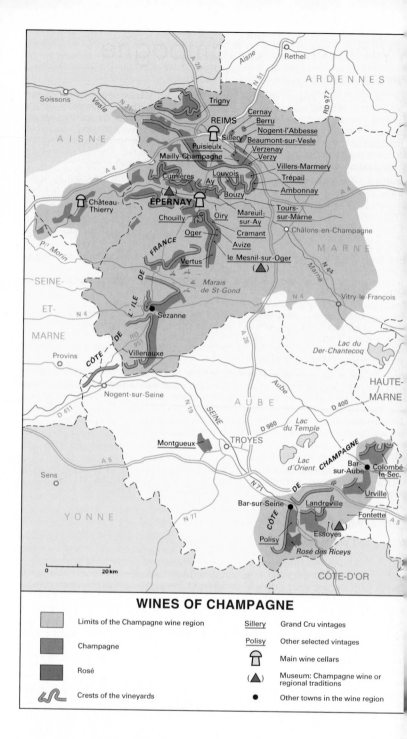

WINES OF CHAMPAGNE

▨	Limits of the Champagne wine region
▨	Champagne
▨	Rosé
∿	Crests of the vineyards

<u>Sillery</u>   Grand Cru vintages

<u>Polisy</u>   Other selected vintages

⌂   Main wine cellars

(▲)   Museum: Champagne wine or regional traditions

●   Other towns in the wine region

A delicate process – Champagne is created through a series of carefully executed steps which take place in the vineyards and in the cellars, where a steady temperature of about 10°C/50°F must be maintained.

Harvest – In October, bunches of grapes are picked and set down in flat trays; they are sorted and carried to the press.

Pressing – The whole grapes are pressed, which results in a white must, even when dark grapes are used. Only the juice obtained by the first pressing (about 2 550l/660gal from 4 000kg/8 800lb of grapes) is used to make true Champagne wine.

Fermentation – The juice is stored in barrels or vats and fermentation is underway by Christmas.

intage and blend – In the spring, the *maître de chais* creates the vintage by blending different still wines, produced by various vineyards in various years. Each Champagne house has its own vintage which respects quality standards. Blendings include wines from the Montagne de Reims (hearty, full-bodied), the Marne Valley (fruity, aromatic wines), the Côte de Blancs (fresh, elegant wines) and the Côte des Bars. Red and white grapes are used in proportions which may vary but are generally about 2/3 to 1/3. Blanc e Blancs sparkling wine is made with only white grapes. Exceptionally, although ever more frequently, Champagne labels bear the vintage year, when the blending includes nly wines of the same year.

econd fermentation and foam – The second fermentation is brought about by adding sugar and selected yeasts to the wine. The wine is drawn and put in very thick bottles which withstand pressure. Under the effects of the yeast (in the form of powder collected from the grape skins), the sugar is transformed into alcohol or carbonised into gas which, when the bottle is uncorked, creates foam. The bottles are set on racks in a cellar for 15 months to three years and sometimes more.

ettling and removing sediment – Over time, a deposit forms and must be eliminated. It is forced to settle in the bottle neck by storing the bottles at an angle, upside down. Each day, one person alone gives a slight turn (1/8 rotation) to as many as 40 000 bottles, and adjusts them for gradually increasing verticality. After five or six weeks, the bottle is fully vertical and all of the sediment has settled around the cork. The cork is then removed and the sediment with it. This process is called *dégorgement*. The bottle is topped off with more of the same wine, which may have had sugar added to make the final product sweeter.

inishing – The corks need to be wired down to contain the pressure of the gas within; then the bottle can be labelled and shipped. Champagne which is already three or four years old will not improve any more in the bottle and should be consumed.

Marketing – Nearly 120 Champagne houses, mostly family-owned, and many dating back to the 18C, produce 70% of all Champagne shipped, with the remaining 30% in the hands of *récoltants-manipulants*, who blend their own wine; there are a few co-operatives as well. Financial backing is necessary for successful operations, because Champagne must be stored – and cared for – for an average of three years before it can be marketed, and thus involves keeping a lot of stock on hand.

Every year, more and more Champagne leaves the region for sale elsewhere. In 1995, over 246 million bottles were shipped; sales projections include 110 million bottles for export outside of France. Production of the region's sparkling wine accounts for just four percent of total French wine production, but in 1997, Champagne generated about 33% of France's $4 billion in earnings from wine exports.

A Merry Widow

Veuve Clicquot-Ponsardin is one of France's best known and best-selling brands of Champagne. The eponymous origin is indeed a *Grande Dame*, Nicole-Barbe Ponsardin. In 1798, she married François Clicquot in a Champagne cellar (the churches had not yet been restored for worship after the Revolution); he left her a widow eight years later. Twenty-seven years old, with a baby daughter and almost no experience in the trade, she took over the family Champagne house, and ran the business until her death in 1866.

She revolutionised the art of blending *(assemblage)* when she developed the technique known as *remuage*. Previously, the wine had to be decanted into new bottles after the second fermentation, an inefficient process which was necessary to remove the sediment, but which reduced precious effervescence. Nowadays, using her technique, the bottles are twisted and tilted so that the dregs settle around the cork, which can then be popped open briefly. A small bit of wine is removed *(dégorgement)*, then the bottle is quickly topped off.

"Champagne", wrote Madame de Pompadour, "is the only wine which leaves a woman beautiful after drinking it. It gives brilliance to the eyes without flushing the face." Good news for merry-makers!

Mulhouse – Hôtel de ville

Sights

ALTKIRCH

Population 5090
Michelin map 87 fold 19 or 242 fold 39

The old town is perched on a hilltop overlooking the Ill Valley. The first settlement wa
established in the valley, then Altkirch was rebuilt on the hilltop at the end of the 12
and belonged successively to the counts of Ferrette *(see p 297)* and the House c
Austria before being ceded to France as a result of the Peace of Westphalia (1648).

SIGHTS

Place de la République – A modern fountain in neo-15C style stands in the centr
of the square; its slender pinnacle shelters a statue of the Virgin Mary, which is a
that remains of the former church.

Hôtel de ville – The town hall dates from the 18C.
On the right stands the bailiff's former residence, adorned with a wrought-iro
balcony, which now houses the Sundgau Museum.

Musée sundgauvien ⊙ – The Sundgau Museum contains collections devoted to th
region's history, archeology and folklore, as well as paintings by local artists (Henne
Lehmann), some fine statues and a model of Altkirch in the past.

Église Notre-Dame – The church was built during the 19C in neo-Romanesqu
style; the north transept contains the remarkable polychrome stone statues of th
"Mont des Oliviers" (Mount of Olives) and a copy of Prud'hon's *Christ* by Henner. I
the south transept, a painting by Oster of Strasbourg depicting St Morand, th
patron saint of Sundgau, being welcomed by the count of Ferrette, hangs above
17C Pietà.

EXCURSIONS

Luemschwiller – *7km/4.3mi northeast towards Mulhouse then right along a coun
try road.*
The village **church** ⊙ houses a beautiful altarpiece, carved and painted in the 15C
the painted wings depict scenes from the life of the Virgin Mary whereas th
carved central panel represents the Virgin between St Barbe and St Catherine.

★Sundgau – *see SUNDGAU.*

AMNÉVILLE

Population 8 926
Michelin map 57 fold 3, 241 fold 20 or 242 folds 5, 9

Access – *Drive along A 31, leave at Hagondange or Mondelange then follow A 4 t
Semécourt Amnéville-les-Thermes.*

Situated at the heart of the Coulange Forest, covering 500ha/1236 acres, this recentl
created spa town has two main assets: a quality environment and good touris
facilities.

Birth of a spa – During the late 1970s, Amnéville was hit hard by the recessio
suffered by the steel industry and the decision was taken for the town to abandon it
industrial tradition and, like its neighbour Hagondange *(see Walibi Schtroumpf p 174*
turn to the service industry. The discovery 900m/2953ft below ground of ferruginou
water at a temperature of 41°C/105.8°F and with therapeutic qualities (for rheuma
tism, traumas and respiratory complaints) pointed to the new activity the town shoul
launch into. The spa centre, opened in 1986, rapidly attracted patients and a
important leisure centre developed around it; it comprises an Olympic-size swimmin
pool and ice-skating rink, a golf course, a casino, a 12 000-seat theatre, a fitnes
centre, known as **Thermapolis**, and an attractive zoo.

★Parc zoologique du bois de Coulange ⊙ – About 900 animals representin
almost 160 different species from various zoos roam around in pens spread abou
a forested area covering 8ha/20 acres. The zoo is committed to internationa
programmes intended to protect endangered species such as the small panda, th
hyena-dog (much feared by plant-eating mammals), the extremely agile spide
monkey, the impressive-looking mandrill and a colony of penguins. There are als
many magnificent big cats: tigers from Siberia and Sumatra, lions from the Atla
mountains, panthers from Iran (there are only 50 wild specimens left), the snov
leppard endangered by its beautiful coat, the strangely graceful serval... A family c
hippopotami, the American buffalo, a reminder of the conquest of the Far Wes
the facetious rhesus monkey from Nepal (the first monkey to have travelled int
space), free-roaming emus hanging on to visitors who are kind to them, are a
equally captivating.

The **Vivarium tropical** houses 200 reptiles in an area covering 1 000m²/1196sq yd where their natural environment has been recreated; crocodiles include a male measuring 4.5m/15ft and weighing 500kg/2 205lb, caymans, varans, water lizards, pythons, anacondas and other snakes.

Penguinland stages a water ballet enacted by otters and penguins moving about underwater.

Audio-visual shows provide more information about the animal world.

Aquarium impérator – Located 300m/328yd from the zoo, this aquarium offers an insight into some aspects of the tropical underwater world: there are species of fish and corals from the Caribbean, other species found only in Australian rivers or in the Amazon Valley, fauna native of Lake Malawi and Lake Tanganika... Several species of sharks share a huge tank.

ANDLAU★

Population 1 632
Michelin map 87 fold 16 or 242 fold 27 – Local map see ROUTE DES VINS

This small flower-decked town, nestling in the green valley of the Andlau River, has retained some old houses and the church of a once-famous monastery. The ridge to the north is crowned with the ruins of the Château du Haut-Andlau *(see p 147)*.

Andlau Abbey – The abbey was founded in 880 by Richarde, the wife of Emperor Charles le Gros (the Fat). According to legend, Richarde had a vision telling her to build a convent on the spot where she would meet a female bear building a shelter for her young. She met the animal in the forest and built the convent there; from then on, a live bear was kept at the convent and passing bear-leaders were always given free lodging and food. Repudiated by Charles in 887, Richarde retired in her convent and died there in 896. She was canonized by Pope Leon IX in 1049.

The abbey declined from the 17C onwards and was finally suppressed during the Revolution.

★ABBEY CHURCH *30 min*

The church is a fine example of 12C architecture, except for the upper part of the steeple which dates from the 17C. The doorway is surmounted by a massive construction. The west front and north side are decorated with a frieze depicting animals, monsters and a mixture of realistic and allegorical scenes.

The **doorway★★**, which is the most interesting part of the building, is adorned with the most outstanding Romanesque carvings in Alsace. Small characters placed on either side support foliated mouldings entwined round animals; several couples, presumably representing the benefactors of the abbey, are framed by the arcading. The lintel is decorated with scenes from the Creation and the Garden of Eden and, on the tympanum, Jesus Christ can be seen giving a key to St Peter and a book to St Paul.

Interior – The church was considerably remodelled inside during the 18C. The chapel above the porch has retained its basic Romanesque structure, although the large window, which replaced the three original Romanesque windows, was opened in 1700.

The pulpit (18C) is supported by a statue of Samson.

The chancel, which is much higher than the nave, is decorated with fine 15C stalls; St Richarde's funeral monument, also dating from the 15C, can be seen against the wall.

The crypt lies beneath the chancel and the crossing. A few features go back to the foundation of the abbey, but most of it dates from the 11C. A hole in the paving is said to mark the spot which the bear indicated as the site of the church. It is guarded by the pre-Romanesque stone statue of a bear.

EXCURSION

Epfig – *6km/3.7mi southeast along D 253 and D 335. Drive through the village and follow D 603 towards Kogenheim.*
Situated at the eastern end of the village, above the Rhine Valley, the **Chapelle Ste-Marguerite**, surrounded by the cemetery, was built in the 11C and 12C. According to legend, it was used by a congregation of nuns, which would explain the addition of a gallery-porch sometime during the 12C. Burned down in 1601, it was completely restored in 1875. The ossuary remains a mystery; one plausible explanation is that it served to house the bones taken out of the cemetery when it became overcrowded.

ARGONNE★

Michelin map 56 folds 19 and 20 or 241 folds 18, 22 and 23

The Argonne region is a geographical entity situated on the border of Champagne a
Lorraine. Its rolling landscapes, its forests and beauty spots are attractive tourist area
The massif which, at its widest point between Clermont and Ste-Menehould, is no mo
than 12km/7.5mi wide, reaches an altitude of 308m/1 010ft south of Clermont. Th
eastern side overlooking the plain forms a considerable obstacle which was always high
coveted. The valleys separating the hillocks are the natural passages through which inv
sions traditionally penetrated the region: the Islettes, Lachalade and Grandpré passes
After the Gallo-Roman period, the Argonne region formed part of the bishoprics «
Châlons, Reims and Verdun. During the Middle Ages, it became a borderland betwee
the Champagne County (incorporated into the kingdom of France in 1285) and th
Holy Roman Empire.
The region was later shared between the king of France and the duke of Lorrain
then between the Champagne, Barrois and Lorraine regions, and was finally split int
three *départements* (Ardennes, Marne and Meuse).
Owing to its geographical position, Argonne was often invaded and witnessed nume
ous battles. In 1792, Prussian troops were held up here after the fall of Verdu
which enabled Dumouriez to get his own troops ready in Valmy and to stop the enem
as he came out of the Argonne passes. During the First World War, the front line ra
for four years between Four-de-Paris, Haute-Chevauchée, Vauquois and Avocour
splitting Argonne into two. Fierce fighting took place near the Vauquois and Beaulie
heights, causing numerous casualties.

ROUND TOUR STARTING
FROM CLERMONT-EN-ARGONNE

77km/48mi – about 4hr – local map below

Clermont-en-Argonne – Clermont is picturesquely situated on a wooded hillsic
above the Aire Valley; the top of the hill reaches 308m/1010ft, the highest point
the Argonne region.
The former capital of the county of Clermontois used to be overlooked by
fortress and surrounded by fortified walls. It belonged in turn to the Holy Rom;
Empire, to the bishopric of Verdun, to the county of Bar and to the duchy «
Lorraine before being joined to the kingdom of France in 1632. Louis XIV late
gave it to the Grand Condé after the castle was razed during the Fronde. The **Égli**
St-Didier ⊙, dating from the 16C is adorned with two Renaissance doorways. No
the Flamboyant Gothic vaulting of the transept and chancel and the modern staine
glass. From the terrace behind the church, the view extends over the Argonr
region and the Hesse Forest.
The **Chapelle Ste-Anne** ⊙ *(access via the path climbing on the right of the church)*,
small edifice erected on the site of the former castle, contains a 16C representatic
of the Holy Sepulchre comprising six statues. The very beautiful Mary Magdalen
which belongs to a painted group depicting the three Marys, is thought to be th
work of Ligier Richier or a sculptor from the same school.
Follow the shaded path leading to the tip of the promontory: the view extend
across the Argonne Forest and the plateau carved by the Aire Valley *(viewing table*
Leave Clermont-en-Argonne on D 998 towards Neuvilly-en-Argonne. From Neuvill
follow D 946. In Boureuilles, take D 212 on the right towards Vauquois. As you ent
Vauquois, follow the surfaced path on the left, which leads to the hillock. Leave the c
and climb along the footpath to the top of the hill.

Butte de Vauquois – Between 1914 and 1918, there was fierce fighting on bo
sides over this hill. A monument marks the site of the former village destroye
during the war. A narrow path running along the ridge and offering views of th
Hesse Forest, the Montfaucon Hill and the Aire Valley, overlooks several mir
craters, 30m/98ft deep. The ground all around is completely churned up and it
still possible to see pieces of barbed wire and chevaux de frise (defensive spikes).
Return to D 38 which leads to Varennes-en-Argonne.

Varennes-en-Argonne – This small town, built on the banks of the River Aire,
famous as the place where Louis XVI was arrested when he tried to flee fro
France with his family during the Revolution. The royal coach was stopped by
handful of soldiers at 11pm on 21 June 1791. The king tried to gain time, hopir
to be freed by his own troops, but the people of Varennes acted promptly and th
royal family was escorted back to Paris by national guards.
The **Musée d'Argonne** ⊙, housed on two levels inside a modern building, featur«
Louis XVI's arrest, arts and crafts of the Argonne region (sigillated ceramics ar
earthenware from Les Islettes and Waly), as well as mementoes from the Fir
World War (underground fighting and the American intervention).
Between the museum and the church, an itinerary lined with seve
explanatory panels commemorates the arrival and the arrest of Louis XV
and his family during the night of 21 to 22 June 1791.
The **Mémorial de Pennsylvanie** is an imposing monument dedicated to American soldie
who died during the fighting which took place in 1918.
There is a lovely view of the River Aire and the surrounding countryside to the nort
Continue along D 38 towards Four-de-Paris.

Abris du Kronprinz – *Drive for 3.5km/2.2mi then take a forest road in a bend. Stop at the end of it and continue on foot along the path on the right; 30m/33yd further on, turn left onto a footpath. A shelter can be seen through the vegetation.*

This blockhouse was used during the First World War by the German Crown Prince and his staff *(not open to the public).*

Return to D 38 then turn left onto the Haute-Chevauchée road.

Haute-Chevauchée – This is one of the main sites of the 1914-1918 War; fierce fighting took place here but today the road offers a pleasant walk through the forest to the Argonne Memorial and the Forestière military cemetery. Trenches and narrow passageways can still be seen in the undergrowth on either side of the road.

Return to D 38 and continue to Four-de-Paris, then take D 2 to Lachalade.

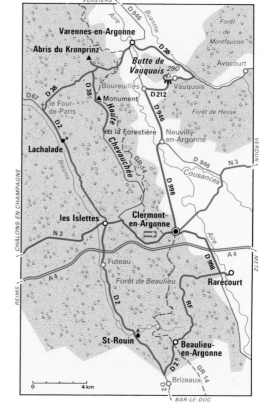

Lachalade – The village is overlooked by the imposing silhouette of a former Cistercian abbey. Two wings of the 17C monastery buildings *(private property)* are still standing.

The 14C **church** looks oddly proportioned, owing to the fact that it is reduced to two bays, the first three having been destroyed by fire at the beginning of the 17C. Note the Flamboyant Gothic rose on the west front: it originally decorated Ste-Vanne abbey in Verdun.

Continue towards Les Islettes.

Les Islettes – This once-thriving village was famous for its tileries, glassworks and above all earthenware factories.

Beyond Futeau, D 2 goes through the Beaulieu Forest.

Ermitage de St-Rouin – St Roding (or Rouin), a 7C Irish monk, settled in Argonne and founded a monastery which preceded the Beaulieu abbey. A "greenery cathedral" lies in a lovely wooded setting. A solitary building intended for pilgrims, welcomes visitors; further on, under the canopy formed by the trees, stands a modern concrete chapel designed by Father Rayssiguier, a disciple of Le Corbusier. The multi-coloured stained-glass windows are the work of a young Japanese artist. A pilgrimage takes place in mid-September.

Continue along D 2 and turn left towards Beaulieu-en-Argonne.

Beaulieu-en-Argonne – This village, brightened up with flowers, occupies a hillock offering fine views of the forested heights. Of the important Benedictine abbey which once stood here, only a few walls remain apart from the huge 13C **winepress★** ⊙, entirely made of oak (except for the hornbeam screw), in which the monks could press 3 000kg/6 615lb of grapes to produce 1 600l/352gal of grape juice.

From Beaulieu-en-Argonne take the forest road running alongside the wine-press building (on the left), continue straight on beyond the Trois Pins crossroads then turn left to Rarécourt.

Rarécourt – The **Musée de la Faïence** ⊙ is housed in a 17C fortified building *(on the right of the road beyond the bridge spanning the River Aire)*. More than 800 earthenware and terracotta pieces from the area (Islettes, Lavoye, Waly, Rarécourt...), dating from the 18C and 19C are exhibited.

From Rarécourt, return to Clermont-en-Argonne along D 998.

69

ASFELD

Population 1 061
Michelin map 56 fold 6 or 241 fold 13

In this village, lying on the south bank of the River Aisne, which once belonged to t
counts of Avaux, Jean-Jacques de Mesmes built an unusual Baroque church.

★**Église St-Didier** – This church is unique: designed in 1683 by the Dominic
priest, François Romain, who built the Pont-Royal in Paris, the brick structu
recalls the shape of a viol. Its vestibule leading to a rotunda is surmounted by
flattened cupola and flanked by four semi-oval chapels. On the outside, a bri
colonnade links the oval peristyle and the rotunda. Inside, sturdy columns suppc
the dome of the cupola whereas, in the upper part, small columns decorate t'
galleries running all round the building. Passages, known as *tournelles* make
possible to walk round the church without going across it.

Basilique d'AVIOTH★★

Michelin map 57 fold 1 or 241 fold 15

This magnificent church, standing in the centre of a remote village near the Belgi
border, offers a striking contrast with it rural setting.

BASILIQUE NOTRE-DAME *about 30min*

The discovery of a statue of the Virgin Mary, believed to perform miracles, led to
pligrimage during the early 12C and to the construction, in warm-coloured stor
of the basilica from the second half of the 13C to the beginning of the 15C wh
the Flamboyant Gothic style prevailed.

The **west doorway** is well proportioned and its design harmonious; the arching
decorated with 70 figures and Christ's Passion is depicted on the lintel. Above t
portal, near the gable, one can see the Last Judgement; note also the statu
representing angels sounding trumpets.

The **south doorway** is dedicated to the Virgin and to Christ's childhood. The low
parts are decorated with carved draperies, in typical Champagne style.

Left of the south doorway stands the **Recevresse**★, a small yet elegant edifice
Flamboyant style, adjacent to the door of the old cemetery and decorated with fi
tracery work. It was meant to receive offerings from pilgrims, hence its name.

Interior – The basilica
very bright inside. There
a walkway (unusual in th
region) and an ambulator
radiating from it are sh;
low chapels fitted betwe
the buttresses which ha
pen to be inside the chur
according to a practice us
in Champagne.

The basilica has retain
several works of popul
art. The elegant pulpit, da
ing from 1538 carved wi
Renaissance motifs st
shows traces of pol
chromy; the central par
depicts the Coronation
the Virgin. Next to it, t
Ecce Homo is flanked by
Pontius Pilate dressed
the court fashion of t;
Holy Roman Empire.

Worth noting in the **chan**
is the 14C high altar dec
rated with the symbols
the four Evangelists. To t
left of the altar, one c
see the ancient statue
Notre-Dame d'Avioth, carv
out of lime c 1110 a
resting on a 15C sto
throne.

B.Kaufmann

Recevresse

70

Note also the 14 polychrome statues placed high against the pillars of the east end, which form a silent court around the Virgin's statue. The Gothic tabernacle on the right of the altar dates from the 15C, its high pinnacle almost touching the top of the arcading forms a frame round it.

Restoration work has brought to light 14C and 15C paintings and frescoes over the chancel screen and vaulting, in particular near the tabernacle, where a Virgin and Child with St John and St Agnes can be seen.

The 18C organ loft has been restored.

BACCARAT

Population 5 015
Michelin map 62 fold 7 or 242 fold 22

∎is small town lying on both sides of the River Meurthe is famous for its crystal-
∎rks founded in 1764.

∎ystalworks – *Not open to the public.* In 1764 King Louis XV allowed the bishop of
∎etz to revive an ancient glass-making tradition; in 1817 the glassworks were turned
∎o crystalworks and since the visit of Charles X in 1828, the works have been
∎pplying kings, presidents and important people throughout the world. There was a
∎ne of great prosperity at the beginning of the 19C and again in the 1950s after the
∎mbre period marked by two World Wars. Today, 1 100 people are employed in the
∎ystalworks (20 of them have been nominated "best workers in France") and 70% of
∎e production is exported to 90 countries including the United States, Italy, Japan, the
∎iddle East and the Far East.

∎ map (in the entrance hall of the museum) shows the importance of the works in
∎00. The workers' district comprised several long buildings. Glassworkers lived near
∎e crystalworks because they had to run to the factory as soon as the bell rang
∎nalling that the crystal had melted.

SIGHTS

Musée du Cristal ⊘ – Located in the directors' house, the museum displays antique and contemporary pieces: 19C opalines, agates, millefiori paperweights, plain, cut or carved glasses, table sets ordered by sovereigns and heads of states. Made from silica, lead oxide (about 30%) and potash, crystal is melted at a very high temperature and then moulded in the same way as glass. For instance, items can be shaped by blowing, then hand cut or carved. From the beginning to the end of the manufacturing process, a simple piece passes through the hands of 20 different persons. In the last room, the various techniques and tools used are illustrated: work under heat, cutting, carving and gilding process.

Église St-Rémy – Built in 1957, the church has an unusual roof with large awnings. The steeple, a 55m/180ft pyramid, stands beside the church. The interior deco-ration, which consists in a huge low relief made up of concrete elements and **stained-glass panels** ★ in Baccarat crystal (more than 50 different colours), illustrates the creation of the world. The tabernacle and christening font lit by two stained-glass windows depicting the Twelve Apostles, are also noteworthy.

EXCURSIONS

Deneuvre – Excavations, carried out between 1974 and 1986 south of this village adjacent to Baccarat, led to the discovery of a Gallo-Roman sanctuary which has been reconstructed in a museum.

Les Sources d'Hercule – In the entrance hall there are explanations, maps, plans and models dealing with the discovery of the site. From the top of the stairs, there is an overall view of the sanctuary with its stelae and pools. Founded in the middle of

---

USEFUL STOPOFF

Magnières: Le Wagon du Pré Fleury – 15km/9mi west of Baccarat. A French Railway carriage has been turned into a restaurant (seating capacity: 48) completed by a large dining area in a metal structure dating from 1910. The cuisine, based on fresh produce, is both French and international. Closed Mondays. ☎ 03 83 72 32 58.

Next door, the whole family can board a *vélorail* and cycle through the Val de Mortagne along the disused railway line. Information and reservation, ☎ 03 83 72 34 73.

the 2C AD, the sanctuary was dedicated to Hercules. Three pools were at t' disposal of those who wished to perform their ablutions. Those whose wishes can true offered ex-votos, i.e. stelae or altars which eventually formed a circle rou the springs. Hercules is represented on most stelae as he was considered as t' protector of the springs.

Fontenoy-la-Joûte – *6km west.* In this typically stretched-out Lorraine villag 18C semi-detached houses have been turned into bookshops and Fontenoy h become a book village with some 15 bookshops, a first-class bookbinder and printing house. An important market takes place on the last Sunday of the mon from April to September.

BALLON D'ALSACE ★★★

Michelin map 66 fold 8 or 242 folds 35, 39

The Ballon d'Alsace is the highest peak (alt 1 250m/4 101ft) of the **Massif du Ball d'Alsace** situated at the southern end of the Vosges mountain range. It belongs to t cristalline part of these mountains where granite predominates and owes its name its rounded shape, although *ballon* could be derived from the name of the Celtic g Bel as there is some evidence that the peak was used as a solar observatory in Cel times.
The massif is clad with dense forests of spruce and fir trees and the undergrowth is parts charming; ravines are pleasantly cool and heights are covered with pastur dotted with Alpine flowers.
The Ballon d'Alsace provides one of the most popular excursions in the region summer as well as in winter (downhill and cross-country skiing).

Access – *From St-Maurice-sur-Moselle in the north or Masevaux in the southea the route is described in the Parc Naturel Régional des BALLONS DES VOSGE From Giromagny, the route is described in the Michelin Green Guide Burgundy-Ju* The path *(30min on foot there and back)* starts from D 465 in front of t' "Ferme-Restaurant du Ballon d'Alsace". It runs through pastures towards the stat of the Virgin. Before Alsace became French once more, the statue stood exactly the border. From the viewing platform, the **panorama★★** extends north to t' Donon, east across the plain of Alsace and the Black Forest and south as far Mont Blanc.

It is possible to go back down along the same path or to continue along the natu trail *(sentier de découverte, 1hr 30min)* where explanatory panels provide adde information about the area's geology, history, fauna and flora.

Preserve the environment! Walk along paths, don't cut through t' forest, and leave wild flowers and plants as you find them.

Parc Naturel Régional des
BALLONS DES VOSGES

Michelin map 62 folds 17 and 18, 66 folds 7, 8 and 9
or 242 folds 27, 31, 34, 35, 38 and 39

The southern Vosges – The Vosges offer contrasting landscapes between the nort south mountain ridge and the rounded summits known as *ballons* reaching altitudes excess of 1 000m/3 281ft (the Grand Ballon peaks at 1 424m/4 672ft).
To the east, glacial cirques open out into deep Alpine valleys. Nearer the Alsati piedmont, the wooded slopes give way to green pastures and then to vineyards.
To the west, the gentler Lorraine slopes are furrowed by a network of valleys a lakes which are the result of major glacial erosion.

The nature park – The natural environment takes on very different aspects: stubb fields, forests, peat bogs, glacial cirques and limestone hills.
Forests, consisting essentially of coniferous trees (silver fir and spruce), cover 60% the total area and are responsible for what is called the "blue line of the Vosges which can be seen on the horizon.
The great diversity of ecosystems accounts for the varied fauna: deer, roe-deer, w boars, chamois and even lynx. Birdlife is also plentiful in forested and mountaino areas (in particular species such as the peregrine, capercaillie and blackbirds). Aqua ecosystems also have a rich fauna (crayfish, common trout, Alpine newt etc) a specific flora.
Villages, farms and museums illustrate agricultural and industrial traditions as well local handicrafts: silver-mine development, weaving, wood-sledging, Munster-chee making.

ere are numerous possibilities of walks and hikes with a wide choice of marked
ths, mountain-bike or cross-country tracks and downhill slopes (la Bresse,
rardmer, Le Markstein, Ballon d'Alsace, Lac Blanc). Paragliding and rock-climbing are
so on offer and themed tours are organised every summer. In addition there is a
oice of nature trails and centres offering an introduction to the environment.
ills and sawmills in the area are open for guided tours and demonstrations.
storic trails, museums and open-air museums deal with the historic and cultural
velopment of the region *(brochures available at tourist offices)*.
e **Maison du Parc**, located in Munster, acts as a central information office.

★ ① COL DU BALLON D'ALSACE

From St-Maurice-sur-Moselle to the Ballon d'Alsace
10km/6mi – allow 1hr

This is the oldest road across the range; it was built during the reign of Louis XV.

St-Maurice-sur-Moselle – This small industrial town (textiles and sawmills) is
close to some remarkable beauty spots as well as the Rouge Gazon and Ballon
d'Alsace winter resorts. It is the starting point of excursions to the Ballon de
Servance and the Charbonniers Valley *(see p 76)*.
On the way up to the Col du Ballon, the road (D 465) offers some fine views of
the Moselle Valley before going through a splendid forest of firs and beeches.

Plain du Canon – *15min on foot there and back.* The path leaves D 465 by an
information panel tied to a tree and runs down towards a forest lodge. Go down
past the lodge and follow a path on the left which meanders upwards. The place
owes its name to a small gun once used by the local gamekeeper to create an echo.
There is a charming view of the wooded Presles Valley over which tower the Ballon
d'Alsace and Ballon de Servance, crowned by a fort.
Beyond **La Jumenterie**, whose name (*jument* means mare) is a reminder of a
horse-breeding centre founded in 1619 by the dukes of Lorraine, there is a fine
view of the Moselle Valley and Ballon de Servance to the right.
The road reaches the high-pasture area.
The **Monument aux Démineurs** by Rivière and Deschler is dedicated to bomb-disposal
experts who died while performing their duty.

Col du Ballon – To the right there is a monument celebrating the racing cyclist
René Pottier *(at the end of the parking area)*. There is a fine view of the summit of
the Ballon d'Alsace, crowned with a statue of the Virgin Mary and, further right, of
the Belfort depression dotted with lakes and the northern part of the Jura
mountains.
A path leads to Joan of Arc's statue.
★**Ballon d'Alsace** – *30min on foot there and back. See BALLON D'ALSACE.*

★ ② DOLLER VALLEY

From the Ballon d'Alsace to Sentheim
28km/17.4mi – allow 1hr

★**Ballon d'Alsace** – *30min on foot there and back. See BALLON D'ALSACE.*
The drive down to the Alfeld Lake is very beautiful. Ahead is the Grand Ballon, the
highest summit in the Vosges mountains (1 424m/4 672ft); later on there are fine
views of the Doller Valley and of the Jura and the Alps.
As the road comes out of the forest, the lake appears inside a glacial cirque.

★**Lac d'Alfeld** – The Alfeld artificial lake (covering an area of 10ha/25 acres and
22m/72ft deep) is one of the most attractive water expanses in the Vosges region.
It ensures that the Doller has a regular flow, particularly when the thaw comes.
The lake is framed by picturesque wooded heights.
The dam, built between 1884 and 1887, is 337m/369yd long and leans against a
moraine left behind by ancient glaciers.

Lac de Sewen – Close to the Alfeld Lake, this small lake is gradually filling up with
peat. Alpine and Nordic plants grow on its shores.
Further downstream, D 466 follows the Doller which flows between high slopes
covered with green pastures alternating with woods of fir trees and beeches. The
valley is overlooked by the Romanesque church of **Kirchberg** perched on a moraine
and, as you enter **Niederbruck**, on the left, by a monumental statue of the Virgin and
Child by Antoine Bourdelle.

Masevaux – *See THANN: Excursion.*
Continue along D 466.

Lauw – An interesting **nature trail** follows the charming Doller River *(1hr 30min)*
which contributed to the agricultural and industrial (sawmill) development of this
small town.

PARC NATUREL RÉGIONAL DES BALLONS DES VOSGES

Legend:

- Information centre
- M — Museum or exhibit
- Historical tour
- Environmental learning centre
- Discovery trail
- Climbing centre
- Off-road bike trail
- Downhill ski area
- Cross-country ski area

0   5 km

ST DIÉ

Bruyères   601 Mont Avison

ÉPINAL

Champ-le-Duc

Granges-s.-Vologne

Barbey

Cha... de R...

★★ RÉ...

Chenimenil

Faucompierre

Archette

HAUTE

Arches

Tête des Cuveaux ★
783

le Tholy

Eloyes

Cascade de Tendon ★

GÉRAR...

D 417

Vallée

St Amé

Vagney

la B...

Remiremont

DE

Vⁱᵉᵉ de la Semouse ★

la Beuille
757

Cornimont

PLOMBIÈRES-LES-BAINS

Cascade du Géhard ★

LA

Saulxures-s-Moselotte

Le Val d'Ajol

Rupt-s-Moselle

MOSELLE ★

Ermitag... Frère J...

So... la...

Fougerolles

M

Col du Mont de Fourche
620

Moselle

le Thillot

Bussang

St Bresson

St-Maurice-s-M...

Raddon

Breuchin

Faucogney-et-la-Mer

Col des Croix
679

Plain du Canon

le Haut-du-Them

3

★★ BALLON DE SERVANCE
1216

1
1178

Servance

Col du Ballon

★★★ BALLON D'ALSACE

Planche des Belles Filles
1148

Mélisey

Plancher-les-Mines

Lepuix

Giro...

Auxelles-Haut

Ronchamp

Ronchamp   Sermamagny

Sentheim – The **Maison de la Géologie** ⊙, opposite the church, houses a fine collection of fossils and minerals.

Sentier géologique du Wolfloch – *Drive along D 466 towards Bussang, then turn rig 300m/328yd after the church and follow the arrows to the starting point of th geological trail. The itinerary extends over a distance of 5km and includes geological sites. Allow 2hr. It is essential to obtain the brochure available at th Maison de la géologie or at the Maison du Parc in Munster.*

Start from the presentation panel and walk to the right along the fields, followir the markings illustrating a fossil.

The path goes across the great Vosges fault and gives an insight into the geo ogy of the region from the Primary Era until today. The fault separates th primary formations, uplifted when the Alps rose, from more recent sediment often rich in fossils, which account for the presence of the sea 100 millic years ago *(see p 18).*

★★ ③ BALLON DE SERVANCE
21km/13mi – allow 1hr 15min

St-Maurice-sur-Moselle – *See p 73.*

Le Thillot – *See MOSELLE: Haute vallée de la Moselle.*

Drive south along D 486 to the Col des Croix then turn left onto D 16. The road ris above the Ognon Valley, offering fine views, before meandering through the forest.

★★**Ballon de Servance** – *Leave the car at the beginning of the military road (r entry) of the Fort de Servance and take a marked path on the right which lea (15min on foot there and back) to the summit of the Ballon (alt 1 216m/3 990ft)* The **panorama** is magnificent: the Ognon Valley, the glacial Plateau d'Esmoulière dotted with lakes and the Plateau de Langres to the west; Monts Faucilles to th northwest; the Moselle Valley further to the right; the Vosges mountain range the northeast and to the east, the nearby rounded summit of the Ballon d'Alsac the foothills of the Vosges mountains stretch to the south and southeast.

④ VALLÉE DES CHARBONNIERS
12km/7.4mi – allow 30min

St-Maurice-sur-Moselle – *See p 73.*

From St-Maurice-sur-Moselle, drive east along the road which follows the Cha bonniers stream.

The inhabitants of this valley are believed to be the descendants of a Swedish an German colony hired by the dukes of Lorraine in the 18C for forestry work an coal mining. In the village of Les Charbonniers, turn left onto the Rouge Gazo road (winter sports); from the **Tête du Rouge Gazon**, there are good views of th Ballon de Servance.

⑤ VAL D'ARGENT

The Vosges mountains are particularly rich in mineral resources, silver, copper an other metals, extracted since the Middle Ages. The mining industry had its heyda during the 16C and 17C and its decline was complete in the middle of the 19C Great efforts have been made in the past few years to restore the region's minin heritage and develop its touristic potential. Today, several protected sites, whic have been restructured, are open to the public.

Round tour from Ste-Marie-aux-Mines
65km/40mi – allow 1hr 30min

Follow N 59 west out of Ste-Marie-aux-Mines through a green valley. The roa then climbs sharply past a war cemetery on the right.

Col de Ste-Marie – From the pass (alt 772m/2 533ft), one of the highest passe in the Vosges mountains, look back towards the Cude Valley and ahead to th Liepvrette Valley, the Plaine d'Alsace and the Haut-Kœnigsbourg Castle.

Roc du Haut de Faite – *From the pass, 30min on foot there and back. Walk north alon a path starting on the right of a gravestone.*

From the top, there is a fine **panorama** of the Vosges summits and the slopes on th Alsatian and Lorraine side.

Return to N 59 and drive towards St-Dié. Turn left onto D 23, 2km/1.2mi beyon Gemaingoutte.

Circuit minier La Croix-aux-Mines – *5.6km/3.5mi walk – allow 2hr 45min.*
Start from the Chapelle du Chipal and follow the panels marked with a black circle against a yellow background and bearing the emblem of the trail (crossed hammer and pickaxe). Miners extracted galena, a mineral ore of lead sulphide mixed with silver, from this site at Le Chipal and others in the area.
Continue along D 23 to Fraize and turn left onto N 415.

Col du Bonhomme – *See Val d'ORBEY.*
On reaching the pass, turn left onto D 148.

★**Le Brézouard** – *45min on foot there and back.*
You will be able to get fairly close to the Brézouard by car if you approach it via the **Col des Bagenelles** *(4km/2.5mi)* which offers a fine view of the Liepvrette Valley.
Leave the car in the parking area, near the "Amis de la Nature" refuge.
The Brézouard and the surrounding area suffered a complete upheaval during the First World War.
From the summit, there is a very wide **panorama★★**: the Champ du Feu and Climont to the north, with the Donon in the background; Strasbourg to the northeast, the Hohneck and Grand Ballon to the south. When the weather is clear, Mont Blanc can be seen in the distance.
Return to Ste-Marie-aux-Mines along D 48.
The road winds its way through the forest then follows the Liepvrette Valley where orchards take over from high pastures.

Sentier patrimoine de Neuenberg – *In Échery.* During the tour of this heritage trail *(short tour: 2hr 30min, long tour: 4hr)*, the mineworkers' tower and the tithe-collector's house, flanked with a turret in characteristic Renaissance style, and a research gallery of the Enigma mine come into view.

St-Pierre-sur-l'Hâte – *Turn right in Échery.* There was once a Benedictine priory in this picturesque hamlet framed by wooded slopes, which has retained an ecumenical **church**, known as the miners' church, built in the 15C-16C and restored in 1934.

Ste-Marie-aux-Mines – This small industrial town, located in the Liepvrette Valley, owes its name to its former silver mines. Today, it is the meeting place of collectors of rocks and fossils who gather for the exhibition and exchange market organised every year during the last weekend in June. Ste-Marie has a famous weaving industry specialising in fine woollen cloth, factory or home made by craftsmen who have been passing their skills on from one generation to the next since the 18C. Twice a year, in spring and autumn, a fabrics fair offers buyers from various countries a choice of fabrics woven in Ste-Marie, in particular tartans and a variety of new textiles mostly intended for the Haute-Couture trade.
The **Maison de Pays** ⊘ *(place du Prensureux)* houses a rich collection of rocks on the ground floor. On the first floor, there is the reconstruction of a workshop where visitors can follow the different stages of the manufacturing process of fabrics. The second floor is devoted to the history of mines and the various techniques used: life-size reconstruction of a mine gallery, models, tools, copies of archives.
The **Mine St-Barthélemy** ⊘ *(rue St-Louis)* organises tours of the galleries hewn out of the rock by 16C miners and the **Mine d'argent St-Louis-Eisenthur** ⊘ presents the various mining sites and techniques used in the 16C.
A **historic trail** *(1hr 30min, booklet available at the tourist office)* enables visitors to discover mansions and miners' houses which show how flourishing the mining industry was in the 16C and early 17C.
Leave Ste-Marie-aux-Mines by D 459 towards Ste-Croix.

Sentier minier et botanique de Ste-Croix-aux-Mines – *A mining and botanic trail (3.8km/2.4mi, allow 2hr 30min) starts on the left of the road as you leave the town, 100m/110yd before the panel marked "les halles".* The trail winds through the Bois de St-Pierremont where several silver mines were located in the 16C. All along the way, panels provide information about the various species of trees.

THE BIRTHPLACE OF PATCHWORK

Every year in September, a historic and artistic exhibition on patchwork and the Amish community takes place in Ste-Marie-aux-Mines. Founded in 1693 in Ste-Marie, the Amish movement emigrated to Pennsylvania in 1740. Amish women used to make up blankets with pieces of fabric and thus initiated the art of patchwork. Lessons in patchwork-making are available and there are lectures on the history of the Amish movement and the various techniques of patchwork-making in several venues throughout the valley.

►► **Vallée de la Liepvrette** ★ – A picturesque stretch of N 59 follows the fresh valley of the Liepvrette River with pastures framed by large forests of firs as far as Sélestat. From Liepvre, it is possible to reach the **Col de Fouchy** *(7km/4.3mi along D 48)*. From the pass, there is a fine view of the Champ du Feu and the Hohwald mountains to the north, the Schlossberg and the ruins of Frankenbourg to the east. Look south for Haut-Kœnigsbourg Castle.

Other itineraries *described in the guide*

★★★ **Route des Crêtes** – *See Route des CRÊTES.*

★★ **Région de Gérardmer** – *See Région de GÉRARDMER.*

★★ **Vallée de Guebwiller** – *See GUEBWILLER.*

★★ **Vallée de Munster** – *See Vallée de MUNSTER.*

★★ **Val d'Orbey** – *See Vallée d'ORBEY.*

★ **Massif du Petit Ballon** – *See Vallée de MUNSTER.*

★ **Vallée de la Thur** – *See Vallée de la THUR.*

★ **Haute vallée de la Moselle** – *See MOSELLE.*

BAR-LE-DUC ★

Population 17 545
Michelin map 56 fold 20, 62 fold 1 or 241 fold 31

Partly built on top of a promontory, Bar-le-Duc is split into two: the Ville Haute or upper town, where the castle of the dukes of Bar once stood, and the Ville Basse or lower town, lying on both banks of the River Ornain, a tributary of the Marne. In the 10C, Bar was already the capital of a county whose influence rivalled that of the duchy of Lorraine, and in 1354 the counts of Bar became dukes. In 1484 the Barrois region was joined to Lorraine, yet managed to retain its autonomy and in 1766 it was united with France. During the First World War, Bar-le-Duc played an important role in the Battle of Verdun.

Today the city is the administrative centre of the Meuse *département* and a commercial town where regular fairs and markets are held. Red-currant jam is a famous speciality.

★ VILLE HAUTE *30min*

This fine ensemble of 16C, 17C and 18C architecture was Bar's aristocratic district. Behind its façade adorned with statues, columns, trophies and gargoyles, each building comprises a mansion, a courtyard and servants' quarters.

Place St-Pierre (AZ) – This triangular open area, overlooked by the elegant west front of the Église St-Étienne, is lined with houses dating from different periods. Three residences standing on the right as you face the church show the evolution of architectural styles from the 15C to the 17C. **No 25**, a timber-framed house with corbelled upper floor, is a good specimen of medieval architecture; whereas **no 21**, formerly the Hôtel de Florainville and today the law courts, has a façade in Alsatian Renaissance style (the graceful wrought-iron balconies were added in the 18C). As

Bar-le-Duc – Le Transi

for the early 17C façade of **no 29**, now occupied by a magistrates' court, it is decorated in strict Classical style: columns and windows surmounted by scrolled pediments.

Église St-Étienne ⊘ (AZ) – This former collegiate church dating from the late 14C has a partly Renaissance west front. It contains several works of art including the famous **"transi"** ★★ by Ligier Richier (in the south transept), which depicts the Prince of Orange, René de Chalon, killed during the siege of St-Dizier in 1544. This powerful work was commissioned by his widow, Anne de Lorraine. It depicts with gruesome realism the contrast between the miserable state of the decomposed body and his triumphant attitude as he looks up to his heart which he is holding up to heaven at arm's length. A Calvary scene, also by Ligier Richier, placed behind the high altar, depicts Christ and the two thieves. In the north transept the *Statue of Notre-Dame-du-Guet* is revered locally. According to legend, it stood by one of the town's gates during the siege of 1440 and warned of a surprise enemy attack. A painting facing the statue illustrates the Crucifixion but, in this case, Jerusalem has been replaced by the upper town as it looked in the 17C.

Place de la Halle (AZ) – It is possible to get a glimpse of the arcades of the former covered market through the gateway of no 3, which has a beautiful Baroque façade, unfortunately damaged.

Take rue Chavée and turn right.

Les Grangettes (AZ E) – This viewpoint offers a pleasant view of the lower town, the hillside and the **clock tower**, which is all that remains of the former ducal castle.

Retrace your steps to place de la Halle and turn left onto rue des Ducs-de-Bar.

Rue des Ducs-de-Bar (AZ) – This former aristocratic high street of the upper town has retained a number of beautiful façades. **No 41**, an interesting example of local 16C architecture, has two friezes decorated with military motifs. **No 47** has retained its gargoyles. At **no 53**, the main door is framed with carved arcading. The façade of **no 73** is adorned with added panels illustrating musical instruments. In a building at the end of the courtyard of **no 75**, one can see a 15C **winepress**.
The street is closed at one end by the façade of the Hôtel de Salm.

ADDITIONAL SIGHTS

Musée Barrois ⊘ (AZ M¹) – Housed in the former tax office and the new castle built in 1567, the museum contains a rich archeological collection covering the period from the Bronze Age to Merovingian times with many Gallo-Roman exhibits including the statue of a goddess from Naix-aux-Forges (Nasium), the stela of an eye specialist from Montiers-sur-Saulx and some Merovingian jewellery from the necropolis at Gondrecourt.
A late-15C hall surmounted by ribbed vaulting houses medieval and Renaissance sculptures (Pierre de Milan, Gérard Richier).

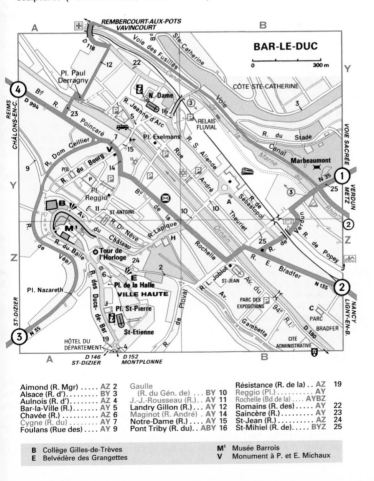

Aimond (R. Mgr)	AZ 2	Gaulle		Résistance (R. de la)	AZ 19
Alsace (R. d')	BY 3	(R. du Gén. de)	BY 10	Reggio (Pl.)	AY
Aulnois (R. d')	AZ 4	J.-J.-Rousseau (R.)	AY 11	Rochelle (Bd de la)	AYBZ
Bar-la-Ville (R.)	AY 5	Landry Gillon (R.)	AY 12	Romains (R. des)	AY 22
Chavée (R.)	AZ 6	Maginot (R. André)	AY 14	Saincère (R.)	AY 23
Cygne (R. du)	AY 7	Notre-Dame (R.)	AY 15	St-Jean (R.)	AZ 24
Foulans (Rue des)	AY 9	Pont Triby (R. du)	ABY 16	St-Mihiel (R. de)	BYZ 25

B   Collège Gilles-de-Trèves
E   Belvédère des Grangettes
M¹ Musée Barrois
V   Monument à P. et E. Michaux

The most noteworthy paintings of the French and Flemish Schools are *Diane an Callisto* by Heindrick de Clerck, the *Temptation of St Anthony* by David Tenier Junior and *Cabaret Scene* by Jan Steen.

A collection of 17C weapons and armours is kept in the former audience room.

The collections of folk art and customs are displayed round a winepress located a no 75 rue des Ducs-de-Bar *(see above).*

In front of the castle, a vast open area, cleared in 1794 when the collegiate churc of St-Maxe was demolished, offers fine views of the lower town, the Collèg Gilles-de-Trèves and a Romanesque gate which was once part of the fortification of the castle.

Collège Gilles-de-Trèves (AY B) – The university college was founded in 1571 b the dean of St-Maxe, Gilles de Trèves, who wished to prevent young aristocrat from going to other universities where the ideas of the Reformation were gainin ground.

The Renaissance façade was remodelled in the 19C but the inner courtyar remained intact. Access is through a long porch with decorated vaulting bearing th inscription in Latin: "Let this house remain standing until ants have drunk th oceans dry and tortoises have gone all the way round the world".

Galleries supported by pillars surround the courtyard. Note the balustrades deco rated with complex carvings which could be Flemish.

Rue du Bourg (AY) – The lower town was essentially a shopping district, the hig street being, from the 16C onwards, one of the most elegant streets of Bar-le-Duc as some richly decorated façades still testify today. **No 26**, dating from 1618, ha window frames adorned with busts of women and sirens and a fine carved wooder door. **Nos 42, 46, 49** and **51** are also noteworthy. **No 49** has retained its gargoyles.

On the corner of rue du Bourg and rue Maginot, a monument picturing a child and a bicycle commemorates Pierre and Ernest Michaux, who invented the velocipede ir 1861.

Église Notre-Dame (AY) – This Romanesque church was restored and remodellec in the 17C following a fire; the steeple dates from the 18C.

In the nave there is a Christ on the Cross by Ligier Richier. A late-15C low relief ir the south-transept chapel depicts the Immaculate Conception: the Virgin, praying beneath God the Father, is surrounded by the symbols of her purity.

Château de Marbeaumont (BY) – This early-20C extravagant castle, which once belonged to the bankers Varin-Bernier, was used by General Pétain as his head-quarters during the First World War.

EXCURSIONS

Rembercourt-aux-Pots – *18km/11mi. Drive north out of Bar-le-Duc along D 11 towards Vavincourt.*

The 15C village **church** has a magnificent **west front** in a successful blend of Flam boyant and Renaissance styles. Admire the wealth of decoration, the shell-shapec recesses and the pagan motifs of the Renaissance frieze. The two towers were never completed. The interior conveys an impression of unity.

Nubécourt – *11km/6.8mi north of Rembercourt.* **Raymond Poincaré** (1860-1934) who was President of the French Republic from 1913 to 1920, is buried in the cemetery.

BAR-SUR-AUBE

Population 6 705
Michelin map 61 fold 19 or 241 fold 38

Situated on the east bank of the River Aube, the town is surrounded by a ring of boulevards, laid on the site of the former ramparts, and has retained many old stone and timber-framed houses.

In medieval times, an important fair took place in Bar-sur-Aube; the region was a lively trading centre at the crossroads of southern and northern Europe.

In 1814, during the Napoleonic Wars, the king of Prussia, the emperor of Austria and the czar of Russia made their headquarters in the Château du Jard.

SIGHTS

Église St-Pierre ⊘ – The west front and south side of this 12C church are lined with a covered gallery (making it look like a *halle* or covered market, hence its name "Halloy"). Ribbed vaulting was later built over the nave and aisles and the chapels were added in the 16C. The high altar was originally in the Clairvaux abbey and the organ in the Remiremont abbey. Some 50 tombstones mark the graves of local lords and wealthy merchants. The 15C polychrome stone statue, known as the *Virgin with the flowers*, is typical of the work produced by the School of Troyes.

Église St-Maclou – This former chapel of the counts of Bar's castle was built between the 12C and 15C and given a Classical front in the 18C. The steeple was the castle's keep.

Cellier aux Moines ⊘ – Situated near the east end of the church, this former townhouse of the monks of Clairvaux *(now a restaurant)* has retained a fine 13C cellar, covered with ribbed vaulting; it was used as their headquarters by the local wine-growers during the 1911 rebellion which enabled the Bar area to continue to give its wine-production the name of Champagne.

EXCURSIONS

Chapelle Ste-Germaine – *4km/2.5mi. Leave Bar-sur-Aube by D 4, southwest of the town, 3km/1.9mi further on, turn left in a bend onto a steep path and continue on foot.* The path leads to a pilgrimage chapel dedicated to Germaine, a virgin martyred by the Vandals in 407. Walk beyond the chapel and around the house to reach the viewing table which offers glimpses of Bar-sur-Aube, the valley, Colombey-les-Deux-Églises and its cross of Lorraine, as well as the Dhuits and Clairvaux forests.

Nigloland ⊘ – *9km/5.6mi. Leave Bar-sur-Aube north by N 19 to Dolancourt.* This leisure park, in a green setting, offers some 15 attractions: family ride in a vintage car dating from 1900, aboard the small train or along the meandering enchanted river. Those who enjoy a thrill will appreciate the Gold Mine Train or the Canadian River. Do not miss the cinema show on the 180° screen or the presentation of the Niglo Company (electronic automata) staged in the theatre of the Canadian Village. A balloon ride enables visitors to get an overall view of the park.
Shops and restaurants make it possible to spend the whole day in the park.

Bayel – *7.5km/4.7mi southeast along D 396.* Bayel is famous for its prestigious **crystalworks** ⊘ founded in 1666 by the Venitian glass-blower Jean-Baptiste Mazzolay. A mixture of sand, lime, soda and lead heated for 12hr in special ovens to a temperature of 1 450°C/2 642°F produces a kind of paste which is ready to be shaped by blowing or casting; all the items are handmade.
Those who are unable to tour the factory can visit the **Écomusée du centre Mazzolay** ⊘, housed in three small workers' cottages *(entrance through the tourist office)*. By means of a series of models, the centre offers an insight into the origins of glass, its various components, the manufacturing process and the different methods used to decorate glass: by guilloche, engraving… A video cassette *(17min)* about the crystalworks, the town and the surrounding area rounds up the visit.
The plain **church** contains a moving 16C polychrome stone **Pietà★**: Mary's simple attitude, the realism of her features and the perfection of the sculpture's outline as well as the harmonious folds of her garment, all point to the work of the Master of Chaource, who also sculpted the famous St Martha housed in the Église Ste-Madeleine in Troyes *(see TROYES)*; a fine 14C Virgin with Child decorates an altar along the north aisle.

Colombé-le-Sec – *About 10km/6mi northeast.* The village has retained an interesting wash-house, thought to date back to the 12C. Although remodelled in the 16C, the church still has a Romanesque lintel, decorated with a Greek cross surrounded by an Easter lamb and a wolf.
The nearby **Ferme du Cellier** ⊘, is a farm built in the 16C over 12C Cistercian cellars, which belonged to the Clairvaux abbey *(see Abbaye de CLAIRVAUX)*.

BITCHE

Population 5 517
Michelin map 57 fold 18 or 242 fold 11

Founded in the 17C and lying at the foot of its famous citadel which used to guard one of the main routes through the Vosges, Bitche is still marked today by the nearby presence of a vast military camp extending northeast to the German border. The plan of this small town is rather unusual wth its main street following the outline of the citadel.

★CITADEL ⊘ *1hr 30min*

Rebuilt by Vauban in 1679, subsequently dismantled, then rebuilt once more in 1741, the citadel successfully repelled Prussian attacks in 1793 and 1870-71. Today, there remain the impressive walls of red sandstone (visible from afar above the dense trees), and the underground structure. The citadel was intended for a garrison of about 1 000 men.

Walk up the ramp and through the vaulted passageway of the norther
entrance towards the top mound crowned by a flagpole *(30min on foot ther
and back)*. There is a panoramic view of Bitche and the wooded heights sur
rounding the town. It is possible, with a pair of binoculars, to spot some c
the armoured domes of the Simserhof structure, which formed part of th
Maginot Line. All along the way, as you walk through the maize of gallerie
and casemates (kitchens, hospital, underground guard-room, officers' quarters)
slides, laser sounds and even smells vividly recreate the siege of the 1870-7
War.

Housed in the former chapel, a museum illustrates the history of the region
note in particular the fine map-model of Bitche in 1794.

The old bakery holds an exhibition about the prosperous Second-Empire period
when there were many thriving industries.

EXCURSIONS

Étang de Hasselfurt – *2km/1.2mi east along N 62*. Swimming facilities an
pleasant walk.

Reyersviller – *5km/3mi west along N 62*. Just beyond the village on the right
stands the impressive **Swedish oak**, said to be more than 400 years old. Accord
ing to legend, the invading Swedes used it as a gallows during the Thirty Year
War.

★**Simserhof** – *See Ligne MAGINOT.*

Ossuaire de Schorbach – *6km/3.7mi northwest along D 962 and D 162B to th
left*.
Near the church there is a small ossuary with Romanesque arcading through which
a pile of bones can be seen.

Michelin publications:
– more than 220 maps, atlases and town plans;
– 12 Red Guides to hotels and restaurants in European countries;
– more than 160 Green Guides in 8 languages to destinations around the world.

BOURBONNE-LES-BAINS✠✠

Population 2 764
Michelin map 62 folds 13 and 14 or 242 fold 33

Already known in Roman times, this spa resort overlooking the Apance Valley became
very popular between the 16C and 18C. It is the foremost spa resort in eastern
France. The hot springs (66°C/150.8°F) are used in the treatment of rheumatism,
arthritis, fractures, osteoporosis and respiratory complaints.

Ville haute – The gatehouse of the former early-16C fortress marks the entrance
to the park of the castle. The **museum** ⊙, housed in the outbuildings, contains 19C
paintings by René-Xavier Prinet, Georges Freset and Horace Vernet *(the Fall of
Constantine)* as well as temporary exhibitions in summer. The **castle**, a fine residence built on the site of the former stronghold and bequeathed to the town as a
gesture of gratitude for treatment received, houses the town hall. There is a fine
view of the lower part of the town and the valley.

There are several fine parks in and around Bourbonne, including the **Parc des
Thermes** (Gallo-Roman remains), the **Arboretum de Montmorency** (230 species of trees
from five continents) and the **Parc animalier de la Bannie** ⊙ *(3.5km/2.2mi southwest
along D 26)* where deer, does and moufflons roam freely.

EXCURSION

Abbaye de Morimond – *16km/9.9mi northwest.* This Cistercian abbey is the
fourth house founded by the Abbaye de Cîteaux in 1115. Owing to its favourable geographical position on the border of Champagne and Lorraine, it spear-
headed the expansion of the Cistercian order in Germany (in the 13C, 213
abbeys were dependent on Morimond).

In this remote dale, only part of the gatehouse and the Chapelle Ste-Ursule
remain; the chapel was remodelled in the 17C, and recently restored. Nearby,
the Morimond Forest is the subject of mysterious legends; a path leads to a
quiet pond.

Château de BRAUX-STE-COHIÈRE ★

Population 61
Michelin map 56 fold 19 or 241 fold 22 (5.5km/3.4mi west of Ste-Menehould)

he buildings were erected in the 16C and 17C by Philippe de Thomassin, who was
overnor of Châlons during the reign of Henri IV; they were designed for a unit of the
ousehold Cavalry whose uniform the king of France wore on the battlefield. In 1792,
eneral Dumouriez made his headquarters here to prepare for the battle of Valmy
gainst the Prussians. The castle was subsequently turned into a farm then used as a
ilitary hospital during the First World War.
oday, the château is the headquarters of the **Association culturelle Champagne-Argonne** and
 used for numerous cultural events: audio-visual show introducing the region, exhibi-
ons, music festival.
very year, celebrations for the "Noël des Bergers de Champagne" include a musical
vening with a procession followed by the midnight mass.

Braux-Ste-Cohière

TOUR ⊘

This vast quadrangle flanked with four corner towers offers a charming view with
its white-striped brick walls reflecting in the deep waters of the moat.
It is possible to walk round the main courtyard and admire the architectural style
of the various buildings: the old stables covered with oak shingles supporting the
tiles, the officers' quarters and its mansard, the dovecote which houses the **Musée
régional d'Orientation** (geology, local history, popular art).
A charming walk takes you through several **gardens** separated by hedges made up
of various species of plants and bushes. Part of the park is used for training
horses.

*The Knight Templars were well established in the area. The octagonal
shape of the dovecote may have been the mark of a building privilege
which was only granted to them.*

BRIENNE-LE-CHÂTEAU

Population 3 752
Michelin map 61 folds 8 and 18 or 241 fold 38

Lying across a flat area, close to the River Aube, Brienne was successfully rebuilt after being partially destroyed in 1940. The town has a famous military camp and airfield and is now a major supplier of cabbage for sauerkraut; one quarter of the cabbages of France are grown here.
Napoleon Bonaparte was a student at the local military school from 1779 to 1784. He returned briefly to Brienne in 1814, at the end of the Napoleonic Wars, when he attacked a coalition of Prussian and Russian troops. Later on, during his exile on the island of St Helena, he recalled with emotion his youthful years in Brienne and left the town a considerable sum of money, which was partly used to build a town hall; the pediment of the building bears the effigy of Napoleon surmounted by an eagle.

SIGHTS *1hr*

*★***Castle** – *Not open to the public*. The imposing white castle crowns the hill overlooking Brienne; built between 1770 and 1778 in typical Louis XVI style, it now houses a regional centre of psychotherapy and can only be seen through the railings of the main gate.

Musée Napoléon ⊙ – Housed in the former military school, the museum contains mementos of Napoleon and relates the various episodes of the French campaign of 1814.
The chapel houses an exhibit of the **Treasuries** ⊙ of nearby churches in the Parc régional de la Forêt d'Orient: sculptures, paintings, and gold plate.

Church – The nave dates from the 14C and the chancel, surrounded by an ambulatory, from the 16C (lierne and tierceron vaulting); the Renaissance stained-glass windows depict interesting scenes: note the story of Noah on the left and the legend of St Crépin and St Crépinien on the right. The bell-shaped stoup goes back to the 16C whereas the christening fonts and the chancel railing date from the 18C.

Covered market – A market takes place regularly beneath the fine 13C timberwork which supports a large tiled roof.

EXCURSIONS

Brienne-la-Vieille – *1km/0.6mi south of Brienne-le-Château along D 443*.
This port used to be the main timber supplier of the capital by the log-floating method. Rough timber would come by cart from the nearby forests of Orient, Temple and Clairvaux. The logs would then be tied together to form floats which would be guided by mariners down the River Aube, then the Seine until they reached Paris.

Écomusée ⊙ – Administered by the Parc régional de la Forêt d'Orient, this museum devoted to the local environment includes the **Boutique** (former smithy which has been left as it was in 1903 and has retained the tools used at the time), the **Maison des jours et des champs** (collection of tools and agricultural machinery showing the evolution of techniques between 1850 and 1950) and the **Maison de l'eau** which will be housed in the mill when the restoration work is finished.

Rosnay-l'Hôpital – *9km/5.6mi north along D 396*.
The 16C **Église Notre-Dame** ⊙ stands on a once-fortified mound, on the banks of the River Voire. Walk along the left side of the church to reach the stairs leading to the vast **crypt**, erected in the 12C but rebuilt in the 16C at the same time as the church above it.

Vallée de la BRUCHE★

Michelin map 87 folds 5, 15 and 16 or 242 folds 23, 24 and 27

The River Bruche takes its source near the Col de Saales and, having furrowed its way between the sandstone and cristalline massifs, flows into the Ill near Strasbourg. On the west bank, in the Wisches area, there are some porphyry quarries. The Bruche supplies several textile factories and sawmills and is partly responsible for the industrial activity which brings life to the Schirmeck and Rothau areas.

FROM SAALES TO SCHIRMECK
41km/25.5mi – allow 2hr

Saales – Situated at the beginning of the Bruche Valley, Saales guards the pass of the same name which gives easy access from one side of the Vosges to the other. Soon after Saales, the road *(N 420)* runs gently down into the picturesque open valley of the Bruche.

Beyond Bourg-Bruche, the dark closely planted firs covering the surrounding heights contrast with the expanses of brightly coloured heather and gorse sloping down to the river.

Near the lively village of **St-Blaise-la-Roche**, the narrow river, lined with aspens and birches, flows tamely through a pastoral landscape.

Every Friday afternoon from mid-June to mid-September, the town hall's covered market is the rendezvous of farmers from the upper Bruche Valley who come to sell high-quality local produce.

Fouday – Jean-Frédéric Oberlin *(see below)* is buried in the small cemetery adjacent to the Lutherian church, which has retained the groined-vaulted apse of the earlier Romanesque church.

Turn right onto D 57.

Vallon du Ban de la Roche – This small valley on the east bank of the Bruche still looks unspoilt.

In 1767, the area was suffering from economic depression (being rather unproductive and having been ruined by several wars), when **Jean-Frédéric Oberlin** (1740-1826) became the new pastor of the small village of Waldersbach, where he remained for the rest of his life. With his wife, he set out to change the life of his parishioners. Helped by local women including **Louise Scheppler**, he created several playschools and prolonged schooling age to 16. He built roads through the valley, set up mortgage societies, developed agriculture and traditional crafts and initiated a small textile industry by acquiring several looms. Today, he is still venerated throughout Alsace.

Waldersbach – The former protestant presbytery of this charming village houses the **Musée Oberlin** ⊙, devoted to the memory of this great philanthropist.

Drive back to rejoin N 420 and turn right to Rothau.

Rocher de la Chatte pendue – *5km/3mi southwest of Rothau to Les Quelles, then 1km/0.6mi along an unsurfaced road (towards La Falle); a panel on the right signals the start of the marked path to La Chatte pendue; it is possible to park at the next bend; 2hr on foot there and back.*

The path climbs through the undergrowth to the top of the plateau (alt 900m/2 953ft) where there is a fine **viewpoint★** with a viewing table.

The **Forêt du Donon**, essentially planted with tall dark conifers and dotted here and there with light-green beeches, offers numerous hiking possibilities.

Turn round and drive back to Schirmeck.

Schirmeck – This small and lively industrial town (metalworks, electronics) stretches along the River Bruche, on the road from Strasbourg to St-Dié. The lovely forests around Schirmeck are the starting point of many hikes.

▶▶**Le Climont★** – *Alt 966m/3 169ft. About 9km/5.6mi east of Saales.* Lovely viewpoint from the summit *(1hr 30min on foot there and back).*

FROM SCHIRMECK TO MOLSHEIM

29km/18mi – allow 30min

Schirmeck – *See above.*

The road *(D 392)* follows the north bank of the Bruche as vineyards and orchards form part of the landscape.

Wisches – This small village marks the border between the French-speaking areas and those where Alsatian dialects are currently spoken.

On the way out of Urmatt, note the huge sawmill on the right.

Niederhaslach – *See DABO-WANGENBOURG.*

Framed by forested slopes, the valley gets narrower as the village of **Heiligenberg** appears perched on a promontory on the north bank.

Mutzig – This charming little city, which was once fortified, has been a garrison town for centuries. There is a lovely fountain and a 13C gate surmounted by a tower.

Antoine Chassepot, the inventor of a rifle named after him, was born in Mutzig in 1833. In 1870, the French infantry was equipped with this rifle, which was far superior to its German counterpart and should have given the French a considerable advantage but a shortage of munitions made the Chassepot useless.

Near the river, the former **Château des Rohan**, named after the bishops of Strasbourg in the 17C, was converted into a weapons factory after the Revolution. Today it is a cultural centre and houses the **Musée régional des armes** ⊙ (firearms – history of the Chassepot – swords, bayonets etc).

From Mutzig to Molsheim, the road runs along the hillside, through vineyards.

★Molsheim – *See MOLSHEIM.*

CHÂLONS-EN-CHAMPAGNE★★

Conurbation 61 452
Michelin map 56 folds 17 and 18 or 241 folds 25 and 26

Formerly known as Châlons-sur-Marne, the town recently resumed its original name of Châlons-en-Champagne.

Two canals, the Mau and the Nau, formed by small arms of the River Marne, meander through the town which is an important crossroads and agricultural market with several food industries (sugar refinery, Champagne wines). To the northeast, an industrial area covering 150ha/371 acres concentrates on agricultural equipment and chemicals.

Châlons is also an administrative and military centre: a number of 17C and 18C mansions confer to the city a certain bourgeois character which contrasts with the charm of its restored timber-framed houses and its old bridges spanning the Mau, such as the three-arched **Pont des Mariniers** (AY 26) dating from 1560 and the **Pont des Viviers** (AY 50) built in 1627, or the 16C **Arche Mauvillain** (BZ 2) spanning the Nau (lovely scalloped vault beneath the boulevard Vaubécourt). The banks of the Marne, lined with beautiful trees, form an attractive sight in the western part of the town.

HISTORICAL NOTES

Catalaunum (Châlons-en-Champagne) was an active Gallo-Roman city named after the Catalauni, a Gallic tribe christianised in the 4C AD. In June 451, the Roman army under the command of General Aetius defeated the Huns led by their powerful chief **Attila**. The exact location of the battle is uncertain, but it was somewhere in the fields around the city of Catalaunum, hence the name of **Champs Catalauniques** which later became a symbol of deliverance from the Barbarian threat.

A site known as the "Camp d'Attila", lying 15km/9.3mi northeast of Châlons, is said to be the place where the Huns camped on the eve of the battle.

During the Middle Ages, the town became an important centre administered by bishops who took an active part in the coronation ceremonies in Reims *(see REIMS p 236)*.

During the Wars of Religion, the town remained loyal to the king who declared it to be the "main town of the Champagne region"; it became the seat of an annexe of the Paris Parliament and, in 1789, the main administrative town of the Marne *département*.

In 1856, a vast military camp was created near the town and a special pavilion was built for **Napoleon III** who often came to watch manœuvres and trials of new weapons as well as to perfect the education of the imperial prince.

★★CATHÉDRALE ST-ÉTIENNE (AZ) *30min*

Before the Revolution, a cloister, attached to the cathedral, stood on the site of the present square. Two royal marriages took place here during the reign of Louis XIV.

Exterior – The north side is in pure Gothic style: the nave, lined with high buttresses supporting double-course flying buttresses, has tall lancet windows; the transept is adorned with an attractive rose window and flanked by a tower with a Romanesque base which belonged to the previous cathedral destroyed by fire in 1230. The massive west portal dates from the 17C.

Interior – The edifice is nearly 100m/110yd long and looks quite imposing in spite of its relatively short chancel. Daylight pours generously into the 27m/89ft high nave which looks particularly elegant with its graceful triforium surmounted by large windows. The west front and the two bays closest to it were erected in 1628 in strict Gothic style.

The cathedral has retained an interesting number of **stained-glass windows★**, which make it possible to follow the progress of the art of stained-glass making between the 12C and 16C, as well as a few works of art in the transept and the chancel:

– The north transept contains 13C stained glass and a rose-window illustrating Jesus' childhood; note also the Renaissance bas-relief depicting a dead body.

– The lower part of the Romanesque tower adjacent to the north transept houses the **Treasury** ⊙ which includes three restored 12C stained-glass panels (representing the Crucifixion and the discovery of St Stephen's relics) and a 12C christening font decorated with a carving representing the Resurrection of the Dead.

– In the chancel stands an imposing baldaquined high altar, dating from the 17C and believed to be the work of Jules Hardouin-Mansart; note the superb Gothic tombstones set all around the chancel. The stained-glass windows above the high altar, dating from the 13C, depict Christ in glory, the Crucifixion and the Holy Mother, accompanied by saints, apostles and prophets.

– Two chapels on the right of the ambulatory contain a 15C painting on wood showing the consecration of the cathedral, Christ restrained by bonds (16C) and Christ in his tomb (17C low relief).

– On the south side, the 13C stained glass in the ninth bay depicts the Christening of Christ, the early 16C stained glass in the seventh bay again shows the Christening of Christ and scenes of his life; in the sixth bay, there is a 15C stained-glass window depicting the Virgin and Child; the next five bays contain early 16C stained glass illustrating the life and martyrdom of St Stephen, the Transfiguration, the Passion, the life of the Virgin Mary and the Creation (note the angel, dressed in a red gown, chasing Adam and Eve out of Paradise).

★NOTRE-DAME-EN-VAUX *1hr 30min*

★**Église Notre-Dame-en-Vaux** ⊘ **(AY F)** – This former collegiate church was built in Romanesque style at the beginning of the 12C, but the vaulting, the chancel and the east end, dating from the late 12C and early 13C, are fine examples of the Early Gothic style. The austere Romanesque west front, flanked by two towers surmounted by lead-covered spires, is reflected in the waters of the Mau Canal; the east end with its ambulatory and radiating chapels is enhanced by two Romanesque towers *(stand on the far side of the place Montseigneur-Tissier in order to get a good overall view)*. The 15C south porch precedes a Romanesque doorway; the statue-columns were mutilated during the Revolution, but the capitals, which were spared, are interesting. There is a peal of 56 bells.
A garden, situated on the north side of the church *(not open to the public)* marks the site of the former cloister.
Enter the church through the south doorway.
The harmonious proportions and simplicity of the **interior★★** are quite impressive. In the nave, there is a marked contrast between the pillars topped by Romanesque capitals and supporting vast galleries and the pointed Gothic vaulting. The chancel is characteristic of the region's architectural style.
The nave is lit by a harmonious set of **stained-glass windows★**. The finest, dating from the 16C, are on the north side. *Walk up the north aisle starting from the west doorway:*
Second bay: the legend of St James (1525) by the master glass-maker from Picardie, Mathieu Bléville, illustrates the battle which took place in 1212 between Christians and Moors (the pilgrims' route to Santiago de Compostela went through Châlons).
Third bay: the Dormition and Coronation of the Blessed Virgin, red and gold symbolising her glory; dated 1526 under the effigy of the donators.
Fourth and fifth bays: legends of St Anne and Mary; Christ's childhood.
Sixth bay: The Compassion of the Virgin Mary, against a blue background dotted with silver stars, is illustrated by a Deposition, a Pietà and Mary Magdalene (1526). *Walk down the south aisle:* past the south doorway, note the two restored stained-glass windows, acquired in the 17C, which depict the legend of St James. At the end of the aisle stands a large 15C wooden crucifix.
Above the west doorway, there is a row of three stained-glass windows, where green and red dominate, surmounted by a mainly blue rose-window, decorated with geometric motifs reminiscent of 13C stained-glass making; they were in fact made in c 1863 by Didron the Elder.

★**Musée du cloître de Notre-Dame-en-Vaux** ⊘ **(AY M¹)** – The cloister museum contains some remarkable sculptures from a Romanesque cloister, discovered in 1960. Built in the 12C next to Notre-Dame-en-Vaux, it was demolished in 1759 by the canons who replaced it with their own quarters. Excavations in the immediate surroundings have made it possible to recreate part of this splendid cloister.
A vast room contains sections of the former fortified wall, the reconstruction of four arcades framed by pillars as well as several valuable exhibits such as carved or ringed columns and 55 **statue-columns★★**: the finest depict prophets, famous biblical characters or saints (Moses, Daniel, Simon and Jesus as a child, St Paul whose face has a wonderful spiritual expression), characters from the Old Testament and from the Middle Ages (kings of Judea, 12C knights in full gear, the governor of Antioch, Olibrius, torturing St Margaret). The transition from the Romanesque to the Gothic style is emphasized by the expressive features of the characters, and the tendency for some of them to be separate from the column. Note a group of storiated capitals depicting episodes of Christ's life and the saints' legends. The four sides of one capital illustrate in succession the Presentation in the Temple, the Flight to Egypt, Jesus' Christening and the Resurrection of Lazarus. Another capital depicts the Wedding at Cana.

ADDITIONAL SIGHTS

Hôtel de ville (AY H) – The town hall was designed in 1771 by Nicolas Durand; the main hall is Doric and the wedding hall is adorned with Louis XVI pilasters of a colossal order.

Bibliothèque ⊘ **(AY E)** – The library is housed in a beautiful 17C residence, once the home of the governors of the city. It was raised by one storey in the 19C. It holds some precious manuscripts and books *(not on display)* such as the **Roman de la**

Rose, a famous 13C allegory in medieval French, and Queen Marie-Antoinette's book of prayers bearing her farewell to her children, written on the day of her execution.

The **Henri-Vendel passageway** leads from the courtyard of the library to the museum. It is lined with a large collection of firebacks.

Musée municipal ⊙ (AY **M²**) – The town museum is organized on two floors. Ground floor: reconstruction of a typical interior from the Champagne region (mid 19C), collection of Hindu deities (16C-17C), 13C recumbent figure of Blanche de Navarre, Countess of Champagne, 15C Head of Christ from the rood screen of Notre-Dame-en-Vaux, three polychrome wooden altarpieces, including one carved around 1500, representing the Passion, and a Head of St John the Baptist by Rodin.

First floor: local archeological finds from the Paleolithic period to the 17C; the Gallic period is particularly interesting. The fine arts gallery contains paintings from the 14C to the 20C: *Winter Landscape* by Josse de Momper (16C), *Gazotte's Portrait* by Perronneau (18C), *Park of St-Cloud Castle* by Daubigny and several works by the local painter, Antral (20C).

The ornithological collection includes some 3 000 birds mostly from Europe.

The last room contains furniture (16C-20C) and tapestries (15C-17C).

CHÂLONS-EN-CHAMPAGNE

Arche-Mauvillain
(Pl. de l') .... BZ 2
Bourgeois (R. Léon) ..... BY
Chastillon (R. de) .... ABZ 6
Croix-des-Teinturiers (R.) AZ 9

Flocmagny (R. du) .... BY 12
Foch (Pl. Maréchal) ...... AY 14
Gaulle (Av. Ch.-de) ...... BZ 15
Godart (Pl.) .... AY 17
Jaurès (R. Jean) .... AZ 20
Jessaint (R. de) .... BZ 22
Libération (Pl. de la) .... AZ 24
Mariniers (Pt. des) ...... AY 26
Marne (R. de la) .... AYZ 27

Martyrs-de-la-Résistance
(R. des) .... BY 29
Ormesson (Cours d') .... AZ 32
Prieur-de-la-Marne
(R.) .... BY 36
République (Pl. de la) ... AZ 39
Récamier (R. Juliette).... AZ 38
Vaux (R. de) .... AY 47
Viviers (Pt. des) .... AY 50

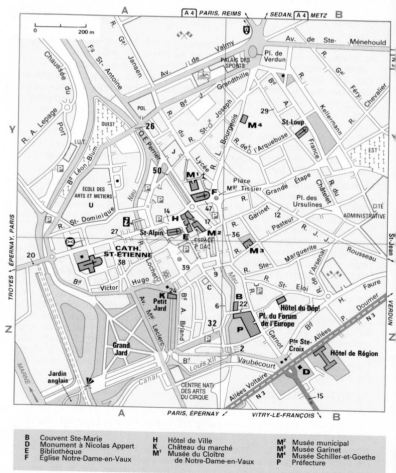

B   Couvent Ste-Marie
D   Monument à Nicolas Appert
E   Bibliothèque
F   Église Notre-Dame-en-Vaux
H   Hôtel de Ville
K   Château du marché
M¹ Musée du Cloître de Notre-Dame-en-Vaux
M² Musée municipal
M³ Musée Garinet
M⁴ Musée Schiller-et-Goethe
P   Préfecture

Église St-Alpin ⊘ (**AY**) – Surrounded by houses on its north and east sides, the church, built between the 12C and 16C, is a mixture of Flamboyant Gothic and Renaissance styles. In the chapels of the south aisle, there are **Renaissance windows** with magnificent *grisaille* stained glass representing the Bishop of Châlons, St Alpin, before Attila (first chapel), Emperor Augustus before the Sibyl of Tibur (third chapel), St John the Baptist (sixth chapel) and, in the south transept, the Miracle of the Loaves and Fishes, and the Miracle at Cana. The precious 15C stained-glass windows of the ambulatory have been restored.

The church contains fine works of art: in the north aisle there is a lovely Christ of Mercy from the 16C French School; in the nave there are several carved tomb-stones, including one going back to the 13C, and the gallery houses an organ case dating from 1762.

Musée Garinet ⊘ (**BZ M³**) – This ancient partly Gothic mansion houses a 19C bourgeois interior, enhanced by paintings from the 14C to 19C; particularly re-markable is the *Flagellation* attributed to Preti and *Ruth strolling in Booz's fields* by Cabanel (in the red room). The second floor contains a collection of some 100 models of French churches and cathedrals.

The Préfecture District (**BZ P**) – The Préfecture occupies the former residence of the royal treasurers of the Champagne region, built between 1759 and 1766; the archi-tects Legendre and Durand's design already points to Louis XVI's sober style. **Marie-Antoinette**, who stopped here on her way to marry the heir to the French throne, came back later, during the Revolution, humiliated after she failed to escape with the king and their children and was arrested in Varennes *(see ARGONNE: Varennes-en-Argonne)*.

Follow rue de Jessaint; on your right you will see part of a 17C convent known as the **Couvent Ste-Marie** ⊘ (**BZ B**); the façade is decorated with fluted pilasters whereas the back, ovelooking the Mau, is built with a mixture of white limestone and red brick. Cross the Mau to reach the **Cours d'Ormesson** (**AZ 32**) dating from the 18C, with lovely views of the Préfecture gardens and the Mau.

Retrace your steps and follow rue Vinetz on the other side of rue Carnot.

The former Couvent de Vinetz, built in the late 17C, now houses the **Hôtel du Département** (**BZ**), the administrative headquarters of the *département*. The façade of the chapel was built to look like a triumphal arch. A steep passageway leads to **place du Forum de l'Europe**; the square is surrounded by old buildings (gallery and timber-framed façade of the convent) and by modern ones (county archives), which are fine examples of style-blend-ing in an urban environment.

Porte Ste-Croix (**BZ**) – This triumphal gateway, erected in 1770 to welcome **Marie-Antoinette**, arriving in France to marry the future Louis XVI, was formerly known as the Porte Dauphine; it was never completed (only one side is decorated with carvings). Beyond the gate, opposite the **Hôtel de Région** (regional adminis-trative headquarters), stands a bronze column (**D**) by the sculptor Ipoustéguy, dedicated to **Nicolas Appert** (1749-1841), who invented a method of preserving food.

Le Jard (**AZ**) – This former grazing field, which formed part of the bishop's estates, was a convenient meeting place. St Bernard probably preached here in 1147 as no doubt did Pope Eugene III who consecrated the church the same year.

Laid in the 18C, the park is crossed by the avenue du Maréchal-Leclerc. It is divided into three sections:

the **Petit Jard**, a landscaped garden in the Napoleon III style, with a flower clock, laid on the site of the former ramparts. It extends along the banks of the Nau across which stands the Porte d'eau of the **Château du Marché** (**K**), a fortified construction which has retained a 16C turret;

Châlons-en-Champagne – Château du Marché

the **Grand Jard**, a vast esplanade lined with chestnut trees; from the footbridge linking it to the Jardin anglais across the canal running along the River Marne, there are pleasant **views** of the cathedral and the Préfecture;

the **Jardin anglais**, an English-style garden laid along the banks of the Marne in 1817.

Église St-Loup ⊘ **(BY)** – The church has a neo-Gothic façade dating from 1886. The 15C nave houses a triptych depicting the Adoration of the Magi, attributed to Van Eyck *(second bay on the left)*, a 16C statue of St Christopher in painted wood *(third bay on the right)*, a 17C painting by Vouet illustrating the Death of Mary Magdalene *(above the sacristy door)*.

Église St-Jean – *Walk along rue Jean-Jacques-Rousseau* (BZ).
The raised area in front of the church allows access to the west part rebuilt in the 14C. The west front flanked by buttresses, is surmounted by a pointed pediment decorated with 17C vases with flames coming out of them. The crossing is surmounted by a massive quadrangular steeple. In the 15C, a small chapel, known as the Crossbowmen's Chapel, was built off the south aisle: the Romanesque nave, covered with wood-panelled barrel vaulting, ends with a raised chancel and a flat apse. The stained-glass windows date from the 19C.

Musée Schiller-et-Goethe ⊘ **(BY M⁴)** – The collections were donated to the museum in 1952 by Baroness von Gleichen-Russwurm, the widow of Schiller's great grandson. They include Meissen and Wedgwood porcelain, vases, clocks, furniture and clothes having belonged to the German poet, together with a model of Schiller's monument by Thorvaldsen in Stuttgart. There are also a few mementoes of Goethe who was a friend of Schiller. The last room contains a bronze statue by Ernest Dagonet depicting the *Marseillaise*.

Within the diocese of Châlons-en-Champagne, the Cathédrale St-Étienne and the Église Notre-Dame-en-Vaux in Châlons, together with the basilica of Notre-Dame-de-l'Épine and several charming country churches, most of them unknown, are open in July and August (a brochure is available in tourist offices and at the diocesan headquarters, 20, rue de l'Abbé-Pierre-Gillet, 51038 Châlons cedex, ☎ 03 26 68 07 03).

Route du CHAMPAGNE★★

Michelin map 56 folds 14–17 or 237 folds 21–23

The map on page 62 shows the region of production of Champagne wine; the text explains how Champagne is made.

The Champagne vineyards, known since ancient times, produce a type of wine famous throughout the world.

The reputation of Champagne grew considerably from the 10C onwards, as a consequence of the fairs which took place during the 12C and 13C and, by the time the Renaissance came, it had spread beyond the borders of France. Yet, up to the 17C, Champagne was a predominantly red wine with a slight tendancy to sparkle. According to tradition, modern Champagne was "invented" by Dom Pérignon, a monk from the Benedictine abbey of Hautvillers, who mixed various local wines. Success was almost immediate: kings, princes and European aristocrats elected Champagne as their favourite drink for festive occasions.

The great Champagne firms were set up in Reims and Épernay from the 18C onwards: Ruinart in 1729, Fourneaux (which later became Taittinger) in 1734, Moët in 1743, Clicquot in 1772, Mumm in 1827...

In fact, the production of Champagne has constantly increased in spite of wars and natural catastrophies.

Champagne can be enjoyed at any time of the day, whatever the occasion. It must be served cold (between 6°C and 8°C/43°F and 47°F) and poured carefully into tall narrow glasses known as *flûtes* or flat wide ones known as *coupes* which enhance its bouquet. Brut Champagne can be served throughout a meal, although many Champagne lovers prefer to drink it as an aperitif or between meals. Sec or demi-sec Champagnes are suitable for dessert.

The authenticity of Champagne is guaranteed by the shape of the bottle and its label which, in addition to the name "Champagne", bears the name of the firm, the capacity of the bottle, the registration number of the Champagne guild preceded by the initials of the wine-grower and the sweetness content: *extra-brut* (or *brut zéro*, driest), *brut*, *extra-dry*, *sec*, *demi-sec*, *doux* (sweetest).

According to the quality of the grapes from which it is made, Champagne is said to be *rosé* (pink), *blanc de blancs* (made solely from white grapes), *blanc de noirs* (less well known, made exclusively from black grapes), *crémant* (its froth is particularly light), vintage Champagne (obtained by mixing wines of the same year but from different vineyards) and prestige Champagne made for specific occasions.

DISCOVERING THE CHAMPAGNE VINEYARDS

The area covered by the Champagne vineyards is well defined: it extends mainly across the Marne *département*, south of Reims, as well as in the southern part of the Aube and Aisne *départements*, around Château-Thierry.

A tour of the vineyards and of the Champagne cellars, often dug through limestone, offers an opportunity of discovering the two main centres of Champagne production, Reims with its magnificent cathedral and Épernay, and of exploring the countryside with its charming wine-growing villages nestling round small Romanesque churches.

The best time to tour the area is usually harvest time, towards the end of September and the beginning of October.

The last day of the harvest is quite an event, marked by a festive meal attended by wine-growers and harvesters.

On 22 January, the feast day of the patron saint of wine-growers, St Vincent, various processions go through the wine-growing villages. The festivities end with a traditional banquet.

The international fair of Champagne-making techniques (VIT'Eff) takes place in Épernay, every other year in May.

Several wine-growing areas are described in detail in this book: the Montagne de Reims, Côte des Blancs, Côte des Bars around Bar-sur-Aube. An itinerary through the most prestigious vineyards is given below.

FROM REIMS TO CHÂTEAU-THIERRY VIA ÉPERNAY

145km/90mi – allow one day

From Reims (see REIMS), drive south along N 51 to Montchenot, then turn left onto D 26 towards Rilly-la-Montagne. The road goes through many wine-growing villages within the **Parc naturel régional de la Montagne de Reims** *(see Parc naturel régional de la MONTAGNE DE REIMS and follow the itinerary from Rilly-la-Montagne to Hauvillers).* In Hautvillers *(see HAUTVILLERS),* the birthplace of Champagne, *drive towards Épernay along RD 386 which crosses D 1.*

From Épernay to Vertus, the **Côte des Blancs** *(see CÔTE DES BLANCS),* which owes its name to the predominant type of vine, known as Chardonnay, producing white grapes, offers a succession of hillside villages such as Cramant, Avize, Oger, Le Mesnil-sur-Oger.

From Bergères-les-Vertus, drive northwest through the Champagne **Brie** *area towards Château-Thierry: turn right onto RD 33 towards Étoges (see ÉTOGES) then continue along D 18 to Montmort-Lucy (see MONTMORT-LUCY) overlooked by its castle. The road follows the Surmelin Valley for a while.*

The castle in Mareuil-en-Brie belonged in the 18C to the count of Coigny whose daughter inspired the young poet André Chénier, guillotined during the French Revolution.

The road then runs through the Vassy Forest, scattered with small lakes, and reaches Dormans *(see DORMANS)* via Igny-Comblizy.

In Dormans, the itinerary reaches the **Marne Valley** *(see Vallée de la MARNE). Drive towards Château-Thierry along the north bank of the meandering River Marne.* The Aisne vineyards which prolong the Marne vineyards, begin in Trélou-sur-Marne. In Barsy-sur-Marne and Jaulgonne, terrace cultivation had to be applied owing to the steep slopes. *Drive through to Château-Thierry via Mont-St-Père, Gland and Bresles.*

There are marked itineraries, dotted with white panels bearing the inscription *"route touristique du champagne"* drawing the motorist's attention to the various information centres *(apply for information at the Comités départementaux du tourisme):*
– Massif de St-Thierry,
– Montagne de Reims,
– Vallée de la Marne,
– Côte des Blancs and Coteaux du Sézannais.
– Côte des Bars, Barséquanais and Baralbin.

Wine-tasting stops at wine-growers, Champagne firms and cooperatives are mentioned.

Museums devoted to wine-growing and wine-making make it possible for visitors to retrace the history of Champagne and to discover the techniques used in making Champagne:
– the local museum and the Musée de la Tradition champenoise (Maison de Castellane) in Épernay.
– the Musée du champagne (Maison Launois) in Mesnil-sur-Oger.
– the Maison de la vigne in Essoyes *(see Admission times and charges).*

The only types of grapes allowed within the Champagne area are:
– the Pinot Noir, a black grape, generous and full of vigour;
– the Pinot Meunier, also a black grape, young and fresh;
– the Chardonnay, a white grape, refined and elegant.

CHARLEVILLE-MÉZIÈRES

Conurbation 67 213
Michelin map 53 fold 18 or 241 fold 10 – Local map p 178

Charleville and Mézières, lying on the banks of the River Meuse, have each retained
their specific character in spite of having been united since 1966.
The middle-class and commercial city of **Charleville** stretches along the north bank of
the river overlooked by Mount Olympus, whereas **Mézières**, an administrative and
military centre, nestles inside a meander of the Meuse.

HISTORICAL NOTES

A Gallo-Roman city destroyed in the 5C by Barbarian invaders stood on the site of
Montcy-St-Pierre; the market town of **Arches** developed on the site of Charleville from
the 9C onwards and acquired a royal palace while Mézières, founded around the year
1000, was just a village; in the 13C, the two neighbouring towns belonged to the
count of Rethel and Nevers.
In 1565, Louis de Gonzague, who belonged to the House of the dukes of Mantua,
acquired the duchy of Nevers and the earldom of Rethel through his marriage to
Henrietta of Cleves. **Charles de Gonzague** (1580-1637) succeeded his father in 1595. In
1606, he decided to turn Arches into the main city of a principality and named it after
himself. Louis XIII granted Charleville the right of free trade with France and the
building of the town was completed in 1627, under the supervision of the architect
Clément Métezeau.
In 1590, a citadel was built to reinforce the strategic position of Mézières and in 1815
the Prussian advance was stopped here for 45 days. During the First World War,
Mézières was the headquarters of the German forces and Kaiser William II stayed in
Charleville on several occasions.

★CHARLEVILLE *2hr*

There were four squares in Charleville in addition to the place Ducale; each one had
its own church and formed a district. Today, the town has retained two of them:
place Winston-Churchill and place de l'Agriculture.

★★**Place Ducale** – Designed by **Clément Métezeau** (1581-1652), the square is characteristic of the Henri IV-Louis XIII architectural style and shows numerous similarities
with the place des Vosges in Paris, which is attributed to Louis Métezeau, Clément's
brother.

Charleville-Mézières – place Ducale

Charleville-Mézières, the capital of puppets

An amateur puppet theatre, known as the *Petits Comédiens de Chiffons*, has been staging shows in the town since 1941. To celebrate its 20th anniversary, the company invited puppeteers from France and other countries. This is how the first international puppet festival in France was born. As it became more and more famous, the festival took the name of **Festival mondial des Theâtres de Marionnettes**, which takes place every three years (the next one is due in 2000) for 10 days, in late September and early October. Courses intended to teach the technique of making puppets have been organised since 1981 and in 1987 the École supérieure national des Arts de la Marionnette, a higher education college, was inaugurated. The Union internationale de la marionnette also has its headquarters in Charleville-Mézières.

A. Nozay/CDT ARDENNES

The square (126m/138yd long and 90m/98yd wide) is still spectacular in spite of the replacement of the duke's palace by the Hôtel de ville in 1843. The statue of Charle de Gonzague, who founded the town in 1606, stands in the centre; the square is lined with arcades surmounted by pink brick and ochre-coloured stone pavilions topped by slate-covered pitched roofs, forming a harmonious and colourful ensemble. Several of these pavilions have been skillfully restored and their dormer-windows fitted with mullioned windows. Each of the four corners of the square was decorated with a dome similar to that at no 9.

★**Musée de l'Ardenne** ⊙ – This modern museum is housed in a group of buildings constructed over 400 years, linked by covered passages and footbridges. The collections are devoted to regional archeology, history and ethnography.

The archeology department, which is the most important, illustrates the first human settlements in the Ardennes, particularly during the Iron Age, the Roman period (stele, 2C mill, ceramics) and the Merovingian period (jewellery and weapons found in the graves of Mézières chieftains).

The first-floor rooms display weapons made in the royal weapon manufacture between 1688 and 1836, documents about the foundation of Charleville (17C relief maps) and an important collection of coins and medals.

The pharmacy (1756) with its 120 earthenware jars decorated with blue motifs, was originally in the former Hôtel-Dieu (hospital) and was still in use 25 years ago.

The top floor houses collections devoted to folk art and traditions: tools used by blacksmiths and slate-quarry workers (in Monthermé, Fumay or Rimogne), nails made in the area during the 18C and 19C, reconstruction of a typical Ardennes interior.

The fine arts section includes sculptures by Croisy *(Four Seasons)* and 19C paintings by Couvelet, Damas and Gondrexon.

A public passageway *(same opening times as the museum)*, which crosses the museum courtyard, links the place Ducale and the place Winston-Churchill.

Horloge du Grand Marionnettiste – *place Winston-Churchill.*
Incorporated into the façade of the Institut international de la Marionnette, this 10m/33ft high brass automaton is the work of Jacques Monestier; its head and eyes are moved by clockwork every hour between 10am and 9pm, a short puppet show depicts an episode of the legend of the Four Aymon Brothers, the twelve scenes being enacted every Saturday at 9pm.

Vieux Moulin – The former ducal mill looks more like a monumental gate than a mill, which is not surprising since it was designed to match the Porte de France in the south, lining up with the main axis of the city. Its imposing Henri IV-Louis XIII façade is decorated with Ionic Italian-style columns.

Musée Rimbaud ⊙ – Housed inside the old mill, the museum contains mementoes of the poet **Arthur Rimbaud** (1854-1891), a native of Charleville: photographs, letters, personal objects, various documents and a portrait by Fernand Léger. *A brief biography of the poet appears on page 58.*

A footbridge, situated behind the museum and overlooking the River Meuse, give access to Mount Olympus.

In Rimbaud's footsteps – The poet's childhood house (7, quai Rimbaud and his college, now the local library (4, place de l'Agriculture) can b seen near the museum; his birthplace (12, rue Bérégovoy) is situate south of the place Ducale and his grave near the entrance of the ol cemetery (avenue Charles-Boutet); a bust of Rimbaud was erected on th square de la Gare in 1901.

Rue de la République – Each pavilion contains two homes under a large slate covered roof. Shops occupy the ground floor on either side of the main doo according to the plans drawn by Charles de Gonzague. There are other simila houses in **rue du Moulin**.

MÉZIÈRES *30min*

Basilique Notre-Dame-d'Espérance – Although it was remodelled over several centuries this basilica is essentially in Flamboyant-Gothic style, except for the belfry-porc erected in the 17C. The interior is grandiose: the central nave is flanked wit double aisles and surmounted by lierne and tierceron vaulting with pendant *(illustration page 35)*. Light pours in through some beautiful abstract **stained-glas windows★**, made between 1955 and 1979 by René Dürrbach who found hi inspiration in a text by Henri Giriat on the theme of the Virgin Mary.
In the 19C, the basilica was dedicated to Notre-Dame-d'Espérance, a black statu of the Virgin standing on top of an altar situated to the right of the chancel.

Ramparts – Part of the medieval ramparts are still standing: Tour du Roy, Tour d l'École, Tour Milart, Porte Neuve, Porte de Bourgogne.

Préfecture – The administrative offices are housed in the buildings of the forme Royal Engineers School (17C-18C).

EXCURSIONS

Mohon – *Drive south out of town towards Reims.*
This industrial town has a 16C church, **Église St-Lié** ⊘, where pilgrims used to flock to see the relics of St Lié. The early-17C west front is decorated with trompe-l'oei motifs.

Warcq – *3km/1.9mi west along avenue St-Julien and D 16.*
The fortified **church** ⊘ has a tower which looks like a keep. Inside it is a hall churc and contains a statue of St Hubert dating from the 18C *(pillar on the left of th altar)*.

St-Laurent – *6km/3.7mi. Drive east out of town along D 979.*
Several marked round tours offer a pleasant walk through this **zoological park** ⊘ covering 45ha/111 acres, where wild boars, deer, roe-deer, goats and moufflons (not forgetting numerous species of birds) roam almost freely.

Ancienne Abbaye de Sept Fontaines – *9km/5.6mi southwest.*
The road (D 39), which follows the delightful Fagnon Valley, offers a fine view of the former abbey dating from the 17C, which has been turned into a hotel.

Launois-sur-Vence – *20km southwest along D 3.*
This small village has retained a 17C posting-house, which made communications between Amsterdam and Marseille easier, particularly after the foundation of Charleville-Mézières. The buildings surrounding the vast inner courtyard include the postmaster's house, the coach house with its beautiful timber frame, the stables, the sheep's pen and the vaulted cider cellar. It is now occupied by the tourist office and a cultural centre which organises many events.

★Vallon d'Élan – *8.5km/5.3mi south. Drive out of Mézières along D 764 to Flize and continue south along D 33 to Élan.*
Although close to the River Meuse, the Vallon d'Élan, with its pasture-covered steep slopes looks like a mountain valley. The Cistercian abbey, founded in 1148, became quite wealthy during the Middle Ages but its prosperity had considerably declined at the time of the Revolution. The Gothic abbey church, with its 17C Classical west front, forms a harmonious architectural ensemble with the abbey manor flanked with elegant turrets (beautiful chestnut timber-work).
At the end of the valley, the 17C **Chapelle St-Roger** stands on the spot where the first abbot, St Roger, liked to meditate. There is a spring nearby.
The **Forêt d'Élan**, covering 872ha/2 006 acres, includes beautiful specimens of oaks and beeches.

On Michelin road maps at a scale of 1:200,000, places with a hotel or restaurant listed in the Red Guide are underlined in red.

CHÂTEAU-THIERRY

Population 15 312
Michelin map 56 fold 14 or 237 fold 21

Château-Thierry lies on both banks of the River Marne and on the slopes of an isolated hill crowned by the former castle; the progress of wine-growing in this part of the Marne Valley has strengthened its links with the Champagne-producing area further east; however, Château-Thierry is mainly famous as the birthplace of the French poet and world famous fable-writer, **Jean de La Fontaine**.

La Fontaine and Château-Thierry – Born in 1621, La Fontaine was more inclined towards rambling than studying. However, he thought he had a religious vocation and entered a seminary, soon discovering that he had made a mistake. He then became a lawyer, came back to Château-Thierry and got married, but he remained a day-dreamer and neglected both his work and his wife. Then one day he heard an officer recite a poem and had a revelation: he had to become a poet himself. At the age of 46, he became Fouquet's official poet and received a regular income from him. However, after Fouquet's arrest, he settled in Paris where he was widely acclaimed until his death in 1695.

For more information on the poet and his Fables, turn to page 56.

TOUR OF THE TOWN

1hr 30min

Start from place de l'Hôtel de ville and walk up the rue du Château to the Porte St-Pierre.

Porte St-Pierre – This is the only one of the four town gates still standing. The main façade is flanked with two round towers.

Château – Go in through the Porte St-Jean and note the embossed decoration which is characteristic of the late-14C style. The former garrison town was razed almost to the ground and the castle turned into a pleasant walking area offering fine views of the town, the Marne Valley and the monument on top of Cote 204 *(see Excursions below)*.
From the Tour Bouillon, where a carved-stone map of the old castle can be seen, a staircase leads down to the lower watchpath.

Portrait of Jean de La Fontaine

Maison natale de La Fontaine ⊙ – This 16C mansion was partly remodelled and now houses the museum devoted to La Fontaine. In addition to private documents, it contains magnificent editions of the *Fables* and *Tales*, including those illustrated by Oudry in 1755 and Gustave Doré in 1868; there is also a collection of various objects decorated with scenes from the *Fables*.
Walk back along the Grande Rue, a lively street lined with old houses.

Caves de champagne Pannier ⊙ – *23, rue Roger-Catillon to the west of the town.* An audio-visual presentation and a tour of the cellars located in 13C stone quarries enable visitors to follow the process of Champagne-making.

EXCURSIONS

Condé-en-Brie – *16km/10mi southeast along N 3 to Crézancy then D 4.*
This small market town has retained an interesting covered market with Doric columns and a **castle** ⊙ rebuilt in the 16C then remodelled in the 18C. It belonged to the Condé family, a junior branch of the House of Bourbon who reigned over France almost continually from the advent of Henri IV (1589) to the abdication of Louis-Philippe (1848).
The interior has retained its 18C decoration and furniture. The **Grand Salon★** is particularly noteworthy with its still-life paintings by Oudry and 17C fresco. Trompe-l'œil canvases by Servandoni hang in the music room. The main staircase was also designed by him. The west wing was decorated by Watteau and his students.

Cote 204 and Bois Belleau – *16km/10mi northwest; allow 2hr. Drive west out of Château-Thierry along N 3 and turn left at the top of the hill along the avenue leading to Cote 204.*

Cote 204 was a very strong position held by the Germans in June 1918. It toc both a French and an American division more than five weeks to dislodge them. A American monument stands at the top.
Fine view of Château-Thierry, the castle and the Marne Valley.
Return to N 3 and, at the crossroads, continue straight on along D 9 to Belleau.

Bois Belleau was taken by the Marines in June 1918. The vast **American cemetel** houses 2 350 graves. The commemorative chapel, looking like a topless Romanesqu tower, bears the names of all the missing soldiers.
The **German cemetery** is situated 500m/547yd further on.
Return to the crossroads where the American cemetery is located and turn right onto narrow road marked "Belleau Wood".

The monument dedicated to the Marines is inside the wood which was the cause o such fierce fighting.

Round tour through the Marne Valley – *47km/29mi; allow 1hr 30min. Leav Château-Thierry southeast along D 969 which follows the meanders of the river.*
The former abbey **church★** ⊘ of **Essômes-sur-Marne** dates from the 13C. The **interior★** is characteristic of early-Gothic architecture. Note the elegant triforium with its narrow twin openings.
Make a detour via Montcourt then turn left onto D 1400.

The road runs through vineyards, offering, between Mont-de-Bonneil and Azy, a interesting **panorama** of a meander of the Marne with the wooded Brie region in the background.
Rejoin D 969 in Azy then turn right in Charly onto D 11 to Villiers-Saint-Denis and lef onto D 842 to Crouttes.

The road offers a wide view of the deep meander of the Marne to the south.

The wine-growing village of **Crouttes** owes its name to its cellars dug out of the rock. Leave the car near the town hall and walk up to the church picturesquely perched above the village.
Return to Charly along D 969 and cross the river; turn left onto D 86 to Nogent-l'Artaud and Chézy.

The road overlooks the Marne and offers fine views of the slopes planted with vines.
Return to Château-Thierry via D 15 and D 1.

CHAUMONT

Population 27 041
Michelin map 62 fold 11 or 241 fold 43

Chaumont-en-Bassigny, situated on the edge of a steep plateau separating the River Suize and the River Marne, was an important trading centre during the Middle Ages.
The counts of Champagne resided in Chaumont from 1228 to 1239, just before Champagne was united with France. The city, which occupies a natural defensive position, has retained part of its medieval character illustrated by the keep of the former feudal castle and the hexagonal 13C Tour d'Arse.
The town of Chaumont owns an important collection of old and contemporary posters and organises several annual events including the Festival international de l'Affiche (International Poster Festival) and Rencontres internationales d'Arts graphiques (International Festival of Graphic Arts).

SIGHTS

Old town – It has retained some old houses with corbelled turrets containing spiral staircases and a few square towers as well as many mansions with carved doorways, middle-class houses surmounted by dormer windows and a few bartizans. Do not miss the turreted houses in rue Guyard and rue Gouthière, the dormer windows in rue St-Jean, the doorways in rue Girardon and the bartizan in rue Bouchardon.
Place de la Concorde, overlooked by the 18C town hall, is surrounded by a network of picturesque narrow streets.

★Basilique St-Jean-Baptiste – The edifice dates from the 13C and 16C. In the 15C, it became a collegiate church and retained its chapter of canons until the Revolution.
The west front, surmounted by two towers dates from the 13C. The **Portail St-Jean**, which opens on the south side, is protected by a stone porch. A fine Virgin with Child is bonded to the upright post; admire the carved door leaves. The tympanum is decorated with a low relief depicting the life of St John the Baptist *(Zachary Visits the Temple, Birth of St John the Baptist*, his *Christening* and his *Beheading)* and surrounded by an archivolt adorned with angels.

The transept and the east end, in Flamboyant Gothic and Renaissance style, date from the 16C. Note the decoration of the doorways and buttresses on each side of the transept.

Inside, the chancel and transept, decorated at the time of the Renaissance, are the most interesting parts of the church, in particular the upper gallery forming a succession of loggias and the keystone pendentives decorating the vaulting. In the north transept, a graceful turret with fine tracery houses a corner staircase. Note the 16C high relief representing the **Tree of Jesse**, carved on the wall of the apsidal chapel close to the arm of the transept.

In the chapel situated at the west end of the nave, on the left-hand side, there is a highly realistic **Entombment★** (1471). The expression and attitude of the eleven life-size characters in polychrome stone are remarkable.

The basilica also contains various paintings and sculptures from the School of Jean-Baptiste Bouchardon, including a high altar in gilt carved wood, a pulpit and a bench from the early 18C.

The "Grand Pardon de peine et de coulpe", initiated by Jean de Montmi-rel (1409-1479) to ward off plague, famine and war, has been celebrated ever since, every time midsummer's day falls on a Sunday, that is to say every five, six or eleven years; the next celebrations will take place in 2001 with processions in the streets, floral decorations in the town centre, theatre performances...

Donjon ⊘ – This square keep, built in the 12C, is all that remains of the former castle of the counts of Champagne; temporary exhibitions and cultural events are held inside.

From the top, there is a fine view of the town and the valley of the River Suize.

Les silos, Maison du livre et de l'affiche ⊘ – The silos have been turned into a multi-purpose cultural centre housing a library, a reference library with multimedia facilities and a poster museum which contains more than 10 000 posters including works by Jules Chéret (1836-1932), Théophile Alexandre Steinlen (1859-1923) and Henri de Toulouse-Lautrec (1864-1901). Themed exhibitions are organised regularly.

Musée ⊘ – Housed in the vaulted rooms of the former palace of the counts of Champagne, the museum displays archeological collections (bronze armour from the 8C BC, Gallo-Roman altar and mosaic, Merovingian sarcoph-

Basilique St-Jean-Baptiste in Chaumont
John the Baptist

agi), paintings from the 16C to 19C (works by Paul de Vos, Sébastien Stosdopff, Nicolas Poussin, François Alexandre Pernot) and sculptures (recumbent effigy of Jean l'Aveugle de Châteauvillain, altarpiece from the Basilique St-Jean and above all fragments of the funeral monument of Antoinette de Bourbon and Claude de Lorraine by Dominique Florentin). A room is devoted to the Bouchardon family: altarpiece from the Chapelle des Ursulines, the *Ascension of the Virgin* carved in wood by Jean-Baptiste Bouchardon and drawings by his son Edme.

The **Salon des expositions** (an annexe of the museum situated near the basilica) exhibits a collection of crèches (nativity scenes with figurines) from the 17C to 20C, made from a variety of materials including wax, wood, glass, terracotta; don't miss the surprising collection of 18C crèches from Naples.

ADDITIONAL SIGHTS

Square Philippe-Lebon – From this square there is a view of the keep, of the ramparts, of the towers of the Basilique St-Jean, of the steeple of the Jesuits' chapel and of the small dome of the town hall.

Chapelle des Jésuites ⊘ – The chapel of the former Jesuits' college contains an altarpiece depicting the Assumption of the Virgin by Bouchardon (at the back of the high altar in gilt carved wood).

As you come out of the chapel, look out for the fountain on the left; it is decorated with a bust of Bouchardon.

★**Viaduct** – *West along avenue du Maréchal-Foch.*
This magnificent structure has 50 three-storey arches; it is 600m/656yd long
towers 52m/171ft above the Suize Valley and carries railway lines right into th
town centre.
It is possible to walk along the first storey which offers a fine view of the valley.

EXCURSION

Prez-sous-Lafauche – *38km/23.6mi northeast along N 74.*
In this village of the upper Marne Valley, there is a **Zoo de bois** ⊙, an unusu
museum of "found art" – a collection of tree branches which resemble people ar
animals and have been placed in funny situations.

*To best enjoy the major tourist attractions, which draw big crowds, try to avoid visiting
the peak periods of the day or year.*

Abbaye de CLAIRVAUX

Michelin map 61 fold 19 or 241 fold 42

On 25 June 1115, St Bernard settled with 11 monks in the remote "Val d'Absinth
and founded one of the four major houses of the new Cistercian order. At the death
the founder abbot in 1153, the Abbaye de Clairvaux had 800 monks and lay brothe
and controlled 69 monasteries; its vast domain extended over more tha
2 000ha/4 942 acres and its considerable influence made it one of the main religio
centres of the Middle Ages.
Difficult times followed the medieval period: for instance, the abbey was ransacked t
the Huguenots during the Wars of Religion; there were also times of religio
decadence or, on the contrary, of spiritual renewal such as the Trappist reform in th
17C. At the time of the Revolution, there were only 26 monks and 10 lay brothers
the abbey which, nevertheless worked 20 000ha/49 422 acres of forests and agricu
tural land and owned important industrial concerns (ironworks).
Confiscated and sold in 1792, the abbey was turned into glassworks, then bought t
the state in 1808 to become a prison. Today, it still belongs to the Ministry of Justi
and several 18C buildings are used for administrative purposes.
However, Clairvaux was partly reopened to the public in 1985.

St Bernard (1090-1153)

Bernard de Fontaine (later known as Bernard de Clairvaux), a young aristocrat
from the Bourgogne region, should have become a soldier to comply with his
family's wishes. Yet, at the age of 21, he entered the Abbaye de Cîteaux
together with his brothers and several uncles and cousins whom he had per-
suaded to follow him. He was only 25 when Étienne Harding, the abbot of
Cîteaux, sent him away with the mission of founding Clairvaux. Being both a
mystic and a fine administrator, Bernard soon embodied the Cistercian ideal: the
strict observance of the rule of St Benedict (prayer and work) which had,
according to him, been relaxed by the Benedictine order.
Deprived of everything, the young abbot encountered immense difficulties: the
harshness of the climate, diseases, physical hardship. For his monks and himself, he set the hardest tasks; "they ate boiled vegetables and drank water, slept
on pallets, had no heating in winter and wore the same clothes day and night".
Yet this new form of spirituality and Bernard's reputation attracted many
enthusiasts and the success of the new abbey was immediate.
The young mystic wanted to reform the whole religious life of his time and he
played a part in many of its aspects: the election of bishops, various councils,
the papal schism, the second crusade which he preached in Vezelay in 1146. His
moral ascendancy gave him a considerable influence in European courts as well
as in Rome where he pushed for the election of Pope Innocent II (1130-1143)
and then Eugene III, a former monk at Clairvaux who was elected pope in
1145.
Shocked by the failure of the Crusade (1148) and by the rise of heretic beliefs,
which he fought without success, he died in 1153 and was canonised in 1174.
St Bernard was one of the strongest personalities of medieval times; his
authoritarian behaviour was inspired by his passionate faith ("the way to love
God is to love him without limit or measure", he said) combined with his taste
for simplicity and voluntary deprivation.

THE MODEL OF ALL CISTERCIAN MONASTERIES

Life in a Cistercian monastery – St Bernard clearly defined and enforced the Benedictine rule laid down before his time. He forbade his monasteries to levy any form of tithe, to receive or purchase land and he imposed upon the monks of Clairvaux (and consequently upon all Cistercian monks) extremely hard living conditions.

The day's timetable was rigorously followed: the monks got up between 1am and 2am, sang Matins and Lauds, then celebrated private masses, recited the set prayers of the canonical hours – prime, terce, sext, none, vesper and compline – and heard the conventual mass. Thus religious services kept them busy for six to seven hours a day and the rest of their time was shared between manual work, intellectual work and the reading of religious texts. The abbot lived among his monks, had his meals with them, presided over all services and meetings of the chapter. He was seconded by a prior who took his place in his absence.

The Rule stressed the importance of working in the fields and Clairvaux soon became a thriving agricultural centre, a pioneer in the expansion of land cultivation, in which the monks excelled. Their system was based on farms, known as *granges*, under the control of the abbey: Clairvaux owned five of them when St Bernard died, 10 at the end of the 12C and 20 in the 14C. In addition to the farm buildings, each *grange* had a dormitory, a refectory, a warming-room and a chapel. Clairvaux next turned to mining and the production of iron, eventually owning some 10 ironworks and becoming in the 18C the most important producer of iron in the Champagne region. The Clairvaux ironworks *(2km/1.2mi from the abbey)* have not stopped working for almost nine centuries. There are also traces of the abbey's former *granges*, the most interesting being the Ferme du Cellier in Colombé-le-Sec *(see p 81)*.

The monastic community included the **monks** who prayed and copied manuscripts and the **lay brothers** who worked in the fields with the help of the **oblates**; the latter were laymen who were allowed to take part in the prayers and worked all their life for the monastery in exchange for their board and lodging.

St Bernard and Cistercian architecture – Simplicity and voluntary deprivation naturally led to a plain and austere architectural style. St Bernard strove to fight against the sumptuosity of so many abbey churches (excessive size, a wealth of ornamentation and interior decoration) and imposed drastic rules: no carved capitals, no stained glass and no steeples. These principles were, of course, applied to Clairvaux; the abbey church, built between 1135 and 1145 then extended from 1154 to 1174, was demolished between 1812 and 1819. Its plan was copied by all the Cistercian houses founded subsequently and in particular by Fontenay in Burgundy. Shaped like a Latin cross, the abbey church was about 100m/328ft long; the nave and the aisles ended in a flat east end lit by three high windows and flanked by four chapels opening onto a vast transept.

Clairvaux and the art of illumination – The abbey workshop produced a wealth of illuminations (almost all of them have been preserved – 1 400 manuscripts – in Troyes' municipal library, *see p 314*) steeped in the Cistercian ideal. The principle of austerity so dear to St Bernard was also applied to the art of illumination: bright colours and imaginative motifs were banned in favour of geometric forms and palettes in more subdued colours such as blue, green, pale red and ochre. However, "St Bernard's Bible" is not totally devoid of fantasy; it includes some picturesque scenes often depicted with shimmering colours.

In the 12C, the Clairvaux manuscripts had an impact on the artistic renewal of the Champagne region comparable to that of the School of Reims. They were copied by monks from all over Europe. It is estimated that, at the end of the 12C, the abbey owned 340 large volumes and that the skins of 300 sheep had been used in the making of the Great Bible alone!

Clairvaux I: monasterium vetus 1115-1135
Clairvaux II: lay brothers' building 1135-1708
Clairvaux III: grand cloître 1708-1792

TOUR OF THE ABBEY ⊘ *allow 2hr*

A high wall, 2.7km/1.6mi long, which encloses an area of 30ha/75 acres, has replaced the fortified wall built by the monks in the 14C.
The way into the estate is through the Porte du Midi. Immediately to the left is the former Hostellerie des Dames and, beyond, the houses and kitchen gardens of Petit Clairvaux; opposite stand the austere monastic buildings of Haut Clairvaux.

Hostellerie des Dames – When Clairvaux was a monastery, women were not allowed to enter the enclosure; therefore the wives of the abbey's visitors had to stay in this building, recently restored.

Petit Clairvaux (Clairvaux I) – The site where Bernard de Clairvaux built his *monasterium vetus* in 1115 is occupied today by the living quarters of the personnel of a nearby penal establishment. The original spring is still visible in the middle of a clump of trees. A few sections of the old walls remain though to remind people that the first monastery was not built of wood as legend would have it.

Abbaye de CLAIRVAUX

Clairvaux – Lay brothers' building

Along the northern part of the surrounding wall stands the 18C Chapelle Ste-Anne which was reserved for outsiders.

Haut Clairvaux (Clairvaux II) – In view of the expansion of the abbey and in spite of the unfavourable advice of Bernard de Clairvaux, Prior Geoffroy de la Roche Vaneau undertook, between 1135 and 1145, the construction of a new monastery at a distance of 300m/328yd from the first. His project was supported by the Count of Champagne, Thibaut II. The lodge of this "new" monastery is today that of the penal establishment. It gives access to the main courtyard which led to the abbey church and the 50 buildings which made up the great Cistercian abbey. It is possible to go into the courtyard and admire the beautiful 18C façades. A small doorway then leads to the lay brothers' courtyard and the buildings of Haut Clairvaux.

★**Bâtiment des convers** – The lay brothers' building is all that remains of Clairvaux II. It comprises a basement cellar and a dormitory in the upper part; both are divided into three naves of 12 bays each. No decoration was allowed to distract the occupants' mind from God. The groined vaulting of the upper floor offers a very sobre white-stone outline whereas the ribbed vaulting of the cellar is supported by octagonal pillars. The building dates from 1140-1160. Note the marks left by stone-masons on the arcading.

Grand cloître (Clairvaux III) – Next comes the wash-house, which has been turned into a canteen. The River Aube was diverted to bring water to the abbey. Further on are the buildings of the new abbey built from 1740 onwards by Abbot Pierre Mayeur round a vast cloister (each side is 50m/164ft long) after the major part of the medieval abbey was demolished.

Clairvaux as a prison – When the abbey became state property in 1808, considerable work was undertaken to turn it into a prison, the largest of its kind in France. The abbey church which had survived the Revolution was almost entirely demolished in 1812 then disappeared completely in 1819. The lay brothers' building became a workshop. The abbot's and prior's mansions lining the main courtyard were used to house the directors. The vast cloister was split into several dormitories which can be seen between the ground floor and the upper floor there, some of the cubicles, designed to give the prisoners some privacy, are still visible.

The tour ends with the monks' refectory, a huge hall (35m/115ft long, 13m/43ft wide and 12m/40ft high) with wood-panelling on the walls.

This dining room served as a prison chapel until 1971; it could hold 1 500 prisoners (standing of course!). Among the famous prisoners held at Clairvaux were the socialist and revolutionary Louis-Auguste Blanqui (1872), members of the Paris Commune, Philippe d'Orléans (1890) and Prince Protopkine (trial of the anarchists from Lyon), deserters from Verdun (1917), many members of the Resistance (1940-1944) of whom 21 were shot, several ministers of the Vichy government (after the Liberation of France) and insubordinate generals during the Algerian War of Independence.

COLMAR★★★

Conurbation 83 816
Michelin map 87 fold 17 or 242 fold 31 – Local map see Route des VINS

The great appeal of Colmar lies in the typical Alsatian character of it streets lined with picturesque houses adorned with carvings and a wealth of ornamentation. Its Musée d'Unterlinden is a must for any visitor. Situated at the heart of the Alsatian vineyards, Colmar is also the starting point of numerous excursions.
The international festival of gastronomy (Festiga), which gathers many culinary talents and presents excellent food products from all over the world, takes place in Colmar (the next one will be held in 2002).

HISTORICAL NOTES

A Frankish town developed in the Rhine Valley, on the banks of the River Lauch, a tributary of the Ill. Emperor Charlemagne, and his son after him, often came to stay. Labourers and craftsmen lived round the royal "villa". In its centre stood a tower with a dovecote which is said to have given its name to the future city: Villa Columbaria (colombe means dove in French), contracted to Columbra and eventually Colmar.
In spite of these peaceful beginnings, Colmar had a troubled history and often had to fight for its freedom. In 1261 the son of a tanner, **Roesselmann**, became the local hero when he bravely led the town militia against the bishop of Strasbourg's soldiers and paid for the city's freedom with his life. Two centuries later, Colmar, together with other Alsatian towns, temporarily came under the rule of the Duke of Burgundy, Charles le Téméraire, and his cruel bailiff, Pierre de Hagenbach. When the latter was at last defeated and taken prisoner, he was condemned to death and the executioner of Colmar was chosen to carry out the sentence. The sword he used is still kept in the Musée d'Unterlinden.
Between 1870 and 1914, when Alsace was occupied by Germany, a talented caricaturist and water colour artist, Jean-Jacques Waltz, better known as **Hansi**, stimulated the town's passive resistance to German influence and kept alive the traditional image of Alsace with his humoristic drawings of grotesque-looking German soldiers and good-natured, likeable peasants and villagers in regional costume.
In late January 1945, French and American troops under the command of **Général de Lattre de Tassigny** attacked one of the last pockets of German resistance, known as the "Colmar pocket" and on 2 February tanks of the French fifth armoured division led by Général Schlesser entered Colmar.

★★MUSÉE D'UNTERLINDEN ⊘ (AY) *2hr*

This museum, situated on place d'Unterlinden through which flows the Logelbach canal, is housed in a former 13C convent whose name means "under the lime trees". The convent changed from the observance of the rule of St Augustin to that of St Dominic and, for 500 years, its nuns were famous for their

---

ON THE TOWN
Guided tours

Guided tours of the old town at 10am, and of the Musée d'Unterlinden at 11.15am, are organised in July and August on Tuesdays, Thursdays and Saturdays and in September on Sundays. Information available from the tourist office.

Tourist train

A small train takes visitors on a 7km/4mi guided tour (35min) through the old town. Departure; quai de la Sinn, Easter to November, 9am to 6pm every half hour.

Entertainment

Between May and September, folkloric displays take place every Tuesday at 8.30pm on place de l'Ancienne-Douane.
Théâtre de la Manufacture, 6, route d'Ingersheim: modern plays, dance shows, music.
Théâtre municipal, place du 18-Novembre: operas, classical plays.

Cheers!

In the **old town**: "Schwendi", 23-25, Grande-Rue, typical Alsatian bar; "Louisiana Club", 3, rue Berthe-Molly, piano-bar, young convivial atmosphere; "Le Club", 12-14, rue Porte-Neuve, English-style pub, 80 different kinds of beer, many cocktails; "Best Bar", Hôtel Amiral, boulevard du Champ-de-Mars.

mysticism and austere way of life. The community was dissolved and the convent turned into barracks before becoming a museum in 1849. Today it is once more famous, but this time for the works of art it contains (Grünewald, Schongauer, Isenmann).

★**Cloître** – The cloister was built in the 13C of pink sandstone from the Vosges mountains. Halfway down the western gallery, one of the arches is larger than the others and more profusely decorated. It stands over what used to be the lavabo; the basin is still visible. In a corner stands an unusual Renaissance well.

Ground floor – The rooms on this floor are devoted to art from the Rhine Valley. There are rich collections of medieval and Renaissance painting and sculpture, as well as minor art forms, with the Retable d'Issenheim as the prize exhibit. *It is advisable to visit rooms 1, 3 and 4 as a preliminary step to the discovery of the masterpiece.*

Rooms 1 and 4 – Sculpture and minor art forms of the medieval and Renaissance periods, 15C and 16C stained glass, statues from St-Martin-de-Colmar, carved-wood altarpiece from Bergheim...

Room 3 – Collection of **Primitive** works from the Rhine region and Germany: predella from Bergheim, panels from the polyptych (1462-1465) of the collegiate church of St-Martin by **Caspar Isenmann** depicting the Passion etc, portrait of a woman by Holbein the Elder, allegorical scene, *Melancholia*, and *Crucifixion* by Cranach the Elder, austere still-life painting with bottles and books, dating from the early 16C and numerous copper engravings by **Martin Schongauer**, an engraver and painter born in Colmar.

Chapelle – *Access via room 4*. The **gallery** of the former Dominican chapel (early-16C sculpture) makes a good viewpoint, enabling visitors to have an overall view of the three central panels and fully appreciate the composition of the famous polyptych.

Works by Schongauer – *Room 5*. The panels of the **Orlier Altarpiece★**, painted c 1470 for the Issenheim convent, are located beneath the gallery. The 24 painted panels of the altarpiece from the Dominican church in Colmar, depicting the **Passion★★** (School of Schongauer) are displayed in the centre of the nave. The reverse side shows scenes from the life of the Virgin.

★★★**Retable d'Issenheim** (Issenheim Altarpiece) – Painted by **Matthias Grünewald** at the beginning of the 16C for the high altar of the monastery at Issenheim, it was taken to Colmar in 1793. Founded in 1298, the monastery was devoted to the cure of patients suffering from ergotism. Around 1500, the prior had the church decorated by the greatest artists of his time.

The polyptych is made up of a carved central part, two fixed panels, two pairs of opening panels and a lower part which also opens. In order to preserve this unique work of art, the different parts were dismantled and are now displayed separately in the chancel. Several models with opening panels have been fixed to the chapel's walls to enable visitors to understand how the altarpiece opened out.

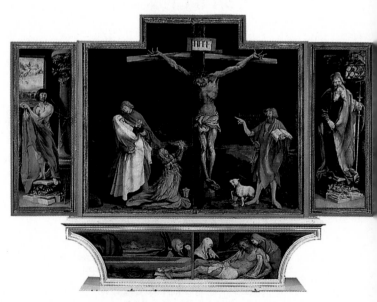

Colmar – The Issenheim Altarpiece

To begin with, the altarpiece is presented in its closed position so that one can measure the full dramatic impact of the **Crucifixion**, one of the most impressive scenes ever depicted by a western religious painting. The predella shows a moving Entombment. On the reverse side, the Annunciation and the Resurrection are represented. The first opening reveals the central part with the Nativity and the Chorus of Angels. The reverse side illustrates the Visit of St Anthony to St Paul and the Temptation of St Anthony.

The second opening shows the carved part of the central panel: three magnificent statues in gilt wood representing St Anthony between St Jerome and St Augustin, believed to be by Nicolas de Haguenau; the lower part, carved in high relief and depicting Jesus among his disciples is believed to be the work of members of Haguenau's School. The statues of a gentleman and a peasant at the feet of St Anthony, stolen in 1823, were returned to their origiinal place in 1985, following an exchange with the Badisches Museum in Karlsruhe, Germany.

As you come out of the chapel, walk up to the first floor.

First floor – The collections on this floor concern the history of Colmar and the region, Alsatian art, furniture, weapons, pewter, gold plate, wrought iron, 18C porcelain and earthenware (Strasbourg). There are also reconstructions of various interiors including the Gothic room, with wood panelling on the walls and ceiling, and the English ladies' drawing room (18C) with its splendid **ceiling**, painted in trompe-l'œil as was the fashion during the Baroque period.

Go down to the basement.

Basement – The Gallo-Roman room contains fragments of the Bergheim mosaic (3C AD). Further on, the two barrel-vaulted naves of the former **cellar** of the convent (13C), admirably preserved, house the archeological collections, from prehistory to the Merovingian period. Two rooms are devoted to modern art: a child's portrait by Renoir; Rouault *(De profundiis, The Child Jesus Among the Doctors)*; Picasso *(Bust of a Seated Woman)*; Viera da Silva, Roger Bissière *(The Forest)*, Léger, Nicolas de Staël *(Anne's Portrait)*, Hélion, Poliakoff.

As you go back through the cloister, look at the reconstruction of a wine-grower's cellar, with 17C winepresses and large casks.

★★ ① OLD TOWN *allow 2hr*

Round tour starting from place d'Unterlinden

Walk along rue des Clefs.

The Hôtel de ville is on the left; this 18C building with pink-sandstone ties belonged to the Abbaye de Pairis *(see Val d'ORBEY)*.

When you reach place Jeanne-d'Arc, turn right onto Grand'Rue.

Église St-Mathieu ⊙ **(BZ)** – This former Franciscan church, which is now a Protestant temple, is decorated with fine 14C and 15C **stained-glass windows**. The most remarkable of them, known as the **Vitrail de la Crucifixion★** (15C) and believed to be the work of Pierre d'Andlau, is located at the top of the south aisle.

Turn left along the side of the temple to reach place du 2-Février lined on the east side by the old hospital.

Ancien Hôpital (BZ) – The façade of this Classical-style edifice is surmounted by a sloping roof with "Alsatian" dormer windows.

Return to Grand'Rue and turn left.

★**Maison des Arcades (BZ E)** – The Renaissance façade (1609), framed by two octagonal turrets, is supported by 10 rounded arches.

In the centre of the square, the **Schwendi Fountain (BZ B)** by a native of Colmar, the sculptor Frédéric-Auguste Bartholdi, commemorates the man who imported the famous Tokay vine into the region *(see KAYSERSBERG)*. Walk past the **Maison du Pèlerin (BZ F)** (1571) to place de l'Ancienne-Douane, a picturesque square lined with timber-framed houses such as the **Maison au Fer Rouge (BZ D)**.

★**Ancienne Douane or "Koifhus" (BZ N)** – This former customs house is the most important civilian edifice in Colmar. There are two separate buildings. The main one dates from 1480. The ground floor was used as a warehouse to stock goods subject to municipal tax. The great hall of the first floor, known as the Salle de la Décapole (the union formed by 10 Alsatian cities), was the meeting place of the representatives of those cities. The second building was added at the end of the 16C.

It is an attractive building decorated with a wooden gallery and flanked by a stair turret with canted corners; on the ground floor, three arches underline the opening and form a passage. Walk through to the other side and admire the fine outside staircase.

Take rue des Marchands opposite the customs house; it is, with Grand'Rue, one of the most picturesque streets in Colmar. The Maison Pfister stands on the right, on the corner of rue Mercière.

COLMAR

Augustins (R. des) .... AZ 2
Ancienne-Douane
  (Pl. de l') .... BZ 3
Boulangers (R. des) ..... AY 4
Cathédrale (Pl. de la) ... ABZ 7
Cigogne (R. de la) .... BZ 8
Clefs (R. des) .... BY
Cloches (R. des) .... BY 9
Consul-Souverain
  (R. du) .... BZ 12
École (R. des) .... BZ 13
Grenouillère (R. de la) ... BZ 14

Haslinger (Pl.) .... BY 15
Herse (R. de la) .... BZ 16
Kléber (R.) .... AY 17
Lattre-de-Tassigny
  (Av. et Pl. de) ...... AYZ 18
Marchands (R. des) .... ABZ 19
Marché-aux-Fruits
  (Pl. du) .... BZ 22
Mercière (R.) .... BZ 23
Neuf-Brisach
  (Rte de) .... BZ 24
Poissonnerie
  (R. et Q. de la) ...... BZ 25
Porte-Neuve
  (R. de la) .... AZ 26
République (Av.) .... AZ

Schongauer (R.) .... BZ 28
Sélestat (R. de) .... BY 29
Serruriers
  (R. des) .... AZ 31
Sinn (Quai de la) .... AY 32
Tanneurs (R. des) ...... BZ 33
Têtes (R. des) .... AY
Unterlinden
  (Pl. et R.) .... AY 34
Vauban (R.) .... BY
4e-Bataillon-de-Chasseurs-
  à-Pied (R. du) .... BY 37
6-Montagnes-Noires
  (Pl. des) .... AZ 38
18-Novembre
  (Pl. du) .... AY 39

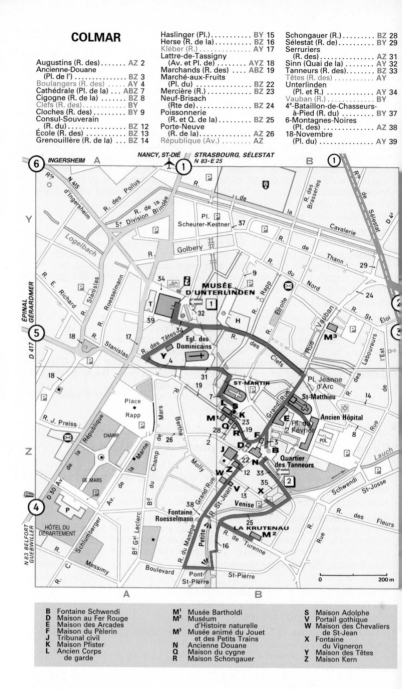

B   Fontaine Schwendi
D   Maison au Fer Rouge
E   Maison des Arcades
F   Maison du Pèlerin
J   Tribunal civil
K   Maison Pfister
L   Ancien Corps
      de garde

M¹ Musée Bartholdi
M² Muséum
      d'Histoire naturelle
M³ Musée animé du Jouet
      et des Petits Trains
N   Ancienne Douane
Q   Maison du cygne
R   Maison Schongauer

S   Maison Adolphe
V   Portail gothique
W   Maison des Chevaliers
      de St-Jean
X   Fontaine
      du Vigneron
Y   Maison des Têtes
Z   Maison Kern

★★**Maison Pfister** (BZ **K**) – A hatter from Besançon had this house built in 1537
decorated with frescoes and medallions, it is the loveliest house in the old town.
The arcaded ground floor is surmounted by an elegant wooden gallery interrupte
on the corner by an oriel window topped by a pyramidal roof.
Next to the Maison Pfister, at no 9, stands a fine house (1609) adorned with
wooden gallery and a corner sculpted figure representing a merchant.
On the left of rue des Marchands, the 15C **Maison Schongauer** (BZ **R**) belonged to th
painter's family.
Note the small house opposite, known as the **Maison au Cygne** (BZ **Q**), wher
Schongauer is said to have lived from 1477 to 1490.
The painter Caspar Isenmann lived a little further on, at no 34.

Musée Bartholdi ⊙ (ABZ **M¹**) – The house where **Frédéric-Auguste Bartholdi** (1834
1904) was born, right in the town centre, is now a museum dedicated to th
sculptor who acquired worldwide fame on account of his Statue of Liberty standin
at the entrance of New York harbour.

In the inner courtyard, a bronze group (1902), *The Main Supports of the World*, symbolises justice, patriotism and labour.

The downstairs rooms contain a majority of works sculpted in Colmar, including four sandstone fragments of allegorical statues intended for the Bruat Fountain (1864), which was demolished in 1940 and a bronze statue entitled *The Art of a Goldsmith*, depicting the sculptor as a goldsmith. The last room is devoted to Jewish art.

On the first floor, his living quarters are furnished exactly as they were during his life (study, music room, dining room with its unusual ceiling decorated with Chinese porcelain and small drawing room) and contain mementoes of the artist. The other rooms display souvenirs of his journey to Egypt (water colours, photographs, terracotta models of *Egypt Enlightening the East*) and models of many public monuments in France (Lion of Belfort, Fontaine des Terreaux in Lyon, Vercingétorix in Clermont-Ferrand...).

The second floor is devoted to his American works, in particular the different stages of the making of the Statue of Liberty.

Schwendi Fountain

Bartholdi's works in Colmar
– Statue of General Rapp, place Rapp
– Monument to Admiral Bruat, place du Champ-de-Mars
– Schwendi Fountain, place de l'Ancienne-Douane
– Wine-grower's Fountain, corner of rue des Écoles and rue du Vigneron.

Walk through the arcades opposite the museum, where the walnut market was held, and look at the façade of the Ancien Corps de garde (guard-house), situated on Place de la Cathédrale.

★**Ancien Corps de garde** (BZ L) – The edifice was built in 1575. The town's magistrate took the oath from the lovely Renaissance loggia decorating the façade and infamous sentences were also proclaimed from there. In the corner stands the oldest house in Colmar, **Maison Adolphe** (BZ S) (1350), which has been restored.

Opposite the former guard-house stands the collegiate church of St-Martin, known as the "cathedral".

★**Collégiale St-Martin** (BZ) – This imposing edifice covered with glazed tiles and decorated with red-sandstone projections was built in the 13C and 14C on the site of a Romanesque church.

Exterior – The west doorway was meant to be flanked by two towers but the south tower alone was completed. It is surmounted by an unusual pinnacle shaped like a Chinese hat and is decorated with a sundial bearing the inscription *Memento Mori*. The central tympanum illustrates Christ as a judge between angels and, below, the Adoration of the Magi. **St Nicholas' doorway**, which gives access to the south transept, is decorated with 13 small statues; the fourth one on the left is the representation of the builder who signed in French, Maistres Humbert. The tympanum, which is Gothic in its upper part and Romanesque in its lower part, shows Christ rising from the Dead and, below, the legend of St Nicholas.

Interior – Flooded with a kind of golden light, the church is impressive on account of its size and the quality of the furniture it contains. The 13C Gothic nave (21m/69ft high), surmounted by a pointed vault without a triforium, is particularly remarkable. The 14C chancel is also noteworthy: an unusual passageway goes round it, linking the chapels and forming a kind of narrow ambulatory. These radiating chapels are decorated with interesting sculptures: a 14C **Crucifixion**★ in the axial chapel, the 15C "Colmar Virgin" and a Last Supper of the same period in the next two chapels on the left.

In the middle of the 18C, a magnificent organ by Silbermann was fitted at the back of the church. The imposing loft is all that remains of the original instrument replaced by a new one in 1974.

On the way out, note two fine 14C stained-glass windows next to the stairs leading to the gallery.

Leave the church by one of the west doors, turn right then left onto rue des Serruriers

Église des Dominicains ⊙ (AY) – Work began on the chancel in 1283, but the main part of the edifice was only completed in the 14C and 15C. Inside, the absence of capitals adds to the impression of loftiness; altars and stalls date from the 18C; but the magnificent **stained-glass windows**★ are contemporary with the construction of the church (superb effigy of King Solomon above the south doorway).

The famous painting by Martin Schongauer, the **Virgin of the Rose Bower**★★, can be seen at the entrance of the chancel; it was painted in 1473. The Virgin and Child form a charming picture against a golden background decorated with white and red rose bushes full of birds.

Walk along rue des Boulangers then turn right onto rue des Têtes.

★**Maison des Têtes** (AY Y) – *At no 19.* This fine Renaissance house (1608) owes its strange name to the numerous carved heads decorating the façade. The graceful gable is underlined by rows of scrolls; oriel windows over two storeys complete the elaborate ornamentation *(see p 43)*. It has now been turned into a hotel and a restaurant.

Return to place d'Unterlinden.

★ ② "PETITE VENISE" (LITTLE VENICE) *allow 45min*

Round tour starting from place de l'Ancienne-Douane

From the square, follow rue des Tanneurs which runs along the canal.

Quartiers des tanneurs – The tanners' district owes its name to its inhabitants who, being near the river, could tan hides and wash them. This activity was discontinued in the 19C. The renovation of the district, completed in 1974, was very successful, in particular along rue des Tanneurs and "petite" rue des Tanneurs (at no 3, lovely house with ashlars underlining the openings). Timber-framed houses were narrow but very high as they had a loft for drying the skins.

Cross the River Lauch to enter the **Krutenau district**, once a fortified outlying area, where many market-gardeners lived; it has retained its picturesque character. These market-gardeners used flat-bottomed boats, similar to Venetian gondolas, to glide along the river.

Turn right along quai de la Poissonnerie.

Cross the next bridge to the corner of rue des Écoles and rue du Vigneron, where the **Fontaine du Vigneron** (BZ X) stands; it was designed by Bartholdi as a celebration of Alsatian wines.

Continue along quai de la Poissonnerie, then rue de la Poissonnerie lined with picturesque fishermen's cottages. It runs into rue de Turenne, the former rue de Krutenau, once the site of the vegetable market.

Museum d'Histoire naturelle ⊙ (BZ M²) – Housed in a 17C building, the natural-history collections of the city of Colmar give a general idea of the region's fauna and forest environment.

The important geology section illustrates more than a billion years of intense activity, which explains the great diversity of the region's landscapes.

An Egyptian room and an ethnographical collection (in particular from the Marquesas Islands) complete the tour.

Take rue de la Herse then turn right onto a narrow street leading to the river.

Pleasant stroll along the bank to Pont St-Pierre. From the bridge, there is a lovely view★ of the "Petite Venise", with the tower of the Église St-Martin in the background.

Below the bridge, **boat tours** ⊙ are available to explore the district further.

Turn right onto rue du Manège leading to place des Six-Montagnes-Noires.

The **Fontaine Roesselmann** (AZ), another of Bartholdi's works, stands on the square. It is dedicated to the town's hero *(see COLMAR: Historical notes)*.

Walk towards the bridge on the right; the river, lined with willow trees, flows between two picturesque rows of old houses.

Colmar – "Petite Venise"

Continue along rue St-Jean.
On the left stands the **Maison des Chevaliers de St-Jean** (**BZ W**), a fine Renaissance building decorated with superposed galleries. A Gothic doorway (**BZ V**) across the street is all that remains of the old medieval building.
A little further, place du Marché-aux-Fruits is lined with the **Maison Kern** (**BZ Z**), in Renaissance style, the lovely Classical façade (in pink sandstone) of the **Tribunal civil★** (**BZ J**) to the left and the Ancienne Douane across the square.

ADDITIONAL SIGHTS

Musée animé du Jouet et des Petits Trains ⊙ (**BY M³**) – Spread on three levels, the museum's collections include numerous railway engines (including the Britannia, British model Pacific 213), trains, dolls in many different materials; collectors will recognize some rare items. One window is given over to a circus theme, with automated figures and fun-fair rides; in another Cinderella's carriage is pulled by four horses using 22 electric motors. On the top floor, trains run around landscaped tracks – guaranteed to appeal to the child in us all.

Maison des vins d'Alsace ⊙ – *12, avenue de la Foire-aux-Vins* – The centre houses four important organisations connected with the wine-growing business. A large relief map shows wine-growing villages and famous vineyards and visitors can get an insight into the work of wine-growers with the help of models and an audio-visual presentation.

EXCURSION

Neuf-Brisach – *15km/9.3mi southeast of Colmar. Leave by ② on the town plan and drive along N 415.*
This octagonal stronghold built by Vauban, Louis XIV's military engineer and architect, has retained its austere 17C character *(illustration page 43)* in spite of the damage incurred during the 1870 siege and the Second World War.

The world's longest walk

The **Paris-Colmar** walk through 171 municipalities and eight *départements* has, since 1981, been a hard test for some 30 of the best hikers in the world. They cover the 520km/323mi in about 70hr (an average of 7.5kph/4.6mph) to arrive on the picturesque place de l'Ancienne-Douane in Colmar where great festivities take place in their honour.
The equivalent feat for women is a walk from Châlons-en-Champagne to Colmar (335km/208mi).

The area within the 2.4km/1.5mi long walls is split into regular plots by a network of streets intersecting at right angles. In the centre stands the Église St-Louis and the vast place d'Armes (parade ground) with a well in each of its four corners.

It is possible to walk along the ditch from the Porte de Belfort (southwest) to the Porte de Colmar (northwest). This pleasant stroll (about 30min) reveals the main elements of the fortifications: bartizaned bastions, ravelins etc.

The **Porte de Belfort**, no longer used as a gate, houses the **Musée Vauban** ⊘ which contains a relief map of the stronghold with a *son et lumière* show.

In summer, the **Association CFTR** ⊘ organises trips aboard steam trains (dating from the 1900s) combined with boat trips (1933) along the Rhine.

Slightly further east *(5km/3mi)*, at **Vogelgrün**, the border-bridge over the Rhine offers a fine **view★** of the river, the hydroelectric power station *(see GRAND CANAL D'ALSACE)* and Vieux-Brisach (Breisach) across the border.

COLOMBEY-LES-DEUX-ÉGLISES

Population 660
Michelin map 61 fold 19 or 241 fold 38

Situated on the edge of the Champagne region and on the borders of Burgundy and Lorraine, Colombey has, since time immemorial, been a stopover on the road from Paris to Basle. However, it became famous through its most illustrious citizen, **Charles de Gaulle**, who had his home at La Boissière from 1933 until his death in 1970. He is buried in the village cemetery, near the church.

In his *Memoirs*, De Gaulle talks about the Champagne landscapes he loved so much *steeped in sadness and melancholy ... former mountains drastically eroded and resigned ... quiet, modest villages whose soul and location have not changed for thousands of years ...*

La Boisserie ⊘ – During the Second World War, La Boisserie was severely damaged by the Germans: part of the roof was destroyed by fire and a wall collapsed. General de Gaulle only returned with his family in May 1946 after having had some work done to the house (a corner tower and a porch were added). It has not changed since that time and continues to preserve the memory of its owner who found it relaxing and conducive to deep thinking about important decisions.

Silence fills my house. From the corner room where I spend most of the day, I embrace the horizon towards the setting sun. No house can be seen over a distance of fifteen kilometres. Beyond the plain and the woods, I can see the long curves sloping down towards the Aube Valley and the heights rising on the other side. From a high point in the garden, I behold the wild forested depths. I watch the night enveloping the landscape and then, looking at the stars, I clearly realise the insignificance of things.

Charles de Gaulle, *Mémoires de guerre*

The public is allowed in the downstairs drawing room, full of mementoes, books, family portraits and photographs of contemporary personalities; in the vast library and the adjacent study where General de Gaulle spent many hours and in the dining room.

Mémorial ⊘ – Inaugurated on 18 June 1972, the memorial stands on the "mountain", which overlooks the village and surrounding forests (including the Clairvaux Forest where St Bernard founded his famous abbey in the 12C) from the great height of 397m/1 302ft.

Every year the Michelin Red Guides publish updated town plans which show
– through routes, by-passes, new streets
– new roads, one-way systems and car parks
– the exact location of hotels, restaurants and public buildings.
Take the stress out of driving in and around town when you travel!

CÔTE DES BLANCS ★

Michelin map 56 fold 16 or 241 folds 21 and 25

Stretching between Épernay and Vertus, the Côte des Blancs or Côte Blanche owes its name to its white-grape vineyards consisting almost exclusively of Chardonnay vines. The refined grapes grown in the area are used to produce vintage and "blanc de blancs" (made solely from white grapes) Champagne.

The majority of the great Champagne firms own vineyards in this area; some of these are even equipped with a heating system to protect the vines from frost.

Like the Montagne de Reims, the Côte des Blancs is a bank sloping down from the edge of the Ile-de-France cliff, facing due east and entirely covered with vines.

The twisting lanes of the villages dotted along the slopes are lined with wine-growers' houses with their characteristic high doorways.

FROM ÉPERNAY TO MONT AIMÉ

28km/17.4mi – allow 1hr 30min

The road described below runs halfway up the slopes, offering general and close-up views of the vineyards, the Montagne de Reims and the vast plain of Châlons.

★**Épernay** – *See ÉPERNAY.*

Leave Épernay south along the Sézanne road to Pierry.

Pierry – The town hall now occupies the house where **Jacques Cazotte** lived; the author of *Le Diable amoureux* ("the Devil in love") was guillotined in 1792.

In Pierry, turn left onto D 10.

This road offers views of Épernay and the Marne Valley on the left.

Cuis –The Romanesque church stands on a platform overlooking the village. From D 10, there are interesting vistas of the Montagne de Reims.

★**Cramant** – This village lies in a pleasant setting, at the heart of an area producing the famous Crémant wine (from the "Pinot blanc Chardonnay" vine) sometimes called "Blanc de Crémant".

Avize – Also famous for its wine, Avize runs a school for future Champagne wine-growers. The 12C church has a 15C chancel and transept. Take a walk above the little town to the west for extended views of the whole area.

Oger – Producing a *premier cru de la Côte Blanche*, one of the area's top quality wines, Oger has a fine church dating from the 12C-13C with a high square tower and flat east end.

Le Mesnil-sur-Oger – This wine-growing village is widely spread out. In the centre of a shaded close stands the Romanesque church with its tower surmounting the crossing and its Renaissance doorway framed by fluted columns. There is an interesting **Musée de la Vigne et du Vin** ⊘ displaying objects, winepresses, tools and machinery which illustrate wine-growing in the past; traditional crafts connected with wine-growing are also dealt with, in particular the production of corks, bottles and barrels.

A small road winds its way across the vineyards to Vertus.

Vertus – This small town surrounded by vineyards was once the property of the counts of Champagne who lived in a castle now demolished except for the Porte Baudet. During the Middle Ages, Vertus, which had several springs, was a busy market town enclosed by a defensive wall. Today, it is a quiet little town dotted with charming squares.

The **Église St-Martin** was built in the late 11C and early 12C. Damaged by fire in 1167, partly destroyed during the Hundred Years War and remodelled several times, it was finally restored after the 1940 fire. The pointed vaulting over the transept and east end dates from the 15C. Note the delicately carved 16C Pietà in the south transept and the 16C stone statue of St John the Baptist near the christening fonts. Stairs lead from the north transept to three 11C crypts; note the capitals of the central crypt, beautifully carved with foliage motifs.

On the way down to Bergères-lès-Vertus, the road affords pleasant views of the surrounding area.

Bergères-lès-Vertus – Small Romanesque country church.

South of Bergères-lès-Vertus, turn right onto the road leading to Mont Aimé.

★**Mont Aimé** – Once part of the Ile-de-France cliff, this isolated hill reaches 237m/778ft. Inhabited since prehistoric times, it was fortified successively by the Gauls, the Romans and the counts of Champagne who built a feudal castle; its ruins are today scattered among the greenery.

On 10 September 1815, a great parade of the Russian army (stationed in the area during the occupation of France by several European countries following the fall of Napoleon) took place at the foot of the hill.

In one of the corners of the old fortifications, a viewpoint *(viewing table)* offers an extended **view** of the Côte des Blancs to the north and of the plain of Châlons to the east.

Route des CRÊTES ★★★

Michelin map 87 folds 17, 18 and 19 or 242 folds 31 and 35

This strategic road was built during the First World War at the request of the French High Command, in order to ensure adequate north-south communications between the various valleys along the front line of the Vosges.

The magnificent itinerary, which continually follows the ridge line, enables motorists to admire the most characteristic landscapes of the Vosges mountains, its passes, its *ballons* (rounded summits), its lakes, its *chaumes* (high pastures where cattle graze in summer) and offers wide panoramas and extended views. In addition it reveals one of the most famous battlefields of the First World War, Vieil-Armand.

Between the Hohneck and the Grand Ballon, the road is lined with *fermes-auberges* (farmhouses turned into inns during the season) where snacks and regional dishes are served from June to October.

The road goes through forested areas constituting half its total distance.

FROM COL DU BONHOMME TO THANN
83km/52mi – allow half a day

Col du Bonhomme – Alt 949m/3 114ft. The pass links the two neighbouring regions of Alsace and Lorraine.

Beyond the pass, the road offers fine vistas of the Béhine Valley to the left, with the Tête des Faux and the Brézouard towering above. Further on, the Col du Louchbach affords a beautiful view of the valley of the River Meurthe to the south.

Turn right at Col du Calvaire.

As it leaves the forest, the road offers views of the Hohneck with the Gérardmer mountains in the distance; in the foreground, the view embraces the Meurthe Valley and the St-Dié Basin.

★**Gazon du Faing** – *45min on foot there and back.* As you reach the summit (1 303m/4 275ft), climb up to a large rock from where an extended panoramic **view** is to be had. In the foreground, the small Étang des Truites, changed into a reservoir by a dam, lies inside the Lenzwasen glacial cirque. Further afield, one can see, from left to right, the Linge, the Schratzmaennele and the Barrenkopf; more to the right, beyond the Fecht Valley and the town of Munster, a long ridge slopes down from the Petit Ballon; to the right of this summit, the silhouette of the Grand Ballon (alt 1 424m/4 672ft) rises in the distance; the twin summits of the Petit Hohneck (alt 1 288m/4 226ft) and Hohneck (alt 1 362m/4 469ft) can be seen further to the right.

Further right still, there is a view of the Rudin and Grand Valtin valleys and of the heights overlooking the upper Meurthe Valley.

Lac Vert – A path starting near the 5km/3mi mark from Col de la Schlucht leads to the Lac Vert, also known as the Lac de Soultzeren. Lichens floating in the water give the lake its characteristic colour.

Col de la Schlucht – Alt 1 139m/3 737ft. The pass links the upper valley of the River Meurthe (which takes its source 1km/0.6mi away from the pass) with that of the River Fecht. Situated at the intersection of the Route des Crêtes and the Gérardmer to Colmar road, La Schlucht is one of the busiest passes of the Vosges mountains. It is also a popular ski resort.

Jardin d'Altitude du Haut-Chitelet ⊘ – Alt 1 228m/4 029. *2km/1.2mi from Col de la Schlucht towards Le Markstein, on the right-hand side of D 430.*
These botanical gardens cover an area of 11ha/27 acres and include a beech wood and a peat bog. Rockeries spreading over more than 1ha/2.5 acres shelter 2 700 species of plants from the main mountain ranges of the world.

Further on, the road offers a fine **view★** of the Valogne Valley, of Lake Longemer and Lake Retournemer. The village of Xonrupt and the suburbs of Gérardmer can be seen in the distance *(viewpoint).*

★★★**Hohneck** – *The steep access path starts from the Route des Crêtes, 4km/2.5mi south of Col de la Schlucht; do not follow the private path which starts closer to the pass (3km/1.9mi) as it is in bad condition. The road is generally closed between the Hohneck and the Grand Ballon from mid-November to mid-March.*
This is one of the most famous and one of the highest summits of the Vosges mountains (alt 1 362m/4 469ft). It is the highest point of the ridge which, before the First World War marked the border between France and Germany.
A splendid **panorama★★★** *(viewing table)* unfolds, encompassing the Vosges from the Donon to the Grand Ballon, the Plaine d'Alsace and the Black Forest. In clear weather, the summits of the Alps are visible.
The road runs through high pastures, known as *chaumes*. The Lac de Blanchemer can be seen on the right, framed in a beautiful wooded setting. Further on there is a magnificent view of the Grande Vallée de la Fecht, followed by the lake and valley of the Lauch with the Plaine d'Alsace in the distance.

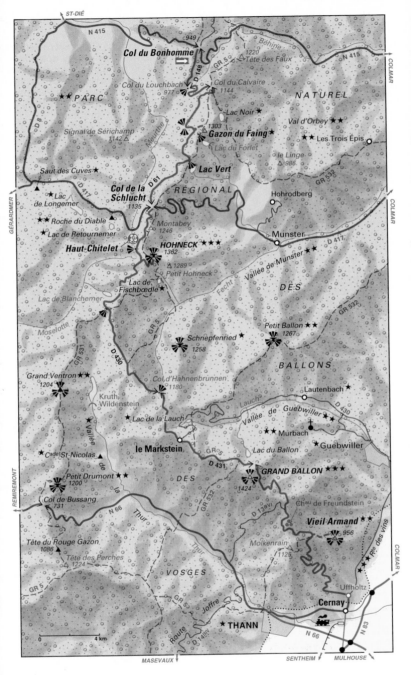

Le Markstein – *See GUEBWILLER: Guebwiller Valley.*

As you drive along the cliff road, there are alternate views of the Thur Valley and Ballon d'Alsace massif on one side and of the Lauch Valley and Petit Ballon on the other. The small **Lac du Ballon** lies inside a funnel-shaped basin.

★★★**Grand Ballon** – *Leave the car by the hotel and follow the path on the left (30min on foot there and back).* There is a radar station at the summit. The Grand Ballon, also known as the Ballon de Guebwiller, is the highest summit (alt 1 424m/4 672ft) of the Vosges mountains. Just below the summit, the Monument des "Diables Bleus" was erected to commemorate the various regiments of *chasseurs* (mountain troops). From the summit of the Grand Ballon, the **panorama**★★★ embraces the southern Vosges, the Black Forest and, when the weather is clear, the Jura mountains and the Alps.

On the way down, there are superb views and a chance to see the ruins of Freundstein Castle.

★★Vieil-Armand – The name was given by the soldiers of the First World War to the foothills of the Vosges (Hartmannswillerkopf) which slope steeply down to the Plaine d'Alsace. This strategic position was one of the most bloody battlefields along the Alsatian front (30 000 French and German soldiers killed). In 1915, attacks and counter attacks were repeatedly launched on its slopes laid waste by the artillery, and the summit, which was turned into a real fortress, was taken time and again.

The **Monument national du Vieil-Armand** ⊙ was built over a crypt containing the remains of 12 000 unknown soldiers; a bronze altar, decorated with the emblems of major French towns, stands on a vast platform.

The **summit** can be reached on foot *(1hr there and back)*. Walk through the cemetery situated behind the national monument, which contains 1 260 graves and several ossuaries. Follow the central alleyway and the path beyond it. Walk towards the summit of Vieil-Armand (alt 956m/3 136ft) surmounted by a 22m/72ft high luminous cross which marks the limit of the French front. Turn right towards the iron cross erected on a rocky promontory to commemorate the volunteers from Alsace-Lorraine. Wide **panorama★★** of the Plaine d'Alsace, the Vosges mountains, the Black Forest and, in clear weather, the Alps. Several commemorative monuments including the monument to the Diables Rouges of the 152nd infantry regiment and the monument to the German mountain troops. Sections of trenches and shelters, mostly German.

Finest viewpoints of the Vosges mountains		
Ballon d'Alsace	★★★	1 250 m
Ballon de Servance	★★	1 216 m
Belmont (rocky knoll)	★★	1 272 m
Brézouard	★★	1 228 m
Champ du Feu	★★	1 100 m
Donon	★★	1 009 m
Galz	★★	730 m
Grand Ballon	★★★	1 424 m
Grand Ventron	★★	1 202 m
Hohkönigsburg	★★	755 m
Hohneck	★★	1 362 m
Hohrodberg	★★	750 m
Montsec	★★	375 m
Mont-Ste-Odile	★★	761 m
Neuntelstein (Rock)	★★	971 m
Nideck	★★	411 m
Petit Ballon	★★	1 267 m
Petit Drumont	★★	1 200 m
Roche du Diable	★★	981 m
Vaudémont	★★	541 m
Vieil-Armand	★★	956 m

On the way down to Uffholtz, the road affords views of the Plaine d'Alsace and of the Black Forest.

Cernay – This small industrial town lies at the foot of Vieil-Armand. It has retained traces of its medieval fortified wall, including the Porte de Thann which houses a small **museum** ⊙ illustrating the wars of 1870, 1914-18 and 1939-45.

From St-André, south of Cernay, it is possible to go on a **tour** ⊙ of the Doller Valley aboard a steam train, over a distance of 14km/8.7mi to Sentheim.

Drive west along D 35.

★Thann – See THANN.

Région de DABO-WANGENBOURG★★

Michelin map 87 folds 14 and 15 or 242 folds 19 and 23

he picturesque Dabo-Wangenbourg region lies on the border of Alsace and Lorraine.
s mountain landscapes, its green valleys, overlooked by ruined castles, and its vast
orests invariably appeal to tourists.
andstone, which is the backbone of the area, is omnipresent and takes on many
napes: long ridges or vertical cliffs, rocky spurs or isolated rocks. Here and there,
olcanic rocks combined with red sandstone add colour to the landscape. A typical
xample of this is the porphyry-rock face of the Nideck waterfall.
he austere sandstone massifs are separated by green valleys and calm rivers flowing
n beds of fine sand.
he ancient and powerful House of Dabo, also known as Dagsbourg, was descended
rom the duke of Alsace Étichon who was the father of St Odile. The most illustrious
member of this dynasty was Bruno de Dabo, born in 1002 in Dagsbourg castle, who
ecame pope under the name of **Leo IX** and was later canonised.
he Peace of Nijmegen (1678), which confirmed the union of France and Alsace,
eprived the counts of Dabo of their lands; their castle was dismantled in 1679 and
azed 11 years later.

FROM THE ZORN VALLEY TO THE BRUCHE VALLEY

110km/68mi – allow half a day

This itinerary, linking the upper valleys of the River Zorn and of the River Bruche,
offers an interesting drive through romantic landscapes with characteristic rocky
escarpments.

★**Saverne** – *See SAVERNE.*

Drive southeast out of Saverne along D 132.

★**Château du Haut-Barr** – *See Château du HAUT-BARR.*

Continue on D 132, then D 38 and D 98 along the Zorn Valley.

★**Vallée de la Zorn** – This pleasant valley, with its slopes covered with beeches and
firs, is traditionally the busiest route through the northern Vosges mountains.
Nowadays, the Marne-Rhine canal and the Paris-Strasbourg railway line run alongside the clear river which flows on a bed of sand and stones.
Beyond Stambach, the ruins of the medieval Château de **Lutzelbourg** stand on a
promontory; 3km/1.9mi past Lutzelbourg, the road moves away from the canal
which, at that point, is equipped with a boat elevator, the first of its type in the
world.

★**Plan incliné de St-Louis-Arzviller** ⊙ – *It is best seen from D 98^C.* Inaugurated in
1969, this boat elevator is equipped with an inclined plane 108.65m/356.46ft long
in order to clear the 44.55m/146ft drop. It replaced 17 locks previously spread
over a distance of 4km/2.5mi alongside the railway, which took a whole day to
negotiate. Instead, a 43m/141ft long ferry-truck going up sideways on rails along
a concrete ramp by a system of counterbalance, transfers barges weighing 350t
from one level to the other in 20min.

★**Rocher du Nutzkopf** – *Accessible by D 98^D from Sparsbrod then a forest track on
the left and finally a footpath signposted on the left (45min on foot there and
back).* From the top (alt 515m/1 690ft) of this strange tabular rock, the view
extends to the Rocher de Dabo, the village of La Hoube and the green valley of the
River Grossthal.

Return to D 98^C then turn right onto D 45.

On approaching Schaeferhof, one can see *(ahead to the left)* the hilltop village of
Haselbourg.
Slightly further on, as the road *(D 45)* rises up the picturesque **Vallée du Kleinthal**,
the Rocher de Dabo comes into view.

Dabo – This popular summer resort lies in a very pleasant **setting**★, at the heart of
a beautiful forested area.

★**Rocher de Dabo** ⊙ – *Signposted "Rocher St-Léon".* This sandstone rock is crowned
by two viewing tables and a chapel dedicated to St Léon (Léon IX) whose statue is
located in the chapel tower. Beneath the tower, to the left of the doorway giving
access to the chapel, a small door opens onto a staircase *(92 steps)*. The **panorama**★
from the top of the tower includes the main summits of the sandstone Vosges
mountains (Schneeberg, Grossmann, Donon etc). There is an interesting view of
the village of Dabo which appears shaped like an X.
Beyond Dabo, the pleasant winding road enters a splendid forest and offers fine
glimpses of the Rocher de Dabo and the surrounding area, of the fertile Kochersberg plateau, of the Plaine d'Alsace and of the green valley of the River Mossig.

113

Obersteigen – This is a pleasant summer resort situated at medium altitude (a 500m/1 640ft). Built of sandstone, the church is the former chapel of an August nian convent founded at the beginning of the 13C. It marks the transition betwee the Romanesque and Gothic styles: rounded arches, crocket capitals; note th ringed columns of the doorway.

Turn left onto D 224.

Vallée de la Mossig – Strange projecting sandstone rocks overlook the Rive Mossig. Strasbourg cathedral is built of sandstone from this area. Beyond Romar swiller, there is a fine view of the sandstone Vosges.

Wasselonne – An old tower is the only part left of the castle overlooking thi former stronghold whose houses are scattered on the slopes of the last foothill c the Kochersberg. The fortifications have completely disappeared except for a tow gate and former keep. The **Protestant church** ⊘ dates from the 18C (organ b Silbermann); in the cemetery *(along the Westhoffen road)*, there is an unusua domed pulpit. The Wasselonne fair *(last Sunday and Monday in August)* is a regiona event, with an impressive procession of floral floats.

Return to D 218 and drive south.

Wangenbourg – This charming summer resort forms an attractive **landscape**★ wit its surroundings of meadows dotted with chalets and forests overlooked by th Schneeberg summit.

The **castle ruins** are accessible on foot *(15min there and back; leave the car in th parking area, 200m beyond the church; walk past a huge lime tree and follow path which prolongs the main street)*. The castle, dating from the 13C and 14C belonged to Andlau abbey. The pentagonal keep and important sections of walls ar still visible. The keep gives access to the platform offering a good overall view c the area. A path, which partly runs along the castle moat, takes you round th huge sandstone outcrop crowned by the ruins. A bridge leads to the old tower.

The surrounding woods are crisscrossed by numerous paths lined with benches a regular intervals.

Beyond Wolfsthal, D 218 climbs up to the beautiful **Haslach Forest**. A pleasant driv leads to the forest lodge then past a stela on the left, which commemorates th building of the road.

Further on *(500m/547yd)*, the road starts winding down towards Oberhaslach Ahead and to the left stands the ruined tower of Nideck castle.

★★**Château and Cascade du Nideck** – *Leave the car in the parking area locate below the forest lodge and follow the signposted footpath (1hr 15min on foot ther and back).*

A 13C tower and 14C keep, standing in a romantic **setting**★★, are all that remain of two castles destroyed by fire in 1636. The German-speaking poet Chamisso d Boncourt, known as Adalbert von Chamisso, celebrated this site in his poems. Fron the top of the tower and the keep, there are fine views of the forest, the Bruch Valley, the Guirbaden castle and the heights of Champ du Feu.

Walk to the right of the keep and follow a path on the left which leads to the waterfal. Bear right beyond a wooden shelter and a small bridge to the viewpoint (ver dangerous in spite of the railing).

From the belvedere, there is a splendid **view**★★ of the glacial valley and the woode chasm into which the waterfall drops from the top of a porphyry wall. In order t see the waterfall, you must continue past the viewpoint along a marked pat *(30min there and back)*.

Return to D 218 and stop 1.2km/0.7mi further on.

Belvédère – The viewpoint is situated 20m/66ft off the road, near a stone marke It offers a fine **view**★ of the Château du Nideck and the valley below. Further on, t the left one can see the steep wooded slopes lining the River Hasel and it tributaries and, in the background, the Bruche Valley and the heights overlooking to the south. The road winds down into the narrow, green valley of the Hase towards Oberhaslach, Niederhaslach and the River Bruche.

Oberhaslach – This village is a place of pilgrimage, particularly lively on th Sunday following 7 November, when pilgrims come to pray St Florent who, in th 7C, was believed to have the power to tame wild animals. Today, he still protect domestic animals but he also intervenes on behalf of pilgrims whatever thei complaints. Numerous grateful acknowledgements testify to his efficiency.

The Baroque chapel, built in 1750 and restored in 1987, stands on the spot wher the saint lived as a hermit before he became the seventh bishop of Strasbourg.

Niederhaslach – The village once had an abbey which, according to legend, wa founded by St Florent in rather comic circumstances: for having cured his daughte King Dagobert granted St Florent as much land as his donkey could pace ou during the time the king spent washing and dressing; on the day in question, th king spent more time than he usually did and the donkey went galloping off, s that St Florent was given a considerable amount of land.

The church, begun in the mid-13C, was almost entirely destroyed by fire in 1287 but the son of Erwin von Steinbach (who designed Strasbourg cathedral), Gerlac, partly rebuilt it in a plain yet elegant Gothic style. The doorway is framed by small statues and decorated with a tympanum illustrating the legend of St Florent curing King Dagobert's daughter.

Note the beautiful 14C-15C stained-glass **windows**★ in the aisles and in the apse. Bishop Rachio's funeral monument can be seen in the chancel, to the left of the main altar; a stone crucifix dating from 1740, flanked by John the Baptist and John the Evangelist, stands on the right. Gerlac's funeral monument and a 14C Holy Sepulchre are housed inside a chapel to the right of the chancel, which contains fine 17C stalls. A pilgrimage in honour of St Florent takes place in November.

D 218 reaches the Bruche Valley.

★**Vallée de la Bruche** − *See Vallée de la BRUCHE.*

Lac du DER-CHANTECOQ ★★

Michelin map 61 fold 9 or 241 fold 34

Created in 1974, this artificial lake is the largest in France (4 800ha/11 861 acres, 1.5 times the area of the Lac d'Annecy). It was intended to regulate the flow of the River Marne and is lined with 77km/48mi of banks including 19km/12mi of dykes; a feeder canal, 12km/7.5mi long, diverts two-thirds of the flow when the river is in spate and another canal supplies the Paris region when the water level is low. The lake fills up slowly during the winter months and empties during the autumn. The level is at its highest in June and at its lowest in November.

This low-lying area was chosen because of the waterproof qualities of its clay soil. Part of the Der Forest (the name means "oak" in Celtic) disappeared beneath the surface of the lake together with the three villages of Chantecoq, Champaubert-aux-Bois and Nuisement. However, the churches of the last two villages were spared.

DRIVE ROUND THE LAKE *83km/52mi − allow 3hr*

Start from Giffaumont where the Maison du Lac (tourist office of Lake Der-Chantecoq) is located.

Giffaumont-Champaubert − The marina can accommodate up to 500 boats. **Boat trips on the lake** ⊘ are organised in summer.

Opposite *(access on foot along the dyke)*, Champaubert church stands alone on a a piece of land jutting out into the lake.

PRACTICAL INFORMATION

Outdoor activities − There are two marinas, one in Nemours and one in Nuisement, water sports facilities in Giffaumont, six beaches with supervised bathing, an area of 650ha/1 606 acres reserved for motor boats and water-skiing, on and off shore fishing, including night fishing, and riding centres.

Excursions:
− walks: 225km/140mi of marked paths forming loops of 5-15km/3-9mi.
− bike tours: 4 itineraries are available.
− mountain-bike tours: 250km/155mi of marked tracks round the lake.
− barouche rides.
− horse or poney rides: treks through the woods.
− tourist-train rides: between Giffaumont harbour and the Maison de l'Oiseau et du Poisson.
− boat trips: starting from Giffaumont harbour.

For nature lovers − All year round, the lake offers visitors the opportunity of watching the changing aspects of nature, in particular when large migrating birds arrive between autumn and spring. More than 270 species have been spotted including cranes, white-tailed eagles, herons, Bewick's swans... There are **observatories** and a nature trail in peaceful areas near Chantecoq, Champaubert, the lakes of Outines and Arrigny.

October to April: cranes, grey lag geese, wigeons, teals, white-tailed eagles...

April to May and mid-August to October: ospreys, sandpipers, terns...

March to August: this is the nesting season for great-crested grebes, herons, mallards...

Information available from the Maison du Lac in Giffaumont.

Grange aux abeilles ⊘ – An exhibition and an audio-visual show enable visitors to appreciate the work accomplished by bees and bee-keepers.

Follow D 13, then D 12 towards Montier-en-Der.

Ferme de Berzillières ⊘ – This entirely restored farmhouse contains a museum of agriculture with 400 pieces of machinery and agricultural tools.

Go back along D 12 and, 500m/547yd further on, turn left towards Troyes then right towards Châtillon-sur-Broué.

Châtillon-sur-Broué – This village is characteristic of the Der area, with its square church steeple and its timber-and-cob houses.

Continue towards the lake.

The road skirts the dyke and runs past the small harbour of Chantecoq.

Opposite the harbour, a path *(parking area at the beginning)* leads to the Maison de l'Oiseau et du Poisson.

Maison de l'Oiseau et du Poisson ⊘ – It is housed in the timber-framed Ferme des Grands Parts, characteristic of the Champagne scenery. It shows various specific environments such as subaquatic life, the four seasons of the lake, migrating birds, with the help of reconstructions, interactive terminals and sound effects.

Two roads run along dykes to allow visitors to spot passing cranes.

West of the lake, a peaceful area has been set aside as a bird sanctuary.

Continue along D 13.

Arrigny – There is a fine timber-framed church in the village.

When you reach the village square, turn left onto D 57 towards St-Rémy-en-Bouzemont. In St-Rémy, take D 58 towards Drosnay. The Ferme aux Grues is located in the hamlet of Isson.

Ferme aux Grues ⊘ – There are explanations about the work undertaken for the preservation of migrating cranes and the study of their migratory habits. An observatory enables birdwatchers to watch cranes feeding on crops and meadows.

Return to Arrigny and follow D 57 towards Eclaron, then turn right in Blaise-sous-Hauteville.

★**Ste-Marie-du-Lac-Nuisement** – A small **Village-musée** ⊘ comprises several timber-framed buildings saved from flooding when the lake was created, including the church of Nuisement-aux-Bois, the school-town hall, the smithy's house where refreshments are available, a dovecote and the Machelignots' barn containing exhibitions on traditional aspects of the Der area: costumes, models of timber-framed houses, reconstructions of workshops. A video-film illustrates the different stages of the creation of the reservoir.

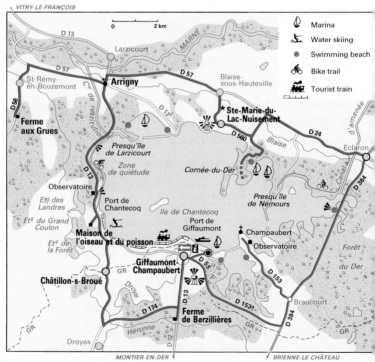

Cranes' migratory habits

Every year in autumn, cranes leave Scandinavia and travel to milder climates in Spain or Africa. They fly over Champagne in successive waves, usually by night, and give out an impressive loud cry. Some of these cranes remain in the region throughout the winter and show a particular liking for meadows situated near a lake. They fly back north in the spring. Thousands of them stop by the **Ferme aux Grues**, near the Lac du Der-Chantecoq, where grain is purposely spread about a large area to attract them.

This large grey bird, with its long neck and long legs, has a wing span of 2m/6.5ft and weighs 4-7kg/9-15lb. It feeds on grain, grass and young shoots as well as insects, molluscs and worms.

Château d'eau panoramique ⊘ – The watertower stands 20m/66ft high and affords views of the lake *(viewing table, telescope and audio-guide)*.
Road D 560 leads to the Cornée du Der, a wooded peninsula jutting out into the lake.
Return to D 24 and turn right to Éclaron, then right again onto D 384.
The road offers a fine view of the lake before entering the Der Forest.
In Braucourt, it is possible to turn right onto D 153 leading to the Champaubert church at the tip of the peninsula of the same name.
Turn right 1.5km/0.9mi beyond Braucourt onto D 153^A.

Château d'eau panoramique ⊘ – From the top (20m/66ft) of this water tower, there are overall views of the lake and the forest *(viewing table, telescope and audio-guide)*.
Continue along D 55 to return to Giffaumont-Champaubert.

Massif du DONON★★

Michelin map 87 folds 14 and 15 or 242 folds 23 and 27

The Donon massif and Donon pass, which mark the boundary between Alsace and Lorraine, had a significant impact on the history and geography of the region. Celts, Romans, Franks and all the Germanic tribes travelling west came through the Donon pass and there is evidence that an ancient god, probably Mercury, was worshipped on the mountain. Geographically, the Donon massif forms the southern part of the sandstone Vosges mountains, reaching their highest point at the Donon summit (alt 1 009m/3 311ft). Numerous streams taking their source near the summit radiate across the splendid forests which cover the massif. A road runs alongside each valley and there are cross-country skiing tracks and skilifts.

THE SARRE ROUGE AND SARRE BLANCHE VALLEYS

Round tour from the Col du Donon – *55km/34mi – allow 2hr*

Col du Donon – Alt 727m/2 385ft.

Donon – Alt 1 009m/3 311ft. *About 1hr 30min on foot there and back.*
It is possible to leave the car at the Donon pass and follow the footpath starting on the right of Hôtel Velléda; alternatively, one can drive for 1.3km/0.8mi along the road branching off D 993 on the right, 1km/0.6mi from the pass; leave the car in the parking area (barrier) and walk the last 2km.
There is a viewing table at the end of each pile of sandstone slabs forming the summit. The **panorama★★** includes the Vosges mountain range, the Lorraine plateau, the Plaine d'Alsace and the Black Forest.
A small temple built in 1869 stands between the two viewing tables and there are Gallo-Roman ruins scattered on the slopes.
A television relay is located 50m/164ft below the summit.
From the Col du Donon, the itinerary follows the **Vallée de la Sarre Rouge** or Vallée de St-Quirin then goes across the Lorraine plateau.
Continue straight on along D 145 and then D 44, ignoring the Cirey-sur-Vezouze road on your left. The itinerary enters the Lorraine region.
The road winds its way down through picturesque scenery, along the narrow wooded valley of St-Quirin, keeping close to the Sarre Rouge which is more of a mountain stream than a river.

Grand Soldat – This hamlet is the birthplace of Alexandre Chatrian (1826-1890), who collaborated with Emile Erckmann (1822-1899) to write a series of novels inspired by Alsatian traditions and legends. They became extremely popular after the annexation of Alsace-Lorraine by Germany in 1871.

Abreschviller – A small **forest train** ⊙, steam or diesel-powered, leads to Grand Soldat (6km/3.7mi).

3km/1.9mi further on, turn left onto D 96ᶠ towards St-Quirin.

Vasperviller – Camped on the first foothills of the Donon, this village offers amateurs of modern sacred art an interesting discovery: a remarkable little church designed in 1968 by the architect Litzenburger, the **Église Ste-Thérèse**. Walk round the church in order to appreciate how the outline of this concrete building is rendered more interesting by a succession of plane and curved surfaces.

The interior, plain yet subtle in design and lit by lovely stained-glass windows (tree of Jesse), comprises three separate areas converging towards the chapel dedicated to St Theresa.

The top of the campanile, open as if to receive the heavenly light, is accessible via an unusual double staircase (75 steps) lined with the Stations of the Cross. Pleasant view of the village and the valley along which runs the St-Quirin road.

St-Quirin – This low-lying village, surrounded by meadows, is overlooked by a Romanesque chapel where a pilgrimage has taken place for centuries. The 18C priory church is surmounted by two towers and a pinnacle crowned by onion-shaped domes. It houses a restored organ made in 1746 by Silbermann.

Drive west out of St-Quirin along D 96 and, 2km/1.2mi further on, turn left onto D 993.

The road follows the **Vallée de la Sarre Blanche** through lovely forests. The area is sparsely populated – with only a few sawmills and forest lodges along the road – but the beauty of the landscape retains the full attention of visitors.

At the end of the tour, you are back in Alsace as you leave the Abreschviller road on your left to return to the Donon pass.

THE PLAINE VALLEY

From Col du Donon to Badonviller – *45km/28mi – 1hr 15min*

Col du Donon – Alt 727m/2 385ft.

On the way down from the pass, the picturesque road runs through a splendid forest of fir trees then offers views of the twin villages of Raon-sur-Plaine and Raon-lès-Leau (note the memorial to escaped prisoners of war and their guides inside the bend to the right).

Raon-sur-Plaine – The village lies amid green meadows, within sight of the Donon. A small road leads up the mountain (4km/2.5mi) to a well-preserved **Roman way** running underwoods over a distance of approximately 500m/547yd.

The **Vallée de la Plaine** or **Vallée de Celles** is dotted with red-roofed houses on the edge of the forest, which add to the charm of the mainly green landscape.

Lac de la Maix – *15min on foot there and back, starting from Vexaincourt; follow a narrow forest road on the left.*

A path runs round this dark green lake overlooked by a chapel.

Between Allarmont and Celles-sur-Plaine, the former **Scierie de la Hallière** ⊙ houses an *écomusée* displaying tools and equipment once used for sawing *(demonstrations in summer)* and for woodwork; interesting waterwheel.

Celles-sur-Plaine is close to the two lakes of Pierre Percée. The **Lac de la Plaine** (36ha/89 acres) has been turned into a leisure and water sports centre (swimming, sailing, rowing, canoeing...)

Take the scenic road which goes round the lakes.

The drive through forests of firs affords fine views during the first part of the climb. The **road★** leads to the tiny village of **Pierre-Percée**. The town hall has an **exhibit area and shop** ⊙ devoted to "art, crafts and regional produce from Lorraine". The road then climbs up to the foot of a ruined castle *(parking area)* perched on top of a knoll, which has retained a 12C keep. From there, extended **views★** of the lake in its romantic setting of hills and forests can be had.

Lac de Pierre-Percée – *Parking area near the Vieux-Pré dam. Walk towards the viewpoint where the construction of the dam is explained on several panels.*

A boat trip aboard the **Vedette "Cristal"** ⊙ offers varied views of the surrounding mountains.

The nature trail of the Roche aux Corbeaux and a **birdwatching post** offer the opportunity of discovering the forest environment *(access by the scenic road)*.

Return to D 182 and continue to Badonviller.

Badonviller – This small industrial town, partly destroyed in August 1914, was, 30 years later, one of the first towns to be liberated by the French Second Armoured Division during the battle of Alsace which began in November 1944.

Use Michelin Maps
With Michelin Guides.

EBERSMUNSTER

Population 445
Michelin map 87 fold 6 or 242 fold 28

, famous Benedictine abbey once stood in this peaceful village. It was believed to have been founded by St Odile's parents, Duke Étichon and his wife *(see Mont STE-ODILE)*. The monastery and the church were destroyed during the Thirty Years War but rebuilt later. A late-18C doorway leads to the former monastery buildings.

★ABBEY CHURCH *15min*

Built c 1725 by Peter Thumb, an architect from the Vorarlberg area, the church can be seen from afar, surmounted by three onion-shaped steeples. The **interior**★★ is considered as the finest example of early-18C Alsatian Baroque art. Daylight pouring in on the brightly painted decoration and stucco work enhances the refined setting and the elegantly carved furniture: Samson supporting the pulpit (late 17C), stalls (late 17C) and their statues (late 19C), confessionals (1727), side altars (1730), organ by André Silbermann (1732). However, one's attention is inevitably drawn to the imposing **high altar** (1728): decorated with numerous gilt carvings and surmounted by a huge baldaquin in the shape of a crown, it almost reaches the chancel vaulting.

Organ and choral concerts, known as "Les Heures musicales d'Ebersmunster", take place in the church every Sunday at 5pm during the month of May.

ÉCOMUSÉE D'ALSACE★★

Michelin map 242 fold 35 – 9km/5.6mi southwest of Ensisheim, in Ungersheim

Some 60 traditional old houses scattered over an area of 15ha/37 acres give an insight into housing in the different rural areas of Alsace.

The wish to preserve the regional heritage was at the origin of this open-air museum: old houses from the 15C to 19C, doomed to be demolished, were patiently located all over Alsace, then carefully taken apart and rebuilt in the new "village". The museum, inaugurated in 1984 and continually expanding, has now turned to the region's industrial heritage with the renovation of the various buildings of the potash mine "Rodolphe" (1911-1930) adjacent to the museum.

During the **tour of the museum** ⊘, past the various timber-framed houses with their courtyards and gardens, grouped according to their original area, Sungdau, Ried, Kochersberg, Bas-Rhin, visitors are able to assess the evolution of building techniques and the location of farm buildings (house, barns, cowsheds) in relation to one another, which changed considerably according to the area and the period.

Characteristic rural buildings such as the fortified house, the chapel, the school and the wash-house, give an insight into social life in traditional Alsatian villages; ancient plant species can be seen growing in their recreated natural environment and there are demonstrations of traditional farming methods. A section of the museum is devoted to funfairs; note in particular the merry-go-round Eden-Palladium, the last of the great Belle-Époque merry-go-rounds in France (1909).

The work of carpenters and stone masons is also evoked together with the evolution of lifestyles in reconstructed interiors including kitchen, alcoves and "stube" (living room containing an earthenware stove).

Écomusée d'Alsace – Fortified house from Mulhouse

ÉCOMUSÉE D'ALSACE

Other buildings house exhibitions or shows on such themes as the Alsatian head dress, water and fire in the home, fishing, recurring feasts. Several workshops are operating: a blacksmith's, a potter's with an impressive wood oven, a cartwright', a distillery, an oil-mill. Cowsheds and stables shelter domestic animals and 12 pair of storks return regularly to nest on the weathered roofs.

Restaurants with shaded terraces, picnic areas, shop (books and handicraft).

USEFUL STOPOFF

Les Loges de l'Écomusée – Situated among a group of timber-framed houses, this hotel includes 40 very comfortable rooms and suites from 355F per person. ☎ 03 89 74 44 94.

La Taverne – This restaurant, open from 7.30am to midnight has a choice of menus based on regional produce from 98F upwards.

The length of time given in this guide
– for touring allows time to enjoy the views and the scenery;
– for sightseeing is the average time required for a visit.

EGUISHEIM★

Population 1 530
Michelin map 87 fold 17 or 242 fold 31 – Local map see Route des VINS p 326

This ancient village is today a lively wine-growing centre; it developed round its 13 castle which has retained part of its imposing wall forming an octagon.
Surrounded by vines and lying at the foot of three famous towers, the village ha hardly changed since the 16C.

Tour of the ramparts – The marked itinerary follows the former watch-path. The narrow paved streets are lined with old houses offering a wealth of architectur features (balconies, oriels, timber frames, pointed gables).

Grand'Rue – The picturesque houses lining this street have wide doorwa' adorned with coats of arms and inscribed with the date. Note also the two love Renaissance fountains.

Church – Inside the modern church, to the right of the entrance, there is a chap beneath the steeple. It contains the old doorway with its 12C tympanum illustra ing Christ between St Peter and St Paul; the procession of Wise Virgins and Foolis Virgins forms the lintel. Beautiful modern stained-glass windows illustrate scenes the life of Léon IX. Fine 19C organ by Callinet.

Eguisheim

★ROUTE DES CINQ CHÂTEAUX

20km/12.4mi round tour including "five castles", plus about 1hr 45min on foot.

Drive to Husseren (see p 329) along D 14. As you come out of the village, turn right onto the forest road, known as the "Route des cinq châteaux"; 1km/0.6mi further on, leave the car in the parking area and walk to Eguisheim's "three castles" (5min uphill).

Donjons d'Eguisheim – Three massive square keeps built of red sandstone and known as Weckmund, Wahlenbourg and Dagsbourg, stand at the top of the hill. They belonged to the powerful Eguisheim family and were destroyed by fire following a 15C war between the burghers of Mulhouse and the aristocracy of the surrounding area *(see MULHOUSE)*. Pope Léon IX was most probably born here *(see Région de DABO-WANGENBOURG)*.

Return to the car and drive on for about 6km/3.7mi.

The narrow road offers fine viewpoints all the way.

Château de Hohlandsbourg – The imposing castle stands on the left; built c 1279, it first belonged to the powerful House of Hapsburg. It was bought in 1563 by Lazare de Schwendi, Emperor Maximilian's personal advisor, who modernised it; it was eventually destroyed during the Thirty Years War. There is a magnificent view of the Pflixbourg keep and Hohneck summit to the west, the Haut-Kœnigsbourg to the north, Colmar and the Plaine d'Alsace to the east. A vast courtyard surrounded by a high granite wall is overlooked on its northern side by the upper castle (Oberschloss) whose fortifications were reinforced in the 14C. On the northern side, a projecting defence work guards the main entrance. Built in the 16C, it was adapted to the use of artillery and could accommodate many guns.

Donjon de Pflixbourg – *A path, branching off to the left 2km/1.2mi further on, leads to the keep.*
The fortress, which was the former Alsatian residence of the representative of the Holy Roman Emperor, came into the possession of the Ribeaupierre family during the 15C. A vaulted water tank can be seen next to the keep. There is a fine view of the Fecht Valley to the west and of the Plaine d'Alsace to the east.

As you rejoin D 417, turn right towards Colmar.
On leaving Wintzenheim (see Route des VINS: From Châtenois to Colmar), turn right onto N 83 then right again onto D 1bis to return to Eguisheim.

ENSISHEIM
Population 6 164
Michelin map 87 fold 18 or 242 fold 35

Excavations undertaken south of the town have revealed that the site was inhabited as far back as the fifth millenium BC. The name of Ensisheim, however, was mentioned for the first time in a document dating from 765. The city acquired fame and became prosperous when it became the capital of the Hapsburgs' territories in Alsace, Baden country and northern Switzerland. When the town was at the height of its fame, more than 200 aristocratic families lived in it. The Thirty Years War brought devastation as the small city was sacked seven times.
After the liberation of Mulhouse on 21 November 1944, Ensisheim was shelled and bombed until it was liberated on 6 February 1945.

SIGHTS

Palais de la Régence – This fine Gothic edifice erected in 1535 was decorated in Renaissance style. On the ground floor, the vaulting of the arcade is decorated with emblems bearing the coat of arms of several Alsatian towns. The façade on the church side is flanked with an octagonal stair turret.

Musée de la Régence ⊙ – In the first room of the museum is exhibited an aerolite (a stony meteorite) which fell on Ensisheim on 7 November 1492. It is believed to be the first fall of an aerolite ever recorded and its size is said to have been impressive (150kg/331lb) but it was gradually reduced to about a third of its original size through the generosity of the town as every important visitor was given a piece of it. The most recent archeological finds are also displayed: ceramics, tools and a child's grave dating from the first period of the Neolithic Age, objects from the Bronze Age and the Gallo-Roman period.
In addition, the museum offers an insight into potash mining in Alsace and in particular the miners' work through a variety of implements and documents.

Hôtel de la Couronne – It is housed in an elegant building dating from 1609, decorated with scrolled gables and a two-storey carved oriel. Turenne, Louis XIV's great general, stayed here in 1675 before his victory at the battle of Turckheim, which led to the Peace of Nimègue and the final union of France and Alsace.

★★**Écomusée d'Alsace** – *9km/5.6mi southwest along D 4 bis to Ungersheim, then D 44 towards Feldkirch Bollwiller; turn left onto D 200 and left again onto D 430 to the open-air museum (see ÉCOMUSÉE D'ALSACE).*

ÉPERNAY ★

Population 26 681
Michelin map 56 fold 16 or 241 fold 21

Épernay is the starting point of excursions into the Marne Valley and the surrounding hills but, above all, it is with Reims, the main wine-growing centre of the Champagne region and the meeting point of three major wine-growing areas: the Montagne de Reims, the Côte des Blancs and the Marne Valley. The town is well provided with green open spaces which add to its appeal. There are many opulent 19C buildings in neo-Renaissance or Classical style, particularly in the district around the avenue de Champagne.

A modern group of buildings was erected to the south, near Mont Bernon. The industrial area extends to the north and east.

★★CHAMPAGNE CELLARS *2hr*

The main Champagne firms, some of them going back to the 18C, line both sides of the avenue de Champagne, above the limestone cliff riddled with miles of galleries which remain at a constant temperature of 9-12°C/48-54°F.

Three of these firms organise tours during which visitors can observe the various stages that Champagne must go through to reach perfection.

Moët et Chandon ⊘ – *18 avenue de Champagne*. Moët et Chandon was the first Champagne firm; its story is linked to that of Hautvillers abbey *(see excursions)* which it owns and to Dom Pérignon whom it honoured by naming its prestigious Champagne after him.

The founder of the firm, Claude Moët, began producing Champagne in 1743. His grandson, Jean Rémy, a close friend of Napoleon, welcomed the emperor several times (one of Napoleon's hats is kept on the premises). Jean Rémy's son-in-law, Pierre Gabriel Chandon, added his name and the firm became known as Moët et Chandon.

In 1962, the family concern was made into a limited company and, since then, the Moët-Hennessy-Louis Vuitton group has been in control of three Champagne firms, Moët et Chandon, Ruinart and Mercier, as well as Hennessy brandy, Rozès porto, Christian Dior perfumes, Louis Vuitton leather goods, Roc cosmetics; it also owns important vineyards in France (850ha/2 100 acres), Brazil, Argentina, California, Australia and Spain. The 28km/17.4mi long cellars, contain the equivalent of 90 million bottles. During the tour, which is very thorough, visitors can observe the various stages Champagne goes through, including *remuage* (moving the bottles round) and *dégorgement* (releasing the deposit).

Mercier ⊘ – *73 avenue de Champagne*. In 1858, Eugène Mercier merged several Champagne firms under his own name. He then had 18km/11.2mi of galleries dug. To celebrate the 1889 World Exhibition, he asked a sculptor from Châlons, named Navlet, to decorate a huge tun with a capacity of 215 000 bottles and placed it on a cart drawn by 24 oxen and 18 horses acting as support in uphill sections of the journey. This exceptional convoy travelled from Épernay to Paris in 20 days; some bridges had to be reinforced and walls demolished along the way. One hundred years later the huge tun, weighing 34t, was put on display in the main hall.

Mercier is the second Champagne producer after Moët et Chandon and it belongs to the same group.

A panoramic lift takes visitors down to the cellars for a ride in a small automatic train along galleries decorated with carvings by Navlet.

De Castellane ⊘ – *57 rue de Verdun*. The 10km/6mi long cellars, the tower and the museum can be visited. The tower, which is 60m/197ft high, is used as an exhibition area devoted to the story of the Castellane family – including the famous art collector Boni de Castellane who married the American millionairess Anna Gould – and of the Mérand family; there is a collection of posters and bottles.

A climb of 237 steps leads to the top which affords an extended view of Épernay and the surrounding vineyards.

The **museum** is devoted to the evolution of the Champagne-making process. Two rooms contain scenes illustrating various aspects of wine-growing such as the cooper's work, looking after the vines, grape-harvesting and pressing. In addition, various sections present printing techniques, regional fauna, posters having a connection with Champagne, several crafts (basketwork, glass-making...) and a rich collection of labels.

ADDITIONAL SIGHTS

Musée municipal ⊘ – *First floor*. This museum is housed in the former Château Perrier, a copy of a castle in the Louis XIII style built in the mid-19C by a wine merchant.

Vin de Champagne – Two rooms illustrate the life and work of a wine-grower and a person in charge of a cellar. Collection of bottles and labels.

Archéologie – An important **archeological collection★** is displayed on the upper floor: funeral objects found in various local cemeteries, reconstructions of graves, remarkable pottery, glassware, weapons and jewellery.

Jardin de l'Hôtel de ville – The town hall stands at the centre of pleasant gardens laid out in the 19C by the Bühler brothers who also designed Lyon's famous Parc de la Tête d'Or.

Jardin des papillons ⊘ – *East of the town, 63 bis avenue de Champagne.*
Butterflies from all over the world flutter among exotic plants and flowers growing in a hot house.

EXCURSIONS

★**Hautvillers** – This attractive village clinging to the southern slopes of the Montagne de Reims *(see Parc naturel régional de la MONTAGNE DE REIMS)* has retained its old houses with their basket-handled doorways and wrought-iron signs. It forms part of the three top wine-growing areas of Ay, Hautvillers and Avenay.

Worth a thousand words

According to tradition, **Dom Pérignon** (1638-1715), who was in charge of the cellars of the Benedictine abbey, was the first to blend various wines to produce a vintage. His knowledge of wine-making was very extensive and he eventually supervised the double fermentation process and initiated the use of corks.

Former abbey church – Founded in 660 by St Nivard, a nephew of King Dagobert, the abbey became one of the finest artistic centres in western Europe; the most beautiful manuscripts of the "**École de Reims**" were produced within its walls. An alleyway at the end of the village leads to the abbey church. Particularly noteworthy is the 17C-18C chancel decorated with carved oak panels, late 18C stalls and large religious paintings including two remarkable works from the School of Philippe de Champaigne: *St Benedict Helping St Scholastic* and *St Nivard Founding Hautvillers Abbey*. A vast chandelier made up of four wheels from winepresses hangs over the high altar. Dom Pérignon's tombstone is located at the entrance of the chancel.

★**Montagne d'Épernay** – *36km/22.4mi round tour – allow 1hr.* The Épernay mountain forms the edge of the Ile-de-France cuesta.
Leave Épernay along RD 51.
The road follows the Cubry Valley with vineyards on both sides of the river.
Pierry – *See CÔTE DES BLANCS.*
As you come to Moussy, look left towards the church of Chavot (13C), perched on a peak.
Turn right 1km/0.6mi beyond Vaudancourt.
Château de Brugny – The castle overlooks the Cubry Valley. Built in the 16C, it was remodelled in the 18C. The square stone keep, flanked by round brick-built bartizans, looks particularly attractive.
In Brugny, take the road leading to St-Martin-d'Ablois.

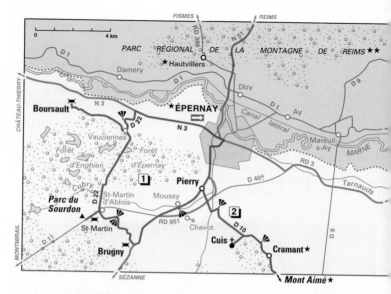

There are interesting **views**★ of the glacial Sourdon cirque, with the church of Chavot on the right, Moussy in the centre and Épernay Forest on the left.
Turn left onto D 11 towards Mareuil-en-Brie.
The famous miniaturist, Jean-Baptiste Isabey (1767-1855), stayed in the 16C **Château de St-Martin**, surrounded by several small waterfalls.
Parc du Sourdon ⊙ – The Sourdon takes its source under a pile of rocks then flows through the park planted with fine trees and forms a series of small pools where trouts can be seen.
Drive back to D 22 and turn left. The road runs through Épernay Forest (private property) and the village of Vauciennes. Turn left towards Boursault.
Château de Boursault – Built in 1848 in neo-Renaissance style for the famous Veuve Clicquot, this vast castle was the venue of magnificent receptions given by Madame Clicquot and later by her grand-daughter, the duchess of Uzès.
Return to Vauciennes and turn left onto D 22 towards N 3.
The road offers fine **views**★ of the Marne Valley, the village of Damery and the Montagne de Reims.

★**Côte des Blancs** – *See CÔTE DES BLANCS.*

★★**Parc naturel régional de la Montagne de Reims** – *See Parc naturel régional de la MONTAGNE DE REIMS.*

ÉPINAL★

Conurbation 50 909
Michelin map 62 fold 16 or 242 forld 30

The town, which occupies a favourable position at an important crossroads, spreads on both banks of the River Moselle. Its famous prints and cotton industry (now declining) once brought prosperity to the town; a factory producing wire, used in making Michelin tyres, has been established north of the town since 1969.

Épinal prints – The enormous success of the Épinal prints lasted for almost two centuries. Most popular prints used to depict religious subjects at the time when Jean Charles **Pellerin** began to illustrate secular subjects such as traditional songs, riddles, La Fontaine's fables and scenes of traditional French life; towards the end of the 19C, the firm even took an interest in publicity. Several well-known artists (Caran d'Ache, O'Galop, Benjamin Rabier...) contributed to this immensely popular form of art.
Once it had been carved on wood (generally peartree wood), the picture was printed on a Gutenberg type of press. The different colours were applied by hand using stencil-plates, a technique which is still used today.
The two world wars and new printing techniques caused the decline of this prosperous business.

Festivities – An ancient tradition, known as the Champs-Golots, is revived on the Wednesday before Easter to mark the end of winter and the general thaw. Children make boats which they parade all lit up on pools situated on rue du Général-Leclerc and on the Plateau de la Justice.
On his feast day, St Nicholas, accompanied by Mr Bogeyman, visits the town's play-schools and gives gingerbread and oranges to all the children.

★OLD TOWN *allow 30min*

★**Basilique St-Maurice** (BZ) – The oldest parts of the basilica date from the 11C (the transept and protruding parts). From the 13C to the Revolution, St-Maurice was both a parish church and the collegiate church of an order of aristocratic ladies. Its architecture denotes various regional influences.

Exterior – The west front overlooking place St-Goëry has a characteristic belfry-porch: the 13C lower part completely surrounds the original Romanesque tower; the doorway dates from 1843.

The 15C doorway on the north side, known as the Portail des Bourgeois, is the main entrance; it is preceded by a deep porch, characteristic of the architectural style of Champagne.

On the south side, there are traces of the former cloister destroyed in 1797.

Interior – The 13C nave is typical of Burgundian churches with its three storeys, arcades, triforium and high windows separated by moulded string-courses; it is prolonged beyond the transept by the bright 14C chancel *(choeur des chanoinesses)*, whose elegant lines are characteristic of Champagne art.

The most noteworthy works of art are a 15C Entombment in the south transept and a 14C statue of the Virgin of the Rose in the adjacent chapel.

Quartier du chapitre – This district has retained a group of houses built for the canonesses in the 17C and 18C. From there, it is easy to reach the medieval defence wall: the base of the towers and part of the red-sandstone wall can now be seen.

Place des Vosges (BZ 56) – This square, lined with arcaded houses, has a definite provincial charm. The 17C former bailiff's house, adorned with a loggia, now an art gallery, stands between a bookshop and a café.

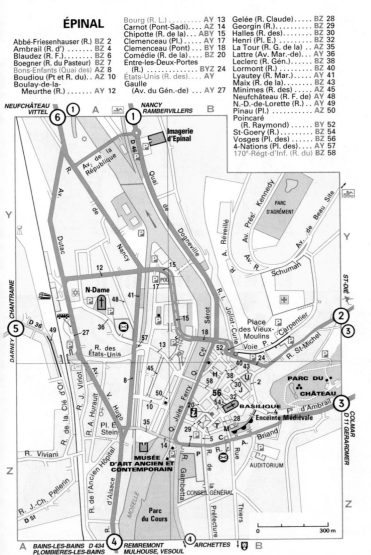

ÉPINAL

Abbé-Friesenhauser (R.) BZ 2
Ambrail (R. d') .... BZ 4
Blaudez (R. F.) .... BZ 6
Boegner (R. du Pasteur) BZ 7
Bons-Enfants (Quai des) AZ 8
Boudiou (Pt et R. du).. AZ 10
Boulay-de-la-
  Meurthe (R.) .... AY 12
Bourg (R. L.) .... AY 13
Carnot (Pont-Sadi).... AZ 14
Chipotte (R. de la)... ABY 15
Clemenceau (Pl.) ..... AY 17
Clemenceau (Pont) ... BY 18
Comédie (R. de la).... BZ 20
Entre-les-Deux-Portes
  (R.) .... BYZ 24
États-Unis (R. des)... AY
Gaulle
  (Av. du Gén.-de) ... AY 27
Gelée (R. Claude)..... BZ 28
Georgin (R.).......... BZ 29
Halles (R. des)........ BZ 30
Henri (Pl. E.) .... BZ 32
La Tour (R. G. de la) .. AZ 35
Lattre (Av. Mar.-de)... AY 36
Leclerc (R. Gén.)...... BZ 38
Lormont (R.) .... BZ 40
Lyautey (R. Mar.)..... AY 41
Maix (R. de la)........ BZ 43
Minimes (R. des) ..... AZ 45
Neufchâteau (R. F. de) BZ 48
N.-D.-de-Lorette (R.) .. AY 49
Pinau (Pl.) .... AZ 50
Poincaré
  (R. Raymond) ...... BY 52
St-Goery (R.) .... BZ 54
Vosges (Pl. des) ...... BZ 56
4-Nations (Pl. des).... AY 57
170e-Régt-d'Inf. (R. du) BZ 58

PELLERIN & Cᵉ, imp.-édit.

L'ILLUSTRE FAMILLE DES JEAN,

IMAGERIE D'ÉPINAL, Nᵒ 1337

Jeanfesse!	J'enseigne.	J'embrasse.	J'embrouille.	Jean pêche.
Jean jean.	Jean rage!!	Ô J'empeste!	Jean chante.	J'emmaillotte.
J'embroche.	J'enfonce.	J'embellis.	Ô J'enlaidis!	J'empoche.
J'empiffre.	J'engraisse.	J'embaume.	J'embête.	J'enfourne.

L'ARBRE D'AMOUR

ADDITIONAL SIGHTS

★**Parc du Château** ⊙ (BZ) – This wooded park, one of the largest in France, covers an area of 26ha/64 acres and includes a "mini zoo". It occupies the site of the former castle, on top of the wooded sandstone hill which stands in the town centre. The medieval gardens have been relaid round the ruins.

★**Musée départemental d'art ancien et contemporain** ⊙ (AZ) – Located at the tip of an island in the River Moselle, the Museum of Ancient and Contemporary Art is housed in a building which allows daylight to flood in through a wide glass panel and a system of footbridges at different levels. On the ground floor are the Gallo-Roman finds dug out from archeological sites in Grand, Soulosse and the Donon as well as from the Merovingian necropolis in Sauville. The museum owns an important collection of coins from the Celtic period onwards. An interesting ethnographic collection is displayed on the first floor.

The paintings department is devoted mainly to the Italian School and French School of the 17C and 18C and to the Northern School. Classical realism is represented by Claude Gellée, Laurent La Hyre, Claude Vignon and **Georges de la Tour** *(Job mocked by his Wife)*. Drawings and water colours by Fragonard, Boucher, Coypel... recreate the carefree spirit of 18C festivities. The Northern School includes such masters as Brueghel, Van Goyen, Van Cleeve and, of course, **Rembrandt** *(Mater Dolorosa)*.

The history of **prints**, from the origin of wood engraving to today, illustrates political, social, religious and military life. The prints come from various French towns, in particular Épinal (the Imagerie Pellerin is the only printing works of its kind still operating in Europe) and from abroad.

The second floor gives an insight into contemporary art, particularly Minimal Art (Carl André, Donald Judd), Arte Povera (Mario Merz) and Pop Art (Andy Warhol).

Parc du Cours (AZ) – In this vast public park, laid out on the east bank of the River Moselle, exotic trees, sometimes more than 100 years old, mingle with typical trees of the Vosges region.

Imagerie d'Épinal ⊙ (AY) – *42 bis quai de Dogneville.*
In 1984, this firm took over from the former Imagerie Pellerin, founded in 1796, which remained in the hands of the Pellerin family for nearly 200 years. The tradition of the famous Épinal prints is being maintained.

In the basement, the **exhibition gallery and shop** displays reprints of old favourites, print albums and contemporary prints. A film illustrates the main events in the development of Épinal prints.

In addition, the **Écomusée** offers an insight into the techniques used by the firm, supported by demonstrations on some of the equipment (colouring machine dating from 1898). The technique of illumination by stencil is also explained.

Église Notre-Dame ⊙ (AY) – Rebuilt between 1956 and 1958, the church has doors decorated with *cloisonné* enamel on a red-copper base, depicting a cross framed by the emblems of the four evangelists above a rainbow and the symbols of the seven planets.

Inside, the horizontal concrete vaulting consists of a chequered pattern of square coffers. Light pours into the chancel through a huge stained-glass window dedicated to the glory of the Virgin Mary.

The Stations of the Cross are a very expressive modern work.

EXCURSIONS

Fort d'Uxegney ⊙ – *5km/3mi northwest by ⑥ on the town plan.*
Uxegney, ovelooking the Avière Valley, was one of the last forts built round Épinal. It was originally stone-built (1882-84) but was later strengthened by the addition of reinforced concrete. This type of fortification is halfway between a bastion, such as those built by Vauban, and the buried fortifications which made up the Ligne Maginot. Since it was never damaged by war, the fort is still intact. From the top, the domes of the various gun turrets can be seen and a vast panorama unfolds.

Cimetière et Mémorial américains – *7km/4.3mi south. Leave Épinal by ④ on the town plan and drive along D 157. The path leading to the cemetery (0.5km/0.3mi) starts on the right 1.8km/1.1mi beyond Donizé.*
The cemetery, which occupies a vast area (20ha/49 acres) on top of a wooded plateau overlooking the River Moselle, houses the graves of 5 255 American soldiers killed during the Second World War. White-marble crosses and Jewish stelae line up on impeccably trimmed lawns behind a chapel and a memorial dedicated to the dead soldiers.

To find the description of a town or an isolated tourist attraction, consult the index.

Notre-Dame de l'Épine ★★

Michelin map 56 fold 18 or 241 fold 26

This basilica, which is as large as a cathedral, has been an important place of pilgrimage since the Middle Ages, when shepherds discovered a statue of the Virgin in a burning thorn bush. Built in the early 15C and gradually extended, the edifice has a Flamboyant Gothic west front and radiating chapels dating from the 16C.

Exterior – The richly decorated west front comprises three doorways surmounted by pointed gables (the highest of these bears a crucifix) and topped by openwork spires; the south spire (55m/180ft high) is ringed by a crown made up of fleurs-de-lis; as for the north spire, demolished in 1798 to make room for a telegraph installation, it was rebuilt in 1868.

Stand a short distance from the doorways to admire the successive levels bearing pinnacles, small spires and gargoyles then walk along the south side of the church to observe the numerous realistic **gargoyles**★ at closer range: they symbolise the vices and evil spirits expelled from the church by the presence of God. They were restored in the 19C and those which were considered too obscene were destroyed. The doorway of the south transept, with deeply splayed sides, is framed by polygonal turrets and adorned with carved draperies similar to those of the main doorway of Reims cathedral; the lintel is decorated with carved scenes depicting the life of John the Baptist. Large rings, set in the stone on either side of the doorway, were used to tie horses; note the Gothic inscription for the attention of travellers: "Good people who are passing by, pray to God on behalf of the deceased".

Interior – It expresses without exaggeration the refined perfection of Gothic architecture. The chancel is closed off by an elegant **rood screen** dating from the late 15C (note the 14C statue of the Virgin under the right-hand arcade) and by a stone screen which is Gothic on the right side and Renaissance on the left. Above the rood screen, a monumental 16C rood beam bears a crucifix flanked by the Virgin and St John.

In the north transept, there is a well which is supposed to have been used during the building of the basilica.

Walking round the chancel (starting from the north side) you will see a Gothic **tabernacle-reliquary** with Renaissance ornamentation, and a small oratory where it was possible for pilgrims to touch the relics including a piece of the True Cross. Further on, a chapel houses a fine 16C **Entombement** by members of the Champagne School.

Château de FALKENSTEIN ★

Michelin map 87 folds 2-3 or 242 folds 11-12
Local map see Parc Naturel Régional des VOSGES DU NORD

The castle, built in 1128 on a sandstone peak overlooking the forest, was struck by lightning and damaged by fire in 1564 then destroyed by the French in 1677 but its ruins are still very impressive.

According to legend, the ghost of a cooper occasionally haunts the cellars at midnight and with a mallet, strikes a number of times corresponding to the number of casks of wine which will be produced during the year.

From Philippsbourg, follow D 87 and D 87ᴬ which lead to a crossroads (3km/1.9mi); leave the car and continue on foot (45min there and back). Follow the second path on the left (marked with blue triangles) for 15min then go up a few steps and turn left then right. Go through a doorway, turn left and walk round the peak on which the castle stands. Go through a second doorway.

On your left you will then see a vast cave carved out of the rock, known as the Salle des Gardes (guards' room), and six recesses all round this cave.

Between the entrance doorway and the cave, there is another small doorway giving access to a flight of steps (with a handrail).

On the way, you will notice several natural caves, where the rockface has been carved by streaming water, as well as several man-made caves.

Further on, beyond a footbridge and some steps, you will see the top of the castle; walk to the viewpoint.

From there, the fine **panorama**★ includes Maimont and the ruins of Schoeneck to the northeast, Waldeck to the northwest, Lichtenberg and Dabo to the southeast and the mountains framing the Bruche Valley to the south.

Read the chapter on art and architecture in the Introduction to best appreciate historic monuments described in this guide.

FÈRE-EN-TARDENOIS

Population 3 168
Michelin map 56 fold 15 or 237 fold 9

ying on the banks of the upper Ourcq, Fère is an important crossroads which both ides fought to control during the second battle of the Marne *(see Introduction p 32).* t was the birthplace of the sculptress Camille Claudel (1864-1943), Paul Claudel's ister and Auguste Rodin's companion.

Church – Erected in the 16C, the church has been extensively restored. Notice the fine doorway on the north side.

Covered market – This is the former grain market built in 1540. The beautiful timberwork (in chestnut wood) rests on large round stone pillars.

EXCURSION

★Château de la Fère – *3km/1.9mi north along D 967. Drive past the private road on the right leading to the Hôtellerie du Château and follow the next alleyway.*
The early-13C fortress belonging to a branch of the royal family was given in 1528, by King Francis I, to the Great Constable of France, Anne de Montmorency, who transformed it into a pleasant residence and built across the moat a monumental bridge in Renaissance style. Louis XIII later took possession of the castle and gave it to Condé, a prince of royal blood; it was eventually passed on to Philippe-Égalité, the head of the younger branch of the Bourbon dynasty, who had it partially demolished.
Go to the east pillar of the monumental bridge and walk up the stairs inside the pillar.

Château de Fère

★★Pont monumental – Built by Jean Bullant for the Great Constable, it is supported by five huge rounded arches and consists of a two-tier gallery; the upper level of this gallery is partly demolished.

Castle ruins – A gate flanked by two small towers leads into the former courtyard. Admire the carefully dressed stonework of the seven round towers.

FISMES

Population 5 295
Michelin map 56 fold 5 or 237 fold 10

Situated at the confluence of the River Vesle and the River Ardre, Fismes was a raditional stopoff for the kings of France on their way to be crowned in Reims. The own had to be rebuilt after the First World War.

RELIGIOUS HERITAGE AROUND FISMES

Round tour of 34km/21mi – allow 1hr

Leave Fismes south along D 386 towards Épernay.

Courville – In medieval times, the archbishop of Reims had a castle here. Excavations have unearthed the lower part of the 12C keep. The presence of the archbishop explains the size of the Romanesque **church** ⊘ overlooking the village. The ancient capitals indicate that the nave dates from the 11C whereas the crossing which supports the high saddleback-roofed tower, the chancel and the side chapel date from the 12C. The original timber-work was replaced by a barrel vault in the 19C.

The road follows the River Ardre, a favourite haunt of anglers, through rur scenery.

In Crugny, turn right onto D 23 to Lagery.

Lagery – On the village square stands a fine 18C covered market next to picturesque wash-house.

Drive west along D 27 towards Coulonges-Cohan.

Abbaye d'Igny – This Cistercian monastery was founded by St Bernard in 1128 a remote valley. The buildings were rebuilt in the 18C and again after the Fir World War in neo-Gothic style.

Return to the intersection with D 25 and turn left.

Arcis-le-Ponsart – This village, which lies in a picturesque site overlooking a sma valley, has a 12C church and a 17C castle.

Continue north along D 25 to Courville and turn left towards Fismes.

Parc Naturel Régional
de la FORÊT D'ORIENT★★

Michelin map 61 folds 17 and 18 or 241 folds 37 and 38

Created in 1970 round the artificial Lac d'Orient, the nature park covers an area c 70 000ha/172 977 acres and comprises 50 municipalities, including Brienne-le-Châtea *(see BRIENNE-LE-CHÂTEAU)* and Vendeuvre-sur-Barse. It lies on the border of tw contrasting areas known as *Champagne crayeuse* and *Champagne humide (see p 2* and it consequently offers visitors a great variety of landscapes. The park aims t preserve the natural environment, in particular the fauna and flora, as well as th cultural and architectural heritage and to promote the economic, social and tourist development of the area.

Forest – The Forêt d'Orient, which formed part of the vast forested Der regic stretching from the Pays d'Othe in the southwest to St-Dizier in the northeas today covers 10 000ha/24 711 acres of wetlands dotted with lakes. It gets i name from the Knights Hospitallers and Knights Templars, known as the Chevalier

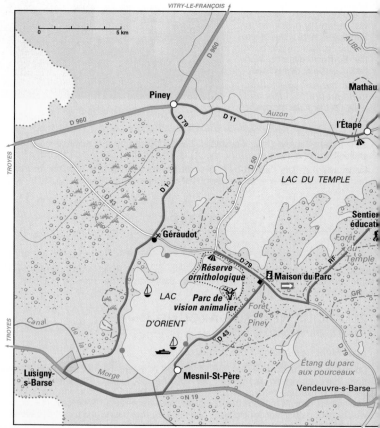

'Orient (Knights from the East), who once owned the area. Follow-
ng the damages caused to the forest during the Second World War,
ew species such as the forest pine, spruce and silver fir were
ntroduced. However, oaks are still the main species in this regularly
lanted forest with varied undergrowth.

ikes – Two long-distance footpaths and several short-distance
nes run through the forest which has become popular with hik-
rs and cyclists alike: itineraries totalling 140km/87mi are
etailed in a topo-guide available from the Maison du Parc.

akes – The park includes three lakes used to regulate the flow of the
River Seine and of the River Aube. The oldest (1966) and largest of the
akes, **Lac d'Orient** covers 2 500ha/6 178 acres and offers many leisure activities such as
ailing and scuba diving. There are two marinas and three sand beaches in Géraudot,
usigny-sur-Barse and Mesnil-St-Père. A scenic road runs round the lake, affording fine
iews, particularly between Mesnil-St-Père and the Maison du Parc.

he **Lac du Temple**, created in 1991 and covering an area of 2 300ha/5 684 acres,
 the rendezvous of anglers and canoeists.

he **Lac d'Amance**, the smallest lake with an area of only 500ha/1 236 acres, is
eserved for motorised water sports such as speedboat and motor-boat racing.
he last two lakes, linked by a canal 1.6km/1mi long, occupy the natural basins of
hree tributaries of the River Aube, the Amance, the Auzon and the Temple.
ngling is allowed in all three lakes except in the northeast creek of the Lac
'Orient which is a bird sanctuary.

TOUR

64km/40mi – allow half a day – start from the Maison du Parc

Maison du Parc ⊙ – This fine traditional timber-framed house was taken apart
and rebuilt in the Forêt de Piney. It is both an information centre about the park
and an exhibition area.

*Drive along D 79 for 3km/1.9mi towards Vendeuvre-sur-Barse then turn left onto the
Route forestière du Temple.*

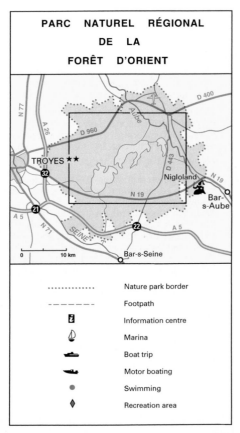

PARC NATUREL RÉGIONAL
DE LA
FORÊT D'ORIENT

.... Nature park border

- - - - - - Footpath

🅑 Information centre

⚓ Marina

🚢 Boat trip

🚤 Motor boating

● Swimming

◆ Recreation area

Sentier éducatif en forêt – This **nature discovery trail** running through the Forêt d
Temple guides visitors among the various species of trees with the help of informa
tive panels.

*Continue along the forest road to Radonvilliers then turn right onto D 11 toward
Dienville.*

Port Dienville, situated on the outskirts of the town, is a leisure and water-sport
centre on the edge of Lake Amance, which attracts amateurs of speedboat an
motor-boat racing. The residential complex, shaped like an ocean liner is framed by
marina (380 moorings) and a bathing and canoeing area.

Dienville – This small town, lying on the banks of the River Aube, has a
impressive stone-built **covered market** and an unusual **church** with a pentagonal aps
and a massive square tower surmounted by a dome. The interior is in a bad stat
of repair; however, note the wrought-iron chancel railing (1768) made by Mathie
Lesueur, the locksmith of Clairvaux abbey.

Continue northwards to Brienne-la-Vieille.

Brienne-la-Vieille – *See BRIENNE-LE-CHÂTEAU: Excursions.*

Return to Radonvilliers along D 11ᴮ then turn right onto D 61 towards Mathaux.

Mathaux – In this small village, there is a lovely timber-framed **church** with
square tower covered with wood shingles.

Drive along D 11ᴬ to l'Étape, then bear right towards Piney (D 11).

Shortly after **l'Étape**, you will see the canal feeding water from the Lac du Templ
back to the River Aube. There are wide **views** of the lake.

Continue to Piney.

Piney – The most noteworthy monument here is the fine 17C wooden covere
market.

Leave Piney by D 79 then follow D 1 to Géraudot.

Géraudot – The village **church** has a wooden porch; the nave dates from the 12
and the chancel from the 16C. The high altar is adorned with a fine Renaissanc
altarpiece in polychrome stone, depicting the Crucifixion and the Resurrection. Not
the 16C stained-glass windows.

*Continue along D 1 and 1km/0.6mi further on turn left onto the road leading t
Lusigny-sur-Barse.*

Lusigny-sur-Barse – At the entrance of the village stands a sculpture (a galvan
ised-steel-and-wood arch, 25m/82ft in diameter spanning the Barse canal) by Klau
Rinke erected on this site in 1986. Through this work, Klaus Rinke, who is th
professor of Constructivist sculpture at the Kunstakademie in Düsseldorf, wished t
celebrate water, a theme illustrated by G Bachelard in his essay *Water and Dreams.*

Mesnil-St-Père – This village, with its timber-and-brick houses, is the mos
important water-sports centre on the shores of the Lac d'Orient; it comprises
marina (300 moorings), a vast beach and sailing schools.
Boat trips ⊘ on the lake are organised on board panoramic motor boats.

Follow D 43 back to the Maison du Parc.

Parc de vision animalier ⊘ – Located on a peninsula (89ha/220 acres) jutting ou
from the eastern shore of the lake, this **wildlife observation area** enables visitors t
discover some of the local fauna.
Two observation points on the edge of the forest offer good views of wild boars
deer and roe-deer roaming around freely. The former eat acorns, roots, rodent
and insects; they remain active day and night, which makes it easier to encounte
them. Deer and roe-deer on the other hand are plant eaters and are mainly activ
at night, which means waiting patiently and silently if you wish to see them.

Go past the Maison du Parc and turn left onto D 79 towards Géraudot.

Réserve ornithologique – This area has been set aside as a **bird sanctuary** fo
waterfowl. An observation point makes it possible to watch moorhens, ducks
black-headed gulls, cranes, herons and wild geese who stop by the lake during thei
annual migrations.

Nature lovers know:

– not to pick flowers, fruit or plants, or gather fossils;

– to take all rubbish and empty cans out of the protected zone;

*– to leave pets, particularly dogs, at home because they might frighte
young wild animals;*

– to stay on the paths, because hillside shortcuts cause erosion.

Région de GÉRARDMER★★

Michelin map 62 folds 17 and 18 or 242 folds 30, 31 and 35

The itineraries described below will enable visitors to discover the western slopes of the Vosges mountains, an area of valleys, lakes and forests, bound in the east by the splendid Route des Crêtes *(see Route des CRÊTES)* running along the ridge line.

Glaciers – The Gérardmer region was deeply marked by glaciers which once covered the Vosges massif *(see p 19)*. One of these, which came down from the Hohneck, filled the valley now occupied by Lake Retournemer and Lake Longemer and joined up with the Moselotte and Moselle glaciers near Remiremont. When it withdrew, it left behind a certain amount of morainic debris which retained the water of the Vologne streaming down the mountain. Downstream from Lake Longemer, the river tried to find an exit through another valley; it dug the gorge known as the Saut des Cuves and flowed towards the Moselle through the Vallée des Granges.

Trapped behind a moraine forming a natural dam, the waters of Lake Gérardmer were diverted and formed the River Jamagne, a tributary of the Vologne. Lake Corbeaux and Lake Blanchemer as well as the small Lake Alfeld and Lake Lispach were also formed after the withdrawal of glaciers.

Textile industry – The cotton industry in the Vosges region was at its height at the end of the 1930s, when there were more than 40 000 workers and 57 000 looms spread over some 250 factories. However, during the past 20 years, fluctuating markets and systematic automation have considerably reduced the area's industrial potential which had brought prosperity to so many valleys of the Vosges. In 1987, 15 major concerns were turning out one third of the French production of cotton and a number of minor businesses were holding on by extending their production to finished products (table linen, clothing).

This area is one of the most actively involved in the textile industry of the whole Vosges region. Gérardmer, where linen weaving has survived, continues to produce household linen, following an old tradition which brought fame to the area. However, bleaching in the fields is no longer standard practice.

★ ① LAKE LONGEMER AND LAKE RETOURNEMER

28km/17.4mi tour – allow 1hr

★**Gérardmer** – Gérardmer owes its fine reputation to its magnificent **setting**★★, its lake, its dark forested mountains and its textile industry. Destroyed by fire in November 1944, a few days before it was liberated, the town was completely rebuilt. Today, it is a popular summer resort, with numerous facilities, hotels and villas scattered among the greenery, and the starting point of many excursions. The tourist office, created in 1875, is the oldest one in France.

Gérardmer's **textile factories** ⊙ are famous for the production of high-quality household linen.

The **Lac de Gérardmer** is the largest lake of the Vosges region (2.2km/1.3mi long, 0.75km/0.45mi wide and 38m/125ft deep); *(for information about angling, see Practical information)*. A **tour**★ round the lake *(6.5km/4mi)* either on foot or by car is a pleasant excursion offering varied views of the lake and its frame of mountains. A **boat trip** ⊙ is a fun excursion; in addition, sailing boats, canoes and pedalos are available for hire.

The nearby ski slopes of **Gérardmer-la Mauselaine-Chaume-Francis-Grouvelin**✳ are accessible to beginners as well as experienced skiers. The ski resort enjoys good snow cover which enhances the appeal of its ski runs (including the longest run of the Vosges massif: 3.9km/2.5mi) and cross-country skiing tracks. There is also a special run for night skiing.

Leave Gérardmer northeast along D 417.

★**Saut des Cuves** – *Leave the car near the Saut des Cuves Hotel. Take the path starting upstream of the bridge and leading to the River Vologne spanned by two footbridges which make it possible to do a short tour.* The mountain stream cascades down over huge granite rocks in a succession of waterfalls; the most important of these is known as the Saut des Cuves. There are fine views of it from several small rocky promontories.

On leaving Longemer, turn right onto D 67.

★**Lac de Longemer** – This lake (2km/1.2mi long, 550m/0.3mi wide and 30m/98ft deep) is surrounded by meadows dotted with low farmhouses with relatively flat roofs *(for information about angling, see Practical information)*.

★**Lac de Retournemer** – This small lake, fed by the waterfalls of the Vologne, is set inside a green basin; its remarkably clear deep-blue waters reflect the trees growing along its shores *(for information about angling, see Practical information)*.

Continue along D 34^D which joins up with D 417 at Le Collet; turn left towards Gérardmer. It is also possible to return to Gérardmer via Xonrupt: turn back by the Lac de Retournemer and follow D 67^A on the left, which skirts the western shore of Lake Longemer.

Région de GÉRARDMER

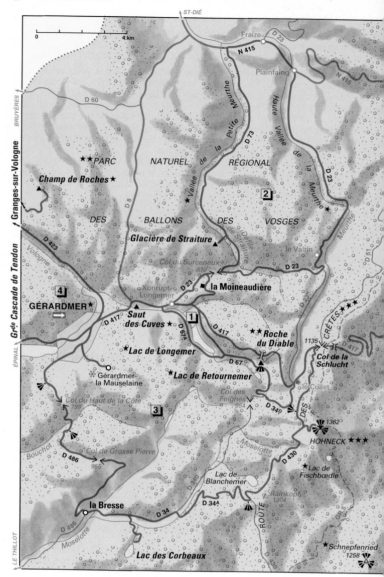

★ ② VALLEYS OF THE MEURTHE AND PETITE MEURTHE

55km/34mi tour – allow 2hr

★**Gérardmer** – *See ① above: Lake Longemer and Lake Retournemer.*
Leave Gérardmer northeast along D 417.

★**Saut des Cuves** – *See ① above.*
Turn left onto D 23 and drive for 2km/1.2mi then turn right.

La Moineaudière – The signposted road leads to the **Domaine de la Moineaudière** ⊘ in a picturesque site on the edge of a spruce forest. There are cacti and other succulent plants, shells, insects, fossils and above all a rich collection of rock including a quartz from Brazil weighing 650kg/1 433lb. Note also the collection of masks and primitive art.

Continue downwards along the forest road which leads to D 417; turn right to return to the intersection with D 23 and turn right again.

The road runs through the forest before reaching the River Meurthe at Le Valtin. The slopes of the **upper valley of the Meurthe** are covered with pastures and forests. Downstream from Le Rudlin, the valley gets narrower and goes through a picturesque gorge. The river supplies several sawmills.

In Plainfaing, turn left onto N 417 then left again onto D 73.

134

On the way back to Gérardmer, the road follows the **valley of the Petite Meurthe**, which, at first, is fairly wide with cultivated fields on both sides but then becomes narrower and forested with sawmills dotted along the river banks. The road then goes through the Straiture gorge whose steep sides are planted with firs.

Glacière de Straiture – A small road branches off to the right; 0.7km/0.4mi beyond this intersection, a path to the southeast makes it possible to cross the river and reach the Glacière de Straiture; a pile of rocks which gets its name from the pieces of ice which can be found between the rocks at the height of summer.

At the end of the gorge, the road crosses the Petite Meurthe, leads to the Col du Surceneux and back to Gérardmer.

★ ③ LA BRESSE – HOHNECK – COL DE LA SCHLUCHT

54km/34mi tour – allow 2hr 30min

★**Gérardmer** – *See* ① *above: Lake Longemer and Lake Retournemer.*
Leave Gérardmer south along D 486.

The road rises through the woods then runs down towards the green valley of the River Bouchot to rise again towards the Col de Grosse Pierre. There are lovely views of the upper valley of the Moselotte and of its tributary, the Chajoux. The slopes, which have been cleared of brushwood, form a pictureque landscape.

La Bresse – This ancient little town scattered across a picturesque valley has always been economically self-supporting thanks to its cheese-making traditions and textile industry; as a result, it remained independent until 1790. Almost completely destroyed in 1944, La Bresse had to be entirely rebuilt.
The **Église St-Laurent**, rebuilt in the 18C, has retained its Gothic chancel. The modern **stained-glass windows** of the nave illustrate the Apostles and the Prophets, whereas those of the chancel depict the Crucifixion with the Assumption on one side and St Laurent on the other. Four windows are devoted to the destruction of La Bresse.

Drive east along D 34.

★**Lac des Corbeaux** – A road, branching off to the right near the Hôtel du Lac, leads to this remote lake (23m/75ft deep) occupying the centre of a glacial cirque with densely forested slopes. A footpath runs all the way round it *(30min; for information about angling, see Practical information).*

Return to D 34 and turn right along the Moselotte Valley. Cross the river, ignoring D 34⁰ on the left, and 2km/1.2mi further on, after a bend to the right, leave the Col de Bramont road and follow the twisting D 34ᴬ, known as the Route des Américains.

As you reach the high pastures, the view extends to the right over the upper valley of the Thur, Wildenstein village and the Kruth-Wildenstein dam.

Turn left onto the Route des Crêtes (D 430) which goes round the Rainkopf summit.

Down on the left, you can see the **Lac de Blanchemer**, lying deep inside a wooded basin and surrounded by meadows *(for information about angling, see Practical information).*
The road then reaches the *chaumes* (high pastures) of the Hohneck.

★★**Hohneck** – *See Route des CRÊTES: itinerary* ②.
Beyond the Hohneck, there are glimpses of Lake Longemer in the distance to the left and later on there are splendid **views**★ of the Valogne Valley, Lake Retournemer and Lake Longemer.

Col de la Schlucht – *See Route des CRÊTES: itinerary* ①.
Turn left onto D 417.

★★**Roche du Diable** – *15min on foot there and back. Leave the car near the Retournemer tunnel and follow a steep path leading to the viewpoint.* The **view**★★ extends to the Valogne Valley, carpeted with lush grass, between Lake Retournemer and Lake Longemer.

★**Saut des Cuves** – *See* ① *above: Lake Longemer and Lake Retournemer.*

④ VALLEYS OF THE TENDON AND OF THE VALOGNE

61km/38mi tour – allow 2hr

★**Gérardmer** – *See* ① *above: Lake Longemer and Lake Retournemer.*
Leave Gérardmer west along D 417.

At the entrance of Le Tholy, turn right onto D 11 towards Épinal and drive for 5km/3mi. Turn left 200m/219yd before the Grande Cascade Hotel and follow the road down to the waterfall (800m/875yd).

★**Grande cascade de Tendon** – This double waterfall drops 32m/105ft in several steps through dense firs.

Further on, as you reach Faucompierre, turn right towards Bruyères along D 30 and D 44. In Bruyères, take the street to the left of the cemetery (towards Belmont), which leads to the foot of mount Avison. Leave the car.

Tour-belvédère du mont Avison – *45min on foot there and back.* This 15m/49 high tower, standing on the summit (alt 601m/1 972ft) of one of the hills sur rounding Bruyères, overlooks the town lying at the intersection of several valley From the platform *(82 steps, viewing table)*, the wide **panorama★** extends to th Tête des Cuveaux, Hohneck and Donon summits.

Drive south along a minor road to Champ-le-Duc.

Champ-le-Duc – The 12C village **church**, built of red sandstone, is a fine examp of primitive Romanesque art from the Rhine region, in spite of being burnt dow by the Swedes in 1635. Note the pillars, alternately massive and slim, beneath th relieving arches, the thick rolls of the vaulting over the crossing, the oven vaulte apse with its three small rounded windows. According to tradition, one of th carved capitals of the crossing depicts a meeting between Emperor Charlemagn and his son Charles in 805.

Continue southeast to Granges-sur-Vologne.

Granges-sur-Vologne – Industrial town: textile factories.

Turn left onto D 31 then right in Barbey-Seroux onto the forest road (second cros. roads) which runs through the Vologne Forest. 2.4km/1.5mi further on, you come another crossroads with a house standing nearby; turn left and leave the ca 150m/164yd further on.

★**Champ de roches de Granges-sur-Vologne** – This horizontal morain 500m/547yd long, cuts through the forest like a petrified river. Its vegetation-fre surface is made up of tightly packed rounded boulders of similar size, which giv the moraine its uniform, almost artificial aspect.

Return to Barbey-Seroux and Granges, then follow D 423 back to Gérardmer.

GIVET

Population 7 775
Michelin map 53 fold 9 or 241 fold 2 – Local map see Vallée de la MEUSE

This border town, guarded by the Charlemont fortress, lies on the banks of the Rive Meuse, at the northern extremity of the Ardennes département jutting out into Belgia territory. **Givet Notre-Dame**, on the east bank, is a former industrial district whereas **Giv St-Hilaire**, on the west bank, is the old town nestling round a church built by Vauba and described by Victor Hugo in derisive terms: "the architect took a priest's or barrister's hat, on this hat he placed an upturned salad bowl, on the base of the sala bowl he stood a sugar basin, on the sugar basin a bottle, on the bottle a sun partl inserted into the neck and finally on the sun he fixed a cock on a spit".

The St-Hilaire district is also a commercial centre as far as place Méhul, prolonged b the Bon Secours district leading to the Belgian border.

Givet's industrial activities include copper tubing, bronze smelting and synthetic tex tiles. The important river harbour is accessible to large Belgian barges for the transfe of goods from French barges, which differ in size.

North of the town, along the Meuse and N 51, you can see a grain silo with a capacit of 80 000t. Stone quarries located between Givet and Foisches produce a bluish ston once used at Versailles.

Givet is the birthplace of the composer, **Étienne Méhul** (1763-1817), essentially know for his operas, which denote Gluck's influence, and for his patriotic songs compose during the Revolution.

From the bridge over the River Meuse, there is a fine overall **view** of the old town, th Tour Victoire and the Fort de Charlemont.

SIGHTS

Tour Victoire ⊘ – In summer, the former keep of the Comtes de la Marck's cast (14C-15C) houses various exhibitions under its pointed vault.

Centre européen des métiers d'art ⊘ – This centre is intended to promot handicraft. It is possible to watch craftsmen at work. Local products are sold in th vaulted cellar, a former 17C custom house.

★**Fort de Charlemont** ⊘ – *The fort is accessible via a narrow road on the left, whic rises through the woods before the first entrance of the military camp.*
This small citadel fortified by Charles V of Spain and named after him, wa redesigned by Vauban as it formed part of the Haurs ring meant to defend Givet Vauban's idea was to cordon off the plateau with bastions, reinforced by ravelin and prolonged by fortified wings, but the project was never completed. Since 196 however, the fort has been used as a commando-training centre. In spite of the ruined state, several buildings have retained an imposing aspect; such is the case o the barrel-vaulted guard-houses opening onto covered passages.

Pointe Est – From the east end of the fort, there are fine **views**★ of Givet, the Meuse Valley, the Mont d'Haurs and the Belgian hills with the Château d'Agimont, which once belonged to the Comte de Paris. The tour includes a long gallery with 5m/16ft thick walls, the casemate with its sophisticated ventilation system, the vast magazine with its pointed brick-built vault and the two 16C bastions.

Fort du Mont d'Haurs – Located on the east bank, this stronghold formed part of the project conceived by Vauban in 1697 at the request of Louis XIV who wanted to defend the bridge at Givet and the fortress of Charlemont on the opposite bank. This fort could accommodate 16 000 to 20 000 men and 2 000 to 3 000 horses. It is the only fortified camp still complete with its monumental gate.

Chemin de fer des Trois Vallées ⊙ – The train overlooks the Meuse Valley between Givet and Dinant in Belgium. It runs past the gardens of the Château de Freyr, through the Moniat tunnel and then across the Anseremme viaduct before reaching Dinant overlooked by the onion-shaped steeple of its collegiate church and its massive citadel.

EXCURSIONS

Grottes de Nichet ⊙ – *4km/2.5mi east.* Situated near the village of Fromelennes, these caves comprise some 12 chambers on two levels, containing numerous concretions (sound effects).

★**Site nucléaire de Chooz (nuclear power stations)** – *6km/3.7mi south. See Vallée de la MEUSE p 181.*

GRAND CANAL D'ALSACE ★★

Michelin map 87 folds 3-10 or 242 folds 16, 20, 24, 28, 32, 36 and 40

River Rhine – The Rhine reaches Alsace slightly downriver from Basle and flows northwards along the eastern edge of the province all the way to Lauterbourg. Although the distance is relatively short, the river drops some 250m/820ft, which accounts for its fast impetuous flow.

In past times, the Rhine used to spread into the surrounding plain and occasionally change course. One of its branches even flowed through Strasbourg; rue d'Or now marks its former route and the rebuilt Ancienne Douane (former custom house) is a reminder of the time (not so long ago) when river craft went through the town. The spates of the Rhine were fearsome; this is the reason why no town, not even Strasbourg, settled on its banks. When the water level rose, local people took turns to watch the dykes day and night. In spite of this, catastrophies were frequent and many an Alsatian village was destroyed by flooding.

Between 1840 and 1878, extensive work was undertaken to prevent flooding. An artificial river bed (200-250m/656-820ft wide) was built to control the river flow. The Rhine has always been an ideal waterway for the promotion of trade between countries bordering the river. In the 8C and 9C, boatmen from Strasbourg sailed downriver to the North Sea in order to sell wine to the English, the Danes and the Swedes. At the end of the Middle Ages, these boatmen controlled the Rhine between Basle and Mainz and theirs was the most powerful guild in Strasbourg. Some 5 000 wagoners, with 20 000 horses at their disposal, carried inland goods unloaded in Strasbourg. Water transport was at its height under Napoleon I and in 1826, the first steamships, operating regular sailings along the Rhine, called at Strasbourg. Unfortunately, dykes built along the Rhine during the 19C to control the river flow caused the river bed to become deeper by 6-7cm/2-3in per year. This, in turn, uncovered rock lying at the bottom of the river and rendered navigation impossible when the water level was low. Water transport consequently declined.

Grand Canal d'Alsace – In order to bring boats and barges back on the Alsatian section of the Rhine and to tap the river's potential of hydroelectric power, the French decided in 1920 to divert part of the river flow to a low-gradient canal and, at the same time, to build several hydroelectric power stations coupled with locks to ensure the continuity of water transport.

The Grand Canal d'Alsace, which includes the four reaches of Kembs, Ottmarsheim, Fessenheim and Vogelgrün, is over 51km/32mi long and 110-140m/361-459ft wide (Suez canal: 100-120m/328-394ft; Panama canal: 91.5m/300ft).

It is interesting to note that water transport on the canal uses only a fourth of the energy required on the Rhine; as a result, 30 000 boats carry a total of 10 million tonnes of freight both ways every year. A road runs alongside the canal.

River harbours – Besides the major port of Strasbourg *(see STRASBOURG)*, there are two other important harbours along this section of the Rhine, Colmar-Neuf-Brisach and Mulhouse-Ottmarsheim, both equipped with extensive port installations and

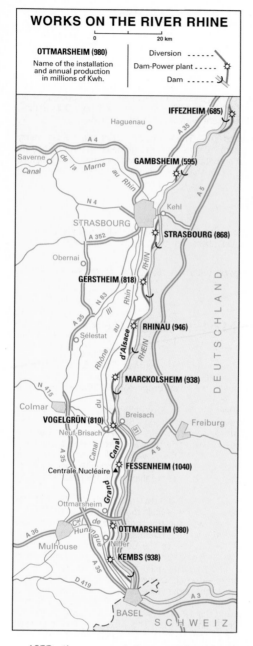

WORKS ON THE RIVER RHINE

0   20 km

OTTMARSHEIM (980)
Name of the installation
and annual production
in millions of Kwh.

Diversion ------
Dam-Power plant -----
Dam -----

Haguenau

IFFEZHEIM (685)

A 4

Saverne

Canal de la Marne au Rhin

GAMBSHEIM (595)

A 5

N 4

Kehl

STRASBOURG

A 352

STRASBOURG (868)

Obernai

GERSTHEIM (818)

N 83

RHIN

DEUTSCHLAND

RHINAU (946)

RHEIN

A 35

Sélestat

Rhin

Canal d'Alsace

N 415

MARCKOLSHEIM (938)

Colmar

Breisach

Freiburg

VOGELGRÜN (810)

Neuf-Brisach

Canal du Rhône au

A 5

Grand Canal

Centrale Nucléaire ▲ FESSENHEIM (1040)

Ottmarsheim

A 36

Cal de Huningue

OTTMARSHEIM (980)

Mulhouse

Niffer

KEMBS (938)

D 419

A 3

BASEL

SCHWEIZ

prolonged by industrial estates
in addition, the linked water
ways formed by the Grand
Canal d'Alsace, the Canal de
Huningue and the Canal du
Rhône au Rhin offer good
communications with the sur
rounding region.

There are guided tours of the
port installations in Strasbourg
and boat trips on the river *(see
STRASBOURG, Port auto
nome)*.

Viewpoints on the Rhine – A
walk along the banks of the
Rhine gives visitors an insight
into the importance of the
international river traffic. The
Pont de l'Europe is, of course
a must for anyone visiting
Strasbourg *(see STRAS
BOURG)*, but it is also easy to
get close to the Rhine between
Lauterbourg and Strasbourg
by following one of the road
branching off D 468. Finally, a
short boat trip along the Rhine
from Strasbourg is probably
the best way to get to know
the river.

★**Bief de Kembs** – This
first reach was completed
in 1932. The small town
of Kembs, which gave its
name to the power sta
tion, was once an impor
tant Roman city. A long
forgotten cement bridge
(uncovered when the canal
was being dug) seems to
contradict the theory that
bridges on the Rhine
were always timber built
so that they could be
burnt in case of invasion.
The dam was the only
one built along the first
four reaches; it diverts
the major part of the
river flow towards the
Grand Canal d'Alsace. A
hydroelectric power station
uses the remaining flow.
Built between 1928 and
1932, the power station was damaged during the Second World War but
repaired in 1945. Today, it produces 938 million kWh every year. The reach
includes the canal and a recently modernised double lock.

A nature reserve covering 150ha/371 acres, known as the **Petite Camargue alsacienne**, lies 9km south of Kembs along D 468 *(parking area near the stadium in
St-Louis-la-Chaussée)*. The aim here is to preserve various ecosystems such as
reedy marshes, copses, ponds, marshland and heaths. Three marked footpaths,
one all the way around the large marsh *(3km/1.9mi)*, offer the opportunity of
observing many species of fauna and flora.

The Canal de Huningue branches off near Niffer towards Mulhouse. The canal and
its access lock form the first section of the Rhine-Rhône link.

Each of the following reaches along the Grand Canal d'Alsace comprises a hydroelectric power station and a double lock, which attracts many curious observers
when in operation.

★**Bief d'Ottmarsheim** – See OTTMARSHEIM.

PRACTICAL INFORMATION

Hydroelectric power stations named below can be visited under the same conditions as the Ottmarsheim power station *(see Admission times and charges)*.

In the Haut-Rhin *département:* Fessenheim, Kembs, Vogelgrün.

In the Bas-Rhin *département:* Gambsheim, Gerstheim, Marckolsheim, Rhinau, Strasbourg.

The Fessenheim, Rhinau and Vogelgrün power stations are open to the public without prior arrangement from 8am to 7pm (5pm from October to March).

The eight locks and dams on the Rhine have information panels explaining the history of the Rhine, the functioning of the hydroelectric power stations and of the locks and the role of the dams.

The dams at Kembs, Rhinau and Strasbourg have been equipped to be used by cyclists and pedestrians as border-crossing points between France and Germany.

★**Bief de Fessenheim** ⊘ – 1956. Situated less than 1km/0.6mi from the Fessenheim lock, it is the first French **nuclear power station** to have used a high-water-pressure reactor; it consists of two units of 900 million watts and was inaugurated in 1977; its annual production is around 12 billion kWh *(an information centre about hydroelectric power is open to visitors).*

The reach is about 17km/11mi long and includes locks similar to those of Ottmarsheim: they have the same length (185m/202yd) but different widths (23m/75ft and 12m/39ft). The power station includes four units with a total capacity of 172 million watts, producing 1 030 million kWh per year.

The **Maison de l'Hydraulique**, situated near the power station, displays models of various water-powered works as well as turbines and other machinery.

★**Bief de Vogelgrün** – 1959. The characteristics of the power station are roughly the same as those of Ottmarsheim and Fessenheim; the reach is 14km/9mi long with locks similar to those of the Fessenheim reach.

The power station consists of four units with a total capacity of 130 million watts and an annual production of 800 million kWh.

Downstream from Vogelgrün, the harnessing of the river includes four more reaches; each one comprises a dam on the river, a feeder canal supplying water to the power station and navigation locks and another canal returning the diverted flow to the Rhine.

The power station is decorated (on the side overlooking the road and on the side overlooking the Rhine) with a huge fresco by Daniel Dyminski from Mulhouse, which covers an area of 1 500m²/1 794sq yd and is entitled *Nix from Vogelgrün*.

Bief de Marckolsheim – Completed in 1961. The power station has an annual production of 928 million kWh.

Bief de Rhinau – 1963. The annual production of the power station totals 936 million kWh.

Bief de Gerstheim – 1967. The power station produces 818 million kWh per year. It was built at the same time as the tidal power station of the Rance estuary in northern Brittany.

Bief de Strasbourg – 1970. The annual production of the power station amounts to 868 million kWh. A regulating reservoir forms a lake covering 650ha/1 606 acres with a water-sports centre at Plobsheim.

Eight power stations have a total capacity of 1 193 million watts and their average annual production amounts to more than 7 billion kWh.

The harnessing of the Rhine was prolonged beyond Strasbourg by a Franco-German project, the power produced being shared between the two countries. The **Gambsheim** power station, situated on the French side and inaugurated in 1974, produces 595 million kWh per year and the **Ifferzheim** power station situated on the German side and completed in 1977 produces 685 million kWh per year.

GUEBWILLER ★

Population 10 942
Michelin map 87 fold 18 or 242 fold 35
Local maps see Route des CRÊTES and Route des VINS

Lying on the south bank of the River Lauch, this small industrial town has retained
wealth of architectural features which testify to its lively past. Throughout the Middl
Ages, vineyards were the main source of wealth of the city and the surrounding area
After it became industrialised in the 19C, its prosperity increased as its textile industr
(silk and cotton) blossomed.

Historical notes – As the administrative centre of the former territory owned by th
nearby Abbaye de Murbach, Guebwiller developed between the 8C and 18C under th
control of the abbots who, because they were princes, were allowed to mint coins i
their castle. In 1275, the abbot granted Guebwiller its own charter and the city wa
allowed to build its own fortifications.
These fortifications turned out to be very useful in 1445, on St Valentine's day, whe
the Armagnacs (opposed to the Burgundians and the English during the Hundred Year
War) tried to take the town by surprise by crossing the frozen moat. A townswoma
named Brigitte Schick gave the alarm; her shrieks were so loud that the attacker
thought the whole population had been warned and they ran away, leaving thei
ladders behind. These are still kept in the Église St-Léger.
In the 18C, the abbey chapter settled in Guebwiller and several religious building
were subsequently built in the town, including the monumental Église Notre-Dam
which gives a fair idea of the wealth of the Church at the time.

SIGHTS

★**Église Notre-Dame** – Built between 1760 and 1785 by the last prince-abbot o
Murbach, this church looks particularly impressive. Its neo-Classical west front i
decorated with statues representing the theological and cardinal virtues. The loft
interior★★ is reminiscent of Roman pomp. The three semicircular apses forming th
end of both transepts and of the chancel are characteristic of Baroque style. Bu
the most striking feature is the high-relief sculpture of the high altar by Sporrer
representing the **Assumption**★★ (1783). Note also, by the same artist, the refined
decoration of the stalls and the organ loft.

★**Église St-Léger** – This church is a good example of late Romanesque architectur
of the Rhine region. The west front, the nave the transept and the aisles date from
the 12C and 13C; the apse and the chancel were completed in the 14C and anothe
set of aisles was added to the first in the 16C.

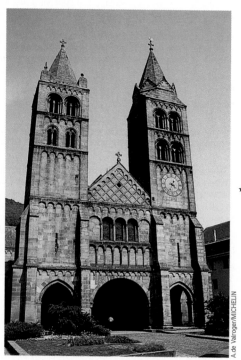

★★**West front** – The porch
flanked by two high towers
and surmounted by blind
arcading and windows, is
open on three sides. The
tympanum of the rounded
central doorway is deco
rated with a representation
of Christ sitting on a
throne and dispensing his
blessings.

Interior – The chancel con
tains fine 18C wood carv
ings. The ladders abandoned
by the Armagnacs in 1445
(see above) hang from the
vault of the south aisle.

★**Hôtel de ville** – Built in
1514 for a wealthy draper
the edifice has mullioned
windows and a five-sided
Flamboyant Gothic oriel. A
16C statue of the Virgin
shelters inside a corner
recess on the right.

**Ancien couvent des Do-
minicains** ⊙ – This convent
was founded in 1294. The
buildings, which had wit
nessed so many historic
events were sold during the
Revolution and became a
factory warehouse and then
a hospital before being

Guebwiller – Église St-Léger

A.de Valroger/MICHELIN

bought by the administrative council of the Haut-Rhin *département* and turned into the **Centre poly-musical des Dominicains** (music centre). The opening of the Jazz Cellar in 1994 has enabled the centre to program a jazz season from September to June, on Fridays and Saturdays.

Église St-Pierre-et-St-Paul – Erected between 1312 and 1340, this Gothic church contains a very fine group of frescoes dating from the 16C and 17C *(restoration underway)*. The acoustics are famous the world over and the nave is the venue of prestigious concerts of classical music from June to September.

During the summer, the music centre organises important exhibitions and small improvised concerts.

> ### Théodore Deck (1823-1891)
>
> This native of Guebwiller was a potter and ceramist of genius. His research led him to discover in 1874 the lost formula of the turquoise blue characteristic of Persian ceramics; this blue was henceforth known as the *Bleu Deck*. Deck also found the secret of the famous Chinese celadon, he reproduced oriental *cloisonné* and succeeded in decorating his ceramics with a gilt background. In his book, *Ceramics*, published in 1887, he disclosed his formulae and offered anyone interested in the subject the benefit of his experience. He was put in charge of the Manufacture nationale de Sèvres and spent the last years of his life perfecting his art and creating new types of porcelain. His funeral monument in Montparnasse cemetery in Paris, where he is buried, was carved by his friend Frédéric Auguste Bartholdi who sculpted the famous Statue of Liberty.

★**Musée du Florival** ⊙ – The museum, housed in the former 18C residence of aristocratic canons from the chapter of Murbach abbey, displays its collections on five levels; these illustrate the geology and history of the Florival Valley, its wine-growing and handicraft traditions and its industrial past. Note in particular a very beautiful 13C Virgin, a 15C altarpiece (remarkably well presented) and a moving 16C Deposition believed to be the work of Quentin Metsys. A spectacular collection of rocks from the Vosges massif occupies the basement. However, the museum no doubt owes its originality to its display of the **works**★ of Théodore Deck, including the decoration of a bathroom and a verandah with glazed tiles depicting bright luxuriant lakeside landscapes, vases coloured in a special blue named after the artist, dishes with a gilt background and a monumental statue in polychrome ceramics representing Bernard Palissy, the 16C master potter.

GUEBWILLER VALLEY

From Guebwiller to Le Markstein *29km – allow 2hr*

Local map see Parc naturel régional des BALLONS DES VOSGES

The **Lauch Valley** or Guebwiller Valley is known as "Florival" ("flower valley") because of its pleasant colourful aspect. Art lovers will find a lot to admire in the lovely Romanesque churches of Murbach and Lautenbach whereas hikers will appreciate the *zone de tranquillité* or "quiet area" *(no cars allowed)* situated at the end of the valley, on either side of D 430 and as far south as D 431, which covers the most interesting part of the Guebwiller Forest.

★**Guebwiller** – *See above.*

Drive out of Guebwiller towards Buhl.

The road follows the River Lauch; on either side, vineyards and woods slope down to the bottom of the wide valley covered with meadows. The picturesque Murbach Valley can be seen on the left.

★**Église de Murbach** – *See MURBACH.*

★**Lautenbach** – The village, which goes back to the 8C, developed round a Benedictine abbey. Today, only the **church**★ remains surrounded by several canons' houses dating from the days when it was a collegiate church.

The Romanesque porch is divided into three parts surmounted by primitive ribbed vaulting. The nave houses a beautiful 18C pulpit and the north aisle a painting on wood from the school of Schongauer. A representation of Christ dating from 1491 marks the entrance to the chancel which has retained a 15C stained-glass window and remarkable 15C stalls (note the detail on the historiated misericords) surmounted by an 18C canopy.

On the left of the church, you can see a cloister gallery dating from the 16C.

Just beyond Linthal, the Lauch Valley becomes narrow and wild.

★**Lac de la Lauch** – This artificial lake (area: more than 11ha/27 acres; depth: 19m/62ft), where angling is allowed *(see Practical information)*, lies inside a wooded glacial cirque. A 250m/273yd long walk has been laid out on top of the dam.

The road enters the forest and rises in a series of hairpin bends, offering glimpse of the valley and of the Grand Ballon.

Drive round the lake and leave the car 2km/1.2mi further on in a bend to the right the follow a path on the left leading to a promontory.

There is a fine view of the Lauch Valley, of the Plaine d'Alsace and of the Blac Forest.

Le Markstein – This winter-sports resort is situated at the intersection of th Route des Crêtes and of the upper Lauch Valley.

HACKENBERG ★

Access – 20km/12.4mi east of Thionville. Leave the town by D 918. The route is sign posted from Metzervisse.

The largest fort of the Maginot Line *(see Ligne MAGINOT)* lies hidden at the heart of forest covering 160ha/395 acres, near the village of Veckring. With its two block houses at the entrance and another 17 spread around, it perfectly illustrates th definition of "fan-shaped forts" given by André Maginot, "forts split into several part placed at strategic points". The fort could accommodate 1 200 men and its powe station could supply a town of 10 000 inhabitants. As for its artillery, it could fire more than 4t of shells per minute!

On 4 July 1940, the crew manning the fort was forced to surrender to comply with the orders brought by the liaison officer of the French government whose member had retreated to Bordeaux. In 1943, the fort housed a factory of mechanical engineer ing worked by Ukrainian women. In November 1944, American tanks had to interven to dislodge German soldiers entrenched in blockhouse no 8.

Tour of the fort ⊙ – Everything here is monumental, which tends to make Hackenberg rather special: the massive blastproof door, the high-vaulted centra station, miles of empty galleries and the huge power station all suggest a useless abandoned metropolis... The lively atmosphere of the brightly shining kitchens, o the impressive sickbay or of the firing headquarters is reconstructed with the help of dummies. The important **museum** displays all kinds of weapons, including a rich collection of machine guns and tommy guns of the two world wars, as well as uniforms of units having taken part in the Battle of France. A small electric train and an elevator lead you to artillery blockhouse no 9, fitted with guns able to fire bombs with a 135mm/5.3in diameter. The gun-turret demonstration is first fol lowed from inside and then from outside, among firing or observation posts and casemates.

In order to understand the strategic importance of the fort, whose defence works overlooked both the Nied Valley and the Moselle Valley, drive up (or walk up if the weather is fine) to the fort chapel surrounded by ancient graves *(2.5km/1.5m. along the road starting from the end of the parking area; in front of the men's entrance, take the surfaced path on the left)*. One can see the two observation towers emerging from the Sierck Forest. Behind the chapel, a path leads to a concrete escarpment (700m/765yd long), a unique defence line reinforced by five blockhouses.

HAGUENAU ★

Population 27 675
Michelin map 87 fold 3 or 242 fold 16

Haguenau lies on the banks of the River Moder, on the edge of the vast Haguenau Forest.

The town prospered in the shadow of the massive castle erected by Frederick I **"Barbarossa"** (Redbeard) of the House of Hohenstaufen, who ruled the Holy Roman Empire from 1152 to 1190. The castle remained one of the favourite residences of the Hohenstaufens in Alsace until the mid 13C. The verses by Longfellow quoted on the opening pages of this book are part of a poem set in Haguenau; it tells the story of a local cobbler.

Haguenau was, for a long time, second only to Strasbourg as a prosperous member of the league of defence known as **Decapolis**, formed by 10 Alsatian cities within the Holy Roman Empire *(see MULHOUSE)*.

SIGHTS

★**Musée historique** ⊙ (BZ M¹) – The history museum is housed in an imposing edifice built at the beginning of the 20C, partly in neo-Gothic and partly in neo-Renaissance style.

The basement contains an important collection of prehistoric and Roman objects found in the region (Haguenau Forest, Seltz).

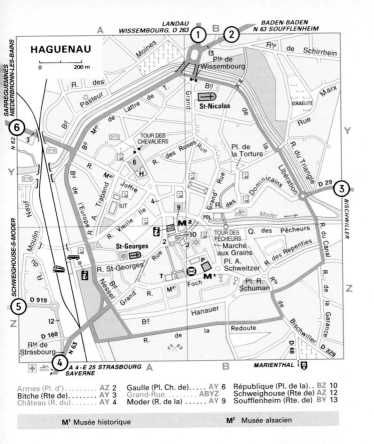

HAGUENAU

0   200 m

Armes (Pl. d') .... AZ 2	Gaulle (Pl. Ch. de) .... AY 6	République (Pl. de la) .. BZ 10
Bitche (Rte de) .... AY 3	Grand-Rue .... ABYZ	Schweighouse (Rte de) AZ 12
Château (R. du) ...... AY 4	Moder (R. de la) ...... AY 9	Soufflenheim (Rte. de) BY 13

M¹ Musée historique   **M²** Musée alsacien

The ground floor is the most interesting level; particularly noteworthy are the remarkable medieval sculptures (predella depicting the Last Supper), which originally adorned the town's monuments. There is also a collection of Alsatian coins and medals, many of them minted in Haguenau, and written works printed in Haguenau between 1489 and 1557.

On the first floor are the collections of local history and ceramics, in particular those produced by the Hannong factory (see STRASBOURG p 289).

Église St-Georges (AZ) – This 12C and 13C church harmoniously combines the Romanesque and Gothic styles. The crossing is surmounted by an octagonal steeple which houses the two oldest bells in France (1268). The buttress of the south transept bears a series of grooves representing the standard measures of length once used in Haguenau.

Inside, the vast nave has retained its Romanesque aspect; it is separated from the aisles by rounded arches resting on massive round pillars. However, the intricate ribbed vaulting and the elegant Gothic chancel, completed in the 13C by sculptors of the Œuvre Notre-Dame in Strasbourg (see STRASBOURG p 290), soften the impression of austerity of the interior.

Several works of art are noteworthy: the stone **pulpit**, carved in 1500 by Veit Wagner, and, opposite, a wooden crucifix carved in 1487 by Clément de Bade for the rood screen demolished in 1628. The south transept contains a composite **altarpiece★** comprising a 19C polychrome central panel carved in neo-Gothic style, representing the Last Judgement, and two side panels painted in 1497 by a local artist, Diebold Martin, which depict the Nativity and the Adoration of the Magi. The north transept houses a 15C altarpiece with a Virgin and Child in its centre. In the chancel, there is an elegant Flamboyant **tabernacle** carved by Friedrich Hammer in 1523, which rises up to the vaulting.

The colourful modern stained-glass windows are the work of Jacques Le Chevallier (between 1956 and 1970).

Église St-Nicolas (BY) – This Gothic church was founded by Emperor Frederick Barbarossa in 1189. It belonged to the Premonstratensians until 1789. The tower is the only part of the original edifice still standing although it was badly damaged in 1944. The chancel and the nave date from c 1300.

From the chancel there is an interesting vista of the long nave with its 10 bays surmounted by ribbed vaulting.

The south aisle contains a 15C wooden Pietà; a door leads to a porch which shelters a sepulchre dating from 1426; next to it stands a late-14C christening font.

The remarkable 18C **woodwork★** *(switch on the light on the left of the chancel,* decorating the pulpit, the organ loft and the choir stalls, was brought to St-Nicolas from the former Abbaye de Neubourg after the Revolution. The other statue superbly carved in wood, which stand at the entrance of the chancel, are fine examples of the Baroque style; they represent the Doctors of the Church: St Augustine, St Ambrose, St Gregory and St Jerome.

Musée alsacien ⊘ (AY M²) – Housed in the restored 15C chancellery, this museum displays various regional collections: on the first floor, there are tools and wooden implements, wrought iron, pewter, paintings mounted under glass, old costumes; on the second floor, visitors can see the "potter's house" (18C-19C) with its workshop, popular prints and the reconstruction of a peasant's home with its kitchen and living room or *stube.*

EXCURSIONS

Forêt de Haguenau – According to legend, **St Arbogast**, entrusted by the king of the Franks with the Christianisation of northern Alsace, stayed in this forest, which was thereafter known as the **holy forest** until the end of the Middle Ages.
The forest covers an area of nearly 14 000ha/34 595 acres as it did in Gallo-Roman times. Today the proportion of evergreens to deciduous tress is: two thirds forest pines and one third deciduous trees, mainly oaks, hornbeams, beeches, and ashes; the forest plays an important role in the economy of the region and offers nature lovers a choice of pleasant footpaths.

Gros Chêne – *6km/3.7mi east of Haguenau. Leave by ② on the town plan.*
This ancient oak or rather what is left of it, stands near a small modern chapel dedicated to St Arbogast; it is the starting point of an interesting botanic trail, a "fitness itinerary" and walks through the forest *(marked paths). Inn and playground for children.*

Walbourg – *10.5km/6.5mi north of Haguenau by ① on the town plan.*
The peaceful village of Walbourg, pleasantly situated at the heart of rolling country-side, owes its name to the foundation in 1074 of a Benedictine abbey dedicated to St Walburga, an English nun who helped to convert Germany to Christianity.
The 15C abbey church is the only part of the abbey still standing. The chancel, surmounted by an intricate ribbed vaulting is lit by five luminous 15C windows. The polished-wood pulpit dates from the 18C.

Soufflenheim *–14km/8.7mi east. Leave Haguenau by ② on the town plan.*
This industrial town is famous for its **ceramic workshops** ⊘ which produce typically Alsatian ceramics with floral decoration against a plain background: oval terrines, dishes, salad bowls, cake tins, jugs etc.
In the former fortified cemetery overlooking the Grand'Rue, you can see a lifesize sculpture of the **Last Supper** after the painting by Leonardo da Vinci; it was modelled in clay by Léon Elchinger and Charles Burger (1871-1942).

Betschdorf – *16.5km/10mi northeast by ① on the town plan.*
This lovely village with its timber-framed houses is famous for its art pottery of grey sandstone with blue decoration: jugs, pots, vases etc. The objects are hand-made and, once dry, they are decorated with a paint brush dipped in cobalt blue, "cooked" at a temperature of 1 250°C/2 282°F and then glazed.
A **museum** ⊘, housed in an old farmhouse, displays an interesting collection of these potteries from the Middle Ages to the present time. There is a reconstructed workshop in the barn.

Hatten: Musée de l'Abri and Casemate d'infanterie Esch – *22km/13.7mi northeast. Leave Haguenau by ① on the town plan. Drive to Hatten via Betschdorf. The museum is in the village; the casemate is situated on the left, 1km/0.6mi beyond Hatten on the way to Seltz. See Ligne MAGINOT p 165.*

Château du HAUT-BARR★

Michelin map 87 fold 14 or 242 fold 19
Local map see Parc Naturel Régional des VOSGES DU NORD

Solidly camped on three huge sandstone rocks overlooking the valley of the River Zorn and the Plaine d'Alsace, the 12C castle was completely remodelled by Bishop Mander-scheidt of Strasbourg who, according to legend, founded the "Brotherhood of the Horn" dedicated to drinking Alsace wine out of the horn of an aurochs!

Access – *5km/3mi. From Saverne, follow rue du Général-Leclerc then D 102 which offers views of the Black Forest. Turn onto D 171 winding through the forest. Park the car near the entrance of the castle.*

Château du Haut-Barr

TOUR OF THE CASTLE *about 30min*

A paved ramp leads from the main gate to a second gateway, beyond which you can see the restored Romanesque chapel on the right and the Restaurant du Haut-Barr on the left. Past the chapel, there is a terrace *(viewing table)*, from which the **view★** extends towards Saverne, the Kochersberg's hills and the Black Forest in the distance, beyond the Rhine Valley.
A metal staircase *(64 steps)*, fixed to the rock face, gives access to the first rock offering similar views.
Return to the restaurant and, immediately beyond it, go up 81 steps to reach the second rock linked by a footbridge, known as the "Pont du Diable", to the third rock. From there, the **view★★** is even better as it offers a 360° panorama including the Vosges mountains, the Zorn Valley (through which flows the canal linking the Marne and the Rhine), the Lorraine plateau and, in clear weather, the spire of Strasbourg cathedral.
A reconstruction of **Claude Chappe's telegraph tower** stands on its original site, 200m/219yd south of the castle: it consists of a relay tower of the famous optical telegraph invented in 1794 by the engineer Chappe and used between Paris and Strasbourg from 1798 to 1852. There is an audio-visual presentation in the small museum.

Château du HAUT-KŒNIGSBOURG ★★

Michelin map 87 fold 16 or 242 fold 27
Local map see Route des VINS

The castle *(see illustration in Architecture and art)*, which is mentioned for the first time in 1147, was built by the Hohenstaufens on a promontory overlooking the Plaine d'Alsace, at an altitude of more than 700m/2 297ft.
This exceptional position enabled the occupants to withdraw easily and to watch all roads leading to Lorraine or crossing Alsace from north to south.
In 1479, it became the property of the Hapsburgs, who had it rebuilt, extended and equipped with a modern defence system. However, 150 years later, these defences did not withstand the attack of the Swedish artillery. The castle was sacked, then burnt down and abandoned for two centuries but its ruins remained imposing until the end of the 19C.
In 1899, the castle was offered by the town of Sélestat to Kaiser William II's daughter who had it restored by Bodo Ebhardt, an architect from Berlin. The restoration work, which lasted from 1900 to 1908, was carried out scientifically with the help of archeological finds and archives.

Access – *The road leading to the castle (2km/1.2mi) branches off D 159 at the intersection of the latter with D 1[B1], near the Haut-Kœnigsbourg Hotel; 1km/0.6mi further on, follow the one-way road on the right, which goes round the castle (it is possible to leave the car on the left).*

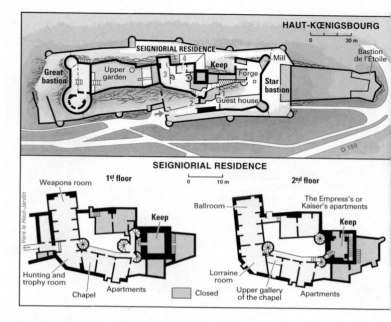

HAUT-KŒNIGSBOURG

SEIGNIORIAL RESIDENCE

1st floor — 2nd floor

TOUR OF THE CASTLE ⏱ *about 1hr*

Beyond the gate and the portcullis, lies the lower courtyard surrounded by the buildings enabling the castle to be self-supporting and withstand a siege: the inn (restaurant, shop and bookshop), the stables, the forge and the mill. A ramp leads to the "lions' doorway" (1) and to the moat separating the seigneurial residence from the rest of the castle. A fortified well (2), 62m/203ft deep, is located on the edge of the rocky promontory, near the residence. On the ground floor of the latter, there is a cellar (3) on the west side and kitchens (4) on the north side.
From the inner courtyard, two spiral staircases lead to the upper floors with two balconies on the south side. The apartments (living room and bedroom) are on the north and south sides. The reception rooms are on the west side: great hall, Lorraine room and guard-room. The keep stands on the east side; its upper levels have been restored. The furniture and weapons (15C-17C) were bought at the beginning of the 20C in order to restore the atmosphere of a castle.

★★**Panorama** – Walk across the upper courtyard to the great bastion for panoramic views including: to the north, the ruins of Franckenbourg, Ramstein and Ortenbourg castles; to the east, across the Rhine, the heights of Kaiserstuhl with the Black Forest behind; to the south, the Hohneck and, on the horizon, the Grand Ballon and Route du Vin; about 200m/218yd to the west, you can see the ruins of Œdenbourg or Petit-Kœnigsbourg.

Région du HOHWALD★★

Michelin map 87 folds 5, 15 and 16 or 242 folds 23 and 27

This region of forests, vineyards and charming villages, lying southwest of Strasbourg, is limited by the Bruche Valley to the north and west, D 424 to the south and the A 35 motorway linking Colmar and Strasbourg to the east. It gets its name from the secluded resort of Le Hohwald.
There are many traces of the area's ancient past, such as the pagan wall round Mont Ste-Odile, believed to have been built by the Celts and reinforced by the Romans, as well as the numerous ruined castles scattered about the countryside.
The Hohwald is traditionally famous for its dense fir forest yet, in the past 200 years, beeches have "invaded" large clearings made by man following a dispute between the towns of Barr and Strasbourg about ownership of the forest.
Vineyards manage to cohabit with this superb forest where raspberries and bilberries grow in abundance. Vines cover the hillsides right up to the villages, and the loess deposits found in the Barr area are ideal for tobacco-growing; further north, hopfields are a familiar sight and the numerous rivers and streams which crisscross the region have favoured the development of sawmills, weaving and spinning mills. This diversity accounts for the traditional prosperity of the region.

★★MONT STE-ODILE
① Itinerary starting from Le Hohwald
24km/15mi – about 1hr – local map and description see Mont STE-ODILE

★★NORTH HOHWALD
② Round tour starting from Le Hohwald
91km/56.5mi – allow one day

★★Le Hohwald – This secluded resort lies at the heart of meadowland surrounded by splendid fir and beech forests offering fine walks. It is also the starting point of a variety of drives through this picturesque area.

The road *(D 425)* follows the wooded Andlau Valley dotted with sawmills. The ruins of Spesbourg and Haut-Andlau castles can be seen high up on the left.

★Andlau – *See ANDLAU.*

Between Andlau and Obernai, the road runs through a hilly area covered with vineyards.

Mittelbergheim – This is a picturesque village clinging to the hillside. Place de l'Hôtel de ville is lined with lovely Renaissance houses with porches and window frames of typical sandstone from the Vosges region. Wine-growing is a long-standing tradition going back to Roman times and the wines of this area are famous.

Barr – *See Route des VINS p 325.*

★Haut-Anlau and Spesbourg castles – *1hr 30min on foot there and back. Drive west along D 854 then, 1.5km/0.9mi beyond Holzplatz, continue on a surfaced path to the left which leads to Hungerplatz forest lodge. Leave the car there and follow the path running along the mountain ridge to the ruins.*
The **Château du Haut-Andlau★**, built in the 14C and restored in the 16C, was lived in until 1806. Today, the imposing ruins include two massive towers and sections of walls with gaping Gothic windows. From the terrace, one can see the vineyard-covered hills, the Plaine d'Alsace and the Black Forest in the distance.
The **Château de Spesbourg★** had an unusually short life for a castle: built of pink granite in the 13C, it was destroyed in the 14C. The square keep overlooks the high walls of the seigneurial residence with its fine twinned windows. There is a beautiful view of the Andlau Valley and the Ungersberg summit to the south.

Gertwiller – This village is famous for its wine and its glacé gingerbread.

Beyond Gertwiller, Landsberg castle can be seen on the foothills of the Vosges with, on the right, the convent of Ste-Odile and, lower down, the ruins of Ottrott's two castles.

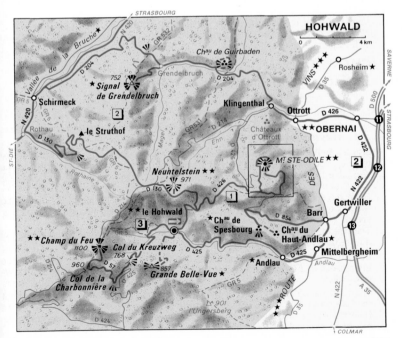

★★Obernai – *See OBERNAI.*

Ottrott – Lying at the heart of vineyards which produce one of the good Alsatian red wines, this village is proud of its two castles, the 12C Lutzelbourg castle with its square building and round tower, and the 13C Rathsamhausen castle, larger and more elaborate than the first.

Coming out of Ottrott towards Klingenthal, you will see, on the site of a former spinning mill, a large aquarium known as **Les Naïades** ⊙, containing more than 3 000 fish from Asia, Africa and South America. A specific natural environment has been recreated in each of the aquarium's tanks (caves, mountain streams, rivers, lakes, estuaries) where you can see exotic species swimming around: shark-fish, piranhas, electric eels, as well as crocodiles from the Nile and sharks...

Klingenthal – This small village was once famous for its weapons factory founded in 1776, which produced fine swords and bayonets.

Drive through the forest along D 204 as far as the Fischhütte inn and leave the car 150m/164yd further on, a path to the right leads (6km/3.7mi there and back) to the ruins of Guirbaden castle.

In spite of being destroyed in the 17C, the 11C **Château fort de Guirbaden** has retained the outer shell of its seigneurial residence and its keep. It offers an extended view of the surrounding forest, of the Plaine d'Alsace and of the Bruche Valley. In summer, the scenery is partly concealed by the luxuriant vegetation.

★Signal de Grendelbruch – *15min on foot there and back.* The wide **panorama★** encompasses the Plaine d'Alsace to the east and, to the west, the Bruche Valley and the Vosges mountain range with the Donon in the foreground, crowned by a small temple.

Further on, the road affords fine views of Wisches, of deep wooded valleys and of the Donon summit, before reaching the picturesque Bruche Valley *(see Vallée de la BRUCHE).*

Schirmeck – *See Vallée de la BRUCHE.*

In Rothau, turn left onto D 130 which follows the Rothaine Valley for 3km/1.9mi then veers suddenly left.

The view soon embraces the whole valley.

A road on the left leads to the gas chamber of the former concentration camp, 1km/0.6mi further, a path branching off to the left, leads to the camp and the Cimetière national des déportés.

Le Struthof – *See Le STRUTHOF.*

The road goes across a plateau, enters the forest and runs down towards La Rothlach.

Leave the car 1.5km/0.9mi beyond La Rothlach and follow a path on the left leading to the Neuntelstein viewpoint.

★★Neuntelstein – *30min on foot there and back.* There is a splendid **view★★** of Mont Ste-Odile, the Ungersberg, Haut-Kœnigsbourg and the Champ du Feu.

Continue along D 130 and, at the intersection with D 426, turn right towards Le Hohwald. A left turn at that point would lead you to Mont Ste-Odile (see Mont STE-ODILE).

★★CHAMP DU FEU

③ Itinerary starting from Le Hohwald

11km/6.8mi – About 30min

★★Le Hohwald – *See round tour ②.*

Leave Le Hohwald along the road which starts opposite the Café-restaurant d'Alsace and crosses the river.

★Grande Belle-Vue (Viewpoint) – *1hr 30min on foot there and back.* After a few minutes, you will get a clear view of Le Hohwald and the surrounding area. *As you reach the former Belle-Vue inn (1km/0.6mi), take a path on the left and climb for 3km/1.9mi through the forest before reaching the high pastures.*

From the summit *(100m/110yd to the left)*, the **view★** extends to Le Climont on the right, the valley of Villé in the foreground and Haut-Kœnigsbourg further ahead.

The rest of the itinerary goes through green meadows and woods then across Col du Kreuzweg (alt 768m/2 520ft) which offers a more open view.

Col du Kreuzweg – From the pass, the view extends over the valleys of the Breitenbach and Giessen rivers framed by mountains and, beyond, over the Liepvrette Valley.

The road *(D 57)* climbs towards the Charbonnière pass, offering superb views of the Villé Valley, the Plaine d'Alsace and the Black Forest. Frankenbourg castle and Haut-Kœnigsbourg castle can be seen from afar, camped on their respective promontories overlooking the plain.

View from Col de la Charbonnière

Col de la Charbonnière – Beyond the heights overlooking the Villé Valley, one can see the Plaine d'Alsace with the Black Forest in the distance.

On reaching the pass, turn right onto D 214 which goes round the Champ du Feu.

★★**Champ du Feu** – The vast **panorama**★★ unfolding from the top of the observation tower includes the Vosges mountains, the Plaine d'Alsace, the Black Forest and, when the weather is clear, the Swiss Alps. The slopes all around are a sought-after ski area. North of the tower, 1km/0.6mi to the left, D 414 leads to the Chalet Refuge and ski slopes of La Serva *(1.5km/0.9mi).*

JOINVILLE

Population 4 754
Michelin map 61 fold 10 or 241 fold 35

This small town nestles between the River Marne, dotted with mills, and a hill crowned by the ruins of a feudal castle which once belonged to the dukes of Guise.

One of the most prominent lords of this barony, established in the 11C, was the famous 13C chronicler, Jean de Joinville (1224-1317), a loyal companion of King Louis IX, better known as St Louis, whom he followed to Egypt in 1248 to take part in the seventh Crusade. He related the events in a chronicle dedicated to St Louis which he wrote when he was already over 80 years old. A 3m/10ft high statue of Joinville, holding a book and a quill pen, by Lescornel, was erected in 1861 in rue Aristide-Briand; the bas-reliefs depict his departure for the crusade, St Louis passing judgement under the oak in Vincennes Forest and the battle of Mansourah in Egypt.

In 1583, during the Wars of Religion, King Philip II of Spain signed an alliance with the heads of the French Holy League, a Catholic extremist group, in the Château de Joinville.

SIGHTS

★**Château du Grand Jardin** ⊙ – The castle owes its name to the fact that it stands at the centre of a large garden. Built by Claude de Lorraine, head of the House of Guise, and Antoinette de Bourbon at the beginning of the 16C, it comprises an elegant edifice surmounted by a high roof and surrounded on three sides by a moat.

The façades are richly decorated with carvings, probably by Ligier Richier and Dominique Florentin, also known as Riconucci, a sculptor from Florence who studied with Primaticcio.

The castle has been restored to its Renaissance splendour. The great hall with its five monumental bays and large ornamental recesses is now the venue of cultural events such as concerts, exhibitions etc.

In the 16C Chapelle St-Claude, note the lovely stone coffered ceiling decorated with floral motifs.

Jardin – The gardens have been recreated as they were in Renaissance times according to written accounts and drawings and now offer pleasant walks: ornamental beds planted with lavender, santolina or medicinal and aromatic herbs, flower beds, an orchard containing more than 70 varieties of fruit trees and a maze are particularly attractive features.

Auditoire ⊙ – This seigneurial tribunal erected in the 16C also served as a prison. The tour starts with the "Chambre des Pailleux" for poor prisoners who slept on straw (*paille* means straw), followed by the "Pistole" accessible to prisoners who could pay a *pistole* (ancient gold coin) for their keep, then the women's quarters. The tribunal and Claude de Lorraine's reception hall are on the second floor. A spiral staircase leads to the loft where the amount of grain tax owed to the local lord was kept: many characters in period dress recreate the atmosphere of the city when it was flourishing.

Église Notre-Dame ⊙ – The church dates from the late 12C and early 13C. Damaged by fire and restored in the 16C, it was parlty rebuilt in primitive style in the 19C. It has retained its original nave (although the vaulting was rebuilt in the 16C) and its 13C aisles.
Note the modillions decorating the lower part of the roof and the 13C doorway under the 19C belfry-porch. The south side has a Renaissance doorway with Corinthian columns and capitals
The church houses a 16C sepulchre denoting a Mannerist influence, an alabaster sculpture in high relief and a reliquary containing "St Joseph's belt" brought back by Jean de Joinville from the Holy Land in 1252.

Chapelle Ste-Anne ⊙ – The chapel (1504) stands in the centre of the cemetery: light pours in through lovely stained-glass windows: red and blue are the main colours used to depict scenes from the life of the Virgin, of St Anne and of St Laurence. Note the 15C **Christ in bonds** in polychrome wood.

EXCURSIONS

Blécourt – *9km/5.6mi south along N 67 to Rupt then right onto D 117.*
This pleasant village has a beautiful Gothic church built in the 12C and 13C whose proportions are remarkable. It contains a Virgin and Child in carved wood dating from the 13C (Champagne School); it was already a place of pilgrimage in Merovingian times and was later mentioned in the chronicles of Jean de Joinville.

Lacets de Mélaire – *19km/11.8mi round tour. Follow D 60; 4km/2.5mi beyond Thonnance-lès-Joinville, take the small road on the right which runs through the woods.*
These hairpin bends with steep slopes offer good views of the wide valley below and the village of Poissons.

Poissons – The village has retained a number of old houses and there are fine views from the banks of the River Rongeant which flows through it. The 16C Église St-Aignan is preceded by a monumental doorway with delicately carved arching forming a beautiful Renaissance ensemble. There is a lovely rood beam inside.

Return to Joinville along D 427 which follows the Rongeant Valley.

KAYSERSBERG★★

Population 2 755
Michelin map 87 fold 17 or 242 fold 31 – Local map see Route des VINS

Kaysersberg is a small charming city with flower-decked houses and a quaint medieval character; it is built on the banks of the Weiss, at the point where the river runs into the Plaine d'Alsace, and surrounded by famous vineyards.
In Roman times, it was already called *Caesaris Mons* (the emperor's mountain) because of its strategic position along one of the most important routes linking ancient Gaul and the Rhine Valley. The appropriateness of this name was confirmed throughout the town's rich history, as it was fortified, protected and developed by more than one

Albert Schweitzer

Born in Kaysersberg on 14 January 1875, Albert Schweitzer became a clergyman, a theologian, a famous organist, a musicologist, a writer and a missionary doctor. After the First World War, he spent most of his life in West Africa where he founded a hospital, occasionally returning to Europe to give organ concerts. He was awarded the Nobel Peace Prize in 1952 and died in 1965 in Lambaréné (Gabon) where his work lives on.

emperor: Frederick II in the 13C, then Rodolph of Hapsburg and Adolph of Nassau who declared it a free city. In 1353, Kaysersberg joined the Decapolis, an alliance between 10 free Alsatian cities *(see MULHOUSE)*. Emperor Charles V encouraged its development and Maximilian nominated **Lazarus von Schwendi** (1522-84) as imperial bailiff. He presented the town with a few vine plants he had brought back from his campaigns in Hungary. These vines from Tokay later contributed to make Kaysersberg one of the finest wine-growing areas in Alsace.

SIGHTS

★**Église** (BZ **L**) – Kaysersberg parish church was built between the 12C and 15C. It stands beside a small square adorned with an 18C fountain surmounted by a 16C statue of Emperor Constantine. The Romanesque west doorway has unusual capitals decorated with pelicans and sirens with two tails, characteristic of Lombard ornamentation. The tympanum depicts the coronation of the Virgin placed between two archangels, St Michael and St Gabriel. Inside, the most striking feature is a large group in polychrome wood representing the Crucifixion, carved in the 15C.

The chancel contains, above the high altar, a wooden **altarpiece★★** in the shape of a triptych, a magnificent work by the Jean Bongartz, the master from Colmar (1518). The central panel depicting the Crucifixion, is surrounded by 12 carved panels illustrating the Stations of the Cross; below, Christ can be seen blessing the people as his disciples surround him. On the reverse side, 17C paintings depict the discovery and glorification of the Holy Cross.

The north aisle shelters a damaged Holy Sepulchre dating from 1514; the most remarkable part is the group representing the holy women, a masterpiece by Jacques Wirt. According to an Alsatian tradition, a slit in Christ's chest is intended for the host during Holy Week.

Note, in the north and south aisles, a statue of St James the Great (1523) and the low relief of the Pietà (1521).

The left window of the west front is decorated with beautiful 15C stained glass by Pierre d'Andlau, depicting Christ on the Cross flanked by the two thieves.

Chapelle St-Michel (BYZ) – The two-storey chapel was built in 1463. The lower level was turned into an ossuary and contains a stoup decorated with a skull. The upper chapel is adorned with frescoes. Note the unusual 14C crucifix in the chancel, to the right of the altar.

Cimetière (BZ **N**) – The soldiers who died during the liberation of the town are buried in this cemetery. Stone fragments strewn around make it look like an archeological museum. A 16C wooden gallery provides a shelter for the unusual cross, known as the "plague cross", dating from 1511.

★**Hôtel de ville** (BZ **H**) – Built in a certain form of Renaissance style characteristic of the Rhine region, the town hall has a lovely façade, a peaceful courtyard and a picturesque wooden gallery.

★**Vieilles maisons** (BZ) – There is a choice of old houses along rue de l'Église, rue de l'Ancien-Hôpital, rue de l'Ancienne-Gendarmerie and rue du Général-de-Gaulle (also called Grand-Rue).

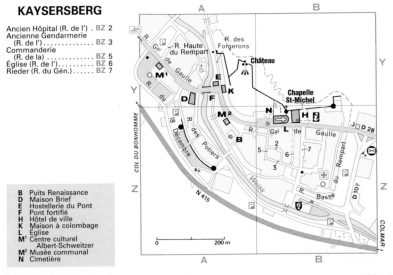

KAYSERSBERG

Ancien Hôpital (R. de l') . BZ 2
Ancienne Gendarmerie
    (R. de l') . . . . BZ 3
Commanderie
    (R. de la) . . . . BZ 5
Église (R. de l') . . . . BZ 6
Rieder (R. du Gén.) . . . . . . BZ 7

B Puits Renaissance
D Maison Brief
E Hostellerie du Pont
F Pont fortifié
H Hôtel de ville
K Maison à colombage
L Église
M¹ Centre culturel
   Albert-Schweitzer
M² Musée communal
N Cimetière

M Guillard/SCOPE

Kaysersberg – Fortified bridge

Puits Renaissance (AZ B) – The Renaissance well dating from 1618, situated in the courtyard of no 54 Grand-Rue, bears a humoristic inscription.

Musée communal ⊙ **(AZ M²)** – Housed in a Renaissance dwelling with a double roof and a stair turret, the museum exhibits medieval religious art (rare 14C opening statue of the Virgin, Christ with branches of palms from the 15C), local souvenirs (16C bell from a town gate used as a belfry), neolithic axes from Bennwihr, the tools of a Roman coppersmith found nearby, various objects connected with a cooper's craft etc.

Hostellerie du Pont (AY E) – Standing on the corner of rue des Forgerons, lined with old houses, this hostel has been restored. It was the former baths. A timber-framed house with open gallery faces the bridge.

★**Pont fortifié (AY F)** – The fortified bridge built in the 15C and 16C is located in a charming setting with old houses all round; an oratory stands on top.

★**Maison Brief (AY D)** – It dates from 1594.

Centre culturel Albert-Schweitzer ⊙ **(AY M¹)** – This cultural centre standing next to Albert Schweitzer's birthplace, displays documents, photos, personal mementoes and souvenirs retracing the life of the great humanist.

Château – *30min on foot there and back.*
From the ruins of the medieval castle there is a lovely general view of the town.

LANGRES ★★

Population 9 981
Michelin map 66 fold 3 or 241 fold 47

A promontory of the Langres plateau forms the remarkable **setting**★★ of this ancient city which was one of the three capitals of Burgundy under the Gauls. Later on it became a bishopric and an advanced post defending the kingdom of France. It is one of the gateways of Burgundy and a tourist stopoff on the north-south European route (A5, A31). The town is near the source of three rivers, the Marne, the Seine and the Aube and four reservoirs supplying the Marne-Saône canal.

Langres is the birthplace of **Denis Diderot**, the 18C philosopher, of **Jeanne Mance**, the missionary who founded Canada's first hospital in Montreal in the mid-17C, and of **Claude Gillot** (1674-1722), the painter who was one of Watteau's masters.

HISTORICAL NOTES

The Lingons, a Gaulish tribe who gave their name to Langres, became Caesar's allies and the town prospered under Roman occupation. However, when Nero died in AD 70, one of their chiefs, by the name of **Sabinus**, tried to usurp the supreme power but failed and, according to legend, he found refuge in a cave close to the source of the Marne *(see p 157)*. He remained there for nine years but was eventually discovered and taken to Rome where he was executed with his wife who wished to share his fate. The city was Christianised in the 3C AD and became a bishopric in the 4C. According to legend, St Didier, who was the third bishop of Langres was made a martyr for having defended the town; after he was beheaded, he picked up his head, left on horseback and died on the spot where a chapel was later built in his honour (now part of the new museum).

Langres and its ramparts

During the Middle Ages, the bishops of Langres became dukes and peers of the realm and some of them were among the king's close advisors.

When Champagne was united with France in 1284, Langres became a royal fortress and played a strategic role on the border of Burgundy, Lorraine and Franche-Comté, a role it resumed in the 19C when the walls were restored (1843-60) and a citadel built (1842-50), reinforced by eight independent forts (1868-1885).

OLD TOWN *1hr 30min*

A **slanting elevator** links the Sous-Bie parking area, situated outside the walls, to the town centre, offering a panoramic view of the town, of the Lac de la Liez and of the Vosges mountains.

A small **tourist train** takes visitors round the old town and the ramparts.

Within the ramparts, visitors strolling along the twisting medieval streets will discover the Cathédrale St-Mammès and a few beautiful old houses as well as numerous decorative features including recesses (15C-19C) which testify to the religious fervour of the town's inhabitants.

From place des États-Unis, enter the town through the **Porte des Moulins** (Z), which used to be the only way into the city on the south side.

Rue Diderot, lined with shops, runs past the **theatre** housed since 1838 inside the former Chapelle des Oratoriens (1676).

Collège (F) – This vast edifice is the former 18C Jesuit college. The Baroque façade of the chapel is surmounted by flame-vases.

Place Diderot (YZ) – This is the town's main square; situated right in the centre, it is adorned with a statue of Diderot by Bartholdi of the Statue of Liberty fame. A plaque has been fixed on the wall of his birthplace located on the corner of rue de la Boucherie.

Denis Diderot (1713-1784)

The son of a cutler, Denis Diderot was a brilliant pupil of the local Jesuit college and he seemed destined for a religious career, but he went on to study in Paris instead and only came back to Langres five times during his life. However he spoke about his native town in his *Letters* to Sophie Volland and in his *Journey to Langres*.

Interested in many subjects, he wrote numerous works, including essays such as *Letters About the Blind for the Attention of Those Who Can See*, for which he was imprisoned in Vincennes, novels *(The Nun)*, satires *(Jacques the Fatalist)*, philosophical dialogues *(Rameau's Nephew)*. He was also an art critic *(Salons)*. Yet his name is first and foremost linked with that of the *Encyclopaedia*, a monumental work which he undertook to write with d'Alembert in 1747 and to which he devoted 25 years of his life. Completed in 1772, the 35-volume *Encyclopaedia* represents the sum total of scientific knowledge and philosophical ideas during the Age of Enlightenment.

For more information on Diderot's life, turn to page 56.

As you walk down rue du Grand-Cloître, admire the view of the Lac de la Liez. Note the 15C timber-framed house at the beginning of rue Lhuillier and, on the corner of rue du Petit-Cloître, a 15C-16C house decorated with a bartizan covered with shingles.

Walk along the south side of the cathedral.

Cloître de la cathédrale ⊙ (**D**) – The cloister, dating from the early 13C, has retained only two galleries which have been restored and glassed-in and now house the municipal library. Inside, the ribbed vaulting rests on slender columns decorated with crocket or leafed capitals.

The centre of the courtyard is adorned with a contemporary sculpture by François Bouillon: a long spiral dotted with "Y"s rises from the well.

★**Cathédrale St-Mammès** (Y) – The cathedral (94m/308ft long and 23m/75ft high) was built during the second half of the 12C but it was subsequently remodelled many times. The primitive west front (12C-13C), destroyed by major fires, was replaced in the 18C by a three-storey Classical façade. If you walk along the north side, you will see a restored Romanesque doorway.

The vast interior is in Burgundian Romanesque style, the nave with its ribbed vaulting marking the transition towards Gothic style. The design and decoration of the triforium are reminiscent of the Gallo-Roman gate of the ramparts.

The first chapel along the north aisle (second bay) has a splendid coffered ceiling and houses an alabaster Virgin and Child by Évrard d'Orléans (1341); note that the bishop who donated the statue is standing next to it. The third bay is decorated with low reliefs representing the Passion, embedded into a fragment of the rood screen built c 1550 by Cardinal de Givry; two other fragments decorate the ambulatory.

Two tapestries displayed in the transept depict the legend of St Mammès. During the 3C, this saint from Cappadocia preached the gospel to wild animals and when Roman guards came to fetch him in order to martyr him, these same wild animals protected him. The cathedral of Langres received from Constantinople some relics of the saint including his head.

The chancel and the apse, built between 1141 and 1153, are the most remarkable parts of the edifice completed during the second half of the 12C and consecrated in 1196.

The capitals of the triforium in the apse are richly decorated with supernatural animals and characters, as well as floral motifs. The radiating chapels were remodelled in the 19C. A 16C sculpture in low relief situated in the ambulatory illustrates the transfer of the saint's relics during a solemn procession round the walls of the city.

Trésor ⊙ – The treasury houses many objets d'art: a reliquary from Clairvaux abbey, believed to contain a piece of the True Cross, a reliquary-bust of St Mammès in vermeil and a small 15C ivory statue of the saint, an enamel evangelistary plate dating from the 13C, a chased-silver box (1615), which is all that remains of the bishop's chapel destroyed during the Revolution.

South tower – *227 steps.* From the top of the *tour sud* (45m/148ft), there is a panoramic view of the town and a vast surrounding area.

Walk across place Jeanne-Mance.

The bronze statue of **Jeanne Mance** (1606-1673) by Jean Cardot stands in the centre of this charming square.

Maison Renaissance (**V**) – This Renaissance house built in the mid-16C has a splendid façade overlooking the garden, adorned with small Ionic and Corinthian columns and friezes representing bucranes, draperies and fruit. An openwork balustrade surrounds the courtyard with a central well.

Follow the side passage (spiral staircase leading to the upper floors) ending rue Cardinal-Morlot and turn right. You will soon see another Renaissance house with twin columns.

Continue to place du Centenaire.

Musée d'Art et d'Histoire ⊙ (Y **M¹**) – The museum is housed in the Romanesque Chapelle St-Didier, where the town's collections have been kept since 1842, and in a vast glass-and-concrete edifice purposely built to display the collections acquired later. These collections, exhibited on four levels, concern archeology and Fine Arts.

The department of prehistory and ancient history includes items discovered during excavations made in the region (Farincourt, Cohons...); note the enigmatic Celtic heads from Perrogney.

The **Gallo-Roman department** ★ displays fragments of stone from various buildings. The *Togatus* or *Consul* is a headless marble statue discovered in Langres during the 17C. *Bacchus's Mosaic* (60m²/72sq yd) was found on the site of the museum in 1985. The numerous stelae and sculptures testify to the importance of this

LANGRES

Barbier-d'Aucourt (R.)....... Y 3
Belle-Allée (La)............. Y 4
Béligné (R. Ch.)............. Y 5
Boillot (R.)................. Y 6
Boulière (R.)............... Y 7
Canon (R.)................. Y 8
Centenaire (Pl. du)......... Y 10
Chambrûlard (R.).......... Y 12
Chavannes (R. des)....... Z 13
Crémaillère (R. de la)...... Y 14
Croc (R. du).............. Z 15
Denfert-Rochereau (R.)..... Z 16
Diderot (R.)............... YZ
Durand (R. Pierre) .... Y 17
Gambetta (R.)............ Y 18
Grand-Bie (R. du)........ Y 19
Grand-Cloître (R. du)...... Y 20
Grouchy (Pl. Col.-de)..... Z 21
Lambert-Payen (R.)....... Y 24
Leclerc (R. Général)...... Y 25
Lescornel (R.)............ Y 26
Longe-Porte (R.).......... X 27
Menec (Place)........... Y 30
Minot (R.)............... Z 31
Morlot (R. Card.)........ Y 32
Roger (R.)............... Y 33
Roussat (R. Jean)........ Y 35
St-Didier (R.)........... Y 36
Terreaux (R. des)....... Y 37
Tournelle (R. de la) ..... Y 39
Turenne (R. de).......... Y 41
Ursulines (R. des)........ Y 43
Walferdin (R.)........... Y 44
Ziegler (Pl.)............. Y 45

CITY GATES

Porte Boulière............. Y
Porte Gallo-romaine .... Y
Porte Henri-IV .... Y
Porte Hôtel-de-Ville (de l') ... Y
Porte Longe-Porte (de) X
Porte Moulins (des) .... Z
Porte Neuve............... Y

TOWERS

Tours Navarre et d'Orval (de) Z
Tour Petit-Saut (du)........ X
Tour Piquante............. X
Tour St-Ferjeux........... Z
Tour St-Jean............. X
Tour Sous-Murs (de)....... Y
Tour Virot................ Y

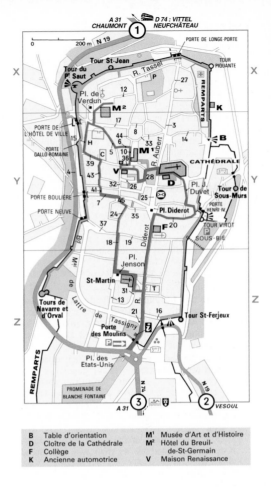

B	Table d'orientation	M¹	Musée d'Art et d'Histoire
D	Cloître de la Cathédrale	M²	Hôtel du Breuil-
F	Collège		de-St-Germain
K	Ancienne automotrice	V	Maison Renaissance

civilization. Note in particular *Bacchus's Altar* in white marble, found in St-Geosmes, the *Wine-Harvest Cart*, the *Horse's head* from Isômes, the *Cobbler's Stela*, the *Barducucullus's Statue* (named after the hooded coat) and the semicircular *Engagement Stela* with four characters. There is also a wide choice of objects of daily life kept under glass.

A small room is devoted to Egyptian art: Canopic jars, sarcophagus, beetle-amulets. Before entering the chapel, note the display of Merovingian objects: damascene sword, belt buckle etc. In the nave there are low reliefs and capitals, coins discovered in the vaulting of the chapel, panels decorated with paintings, ceramics from Aprey and knives from Langres.

Painting from the 17C and 18C is represented by Jean Tassel and his students *(Mucius Scaevola in Front of Porsenna...)* and Jean Michelin, whereas local sculpture is illustrated by Edmé Bouchardon, Pierre Petitot and Antoine Besançon. The 19C room displays the works of Jules-Claude Ziegler, a native of Langres, who was at once a painter, a ceramist and a photographer, as well as paintings by Courbet, Corot *(Christ on the Mount of Olives)*, Van de Champ, Berger, Jules-René Hervé, Charles Duvent...

Follow rue Boillot then turn right onto rue Charles-Beligné to reach place de l'Hôtel-de-ville.

Hôtel de ville – The town hall has retained its impressive 18C façade with a protruding central part of the colossal order.

Continue to place de Verdun and rue Chambrûlard.

Musée du Breuil-de-St-Germain (XY M²) – This museum is housed in a private mansion comprising a Renaissance building (elaborate doorway and dormer-windows) and a graceful pavilion of the late 18C, bequeathed by Madame Du Breuil-de-St-Germain, hence its name.

Inside, there is a collection of ceramics (Aprey) and porcelain (Giey-sur-Aujon) and some fine furniture. One room is devoted to Diderot and another one to Claude Gillot.

Retrace your steps and follow rue du Croc.

Note the ruins of the former chapel of the Ursuline convent (17C), showing a wealth of ornamentation.

Follow rue des Ursulines on the right, then turn left onto rue Boulière.

Continue along rue Lambert-Payen and rue Gambetta leading to the charming place Jenson.

Église St-Martin (Z) – This 13C church, remodelled in the 18C following a fire, is surmounted by an elegant campanile of the same period. It contains a few works of art: a 16C Christ on the Cross in carved wood above the high altar, a 16C stone group representing the Holy Trinity in the south transept and a sculpture in high relief illustrating St Martin's Charity above the door of the sacristy.

Take rue Minot leading to rue Diderot and the Porte des Moulins.

★★WALK ALONG THE RAMPARTS *4km/2.5mi – about 1hr 30min*

The watchpath offers a pleasant walk round the town and a magnificent panorama including: to the east the Marne Valley, the Lac de la Liez and the Vosges mountains when the weather is clear, to the north the Colline des Fourches crowned by a chapel, to the west the slopes of the Bonnelle Valley and further afield the Plateau de Langres and its wooded slopes. The ramparts have retained seven gates and 12 towers showing the evolution of fortifications from the Hundred Years War to the 19C. Only the most important of these are described below.

Start from place des États-Unis south of the old town.

– **Porte des Moulins** (1647): this is the monumental entrance to the city; its style is characteristic of Louis XIII's military architecture and it is surmounted by a dome covered with shingles of chestnut-wood. The ornamentation includes an allegorical representation of French victories at the end of the Thirty Years War: chained enemies, helmets and trophies.

– **Tour St-Ferjeux** (c 1469-1472): specially adapted to artillery warfare, its terrace can accommodate heavy guns. The two vaulted rooms with walls 6m/20ft thick house eight casemates. From the platform, the view extends to the surrounding countryside and there are beautiful vistas of the ramparts. A polished-steel sculpture by the Dutch artist Eugene Van Lamsweerde, entitled *Air*, dedicated to Gaston Bachelard *(see BAR-SUR-AUBE)*, stands on the tower.

– **Tour Virot**: this semicircular tower used to defend the "Sous-Murs" district, an area below the walls of the city (hence its name) where many tanners used to live. It was surrounded by its own wall reinforced by the **Tour des Sous-Murs** (1502) which can still be seen.

– **Porte Henri IV** (1604): this gate, which gave access to the Sous-Murs district, has retained traces of its defence system (ditch, drawbridge, portcullis).

– **Viewing table** (B): from this point, the view encompasses the Sous-Murs district below, surrounded by its own wall, and the ramparts on either side; the Lac de la Liez and the Vosges mountains can be seen in the distance.

– From 1887 to 1971, a rack-railway linked the station located in the valley to the town, with a difference in height of 132m/433ft. The old railcar can still be seen (K).

Tour Piquante: this tower looks more like a polygonal bastion flanked by a small bartizan.

Porte Longe-Porte: once adorned with a Gallo-Roman arch, this gate was fitted with a drawbridge whose piers are still standing.

Tour St-Jean: built on a rocky spur, this former gun tower was fitted as a military dovecote in 1883.

Tour du Petit-Sault (c 1517-1521): this elongated gun tower with very thick walls, contains two vaulted rooms linked by a large staircase. From the terrace *(viewing table)*, there is a view of the Bonnelle Valley and of the Plateau de Langres.

Porte de l'Hôtel-de-ville: standing on a rocky spur, this gate has retained its 17C guard-room.

Porte gallo-romaine (1C AD): set within the walls, this gate was used as a tower in medieval times.

Porte Boulière and tour St-Didier (mid-15C): the gate was remodelled in the early 20C, but the tower has retained its medieval character.

Porte Neuve or Porte des Terreaux (1855): this is the most recent of the gates; it is crowned with neo-Gothic machicolations and there are traces of the drawbridge.

Tours de Navarre et d'Orval ⊙: The former gun platform of the Tour de Navarre was covered with chestnut timberwork in 1825; it is the most powerful of them all. It is reinforced by the Tour d'Orval whose spiral ramp enabled soldiers to wheel heavy guns up to the summit of the Tour de Navarre.

LAND OF THE FOUR LAKES

Four reservoirs were created at the end of the 19C and beginning of the 20C in order to supply the Marne-Saône canal. They offer relaxation, pleasant walks in wooded surroundings and a choice of water sports as well as the possibility to fish for pike, carp and perch.

During the summer, the surface of these reservoirs may shrink and the extremities are then turned into reedy marshland sheltering an interesting fauna and flora.

Lac de la Liez – *5km/3mi east of Langres.* This is the largest of the four lakes (270ha/667 acres); it is possible to walk along its earth dyke (460m/503yd long and 16m/53ft high) which affords views of the fortified town of Langres.

The lake offers safe bathing *(supervised in July and August)*, angling, sailing and water sports *(rental facilities and sailing school)* near Peigney. Birdwatching is also rewarding (herons) at the end of the reservoir reached via the villages of Lecey and Orbigny-au-Val or via the footpath running round the lake.

Lac de la Mouche – *6km/3.7mi west of Langres.* This is the smallest of the four lakes (94ha/232 acres); it is overlooked by two villages, St-Ciergues in the north and Perrancey-les-Vieux-Moulins in the south, linked by a scenic road which runs over the dyke (410m/448yd long and 23m/75ft high).

Lac de Charmes – *8km/5mi north of Langres.* The earth dyke here is 362m/395yd long and 17m/56ft high and the elongated lake covers 197ha/487 acres. An area has been set aside for bathing and the reservoir also supplies Langres and nearby municipalities with drinking water.

Lac de la Vingeanne – *12km/7.5mi by ③ on the town plan along N 74.* A footpath (8km/5mi) runs all the way round this lake (190ha/250 acres) which has the longest dyke (1 254m/1 371yd). A great number of migrating birds nest or just rest in the reedy marshland.

There is a large well-appointed beach and the lake is paradise for windsurfers.

Source de la Marne – *15km/9.3mi round tour and 15min on foot there and back. Leave Langres by ③ on the town plan along N 74 then follow D 122 on the left towards Noidant-Chatenoy; 2.5km/1.5mi further on, turn left onto D 290 towards Balesmes-sur-Marne; drive for another 1km/0.6mi and turn right towards the parking area; a path on the left leads down to the source of the River Marne (400m/437yd).*

The Marne springs from a kind of vault closed by an iron door. Nearby, you can see the cave where Sabinus hid for nine years as well as a few fine rocks.

Return to Langres via Balesmes-sur-Marne; drive along D 193 (towards St-Vallier) for 1km/0.6mi and turn left onto D 17 which crosses the Marne-Saône canal and joins N 19.

You can watch the canal disappear into a **tunnel** (4.8km/2.5mi long), which is so narrow that an alternating traffic system has been installed.

EXCURSIONS

Faverolles, Mausolée gallo-romain – *10km/6mi by ④ on the town plan along N 19 to Rolampont, then left along D 155 and D 256.* The ruins of this mausoleum were discovered in 1980 in the forest, 3.5km/2.2mi outside the village *(it is possible to visit the excavation site during the course of a walk through the forest).* Erected in 20 BC, it was more than 20m/66ft high and comprised three tiers of the Corinthian order. By its shape and function (it is a cenotaph dedicated to a deceased person), it is comparable to the mausoleum situated in St-Rémy-de-Provence.

Fragments of the mausoleum are displayed in an **Atelier archéologique** ⊙: sculpture in high relief representing a bird of prey, two rampant lions, funeral masks...

Fort du Cognelot ⊙ – *10km/6.2mi by ② on the town plan then D 17 on the right.* This is one of eight forts built round Langres after the 1870 war to defend France's eastern border. It was built between 1874 and 1877. Casemates for 600 men were grouped round two courtyards together with magazines, stores for food supplies, equipment and artillery.

Château du Pailly ⊙ – *12km/7.5mi by ③ on the town plan along N 74 and D 122 to Noidant-Chatenoy then left onto D 141.* An elegant Renaissance residence was built in 1560 round a feudal castle by Marshal de Saulx-Tavannes. Only three of the four buildings have survived. The most remarkable parts are the balconied façade overlooking the main courtyard and, to the left, the spiral staircase with an openwork turret. The entrance pavilion, rebuilt in the 18C in similar style, located in the left-hand corner, with its vermiculated stone base, its two fluted storeys and elaborate decoration, shows how strong the craze for Renaissance art was.

The "**Salle dorée**" of the 15C keep has a remarkable French-style ceiling and two monumental fireplaces.

Cascade de la Tuffière – *14km/8.7mi by ④ on the town plan along N 19 t* *1km/0.6mi beyond Rolampont then left onto D 254; follow the arrows.* The waterfall owes its name to the tufa concretions formed by the calcareous spring water streaming down huge natural steps in a wooded setting. A footpath runs round the site.

Andilly-en-Bassigny – *22km/13.7mi by ① on the town plan along D 74 to the La des Charmes then, just beyond, turn right onto D 35.*

Gallo-Roman excavations ⊙ – The Andilly villa is a remarkable example of self-supporting economy under Roman occupation. It comprises the master's house, the baths and the fishpond, the servants' quarters and the craftsmen's workshops.

The **baths** include a cold room, a changing room, part of an individual pool, a warm room with part of a hypocaust, a semicircular hot pool with bench and side steps, an octagonal steam bath, a rectangular cold pool with bench and access steps. These baths were splendidly decorated as can be seen from the marble facing at the base of the walls, from the magnificent sculpture (woman's head wearing a crown of flowers) and from the fragments of a painted ceiling.

In the craftsmen's area below, various workshops have been identified: tilers', stone masons', potters', painters' and masons'.

The villa was a thriving production centre which survived successive invasions from the east as the presence of a Merovingian necropolis shows.

The finds are exhibited in a small **museum**.

Fayl-Billot – *26km/16mi by ② on the town plan along N 19.* Situated on the border of the Plateau de Langres and Plateau de Haute-Saône, this large farming village lies on the edge of a lovely forested area which offers pleasant walks (Forêt de Bussières). Cane furniture and wickerwork are a speciality of Fayl-Billot. The national school, which houses three **exhibition rooms** ⊙ displaying the creations of the students, upholds handicraft traditions.

PLATEAU DE LANGRES

Itinerary from Langres to Arc-en-Barrois
58km/36mi – 2hr

The Plateau de Langres is covered with forests and heathland and dotted with caves, dolines and numerous resurgent springs owing to the underground layers of clay. The watershed between the Paris Basin, the Rhine Valley and the Rhône Valley is situated on this plateau and the Seine, the Aube, the Marne and the Meuse all take their source in the area.

Leave Langres by ③ on the town plan along N 74.

Sts-Geosmes – The 13C **church** ⊙, dedicated to three saints martyred on this site, is built over a 10C crypt with three naves.

Follow D 428 towards Auberive.

Beyond the village of Pierrefontaines, the road runs near the Haut-du-Sec (alt 516m/1 693ft), the highest point of the Plateau de Langres, before entering the Forêt d'Auberive.

A few kilometres further on, turn left onto the Acquenove forest road. The source of the River Aube is signposted.

Source de l'Aube – The Aube wells up in a pastoral setting with picnic facilities.
Drive to Auberive along D 20 then D 428.

Auberive – An ancient Cistercian abbey, founded in 1133 on the initiative of St Bernard, stands in a wooded setting near the source of the Aube. The only Romanesque features left are the chancel of the abbey church (1182), surmounted by pointed barrel vaulting and ending with a flat east end as in Fontenay, and the doorway of the chapter-house.

Along the road to Châtillon, one can see the abbey buildings rebuilt in the 18C through the elegant wrought-iron railing by Jean Lamour, who also made the railings of place Stanislas in Nancy *(see NANCY)*.

On the way out of Auberive, turn right onto D 20 which follows the River Aube.

★**Cascade d'Étufs** – *Leave the car in the parking area.* Soon after Rouvres-sur-Aube, an alleyway branches off D 20 on the left and leads to a private property; go round the right side of it to reach the waterfall. Water wells up from the hillside in a lovely shaded site and forms several successive waterfalls.

Continue on D 20 to Aubepierre-sur-Aube then turn right onto D 159 towards Arc-en-Barrois.

Arc-en-Barrois – Nestling at the bottom of a valley and surrounded by forests, this small town is a lovely place to stay in.

The Église St-Martin was altered in the 19C and one has to go round the edifice to discover the old 15C doorway: the tympanum, located under a three-lobed arch, is decorated with a representation of Christ on the Cross between the church and the synagogue. The chapel situated on the right of the entrance houses a 17C sepulchre.

LUNÉVILLE★

Population 20 682
Michelin map 62 fold 6 or 242 fold 22

Lunéville spreads its wide streets, its vast park and its beautiful monuments, designed in the 18C, between the River Meurthe and its tributary, the Vezouze. The ceramic factory, which King Stanislas promoted to the rank of royal manufacture, specialises in tableware. At the beginning of the 18C, the duke of Lorraine, **Leopold**, often stayed in the town. He greatly admired Louis XIV and commissioned Germain Boffrand, a student of Mansart, to build the castle using Versailles as his model. The duke enjoyed dancing, gambling and the theatre as well as hunting and he attracted to his small-scale Versailles the aristocracy of Lorraine.

Later on, Lunéville was the favourite residence of King Stanislas *(see NANCY)* who remodelled the park and redecorated the castle. Writers and artists, among them Voltaire, Montesquieu, Saint-Lambert and Helvetius flocked to his court. Stanislas died in the castle on 23 February 1766.

★CHÂTEAU (A) *45min*

This imposing castle surrounds a vast courtyard open on the west side *(see Introduction: Architecture and art)* which has in its centre the equestrian statue of General de Lasalle killed at the battle of Wagram. The central building has two monumental staircases and is flanked by two small wings separated by porticoes from the larger wings lining the main courtyard. The **chapel** ⊙ is modelled on its counterpart in Versailles.

Musée ⊙ (**M¹**) – The museum houses an important collection of ceramics from Lunéville and St-Clément, the pharmacy of Lunéville's hospital, terracotta statuettes by Paul-Louis Cyfflé, a unique collection of ink portraits by Jean-Joseph Bernard (18C), Flemish painted-leather hangings (17C) and Art Nouveau objects dating from c 1900 (glassware from the Muller Brothers' glassworks).

The works of Georges de la Tour, painted in Lunéville between 1620 and 1652 are illustrated in an audio-visual programme.

Lunéville ceramic
"Bébé", King Stanislas's dwarf

★**Parc des Bosquets** (AB) – Laid out at the beginning of the 18C by Yves des Hours, the park was successively embellished by Leopold and Stanislas. When the latter died, the castle and the park were taken over by the army and most of the pools were filled in. In 1936, it became the property of the town. In 1946, the groves were given back their original 18C design with flower beds, statues and fountains; at the same time, the terrace reappeared.

LUNÉVILLE

Banaudon (R.)	A	2
Basset (R. R.)	B	3
Bosquets (R. des)	B	4
Brèche (R. de la)	B	5
Carnot (R.)	B	7
Castara (R.)	A	9
Chanzy (R.)	A	10
Charier (R. G.)	A	13
Charité (R. de la)	A	15
Château (R. du)	A	16
Erckmann (R.)	B	18
Gaillardot (R.)	A	20
Gambetta (R.)	B	21
Haxo (R.)	B	23
Lebrun (R.)	B	25
Leclerc (R. Gén.)	A	27
Léopold (Pl.)	AB	28
République (R.)	A	30
St-Jacques (Pl.)	A	32
St-Rémy (Pl.)	B	36
St-Marie (R.)	A	37
Sarrebourg (R. de)	A	39
Templiers (R. des)	A	41
Thiers (R.)	A	43
Viller (R. de)	A	48
2e-Div.-de-Cavalerie (Pl. de la)	A	50

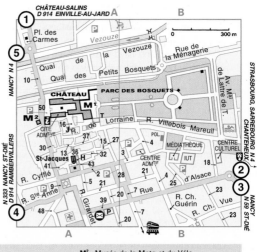

M¹ Musée   **M²** Musée de la Moto et du Vélo

ADDITIONAL SIGHTS

Église St-Jacques (A) – This Baroque abbey church was built between 1730 and 1747 by Boffrand and Héré. The façade is flanked by two round towers surmounted by statues of St Michael *(left)* and St John Nepomucenus *(right)*, the chaplain of Emperor Wenceslas who had him drowned for refusing to reveal the empress' confession. On the pediment, a statue representing Time supports a clock. Inside, note the Regency **woodwork★** (tambour of the main doorway, choir stalls, pulpit), a Pietà in polychrome stone dating from the 15C *(on the left of the chancel)* and fine works by Girardet: the christening of Clovis at the end of the apse, St Joseph carrying Jesus as a child and a cruciifix opposite the pulpit. Before leaving, do not miss the attractive gallery and organ loft (cleverly concealing the pipes) designed by Héré in 1751.

Musée de la Moto et du Vélo ⊘ (A M²) – This museum houses more than 200 different types of bicycles and motorbikes with two or three wheels, the oldest dating from 1865. Some are quite rare like the motorbike of an English parachutist (1943) weighing only 43kg/95lb or the bicycle fitted with an auxiliary diesel engine of 18cc (1951) or the bike with a wooden frame dating from 1910.

LUXEUIL-LES-BAINS⚓

Population 8 790
Michelin map 66 fold 6 or 242 fold 38

Luxeuil is a well-known spa resort specialising in the treatment of gynecological and venous problems and offering visitors a wide choice of activities (concerts, casino, tennis, golf, swimming).
The town has a wealth of red-sandstone architecture and a former abbey founded by **St Columba**, an Irish monk who arrived in France in 590 with 12 companions. Having lectured the duke of Burgundy about his dissolute life, he was expelled from the country and forced to take refuge in Bobbio (Italy).

SIGHTS

★**Hôtel du cardinal Jouffroy** – Abbot of Luxeuil, then archbishop of Albi and finally cardinal, Jouffroy was King Louis XI's favourite until the end of his life. His house (15C), the finest in Luxeuil, successfully combines the Flamboyant-Gothic style (windows and gallery) with the Renaissance style (16C corbelled turret surmounted by a lantern). Madame de Sévigné, who described life at the court of Louis XIV in famous letters to her daughter, and the Romantic poet Alphonse de Lamartine lived in this house.
Note the carving on the third keystone under the balcony: it illustrates a group of three rabbits; the artist has carved only three ears in all yet each rabbit appears to have two ears.

★**Musée de la Tour des Échevins** ⊘ – The museum is housed in an imposing 15C crenellated building whose general appearance is in striking contrast with the exterior decoration and the elegant loggia in the Flamboyant-Gothic style. On the ground floor and first floor are displayed several splendid stone funeral monuments from the Gallo-Roman period, when the town was called Luxovium, as well as votive **stelae★**, inscriptions, a Gaulish ex-voto, sigillate pottery etc. The second and third floors house the **Musée Adler** with paintings by J Adler, Vuillard and Pointelin. From the top of the tower *(146 steps)*, there is an overall **view** of the town and of the Vosges, Jura and Alps in the distance.

★**Ancienne abbaye St-Colomban** ⊘ – The majority of the abbey buildings have been preserved and have recently been restored.

Basilique – The present edifice was built in the 13C and 14C on the site of an 11C church. The west tower is the only one left of the three original towers; rebuilt in 1527, it was raised in the 18C. The apse was remodelled by Viollet-le-Duc in 1860. From place St-Pierre, one can see the north side of the church and the modern statue of St Columba. A doorway in the Classical style gives access to the interior in the Burgundian Gothic style. Note the impressive organ case supported by a telamon resting on the floor, decorated with splendid carved medallions. The pulpit with its refined Empire-style decoration contrasts with the general architectural style of the church; it dates from 1806 and was originally in Notre-Dame cathedral in Paris. There are some interesting 16C stalls in the chancel. In the south transept, one can see the reliquaries of St Columba and of one of his companions, St Gall who founded St-Gall abbey in Switzerland. In the north transept stands the 14C statue of St Peter.

Cloître – Three of the four red-sandstone galleries have been preserved: the bay with three windows surmounted by an oculus dates from the 13C, the others were rebuilt in the 15C and 16C.

Conventual buildings – They include the 17C-18C "monks' building", situated south of the church, and the 16C-18C abbot's palace on place St-Pierre, which is now the town hall.

★Maison François I –This Renaissance edifice is not named after the king of France but after one of the abbots of Luxeuil abbey.

Maison du Bailli – This building dates from 1473. The courtyard is overlooked by a Flamboyant stone balcony and a crenellated polygonal tower. A **museum** ⊘ devoted to the historian, geographer and economist Maurice Baumont is housed inside.

Thermes – The baths, rebuilt in red sandstone during the 18C, are surrounded by a lovely shaded park and include a very modern **fitness centre** open to everyone.

Sentier des Gaulois – A 4km/2.5mi long footpath, known as the "path of the Gauls", starts from the baths and enables visitors to discover the history of the town and its monuments.

Ligne MAGINOT★

Michelin map 56 and 57 or 241 and 242

etween the two world wars French people put all their pride and trust in this mighty northeastern shield" which did not, as we know, fulfil the mission assigned to it by he war minister Paul Painlevé and his successor André Maginot (1877-1932).

he new frame of mind of France's politicians, who concentrated purely on defence nd the need to protect the territories regained as a result of the First World War, led, s early as 1919, to the elaboration of a defensive perimeter skirting the new borders. lodern warfare with tanks, aircrafts and the use of gas ruled out a defence system ased on isolated strongholds or forts and a network of open trenches. Instead, plans vere drawn to divide the length of the border into fortified areas consisting of a ontinuous frontline, 20-60km/12-37mi long, and underground fortifications adapted o modern warfare. Once completed, the Maginot Line consisted of mixed large works, ifantry or artillery small works, shelters, strings of casemates and, behind a flood one, simple pillboxes linked by barbed wire, minefields or anti-tank ditches and upporting one another by crossfire.

Block 9 – Armour-plated airlock and railway

Troops were meant to fill in the gaps between these fortified areas. The project wa launched on 14 January 1930 when France's economy began to recover.

France's "eastern wall" – The number of works built in less than 10 years i amazing: 58 works along the northeast border, including 22 large works, and 50 i the Alps; in addition, there were about 400 casemates and shelters for the infantry 150 revolving turrets and one 1 500 fixed cupolas with special armour-plating crowned the superstructures in reinforced concrete, the only parts of the fortification which could be seen.

From the very beginning however, the project was cut back owing to lack of funds the number of works built was considerably reduced and infantry weapons ofte replaced the artillery initially planned.

From 1935 onwards, it was clear that the original purpose was being thwarted several large works were replaced by pillboxes and casemates, artillery from the Firs World War was substituted for ultra-modern technology deemed too costly, and ther were too few anti-tank guns.

The Maginot Line did not form a continuous network of underground galleries; eac work was separate from its neighbours. The different works were originally identifie by a code number, for instance A10 for Immerhof or A19 for Hackenberg. Later or they were given the name of the place where they stood or occasionally the name c one of their defenders.

Large works were linked to an ammunition dump by electrified railway lines, toda used by visitors along the galleries.

Overground blocks were built of reinforced concrete; the thickness of their back wall turned out to be insufficient when they were attacked from the rear in 1940 Underground structures, below 20m/66ft, were built of stone, which was less costly. The size of the garrison, known as "the crew", depended on the size of the fortifie work: around 15 men for a small casemate such as that of Dambach-Neunhoffen an nearly 1 100 men for Hackenberg or Guentrange. They were elite troops, created i 1933, specially trained to man forts.

Defeat – Owing to the fact that the Maginot Line did not extend along the norther border of France for political as well as economic reasons, that it was not used as base from which to launch an offensive during the "phony war" and that it wa deprived of part of its troops at the crucial moment, being thus reduced to its garriso (which never exceeded 30 000 men), the crews put up a glorious yet vain resistanc to the German onslaught of May-June 1940 and, although they remained undefeated they were forced to surrender once the armistice had been signed.

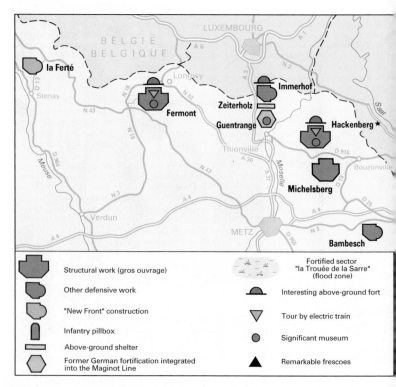

SIGHTS

The various works are described from the northwest to the southeast, from the Ardennes to the Rhine.
Visits often last 2hr. Wear warm clothing and walking shoes.

During the "cold war", some of the existing structures formed part of NATO's defence system. In 1965, the French army decided to stop maintaining the whole of the Maginot Line. Some of the works were ceded to private owners, associations or municipalities who restored them and opened them to the public. The first to be opened in 1972 was the Marckolsheim casemate; since then another dozen or so have been opened to the public.

Petit ouvrage de Villy-la-Ferté ⊙ – *18km/11mi northwest of Montmédy along N 43 and D 44.*
This is one of the "new front" constructions built from 1935 onwards and including technical improvements such as zigzag entrances, revolving firing positions offering more protection, "mixed-gun" cupolas equipped with machine guns and extremely precise anti-tank guns. Villy was meant to be the main western work of the Maginot Line, defending the Chiers Valley; however, it was eventually reduced to a couple of infantry blocks linked by a gallery running more than 30m/98ft below ground and flanked by two artillery casemates (one of these stands on the side of the road opposite the access path).
On 18 May 1940, the fort, which was no longer defended from the outside was encircled by German sappers; the whole crew (more than 100 men), who took refuge in the badly ventilated underground gallery, died of suffocation.
Outside, close to the field of anti-tank obstacles, a monument recalls the sacrifice of these men. The overground constructions bear the mark of the attack: damaged cupolas, turret overturned by an explosion.

Gros ouvrage de Fermont ⊙ – *13km/8mi southwest of Longwy along N 18 and D 172 to Ugny, then right onto D 17[A] and left onto D 174.*
This large work occupying the most western position along the Maginot Line comprised two entrance blocks and seven combat blocks, including three equipped with artillery. In front of the fort, there is a monument dedicated to the "fortress troops" and a shed housing a museum of heavy equipment.
Ammunition elevators and small electric trains convey visitors to Block 4, an imposing artillery casemate covered with a concrete slab (3.5m/11.5ft thick which represents the maximum protection along the Maginot Line) and fitted with 75mm/3in guns. The tour of the barracks is very interesting: it has been left as it

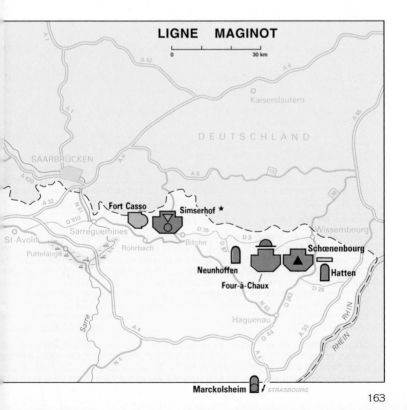

was in 1940 and consists of kitchens, a bakery, a cold room, a sick bay, dormito- ries, NCOs' and officers' quarters, showers, soldiers' quarters etc. The tour of th overground installations includes revolving turrets, cupolas with periscopes an automatic rifles, cupolas equipped with grenade-launchers and casemates. Damag caused by fighting which took place in 1940 is clearly visible: submitted to heav shelling, then attacked by assault troops from 21 June onwards, Fermont did no suffer defeat but was compelled to surrender six days later by the French hig command.

Fort de Guentrange ⓧ – *2km/1.2mi northwest of Thionville. Leave town alon allée de la Libération then turn right towards Guentrange.*
This former German stronghold, built between 1899 and 1906 and occupied b French troops in 1918, was integrated into the Maginot Line in 1939-40 as support work for the Thionville fortified area. Some of its technical advantage were adopted throughout the Maginot Line: electrical machinery, telephone trans missions etc. Besides the power station and its eight diesel engines, still in workin order, the most spectacular feature of the fort is the 140m/153yd long barrack on four levels, suitable for 1 100 men. Note that the revolving turrets fitted wit 105mm/4in guns were not retractable. Several rooms contain detailed informatio about the fort.

Abri du Zeiterholz ⓧ – *14km/8.7mi north of Thionville. Drive towards Longw then turn right onto D 57. Go through Entrange and follow the signposts from th chapel.*
The Zeiterholz is the only shelter along the Maginot Line that can be visited; it wa built of reinforced concrete on two levels as an overground shelter, quite differen from "cave shelters" in which men were accommodated in underground areas. It occupants were entrusted with the defence of pillboxes scattered between th larger works and casemates. The barracks, which have been well preserved, ar being gradually refitted and reconstructed scenes are displayed throughout.

Petit ouvrage de l'Immerhof ⓧ – *From the Zeiterholz shelter, go to Hettange Grande via Entrange-Cité then turn left onto D 15 (signpost) which leads to th Immerhof.*
This is one of only two works along the Maginot Line (and the only one open t the public), which were built overground owing to the lie of the land and com pletely covered with concrete. Bedrooms, sick bay, washrooms etc are in excellen condition because the fort was, for a long time, used by NATO as one of it headquarters. The revolving turret of the artillery block, fitted with 81mm/3i mortars, is activated for the benefit of visitors who can also see a grenade launching turret and other turrets for simultaneously operating machine gun During the tour of overground structures, note the false cupolas intended t deceive the enemy.

★**Gros ouvrage du Hackenberg** – *20km/12.4mi east of Thionville. See HACKEN BERG.*

Gros ouvrage du Michelsberg ⓧ – *22km/13.7mi east of Thionville along D 91 (access from the village of Dalstein). From Hackenberg, drive east along D 60, tur right onto D 60^B then left onto D 118^N to Dalstein.*
The fort successfully withstood the attack launched against it on 22 June 194 thanks to its own fire-power and crossfire from nearby forts, in particular Hacker berg situated 6km/3.7mi away. The crew only left Michelsberg on 4 July by orde of the French high command and was granted military honours.
The barracks were, for a while, used for growing mushrooms but the fort has no been restored and includes an entrance block, two infantry and three artiller blocks. Artillery block no 6 comprises the famous turret fitted with a 135mm/5i gun which smashed the German attack on 22 June 1940; the gun, which weigh 19t and is still in good condition, was the largest gun along the Maginot Line.

Groupe fortifié l'Aisne – *See METZ: Excursions.*

Petit ouvrage du Bambesch ⓧ – *9km/5.6mi west of St-Avold along N 3.*
This is a good example of a work which was gradually modified owing to th shortage of funds: the number of blocks was reduced as was the artillery and th flanking support... The fort, thus limited to three infantry blocks, was attacke from the rear with heavy guns on 20 June 1940 and the cupolas were burst open The crew, having heard of the tragedy of Villy-la-Ferté, chose to surrender.
The galleries, situated 30m/98ft below ground, are reached by a staircase. Th tour includes the barracks and combat blocks. The machine-gun turret is partic ularly narrow. Block no 2 bears the marks of the German assault of June 1940.

Zone inondable de la Trouée de la Sarre – Situated between two large fortifie sectors of the Maginot Line, that of Metz and that of the Lauter, the area extendin from Barst to Wittring and limited in the north by the Sarre region under Frenc administration, was not defended by fortified works but by a flood zone controlle by a system of dyked reservoirs. When the Sarre became German once more in 1935, this system was reinforced by a network of pillboxes and anti-tank obstacles.

Drive from St-Avold along N 56 to Barst (8km/5mi), turn right past the church then twice left onto rue de la Croix and the first path.

The path is lined with a variety of characteristic pillboxes (about a dozen in all), of the type built after 1935.

Leave the path and take the next one on the right; park the car.

Some 50m/164ft below the level of the lake, the concreted railway carriage is the last anti-tank obstacle of the Trouée de la Sarre.

Drive east out of Barst.

Between Cappel and Puttelange-aux-Lacs, the road overlooks some of the reservoirs which were used to flood the area.

Rohrbach-lès-Bitche, Fort Casso ⊙ – *18km/11mi east of Sarreguemines along N 62. Turn left onto D 84 1km/0.6mi before Rohrbach.*
This "new front" work *(see characteristics under Villy-la-Ferté above)*, named after one of its defenders, Lieutenant Casso, who became a general in the Paris fire-brigade, has some interesting features: roughcast buildings, hammocks in the dormitories, mixed-weapon turret (the structure dates from the 1914-18 war) and machine-gun turret in working order.
The well-preserved structures are gradually being refitted: firing station, telephone exchange etc.
Attacked on 20 June 1940, Fort Casso was able to resist with the support of the guns of Simserhof and to avoid the fate of Villy-la-Ferté but the crew was eventually ordered to surrender.

★**Gros ouvrage du Simserhof** – *4km/2.5mi west of Bitche along D 35 then the military road starting opposite the former barracks of Légeret.*
This is one of the most important works of the Maginot Line *(see SIMSERHOF)*.

Casemate de Dambach-Neunhoffen ⊙ – *Between Neunhoffen and Dambach, 20km/12.4mi east of Bitche along D 35, then right onto D 87 and D 853.*
This very basic model, consisting of a small concrete block on one level, defended one of the 12 dykes of the flooding system of the Schwarzbach Valley.
Having been abandoned, it was plundered after the war but has been gradually refitted during the past few years. Note the ventilation system, hand operated (or by pedalling) since the fort was not equipped with electricity.

Lembach, Four à Chaux ⊙ – *15km/9.3mi west of Wissembourg along D 3 then D 27 on the way out of Lembach.*
This medium-size artillery work (6 combat blocks and 2 entrances, crew: 580 men) is still in good condition and has retained its original equipment: barracks, HQ, telephone exchange, power station, central heating and hot-water supply...
The tour of a combat block includes a demonstration of a revolving turret fitted with a 75mm/3in gun, illustrating a modernised version of the forts surrounding Verdun. The fort has an original feature: an inclined plane fitted with a rack, used for the transport of small trucks between the fort and the entrance of the ammunition dump below.
Outside, visitors can see part of the anti-tank obstacles.

Ouvrage d'artillerie de Schœnenbourg ⊙ – *12km/7.5mi south of Wissembourg along D 264. Follow the signposts.*
This fort was one of the main components of the Haguenau fortified sector; its design took into consideration the experience gained at Verdun from 1916 to 1918. When it was completed in 1935, it was considered that no known weapon could have the advantage over this type of fort. The tour takes visitors round some of the underground structures: communications galleries (totalling more than 3km/1.9mi, running 18-30m/59-125ft below ground), kitchen, power station, air-filtering system, barracks and HQ, as well as an artillery block with its revolving turret.
On 20 June 1940, Schœnenbourg, having withstood the assault of a German division, was attacked by bombers and heavy mortars. No other work was submitted to such fire power, yet this fort managed to hold on until the armistice was signed.

Hatten – *22km/13.7mi northeast of Haguenau along D 263 then right onto D 28. From Schœnenbourg (14km/8.7mi), drive to Soultz-sous-Forêts along D 264 then turn left onto D 28.*

Musée de l'Abri ⊙ – The half-buried casemate provided shelter for the troops defending areas situated between fortified works of the Maginot Line: soldiers' sleeping quarters, officers' room, food-supply storeroom, kitchen... Some of the rooms display French, American and German military equipment (uniforms, weapon photos). There is also an open-air display of vehicles including a T34 Russian tank a Sherman tank, some jeeps, lorries...

Casemate d'infanterie Esch ⊙ – This casemate was situated at the heart of the battl which took place in January 1945 between American and German tanks, devastatin Hatten and the nearly villages.

The reconstruction of the soldiers' quarters, a firing chamber and a small museun (uniforms, weapons, various equipment...) are a lively illustration of the Magino Line's defensive system. The section of a model of an artillery block with revolving turret helps to explain how the main underground forts worked.

Marckolsheim, Mémorial Musée de la Ligne Maginot du Rhin ⊙
15km/9.3mi southeast of Sélestat along D 424. Leave Marckolsheim by D 10.
On the esplanade, there is a display of a Soviet gun, a Sherman tank, a machine gun truck and a half-track. Inside the eight compartments *(beware of the met steps)* of the casemate, there are weapons and objects connected with the battle o 15-17 June 1940 when the casemate was bravely defended by 30 men. Hitle visited it after the battle.

To best enjoy the major tourist attractions, which draw big crowds, try to avoid visiting c the peak periods of the day or year.

MARMOUTIER ★

Population 2 234
Michelin map 87 fold 14 or 242 forl 19

Marmoutier's former abbey church is one of the most remarkable examples of Roma nesque architecture in Alsace.

The abbey was founded by St Leobard, a disciple of St Columba *(see LUXEUIL-LES BAINS)*. Endowed with royal possessions, the abbey soon acquired fame and in the 8 it was named Maurmunster after one of its abbots, Maur. In the 14C, the abbots ha an enormous spiritual and worldly influence. Craftsmen and farmers lived in th shadow of the abbey and one of the oldest Jewish communities in Alsace was mos probably called in by the abbots to deal with the abbey's trading activities. In 1792 during the Revolution, the abbey was abolished and the monks dispersed.

★★ABBEY CHURCH *30min*

The west front, the narthex and the towers date from the 11C and 12C; the nav was built in the 13C and 14C. The chancel is much more recent (18C). The **we front★★** *(see Introduction: Architecture and art)* is the most interesting part of th edifice. Built in local red sandstone, it consists of a heavy square belfry and tw octagonal corner towers. The only decorative features are Lombard strips unde lining the outline of the edifice.

The porch has a central ribbed vault with a barrel vault on either side.

Interior – The narthex, surmounted by several domes, is the only Romanesqu part of the interior.

The transept houses some funeral monuments built in 1621 and the chance contains beautiful carved wooden furniture: stalls in Louis XV style with charmin angels and four canopies surmounted by foliage and branches; note also the fou large Baroque altars (second half of the 18C) including two unusual corner one surmounted by a concave pediment. The pulpit dates from the 16C; the orgar built by Silbermann in 1710, is one of the finest in the whole of Alsace.

Traces of a **Merovingian church** were found beneath the transept *(access through th crypt; entrance in the south transept).*

ADDITIONAL SIGHTS

Musée d'Arts et Traditions populaires ⊙ – The folk museum is housed in timber-framed Renaissance building dating from 1590; the ground floor has a early-17C polychrome ceiling. The collections illustrate Alsatian rural life in th past: reconstructions of interiors *(stube, kitchen...)*, craftsmen's workshops (black smith, cooper, stonemason...). In addition, there is a large collection of terracott cake pans as well as numerous Jewish religious objects.

Sindelsberg – *1.5km/0.9mi northwest along the old Saverne road and a sma surfaced road on the left.* Stand near the former monastery church (13C-14C) t admire the lovely bird's-eye view of Marmoutier.

MARSAL

Population 284
Michelin map 57 fold 15 or 242 fold 18

tuated in the western part of the Parc Naturel Régional de Lorraine, an area once
able to flooding, this village has retained numerous Gallo-Roman ruins and a section
f its defensive wall fortified by Vauban in the 17C, including an elegant gate, the
orte de France, which has been restored.

Maison du Sel ⊘ – The salt museum relates the history of this precious commodity, gathered since Antiquity in the salt mines of the Seille Valley.

Ancienne collégiale – This 12C collegiate church, built without a transept, like a
basilica, has a Romanesque nave and a Gothic chancel.

EXCURSIONS

Vic-sur-Seille – *7km/4.3mi west along D 38*. The administration of the diocese of
Metz and the residence of the bishop were established here from the 13C to 17C.
Visitors can still see the ruins of the bishop's castle. Vic was a prosperous little
town in the 15C-16C thanks to its salt mines and it is well known by art lovers as
the birthplace of **Georges de La Tour** (1593-1652).
The 15C Gothic Maison de la Monnaie (mint) and the former Carmelite convent
dating from the 17C stand on place du Palais.
Note, on the north side of the 15C-16C church, an interesting doorway with a
lintel illustrating the legend of a hermit known as St Marian; inside, the tall 15C
statue of the Virgin and Child is worth seeing; it decorates the entrance of the
chapel dedicated to Notre-Dame-de-Bonsecours, to the left of the chancel.

METZ ★★

Population 193 117
Michelin map 57 folds 13 and 14 or 242 folds 9 and 10

tuated between the Côtes de Moselle and the Plateau lorrain, Metz occupies a
trategic position at the confluence of the Seille and the Moselle, which temporarily
ivides into several arms as it flows through the town. Metz is therefore a major
nction at the heart of Lorraine (railway lines, roads and motorways, waterways and
r traffic).
n the past, Metz played an important role as a religious centre (with nearly 50
hurches) and a military stronghold; the wealthy medieval city has become an adminis-
ative and intellectual centre, with its university founded in 1972 and its European
cological Institute, but it is, above all, a large commercial town.
Metz is also an attractive tourist centre with a choice of pleasant walks and interesting
monuments, including one of the finest Gothic cathedrals in France.

PRACTICAL INFORMATION

Guided tours

The tourist office organises daily guided tours at 3pm from Monday to Saturday.
Tours of the town in a barouche, a taxi or a small tourist train start from place
d'Armes.
Boat trip: Croisière du Val de Lorraine; boarding: quai des Régates, time:
45min, ☎ 03 83 24 39 24.
Guided tours by night, either on foot (30min or 1hr) or by coach (1hr) start
every Saturday at 10pm during the summer season.

Accommodation

"Bon week-end à Metz" (a similar offer is available in many French towns): a
second hotel night is offered to tourists at weekends, together with presents
and reductions for guided tours and museum admission fees. A list of hotels
with booking procedure is available from the tourist office.

On the town

Place St-Jacques: pavement restaurants and cafés such as "Le Beverley" or "Le
Village".
Rue du Palais: "Brasserie du Palais", café "Au Duc".
Place de la Cathédrale: the café "A la Lune" affords an interesting view of the
illuminated cathedral.
Place de Chambre: several convivial restaurants, where one can start an evening
on the town, line this square situated below the cathedral.

HISTORICAL NOTES

In the 2C AD, Metz was already an important Gallo-Roman trading centre with 40 00
inhabitants and a 25 000-seat amphitheatre. It soon became a bishopric and, in 275
fortifications were built round the city to ward off Germanic invasions.

The names of three saints are associated with that of Metz. According to legend, **S
Livier** fought the Huns and tried to convert them to Christianism but Attila had him
beheaded; the saint then picked up his head and climbed a mountain where he wa
buried. **St Clement** was the first bishop of Metz; there he slew the "Graoully", a hideou
snake with poisonous breath. As for **St Arnoult**, he was a prominent 7C politician and
family man who, at the people's request, agreed to become the bishop of Metz whil
his wife took refuge in a convent.

In the 12C, Metz became a free city and the capital of a republic whose citizens wer
so wealthy that they often lent money to the dukes of Lorraine, the kings of Franc
and even the Holy Roman emperors.

In 1552, the French king, Henri II, annexed the three bishoprics of Metz, Toul an
Verdun. The Holy Roman Emperor, Charles V, then besieged Metz but all his attempt
to take the city were thwarted by the young intrepid François de Guise.

During the 1870 war with Prussia, part of the French army was encircled in Metz an
eventually surrendered, its general being booed by the population.

On 19 November 1918, French troops entered the town after 47 years of Germa
occupation.

In 1944, Metz was at the heart of heavy fighting once more as it lay on the path c
the advancing American third army. It was bitterly defended for two and a half month
by the German forces stationed in the town; the surrounding forts were pounded b
heavy allied artillery but the town was spared in memory of La Fayette who com
manded the garrison in 1777. American troops eventually entered Metz on 1
November 1944, 26 years to the day after French troops had entered the town at th
end of the First World War.

★★★CATHÉDRALE ST-ÉTIENNE ⊘ (CDV) *1hr 30min*

The 18C unfinished bishop's palace, standing on the cathedral square, now house
the market. The entrance of the cathedral in on **place d'Armes** (**DV 5**). The squar
was designed in the 18C by Jacques François Blondel on the site of the forme
cloister. The **town hall** (**H**), facing the south side of the cathedral, has an elegan
Louis XVI façade with two pediments. The two remaining sides of the square ar
lined with the district hall, a former guard-house whose pediment is decorated wit
trophies, and with the regional parliament, now a residential building.

In the 12C, there were two separate churches on this spot: Notre-Dame-la
Ronde and St-Étienne; a narrow street ran between them. Rebuilt under
common vault, they became the Cathédrale St-Étienne.

In the 18C, when the whole district was remodelled in the French Classica
style, a doorway was added to commemorate the recovery of Louis XV. Durin
the Revolution, the cathedral became state property and was up for letting. Th
statues decorating the doorways and most of the monuments inside the cathe
dral were destroyed.

At the beginning of the 20C, the Louis XV doorway was replaced by a neo
Gothic doorway with a porch, decorated on the outside with statues of the
prophets (one of these, the furthest on the right, was modelled on Empero
William II). In 1940, the moustache was removed to eliminate any resemblance

Exterior – One is impressed by the harmonious proportions of the cathedra
built of yellow stone from Jaumont like several other edifices in Metz. Th
north and south sides are most remarkable. In order to appreciate the sout
side, it is better to stand on the pavement running along the town hall on th
opposite side of the square.

Towers – The church is flanked by two symmetrical towers, the chapter tower on th
north side and the Tour de Mutte on the south side; both built from the 13C
onwards.

The **Tour de Mutte** ⊘ owes its name to the famous bell known as Dame Mutte
dating from 1605 and weighing 11t, which belongs to the town; the name i
derived from the verb *ameuter* which originally meant "to call for a meeting". Th
bell used to ring for all major events and even today, it sounds the 12 strokes o
midday and every quarter hour on election days.

Doorways – The Virgin's portal and porch, located to the left of the Tour de Mutte
were reconstructed from the 13C doorway which was walled up in the 18C.

The sides of the Notre-Dame-la-Ronde portal (second bay on the north side) ar
decorated with carved draperies and small 13C bas-reliefs: note the supernatura
animals on the left, which are reminiscent of medieval bestiaries and, on the right
the scenes from the life of King David, St Margaret and St Stephen.

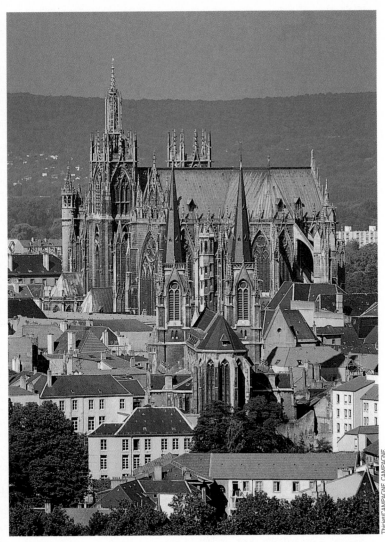

Metz cathedral

Interior – The most striking feature is undoubtedly the height of the nave (41.77m/137ft), dating from the 13C and 14C. The impression of loftiness is enhanced by the fact that the aisles are rather low. This nave is, with that of Amiens Cathedral and after the chancel of Beauvais cathedral, the highest of any church in France. Light pours in generously into the nave, the chancel and the aisles.

A frieze decorated with draperies and foliage runs all the way round the edifice, between the triforium and the impressively large high windows.

Note the overhanging 16C choir organ (1) situated at the end of the nave, on the right-hand side. Its unusual position enhances its outstanding acoustic features.

The **stained-glass windows**★★★ form a splendid ensemble covering more than 6 500m²/7 774sq yd. They are the work of famous as well as anonymous artists, completed or renewed through the centuries: 13C and 14C (Hermann from Munster), 16C (Theobald from Lyxheim, followed by Valentin Bousch), 19C and 20C (Pierre Gaudin, Jacques Villon, Roger Bissière, Marc Chagall).

The west front is adorned with a magnificent 14C rose-window measuring 11.5m/38ft in diameter. There is also a 14C stained-glass window by Hermann from Munster, which unfortunately lost its base part when the large doorway was built in 1766.

The Chapelle Notre-Dame (second bay along the south aisle) is the former chancel of the collegiate church of Notre-Dame-la-Ronde.

In the first bay of the north aisle (2), there is a porphyry basin which originally belonged to the Roman baths, a 16C statue of the Virgin and Child, known as Notre-Dame-de-Bon-Secours and, above the statue, a fine stained-glass window dating from the 13C.

The abstract stained glass (3) decorating the tympanums beneath the two towers (fourth bay) is the work of R Bissière (1959).

In the fifth bay along the south aisle, the 15C chapel of the Holy Sacrament has interesting star-like vaulting. The stained glass dating from 1957 is the work of Villon.

The openwork design of the edifice is even more apparent in the **transept** built at the end of the 15C and beginning of the 16C. There are two huge stained-glass windows (33.25m/109ft high and 12.75m/42ft wide): that in the north part of the transept (4), dating from the early 16C and decorated with three roses, is the work of Theobald from Lyxheim; that in the south part of the transept (5), dating from the Renaissance, is by Valentin Bousch, an artist from Strasbourg. These two windows, covering an area of 425m²/508sq yd, light up the cathedral in a remarkable way.

The eastern wall of the south part of the transept has the oldest stained-glass windows (6) which illustrate six scenes from the life of St Paul (13C). Note the starlike vaulting of the middle part of the transept.

The stained-glass window in the western wall of the north part of the transept, designed by

CATHÉDRALE ST-ÉTIENNE

Former church N.-D.-la-Ronde

Rue du Vivier

N

Ambulatory

Tour de la Boule d'Or   9   CHANCEL   Tour de Charlemagne

Treasury (Large Sacristy)   9

8

Crypt   6

4

TRANSEPT   5

7

Place d'Armes

1

NAVE

Chapelle du Saint-Sacrement

St-Étienne

Tour du Chapitre   3   3   Tour de Mutte

Chapelle Notre-Dame

Portail de N.-D.-la-Ronde

Place

2

Portail de la Vierge

Grand Portail

Place de la Cathédrale

0   15m

Chagall in 1963, depicts scenes from the Garden of Eden (7).

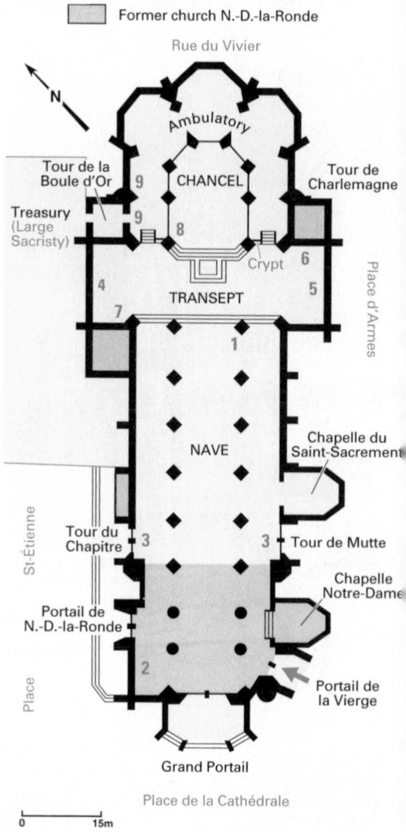

The 16 lancet windows of the triforium, also by Chagall, make up a double fresco illustrating flowers or birds from the Garden of Eden (1968).

The **chancel** was considerably raised when it was rebuilt in the 16C; it is lit by splendid stained-glass windows by Valentin Bousch.

On the left, St Clement's episcopal throne (8), carved out of a cipolin-marble column, dates back to Merovingian times.

In the ambulatory, two stained-glass windows by Chagall (9) can be seen above the sacristy door and the door leading to the Tour de la Boule d'or on the left. Designed in 1960, they illustrate scenes from the Old Testament (Jacob's Dream, Abraham's Sacrifice, Moses and David).

The **crypt** ⊘ was adapted in the 15C to be used as a base for the new chancel. It looks more like a low church than a crypt, having retained in its central part some elements from the 10C Romanesque crypt. It also contains the damaged tympanum of the 13C Virgin's doorway as well as various objects, carvings and reliquaries from the treasury. Note in particular a 16C **Entombment**, originally in the church of Xivry-Circourt, and hanging from the vaulting, the famous "Graoully", the legendary dragon slain by St Clement which used to be carried in procession round the town until 1785.

What is left of the **treasury** ⊘ is kept in the 18C sacristy, decorated with Louis XV woodwork.

The most remarkable items include St Arnoult's gold ring (primitive Christian art), a 12C enamel reliquary, 12C and 13C ivory crosiers, Pope Pie VI's mule, precious religious objects such as a 17C ivory crucifix, a 19C silver Virgin, a ciborium decorated with enamel and a portable altar.

The "Gueulard", a 15C carved-wood head, originally decorating the organ, used to open its mouth (hence its name) when the lowest note was sounded.

★★MUSÉES DE LA COUR D'OR ⊘ (DV M¹) *allow 2hr*

The museums are housed in the buildings of the former Couvent des Petits Carmes (17C), of the Grenier de Chèvremont (15C) and in several rooms which link or prolong this monumental ensemble. Elements of the antique baths are displayed in situ in the basement.

Extended in 1980, the museums were organised along the most modern lines and offer a unique journey into the past.

★**Section archéologique** – The exhibits, which were mostly found during excavations in Metz and the surrounding region, testify to the importance of the city, a major road junction in **Gallo-Roman times** and a thriving cultural centre during the Carolingian period.

Social life during the **Gallo-Roman period** is illustrated by remains of the large baths, of the town wall and of the drainage system as well as by objects of daily life (meals, garments, jewellery, trade) and sculptures: statuettes of gods, winged Victory (2C AD), funeral monuments.

Religious life before the spread of Christianism is represented by the high Merten column surmounted by Jupiter slaying a monster and a large carved retable (Mithraeum) showing the god Mithra sacrificing a bull.

Various glass-cases are devoted to the methods of producing ironwork, bronzework, ceramics and glasswork.

Metz was the capital of Austrasia during the **Merovingian period** illustrated by graves, sarcophagi and tombstones bearing Christian emblems, jewels and objects of daily life (crockery), damascened metal objects.

In the rooms devoted to **paleo-Christian archeology**, there is an important ensemble dating from the early Middle Ages, surrounding the chancel of St-Pierre-aux-Nonnains. This stone screen comprises 34 carved panels admirably decorated and extremely varied. Note in particular the panel depicting Christ consecrating bread and wine.

"Architecture et cadre de vie" – Exhibits in this section illustrate daily life, building techniques and decorative styles in the past, up to the Renaissance period. There are reconstructed façades (front of a house decorated with four busts) and characteristic architectural features (windows, doors, roofs, staircases).

The roofs of traditional medieval and Renaissance houses were hidden by the façades adorned with gargoyles and stone gutters. Several mansions and ordinary houses have been reconstructed round the museums' courtyard.

The **Grenier de Chèvremont**★ is a well-preserved edifice dating from 1457, once used to store the tithe taken on cereal crops. Particularly striking are the monumental façade, the crenellated top, the stone arcades supporting the oak timberwork and the large paving stones covering the ground.

The ground floor houses a beautiful collection of regional religious art: Pietà, Virgin lying down, Crucifixion, 15C statues of St Roch and St Blaise, St Agatha's altarpiece.

There are some craftsmen's workshops nearby.

Two stunning early-13C ceilings from the Hôtel de Voué, painted in tempera on oak panels, decorate adjacent rooms; they represent an imaginary or mythical bestiary.

La Cour d'or, Musées de Metz

Metz – Grenier de Chèvremont

Do not miss the fine Baroque staircase, the 15C ceiling decorated with heraldic motifs and Renaissance murals discovered in 1982.

Beaux-Arts – *First and second floors.* Interesting paintings of the French School (François de Nomé, Delacroix, Corot, Gustave Moreau), of the German School (*Adoration of the Magi* by H Schuchlin, 15C), of the Flemish School (Van Dyck) and of the Italian School. The School of Metz (1834-1870) is mainly represented by its leading exponent, the painter, pastellist and stained-glass artist Laurent-Charles Maréchal.

The modern-art gallery contains works by Bazaine, Alechinsky, Estève, Dufy, Soulages and Manessier.

Collection militaire – Gathered by Jacques Onfroy de Bréville (JOB), who specialised in the illustration of school manuals and history books, this collection consists of weapons, uniforms and accessories from the late 18C and from the 19C.

The modern-art gallery contains works by Bazaine, Alechinsky, Estève, Dufy, Soulages and Manessier.

Collection militaire – Gathered by Jacques Onfroy de Bréville (JOB), who specialised in the illustration of school manuals and history books, this collection consists of weapons, uniforms and accessories from the late 18C and from the 19C.

171

★ESPLANADE (CV) *30min*

This is a splendid walk laid out at the beginning of the 19C on the site of one of the citadel's moats: from the terrace, there is a fine view of Mount St-Quentin crowned by a fort and of one of the arms of the River Moselle.

★Église St-Pierre-aux-Nonnains ⊙ (CX E)

– Around 380-395, during the reign of Emperor Constantine, a **palæstra** or gymnasium was built on this site. When Attila plundered the town in 451, the edifice was partially destroyed, but the walls built of rubble stones reinforced at regular intervals by ties of red bricks were spared and used again in the building of a chapel c 610-620. The nuns, settled here by order of Duke Éleuthère, followed the rule of St Columba *(see LUXEUIL-LES-BAINS)*. Fragments of the **chancel** added to the edifice at that time, which are fine examples of Merovingian sculpture, are kept in the Musée de la Cour d'or. Around 990, the abbey, which followed the Benedictine rule, was reorganised and the vast

METZ

Allemands (R. des)	DV 2
Ambroise	
Thomas (R.)	CV 3
Armes (Pl. d')	DV 5
Augustins (R. des)	DX 6
Chambière (R.)	DV 10
Chambre (Pl. de)	CV 12
Champé (R. du)	DV 13
Chanoine-Collin (R.)	DV 15
Charlemagne (R.)	CV 17
Chèvre (R. de la)	DX 19
Clercs (R. des)	CV
Coetlosquet (R. du)	CX 22
Coislin (Pl.)	DX 23
Enfer (R. d')	DV 25
En Fournirue	DV

Fabert (R.)	CV 26
Faisan (R. du)	CV 27
Fontaine (R. de la)	DX 29
Gaulle	
(Pl. du Gén.-de)	DX 31
Gde-Armée (R. de la)	DV 34
Hache (R. de la)	DV 39
Jardins (R. des)	DV
Juge Pierre Michel	
(R. du)	CV 46
La Fayette (R.)	CX 47
Lasalle (R.)	DX 49
Lattre-de-T. (Av. de)	CX 51
Leclerc-de-H. (Av.)	CX 52
Mondon (Pl. R.)	CV 57
Paix (R. de la)	CV 61
Palais (R. du)	CV 62
Parmentiers (R. des)	DX 63
Petit-Paris (R. du)	CV 65

Pierre-Hardie	
(R. de la)	CV 66
Prés.-Kennedy (Av.)	CX 73
République (Pl. de la)	CX 75
St-Eucaire (R.)	DV 76
St-Gengoulf (R.)	CX 78
St-Louis (Pl.)	DVX
St-Simplice (Pl.)	CV 80
St-Thiébault (Pl.)	DX 82
Ste-Marie (R.)	CV 84
Salis (R. de)	CX 86
Schuman (Av. R.)	CX
Serpenoise (R.)	CV
Sérot (Bd Robert)	CV 87
Taison (R.)	DV 88
Tanneurs (R. des)	CV 90
Tête d'Or (R. de la)	DV
Trinitaires (R. des)	DV 93
Verlaine (R.)	CX 97

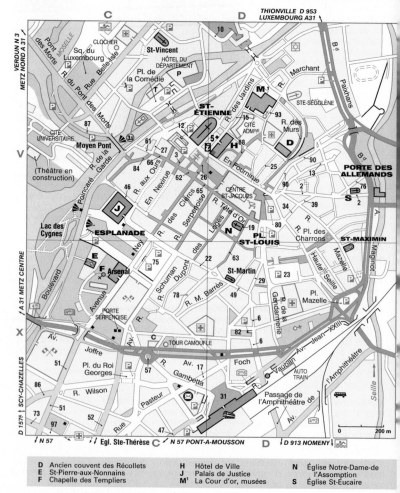

D	Ancien couvent des Récollets	**H**	Hôtel de Ville	**N**	Église Notre-Dame-de-l'Assomption
E	St-Pierre-aux-Nonnains	**J**	Palais de Justice		
F	Chapelle des Templiers	**M¹**	La Cour d'or, musées	**S**	Église St-Eucaire

chapel was split into three naves by rounded arcades. During the Gothic period, the naves were covered with pointed vaulting and an elegant cloister (one side of which is still standing) was added to the conventual buildings in the 15C.

The former palaestra was damaged by Emperor Charles V's artillery during the 1552 siege of Metz and was eventually included in the new citadel. **Excavations** undertaken in the 20C enabled archeologists to discover the level of the Roman floor and to reconstruct the history of this ancient building which is believed to be the oldest church in France. Important repair work has made it possible to restore the volume of the 10C nave and the timber work which covered it.

Chapelle des Templiers ⊘ (**CX F**) – This chapel, built at the beginning of the 13C by the Knight Templars established in Metz since 1133, marks the transition between the Romanesque and Gothic styles. The building is shaped like an octagon, each side except one having a small rounded window; the last side opens onto a square chancel prolonged by an apse. Buildings of this type are rare and this chapel is, in fact, the only one of its kind in Lorraine. The paintings are modern except one which decorates a recess on the right (14C).

Arsenal ⊘ (**CX**) – The walls of the 19C arsenal were partially used to build this ultra-modern centre dedicated to music and dance.

Designed by Ricardo Bofill, the large hall fitted with a central stage was intended for a variety of shows. Its special shape and its elaborate acoustics were inspired by the Musikverein in Vienna. Surrounded by warm wood panelling, the 1 500 spectators get the impression that they are at the centre of a huge musical instrument.

Palais de Justice (**CV J**) – Built in the 18C, during the reign of Louis XVI, this edifice was intended to be the military governor's palace but the Revolution changed all that. Sentry boxes on either side of the entrance remind visitors of the military origins of the building. In the courtyard, there are two interesting bas-relief sculptures: one shows the Duc de Guise during the 1552 siege of the town, the other celebrates the 1783 peace treaty between England, France, the USA and Holland.

The great staircase is decorated with splendid wrought-iron banisters.

RELIGIOUS CITY

★★**Cathédrale St-Étienne** (**CV**) – *See p 168.*

★**Église St-Pierre-aux-Nonnains** (**CX E**) – *See p 172.*

Chapelle des Templiers (**CX F**) – *See p 173.*

★**Église St-Maximin** (**DX**) – The beautiful chancel of this church, which dates from the 12C like the crossing and the tower, is decorated with stained-glass windows by Jean Cocteau. Note also the 14C-15C Chapelle des Gournay, named after a prominent local family, which opens onto the south transept through two basket-handled arches; a fine carved Christ's head decorates the central pillar at the entrance of the chapel.

Église St-Martin (**DX**) – A Gallo-Roman wall, once part of the town's fortifications, forms the base of the church; it is visible on both sides of the entrance. The most attractive feature of this 13C church is its very low **narthex★** whose three sections, covered with pointed vaulting resting on four Romanesque pillars surrounded by colonnettes, open onto the lofty nave. The 15C transept and chancel have stained-glass windows dating from the 15C, 16C and 19C, an organ case in the Louis XV style, 15C, 16C and 18C tombstones and a fine sculpture representing the Nativity (in the north transept).

Église Notre-Dame-de-l'Assomption (**DV N**) – This Jesuit church was erected in 1665 and the west front was completed in the 18C. The interior, decorated in the 19C, is lined with rich wood panelling. The Rococo confessionals come from the German city of Trier, as does the Baroque organ built by Jean Nollet.

Église St-Eucaire (**DV S**) – The fine square belfry dates from the 12C and the west front from the 13C. The Romanesque crossing was remodelled in the 14C and 15C. The small 14C nave with its huge pillars looks out of proportion. The aisles, lined with low arcades, lead to unusual 15C chapels, surmounted by pointed vaulting converging on carved corbels.

Ancien couvent des Récollets ⊘ (**DV D**) – This former convent now houses the European Ecological Institute. The 15C cloister has been restored.

Église St-Vincent ⊘ (**CV**) – The Gothic chancel of the church, flanked by two elegant steeples, is in striking contrast with the west front, rebuilt in the 18C and reminiscent of that of St-Gervais-St-Protais in Paris.

Église Ste-Thérèse-de-l'Enfant-Jésus (**CX**) – *Entrance along avenue Leclerc-de-Hauteclocque.* Consecrated in 1954, this large church, topped by a 70m/230ft mast known as the "pilgrim's staff", has an imposing nave and fine stained-glass windows by Nicolas Untersteller.

ADDITIONAL SIGHTS

★**Porte des Allemands** (DV) – This massive fortress, which formed part of the town walls running along the Moselle and the dual-carriageway ringroad south and east of Metz, straddles the River Seille. It gets its name from an order of German hospitallers established nearby in the 13C.

There are in fact two gates: the first one, dating from the 13C and standing on the town side, is flanked by two round towers topped with slate pepper-pot roofs; the other tower, facing the opposite way, dates from the 15C and has two large crenellated towers. A 15C arcaded gallery links the four towers. The edifice was remodelled in the 19C.

North of the Porte des Allemands, the fortified wall continues for another 1.5km/0.9mi, with numerous towers at regular intervals: Tour des Sorcières (Witches' Tower), Tour du Diable (Devil's Tower), Tour des Corporations (Guilds' Tower). A path follows the ramparts, first along the Seille then along the Moselle.

★**Place St-Louis** (DVX) – Situated at the heart of the old town, the rectangular place St-Louis is lined on one side with buttressed arcaded buildings dating from the 14C, 15C and 16C, which once housed the money-changers' shops. At the end, on the corner of rue de la Tête-d'Or, note the three golden Roman heads protruding from the wall, which gave its name to the street.

★**Moyen Pont** (CV) – Pleasant view of the arms of the River Moselle, of the islands, of the neo-Romanesque protestant church (1901) and of the two small bridges reflecting in the water.

The 18C **theatre** (T) overlooking place de la Comédie, is the oldest in France; nearby stands the **Hôtel du Département** (P), also dating from the 18C.

★**Place du Général-de-Gaulle** (DX 31) – The **station** (1908) a huge neo-Romanesque edifice (300m/328yd long), profusely decorated (capitals, low-relief sculptures), is one of several buildings erected by the Germans at the beginning of the 20C to assert the power of their empire. The vast pedestrianised semicircular area in front of the station is lit by lamp posts designed by Philippe Stark.

EXCURSIONS

★**Walibi Schtroumpf** ⊘ – *15km/9mi north. Accessible by train from Metz on the Nancy-Luxemburg line; station: Walibi Schtroumpf. By car, drive along the Paris motorway to the Semécourt exit then follow signposts for 2km/1.2mi to the parking area.*

This vast leisure park offers visitors of all ages a journey with Walibi, the friendly kangaroo, and the Schtroumpfs, the famous blue characters of Peyo's comic strip. There is a wide choice of shops, snacks and restaurants, so that visitors can easily spend a whole day in the park.

Attractions include the Réaktor, a huge wheel with a loop-the-loop track, the **Odisséa**, a buoy tossed about among the rapids, the Waligator which splashes 12m/39ft down a waterfall and the Aquachute, a huge water slide. There is a

In France, a "Smurf" is a "Schtroumpf"

guaranteed thrill on a vertigineous roller-coaster circuit, the Comet Space, which includes a loop-the-loop and two spiral dives, or on the **Anaconda**, the longest and highest wooden roller coaster in Europe.
For children there are mini jeeps (Convoy-Race), dodgems (Meteore), a musical merry-go-round (Maestro), Arkel marsh (marais d'Arkel) and its giant frogs.

Scy-Chazelles – *4km/2.5mi west along D 157A (CX) then turn right.*
Robert Schuman's house ⊙ is located in the village, near the 12C fortified church where the "father of Europe" (1886-1963) is buried. This austere building, characteristic of Lorraine, conveys an impression of calm and serenity which this generous and modest man found conducive to meditation. His library, his diplomas and decorations are among Schuman's personal mementoes.
In the park, beyond the terrace, there is a sculpture by Le Chevallier entitled *The European Flame.*

Château de Pange ⊙ – *10km/6mi east along D 999, D 70 and D 6.*
Built between 1720 and 1756 on the site of an ancient fortress, along the banks of the Nied, a small tributary of the Moselle, the castle has retained its plain Classical façade.
The dining room in the Louis XV style is still decorated with green wood panelling and a primitive regional stove.

Vallée de la Canner ⊙ – *Departure from Vigy, 15km/9mi northeast along D 2 then D 52.*
From Vigy to Hombourg *(12km/7.5mi)*, a small tourist train, pulled by a real steam engine, follows the remote Canner Valley through a densely forested part of the Lorraine plateau.

Groupe fortifié de l'Aisne ⊙ – *14km/8.7mi south along D 913.* The former Wagner fortress, built by the Germans between 1904 and 1910, formed part of the outer defences of Metz. Renamed Aisne after 1918, it was not, unlike Guentrange, incorporated into the Maginot Line *(see Ligne MAGINOT)*; during the Second World War, it was only used to store torpedo heads.
This type of fortified complex replaced massive fortresses at the end of the 19C; it consisted of several works linked by underground galleries. The Aisne for instance comprises four infantry blocks with up to three levels of underground barracks, three artillery blocks fitted with revolving turrets suitable for heavy guns and about 15 armor-plated observatories.

Sillegny – *20km/12.5mi south along D 5.*
This village of the Seille Valley has a small 15C **church**, which looks unassuming but is entirely covered with **murals** ★ dating from 1540. Note the warmth of the colours and the great number of naive details of these murals representing the Apostles, the Evangelists, the Tree of Jesse *(in the chancel on the right)*, the Last Judgement above the entrance and the huge St Christopher, 5m/16ft high.

Gorze – *18km/11mi southwest along D 57, then right onto D 6^B.*
This village, which developed round a Benedictine abbey founded in the 8C and destroyed in 1552, has retained a number of old Renaissance residences dating from the 17C and 18C. The surrounding forest offers a choice of fine walks along a network of marked paths.
The **Maison de l'Histoire de la Terre de Gorze** ⊙ relates episodes of Gorze's prosperous past, in particular the harnessing of the springs by the Romans during the 1C AD, the construction of a bridge-aqueduct (model) and the Benedictine foundation.
The **Église St-Étienne** is Romanesque on the outside and early Gothic (late 12C and early 13C) inside, with characteristic features of the Rhine region. The central belfry dates from the 13C; note the absence of flying buttresses and the narrow windows. The tympanum of the north porch is decorated with a 13C Virgin between two praying figures. The tympanum of the small adjacent doorway shows a late-12C Last Judgement. The chancel is decorated with fine woodwork and 18C biblical paintings. Note the large wooden crucifix, attributed to Ligier Richier, on the inside of the north doorway.
The former **abbatial palace**, built in 1696, is a Baroque edifice designed by Philippe-Eberhard of Lowenstein and Bavaria; note the staircase and the fountains decorated with mythological scenes, as well as the chapel adorned with Baroque motifs.

Aqueduc romain de Gorze à Metz – *12km/7.5mi southwest. Drive along N 3 to Moulins then continue along D 6 to Ars-sur-Moselle.*
Seven arches of this 1C AD Roman aqueduct, which spanned the Moselle, are still standing alongside D 6, south of **Ars-sur-Moselle** (west bank). Excavations have revealed pipes and sections of masonry. In **Jouy-aux-Arches** (east bank), another 16 arches, in a better state of preservation, span N 57.

‡‡ **Amnéville** – *21km/12.4mi north along D 953. See AMNÉVILLE.*

Vallée de la MEUSE

Michelin maps 53 folds 8, 9, 18, 19, 56 fold 10, 57 folds 1, 11, 12, 62 folds 3, 13
or 241 folds 2, 6, 10, 14, 15, 19, 23, 27 and 31

The River Meuse takes its source in the foothills of the Plateau de Langres, not far from Bourbonne-les-Bains, at an altitude of only 409m/1 342ft; it flows into the North Sea 950km/590mi further on, forming with the Rhine a common delta along the coast of the Netherlands where it is known as the Maas.

The course of this peaceful river often changes, for instance when it flows along the bottom of the ridge known as the Hauts de Meuse, or crosses a large alluvial plain (beyond Dun-sur-Meuse), or meanders through the Ardennes.

The section from Charleville-Mézières to Givet is the most picturesque part of the river's journey through France: the Meuse has dug its deep and sinuous course through hard schist, which is sometimes barren and sometimes forested (hunting for wild boar and roe-deer is a favourite pastime in the area). The railway line linking Charleville and Givet follows the river which is linked to the Aisne by the Canal des Ardennes dug in the mid 19C. River traffic is reduced to barges not exceeding 300t because the rate of flow is insufficient and the river bed not deep enough in places, whereas downriver from Givet, the river has been adapted to allow barges of up to 1 350t through.

Cruises and boat trips are organised from Charleville-Mézières, Monthermé and Revin (see Practical information).

FROM COMMERCY TO CHARLEVILLE
196km/122mi – allow 1 day

Commercy – Commercy occupied a strategic position on the west bank of the River Meuse and the number of fortified houses and churches still standing are a reminder of the constant threat of invasion the whole area lived under in the past. The town has retained an ancient metalwork tradition and a biennial exhibition of contemporary art takes place in the castle as part of a competition known as "l'Art du Fer". Small soft cakes called *madeleines*, a speciality of Commercy, are the product of a prosperous industry.

An imposing horseshoe esplanade precedes the **Château Stanislas** ⊘ situated along the axis formed by rue Stanislas and the alleyway lined with lime trees which leads to the Commercy Forest. Dating from the Middle Ages, the castle was rebuilt in the 17C for the Cardinal de Retz and redesigned by Boffrand and d'Orbay for the Prince de Vaudémont at the beginning of the 18C. It was used as a hunting lodge by the dukes of Lorraine before becoming the property of Stanislas Leszczynski, King Louis XV's father-in-law, who commissioned E Héré to relay the gardens (which no longer exist) and the horseshoe esplanade. Severely damaged by fire in 1944, the castle was completely restored and now houses the town hall.

The former municipal baths, dating from the 1930s, have been turned into the **Musée de la Céramique et de l'Ivoire**, which houses a fine collection of ceramics together with European and Asian ivories.

From Commercy, D 964 follows the Meuse almost as far north as Sedan, twisting through meadows along the west bank to Sampigny, then cutting across a meander of the river towards St-Mihiel and continuing along the east bank.

★**St-Mihiel** – *See ST-MIHIEL.*

To the right is the ruined fort of Troyon, bitterly defended in 1914.

Génicourt-sur-Meuse – The church is a fine example of the Flamboyant-Gothic style. It contains beautiful 16C stained-glass windows by members of the School of Metz, a high altar surmounted by a retable depicting the Passion and, on its right, another altar dating from 1530. The interesting wooden statues of the Calvary are believed to be the work of Ligier Richier; 16C frescoes were discovered in June 1981.

In Dieue-sur-Meuse, cross the Canal de l'Est and the Meuse and turn right onto D 34.

Dugny-sur-Meuse – In the village, there is a fine 12C Romanesque **church** ⊘, now deconsecrated; this edifice of moderate proportions is surmounted by a massive square belfry decorated with a row of arcading resting on colonnettes and topped by timber hoarding. Inside, the large square pillars of the nave are not surprisingly support timber vaulting (a common practice in the Rhine region) since, in the mid 12C, Lorraine formed part of the Holy Roman Empire.

★★**Verdun** – *See VERDUN.*

Rejoin D 964 and continue along the east bank.

Dun-sur-Meuse – The oldest part of this small town is built on a picturesque hilltop, on the edge of the Lorraine plateau. It was considerably damaged when it was liberated by American troops in November 1918. From the open space in front of the 16C church, there is an extended view of the Meuse Valley.

Cross the canal and the river 3km/1.9mi north of Dun to reach Mont-devant-Sassey.

Mont-devant-Sassey – The village lies at the foot of a hill on the west bank of the river. An interesting 11C church, remodelled later, stands on the hillside. During the 17C wars, it was turned into a fortress. The building, characteristic of the Rhine region, has square towers over the transept and a raised east end built over a crypt. Preceded by a Gothic porch decorated with statues in naive style, the monumental 13C doorway, dedicated to the Virgin, is similar in design to those of the great Gothic cathedrals: a damaged bearing shaft supports a tympanum consisting of three historiated bands, framed by four recessed arches decorated wiith carved characters.

Drive north along D 30 to Laneuville-sur Meuse, then northwest to Beaumont-en-Argonne; turn left onto D 4 to reach the Parc de vision de Belval.

★**Parc de vision de Belval** ⊙ – Situated in the grounds of a former Augustinian monastery, this wildlife park covers 600ha/1 483 acres of meadows, woods and lakes at the heart of the Belval Forest. All the animals live or used to live in this natural environment a few hundred years ago: wild boars, deer, roe-deer and also moufflons, bisons and bears which have now disappeared. During the 6km/3.7mi drive round the park, it is possible to stop, go on short hikes and watch the animals roaming around almost freely from watchtowers and hidden observation points. Mallards and herons live on the lakes.

Return to Laneuville and cross the river towards Stenay.

Stenay – This former stronghold situated on the east bank of the river and of the canal, is a small industrial centre with a paper factory and steelworks. The town's fortifications were modified by Vauban at the request of Louis XIV who had them dismantled a few years later in 1689. The Kronprinz had his headquarters in the town for 18 months between 1914 and 1918.

Stenay – Musée de la Bière

The vast **Musée européen de la Bière** ⊙ (European Beer Museum) is housed in the former supply stores of the 16C citadel turned into a malt factory in the 19C. Explanatory panels, maps, models, objects and tools help to inform visitors about the history and technique of beer-brewing since ancient times. The uninitiated discover how brewers make beer from simple ingredients such as spring water, barley turned into malt and hops which give beer its characteristic bitter flavour.

The 16C residence of the former governor of the citadel, situated on the edge of town, houses the **Musée du pays de Stenay** ⊙ (collections of archeology as well as arts and crafts).

★**Mouzon** – *See MOUZON.*

In Douzy, turn left onto N 43 to Bazeilles.

Bazeilles – Bitter fighting took place here in September 1870, before Sedan capitulated. The **Maison de la dernière cartouche** ⊙ (House of the last round of ammunition), where a group of French soldiers resisted to their last round, is now a

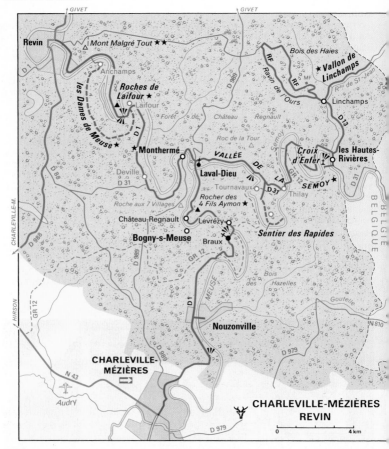

museum containing many French and German exhibits gathered on the battlefield together with photocopies of letters sent by Gallieni to his family giving details about the fighting. A nearby ossuary contains the remains of some 3 000 French and German soldiers.

The 18C **castle** ⊘, built in the Rococo style for a wealthy draper from Sedan stands beyond an elegant wrought-iron gate flanked by stone lions. In the French-style gardens there are two charming pavilions, an oval-shaped orangery (now a restaurant) and a dovecote as well as the former stables turned into a hotel.

Sedan – *See SEDAN.*

From Sedan, follow D 764 to Charleville-Mézières.

Charleville-Mézières – *See CHARLEVILLE-MÉZIÈRES.*

★★FROM CHARLEVILLE TO GIVET *84km/52mi – allow 6hr*

The Meuse meanders through the forested Ardennes region and a scenic road *(D 1, D 988 and N 51)* follows the sinous course of the river closely.

Charleville-Mézières – *See CHARLEVILLE-MÉZIÈRES.*

From Charleville drive along D 1 which runs towards the river.

View of Nouzonville.

Nouzonville – This industrial centre (metalworks and mechanical industries), situated at the confluence of the Meuse and the Goutelle, follows a long-standing nail-making tradition introduced in the 15C by people from Liège running away from the duke of Burgundy, Charles the Bold.

Bogny-sur-Meuse – Bogny-sur-Meuse, which stretches for 10km/6mi along the river, evolved in 1967 from the merging of three villages, Braux, Levrézy and Château-Regnault. There are several marked footpaths starting from the tourist office. The **Sentier Nature et Patrimoine du Pierroy** (the Pierroy Nature and Heritage Trail) leads past typical geological features (conglomerate and schist) and the remains of quartzite quarries, offering fine views of the Meuse Valley.

Continue along D 1 to Braux.

Braux – The former collegiate **church** has retained its Romanesque apse, chancel and transept but the nave and the aisles date from the 17C and 18C. Note the rich 17C marble altars with low-relief sculptures and above all the fine 12C christening font, carved out of blue stone from Givet and decorated with grotesques.

Cross the River Meuse.

From the bridge, there is an interesting vista on the left of the Rocher des Quatre Fils Aymon.

Levrézy – A former factory houses a **Musée de la Métallurgie** ⊙ which illustrates the making of nuts and bolts with tools and machines still in working order (forge, planing and milling machines...).

Château-Regnault – Once the main centre of a principality, Château-Regnault had its castle razed to the ground by Louis XIV. The village lies at the foot of the **Rocher des Quatre Fils Aymon★** whose outline formed by four sharp points suggests the legend of the Four Aymon Brothers escaping from Charlemagne's men on their famous horse "Bayard".

The **Centre d'exposition des minéraux** ⊙ displays rocks from the Ardennes region together with fossils from various parts of the world.

Platelle des Quatre Fils Aymon – This artificial ledge fitted as a play area is overlooked by the monument of the Four Aymon Brothers. There is a view of the meanders of the Meuse, of the factories lining its course, of workers' housing estates and of private mansions.

Continue along D 1 which runs beneath the railway line before crossing the Semoy which flows into the Meuse at Laval-Dieu.

Laval-Dieu – This industrial suburb of Monthermé grew round an abbey of Premonstratensians established here in the 12C. The former abbey church stands on a peaceful wooded site. The massive 12C square belfry, built of schist, contrasts with the elegant late 17C west front, brick built with stone surrounds. Note the flat east end, decorated with Lombardy banding, the only one of its kind in the region.

★**Vallée de la Semoy** – *See Vallée de la SEMOY.*

★**Monthermé** – *See MONTHERMÉ.*

In Monthermé, the road (D 1) crosses back to the west bank, running close to the hill topped by the Roche aux Sept Villages (see MONTHERMÉ) and goes through Deville before reaching Laifour.

★**Roches de Laifour** – This promontory rises 270m/886ft above the river bed; its schist slopes dropping steeply towards the river are a striking feature of this wild landscape.

From the bridge, there is an impressive **view★★** of the Roches de Laifour and Dames de Meuse.

Meander of the Meuse at Monthermé

★**Dames de Meuse** – This ridge line sloping steeply down to the river, forms a black gullied mass whose curve follows the course of the Meuse; it reaches the altitude of 393m/1 289ft at its highest point and rises 250m/820ft above the river bed. According to legend, it owes its name to three unfaithful wives turned to stone by God's wrath.

A **path** branches off D 1 south of Laifour, climbs to the Dames de Meuse refuge and reaches the edge of the ridge *(2hr on foot there and back)*; the walk affords a fine **view**★★ of the valley and the village. From there, another path follows the top of the ridge and leads to Anchamps *(about 2hr 30min on foot)*.

Drive along D 1 which crosses the Meuse.

This road offers impressive views of the Dames de Meuse.

Revin – Revin occupies an exceptional position within two deep meanders of the Meuse; the old town nestles round its 18C church, inside the northern meander whereas the southern meander shelters the industrial district with its factories specialising in the production of domestic appliances and bathroom units. There are a few 16C timber-framed houses along quai Edgar-Quinet; note in particular the **Maison espagnole** ⊙ on the corner of rue Victor-Hugo, which has been turned into a museum holding a yearly exhibition about traditions and customs of the Ardennes. A building situated on the edge of the **Parc Maurice-Rocheteau** ⊙ houses a **Galerie d'art contemporain** ⊙ (contemporary-art gallery) including works by Goerges Cesari (1923-1982).

★★**Mont Malgré Tout** – *3km/1.9mi east then 1hr on foot there and back. On the outskirts of Revin, the winding Route des Hauts-Buttés rises 300m/984ft to the Monument des Manises standing on the roadside.*

From the **Monument des Manises**, dedicated to the members of the "maquis des Manises" resistance group, there is an interesting bird's-eye view of Revin and the surrounding area.

The viewing-platform of La Faligoette also offers an interesting view of Revin and of the meanders of the Meuse.

Park the car 400m/437yd from a signpost bearing the inscription "Point de vue à 100m". The footpath begins here (1hr on foot there and back).

The steep path leads to a television relay. From there it is possible to walk through a thicket of birch and oak trees and reach a higher viewpoint (alt 400m/1 312ft) offering a wide **view** of Revin, the meanders of the Meuse, the Dames de Meuse across the river to the south and the Vallée de Misère to the west *(see ROCROI)*.

Return to Revin and turn right onto D 988.

The road runs close to the river through the narrow Meuse Valley.

Fumay – The old town, with its twisting narrow streets, occupies a picturesque position on a hillside within a deep meander of the Meuse. From the bridge there is a pleasant view of this group of old houses.

Four Brothers and their Legendary Steed

The deep and impenetrable Ardennes Forest is the favourite haunt of wild animals, of pagan spirits and fantastic creatures. Among the many legends which flourish in the thick woods, the most famous is undoubtedly the legend of *The Four Aymon Brothers*, sometimes called *The Tale Renaud de Montauban*, which relates the feats of four brave knights astride their mighty horse, **Bayard**.

Aymon was the Duke of Dordogne and an ardent supporter of Charlemagne. In a complicated dispute, the duke's brother killed a son of Charlemagne, and was then killed himself by supporters of the king. Aymon's four sons, handsome and valiant (as legend must have it), could not suffer their uncle's murder and finally had to flee; their mother thoughtfully provided them with the family treasury. They established themselves in the thick forest of the Ardennes in a castle, Montfort, built into the rocky cliff above the Meuse.

This epic can be compared to the *Chanson de Roland*, the earliest master-peice of the French *chansons de gestes* ("songs of deeds"), which formed the core of the Charlemagne legends.

Numerous episodes were gradually added to the simple story which, in the 13C, became a poem intended to be read. The 15C prose version is a precursor of the novel form.

Precious manuscripts, incunabula and old editions of this work are kept with the archives of the *département*, and many place names recall their heroic exploits.

The **Musée de l'Ardoise** ⊙ (Fumay is known for its blue slate), housed in the former Carmelite convent, illustrates the hard work of miners extracting schist during the past 800 years. The last two mines closed down in 1971.

The low-relief sculpture (avenue Jean-Jaurès), dedicated to the memory of these miners, is the work of Georges-Armand Favaudon.

Continue along N 51 towards Givet until you come within sight of the station and bridge at Haybes.

Haybes – From Haybes bridge there is a lovely view of this attractive resort which offers numerous possibilities of walks, in particular to the viewpoint at **La Platale** *(2km/1.2mi from Haybes along the scenic Morhon road; picnic area)*, which affords a close-up view of Fumay, and to the viewpoint of **Roc de Fépin** *(8km/5mi east along D 7; access signposted)*.

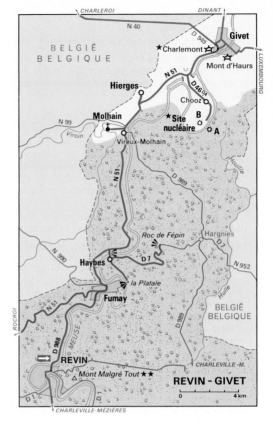

The main N 51 leads to **Vireux-Molhain**, lying in a pleasant setting at the confluence of the Meuse and the Viroin. Excavations on Mount Vireux have revealed a Gallo-Roman and medieval site. Part of the medieval walls and a 14C bread oven can be seen.

Ancienne collégiale de Molhain – Built over a 9C-10C crypt and remodelled in the 18C, this former collegiate church has interesting interior decoration (Italian stuccowork, furniture). Note the 17C altarpiece over the high altar, depicting the Assumption, a 16C Entombment, 14C-16C statues, 13C-18C tombstones.

Turn left towards Hierges 2km/1.2mi beyond Vireux-Molhain.

Hierges – The village, which has retained a few 17C houses and a 13C mill, is overlooked by the ruins of a castle built between the 11C and the 15C, once the seat of a barony. The austerity of its fortress-like aspect is tempered by its Renaissance features (brick ornamentation of the towers).

The road (N 51) reaches the Chooz meander.

★**Site nucléaire de Chooz** ⊙ – It consists of two nuclear power stations, **Chooz A** which stopped producing electricity in 1991 after 24 years and **Chooz B**, situated inside the meander of the river and completed in 1996, which comprises two units producing 1 450 million watts each. Chooz B will eventually produce, together with the power station at Nogent, almost 10% of the total French needs. Technological innovations include an entirely computerised control room and a new, very powerful turbine called "Arabelle".

An information office, situated at the entrance of the site, has a display of explanatory panels and models about the production of electricity and nuclear energy.

Return to N 51 and drive towards Givet past black-marble quarries.

Givet – See GIVET.

In this guide town plans show the main streets and the way to the sights; local maps show the main roads and the roads on the recommended tour.

MOLSHEIM ★

Population 7 973
Michelin map 87 folds 5 and 15 or 242 folds 23 and 24
Local map see Route des VINS

This charming old town lies in the Bruche Valley, at the heart of a wine-growing area which produces the famous Riesling. The Messier-Bugatti factory, specialising in landing gear *(not open to the public)* is located on the outskirts of town, along the Sélestat road.

SIGHTS

★**Metzig** – This graceful Renaissance building was built in 1525 by the butchers' guild whose meetings were held on the first floor, the ground floor being occupied by butchers' shops. It looks typically Alsatian with its scrolled gables and its double flight of steps leading to the belfry-loggia. On either side of the jack clock (1537), two angels strike the hours. An elegant carved-stone balcony runs along the façade and the sides at first-floor level.

The centre of the square is decorated with a fountain consisting of two superposed basins and an impressive lion bearing the arms of the city.

★**Église des Jésuites** – The church belonged to the famous Jesuit university founded in 1618 by Archduke Leopold of Austria, who was the bishop of Strasbourg at the time. The fame of this university, which included a faculty of theology and philosophy spread far and wide. The Cardinal de Rohan transferred it to Strasbourg in 1702 in order to counteract the influence of the town's protestant university.
Although it was built between 1615 and 1617, the edifice was designed in the Gothic style. The harmonious proportions of the interior, the wide gallery and the fishnet vaulting draw the visitor's attention. The two **transept chapels** are adorned with stuccowork, gilt ornamentation and 17C-18C paintings depicting the life of St Ignatius and of the Virgin. St Ignatius' chapel contains white-sandstone fonts dating from 1624 as well as several early-15C tombstones. The Virgin's chapel contains a fine polychrome recumbent effigy of Jean de Durbheim, who was the bishop of Strasbourg from 1306 to 1328.
The pulpit (1631) and the doorways (1618), particularly the sacristy doorway, are decorated with fine carvings. The Silbermann organ dates from 1781.
The north entrance houses the Carthusian Cross, a beautiful stone cross dating from the late Middle Ages.

Musée de la Chartreuse ⊙ – The priory of the former Carthusian monastery (1598-1792) houses a museum devoted to the history of Molsheim and its region, from prehistoric times to today.
Objects discovered on the archeological sites of Dachstein, Achenheim and Heiligenberg-Dinsheim (sigillate ceramics) testify to the presence of man from the paleolithic period to Merovingian times. With the arrival of Jesuits, Capuchins and above all Carthusian monks in the 17C, the town soon became the religious capital of Alsace. A general map dating from 1744 shows the importance of the Carthusian monastery which spread over 3ha/7.4 acres within the town. Part of the cloister has been restored and two monks' cells, divided into three rooms each, have been reconstructed with the original furniture.

In another building, the **Bugatti Foundation** displays mementoes of the family and a few models of cars built here between the two world wars.

Tour des Forgerons – This 14C fortified gate, located in rue de Strasbourg, houses one of the oldest bells in Alsace, dating from 1412.

Maison ancienne – A beautiful timber-framed Alsatian house with wooden oriel (1607) and finely decorated windows can be seen along rue de Saverne.

Ettore Bugatti

A native of Italy, Ettore Bugatti (Milan 1881-Neuilly 1947) gave up his fine arts studies to devote himself to mechanical engineering. At the age of 17 he was engaged as an apprentice in a cycle factory. At the age of 20 he designed his first car which was awarded the major prize of the town of Milan. He next worked with Baron de Dietrich in Niederbronn and then became the partner of Mathis with whom he built the Hermès Simplex in 1904. In 1909, he founded his factory in Molsheim and in 1911, with his unique gift as an engineer and an artist, he designed and built a small car which later became the BB Peugeot, nicknamed Bébé.

Parc naturel régional de la
MONTAGNE DE REIMS★★

Michelin map 56 folds 16 and 17 or 241 fold 21

The Montagne de Reims is a picturesque massif covered with vineyards and woods and offering a wide choice of pleasant sites.

Forest and vines – The Montagne de Reims is a section of the Ile-de-France cliff jutting out between the Vesle and the Marne towards the plain of Champagne. The Grande Montagne (high mountain) extends east of N 51 whereas the Petite Montagne (small mountain) spreads to the west of N 51. The highest point of the massif (287m/942ft) is located south of Vezy but, apart from Mont Sinaï (alt 283m/928ft) and Mont Joli (alt 274m/899ft), there are no distinct summits. The Montagne de Reims would be more appropriately described as an uneven limestone plateau covered with sand and marl deposits, with occasional depressions filled by lakes or chasms leading to the formation of underground rivers.

Wild boars and roe-deer roam freely through the vast forest of oaks, beeches and chestnuts, which covers an area of 20 000ha/49 422 acres. The north, east and south slopes, gullied by erosion, are covered with 7 000ha/17 298 acres of vineyards producing some of the best Champagnes.

Parc naturel régional de la Montagne de Reims – Created in 1976, the nature park extends over an area of 50 000ha/123 555 acres between the towns of Reims, Épernay and Châlons-en-Champagne and includes 68 villages and hamlets of the Marne *département*. The forest, consisting essentially of deciduous trees, covers more than a third of the park's area; part of it, south of Verzy, is a biological reserve.

There are numerous possibilities and facilities for exploring the park: footpaths starting from Villers-Allerand, Rilly-la-Montagne, Villers-Marmery, Trépail, Courtagnon and Damery; walks along the canal running alongside the Marne, picnic areas, viewpoints in Ville-Dommange, Hautvillers, Dizy, Verzy and Châtillon-sur-Marne.

In addition to the sights listed in the itinerary, **Olizy** has a small **Musée de l'Escargot de Champagne** ⊙ (snail museum) and offers a tour of a snail farm.

The Maison du parc in **Pourcy** organises numerous cultural and outdoor activities every year. There are other information centres about the park in **Hautvillers** and **Châtillon-sur-Marne**.

TOUR STARTING FROM MONTCHENOT

100km/62mi – allow half a day

Drive along D 26 towards Villers-Allerand.

The road, which follows the northern ridge of the Montagne de Reims, winds its way through vineyards and the prosperous villages of the Champagne countryside.

Faux de Verzy

S Chirol

183

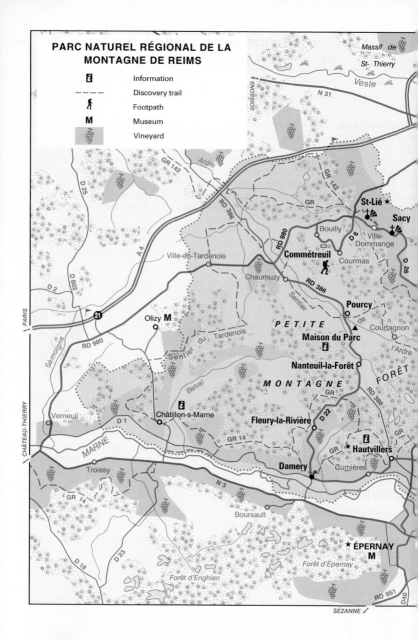

PARC NATUREL RÉGIONAL DE LA MONTAGNE DE REIMS

🛈 Information
- - - - Discovery trail
🚶 Footpath
M Museum
Vineyard

Rilly-la-Montagne – A number of wine-growers and Champagne merchants have brought prosperity to this village. In the church, note the 16C stalls carved with motifs connected with wine-growing.

From Rilly there are fine walking possibilities on the slopes of **Mont Joli** through which goes the railway tunnel (3.5km/2.2mi long) of the Paris-Reims line.

Mailly-Champagne – 1km/0.6mi beyond Mailly-Champagne whose vineyards slope down into the plain, there is an interesting **Carrière géologique** ⊘ (geological quarry) showing a complete cross section of the Tertiary formations of the eastern Paris Basin. From the road, one can spot, at the top of the hill to the right, a contemporary sculpture by Bernard Pages celebrating the Earth.

Verzenay – A windmill can be seen among the vines just before the village. From the esplanade on the roadside, there is a **view**★ of the vast expanse of vineyards with Reims and the Monts de Champagne beyond.

Verzy – This ancient wine-growing village developed under the protection of the Benedictine abbey of St-Basle, founded in the 7C by the archbishop of Reims, St Nivard, and destroyed in 1792.

★**Faux de Verzy** ⊘ – In Verzy, take D 34 towards Louvois. On reaching the plateau, turn left onto the "Route des Faux". From the parking area, follow the path over a distance of about 1km/0.6mi. The "Faux" (from the Latin fagus meaning birch) are

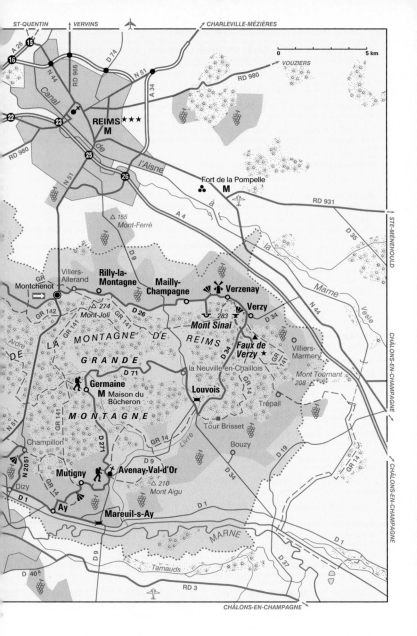

twisted and stunted birches as seen in the photograph on page 183. This is the result of a genetic phenomenon, probably reinforced by natural layering. The site is now a biological reserve with footpaths, a playground and picnic area.

Mont Sinaï – *Parking area on the other side of D 34. Walk along the forest road and, 200m/219yd further on, turn right onto a very wide path (30min there and back).* A casemate situated on the edge of the ridge marks the observation post from which General Gouraud studied the positions and the terrain during the battle of Champagne in 1918. There is an extended view of the area towards Reims and the Champagne hills.

Return to D 34 and continue towards Louvois.

Louvois – Erected by Mansart for Louis XIV's minister, the **castle** *(not open to the public)* became the property of Louis XV's daughters. This splendid residence surrounded by a park designed by Le Nôtre was for the most part demolished between 1805 and 1812. From the gate of the park, it is possible to see the present castle which consists of a pavilion partly rebuilt in the 19C.

Drive north along D 9 to Neuville-en-Chaillois then turn left onto D 71 which goes through the forest.

Germaine – A small museum, the **Maison du bûcheron** ⊙, created by the nature park, is devoted to all the aspects of forestry (marking, clearing, cutting, felling, carrying) and its corresponding skills. Nearby, there is a nature trail through the forest.

Follow D 271 to Avenay-Val-d'Or.

Avenay-Val-d'Or – The **Église St-Trésain** ⊙, dating from the 13C and 16C, has a fine Flamboyant west front, a 16C organ in the south transept and pictures from a Benedictine abbey destroyed during the Revolution. A discovery trail starting from the station *(brochure available from the Maison du Parc)*, enables visitors to discover a rural community.

Follow D 201 opposite the station and immediately after the railway line, take the small road which climbs through the vineyards to Mutigny.

Mutigny – Stand near the simple rural church, situated on the edge of the ridge, to get a good view of Ay and the Côte des Blancs on the right, Châlons and the plain straight ahead.
On the way down to Ay, there are glimpses of Épernay and the Côte des Blancs.

Ay – This ancient city, well-known in Gallo-Roman times and well-liked by several French kings including Good King Henri (IV), lies in a secluded spot at the foot of a hill among famous vineyards.
Gosset, the Champagne firm whose founder is listed as a wine-grower in the city's records of 1584, prides itself in being the oldest firm in the whole Champagne region.

In Ay, turn left onto D 1 to Mareuil-sur-Ay.

Mareuil-sur-Ay – The castle was erected in the 18C and the estate was bought in 1830 by the duke of Montebello who created his own make of Champagne.

Return to Ay and continue to Dizy.

Between Dizy and Champillon, the road rises through endless vineyards. There is a good view★ of those vineyards, of the Marne Valley and of Épernay from a terrace on the side of the road.

★**Hautvillers** – *See ÉPERNAY: Excursions.*

Damery – Damery offers fine walks along the banks of the River Marne; the 12C-13C church once belonged to the Benedictine abbey of St-Médard de Soissons. The Romanesque nave is lit by lancet windows. Note the carved capitals of the pillars supporting the belfry: they represent an interesting bestiary against a background of foliage and intertwined stems. The organ case and the chancel railing date from the 18C.

Turn right towards Fleury-la-Rivière.

Fleury-la-Rivière – The walls of the **Coopérative vinicole** ⊙ (wine-growers' cooperative society) are decorated with a huge frescoe by Greg Gawra, which depicts the history of the Champagne region.

Nanteuil-la-Forêt – There was once a Templars' priory in this remote place hidden inside a narrow vale and surrounded by a forest.

Pourcy – The **Maison du Parc** ⊙, built in the Ardre Valley, houses the offices of the nature park as well as an information centre. Designed by Hervé Bagot, it is reminiscent of farm buildings surrounding an enclosed courtyard.

Beyond Chaumuzy, turn right onto RD 980 then right again towards Bouilly.
Continue to the parking area known as "Aire de l'étang", at the entrance of Courmas.

The **Domaine de Commetreuil**, which belongs to the nature park, offers many possibilities of fine walks.

Turn left onto D 6.

★**Chapelle St-Lié** – This chapel, dating from the 12C, 13C and 16C, stands on a mound near Ville-Dommange, at the centre of a copse which was probably a holy grove in Gallo-Roman times. Note the wrought-iron cross on the edge of the wood. Dedicated to a 5C hermit, the chapel is surrounded by its cemetery.
There is an extended view★ of Ville-Dommange, the ridge, Reims and its cathedral and the plain as far as the St-Thierry massif.

Sacy – The Église St-Rémi has an 11C east end and a 12C square belfry. From the adjoining cemetery there is a fine view of Reims.

The towns and sights described in this guide are shown in black on the maps.

MONTHERMÉ ★

Population 2 866
Michelin map 53 fold 18 or 241 fold 6 – Local map see Vallée de la MEUSE

Situated just beyond the confluence of the Semoy and the Meuse, this lively little town is the ideal centre from which to explore the valleys of these two rivers. The old town (vieille ville) and new districts are separated by the River Meuse; from the bridge linking them, there is a fine overall view of Monthermé.

Vieille ville – A long street lined with old houses runs through the old town and leads to the fortified **Église St-Léger** ⊘ (12C-15C), built of fine stone from the Meuse region. Inside there are 15C frescoes, a Romanesque christening font and an 18C pulpit.

EXCURSIONS

★**Roche à Sept Heures** – *2km/1.2mi along the Hargnies road then left at the top of the hill onto the tarmacked path.* From this rocky spur, there is a bird's-eye **view**★ of Monthermé and the meander of the Meuse with Laval-Dieu upstream and, further away, Château-Regnault and the Rocher des Quatre Fils Aymon.

★★**Longue Roche** – *The tarmacked path continues beyond the Roche à Sept Heures for a further 400m/437yd to a parking area. From there, you can walk to the viewpoint (30min there and back).* This is another rocky spur (alt 375m/1 230ft) overlooking the Meuse. A path running along the ridge offers bird's-eye views of the valley from different angles. The **panorama**★★ is wilder and sharper than that of the Roche à Sept Heures.

★★**Roc de la Tour** – *3.5km/2.2mi east then 20min on foot there and back. The access road branches off D 31 on the left as you leave Laval-Dieu; it rises through the wooded vale of a stream (the Lyre). Leave the car and follow the footpath.* This ruin-like quartzite spur surrounded by birches stands in a dramatic setting overlooking the Semoy and affords a panoramic **view**★★ of the wooded heights of the Ardennes massif.

★★**Roche aux Sept Villages** – *3km/1.9mi south. Follow the Charleville road (D 989).*
As the road rises, the view gradually extends over the valley.
Steps climb this rocky peak rising above the forest. From the top there is a remarkable **view**★★ of the meandering River Meuse lined with seven villages from Braux to Deville. Next to Château-Regnault stands the jagged Rocher des Quatre Fils Aymon.

★**Roche de Roma** – Alt 333m/1 093ft. *The road continues to climb beyond the Roche aux Sept Villages; at the top, a path leads to the viewpoint of the Roche de Roma.* **View**★ of the meander of the Meuse between Monthermé and Deville.

MONTIER-EN-DER

Population 2 023
Michelin map 61 fold 9 or 241 fold 34

Destroyed by intensive shelling in June 1940, Montier-en-Der was completely rebuilt and now boasts pleasant public gardens.
The town developed round a Benedictine monastery established on the banks of the River Voire. It is the capital of the **Der**, a low-lying area of sand and clay, covered with oak forests (*Der* means "oak" in Celtic language) until medieval monks undertook to deforest it; the Der Forest in the north east is all that remains of the original forests. Pastures where horses and cattle graze alternate with woods and lakes where wildlifeabounds. Villages set in ancestral orchards have retained their characteristic features: low timber-framed houses with cob walls, the church steeple rising to a shingled point above one and all.

SIGHTS

Église Notre-Dame – This is the former church of the monastery founded in Montier in 672, which followed the rule of St Columba (an Irish monk who founded Luxeuil abbey, see LUXEUIL-LES-BAINS). The present edifice was built between the 10C and 13C. Damaged by fire in June 1940, it was remarkably well restored. The conventual buildings were razed in 1850.

The **nave** is the oldest part of the building: eight rounded arches rest on low rectangular piers. Above, there is a row of twinned openings separated by cylindrical or polygonal colonnettes. Above them are the clerestory windows. The timber vaulting is a copy of the 16C vaulting.

The **chancel★** (12C-13C) is a splendid example of Early Gothic in the Champagne region. It consists of four-storey elevations:
– main arcades resting on twinned columns decorated with strange grotesques,
– upper gallery with twinned arches surmounted by an oculus,
– triforium with trefoil arches,
– clerestory windows separated by colonnettes.

A row of columns separates the radiating chapels from the ambulatory; the deep apsidal chapel is surmounted by an elegant ribbed Gothic vault.

Haras ⊙ – This stud farm, situated on the site of the former abbey, on the left of the church, looks after some 40 stallions and 15 horses for various riding clubs.

EXCURSIONS

★★Lac du Der-Chantecoq –
See Lac du DER-CHANTE-COQ.

★CHURCHES OF THE DER AREA

60km/37mi tour starting from Montier-en-Der – allow 3hr

Drive out of Montier-en-Der along the Brienne road.

Ceffonds – The **Église St-Rémi**, rebuilt round its Romanesque belfry at the

> ### Horse Sense
>
> The Ardennes horse is one of most sought-after breed of draught horses in France. This small, tough, calm and docile horse is essentially bred in northeast France, that is Champagne, Ardennes, Lorraine and Alsace. It is extremely useful on farms, in the fields and in forests but is also used for leisure activities (riding, barouche trips, horse-drawn caravaning, touring along bridle paths).
>
> A competition, which takes place in Sedan every September, brings together the best representatives of the Ardennes breed.

beginning of the 16C, stands in the disused cemetery which has retained a 16C stone cross. The church is entered through a Renaissance doorway added to the west front in 1562. Note, on the inside wall, the interesting 16C mural depicting St Christopher and, in the first chapel on the south side, the unusual stone christening fonts; on the north side, the Holy Sepulchre chapel contains a 16C Entombment including 10 polychrome stone statues.

The transept and the chancel are decorated with fine 16C **stained-glass windows★** made in the famous workshops of the city of Troyes: in the chancel, you can see from left to right St Rémi's legend, Christ's Passion and Resurrection and the Creation; in the transept, to the left of the chancel, the legend of St Crépin and St Crépinien, patron saints of tanners and cobblers who made a present of the stained glass to the church; in the transept, to the right of the chancel, a Tree of Jesse;

As you come out of the church, look at the old timber-framed house.

Turn back towards Montier-en-Der then left onto D 173.

Puellemontier – Timber-framed houses are scattered in the fields. The **church** is surmounted by a slender pointed steeple; the nave dates from the 12C but the chancel is more recent (16C); in the south transept, two 16C statues of St Cyre and St Flora stand on either side of a stained-glass window representing a Tree of Jesse (1531), one of several fine stained-glass windows made in the workshops of Troyes in the 16C.

Continue along D 173 then D 62 to Lentilles.

The road runs close to the peaceful **Étang de la Horre** (250ha/618 acres), lined with tall grass.

★Lentilles – This is a typical Der village with a well-ordered street plan and low timber-framed houses. the church is a fine 16C edifice whose timber frame is strengthened by horizontal and oblique timbers. The pointed octagonal spire is covered with shingles and the wooden porch is surmounted by a statue of St James.

Follow D 2 to Chavanges.

Chavanges – The church, dating from the 15C and 16C, has a 12C doorway; it contains several interesting 16C stained-glass windows and statues from the 14C to 16C.
Opposite the church, there is a splendid 18C timber-framed house flanked by a square turret.

Drive east along D 56 to Bailly-le-Franc.

Bailly-le-Franc – Hardly restored during the past centuries, the church has remained the simplest and most authentic of all the churches of the Der region.

Follow D 127 to Joncreuil.

Joncreuil – The church, surmounted by an imposing timber-framed steeple, has a Romanesque nave and a 13C chancel.

Arrembécourt – Note the carved doorway of the church and, inside, the stained-glass window depicting the Crucifixion.

Continue along D 6 then D 58.

Drosnay – This village has retained a few timber-framed buildings including some houses and the church which contains a carved-wood altarpiece over the high altar.

Drive along D 55 to Outines.

Bailly-le-Franc – Village church

Outines – This is a typical Der village with its timber-framed cob-wall houses and its church surmounted by a pointed steeple covered with shingles.

Châtillon-sur-Broué. – *See Lac du DER-CHANTECOQ.*

Droyes – The brick-built church comprises a Romanesque nave and a 16C chancel.

Take D 13 to return to Montier-en-Der.

Churches are floodlit every night from May to September, at weekends only during the rest of the year. Other churches and some edifices situated round the Lac du Der-Chantecoq are also floodlit: Éclaron, Giffaumont, St-Rémy-en-Bouzemont, Larzicourt, Arrigny and the museum-village of Ste-Marie-du-Lac-Nuisement.

MONTMÉDY

population 1 943
Michelin map 57 fold 1 or 241 fold 15

There are two towns in one: Montmédy-Bas (lower town) and Montmédy-Haut (upper town), fortified during the Renaissance and remodelled by Vauban, which has retained its ramparts.
Montmédy belonged to the duke of Burgundy, to the Hapsburgs and to Spain before being ceded to France in 1659. It was then that Vauban altered the town's defence system.

MONTMÉDY-HAUT

The upper town is perched on an isolated peak. On the north side, two successive gates fitted with drawbridges and an archway lead inside the walled town.

★**Citadelle** ⊘ – A walk along the ramparts, past glacis, curtain walls, bastions and underground passages, gives a good idea of the complexity and ingenious design of the citadel's defence system. From the top of the ramparts, the **view** extends over the lower town, the Chiers Valley and numerous surrounding villages.

189

Musées de la Fortification et Jules Bastien-Lepage ⊙ – Situated at the entrance of the citadel, these museums are devoted respectively to the history of fortifications (models, historic documents, audio-visual presentation) and to the life and work of a native of the region, the painter Jules Bastien-Lepage (1848-1884).

Église – This vast church dating from the mid 18C has retained its stalls and woodwork decorating the chancel.

EXCURSIONS

★★**Avioth** – 8.5km/5.3mi north along D 110. See Basilique d'AVIOTH.

Marville – 12.5km/7.8mi southeast along N 43.
Founded in Gallo-Roman times under the name of Major villa, Marville is situated on a promontory jutting out between the valleys of the Othain and the Crédon. It was under Spanish rule during the first half of the 17C while being granted the privileges of a free city. There are a few 16C and 17C houses to be seen along the Grand'Rue, walking towards the Grande-Place.
The building of the **Église St-Nicolas** was started in the 13C, but the major part of the edifice is in 14C Gothic style and includes a five-bay nave with aisles on either side. Wealthy merchants and corporations had chapels added towards the end of the 15C. Note the early-16C balustrade of the organ loft and, in the chapel situated in the south transept, the beautiful Virgin (13C-14C), which once decorated the west portal.

Cimetière de la chapelle St-Hilaire ⊙ – The tarmacked path leading to the cemetery branches off N 43. Situated at the top of the hill, the cemetery of the former Église St-Hilaire contains some interesting funeral monuments (now mostly inside the chapel). Note, in particular, a Christ in bonds and above all a beautiful Pietà with the statues of the apostles decorating the base. The walled ossuary is said to house 40 000 skulls.

Louppy-sur-Loison – 14km/8.7mi south. Leave Montmédy by N 43 towards Longuyon then turn right in Iré-le-Sec.
The Renaissance **castle** ⊙ built at the beginning of the 17C by Simon de Pouilly, who was the governor of Stenay (see Vallée de la MEUSE), is still owned by his descendants. The tour of the exterior enables visitors to admire the dovecote, the chapel and some richly carved doorways.
Ruins of a fortress can be seen near the church.

MONTMIRAIL

Population 3 812
Michelin map 56 fold 15 or 237 folds 21 and 22

The low roughcast houses of this once fortified town cling to the slopes of a promontory overlooking the rural valley of the Petit Morin.
Paul de Gondi, who later became the famous **Cardinal de Retz**, was born in Montmirail castle in 1613. After the death of Cardinal Richelieu and Louis XIII, this dangerous schemer used his ecclesiastical influence to destabilise the regency of Anne of Austria during Louis XIV's childhood. The 17C brick-and-stone castle was acquired in 1685 by one of Louis XIV's ministers, the **Marquis de Louvois**, who remodelled it, had French-style gardens laid and invited the king. His great-granddaughter married the Duc de La Rochefoucauld whose descendants still own the castle.
A column surmounted by a gilt eagle (4km/2.5mi northwest of Montmirail along RD 933) commemorates one of the last battles won by **Napoleon** in 1814 over Russian and Prussian troops.
A century later, in September 1914, the German army commanded by Von Bülow was attacked here by French troops under the command of Foch and Franchet d'Esperey who managed to stop the German advance.

VALLÉE DU PETIT MORIN

38km/24mi drive from Verdelot to Baye – allow 2hr

This tributary of the Marne, which takes its source in a marshland area east of Montmirail (see Marais de ST-GOND), flows through undulating meadows, marshy in places, dotted with groves and rows of poplars. Traditional houses, with roughcast walls underlined by brickwork and roofs covered with flat brown tiles, nestle round village churches.

From Montmirail, drive west along D 933 to Viels-Maisons then turn left onto D 15 to Verdelot.

Verdelot – The imposing **church** ⊙, dating from the 15C-16C, stands on the hillside. Note the intricate vaulting and the height of the aisles almost level with the chancel vaulting. On either side of the chancel, there are small statues of St Crépin and St Crépinien, patron saints of cobblers, to whom the church is dedicated. A sitting Virgin in carved walnut (Notre-Dame-de-Pitié de Verdelot), forming part of a 19C altarpiece, is reminiscent of 12C or 13C representations of the Virgin carved in the Auvergne and Languedoc regions.

Drive east along D 31, then D 20 and D 241, which follow the Petit Morin.

The valley widens and Montmirail appears, perched on its promontory.

Montmirail – *See above.*

From Montmirail, drive into the valley then continue eastwards along D 43.

The road goes through charming villages.

Abbaye du Reclus ⊙ – A holy hermit called Hugues-le-Reclus, retired to this remote vale (c 1123) and gave it his name. In 1142, St Bernard founded a Cistercian abbey which was partly destroyed during the Wars of Religion then rebuilt. Parts of the 12C abbey (east gallery of the cloister, chapter-house, sacristy) were discovered beneath the present monastery building.

Beyond Talus-St-Prix, turn left towards Baye.

Baye – This village lies in the valley of a tributary of the Petit Morin. St Alpin, a native of Baye who became bishop of Châlons, was buried in the 13C church. The 17C castle has retained a 13C chapel believed to have been designed by Jean d'Orbais.

MONTMORT-LUCY

Population 583
Michelin map 56 folds 15 and 16 or 237 fold 22

Occupying a pleasant site overlooking the River Surmelin, Montmort is the ideal starting point of excursions through the valley and the surrounding woodland area dotted with picturesque lakes.

Château ⊙ – Standing on high ground, the castle occupies a commanding position above the Surmelin Valley. Some parts date from the 12C, but the castle was rebuilt at the end of the 16C. It belonged at one time to Pierre Rémond de Montmort (1678-1719), an esteemed mathematician who published an essay on games of chance. In 1914, it was here that General von Bülow ordered the retreat from the Marne *(see MONTMIRAIL).*

The edifice, which shows a fine brick bond with white-stone facing, still retains a certain feudal aspect with its 14m/46ft deep moat. During the tour, visitors can admire the well-preserved bread oven, a beautiful Renaissance doorway (1577), the guards' room and the kitchens. The lower part of the castle can be reached by a ramp designed for horses, similar to that of Amboise Castle.

Église – Still surrounded by a cemetery, the church has an interesting porch, a Romanesque nave, a 13C transept, a second transept and an early-16C chancel (stained-glass windows of the same period). In the nave there is an 18C pulpit.

EXCURSIONS

Étoges – *6km/3.7mi southeast along D 18.*
Étoges is a wine-growing village close to the Côte des Blancs. There is a fine view of the elegant 17C castle from the bridge spanning the moat: pink-brick buildings with white-stone ties and facings, high French-style roofs covered with pale-purple slates. The edifice was restored in 1991 and turned into a hotel.
The 12C church, remodelled in the 15C and 16C, has a Gothic rose-window and a Renaissance doorway; it contains several 16C recumbent figures.

Forêt de la Charmoye – *12km/7.5mi round tour through the Charmoye Forest; about 30min.*
Drive east along D 38.

The road follows the green secluded valley of the Surmelin, runs past the Château de la Charmoye, a former abbey, and enters the Charmoye Forest.

Take the first road on the right towards Étoges; it goes through thick woods; turn right again onto D 18 to Montmort.

There is a picturesque view of the pink castle with its bluish roof.

Orbais-l'Abbaye – *9.5km/5.9mi northwest of Montmort along D 18, then left onto D 11.*
An important Benedictine abbey was founded here in the 7C. The village makes a pleasant outing and can also be the starting point of excursions through the Surmelin Valley and Vassy Forest. The **church★** ⊙ includes the chancel and transept of the former abbey church as well as two bays from the original nave (one being used as a porch, the other forming part of the interior). The other bays and the

west front flanked by two towers were destroyed in 1803. The building of the church (end of the 12C and 13C) was most probably supervised by Jean d'Orbais, one of the master builders of Reims cathedral.

As you walk round the edifice, note the unusual positioning of the flying buttresses of the transept and of the apse which meet on the same abutment; the slender spire surmounting the crossing date from the 14C.

Inside, the **chancel**★, with its ambulatory and radiating chapels, is considered as the prototype of that of Reims cathedral; the sanctuary is remarkably well designed: pointed arcades supporting a lofty triforium and clerestory windows surmounted by oculi.

The entrance of the transept, which replaces the nave, is furnished with early-16C stalls: the parcloses are decorated with representations of the apostles except the first two which depict a Tree of Jesse on the right and the Virgin on the left. The misericords and cheeks are carved with amusing figures. The axial chapel contains a 13C stained-glass window illustrating scenes from the Old Testament.

The well-preserved monastery buildings include a fine 13C hall, used as a winter chapel.

Fromentières – *11km/6.8mi southwest. Leave Montmort by RD 951 towards Sézanne; in Champaubert, turn right onto RD 933 to Fromentières.*

The plain village church contains a monumental Flemish altarpiece, carved and painted at the beginning of the 16C, which was bought by the vicar in 1715 for a very modest sum. The signature, a "severed hand", is the legendary emblem of Antwerp. The altarpiece is behind the high altar. The paintings decorating the side panels depict episodes of the New Testament whereas the central panel comprises three tiers of delicately carved scenes; the refined expressive figures, originally painted with bright colours against a gilt background, illustrate Christ's life and Passion.

La MOSELLE

Michelin maps 62 folds 4, 5, 15, 16 and 66 folds 7, 8 or 242 folds 5, 6, 30, 34, 35

The River Moselle takes its source in the Vosges mountains, near Bussang *(see Upper valley of the Moselle below)* and soon turns into a peaceful river meandering through rural landscapes. Neuves-Maisons marks the beginning of the Côtes de Moselle and of a vast industrialised region centred on the extraction of iron ore, with two highly concentrated areas, one along the Fensch and Orne valleys *(see THIONVILLE)*, the other round Longwy (Chiers Valley). Between Neuves-Maisons and Thionville, the Moselle is therefore lined with industrial towns where foundries, steelworks, sheet-metal works and wireworks are traditionally established.

Harnessing the Moselle – An international agreement signed in 1956 by France, the Federal Republic of Germany and the Grand Duchy of Luxemburg launched a vast harnessing project intended to open the section of the Moselle from Koblenz to Thionville to 3 000t convoys. It was inaugurated in 1964. Further harnessing work undertaken upstream as far as Neuves-Maisons was completed in 1979.

Harbour activities in Thionville-Illange, Mondelange-Richemont, Hagondange, Metz, Nancy-Frouard and Neuves-Maisons are essentially connected with the unloading of coal, iron ore and fertilizers and with the loading of metalwork, slag, cereals, foodstuffs and building materials.

Pleasure cruising and water sports have expanded rapidly along the Moselle which now has several stretches of smooth water equipped for sailing, canoeing, water skiing etc. In addition, efforts to reduce the pollution have led to an increase in the fish population. Finally, cycle paths have been laid along the river banks.

★UPPER VALLEY OF THE MOSELLE

101km/63mi – allow 4hr 30min – Local map see p 74

This itinerary follows the Moselle upstream from Épinal to Bussang where it takes its source, at the heart of the Vosges mountains.

★Épinal – *See ÉPINAL.*

From Épinal, a scenic road follows the east bank of the river, offering lovely vistas of the Moselle and running past striking sandstone escarpments just before reaching Archettes.

In Archettes, cross over to the other bank.

Arches – Arches is known for its traditional paper industry; a paper mill was already operating here in 1469. **Beaumarchais**, the famous playwright, author of the *Barber of Seville* and the *Marriage of Figaro*, bought the mill in 1779 in order to produce the necessary paper for the complete edition of Voltaire's works. As most of the great philosopher's writings had been banned in France, he set up a printing press in Kehl (across the Rhine from Strasbourg). This resulted in two editions, both known as the "Kehl editions", which are today much sought after by book lovers. The factory now turns out high-quality paper for books and prints as well as drawing paper, special paper and industrial paper.

Eloyes – This small town has thriving textile and food-processing industries.

★**Tête des Cuveaux** – *5km/3mi east of Eloyes, then 30min on foot there and back. Follow the road leading to the ridge line marked by a spruce forest and leave the car in the parking area (picnic area).*
Walk to the right along the ridge line to a viewpoint *(viewing table at the top)*. There is a beautiful **panoramic view**★ of the Moselle Valley, the Plateau lorrain and the Vosges mountains.
After driving through several industrial centres and getting past the moraine left behind by the Moselle glacier, which raised the bottom of the valley, one reaches Remiremont. The road offers fine views of the town and of the wooded heights surrounding it.

Remiremont – *See REMIREMONT.*
A lovely drive through the forest leads to the ridge *(D 57)* which, from Remiremont to Col des Croix, separates the deep and wide furrow followed by the Moselle from a vast glacial plateau dotted with small lakes and drained by tributaries of the Saône.
The road affords glimpses of the slopes on both sides of the ridge.

La Beuille – *Drive 6km/3.7mi along D 57 then turn left onto a tarmacked path leading to the parking area overlooking the Chalet de la Beuille, a refuge owned by the Amis de la Nature (Nature Lovers Association).* From the terrace-viewpoint at the chalet, there is a fine **view**★ of the Moselle Valley and of the Ballon d'Alsace in the distance.
At Col des Croix, turn northeast onto D 486 to Le Thillot, ignoring D 16 which winds its way past the Ballon de Servance down to Plancher-les-Mines.

Le Thillot – Many tourists go through this lively industrial centre (weaving, spinning, tanning, industrial woodwork) on their way to visit the surrounding area and the highest summits of the Vosges mountains.

St-Maurice-sur-Moselle – *See Parc Naturel Régional des BALLONS DES VOSGES p 73.*
Between St-Maurice and Bussang, morainic deposits at the bottom of the valley have created a lanscape of rolling hills crowned by wooden-gabled farmhouses.

Bussang – Bussang, lying in a picturesque setting near the source of the River Moselle, is both a summer and winter resort.
The **Théâtre du Peuple** (folk theatre) founded in 1895, consists of a mobile stage using nature as its background and can seat 1 100 spectators. The actors, many of them local inhabitants, give performances of folk plays as well as plays by Shakespeare, Molière etc.

★★**Petit Drumont** – *15min on foot there and back. Turn onto the forest road branching off D 89 just before the Col de Bussang.*
At that point, you are barely 100m/110yd from the **source of the Moselle** (alt 715m/2 346ft – monument by Gilodi, 1965).
Leave the car near the inn and follow the path which rises through high pastures.
At the summit of Petit Drumont (alt 1 200m/3 846ft), there is a viewing table forming two semicircles. The **panorama**★★ extends from the Hohneck to the Ballon d'Alsace. The Swiss Alps can be seen to the south when the weather is clear.

Col de Bussang – At the pass (alt 731m/2 398ft) stands the monument marking the source of the Moselle, which at this point is no more than a small stream. It soon swells to a powerful torrent to reach the size of an impressive river by the time it flows through Rupt-sur-Moselle. Having become definitely tamer, it then meanders through wooded hills towards Remiremont and Épinal.
From the pass, you can drive down towards the Thur Valley (see Vallée de la THUR).

FROM THIONVILLE TO SIERCK-LES-BAINS
49km/30mi – allow 1hr 30min

This itinerary explores the hilly countryside lying on the north bank of the Moselle, between the thriving industrial town of Thionville and the peaceful ancient city of Sierck.

Thionville – *See THIONVILLE.*
From Thionville, drive north along N 53.

Roussy-le-Village – The modern Église St-Denis (1954), built of stone and concrete contains interesting carvings by Kaeppelin and stained-glass windows by Barillet.
Drive southeast along D 56 then turn right onto D 57 to Boust.

Boust – Standing on high ground, the stone-built Église St-Maximin (1962), designed by Pingusson, has a remarkable circular nave prolonged by a long chancel flanked by a campanile.
Return to D 56.

Usselkirch – The cemetery stretches along the road on the right. Inside stands solitary Romanesque tower, which is all that remains of the 12C church; the mai alleyway is lined with the eight Stations of the Cross carved in stone in the 17C or 18C

On the way to Cattenom, you can see, on your right, the 165m/541ft cooling tower of the **Centre nucléaire de production de Cattenom** ⊘ which comprises four units with a output of 1 300 million watts each. The centre produces 30 billion kWh every yea

Just before Cattenom (Romanesque belfry) turn left onto D 1 then left onto D 62 a you reach Fixem.

Rodemack – From its prosperous medieval past, this ancient city, situated 5km/3mi from the border between France and Luxemburg, has retained an impos ing fortress restored in the 17C and a fortified gate with two round towers. The grey-roughcast village houses with arched windows, the cellars and barn entrance are all characteristic of the architectural style of the Lorraine region. The simple church, dating from 1783, contains interesting statues and furniture.

Like many villages in the region, Rodemack has its *Bildstöcke* (votive crosses); ther is one on place de la Fontaine and another on the corner of the road leading to th 19C castle overlooking the village.

Return to Fixem and drive straight on past the church to join D 64.

Haute-Kontz – From the terrace in front of the church, which has an 11C belfry there is a fine **view** of a meander of the Moselle and of the village of Rettel on th opposite bank.

The road runs alongside the Moselle to Contz-les-Bains then crosses the river t reach Sierck-les-Bains.

Sierck-les-Bains – *See SIERCK-LES-BAINS.*

MOUZON ★

Population 2637
Michelin map 56 fold 10 or 241 folds 10 and 14

This small town, lying on the banks of the River Meuse, was originally a Gaulis trading centre (Mosomagos) then a Roman military post. The Frankish king Clovi offered it to St Remi (who had christened the king c 498), and it later became favourite residence of the archbishops of Reims. United with France in 1379, Mouzo was besieged by the Holy Roman Emperor Charles V in the 16C, by the Spaniards an by Condé in the mid 17C. The fortifications were demolished in 1671 except for th 15C **Porte de Bourgogne**. The last factory to produce industrial felt is based in Mouzon.

SIGHTS

★**Église Notre-Dame** – The construction of this ancient abbey church, started at th end of the 12C and was completed in just over 30 years, except for the towers which were built in the 15C (north tower) and 16C (south tower). The west-fron central doorway is richly carved: Virgin and Child on the upright post and, on th tympanum (from left to right and bottom to top), the Death of the Virgin, th Martyrdom of St Susanna and St Victor of Mouzon, the Visitation, the Coronatio of the Virgin, the Annunciation.

The interior *(see page 38)* is imposing. The nave and the chancel rest on massiv round piers, as in Laon cathedral on which Mouzon is modelled. The upper galler goes all the way round the nave and the chancel, above the ambulatory and th radiating chapels. The 18C furniture is noteworthy, in particular the organ and th carved-wood organ case (1725), the only remaining example of the work c Christophe Moucherel in northern France.

The late-17C conventual buildings, situated to the left of the church, have bee turned into a pensioners' home. The French-style gardens offer a pleasant walk.

Musée du Feutre ⊘ – The Felt Museum, housed in one of the abbey's forme farmhouses, is devoted to the history and manufacture of felt from its tradition use in daily life (carpets and coats of nomadic stockbreeders in Turkey an Afghanistan) to its industrial use (floor coverings, filters) or its more current us (hats, slippers, decorative objects). The reconstruction of a production line (on reduced scale) helps visitors to understand the manufacturing process. There is a exhibition of contemporary designs as well as workshops for children and adults.

Musée de la Tour de la Porte de Bourgogne ⊘ – This small museum illustrate 2 000 years of local history and includes finds from the Flavier archeological site.

EXCURSION

Site gallo-romain du Flavier – *4km/2.5mi southeast on D 964 to Stenay.*
The remains of a Gallo-Roman sanctuary, discovered on this site in 1966, includ the foundations of three small temples *(information panels).*

Situated on the northern foothills of the Sungdau, Mulhouse has several attractive features including its rich past as an independent republic, its strong industrial tradition and its prestigious museums.

This modern and dynamic town has, since 1975, been the seat of the Université de Haute-Alsace, which specialises in high technology, working on the principle of close links between training, research and industry.

From the top of the Tour de l'Europe (FY) *(tearoom, revolving restaurant)*, there is a good overall **view** of the town and the surrounding area.

MULHOUSE: CITY AND REPUBLIC

A passion for independence – From the 12C onwards, Mulhouse strived to liberate itself from its feudal bonds and in 1308 it acquired the status of an imperial city, thus becoming a virtually independent republic, acknowledging the Holy Roman Emperor as its sole suzerain. Encouraged by the latter, Mulhouse formed, with nine other imperial cities, a league of defence against the power of the nobility, known as **Decapolis**.

In the mid 15C, the town's guilds became politically powerful; they installed a kind of oligarchic government and the Republic freed itself from imperial control. In 1515, under threat from the Hapsburgs' territories which completely surrounded it, Mulhouse left Decapolis and entered into an alliance with the **Swiss cantons**, an inspired decision which placed the town under the protection of the kingdom of France: the intervention of Henri IV in favour of his allies and the cession to France of the Hapsburgs' possessions in Alsace under the treaty of Westphalia (1648) enabled the Republic to retain its independence. Even the revocation of the Edict of Nantes in 1685 did not really threaten this bastion of calvinism which remained the only Alsatian territory not under French control after the Sun King had annexed Strasbourg in 1681.

In the 18C, low custom duties imposed on goods entering France and the possibility for Mulhouse to trade freely with foreign states, favoured the town's commercial activities and encouraged it to launch into industrial expansion.

Calvinist citadel – In 1524, the Republic's government adopted the principles of the Reformation and a little later on adhered to Calvinism. As a consequence, theatrical performances were banned, inns had to close at 10pm and the citizens' clothing had to be discreet in style and colour. However, the spirit of the new religion also had its positive aspects: it spurred industrial development and prompted original social and cultural initiatives.

ON THE TOWN

Theatres and concert halls

The **Filature** (20 allée Nathan-Katz) is a cultural centre which stages performances with the Orchestre symphonique de Mulhouse and the Ballet du Rhin and gives regular concerts, opening its doors to major national ensembles.

In the **Théâtre de la Sinne** (39 rue de la Sinne), theatre companies such as the Tréteaux de Haute-Alsace (intended for a young audience), the Théâtre alsatien and numerous regional theatrical associations perform in turn.

L'**Entrepôt** (50 rue du Nordfeld) is an exhibition and conference centre and a place where café-concert shows are presented and the Théâtre de la Ruelle gives performances of its recent creations.

The **Noumatrouff** (57 rue de la Mertzau) organises shows for youngsters as well as various music shows.

Bars, cafés and discotheques

The **Brasserie O'Neil**, place des Victoires, specialises in beer; the **Taverne des chevaliers teutoniques**, passage Teutonique, sells well-known Alsatian wines by the glass; the **Brasil Café**, rue du Raisin, serves cocktails and punch to the sound of South-American music; **L'Aiglon**, avenue Auguste-Wicky, is an American bar; **Charlie's Bar**, rue de la Sinne, is the lively piano-bar of the Hôtel du Parc; the **Glen Coe**, 143 avenue de Colmar, serves a wide choice of beers and nearly 40 different whiskies in a typical Scottish setting; the **Club 1900**, 3 rue des Halles, is a discotheque which organises themed evenings on Thursdays and becomes a traditional dance hall on Sundays; the **Caesar Palace**, the largest discotheque in the area, is situated on rue Vauban.

Union with France – In 1792, the new French Republic imposed a commercial blockade on Mulhouse and the town opted for union with France. During the union festivities which took place in 1798 on place de la Réunion, the flag of the city was rolled inside a case bearing the colours of the French flag and the following inscription was written on the case: *La République de Mulhouse repose dans le sein de la République française (the Republic of Mulhouse Rests in the Bosom of the French Republic).*

Together with the rest of Alsace, Mulhouse was German from 1870 to 1918 and from 1940 to 1944. It took the French first armoured-car division two months to completely liberate the town.

★PLACE DE LA REUNION,
the historic centre of Mulhouse

★★**Hôtel de ville** (FY H¹) – Erected in 1552 by an architect from Basle in a kind of Renaissance style characteristic of the Rhine region and decorated on the outside by artists from the Constance area, this edifice is unique in France. In 1698, Jean Gabriel, a native of Mulhouse, designed an entirely new decoration (adding the allegorical figures for instance) which is still admired today. The shields bearing the arms of the Swiss cantons, which decorate the façade on either side of the covered steps leading to the entrance, are a reminder of the historic ties linking the city and the Swiss Confederation.

On the right side of the building, you can see a grinning stone mask similar to the *Klapperstein* or gossips' stone weighing 12-13kg/26-28lb, which was tied to the neck of slanderers condemned to go round the town riding backwards on a donkey. This punishment was used for the last time in 1781.

The tour of the history museum shows part of the interior of the town hall, in particular the **council chamber** on the first floor, once the council chamber of the Republic's government and now the municipal council chamber.

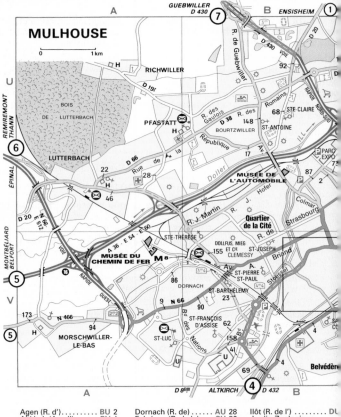

Agen (R. d')	BU 2	Dornach (R. de)	AU 28	Ilôt (R. de l')	DU
Altkirch (Av. d')	BV 4	Fabrique (R. de la)	CU 36	Jardin-Zoologique	
Bâle (Rte de)	CU 7	Frères-Lumière		(R. du)	CV
Bartholdi (R.)	CV 8	(R. des)	BV 41	Juin (R. A.)	CU
Belfort (R. de)	AV 9	Gambetta (Bd Léon)	CV 42	Katz (Allée Nathan)	CL
Belgique (Av. de)	CU 12	Gaulle		Kingersheim (R. de)	BU
Bourtz (R. Sébastien)	BU 17	(R. du Gén. de)	AU 46	Lagrange (R. Léo)	BV
Briand (R. Aristide)	AU 22	Hardt (R. de la)	CU 51	Lefèbvre (R. de)	BV
Brunstatt (R. de)	BV 23	Hollande (Av. de)	CU 57	Lustig (R. Auguste)	BV
Bolflfus		Ile-Napoléon (R. de l')	CU 58	Mer-Rouge	
(Av. Gustave)	CV 27	Illberg (R. de l')	BV 62	(R. de la)	AV

★★Musée historique ⊘ **(FY)** – The rich and varied collections of this museum, carefully displayed to take into account the building and its past, illustrate the history of the town and daily life in the region.

The first floor was the official floor of the government of the Republic; it houses the medieval collections.

On the second floor, there are various objects of historic interest: paintings, manuscripts, weapons, furniture... including the original Klapperstein and the **silver-gilt cup** offered by the town to the representative of the French government in 1798 when Mulhouse was united with France. Daily life in the 18C and 19C is illustrated by the reconstruction of various drawing rooms; note an unusual bed concealed as a painted cabinet and a large blue-and-white-ceramic stove.

The former **corn loft** (access from the second floor across a footbridge built in the 18C), contains a collection of toys: doll's houses, outfits, crockery, games. The folk-art gallery houses reconstructions of regional interiors (kitchen and bedroom from the Sungdau area), pottery, woodcarvings etc. Note the monumental mechanical piano dating from the beginning of the 20C and an 18C sledge.

The loft itself (early-16C timber work) contains collections of coins and medals, gold plate, pewter and shop signs.

The third floor houses archeological collections, from prehistoric to Gallo-Roman times, including neolithic jewellery.

Temple St-Étienne ⊘ **(FY)** – This neo-Gothic building has retained several 14C **stained-glass windows★** from the previous church demolished in 1858; the most interesting, inspired by the *Salvation Mirror*, a famous work dating from 1324, illustrate the concordances between the Old and the New Testaments.

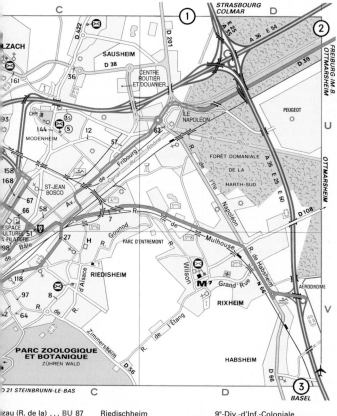

...zau (R. de la) ... BU 87
...rrand (Av. F.) ... BV 90
...ouse (Fg de) ... BU 92
...ouse (R. de)
...ZACH .... CU 93
...ouse (R. de)
...ORSCHWILLER-
...BAS. .... AV 94
...ting
...Emilio) .... CV 97
...feld (R. du) ..... CV 98

Riedischheim
  (Av. de). .... CV 118
Sausheim (R. de)... CU 144
Soultz (R. de) ...... BU 148
Thann (R. de) ...... BV 155
Vauban (R.)......... CU 158
Vosges (R. des) .... BCU 161
Wyler
  (Allée William) .... CU 168
1re-Armée-Française
  (R.) .... AV 173

9e-Div.-d'Inf.-Coloniale
  (R.) .... CV 175

M⁷ Musée
   du Papier peint
M⁸ Électropolis :
   musée de l'énergie
   électrique

Musée des Beaux-Arts ⊘ (FZ **M⁴**) – *A stone's throw from place de la Réunion.*
The fine arts museum contains works by Brueghel the Younger, Teniers, Ruysdael
Boucher and other 17C and 18C painters; 19C landscapes and mythological scenes
(Boudin, Courbet, Bouguereau); paintings by Alsatian artists: nudes and portraits by
Henner (1829-1905), landcapes and still-life paintings by **Lehmann** (1873-1953)
bright compositions by **Walch** (1896-1948).

THE "TOWN WITH A HUNDRED CHIMNEYS"

In 1746, three natives of Mulhouse, Samuel Koechlin, Jean-Jacques Schmaltzer and
Jean-Henri Dollfus, founded a manufacture of pattern-printing on fabric. These
fabrics, known as *indiennes* because they used to be made in India, were ther
extremely popular. The union with France gave a boost to the industrial development of Mulhouse which was nicknamed "the town of the hundred chimneys". A
the beginning of the 19C, the town diversified its activities: spinning, weaving
chemicals and mechanical engineering soon employed 1 000 workers. Rows of
factories lined the Chaussée de Dornach and the Steinbachlein. It was this anarchic
growth which prompted the two contrasting attempts at urban planning: the
"Nouveau Quartier" (new district) and the working-class garden-cities.

The "Nouveau Quartier" and the Société Industrielle – A new residential
complex intended for young industrialists was built from 1827 onwards on the
edge of the old town centre. Known as the **"Nouveau Quartier"**, it consisted of
arcaded buildings modelled on those of rue de Rivoli in Paris, surrounding a central
triangular garden, place de la Bourse; the Société Industrielle stands along the small
side of the triangle.
Founded in 1825 by 22 industrialists, including Koechlin, Schlumberger, Dollfus
Zuber, the **Société Industrielle de Mulhouse** aimed to promote and spread industrial
development but it also set out to play a role in the intellectual and artistic life of
the town by creating museums *(see below)* and to further education with the
opening of schools of chemistry, weaving, spinning and commerce (the first one of
its kind in France); in addition, it carried out a study of working-class housing
conditions as early as 1851.

Working-class garden-cities – Social urban planning launched by the Société
Industrielle was a novelty in Europe. From 1855 onwards, the "Cité de Mulhouse
and the "Nouvelle Cité" were built on both sides of the Ill diversion canal. Each
family had lodgings with a separate entrance and a small garden. A leasing system
enabled workers to become property owners. The availability of public services was
remarkable for the time. The Quartier de la Cité, which has been preserved round
the Église St-Joseph, is worth a visit, as the small houses (although many have
been transformed and enlarged) and their carefully tended plots are an eloquent
illustration of the ideals which once united industrial growth and popular welfare.

THE "TOWN WITH TWELVE MUSEUMS"

With its dozen museums and themed parks mainly devoted to industry and tech
nology, Mulhouse is a must for people with enquiring minds. This exceptional
concentration was the result of the philanthropic action of the Société Industrielle
convinced that museums contributed to the "moral improvement" of society. The
Museum of Industrial Design (later to become the Museum of Printed Fabrics) was
created as early as 1857; next came the Natural History Museum, the zoo, the Fine
Arts Museum... Recent creations, some of them unique in France, have completed
and enriched this pioneering work.

★★★Musée national de l'Automobile collection Schlumpf ⊘ (BU)

This fabulous collection of 500 vintage cars (not all of them are on permanent
display) was gathered with passionate enthusiasm over a period of 30 years by the
Schlumpf brothers, who owned a wool-spinning mill in the Thur Valley upstream of
Thann.
The textile recession, social unrest, the unwise acquisition of many expensive car
led to bankrupcy and a legal judgement enabled an association to acquire the
museum which was opened to the public in 1982.
The collection illustrates more than 100 years of motor-car history, from the
steam-driven Jacquot of 1878 to the Citroën Xenia of the year 2000; 98 European
makes and some rare, even unique specimens are displayed. The models are usually
in working order and several belonged to celebrities such as President Poincaré
(Panhard X26), King Leopold of Belgium (Bugatti 43 roadster sport) or Charlie
Chaplin (Rolls Royce Phantom III limousine).
Cars are exhibited along alleyways lined with turn-of-the-century lamp-posts; many
of them can be regarded as authentic works of art such is the refinement of their
bodywork (Peugeot 174 saloon, 1924), the smoothness of their aerodynamic line
(Bugatti Model 46, streamlined saloon, 1933), the finish of their wheels and hub

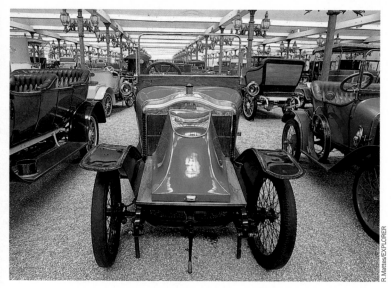

Vintage cars in the Automobile museum

(Gardner-Serpollet), the design of their radiator grill (Alfa Romeo saloon, 1936), the elegance of their radiator stoppers (Hispano-Suiza's stork) and the quality of their accessories (Renault NM small coupé, 1924).

The Bugatti section is something of a collection within the collection. Bugatti who settled in Molsheim in 1909 was extremely demanding regarding quality, reliability and finish (hence his 340 patents and 3 000 racing victories); this is illustrated by some 120 racing cars, sports cars and luxury cars.

The gems of this outstanding collection are two Bugatti Royales: a limousine and the "Napoleon coupé", Ettore Bugatti's personal car, sometimes considered as the most prestigious car of all times.

Other makes include Panhard et Levassor (the 1893 model was the first car to be presented on a catalogue with options), Mercedes (the 300SL GT saloon), Alfa Romeo (the light *Disco volante*, 1953; only three copies were made), Rolls-Royce (the legendary Silver Ghost, of which one model had silver plated accessories), Porsche, Ferrari, Gordini...The museum also follows the evolution of the three major French manufacturers before the Second World War and gives details of all the other makes which disappeared owing to the tendancy to concentrate which characterized the car industry (Ravel from Besançon, Zedel from Pontarlier, Vermorel from Villefranche-sur-Saône, Clément-Bayard from Mézières, Pilain from Lyon).

The technology of modern cars and tyres is explained in another building.

★Musée français du Chemin de fer ⊙ (AV)

Before starting on a tour of the railway museum, visitors can get acquainted with railways at the **Musée-express**, through models, games and interactive programmes.

The French Railways (SNCF) collection, splendidly displayed, illustrates the evolution of railways from their origin until today. Apart from engines and rolling stock, there is an important section devoted to various equipment: signals, rails, automatic coupling, shunting, level-crossing keeper's hut, swing bridge etc. The main hall invites visitors to get personally involved by means of video films, animated presentations; footbridges offering a view inside carriages, pits making it possible to walk beneath engines, driver's cabins open for inspection...

Mulhouse – French Railway Museum

199

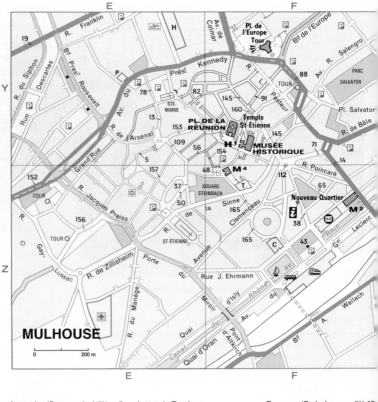

MULHOUSE

0   200 m

Augustins (Passage des)	EY	5	Lattre-de-Tassigny			
Bonbonnière (R.)	EY	13	(Av. Mar. de)	FY	71	
Bonnes-Gens (R. des)	FY	14	Lorraine (R. de)	EY	78	
Briand (Av. Aristide)	EY	19	Maréchaux (R. des)	EY	82	
Colmar (Av. de)	FY		Metz (R. de)	FY	88	
Fleurs (R. des)	EZ	37	Moselle (R. de la)	FY	91	
Foch (Av. du Mar.)	FZ	38	Prés.-Kennedy			
Gaulle (Pl. Gén. de)	FZ	43	(Av. du)	EFY		
Guillaume-Tell (Pl.)	EFZ	48	Raisin (R. du)	EY	109	
Halles (R. des)	EZ	50	République (Pl. de la)	FY	112	
Henriette (R.)	EY	56	Sauvage (R. du)	FY	145	
Joffre (Av. du Mar.)	FZ	65	Stoessel (Bd Charles)	EZ	152	

Tanneurs (R. des)	EY	15
Teutonique (Passage)	FY	15
Tour-du-Diable (R.)	EZ	15
Trois-Rois (R. des)	EZ	15
Victoires (Pl. des)	FY	16
Wicky (Av. Auguste)	FZ	16

H¹ Hôtel de ville
M² Musée de l'Impression
     sur étoffes
M⁴ Musée des Beaux-Arts

The panorama of steam engines which spans more than 100 years includes famou
engines such as the Saint-Pierre, built of teak, which ran between Paris and Roue
from 1844 onwards, the very fast Crampton (1852) which already reached speed
of around 120kph/75mph and the 232 U1 (1949), the last operating stear
engine. The museum also boasts the drawing-room carriage of Napoleon III'
aides-de-camp (1856) decorated by Viollet-le-Duc, a Pullman carriage (1926)
which formed part of the luxury train called "Flèche d'Or" running between Pari
and London, a sleeping car (1929) of the "Calais-Méditerranée-Express" or "Trai
Bleu" and the French President's carriage (1925) decorated by Lalique and fitte
with a solid-silver washbasin... In striking contrast, the bottom of the rang
includes one of the fourth-class carriages of the Alsace-Lorraine line.

Among electric engines there is the first electrically powered engine (1900), know
as the "boîte à sel" (salt box), designed to convey trains between the Orsay an
Austerlitz stations in Paris, and the famous BB 9004, which set the rail spee
record in 1955.

Note also the famous Bugatti "Presidential" railcar inaugurated by President Alber
Lebrun and the XM 5005 railcar running on tyres.

Goods transport is represented by the unusual self-powered luggage van of th
St-Gervais to Vallorcine line in the Alps, which, at the beginning of the century
carried the heavy luggage and skis of winter sports enthusiasts; a special wago
designed to carry wine from southern France; double-decker wagons with ope
upper deck, operating in the Paris suburbs until 1931.

Musée du Sapeur-Pompier – Housed under the same roof, the Fire Brigad
Museum displays some 20 hand pumps, the oldest dating from 1740, steam
powered fire engines, others dating from the early 20C, uniforms, weapons and
big collection of helmets.

There is also a reconstruction of the fire brigade watchtower in Mulhouse and c
the telephone exchange of the former fire station.

★★Parc zoologique et botanique ⊙ (CV)

This zoological and botanical garden, covering an area of 25ha/62 acres and sheltering more than 1 000 animals, aims at preserving, breeding and studying rare and endangered species by collaborating with other zoos and various agencies. This policy was launched with the arrival in 1980 of lemurs from Madagascar, followed by Prince Alfred's deer, of which only a small number had survived on two Philippine islands, then white-backed tapirs, wolves, panthers and rare primates from South America (tamarins, capuchins) housed in a building specially adapted for them in 1993.

Gibbons from China and Vietnam are a typical example of an endangered species placed under the protection of the park. The spectacular regression of this primate in its natural environment can be explained by deforestation and excessive hunting. These agile animals, with their characteristic cry, are extremely popular inmates of the zoo. Other interesting animals include sea-lions, jackass penguins, pythons... The large botanical collection is an array of rare species in beautifully landscaped areas.

A 20m/66ft viewing tower (Tour du Belvédère, *110 steps*), situated 300m/328yd southwest of the zoo *(along rue A-Lustig and rue A-de-Musset)*, offers a beautiful panorama of Mulhouse, the Black Forest, the Jura mountains and even the Alps when the weather is clear.

Other main museums

For a description of the Musée historique and Musée des Beaux-Arts, see Place de la Réunion p 196.

★**Electropolis: Musée de l'énergie électrique** ⊙ (AV M[8]) – A large masonry cube and an elliptical gallery surrounding it are the unusual setting of the exhibition showing the different stages of the production of electricity and its various uses. Many themes are dealt with: music, domestic appliances, computer science, laser, electronic toys, radio, satellites... Experiments and interactive games help to introduce the amazing world of electricity to visitors.

The "Galerie de Jupiter", 80m/88yd long, provides models of the different stages of production, the means of "transporting" electricity and its numerous uses.

Note the Sulzer steam engine coupled to a BBC alternator, which was one of the first to produce electricity.

The "Maison de l'électricité" occupying one of the pavilions in the garden, gives visitors an insight into tomorrow's comfort.

★**Musée de l'Impression sur étoffes** ⊙ (FZ M[2]) – Founded in 1955, the Museum of Printed Fabric displays textile collections gathered by industrialists and gradually enriched: three million samples, nearly 50 000 pieces (various lengths of fabric, bedcovers, shawls...). The rare and fragile samples are displayed in thematic exhibitions. The museum also illustrates the birth and development of the industry: engraving and printing techniques are explained, and impressive machines used throughout the ages are employed for regular demonstrations.

The museum shop which reprints original motifs offers a choice of tablecloths, shawls, scarfs, handkerchiefs and various accessories, along with books and stationery. This museum and its lovely shop are a must for anyone interested in fashion or interior design or the history of decorative arts.

Musée du Papier peint, Rixheim

Panoramic wallpaper on an Egyptian theme

201

★**Musée du Papier peint** ⊙ (DV **M**[7]) – *In Rixheim, 6km/3.7mi east towards Basle, see town plan p 197.*
The Wallpaper Museum, inaugurated in 1984, is housed in the right wing of the former headquarters of an order of Teutonic knights where, c 1790, Jean Zuber set up a wallpaper factory, still operating. The collection comprises some 130 000 documents. The museum also owns a priceless set of wallpaper from the Réveillon manufacture in Paris, which was plundered by Revolutionaries in 1789.
The huge printing presses, able to print up to 16 colours, are on the ground floor. The first floor is devoted to themed temporary exhibitions. The second floor houses a superb **collection**★★ of panoramic wallpaper exported throughout the world (but mainly to North America) during the 19C. Vast landscapes painted with fresh colours include views of Switzerland (1802), Hindoustan (1807), Eldorado and North America. Another panoramic view, entitled *Zones terrestres* (the World's regions, 1855), mixes views of a polar sea, Switzerland, Algeria, Bengal and Canada. The 21 rolls of this vast composition made use of 2 047 plates.

★★**Écomusée d'Alsace** – *14km/8.7mi north. See ÉCOMUSÉE D'ALSACE.*

Vallée de MUNSTER★★

Michelin map 87 folds 17 and 18 or 242 folds 31 and 35

Irish monks arrived in the area in the 7C to complete the Christianisation of Alsace and founded an abbey which gave its name to the village growing in its shadow (Munster comes from the Latin word for monastery). The village developed into a town, freed itself from the authority of the abbots and formed, with nine neighbouring villages, an independent municipality which became a member of Decapolis *(see MULHOUSE)*.
The Revolution ruined the abbey and dissolved the agreement uniting the villages of the Munster Valley which continued to live on its traditional cheese industry and on the textile industry introduced in the area in the 18C by André Hartmann.
Further up the Fecht Valley, to the south of Munster, the rounded summit of the Petit Ballon, also known as **Kahler Wasen**, stands in an area of high pastures where herds spend the summer and Munster cheese is made.

FROM COLMAR TO LAKE FISCHBOEDLE

33km/21mi – about 1hr – local map see p 75

★★★**Colmar** – *See COLMAR.*

Leave Colmar by ⑤ *on the town plan and continue along D 417.*

Straight ahead, on a hilltop, you can see the three keeps of Éguisheim and, on a height to the right, the hotels and villas of Les Trois-Épis overlooked by Le Galz and its commemorative monument. The road enters the wide **Vallée de la Fecht** and the ruins of the high keep of Pflixbourg castle, crowning a wooded knoll, soon come into view. The bottom of the valley, covered with meadows, becomes gradually narrower as the heights on either side get higher and higher.
The lower part of the sunny northern slopes is covered with vineyards.

Soultzbach-les-Bains – This peaceful medieval city, known for its spa, has a wealth of timber-framed flower-decked houses. A **historic trail** *(2km/1.2mi, 1hr 30min, brochure available from the tourist office)*, lined with 16 information panels, acquaints visitors with the history and traditions of the village.
The 17C **Chapelle Ste-Catherine** contains two interesting paintings (1738) by Franz-Georg Hermann, *Our Lady of Solace* and *St Nicholas of Tolentino*. The isolated parish **church** ⊙, extensively restored, houses three remarkable gilt **altars**★★ in carved wood made between 1720 and 1740. In the chancel, on the left, there is a fine 15C tabernacle carried by St Christopher. The Callinet organ dates from 1833.

Gunsbach – Albert Schweitzer spent part of his childhood in this village where his father was the vicar until his death in 1925. Schweitzer regularly came back here and had a house built after he won the Goethe prize in 1928; this is now a **museum** ⊙ housing furniture, books, photos, music, sermons and other mementoes of the great man.
There is an interesting **walking itinerary** *(4km/2.5mi, about 2hr 30min)* on the theme of "water" along the banks of the Flecht lined with explanatory panels. The southern slopes of the Flecht Valley are entirely forested. In Munster, the river divides into two arms, the Grande and Petite Flecht.

Munster – The only remaining wing of the former abbots' palace, situated south of the market square, is now the headquarters of the **Parc naturel régional des Ballons des Vosges**. The **Maison du Parc** suggests various activities to discover this fascinating environment and presents a permanent exhibition covering 600m²/718sq yd and illustrating the main feature of the park with the help of models, dioramas, video films and interactive terminals. Munster is also the starting point of excursions to the Petit Ballon *(see From Munster to the Petit Ballon below)*.

Continue along D 10 which follows the Grande Flecht Valley, offering ever finer views of the wooded slopes on either side as it penetrates deeper into the mountain.

Muhlbach-sur-Munster – The **Musée de la Schlitte** ⊘ stands on the village square, opposite the train station; which shows a reconstruction of the traditional natural environment in which sledges would carry timber from the dense forests of the Vosges mountains *(see Introduction p 21)*.

In Metzeral, take D 10^{VI}; turn right 1km/0.6mi further on, cross the river and leave the car. The footpath *(3km/1.9mi, about 1hr)* rises through the wild glacial valley of the Wormsa and reaches the Lac de Fischbœdle.

★**Lac de Fischbœdle** – Alt 790m/2 592ft. This almost circular lake, barely 100m/328ft in diameter, is one of the most picturesque lakes of the Vosges region. It was created c 1850 by Jacques Hartmann, the Munster industrialist. Rocks and firs reflecting in the water form a splendid setting. The Wasserfelsen stream supplying the lake forms a lovely waterfall at the time of the thaw.

Lac de Schiessrothried – *1hr on foot there and back along the winding path starting on the right as you reach Lake Fischbœdle. It is directly accessible by car from Muhlbach along D 310.* The lake, which covers 5ha/12 acres, now a reservoir, lies at an altitude of 920m/3 018ft, at the foot of the Hohneck summit.

Beyond Metzeral, follow the itinerary "From Munster to Le Markstein" (below) if you wish to join the Route des CRÊTES 3km/1.9mi before Le Markstein.

FROM MUNSTER TO COL DE LA SCHLUCHT

32km/20mi – about 1hr 30min – Local map see p 75

Munster – *See From Colmar to Lake Fischbœdle above.*
From Munster, drive northwest along D 417 then turn onto D 5^{B1} which winds its way up to Hohrodberg.

Hohrodberg – This summer resort spreads along sunny slopes which afford an extended **view**★★ to the southwest of Munster, its valley and, from left to right, the summits rising in the background from the Petit Ballon to the Hohneck. During the climb, stop by the picnic area and walk along the road as far as the bend.

Le Collet du Linge – On the right-hand side of the road lies a German military cemetery.

Le Linge – *30min.* Memorial and museum.
In 1915, following fierce fighting, French troops secured their position on the western slopes of the Linge and Schratzmaennele, close to German troops which occupied the summit. Walk to the right to reach the summit of the Linge, quite close, through what is left of the German position and of the trenches dug out of sandstone.

Continue along D 11^{VI} which soon overlooks the Orbey Valley.

Col du Wettstein – The cemetery contains the graves of 3 000 French soldiers.

D 48 then runs down into the valley of the Petite Fecht and joins up with D 417 near Soultzeren.
The road winds up towards Col de la Schlucht offering better and better views first of the Fecht Valley and then of the Petite Fecht Valley. The Hohneck can be seen to the south. The road leading to Lac Vert *(see Route des CRÊTES: Itinerary* ❶*)* branches off on the right just before a bend. The road then runs through a forested area, affording glimpses of the Plaine d'Alsace and of the Black Forest and finally overlooks the splendid glacial cirque where the Petite Fecht takes its source.

Col de la Schlucht – At the pass, D 417 joins up with the Route des Crêtes *(see Route des CRÊTES)*.

FROM MUNSTER TO THE PETIT BALLON

17km/11mi – about 2hr – Local map see p 75

Munster – *See From Colmar to Lake Fischbœdle above.*
Drive out of Munster along D 417 towards Colmar then turn right 5km/3mi further on and follow D 40.
Beyond Soultzbach, a scenic road *(D 43)* on the right follows the verdant pastures and forests of the Krebsbach Valley.
In **Wasserbourg**, turn onto a forest road leading to an inn *(Auberge Ried)* where there is a fine view of the Hohneck summit. After going through a wood, the road comes out into the open again. The Kahler Wasen farm-restaurant stands on pastureland and the **view**★ extends down the Fecht Valley towards Turckheim and, beyond, across the Plaine d'Alsace.

★★**Petit Ballon** – *Alt 1 267m/4 157ft. 1hr 15min on foot there and back from the Kahler Wasen farm-restaurant.*
The **panorama** is superb: the Plaine d'Alsace, the Kaiserstuhl hills and the Black Forest to the east; the Grand Ballon massif to the south; the valleys of the two Fecht rivers to the north and west.

Vallée de MUNSTER

FROM MUNSTER TO LE MARKSTEIN

22km/14mi – about 1hr 15min – Local map see p 75

Munster – *See From Colmar to Lake Fischbœdle above.*
Drive west out of Munster along D 10.

Muhlbach – *See From Colmar to Lake Fischbœdle above.*
Continue along D 10 beyond Metzeral towards Sondernach.

Beyond Sondernach, the road rises through pastures framed by woods. Just before a bend to the left, look towards the grass-covered summit of the Petit Ballon. The winding road enters the forest; from the second hairpin bend, there is a fine view of the Munster Valley and of Hohrodberg halfway up the mountainside. A little further on, the view embraces the Fecht Valley with Sondernach in the foreground, Metzeral further away and Hohrodberg and the Vosges summits in the distance. The nearby rounded Petit Ballon towers above the whole area. The road leading to Schnepfenried branches off to the right in a deep bend.

★**Schnepfenried** – This popular winter sports resort is equipped with several ski lifts. There is a beautiful **panorama**★ of the Hohneck massif to the north with the Schiessrothried dam and lake lower down on the slopes of the mountain; Munster can also be seen to the right. From the summit of Schnepfenried (alt 1258m/4 127ft), just south of the resort, which is accessible on foot *(1hr there and back)*, there is a panoramic **view**★ of the range from the Grand Ballon to the Brézouard, of the Fecht Valley, of the Black Forest and, when the weather is perfectly clear, of the Bern Oberland.
The road (D 27) continues to rise through woods and finally reaches the high-pasture area; fine view of the Hohneck to the right. Further on, it joins up with the Route des Crêtes affording a wide view of the Thur Valley.
Turn left onto the Route des Crêtes. As you pass beneath a ski lift, you will catch a glimpse of Lac de la Lauch below, of the Guebwiller Valley and of the Plaine d'Alsace in the distance.

Le Markstein – *See GUEBWILLER: Guebwiller Valley.*

THE VOSGES SUMMITS
Le Donon 1 009m/3 310ft
Champ du Feu 1 100m/3 609ft
Ballon de Servance 1 216m/3 990ft
Ballon d'Alsace 1 250m/4 101ft
Petit Ballon or Kahler Wasen 1 267m/4 157ft
Le Hohneck 1 362m/4 469ft
Grand Ballon or Ballon de Guebwiller 1 424m/4 672ft, highest summit.

FROM LE MARKSTEIN TO MUNSTER

39km/24mi – about 1hr 15min – Local map see p 75

For a description of the itinerary from Le Markstein to Lautenbach, see GUEBWILLER: Guebwiller Valley.

★**Lautenbach** – *See GUEBWILLER: Guebwiller Valley.*
Turn back at the church and drive out of Lautenbach, turning right onto the forest road leading to the Col de Boenlesgrab.

The road rises steeply and, after two hairpin bends, it affords a fine view of the Lauch Valley and of the Grand Ballon.
A path, starting on the left of the restaurant situated at the pass, leads to the Petit Ballon.

★★**Petit Ballon** – *2hr on foot there and back from the pass.*
From the pass, a stony path goes through the forest then across high pastures, offering a fine **view** of Wasserbourg and the Krebsbach Valley to the right, with the Trois-Épis in the background. The path goes past the Strohberg inn two thirds of the way to the summit. Walk across a small gate and follow the path on the left right up to the summit *(for a description of the beautiful panoramic view, see From Munster to Petit Ballon above).*
Return to the car at the Col de Boenlesgrab.

The forest road leading to the Firstplan crossroads runs through a forest of mature beeches and firs. Halfway there, there is a fine view of the Krebsbach Valley and the Fecht Valley. Then, as the road winds its way down towards Soultzbach, it affords some glimpses of the rounded summit of Petit Ballon.
Shortly beyond Soultzbach, turn left onto D 417 towards Munster.

Munster – *See From Colmar to Lake Fischbœdle above.*

Église de MURBACH ★★

Michelin map 87 fold 18 or 242 fold 35

The village of Murbach, lying in a remote wooded valley, nestles round the former abbey church of the famous Murbach abbey, whose Romanesque style is characteristic of the Rhine region.

Founded in 727 the abbey was generoulsy endowed by Count Eberhard, a powerful Alsatian lord and by the 9C it was already rich and famous; its library was remarkable and it owned property in more than 200 places from Worms to Lucerne. "As proud as the Murbach hound" soon became a popular saying, referring to the black hound decorating the coat of arms of the abbey. From the 12C onwards, the abbots of Murbach were also princes of the Holy Roman Empire and the monks were all aristocrats. Considering the number of castles under its control, the abbey was certainly a powerful feudal lord and its mint worked from 1544 to 1666. In 1789, the peasants of the St-Amarin Valley, wishing to shake off the abbey's authority, plundered the castle at Guebwiller, where the abbey had been transferred in 1759.

CHURCH *15min*

The 12C church is now reduced to the chancel and the transept surmounted by two towers, the nave having been demolished in 1738.

The **east end**★★ is the most remarkable part of the edifice. Its flat wall, which projects slightly, is richly decorated in its upper section. A gallery with 17 different colonnettes can be seen above two tiers of windows.

The tympanum of the south doorway, with its low-relief carvings depicting two lions facing each other framed by palmettes and foliated mouldings, is reminiscent of certain oriental works. Inside, in the chapel situated to the left of the chancel, lies the sarcophagus of the seven monks killed by Hungarians in 926. A recess in the south transept contains the 14C recumbent figure of Count Eberhard.

On leaving the abbey church, walk (note the Stations of the Cross below) to the Chapelle Notre-Dame-de-Lorette (1693) offering views of the church and the surroundings through trees and shrubs.

Murbach – The church

EXCURSION

Buhl – *3km/1.9mi east.* The large neo-Romanesque **church** of this lively village (metalworks and plastics) houses one of the few sizeable painted triptychs in Alsace (7m/23ft wide) to be found outside a museum. The **Buhl altarpiece**★★ was probably made c 1500 by artists from the school of Schongauer *(see COLMAR: Musée d'Unterlinden)* for the Dominican convent in Colmar. The superb central Crucifixion is framed by four scenes depicting Christ's Passion. On the other side, the Last Judgement is represented between episodes of the Virgin's life.

To choose a hotel, a restaurant, a campsite ...
Michelin Red Guide to France
Michelin Red Guide Paris and Environs
Michelin Camping Caravaning France.

NANCY ★★★

Conurbation 310 628
Michelin map 62 folds 4 and 5 or 242 folds 17 and 18

The former capital of the dukes of Lorraine offers visitors the elegant harmony of its 18C town planning, its aristocratic architecture and beautiful vistas.

Nancy is also an important intellectual centre with several scientific and technical institutes, its higher school of mining engineering, its national centres of forestry research and study, as well as its cultural centre and theatre housed in a former tobacco manufacture.

The town has retained a remarkable ensemble of buildings erected at the turn of the 20C, which are fine examples of the decorative style of the **École de Nancy** *(see p 212)*.

HISTORICAL NOTES

The foundation of Nancy goes back to the 11C. The site chosen by Gérard d'Alsace, the first hereditary duke of Lorraine, to build his capital was a piece of land flanked by two marshes where he had a fortress erected. Nancy's only real advantage was that it was located at the centre of the duke's land. At first the new capital consisted of the ducal castle and a few monasteries.

In 1228, Nancy was destroyed by fire and rebuilt almost immediately. In the 14C, what is now the old town was surrounded by a wall of which only the Porte de la Craffe has survived.

In 1476, Charles the Bold, Duke of Burgundy, occupied Lorraine which was lying between Burgundy and Flanders (both belonging to him) but the following year, Duke **René II** returned to Nancy and stirred a rebellion. Charles then lay siege in front of the town; he was killed at St-Nicolas-de-Port *(see ST-NICOLAS-DE-PORT)* and his body was found later in a frozen lake, half eaten by wolves.

The distinctive **Croix de Lorraine** *(also see p 54)*, with two crosspieces, was a reminder of Duke René's illustrious ancestors, his grandfather "good King René", Duke of Anjou and Count of Provence, and a more remote ancestor and founder of the dynasty, the brother of Godefroy de Bouillon who led the first Crusade and became king of Jerusalem. Used as a distinguishing mark by René II's troops on the battlefield of Nancy, the cross later became a patriotic symbol *(see Colline de SION-VAUDÉMONT)*. In July 1940 it was adopted as the emlem of the Free French Forces.

Gradually becoming more powerful, the dukes of Lorraine set out to develop their capital city. A new palace was erected and, at the end of the 16C, Duke Charles III built a new town south of the old one. At the same time, Nancy became an important religious centre and, in the space of 40 years, 13 monasteries were founded. However, the **Thirty Years War** stunted Nancy's economic growth as illustrated by **Jacques Callot**'s engravings entitled "Misfortunes of War". When peace returned, Duke Leopold undertook the building of the present cathedral designed by **Germain Boffrand** (1667-1754), who also built several mansions north of place Stanislas.

In the 18C, François III exchanged the duchy of Lorraine for the duchy of Tuscany. Louis XV, King of France, seized the opportunity and gave Lorraine to his father-in-law, **Stanislas Leszczynski**, the deposed king of Poland, on the understanding that the duchy would naturally become part of the kingdom of France after Stanislas' death. Stanislas was a peaceful man who devoted himself to his adopted land, embellished his new capital and made it into a symbol of 18C charm and elegance with the magnificent square which bears his name in its centre. He chose artists of genius such as Jean Lamour, who made Nancy's superb wrought-iron railings.

Between 1871 and 1918, Nancy welcomed refugees from the nearby regions occupied by the Germans and a modern town developed next to the three already existing, the old town, the dukes' town and Stanislas' town. The new industrial town expanded rapidly and its population doubled in the space of 50 years.

In 1914, Nancy was narrowly saved from occupation but was shelled and bombed throughout the war.

Occupied in 1940, Nancy was liberated in September 1944 by General Patton's army, with the help of the Résistance.

★★★PLACE STANISLAS AND NEARBY *allow 2hr*

★★★**Place Stanislas** (BY) – The collaboration between the architect, **Emmanuel Héré**, and the craftsman who made the railings, **Jean Lamour**, resulted in a superb architectural ensemble (1751-60) characterised by the perfect harmony of its proportions, layout and detail. Place Stanislas forms a rectangle with canted corners, measuring 124m/136yd by 106m/116yd. Louis XV's statue which stood in its centre was destroyed during the Revolution and in 1831 a statue of Stanislas replaced it and the square was renamed after him.

Railings – The partly gilt wrought-iron railings, a model of delicacy and elegance, decorate the canted corners of the square as well as the beginning of rue Stanislas and rue Ste-Catherine. Each railing on the north side forms a triple portico framing the Poseidon and Amphitrite fountains by Guibal, a sculptor from Nîmes.

ON THE TOWN
Guided tours

Guided tours of the town are organised all year round on Saturdays at 4pm (except in January, February and December) in July and August daily. It is also possible to rent a walkman. Apply at the tourist office. Alternatively, five itineraries with prerecorded commentaries are available for visitors who wish to explore Nancy by taxi (1hr approximately). Information: Taxis de Nancy ☎ 03 83 37 65 37 or the tourist office.

The tourist office also proposes a special pass called "**Clé de la ville**", which gives access to the city's main sights for a fixed charge.

From May to September, visitors can tour the old town and the 18C town aboard a tourist train. Departure from place de la Carrière every hour from 10.30am (10am in July and August). There is also a night tour starting at 9pm in July and August.

Entertainment

The Opéra de Nancy et de Lorraine, the Ballet national de Nancy et de Lorraine, the Association de musique ancienne de Nancy, the Ensemble Stanislas, the Orchestre symphonique et lyrique de Nancy, the Association lorraine de musique de chambre, Gradus Ad Musicam and La Psalette de Lorraine organise numerous concerts and shows in various venues in town:
– Opéra, place Stanislas.– Théâtre de la Manufacture,
– Ballet, 3, rue Henri-Bazin.10, rue Baron-Louis.
– Salle Poirel, rue Victor-Poirel.– Hôtel de Lillebonne,
– Zénith, rue Zénith à Maxéville14, rue du Cheval-Blanc.
Apply at the tourist office for the programme of coming events.

Cafés, bars and restaurants

Two **Art Nouveau** establishments are worth looking up:
– Brasserie Excelsior, 50, rue Henri-Poincaré.
– Capucin Gourmand, 31, rue Gambetta.
On the pedestrianised **Place Stanislas**, there are many pavement cafés offering musical entertainment daily from 8.30pm in July and August.
In **Rue des Maréchaux**, a small but pleasant pedestrianised street, there are many traditional and gourmet restaurants.
Rue de la Primatiale is a tiny street lined with convivial small restaurants and wine bars.

Pavilions – The square is surrounded by five tall pavilions and two one-storey pavilions; this emphasises the impression of space and harmony. The façades designed by Emmanuel Héré are elegant, graceful and symmetrical without being monotonous. The wrought-iron balconies by Lamour enhance the richness and elegance of the ensemble.

★★**Musée des Beaux-Arts** ⊘ (BY M²) – The Museum of Fine Arts, housed in one of the pavilions of place Stanislas prolonged in 1936 by a modern pavilion, contains rich collections of painting from the 14C to the present day, of sculpture and of graphic art. The museum was extended again between 1996 and 1998.

The ground floor displays the collection gathered from 1919 to 1930 by the art collector Henri Galilée, including works by Bonnard, Vuillard, Dufy, Utrillo, Modigliani, as well as a portrait of *Méry Laurent* by Manet and the *Cliff at Étretat* by Monet.

One room is entirely devoted to the Daum collection, a magnificent group of 200 pieces of glassware and crystal.

Modern art is essentially represented by Cubist works including sculptures by Duchamp-Villon, Zadkine, Laurens and Lipchitz.

The first floor exhibits works by the Italian primitives as well as Perugino *(The Virgin, The Child Jesus and St John)*, Tintoretto, Pietro da Cortona and Caravaggio *(The Annunciation)*. Also noteworthy is the collection of 17C Flemish, Dutch and Rhenish landscapes, *The Transfiguration* by Rubens and several paintings by Jordaens. Among the portraits and other paintings of the 17C and 18C French schools, the most remarkable are *Love Taking Its Revenge* by Vouet, *Pastoral Landscape* by Claude Lorrain, *Aurora and Kephalos* by Boucher, and works by Van Loo and De Troy.

The second floor, devoted to 19C French painting, houses the famous *Battle of Nancy* by Delacroix and two luminous paintings by Emile Friant, a native of Nancy *(All Saints' Day, Idyll on the Bridge)*.

The department of graphic art holds temporary exhibitions and alternate displays of prints by Jacques Callot and drawings by Grandville.

NANCY

Adam (R. S.) . . . . . . BX 2
Albert-Ier (Bd) . . . . DV 3
Anatole-France
  (Av.) . . . . DV 6
Armée-Patton (R.) . . DV 7
Auxonne (R. d') . . . DV 8
Barrès (R. Maurice) CY 10
Bazin (R. H.) . . . . . . CY 13
Bénit (R.) . . . . BY 14
Blandan
  (R. du Sergent). DX 15
Braconnot (R.) . . . BX 19
Carmes (R. des) . . BY 20
Chanoine-Jacob (R.) AX 23
Chanzy (R.) . . . . . . AY 24
Cheval-Blanc (R. du) BY 25
Clemenceau (Bd G.) EX 26
Craffe (R. de la) . . AX 27
Croix de Bourgogne
  (Espl.) . . . . AZ 28
Dominicains
  (R. des) . . . . BY 29
Foch (Av.) . . . . DV 33
Gambetta (R.) . . . . BY 35
Gaulle (Pl. Gén.-de) BX 36
Grande-Rue . . . . BXY 37
Haussonville (Bd d') DX 38
Haut-Bourgeois (R.) AX 39

Héré (R.) . . . . BY 40
Ile de Corse (R. l') CY 41
Jaurès (Bd Jean) . EX 43
Jeanne-Arc (R.) . . DEX 44
Keller (R. Ch.) . . . . AX 46
Linnois (R.) . . . . . . EX 49
Louis (R. Baron) AXY 50
Loups (R. des) . . . AX 51
Majorelle (R. Louis) DX 52
Maréchaux (R. des) BY 53
Mazagran (R.) . . . . AY 54
Mengin (Pl. Henri) BY 55
Molitor (R.) . . . . . . CZ 60
Mon Désert (R. de) ABZ 61
Monnaie (R. de la) BY 62
Mouja (R. du Pont) BY 64
Nabécor (R. de) . . EX 65
Oudinot (R. Mar.). EX 68
Poincaré (R. H.) . . AY 69
Poincaré (R. R.) . . AY 70
Point-Central . . . . . BY 72
Ponts (R. des) . . . BYZ 73
Primatiale (R. de la) CY 74
Raugraff (R.) . . . . . BY 75
St-Epvre (R. de la) BY 82
St-Dizier (R.) . . . . . BY
St-Georges (R.) . . . CY
St-Jean (R.) . . . . . . BY
St-Lambert (R.) . . DV 84
St-Léon (R.) . . . . . . AY 85
Source (R. de la) . AY 99

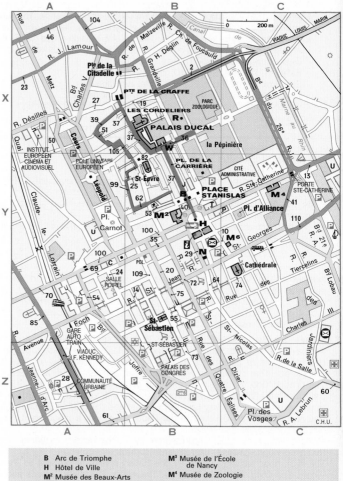

B Arc de Triomphe	**M³** Musée de l'École
H Hôtel de Ville	de Nancy
M² Musée des Beaux-Arts	**M⁴** Musée de Zoologie

Hôtel de ville ⊘ (**BY H**) – The town hall was erected between 1752 and 1755. The pediment is decorated with the coat of arms of Stanislas Leszczynski: Polish eagle, Lithuanian knight, Leszczynski buffalo.

The staircase is enhanced by a handrail and banisters by Jean Lamour. It leads to the Salon Carré adorned with frescoes by Girardet then to the Grand Salon, inaugurated by Empress Eugénie in 1866, followed by the Salon de l'Impératrice. These rooms offer a splendid vista which includes place Stanislas, place de la Carrière and the Palais du Gouvernement.

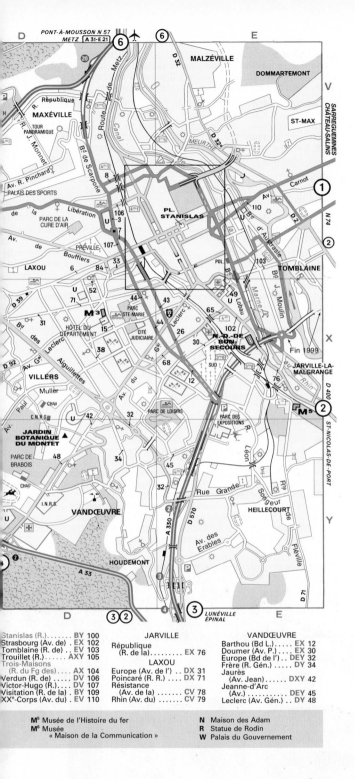

Stanislas (R.)	**BY** 100	
Strasbourg (Av. de) . .	**EX** 102	
Tomblaine (R. de) . . .	**EV** 103	
Trouillet (R.)	**AXY** 105	
Trois-Maisons		
(R. du Fg des)	**AX** 104	
Verdun (R. de)	**DV** 106	
Victor-Hugo (R.)	**DV** 107	
Visitation (R. de la) . .	**BY** 109	
XXᵉ-Corps (Av. du) . .	**EV** 110	

JARVILLE
République	
(R. de la)	**EX** 76

LAXOU
Europe (Av. de l') . .	**DX** 31
Poincaré (R. R.)	**DX** 71
Résistance	
(Av. de la)	**CV** 78
Rhin (Av. du)	**CV** 79

VANDŒUVRE
Barthou (Bd L.)	**EX** 12
Doumer (Av. P.)	**EX** 30
Europe (Bd de l') . .	**DEY** 32
Frère (R. Gén.)	**DY** 34
Jaurès	
(Av. Jean)	**DXY** 42
Jeanne-d'Arc	
(Av.)	**DEY** 45
Leclerc (Av. Gén.) . .	**DY** 48

M⁵ Musée de l'Histoire du fer	**N** Maison des Adam
M⁶ Musée	**R** Statue de Rodin
« Maison de la Communication »	**W** Palais du Gouvernement

Walk along rue Héré facing the town hall; it leads to the Arc de Triomphe.

★**Arc de Triomphe** (**BY** B) – This deep triumphal arch, built between 1754 and 1756 in honour of Louis XV, is modelled on Septimus Severus's arch in Rome. The decoration of the main façade facing place Stanislas is a glorification of war and peace, both aspects of Louis XV's reign.
On the parkside, to the right, there is a monument dedicated to Héré and on the left a monument dedicated to Callot.

★**Place de la Carrière** (BY) – This elongated square dates from the time of the dukes of Lorraine; originally used for cavalry drills, it was remodelled by Héré and is now lined with beautiful 18C mansions. Fountains decorate the corners and at each end there are railings by Lamour, adorned with lanterns.

★**Palais du Gouvernement** (BX **W**) – Facing the Arc de Triomphe across place du Général-de-Gaulle and place de la Carrière, this edifice is the former residence of the governors of Lorraine. The peristyle is linked to the other buildings of the square by an ionic **colonnade**★ surmounted by a balustrade decorated with vases. The columns are separated by busts of mythological characters.

Walk along the right side of the Palais du Gouvernement and enter la Pépinière.

La Pépinière (BCX) – This fine 23ha/57 acre open space includes a terrace, an English garden, a rose garden and a zoo. Note the statue of the artist, Claude Gellée, known as le Lorrain, by Rodin (BX **R**).

★**Église and Couvent des Cordeliers** ⊘ (BX) – The Franciscan convent and the adjacent church were erected in the 15C on the initiative of Duke René II; after being restored, they partially regained their original aspect.

★**Église** – The church has only one nave as is usual for the church of a mendicant order. All the dukes are buried in the crypt. Most of the funeral monuments are the works of three great Renaissance artists, native of Lorraine: Mansuy Gauvain, Ligier Richier and Florent Drouin.

A chapel on the left-hand side contains the **recumbent figure of Philippa of Gelderland**★★, René II's second wife, carved in a fine tuffa, one of the finest works of Ligier Richier. Against the south wall (near the high altar), note the funeral recess of **René II's funeral monument**★, carved by Mansuy Gauvain in 1509. The effigy of Cardinal de Vaudémont (d 1587) is the work of Florent Drouin. The latter is also the author of a remarkable Last Supper, a low-relief sculpture after the famous painting by Leonardo da Vinci. The chancel contains a carved altarpiece over the high altar (1522), 17C stalls and an 18C wrought-iron lectern bearing the emblems of Lorraine. Paintings include Notre-Dame-de-Lorette believed to be the work of Guido Reni and works by R Constant, a native of Lorraine.

★★DUCAL PALACE AND OLD TOWN *about 2hr*

★★**Palais ducal** (BX) – Dating from the second half of the 13C, the palace was in ruins when René II had it rebuilt after his victory over Charles the Bold of Burgundy.

In the 16C, Duke Antoine had the Porterie (gateway) completed together with the Galerie des Cerfs (Deer Gallery). In 1792, the palace was ransacked and skillfully restored in 1850. The northern part was entirely rebuilt.

The plain façade overlooking the Grande-Rue enhances the elegant and rich decoration of the **Porterie**★★. Above this remarkable gate, in a mixture of Flamboyant Gothic and Renaissance style, stands the equestrian statue (reconstructed) of Antoine de Lorraine surmounted by a Flamboyant gable.

Nancy – The gateway of the Ducal palace

At first-floor level, three balconies decorated with a Flamboyant balustrade are supported by carved corbels.

The façade overlooking the gardens is adorned with a fine Gothic gallery prolonging a vast vaulted vestibule.

The former Ducal palace houses the very interesting Historical Museum of Lorraine.

★★Musée historique lorrain ⊘ – *Entrance: no 64 Grande-Rue.*
The museum contains a wealth of exceptional documents illustrating the history of Lorraine, its artistic production and its folklore.

The pavilion at the bottom of the garden houses an **archeological gallery** concerned with prehistory, the Celtic period, Gallo-Roman and Frankish times. *Walk across the garden.* The collections displayed on the ground floor of the main building illustrate the history of Lorraine from the Middle Ages to the 16C (sculptures). There is also a Musée de Pharmacie.

On the first floor, the Galerie des Cerfs, 55m/180ft long, contains mementoes of the House of Lorraine, from the 16C to the mid 18C, as well as tapestries from the early 16C, paintings by Jacques Bellange *(Stigmatization of St Francis of Assisi, Mary Magdalene in Ecstasy)*, **Georges de La Tour** *(Woman with a Flea, Discovery of St Alexis's Body, Young Smoker, St Jerome Reading)*, Charles Mellin *(Abel's Sacrifice, St Francis of Paola Praying, Magdalene)* and Claude Deruet *(Portrait of Madame de Saint-Baslemont)*, as well as etchings and drawings by **Jacques Callot** (practically his entire output of engravings and 330 copperplates).

Still on the first floor, the history of Lorraine during the lifetime of dukes Charles V, Leopold and Francis III is illustrated by numerous paintings, documents, miniatures, ceramics from eastern France (Niederviller, Lunéville, St-Clément), biscuits and terracottas and sculptures by Clodion.

The second floor is devoted to Lorraine and Nancy during the lifetime of Stanislas: his foundations, his creations including the square which bears his name, as well as to political, military and literary history from the Revolution to the Empire. One room contains a collection of Jewish objects.

The third floor is concerned with Lorraine from the Restauration to the Third Republic, in particular the First World War and Maréchal Lyautey, a native of Nancy.

★Chapelle ducale – On the left of the chancel. Built from 1607 onwards over the tomb of the dukes of Lorraine, the octagonal chapel was modelled on the Medici Chapel in Florence at the request of Charles III. Its walls are framed by 16 columns in front of which are seven black-marble cenotaphs. On each of these are placed the emblems of sovereignty. Jean Richier, a nephew of Ligier, and the Italian artist Stabili were responsible for the building; the coffered cupola is the work of Florent Drouin.

Couvent – The cloister and some of the rooms of the former monastery were restored and now house a rich **Musée d'Arts et Traditions populaires** (Museum of Folk Art and Traditions) which contains reconstructions of interiors (kitchen and bedroom) furnished in regional style and a wealth of objects of daily life, craftsmen's tools, kitchen utensils, lighting and heating equipment (enamelled ceramic tiles), models, maps, photos and paintings.

★Porte de la Craffe (BX) – This gate, which formed part of the 14C fortifications, is decorated with the thistle of Nancy and the cross of Lorraine (19C). The opposite façade is in Renaissance style. The gate was used as a prison until the Revolution.

To the north stands the **Porte de la Citadelle** (AX) which used to secure the old town. This Renaissance gate is decorated with low-relief sculptures and trophies by Florent Drouin.

Retrace your steps then turn right onto rue Haut-Bourgeois.

Admire the Hôtel de Fontenoy *(no 6)* designed by Boffrand at the beginning of the 18C, the **Hôtel Ferrari** *(no 29)* also by Boffrand with an emblazoned balcony, a monumental staircase and Neptune fountain in the courtyard, the Hôtel des Loups *(no 1 rue des Loups)* again by Boffrand and the Hôtel de Gellenoncourt *(no 4)* with a Renaissance doorway.

Walk across place de l'Arsenal (16C arsenal at no 9, decorated with trophies) towards rue Mgr-Trouillet and look at the Renaissance **Hôtel d'Haussonville** with its outside galleries and Neptune fountain. Continue to place St-Epvre adorned with the equestrian statue of Duke René II by Schiff.

Basilique St-Epvre – Built in the 19C, in neo-Gothic style, this imposing church is dedicated to a 6C bishop of Toul. Its elegant west front is preceded by a monumental staircase (a present from the emperor of Austria).

Turn right onto rue de la Charité then right again onto rue du Cheval-Blanc.

The **Hôtel de Lillebonne** *(no 12 rue de la Source)*, with its fine Renaissance staircase, houses the American library. Next door at no 10, note the unusual doorway of the Hôtel du Marquis de Ville, decorated with a bearded head. Rue de la Monnaie on the left (the Hôtel de la Monnaie at no 1 was built by Boffrand) leads to place de La Fayette adorned with a statue of Joan of Arc by Frémiet, a replica of the statue which can be seen in Paris.

Follow rue Callot to the Grande-Rue: on the corner note the 17C turret.

★★MUSÉE DE L'ÉCOLE DE NANCY ⊘ (DX M³)

Housed in an opulent turn-of-the-century residence, this museum offers a remarkable insight into the renewal movement in the field of decorative arts which took place in Nancy between 1885 and 1914 and became known as the **École de Nancy** *(see p 51)*.

Finding its inspiration in nature, this movement blossomed under the leadership of **Émile Gallé**.

The museum contains an important collection of exhibits characteristic of this movement: carved and inlaid furniture by Émile Gallé, Louis Majorelle, Eugène Vallin, Jacques Gruber and Émile André; book bindings, posters and drawings by Prouvé, Martin, Collin and Lurçat; glassware by Gallé, the Daum brothers and Muller; ceramics also by Gallé as well as by Bussière and Mougin; stained glass by Gruber.

Several complete furnished rooms, including a splendid **dining room** by Vallin (painted ceiling and leather wall-covering with delicate floral motifs by Prouvé) show the changing styles of middle-class interiors at the turn of the 20C. On the first floor, there is an interesting bathroom decorated with ceramics by Chaplet, a businessman's office comprising leatherwork with floral motifs, seats, a bookcase and a monumental filing cabinet. A few pieces of furniture by Hector Guimard, who did not belong to the Nancy movement but took part in a similar renewal of decorative arts, complete the collection.

The aquarium, situated at the bottom of the garden, is a strange circular edifice designed by Weissenburger, who seems to have drawn his inspiration from 18C follies.

Musée de l'École de Nancy – Art Nouveau window by Henri Bergé

ADDITIONAL SIGHTS

★**Église Notre-Dame-de-Bon-Secours** (EX) – *Avenue de Strasbourg.*
Built in 1738 for Stanislas by Emmanuel Héré, on the site of René II's chapel commemorating his victory over Charles the Bold (1476), this church is a well-known place of pilgrimage. Note the Baroque west front.

The richly decorated interior includes carved confessionals in the Louis XV style, railings by Jean Lamour and a splendid Rocaille pulpit. The chancel contains **Stanislas' tomb★** and the monument carved by Vassé for the heart of Marie Leszczynska, Louis XV's wife, on the right-hand side and, on the left, the **mausoleum of Catherine Opalinska★**, Stanislas' wife. Note the 19C stalls behind the altar and the statue of **Notre-Dame-de-Bon-Secours**, carved in 1505 by Mansuy Gauvain: this representation of the merciful Virgin conceals inside its coat some 20 small characters, both lay and religious.

Musée de Zoologie ⊘ (CY M⁴) – On the ground floor is the **tropical aquarium★** which comprises 70 ponds full of numerous species of fish, from Asia, Africa, the Red Sea, the Indian and Pacific oceans and the Amazone basin.
The first floor houses a collection of over 10 000 stuffed animals.

Art Nouveau architecture in Nancy

Much of Nancy's architecture (commercial buildings, villas, houses) was influenced by the Art Nouveau movement. Interesting examples are listed below:

– **3 rue Mazagran**: Brasserie Excelsior built in 1910 and decorated by Majorelle.

– **1 boulevard Charles V**: house built for himself by Weissenburger in 1904 with decorations and wrought-iron work by Majorelle.

– **86 rue Stanislas**: house built in 1906 by Eugène Vallin.

– **5 avenue Foch**: building belonging to the regional newspaper *L'Est Républicain* and dating from 1912.

– **40 rue Henri-Poincaré**: Chamber of commerce, designed by members of the École de Nancy in 1908, with wrought-iron work by Majorelle and stained glass by Gruber.

– **9 rue Chanzy**: BNP bank, built in 1910, wrought-iron work by Majorelle.

– **2 rue Bénit**: this shop, dating from 1900-1901, was the first metal-framed building to be erected; the stained glass is the work of Gruber.

– **42-44 rue St-Dizier**: block of flats built in 1902 by Georges Biet and Eugène Vallin.

– **7 bis rue St-Georges**: Crédit Lyonnais building with stained glass by Gruber (1901).

– **92-92 bis quai Claude-le-Lorrain**: semi-detached houses built by Émile André in 1903.

– **1 rue Louis-Majorelle**: Villa Majorelle *(not open to the public)*.
This house whose real name is Villa "Jika", was designed in 1899 by the Parisian architect Henri Sauvage (1873-1932) and built in 1901 for Louis Majorelle. Originally, it stood in a large park on the edge of town. It is possible to walk through the garden surrounding the villa.

– **24 rue Lionnois**: The house of the printer Jules Bergeret was built in 1903-1904 and decorated with stained glass by Gruber and Janin.

A brochure entitled *École de Nancy, itinéraire Art Nouveau* (available from the tourist office) suggests five itineraries which will help you discover the town's architectural heritage. Audio-guided tours of Art Nouveau districts are also available (apply to the tourist office, cost 35F, deposit 300F).

★Jardin botanique du Montet ⊘ (DY) – Situated in a vale, near the university's college of science, the botanical gardens cover an area of 25ha/62 acres including hot houses extending over 2 000m²/2 392sq yd. The gardens contain some 15 thematic collections: Alpine, ornamental, medicinal plants, an arboretum etc; 6 500 species grow in the hot houses: orchids, insect-eating and succulent plants... In their role as National Botanical Conservatory, the gardens also contribute to the preservation of endangered species in the Alsace-Lorraine region and in the French overseas territories.

Place d'Alliance (CY) – Designed by Héré, the square is lined with 18C mansions and adorned with a fountain by Cyfflé, commemorating the alliance pact signed by Louis XV and Maria-Theresa of Austria in 1756.

Maison de la Communication ⊘ (CY M⁶) – The museum illustrates the history of telecommunications over the past 200 years with the help of objects, documents, reconstructions of historic scenes, technical demonstrations... 1793 saw the advent of Chappe's aerial telegraph and 1876 the birth of the telephone. The museum also exhibits models of telephone exchanges in working order, the reconstruction of a post office of the 1920s, submarine telegraph and telephone cables, toys and old documents.

Cathédrale (CY) – This imposing edifice was erected during the first half of the 18C. Inside, the superb railings of the chapels are the work of Jean Lamour and François Jeanmaire, and the graceful Virgin and Child which can be seen in the apse was carved by Bagard in the 17C. The sacristy houses the **treasury** ⊘ containing, among others, the ring, the chalice, the paten, the comb and the evangelistary of St Gauzelin, who was bishop of Toul during the first half of the 10C.

Maison des Adam (BY N) – *57 rue des Dominicains.*
This is the elegant home of the Adam family, who were renowned sculptors in the 18C and decorated the house themselves.

Église St-Sébastien (BY) – *Place Henri-Mengin.*
This hall-church is the masterpiece of the architect Jenesson; consecrated in 1732, it has a striking concave Baroque **façade**★ decorated with four large low-relief carvings. Inside, the three naves are surmounted by unusual flattened vaulting resting on massive Ionic columns. Eight huge windows let light into the church. The chancel has retained some elegant woodwork. The side altars are the work of Vallin (École de Nancy).

EXCURSIONS

Musée de l'Aéronautique ⊙ – *2km/1.2mi. Leave Nancy by ② on the town plan, towards Nancy-Essey airport where the museum is located.*

On 31 July 1912, a Farman biplane left Nancy with three postal bags on its way to Lunéville where it landed a few minutes later. This flight marked the beginning of the French air postal service. The museum is a reminder of the role played by Nancy during this pioneering period.
Some 40, mostly military aircraft, exhibited in a purpose-built edifice, show the spectacular technological evolution which took place from 1930 onwards and commemorate historic events. Note, in particular, the Douglas DC 3, which carried the airborne troops at the time of the Normandy landings, the Gloster "Meteor", the only jet plane used by the Allies during the Second World War (particularly against the V1s which attacked England), the anti-submarine Loockheed PV2 "Neptune" with its characteristic central radome, the Dassault MD 450 "Ouragan", the first French jet fighter, the Loockheed F 104-G "Superstarfighter" used for training the first American astronauts, the Fouga CM 70 "Magister" and its famous tailplane shaped like a butterfly, flown from 1964 to 1980 by the French aerobatics specialists of the "Patrouille de France", not fogetting the safe and hard-wearing "Caravelle".

Musée de l'Histoire du fer ⊙ (EX M⁵) – Located in **Jarville-la-Malgrange**, the museum is housed in a building which illustrates the role of metallic architecture in contemporary design. The ground-floor gallery recalls the importance of iron in the universe and explains some physical and chemical facts about iron, cast iron and steel. The machinery section contains a small steam engine called "Boyotte".
The basement illustrates iron working and the uses of iron from prehistoric times to the Middle Ages, including techniques used to make weapons during the Gaulish period, as well as various processes such as Merovingian damascening.
The vast collections displayed on the first and second floors (begin with the second floor) are connected with the evolution of metalwork from the Renaissance until today: models, reproductions of paintings (with commentaries) depicting ironworks, smithies, cast-iron and iron objects etc.

★★**St-Nicolas-de-Port** – *12km/7.5mi. Leave Nancy by ② on the town plan. See ST-NICOLAS-DE-PORT.*

Chartreuse de Bosserville – *5km/3mi. Leave Nancy by ② on the town plan. In Laneuville, immediately after the bridge on the Marne-Rhine canal, turn left onto D 126.*

The road veers to the right, offering a fine overall view of the Chartreuse de Bosserville before crossing the Meurthe.

Turn left onto D 2; 1km/0.6mi further on, an alleyway lined with plane trees leads to the Chartreuse de Bosserville. Not open to the public.

Founded in 1666 by Duke Charles IV, this former Carthusian monastery is now occupied by a technical college. Built on a terrace overlooking the Meurthe, the edifice, with the chapel in its centre, comprises a long imposing 17C-18C façade flanked by two perpendicular wings. A splendid stone staircase leads up to the terrace. Bosserville was used as a military hospital from 1793 to 1813 and many French and foreign soldiers died there. Hundreds of bodies were deposited in the former lakes of Bois Robin.

Château de Fléville ⊙ – *9km/5.6mi southeast. Leave Nancy along A 33 and continue to the Fléville exit (8km/5mi).* The present edifice, erected in the 16C, replaced a 14C fortress of which only the square keep remains.
Once across the former moat, you are in the main courtyard. A balcony with a balustrade runs along the beautiful Renaissance façade of the central building. The tour of the interior includes the dukes of Lorraine's hall, Stanislas' bedroom, the 18C chapel, as well as several bedrooms decorated with paintings and furnished in the Louis XV, Regency or Louis XVI styles.
After the visit, take a walk round the outside of the castle through the landscaped park.

Parc de loisirs de la forêt de Haye – *9km/5.6mi west. Leave Nancy by ⑤ on the town plan and continue along D 400. There is an information centre near the entrance on the right.*
This leisure park lies at the heart of the Haye Forest, a vast area of rolling hills covering 9 000ha/22 240 acres, used as hunting grounds by the dukes of Lorraine. Mostly planted with beeches, the park includes several sports grounds, tennis courts, playgrounds, picnic areas, and marked itineraries for walking or running. It is also the starting point of long hikes, as well as riding and mountain-bike tours *(130km/81mi)* through the forest.

Musée de l'Automobile ⊙ – The museum houses about 100 vehicles of different makes, dating from 1898 (such as the Aster of 1900) to 1989; note the collection of GT saloon cars of the 1960s, radiator stoppers and advertising posters.

NEUFCHÂTEAU

Population 7 803
Michelin map 62 fold 13 or 241 fold 39

Situated at the confluence of the Meuse and the Mouzon, this ancient town has retained a number of old houses, mainly from the 17C and 18C round place Jeanne-d'Arc and along the adjacent streets. Neufchâteau owes its name to the former castle of the dukes of Lorraine destroyed together with the 18C fortifications. Having received its charter in 1123, it became the first free city of the duchy of Lorraine and enjoyed considerable prosperity from the 13C to 15C. This thriving market town also became a busy industrial city specialising in period furniture and food-processing. Its annual fair, which takes place in mid-August, is one of the oldest fairs in the Vosges region.

SIGHTS

Hôtel de ville – This late-16C edifice, has retained a fine Renaissance doorway; inside, there is a beautiful, richly decorated **staircase★** dating from 1594 and 14C cellars with pointed vaulting.

Église St-Nicolas ⊙ – The church stands on the mound where the dukes of Lorraine's castle also stood and, because of the difference in ground level, it consists of two superposed churches.
The doorway and tower of the upper church are modern, but the nave dates from the 12C and 13C. The five-sided apse was added in 1704.
The side chapels contain funeral monuments of wealthy 15C and 16C burghers; note the late-15C polychrome **stone group★** representing the anointing of Christ, a 15C Virgin with grapes, two 17C stone altarpieces, an organ case by Trenillot dating from 1684 and an 18C pulpit.
The three-naved lower church extends under the chancel of the upper church; it has retained interesting Romanesque capitals and a group of polychrome statues of the 16C-18C.

Église St-Christophe ⊙ – Part of the church goes back to 1100, but most of it dates from the 13C: the arcading of the west front resting on slender colonnettes denotes a Burgundian influence. On the south side, the christening-font chapel, originally a funerary chapel, was added in the 16C; admire the beautiful lierne and tierceron vaulting.
In the nave, there is a pulpit in the Louis XV style and in the chancel some paintings and woodwork in the Louis XVI style.

EXCURSIONS

St-Élophe – *9km/5.6mi north. Leave Neufchâteau along N 74.*
The church ⊙, standing on the edge of a plateau, at the end of the village, was remodelled several times. The massive belfry dating from the 13C contrasts with the early-16C nave, lit by the tall windows of the apse and containing the recumbent figure of St Élophe, who evangelised Lorraine and was martyred in the 4C. The monumental statue (7m/23ft) of the saint, which used to stand on top of the belfry, dates from 1886.
From the square in front of the church, there is a fine view of the Vair Valley, of the Bois-Chenu basilica and of Bourlémont castle. It is possible to take a **walk** in the footsteps of St Élophe to the fountain where he washed his head after having been decapitated, then on to la Reculée, a split in the rock where he is supposed to have hidden and finally to a stone in the cemetery, known as la Chaire, where he is said to have collapsed.
A small **museum** ⊙ housed inside the town hall also recalls St Élophe.
A pilgrimage takes place every year on the third Monday in October.

★ **Domrémy-la-Pucelle** – *9km/5.6mi along D 164. See VAUCOULEURS: Excursions.*

Pompierre – *12km/7.5mi south along D 74 then left onto D 1.*
The **Église St-Martin**, rebuilt on the roadside in the 19C, has retained its 12C Romanesque **doorway★**. Superbly carved recessed arches frame the three historiated bands of the tympanum depicting: the Massacre of the Innocents, the Flight to Egypt, the Message brought to the Shepherds, the Adoration of the Magi and Jesus entering Jerusalem. The capitals and colonnettes are also elaborately decorated.

Grand – *22km/13.7mi west. Drive north out of Neufchâteau along D 53 then turn left onto D 3 to Midrevaux. From there, D 71^E leads directly to Grand.*

In Roman times, Grand, which was then called Andresina, was a kind of water sanctuary dedicated to Apollo Grannus; the healing and oracular powers of this god attracted crowds of pilgrims including one or two emperors such as Caracalla in AD 213 and Constantine in AD 309.
Excavations have revealed some 60 different kinds of marble from all over the Empire, which testify to the splendour of the town's equipment.
Several kilometres of piping brought fresh water to the sacred pool, over which the present parish church stands. However, a **section of piping** ⊙ (80m/88yd long) gives a good idea of what this intricate network was like.
The **amphitheatre** ⊙, built c AD 80 in the shape of half an oval, could contain 17 000 spectators who came to watch gladiators fight; it was abandoned at the end of the 4C but part of the walls and some arcades were saved; tiers have recently been rebuilt so that the amphitheatre can be used once more.
A huge **mosaic** ⊙ (224m²/268sq yd), dating from the first half of the 3C AD, one of the best preserved Roman mosaics ever found, was discovered in Grand; it used to pave the ground of a basilica. In the centre are two characters sometimes thought to represent a pilgrim and a priest of Apollo Grannus. Various animals decorate the corners and the apse is adorned with geometric motifs.

NEUWILLER-LÈS-SAVERNE ★

Population 1 116
Michelin map 87 fold 13 or 242 fold 15
Local map see Parc Naturel Régional des VOSGES DU NORD

Situated on the forested foothills of the northern Vosges mountains, this pleasant village has retained several fine balconied houses and two interesting churches, including the Romanesque abbey church of one of the richest abbeys in Alsace.

★ÉGLISE ST-PIERRE-ET-ST-PAUL *allow 30min*

The original church was remodelled in the 9C to receive the relics of the bishop of Metz, St Adelphus. The oldest part is the crypt, the two superposed chapels, dating from the 11C are located behind the chancel. The chancel, the transept and the first bay of the nave were built in the 12C, the nave being completed in the 13C. The belfry dates from 1768. The upper parts of the edifice are Romanesque. There are two doorways on the north side facing a vast square surrounded by canons' houses: on the right, a 13C doorway, framed by the statues of St Peter and St Paul, and on the left a 12C doorway with a fine tympanum depicting Christ giving his blessing.

Interior – The gallery and the organ situated at the extremity of the nave date from 1773-1777.
At the west end of the south aisle, the 13C tomb of St Adelphus rests on top of eight tall columns, which enabled the congregation to pass beneath the saint's tomb. Walk up the south aisle to the south transept which contains a 15C "sitting" Virgin★ and, in the transept chapel, another late-15C statue of the Virgin. The chancel is decorated with 18C woodwork.
The north transept houses a polychrome Holy Sepulchre dating from 1478. Note a small "hole" in Christ's chest, where the host was kept during holy week. Above the group formed by the three Marys carrying perfume vases and surrounding Christ's body, the recess of a Flamboyant Gothic gable contains a 14C statue of the Virgin. The Romanesque christening fonts are located in the north aisle.

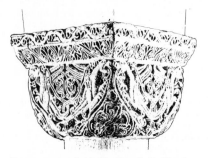
Romanesque capital in the Chapelle St-Sébastien

★**Superposed chapels** – They were both built in the 11C and their plans are identical. Round piers support the vaulting. The base of the columns are similar in both chapels; however, the cubic-shaped capitals of the lower chapel are plain whereas those of the upper chapel, dedicated to St Sebastian, are carved with beautiful motifs. In addition, this chapel houses remarkable tapestries ⊘★★. The four panels dating from the 15C depict St Adelphus' life and the miracles he accomplished. The well-restored tapestries form a charming ensemble whose naive style and beautiful colours are most attractive.

ADDITIONAL SIGHT

Église St-Adelphe ⊘ – This church, characterictic of the transition between the Romanesque and Gothic styles (12C-13C), now belongs to the Lutheran Church.

NIEDERBRONN-LES-BAINS‡‡

Population 4 372
Michelin map 87 fold 3 or 242 fold 16
Local map see Parc Naturel Régional des VOSGES DU NORD

This spa is an excellent holiday resort and the ideal starting point of hikes and excursions in the nature park of the northern Vosges region *(see Parc Naturel Régional des VOSGES DU NORD)*.
Lying at the heart of a hilly area, the town grew up around the mineral springs. Founded by the Romans c 48 BC and destroyed in the 5C AD, when barbarian tribes swept across western Europe, it was restored in the 16C by Count Philip of Hanau; his work was continued in the 18C by the Dietrich family.
During the second half of the 19C, the resort became quite popular and as many as 3 000 people took the waters in 1869. The Dietrich metalworks prospered during the same period and today, they are the city's main job provider.
Damaged during the Second World War, the town is booming again and some 4 000 people take the waters every year.
There are two springs:
– the **Source Romaine** (Roman spring) which gushes forth in the town centre, in front of the municipal casino, recommended for various forms of rheumatism;
– the **Source Celtic** (Celtic spring) relatively low in mineral content, bottled since 1989.

SIGHTS

Maison de l'Archéologie ⊘ – Modern display of local archeological documents. One room is devoted to cast-iron stoves, which have been the speciality of Niederbronn for over 300 years.

Cimetière allemand – This German military cemetery occupies a peaceful position on top of a rounded hill overlooking the town; 15 400 soldiers of both world wars are buried here.

Château de Wasenbourg – *West of the town. 1hr 15min on foot there and back. Start from the station and follow the alleyway lined with lime trees. Walk under the bypass and turn left onto the "sentier promenade et découvertes" (discovery trail).*
It leads to the ruins of the 13C castle. Fine view of Saverne to the southwest and of the southeastern part of Alsace.
Nearby, to the northwest, there are traces of a Roman temple.

EXCURSIONS

Châteaux de Windstein – *8km/5mi north. See Parc Naturel Régional des VOSGES DU NORD p 339.*

★**Château de Falkenstein** – *10km/6.2mi northwest, then 45min on foot there and back. Leave Niederbronn along N 62 towards Bitche; in Philippsbourg, turn right onto D 87 then left onto D 87ᴬ 1.5km/0.9mi further on. See FALKENSTEIN.*

Wintersberg – *15km/9mi roundtour. Drive northwest out of Niederbronn along N 62 and, after 1.5km/0.9mi, turn right towards the Wintersberg, the highest point of the northern Vosges mountains (580m/1 903ft).*
From the tower there is a fine panorama of the lower Vosges region and of the plain.
Come down along the western slopes of the mountain.

NOGENT-SUR-SEINE

Population 5 500
Michelin map 61 folds 4 and 5 or 237 fold 33

This small town, lying on both banks of the Seine and on an island linked to the river bank by a watermill, is overlooked by mills, silos and the cooling towers of the nuclear power station (Centre nucléaire de production d'électricité de Nogent-sur-Seine ⊙).

SIGHTS

Église St-Laurent – Built in the 16C, the church offers a pleasant blend of Flamboyant Gothic and Renaissance styles. An imposing tower rising on the left of the main doorway is decorated in the Renaissance style and surmounted by a lantern which supports the statue of St Laurent holding the instrument with which he was roasted alive.
The Renaissance aisles have large windows and the buttresses are adorned with carved capitals and gargoyles. Note the fine pediment of the south doorway.
Inside, the Renaissance chapels contain a few works of art including a painting depicting the Martyrdom of St Laurent believed to be by Eustache Lesueur (fifth chapel along the south aisle) and a large carved altarpiece bearing the emblems of the Virgin Mary (fifth chapel along the north aisle).

Musée Paul-Dubois-Alfred-Boucher ⊙ – The archeological collection consists of finds excavated in the area: Gallo-Roman pottery found in Villeneuve-au-Chatelot, coins... On the first floor, there are paintings and plaster casts by regional artists including the two sculptors after whom the museum is named.

Quais – From the embankment along the north bank of the Seine, near the house known as the "Maison d'Henri IV", there is a pleasant view of the river and the town.

EXCURSIONS

Château de la Motte-Tilly

*★**Château de la Motte-Tilly** ⊙ – 6km/3.7mi southwest along D 951.
The castle was opened to the public following the bequest of the Marquise de Maillé (1895-1972), an archeologist and art historian. The family furniture was restored and added to with a preference given to the 18C.
Although simple in style, the edifice has a certain nobility. It was built in 1754 on a natural terrace overlooking the Seine by the Terray brothers; one of them, a priest (1715-1778), was one of Louis XV's finance ministers.
The main features of the south façade, facing the road from Nogent-sur-Seine to Bray, are the unusually high roofs and the arcading linking the main building to the pavilions. The ground-floor reception rooms are beautifully furnished and decorated with painted woodwork which adds to the impression of intense luminosity and refined atmosphere. Two rooms on the first floor recall the benefactress, her bedroom with its green decoration and the Empire-style bedroom of her father, the Count of Rohan-Chabot.
After the tour of the castle, walk to the north side with its characteristic stone-built central part and admire the park with its beautiful ornamental lake and canal.

Ancienne abbaye du Paraclet ⊙ – 6km/3.7mi southeast along N 19 and D 442.
Abélard retired to this remote place with one companion after the Church had condemned his teaching in 1121. He built a modest oratory with reeds and straw and was soon joined by a group of students who camped round the oratory and

helped rebuild it in stone. **Héloïse** became the abbess of Le Paraclet in 1129. There is nothing left of the abbey except a cellar located beneath some farm buildings. Behind the chapel, an obelisk marks the site of the crypt where Abélard and Héloïse were buried. Moved in the 15C to the main church of Le Paraclet, their remains were taken away during the Revolution and now rest in the same grave in the Père-Lachaise cemetery in Paris. *(Turn to page 29 for more information on Abélard and Héloïse.)*

Villenauxe-la-Grande – *15km/9.3mi north along D 951.*
This small town is situated on the Ile-de-France cuesta *(see p 21)*, among rolling hills of fertile soil with outcrops of white limestone. The **church**, built of local sandstone, is plain on the outside. The 16C tower rises above the north aisle and the badly damaged Flamboyant doorway is decorated with the effigies of St Peter and St Paul. The most striking part of the interior is the Gothic chancel and its 13C ambulatory. The panelled vaulting is supported by tall arcades resting on round piers. The **ambulatory★** is lit by twin windows surmounted by five-foiled oculi. The arcades of the nave are wider and less elaborately decorated than those of the chancel and the pointed vaulting is loftier. The south aisle has fine pendentives.

OBERNAI★★

Population 9 610
Michelin map 87 fold 15 or 242 folds 23 and 24
Local map see Région du HOWALD and Route des VINS

Obernai, nestling at the foot of Mont Ste-Odile, is a pleasant holiday resort. The old town, with its narrow winding streets lined with rows of pointed gables, is still partly surrounded by its ramparts.

St Odile's city – Odile was the daughter of Étichon, Duke of Alsace, who, in the 7C, had his residence in Obernai, called Ehnheim at the time.
The town, which grew up around the abbey founded by St Odile, became a possession of the Holy Roman Emperor in the 12C and built its own fortifications. In the 14C, it joined Decapolis *(see MULHOUSE)* and successfully held on when attacked by the Armagnacs and later by the Burgundians led by Charles the Bold. Obernai had its heyday in the 16C just before the Thirty Years War practically ruined it.
It was eventually annexed by Louis XIV in 1679.

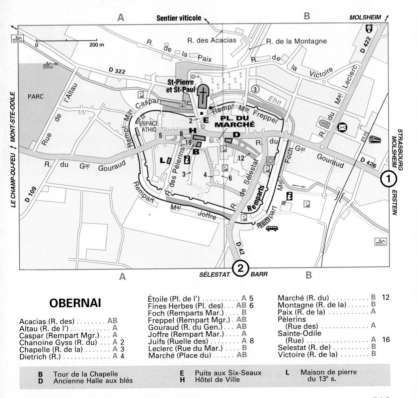

OBERNAI

Acacias (R. des)	AB	Étoile (Pl. de l')	A 5	Marché (R. du)	B 12
Altau (R. de l')	A	Fines Herbes (Pl. des)	AB 6	Montagne (R. de la)	B
Caspar (Rempart Mgr.)	A	Foch (Remparts Mar.)	B	Paix (R. de la)	A
Chanoine Gyss (R. du)	A 2	Freppel (Rempart Mgr.)	AB	Pèlerins	
Chapelle (R. de la)	A 3	Gouraud (R. du Gen.)	AB	(Rue des)	A
Dietrich (R.)	A 4	Joffre (Rempart Mar.)	A	Sainte-Odile	
		Juifs (Ruelle des)	A 8	(Rue)	A 16
		Leclerc (Rue du Mar.)	B	Selestat (R. de)	B
		Marché (Place du)	AB	Victoire (R. de la)	B

B	Tour de la Chapelle	**E**	Puits aux Six-Seaux	**L**	Maison de pierre
D	Ancienne Halle aux blés	**H**	Hôtel de Ville		du 13ᵉ s.

★★PLACE DU MARCHÉ *30min*

The golden hues of the buildings surrounding it add to the charm of the picturesque market square; in its centre, a fountain dating from 1904 is surmounted by
a statue of St Odile.

★**Hôtel de ville** (**H**) – The town hall has retained some features from the 14C-17C
in spite of being remodelled and extended in 1848; the façade is adorned with an
oriel and a beautifully carved balcony, both added in 1604.

★**Tour de la Chapelle** (**B**) – This 13C belfry was the tower of a chapel now reduced
to its chancel. The last storey, dating from the 16C, is Gothic; the spire, which
soars 60m/197ft into the sky, is flanked by four openwork bartizans.

★**Ancienne Halle aux blés** (**D**) – The old covered market dates from 1554.

ADDITIONAL SIGHTS

★**Maisons anciennes** – Most of them are to be found near the town hall, the old
market, or along rue du Marché and round place de l'Étoile.
In rue des Pèlerins, there is a three-storey stone house dating from the 13C (**L**). At
the back of the town hall, the picturesque rue des Juifs is worth the detour. On the
corner stands a fine timber-framed house with a wooden footbridge.

Puits aux Six-Seaux (**E**) – This elegant Renaissance well is surmounted by a
baldaquin resting on columns and crowned by a weather cock dating from 1579.
Six pails hang from the three pulleys.

Market day in Obernai

Église St-Pierre-et-St-Paul – This imposing neo-Gothic church, built in the 19C,
houses, in the north transept, a Holy Sepulchre altar (1504) and a reliquary
containing the heart of the bishop of Angers, Charles Freppel, a native of Obernai,
who died in 1891 and asked in his will that his heart be returned to the church of
his native town once Alsace became French again. His wish was fulfilled in 1921.
Note also the four stained-glass windows dating from the 15C, believed to be the
work of Pierre d'Andlau or his pupil Thibault de Lyxheim. The chapel dedicated to
St Odile contains a modern triptych.

Ramparts – It is pleasant to walk along the ramparts lined with a double row of
trees. The best-preserved part of the inside wall, once reinforced by more than 20
towers, is the Maréchal-Foch section.

Sentier viticole – *3.6km/2.3mi round tour, 1hr 30min on foot. Parking area near
the memorial ADEIF, a tall cross 12m/40ft high.*
A marked footpath leads through part of the vineyards covering 250ha/618 acres.

Val d'ORBEY ★★

Michelin map 87 fold 17 or 242 fold 31

The round tour of the Val d'Orbey starts from the northern extremity of the Route des Crêtes (see Route des CRÊTES). It is one of the finest excursions in the Trois-Épis area, which takes in the austere landscapes of the Lac Noir and the Lac Blanc contrasting with the picturesque valleys of the River Béhine and the River Weiss and leads to Le Linge, one of the most dramatic battlefields of the First World War.

Abbaye de Pairis – Situated 3km southwest of Orbey, Pairis is now just a hamlet surrounding a hospital, which was built on the ruins of the former abbey founded in 1136 by Cistercian monks.
Pairis remained a place of pilgrimage for several hundred years. The monks were known for their holiness and their learning. One of them, Martin, was chosen by Pope Innocent III to preach the Crusade and he followed the crusaders to the holy land. The monastery was destroyed during the Revolution.

FROM LES TROIS-ÉPIS TO LE BONHOMME

40km/25mi – allow 5hr – local map see Parc Naturel Régional des BALLONS DES VOSGES

★★**Les Trois-Épis** – This resort is the ideal starting point of numerous hikes and drives for those who are keen to explore the mountains or visit interesting towns, castles and battlefields. An event which took place in 1491 led to a famous pilgrimage which is at the origin of les Trois-Épis. A blacksmith on his way to market stopped for a while to pray in front of a picture of the Virgin Mary fixed to an oak tree when suddenly the Virgin appeared and spoke to him; in her left hand she held a piece of ice as a symbol of the great misfortunes which the area would have to endure if its inhabitants persisted in their wicked ways and in her right hand she had three ears of corn *(épis de maïs)* as a symbol of the rich harvests which would reward them if they repented. The blacksmith was entrusted with the task of warning the inhabitants but once he got to market he kept quiet. However the sack full of wheat which he had just bought suddenly became so heavy that no one could lift it; the blacksmith immediately remembered the warning and told the inhabitants about his vision. They all swore to amend their ways and decided to build a sanctuary on the spot where the oak tree stood.

★★**Le Galz** – *1hr on foot there and back.* At the summit a huge monument by Valentin Jæg commemorates the return of Alsace to France in 1918. The view extends over the Plaine d'Alsace, the Black Forest, the Sundgau and the Jura mountains.
From les Trois-Épis drive west along D 11 for 3km/1.9mi then turn left onto D 11VI.

Le Linge – *See Vallée de MUNSTER p 203.*
Turn right at Collet du Linge then, leaving the Glasborn path on your left, continue to the Col du Wettstein (war cemetery) and turn right.

Beyond the pass, the twisting road offers fine views of the Val d'Orbey.
Leave Pairis on your right and continue along D 48II then turn left towards the Lac Noir.

★**Lac Noir** – *Parking space by the lake.* The Lac Noir and the Lac Blanc were linked in 1930 by joint hydroelectric installations. The power station built on the north shore of the Lac Noir is connected by a pressure pipeline to the Lac Blanc situated 100m/328ft higher up. Water from the Lac Noir is pumped into the Lac Blanc during the night so that it can work the turbines of the power station during peak hours.
The Lac Noir (alt 954m/3 130ft) lies inside a glacial cirque. A moraine reinforced by a dam retains the water on the east side; the lake is otherwise surrounded by high granite cliffs which contribute to the austerity of the landscape.
To walk round the lake (1hr there and back to the viewpoint), start from the parking area and follow a path on the left which rises towards a rocky promontory. From there, the **view**★ *embraces the whole lake and extends towards the Pairis Valley and the Plaine d'Alsace. The path then continues to rise among the cliffs affording more fine views of the glacial cirque filled by the lake.*
Return to D 48II and turn left.

★**Lac Blanc** – Alt 1 054m/3 458ft. The road skirts the Lac Blanc, offering beautiful views of the glacial cirque which forms the setting of the lake (area: 29ha/72 acres, depth: 236ft). A strange rock, shaped like a fortress and known as the **Château Hans**, overlooks the lake. The high cliffs surrounding it are partly forested.
The road joins the Route des Crêtes at the Col du Calvaire. Turn right; the road enters the forest.

The road affords glimpses of the Béhine Valley, over which towers the Tête des Faux, before reaching the Col du Bonhomme.

Col du Bonhomme – Alt 949m/3 114ft. This pass links Alsace and Lorraine via the Col de Ste-Marie in the north and the Col de la Schlucht in the south *(see also Route des CRÊTES)*. The twisting road leading down from the pass into the Béhine Valley offers fine views of the valley with the Brézouard summit in the distance and the Tête des Faux quite near to the right.

Le Bonhomme – This pleasant resort was three times caught in heavy fighting during the two world wars.

WELCHE COUNTRY

From le Bonhomme to les Trois-Épis *29km/18mi – allow 2hr –*

Local map see Parc Naturel Régional des BALLONS DES VOSGES

From le Bonhomme, the itinerary goes through Welche country, a kind of French enclave (linguistically speaking) in Alsatian country.

Le Bonhomme – *See above.*
The road passes beneath a rocky spur topped by the ruins of Gutenburg castle.

Lapoutroie – In this village there is a small **Musée des Eaux-de-Vie** ⊙ (liqueurs and traditional distillery), housed in a former posting house dating from the 18C.

Continue along N 415 towards Kaysersberg, past the intersection with D 48 (round about), then turn immediately left onto D 11IV leading to Fréland.

Fréland – The name means "free land"; miners from Ste-Marie-aux-Mines *(see Parc Naturel Régional des BALLONS DES VOSGES: Val d'Argent)* enjoyed the right to cut timber.

Maison du Pays Welche ⊙ – Local people have gathered objects illustrating the region's traditions and displayed them in a former presbytery dating from the 18C. The setting and the local way of life are carefully recreated.

Return to N 415 and to the roundabout where you turn left onto D 48 towards Orbey.

Orbey – This village, which includes several hamlets, stretches along the green valley of the River Weiss; the heights overlooking the valley, crisscrossed by paths are ideal hiking country.
Beyond Orbey, the road *(D 11)* rises up a narrow valley past Tannach then, after a deep bend, it winds its way up offering fine views of the Weiss Valley overlooked by the Grand Faudé.
Further on it continues along a different slope revealing the Walbach Valley ahead with Le Galz and its monument behind and the Plaine d'Alsace in the distance. Leaving Labaroche on your left, you will soon notice the Grand Hohnack straight ahead and, quite close on your right, the conical summit of Petit Hohnack.
Les Trois-Épis lies 3km/1.9mi beyond the intersection of D 11 and D 11VI.

For a quiet place to stay, consult the annual Michelin Red Guide France which offers a selection of pleasant and quiet hotels in a convenient location.

OTTMARSHEIM

Population 1 897
Michelin map 87 fold 9 or 242 fold 40 – Local map see GRAND CANAL D'ALSACE

This village, situated on the edge of the vast Harth Forest, acquired fame through its church, a unique example of Carolingian architecture in Alsace. Nowadays, Ottmarsheim is also known for its hydroelectric power station, the second of eight such power stations along the Grand Canal d'Alsace *(see GRAND CANAL D'ALSACE)*.

★**Église** – The church was consecrated by Pope Léon IX c 1050. It is a very unusual octagonal edifice, a reduced model of the Palatine chapel in Aachen (Aix-la-Chapelle). This type of circular or octagonal construction, characteristic of Carolingian architecture, is very rare. For a long time, it was thought to be a kind of pagan temple or baptistery. In fact, the Ottmarsheim building is the church of a Benedictine abbey founded in the mid 11C.
The upper part of the belfry dates from the 15C as does the rectangular chapel on the southeast side, whereas the Gothic chapel was built in 1582 on the left side of the apse. The interior is designed in the shape of an octagon surmounted by a cupola. To the left of the square apse, a wrought-iron gate gives access to the Gothic chapel; above the entrance are seven 18C funeral medallions.
The church has retained some 15C murals depicting St Peter's life and Christ in glory presiding over the Last Judgement.

★**Centrale hydro-électrique** ⊙ – The Ottmarsheim hydroelectric power station, the reach and the locks built between 1948 and 1952 form the second section of the Grand Canal d'Alsace, which was the first stage of the harnessing-of-the-Rhine project *(see GRAND CANAL D'ALSACE)* between Basle and Lauterbourg.

Locks – They are of equal length (185m/202yd) but of different widths (23m/75ft and 12m/40ft). They are closed by angled gates upstream and by lifting gates downstream.

The control room overlooks the two locks.

The whole operation takes less than half an hour: 11min in the small lock and 18min in the large lock.

Power station – The engine room is vast and light. The four units have a total output of 156 million watts and produce an average of 980 million kWh every year.

La PETITE-PIERRE ★

Population 623
Michelin map 87 fold 13 or 242 fold 15
Local map see Parc Naturel Régional des VOSGES DU NORD

Situated at the intersection of several major routes, la Petite-Pierre, also known as Lützelstein or Parva Petra, prospered during the Middle Ages, was later fortified by Vauban, Louis XIV's military engineer, and then no longer maintained as a stronghold after 1870. Today, it is a popular summer resort at the heart of the forested massif of the low Vosges and the starting point of more than 100km/62mi of marked footpaths *(information panel inside the town hall)*.

OLD TOWN

Walk up a steep path past an outwork and follow the high street.

Chapelle St-Louis – Built in 1684 and once reserved for the garrison (funeral monuments of former governors and military chiefs), the chapel now houses the interesting **Musée du Sceau alsacien** ⊙ (Museum of Alsatian seals), illustrating the history of Alsace through numerous reproductions of seals which used to be the distinguishing marks of cities, stately homes, important people or families, crafts or guilds, religious orders or chapters etc.

Église – The belfry and the nave were rebuilt in the 19C, but the Gothic chancel dates back to the 15C. It is decorated with **murals** of the same period depicting the Coronation of the Virgin, the Temptation of Adam and Ève, the Last Judgement etc. Since 1737, the church has been used for Catholic and Protestant offices.

Château – Built in the 12C, the castle was remodelled several times, in particular in the 16C, at the instigation of Georg Hans von Veldenz, the Count Palatine of the Rhine region. The castle has, since 1973, been the headquarters of the **Parc naturel régional des Vosges du Nord**.

Maison du parc ⊙ – Skilfully displayed (reconstructions, games, slide shows) in six thematic multimedia rooms, the **permanent exhibition** entitled "Nouveaux Espaces" (New Spaces) helps visitors to discover the historic, cultural and technical heritage of the Parc as well as its natural diversity (fauna and flora). Nature park management issues (protection of the environment, fight against pollution) are also explained.

Follow rue des Remparts which offers views of the surrounding countryside and forested heights.

"Magazin" ⊙ – This former 16C warehouse, which forms part of the ramparts, houses a small **Musée des arts et traditions populaires**; the museum of folk art and customs displays an interesting collection of tins for specific cakes such as *springerle* (aniseed cake) and *lebkuche* (gingerbread).

Continue along rue des Remparts leading back to the high street.

Maison des Païens – This Renaissance house, situated in the gardens of the town hall, was built in 1530 on the site of a Roman watchtower.

EXCURSION

Parc animalier du Schwarzbach – *Access via D 134, by the Loosthal forest lodge, between La Petite-Pierre and Neuwiller.* This wildlife park offers the opportunity to observe red deer (one of the most interesting large species of the northern Vosges) in its natural surroundings. Visitors enjoy the view from an observation tower.

Further on, a **nature trail** reveals the diversity of the northern Vosges environment (trees, ecological forestry, geology, fauna). There are two separate itineraries: one is 1.8km/1mi long *(45min)*, the other is 4km/2.5mi long *(2hr)*; both offer fine views of the surrounding area.

PFAFFENHOFFEN

Population 2 285
Michelin map 87 fold 3 or 242 fold 16

Once the main centre of the bailiwick of Hanau-Lichtenberg, Pfaffenhoffen was forti
fied in the 15C to guard the south bank of the River Moder and became in the 16C
one of the rallying points of rebellious peasants *(see SAVERNE)*. Today the small
industrial town (shoes, metalworks) has retained part of its fortifications, a Catholic
church with a 15C Gothic nave and 13C crypt and a synagogue dated 1791, the oldest
Alsatian synagogue to have remained intact.

Regimental memento

★**Musée de l'Imagerie peinte et populaire alsacienne** ⊙ – *38 (first floor) rue du
Dr-Albert-Schweitzer (high street).*
The museum illustrates the long-standing Alsatian tradition of picture-painting
through rich collections of hand-painted pictures (on paper or vellum, on the back
of glass plates or on objects) by ordinary people or by local painters.
There are religious pictures intended to encourage prayers (representations of God
and various saints or decorated religious texts), to protect houses, cattle and crops
(pictures of patron saints such as St Agatha or St Wendelin); "memento" pictures
illustrate important events in peoples' lives (birth, first communion or confirmation,
friendship, military service, wedding and death of loved ones).
Religious pictures were traditionally hung in the *Herrgottswinkel* (God's corner) in
Catholic homes or in the *Biwelseck* (Bible corner) in Protestant homes.
Many of these pictures are touchingly naive, such as the bouquet of flowers sent in
1871 to Marguerite Finck by her fiancé: there are three main colours, red for
passion, green for hope and blue for faithfulness.
The first room contains pictures mounted under glass; most are very old yet note
how bright the colours are. Among them are the two oldest pictures mounted
under glass known in France: one depicts St Frances, the other St Xavier.
The second room also contains a collection of pictures mounted under glass, but
these, known as *églomisés*, have black backgrounds and gilt decorations and texts.
They are intended to adorn oil-lamp or candle-lit rooms and date from the Second
Empire (1852-1870).
The third room displays most of the "memento" pictures (17C-19C): christening
letters, decorated texts connected with confirmation, wedding or death, mementoes
of first-communion day, pictures of love, friendship books and even decorated
notarial deeds.
In the fourth room there are minutely executed paper cut-outs, ex-votos, pictures
of patron saints, banners, small religious pictures, some dating back to the 17C
and reliquaries.
The next room houses a collection of *Goettelbriefe* or christening wishes, one of
the oldest traditions in Alsace, which lasted for nearly 400 years.
In the last room toy soldiers from Strasbourg are exhibited; they were hand-
painted in the 18C. Nearby, there are decorated conscription mementoes and
multicoloured regimental mementoes.

Hôtel de ville – The façade is adorned with a medallion of Dr Schweitzer, who was made a freeman of the city. In the hall there is an exhibition of the work (sculpture, figurative painting in the style of Impressionism) of a native of Strasbourg, Alfred Pauli (1898-1988).

Maisons anciennes – The town has retained many half-timbered houses dating from the 16C to 19C, particularly in rue du Docteur-Schweitzer and rue du Marché.

EXCURSION

Cimetière juif d'Ettendorf – *6km/3.7mi southwest along D 419A and D 25, first road on the right. Drive through the village and follow a small road running parallel to the railway line which leads to the cemetery (500m/547yd).*
This is the oldest Jewish cemetery in Alsace; it spreads over a large area, on the hillside, blending perfectly well with the landscape.
Continue northwest along D 735 to Buswiller (2km/1.2mi).

Buswiller has retained some fine timber-framed houses. In the high street, note the carved gable of no 17, painted in cobalt blue; the house, dated 1599, was spared by the Thirty Years War.

PLOMBIÈRES-LES-BAINS‡‡

Population 2 084
Michelin map 62 fold 16 or 242 fold 34

Plombières stretches along the narrow and picturesque valley of the River Augronne. It is a renowned spa and a pleasant holiday resort. Water from the mineral spring is used in the treatment of diseases of the digestive system and various forms of rheumatism.

A fashionable spa – The Romans built imposing baths in Plombières and the spa flourished until it was destroyed by barbarians during the great wave of invasions from the east. Revived in the Middle Ages, the resort has steadily developed and welcomed many a famous person.
The dukes of Lorraine were, of course, regular visitors. Montaigne took the waters in 1580 and Voltaire spent several summers there. Louis XV's daughters stayed in Plombières for two consecutive seasons accompanied by a great many followers. Napoleon's wife Josephine and her daughter Queen Hortense also spent some time in Plombières. In 1802, an American engineer named Robert Fulton gave a demonstration of the first steamship on the River Augronne, in front of the empress. Napoleon III stayed in Plombières several times and decided to embellish the town. In 1858, he met the Italian minister, Cavour, and together they planned Italy's future and agreed on Nice and the Savoie being united to France.

SIGHTS

Spa town – The historic baths and thermal establishments can be seen along the town's lively high street, rue Stanislas and rue Liétard.
The **tour** ⊘ begins with the **Bain Stanislas**, built between 1733 and 1736. Next comes the **Étuve romaine**, discovered during excavations in 1856.
One of the finest 18C houses (note the wrought-iron balconies) is the **Maison des Arcades**, built in 1762 by Stanislas Leszczynski whose coat of arms is carved on the façade. On the ground floor, beneath the arcades and behind a wrought-iron railing, the Crucifix spring was, for a long time, a public fountain.

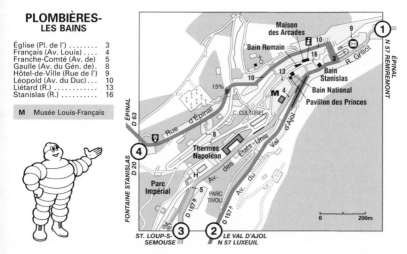

PLOMBIÈRES-
LES BAINS

Église (Pl. de l') 3
Français (Av. Louis) 4
Franche-Comté (Av. de) 5
Gaulle (Av. du Gén. de) . 8
Hôtel-de-Ville (Rue de l') 9
Léopold (Av. du Duc) . . . 10
Liétard (R.) 13
Stanislas (R.) 16

M   Musée Louis-Français

Nearby is the **Bain romain**, in a basement (staircase at the end of the square); th
vestibule shaped like a rotunda has retained important traces of the Roman poc
(tiers and statue of Emperor Augustus).

Further along on the left, the **Bain national**, built at the request of Napoleon (bust o
the emperor) and rebuilt in 1935, has retained its façade in the First Empire styl
(1800-1814). In the hall, the pump room is still in use.

The **Thermes Napoléon** wer
erected by Napoleon II
whose statue decorates th
entrance. The vast hall i
reminiscent of the Caracall
Baths in Rome.

A **historic trail** *(about 2h*
booklet available from th
tourist office) helps visitor
to discover the architectur
of the spa town and the ce
lebrities and artists wh
stayed in it.

Musée Louis-Français ⊙
(**M**) – The museum contain
paintings by Louis Français,
native of Plombières, and hi
friends from the Barbizo
School: Corot, Courbet
Diaz, Harpignies, Monticell
Troyon...

Parc impérial – The par
was laid by Baron Hauss
mann. It contains beautifu
trees and some rare specie

> ### Plombières ice cream
>
> This ice cream, flavoured with kirsch and
> glacé fruit, was supposed to have been
> invented accidentally in 1858 by a chef pre-
> paring a dessert ordered by Napoleon III for
> his guests during his famous visit to Plom-
> bières. The cream having turned out
> wrong, the chef added some kirsch and
> glacé fruit to it. This saved the day and the
> guests were delighted. It so happened that,
> in 1798, an Italian confectioner was already
> serving a similar kind of ice cream in the
> Paris region; it was called "Plombières"
> because it was left to set in lead *(plomb)*
> moulds. The name was originally spelt
> without an "s" but it was eventually con-
> fused with the name of the town where it
> became a speciality.
>
> The tradition lives on at Fontaine Stanislas
> where the ice cream is still handmade.

Pavillon des Princes ⊙ – Built during the Restauration (1814-1830) for member
of the royal family, the pavilion houses an exhibition devoted to the Second Empire

EXCURSIONS

Fontaine Stanislas – *3.5km/2.2mi southwest. Leave Plombières by ④ on the tow*
plan, along D 20; 1km/0.6mi further, turn left twice.

Very pleasant drive through the beech forest.

1.5km/0.9mi after the last turn, take the path on the left leading to the Fontain
Stanislas.

From the terrace of the hotel, there is a fine view of the valley where fields an
woods alternate. Nearby, a small spring gushes forth from a rock covered wit
inscriptions dating from the 18C and beginning of the 19C.

⁜ **Bains-les-Bains** – This spa resort lies on the banks of the Bagnerot, at the hea
of a forested region; there are many possibilities of walks and cycle tours in th
surrounding area. Water gushing forth from 11 springs, at temperatures varyin
from 25-51°C/77-124°F, is mainly used in the treatment of rheumatism an
cardiovascular diseases. The **Bain romain**, rebuilt in 1845, stands on the site of th
springs harnessed by the Romans, whereas the **Bain de la Promenade**, dating fro
1880 and remodelled in 1928, houses the pump room. From the Chapelle Notre
Dame-de-la-Brosse, situated 500m east along D 434, there is a pleasant **view** of th
hills overlooking the Bagnerot Valley.

★AUGRONNE AND SEMOUSE VALLEYS

33km/21mi round tour – allow 1hr

Leave Plombières by ③ on the town plan, along D 157bis.

Vallée de l'Augronne – The road follows the river through pastureland an
forested areas.

In Aillevillers-et-Lyaumont, drive north along D 19 to la Chaudeau then turn right on
D 20 which follows the Semouse Valley upstream.

★**Vallée de la Semouse** – This green and peaceful valley with densely foreste
slopes is deep and sinuous and barely wide enough for the river to flow throug
although there are here and there a few narrow strips of pastureland. Wirework
rolling mills and sawmills once lined the river, making use of its rapid flow (on
one of those mills has survived at Blanc Murger).

Turn right onto D 63 which leads back to Plombières.

The road runs rapidly down towards Plombières, offering a fine view of the tow

VALLÉE DES ROCHES *47km/29mi round tour – allow 2hr*

Leave Plombières by ① on the town plan and drive northeast along N 57.

The road soon leaves the picturesque Augronne Valley to climb onto the plateau marking the watershed between the Mediterranean and the North Sea, it then runs down towards Remiremont and the Moselle Valley.

Remiremont – *See REMIREMONT.*

Drive south out of Remiremont along D 23.

The road rises through a green vale then enters the forest.

3.5km/2.2mi further on, turn left onto D 57.

Just beyond la Croisette d'Hérival, turn right onto a surfaced forest road which winds its way through the Hérival Forest dotted with rocks.

Shortly after leaving the road to Girmont and an inn on your left, you will reach the Cascade du Géhard.

★**Cascade du Géhard** – The waterfall is situated below the level of the road, to the left. Foaming water cascades down into a series of potholes. The effect is particularly striking during the rainy season.

Continue past the forest lodge on your left and the path to Hérival on your right and turn left onto the road which follows the Combeauté Valley, also known as the Vallée des Roches.

Vallée des Roches – The deep narrow valley is framed by magnifiicent forested slopes.

Shortly after entering the village of Faymont, turn right near a sawmill and leave the car 50m/55yd further on; continue on foot along a forest road leading to the Cascade de Faymont (300m/328yd).

Cascade de Faymont – The waterfall, set among coniferous trees and rocks, forms a remarkable picture.

Le Val-d'Ajol – The municipality of Le Val-d'Ajol includes more than 60 hamlets scattered along the Combeauté Valley and Combalotte Valley which have retained their traditional industrial activities (metalworks, weaving, sawmills).

Turn right towards Plombières.

Continue 1.8km/1.1mi beyond a hairpin bend to the right, the road offers a fine view of the valley on your right.

Soon after, a path branching off on the left climbs up to La Feuillée Nouvelle (100m/109yd).

La Feuillée Nouvelle – From the platform there is a fine bird's-eye **view**★ of Le Val-d'Ajol.

Continue past the swimming pool at Le Petit Moulin on your left and follow N 57 back to Plombières.

PONT-À-MOUSSON ★

Population 14 647
Michelin map 57 fold 13 or 242 fold 13

Pont-à Mousson developed from the 9C onwards round the bridge built across the Moselle, beneath a knoll crowned with a fortress. This strategic position accounts for the heavy shelling which the town was subjected to in 1914-1918 and in 1944.
A foundry belonging to the St-Gobain group, situated between the Moselle canal and N 57, produces water and gas pipes.
The town is the headquarters of the **Parc naturel régional de Lorraine**.

HISTORICAL NOTES

The Reformation made rapid progress in Lorraine during the course of the 16C and, as a countermeasure, Charles III founded in 1572 the University of Lorraine which he based in Pont-à-Mousson. The abbeys of Metz, Toul and Verdun were responsible for the upkeep of the university run by Jesuits which encountered immediate success. Following its transfer to Nancy in the 18C, it was replaced by a royal military school. In early September 1944, the American army led by General Patton, coming from Verdun, met a German armoured division defending the bridge on the River Moselle. The Americans bombed the town on 3 September and entered it the next day. However, having blown up the bridge, the German troops took up a commanding position on the Butte de Mousson and for two weeks Pont-à-Mousson and the nearby village of Mousson were pounded by artillery fire from both sides. The Americans eventually crossed the river a few kilometres upstream and dislodged the Germans on 8 September.

★ANCIENNE ABBAYE DES PRÉMONTRÉS ⊘ *allow 1hr*

The former Premonstratensian abbey is a rare example of 18C monastic architecture. In 1964 it became a **cultural centre** and it is also now the headquarters of the European Centre of Sacred Art.

Façade – The three-storeys of the restored façade are underlined by elegant friezes.

Conventual buildings – Several rooms formerly used by the monks surround a lovely cloister: warming-room, refectory, chapter house, sacristy, former chapel etc. The three **staircases**★ are particularly noteworthy: the small spiral-shaped staircase, situated in a corner of the cloister near the warming-room, is very elegant; on the other side of the chapel (used as a concert hall), the oval Samson staircase is one of the finest features of the abbey; as for the great square staircase, located on the right of the sacristy, it is concealed by a beautiful wrought-iron handrail and matching banisters.

Ste-Marie-Majeure – The former abbey church consists of a nave, flanked by two aisles of almost similar height, supported by Baroque transverse arches resting on Corinthian capitals. The piers are slightly curved. Note traces of Baroque ornamentation in the chancel. The recesses, located on either side of the chancel, contain sculpted groups. A moving floor makes it possible to turn the church into a theatre or conference room.

The old abbey is now a cultural centre

ADDITIONAL SIGHTS

★**Place Duroc** – The square is surrounded by 16C arcaded houses. In its centre stands a monumental fountain, offered to the town by American ambulance service. There are several remarkable buildings in the vicinity: the **Maison des Sept Péchés Capitaux** (House of the Seven Deadly Sins), adorned with lovely caryatides representing the various sins and flanked by a Renaissance turret, where the dukes of Lorraine used to stay, and the town hall.

Hôtel de ville ⊘ – This 18C edifice decorated with a pediment is surmounted by monumental clock supported by two eagles; one of these wears the cross of Lorraine round its neck. The interior is adorned with fine woodwork *(meeting hall, second floor)*, 18C tapestries after drawings by Le Brun illustrating the epic life of Alexander the Great *(wedding hall, first floor)* and mythological scenes *(council chamber, second floor)*.

Église St-Laurent – The chancel and the transept date from the 15C and 16C. The central doorway and the first two storeys of the tower date from the 18C, the rest of the west front being completed in 1895.
The south aisle contains a 16C representation of Christ and the polychrome triptych of a 16C altarpiece from Antwerp; in the north aisle, you can see a 16C Pietà from the collegiate church of Ste-Croix and a statue of Christ carrying his cross by Ligier Richier; the chancel is decorated with fine 18C woodwork.

Maisons anciennes – The house at no 6 rue Clemenceau has a picturesque inner yard, restored to its original appearance, with a Renaissance well, a balcony and regional furniture; no 9 rue St-Laurent has a balcony overlooking the courtyard; no 11 has a brick façade with stone ties; no 19 is a Renaissance house built in 1590 and no 39 is the birthplace of General Duroc, one of Napoleon's faithful generals. The Renaissance house at no 2 rue de la Poterne has a beautiful doorway with delicately decorated door leaves.

Église St-Martin – The church was built in the 14C and 15C and extended by means of side chapels in the 17C and 18C. The 15C west front is flanked by two dissimilar towers.

Inside, note the 18C carved pulpit and the former rood screen now used as an organ loft. In the south aisle, there is a Flamboyant Gothic funerary recess containing two recumbent figures: that of a 13C knight (the best-preserved of the two) and that of a 15C lady. In the chancel, seven 18C paintings are surmounted by seven reliquaries. In the north aisle, you can admire an Entombment comprising 13 characters by early-15C artists from Champagne and Germany (note the dress of the three soldiers asleep in the foreground); Ligier Richier was probably influenced by this work when he made the St-Mihiel Entombment half a century later.

Ancien Collège des Jésuites – This former Jesuit college is now a secondary school. The edifice originally housed the university founded in the 16C; it was severely damaged and had to be rebuilt (note the 17C doorway in the centre of the right wing).

The fine courtyard has regained its original appearance.

EXCURSIONS

★Butte de Mousson – *7km/4.3mi east then 15min on foot there and back. Drive north out of Pont-à-Mousson along N 57 for 200m/219yd then turn right onto D 910 and, 3km/1.9mi further on, turn left towards Lesménils in order to reach D 34; turn right towards Mousson.*

A modern chapel stands at the top of the knoll as do the ruins of the feudal castle of the counts of Bar. From the viewpoint *(parking area)*, there is a fine **panorama★** of Lorraine and Moselle.

Signal de Xon – *4km/2.5mi northeast. Drive north out of Pont-à-Mousson along N 57 and turn right onto D 910 then left 3km/1.9mi further on towards Lesménils and left again at the top of the hill. Continue for 1km/0.6mi and leave the car to reach the Signal de Xon on foot.*

From the summit there is a fine view of Pont-à-Mousson and the Moselle Valley.

Vallée de l'Esch – *17km/10.6mi southwest. Drive south out of Pont-à-Mousson along N 57. In Blénod, take the second road on the right after the church. It leads to Jezainville.*

As you enter Jezainville, turn round to catch a glimpse of the Butte de Mousson right behind you and of the Blénod power station on the right, with four units of 250 million watts each.

The road enters the charming Esch Valley, at the heart of an area known as "Little Switzerland". The narrow road sometimes runs level with the small river winding its way across pastures and at other times climbs up a hill offering views of the pleasant green scenery.

Griscourt – This is a small pastoral village. From the east end of the church, the view embraces a restful landscape of green pastures.

From Griscourt to Martincourt, the road follows the edge of the forest along the Esch Valley.

Prény – *13km/8mi north. Leave Pont-à-Mousson along D 958 then turn right onto D 952. In Pagny-sur-Moselle, turn left onto D 82.*

The substantial ruins of a 13C castle dismantled by order of Richelieu stand on a hill (365m/1 197ft) overlooking the village. The towers linked by a high curtain wall formed an imposing fortress. It was the residence of the dukes of Lorraine before they moved to Nancy. The castle was finally abandoned at the beginning of the 18C. From the ruins, there is a fine view of the Moselle Valley.

Sillegny – *15km northeast. See METZ: Excursions.*

PROVINS ★★

Population 11 608
Michelin map 61 fold 4 or 237 fold 33

Whichever way one approaches the medieval town of Provins, the outline of the Tour César and the dome of the Église St-Quiriace can be seen from afar. The lower town lies on the banks of the Voulzie and the Durteint, beneath the promontory on which stand the romantic ruins celebrated by Balzac and painted by Turner. The formidable ramparts are the backdrop for medieval festivals and demonstrations in the summer months.

Clay from the Provins Basin, extracted from open quarries since time immemorial, supplies potters as well as brick and tile manufacturers with a complete range of raw materials.

HISTORICAL NOTES

The lower town developed from the 11C onwards round a Benedictine priory built on the spot where the relics of St Ayoul (or Aygulf) were miraculously found.

Under the leadership of Henri I (1152-1181), Count of Champagne, known as "the Liberal", Provins became a prosperous trading town and one of the two capital cities of Champagne.

The Provins fairs – The two fairs, held in Provins from May to June and from September to October, were, with those of Troyes, the most important of the Champagne fairs. There were three stages to each fair: first of all there was the display during which traders showed their merchandise, comparing prices and quality; next came the sale during which goods changed hands; the payment of the goods came last and, for this operation, sellers and buyers needed the help of money changers, notaries and **fair keepers**. The latter were initially police officers responsible for the prevention of theft and fraud, but by the 13C they had acquired real judicial power.

During the fair, the city looked like a huge market hall full of a colourful crowd of people from northern regions as well as from the Mediterranean. Transactions were made in local currency, hence the growing importance of Italian bankers who could calculate complex exchange rates; by the end of the 13C, they had taken control of the fairs and money changing took precedence over the sale of goods. The first annual fair, which was the most important, took place on the hilltop, near the castle, the second near the Église St-Ayoul.

Medieval town – Two separate towns developed simultaneously: the "Châtel" or upper town and the "Val" or lower town. They were later included within the same fortifications. In the 13C the city already had a large population of more than 10 000 inhabitants. Apart from numerous merchants, there were weavers, fullers, dyers, cloth-makers, shearers, without forgetting money changers, guards entrusted with police duties and other judicial representatives of the counts of Champagne. Numerous inns, shops and a thriving Jewish community added to the town's cosmopolitan atmosphere.

The counts of Champagne stayed in Provins for long periods and were surrounded by a lively court. Thibaud IV (1201-1253), known as the "Chansonnier", encouraged the arts and wrote songs which range among the best 13C literature.

In the 14C, the town's activities declined and the fairs were supplanted by those of Paris and Lyon. The Hundred Years War confirmed the end of economic prosperity for Provins.

Common rose from Provins
by Pierre-Joseph Redouté

Roses – According to tradition, it was **Thibaud IV** who brought red rose bushes back from the seventh crusade and began growing them in Provins. Edmund of Lancaster (1245-1296), the king of England's brother, married Blanche of Artois, the widow of the count of Champagne, and was for a while suzerain of Provins. He then added a red rose, a rare flower at the time, to his coat of arms. One hundred and fifty years later, during the War of the Roses, the House of Lancaster, whose emblem was a red rose, fought the House of York, whose emblem was a white rose for the throne of England.

During the Middle Ages, rose petals were used in medicine.

Nowadays, roses have become popular once more and rose lovers should visit Provins in June when the town's rose bushes are in full bloom, in particular in the **Pépinières et Roseraies J Vizier** ⊙ (EY), in rue des Prés.

★★VILLE HAUTE *1hr 30min*

Follow the street branching off avenue du Général-de-Gaulle and leave the car in the parking area. Continue on foot to the Porte St-Jean where the tour of the upper town begins.

Porte St-Jean (DY) – This massive gate, dating from the 13C, is flanked by two wedge-shaped towers partially concealed by buttresses added in the 14C to support a drawbridge. The stones are cut in such a way as to protrude and thus offer more resistance to impacts. The defence system also included a studded wooden portcullis sliding up and down in deep grooves, which are still visible, and a heavy

PROVINS
VILLE HAUTE

Bourreau (Sentier du)	EZ 9
Capucins (R. des)	EZ 12
Chapelle-St-Jean (R.)	DY 17
Clemenceau	
(R. Georges	DZ 22
Collège (R. du)	EY 23
Couverte (R.)	DY 28

Desmarest (R. Jean)	DZ 29
Enfer (R. de l')	EZ 32
Gambetta (Bd)	EZ 38
Jacobins (R. des)	EY 44
Madeleine (R. de la)	DY 49
Moulin de la Ruelle (R.) ..	DY 53
Opoix (R. Christophe)	EZ 57
Ormerie (R. de l')	DY 58
Palais (R. du)	EY 59
Petits Lions	
(R. des)	EY 62

Pie (R. de la)	EZ 63
Pompidou (Av. Georges).	EZ 67
St-Quiriace (Pl.)	EZ 77
Vieux Minage (R. du)	DY 83

K	Hostellerie de la Croix d'Or
L	Hôtel des Lions
N	Hôtel de Vauluisant

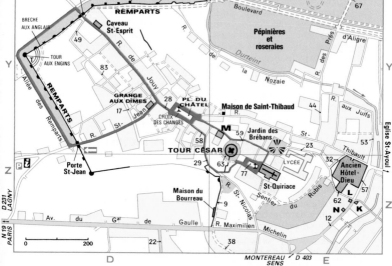

double-leafed door opening on the town side, itself reinforced by a bar. The guard-rooms on either side of the gate were linked by an underground passage and by an upper gallery. A watchtower surmounting the gate was taken down in 1723.

★★Remparts (DYZ) – The 12C-13C fortifications of the upper town, the oldest in Provins, are a fine example of medieval military architecture. The most interesting section stretches from the Porte St-Jean to the Porte de Jouy. The wall overlooking the dry moat is reinforced by square, rectangular, semicircular or wedge-shaped towers.

The imposing corner tower, known as the "Tour aux Engins", which links the two curtain walls, owes its name to a nearby barn where war machines were kept. Its walls are nearly 3m/10ft thick.

The upper part of the wall extending from the Tour aux Engins to the Porte St-Jean is pierced with loopholes; the glacis starts sloping outwards halfway down the wall.

From the Tour aux Engins to the Porte de Jouy, there are five defence works; the Brèche aux Anglais located between the first two, is a breach made by the English in 1432, during the Hundred Years War.

The 12C Tour de Jouy is reduced to its wedge-shaped base; on the right you can see part of the crenellated wall which has been reconstructed.

Follow rue de Jouy.

The street is lined with a variety of picturesque houses, low tiled-covered ones and higher ones with corbelled upper storeys. The **Caveau St-Esprit** (DY), which is used for certain events, formed part of a hospital destroyed by fire in the 17C.

★Place du Châtel (DY) – This vast rectangular area is lined with houses full of old-world charm. Walk around it in a clockwise direction to get a closer look at the most interesting medieval houses: on the southwest corner stands the 15C timber-framed Maison des Quatre Pignons, on the northwest corner, the 13C Maison des Petits-Plaids, where the provost used to render justice and which has retained a fine lower room with pointed vaulting; on the north side, the Hôtel de la Coquille, whose rounded doorway is decorated with a scallop shell, the emblem of pilgrims on their way to Santiago de Compostela; on the northeast corner, the ruins of the 12C Église St-Thibault; lower down, in rue St-Thibault, the house (EY) where, according to legend, St Thibault, the son of a count of Champagne, was born in 1017.

In the centre stands the Croix des Changes, on which edicts were posted; nearby there is an old well with a wrought-iron superstructure.

Continue along rue du Palais.

Musée de Provins et du Provinois ⊙ (EY) – The museum is housed in one of the oldest houses in Provins, known as the "Maison romane", whose curved façade has three Roman-arched openings. The lower one is framed by a diamond fret and the twinned upper ones are separated by a colonnette.

A low door leads to the cellar containing capitals and Merovingian sarcophagi displayed round an 11C pier.

The ground floor houses interesting **collections of sculpture and ceramics★**. Stone and polychrome carved-wood statues, most of them from demolished churches, are valuable examples of medieval and Renaissance art in the Provins region. The collection of ceramics illustrates the great quantity and diversity of the local production since prehistoric times: Neolithic pottery, Gallo-Roman tiles, fragments of sigillate bowls and goblets (stamped with seals and hallmarks), funeral vases, floor tiles with inlaid decoration (12C-13C), glazed jugs, finials. Iron-Age and Bronze-Age jewellery, Merovingian buckles in damascened iron and sarcophagi decorated with fishbone patterns are also exhibited.

Jardin des Brébans (EY) – From the public garden laid over a mound, there is a striking view of the nearby Église St-Quiriace and, next to it, of the Lycée (high school) built on the site of the former palace of the counts of Champagne which dated from the 12C and used to house one of the oldest colleges in France.

PAST IS PRESENT IN PROVINS

Medieval festival	1st weekend in June
Sound and Light show	1st and 2nd weekend in June
Jousting tournaments	June, July and August
"Les aigles de Provins"	March to October
Falconry demonstrations	
with medieval flair	
"À l'assaut des remparts"	Easter to 1 November
Medieval warfare demonstrations	

Contact the tourist office for more details.

Collégiale St-Quiriace (EZ) – The collegiate church dates from the 11C. The construction of the present edifice began around 1160 on the initiative of Henri the Liberal. In 1176, the chapter comprised 44 canons who maintained a thriving cultural centre. The church was surmounted by a dome in the 17C and the building was then considered to be completed although the nave only consisted of two bays. The isolated belfry collapsed in 1689. On the square, shaded by lime trees, a cross marks the spot where it stood.

The **chancel★** and square ambulatory were the first parts to be erected (second half of the 12C). Note early-Gothic features such as the rounded arcading of the blind triforium. The south bay of the chancel was surmounted in 1238 by an octopartite vault (formed by assembling four diagonal arches), characteristic of the region. Flying buttresses were then built on the outside to strengthen the vaulting. The bays of the triforium in the north transept and the nave have a more varied pattern which corresponds to a later design (building went on until the 16C). The dome rests on pendentives decorated with stuccowork representing the evangelists.

★★**Tour César** ⊙ (EY) – This splendid 12C keep (44m/144ft high), flanked by four turrets is the emblem of the town. It was once linked to the fortifications of the upper town. Its pyramidal roof dates from the 16C.

Walk beneath the archway and take the stairs on the right leading to the information desk then keep left and walk round the tower.

The skirt which surrounds the base of the tower was added by the English during the Hundred Years War to accommodate a number of guns.

On the first floor, the octagonal guard-room (11m/36ft high) is surmounted by ribbed vault crowned by a cupola with a hole in it, which was used to supply soldiers on the upper floor and to collect information from the lookouts. Watch paths running all the way round lead to former cells. The governor's bedroom is located at the foot of the stairs leading to the upper gallery.

From the once-covered gallery, which surrounds the keep, the **view★** extends over the city and the countryside beyond: to the west, the upper town within its fortifications, to the north, the former **Couvent des Cordelières** (Franciscan convent) founded in the 13C by Count Thibaud IV, which now houses an annexe of the French National Library.

The next floor is reached up a narrow staircase. The bells of St-Quiriace have been housed under the fine 16C timber work since the church lost its belfry.

Return to place du Châtel along rue Jean-Desmarets and rue de l'Ormerie. Continue along rue Couverte then turn left onto rue St-Jean.

***Grange aux Dîmes** ⊙ (DY) – This military-looking 13C building once belonged to the canons of St-Quiriace, who used to let it to merchants during the annual fairs. When the fairs were discontinued, the building was used as a tithe barn.

The ground floor consists of one vast hall, covered with ribbed vaulting resting on two rows of round piers topped by capitals with foliage motifs. An exhibition illustrates Provins at the time of the Champagne fairs.

The basement houses two Gothic cellars once used as storehouses.

ADDITIONAL SIGHTS

Église St-Ayoul – In 1048, Count Thibaud I founded a monastery in St-Ayoul. The church completed in 1084 was badly damaged by fire in 1157 and only the transept was saved. It was rebuilt almost immediately. The three doorways stand out from the west front whose gable is pierced by three 13C windows. The headless Romanesque statues decorating the central doorway are reminiscent of those which decorate the portal of St-Loup-de-Naud *(see Excursions below)*.

Bronze statues by Georges Jeanclos replacing the missing carved figures blend successfully with the remaining medieval sculptures. The tympanum illustrates Christ in glory set within a mandorla and accompanied by two evangelists; on the lintel, three episodes of the Virgin's life are depicted: the Annunciation, the Visitation and the Dormition; the bearing shaft is adorned with Abraham's Sacrifice.

The nave contains a wealth of beautiful woodwork by Pierre Blasset (1610-1663): the high altar and altarpiece, panelling and carved coffers in the aisles.

In the north aisle, there is a 16C **group of statues**★★ carved out of marble enhanced with gold and depicting a graceful Virgin with two musician angels clad with beautifully draped clothes.

Tour Notre-Dame-du-Val – This belfry, standing within the ruins of the former Porte Bailly, is all that remains of the collegiate church founded in the 13C by Countess Marie de Champagne and rebuilt in the 15C-16C. The tower, surmounted by a lantern houses the bells of St-Ayoul whose Romanesque belfry has lost its spire.

Église Ste-Croix ⊙ – According to local tradition, the church owes its name to the fact that Thibaud IV entrusted the church with a fragment of the True Cross he had brought back from the seventh Crusade. A second aisle in Flamboyant style was added

Provins – Tour César

PROVINS

on the north side in the 16C; inside, it is separated from the original one by fine spiral columns. The Romanesque belfry, surmounted by a modern spire, towers above the crossing. Note the modillioned cornice reminiscent of the Burgundian style.

The left doorway of the three-gabled west front is richly decorated in the Flamboyant and Renaissance styles. Flanked by two pilasters surmounted by crocket pinnacles, it consists of a surbased arch beneath an archivolt festooned with small trefoil arches. The gable is framed by statues. Foliage, grapes and grotesques complete the decoration.

Ancien Hôtel-Dieu (EZ) – This former hospital was originally a palace founded in the 11C by Count Thibaud I for the countesses of Blois and Champagne. Remodelled several times, the building has retained its 13C Gothic doorway, a Romanesque doorway with a rounded arch supported by two colonnettes and a 12C vestibule surmounted by groined vaulting, which houses an interesting Renaissance altarpiece in carved stone depicting the Virgin and Child implored by a kneeling donor.

Souterrains ⊙ – *Entrance in rue St-Thibaud, on the left of the doorway of the former Hôtel-Dieu* (EZ). Provins has a very dense network of underground passageways. Those which are open to the public were dug out of a layer of tuffa situated at the base of the promontory on which the upper town is built. They are accessible through a groin-vaulted low room in the Hôtel-Dieu. Following a geometric pattern, they are lined with cells and the rockface is covered with numerous graffiti from various periods. Their purpose remains a mystery.

Vieux hôtels – There are three interesting 13C inns in the vicinity of the Hôtel-Dieu. The **Hostellerie de la Croix d'Or** (EZ **K**) with twinned pointed windows stands at no 1 rue des Capucins; facing it is the **Hôtel des Lions** (EZ **L**) with a carved timber-framed façade. A little further on, you can see the **Hôtel de Vauluisant** (EZ **N**), once used by monks from Cîteaux; note the first-floor pointed windows flanked by colonnettes and surmounted by trefoil arches.

Maison du Bourreau (EZ) – This house, built astride the curtain wall linking the fortifications of the upper and lower towns, was the residence of the official executioner of Provins. Note the decorative oculus on the southeast gable.

EXCURSIONS

★**Saint-Loup-de-Naud** – *9km/5.6mi southwest.* The early-11C **church**★ belonged to a Benedictine priory. The porch and the two adjacent bays of the nave date from the 12C. The **doorway**★★, sheltered by the porch, is remarkably well preserved; it is reminiscent of the royal doorway of Chartres cathedral: the tympanum is decorated with a Christ in Glory surrounded by the emblems of the Evangelists, the apostles framed by arcading adorn the lintel, statue-columns line the embrasures and various characters decorate the recessed arches of the archivolt. The St-Loup

sculptures mark the beginning of a transition in architectural style which eventually led to Gothic realism.

The evolution is even more obvious inside: the early Romanesque style of the chancel switches to early Gothic in the nave which includes two 12C bays with ribbed vaulting next to the porch followed by two older bays, one of them surmounted by barrel vaulting, the other by groined vaulting. The crossing is covered by a dome whereas the transept itself, in line with the nave, is also surmounted by barrel vaulting. The 11C barrel-vaulted chancel is prolonged by an oven-vaulted apse.

Voulton – *7km/4.3mi north along D 71.* The imposing Gothic church has a saddleback-roofed belfry. In the nave, massive piers surrounded by engaged columns alternate with plain round piers. Note the octopartite vaulting surmounting the last bay before the chancel.

Beton-Bazoches – *18km/11mi north along D 55.* In this village, you can see a huge **cider press** ⊙ built in 1850 which was worked by a horse.

St-Loup-de-Naud – Columns on the church doorway

REIMS ★★★

Population 206 362
Michelin map 56 folds 6 and 16 or 241 fold 17

This ancient university town lying on the banks of the River Vesle is famous for its magnificent cathedral, where French kings were traditionally crowned, as well as the Basilique St-Remi. Reims is also, together with Épernay, the capital of Champagne and most cellars are open to the public.

The town, surrounded by a ring of boulevards laid out in the 18C, was badly damaged in 1914, when 80% of the buildings were destroyed. It has, since then, considerably expanded and some of its vast suburbs stretch as far as the edge of the vineyards.

Allow at least one day to see the city's main sights.

HISTORICAL NOTES

The origins of Reims go back to pre-Roman times when it was the fortified capital of a Gaulish tribe, the Remes. After the Roman conquest, it became a thriving administrative and commercial city with many public buildings. The **Porte de Mars** and the **Cryptoportique** are the only two to have survived to this day. From the 3C onwards, the town's strategic position increased its military importance as the Romans desperately tried to stop invading hords from the east. At the same time, Reims became a christian city and the first cathedral was built.

Then came the conversion of **Clovis**, the proud king of the Franks, who was baptized by the bishop of Reims, **Remi** (440-533), on Christmas day shortly before the year 500. The whole population rejoiced and led a procession from the former imperial

---

VISITING TIPS

Tours of the town

The tourist office is housed in the restored house of the chapter's treasurer near the cathedral, 2 rue Guillaume-de-Machaut, ☎ 03 26 77 45 25.

Daily guided tours of the cathedral in July and August: 1hr 30min.

— Audio-guided tours (cassettes in English) of the town and the cathedral are available during the rest of the year.

— Tours of the town in a barouche in July and August daily except Tuesday and rainy days; departure between 2pm and 7pm from the square in front of the cathedral; choice of three itineraries; time: about 30min.

— Tours of the town aboard a tourist train: weekends and holidays in May and June, daily in July and August; departure between 2pm and 7pm from the square in front of the cathedral; time: about 30min.

Events

— January and February: Traditional circus performances in one of the few remaining permanent circuses.

— June: Les Fêtes Johanniques, a Joan of Arc Festival in a superbly recreated medieval atmosphere, and les Sacres du Folklore, a prestigious folk festival.

— Late June to early October: music and light show at the Basilique St-Remi.

— July and August: Flâneries musicales d'Été (free concerts) in the town's museums, gardens and churches.

"Techniscénies" at the cathedral: High-tech sound and light shows.

Bars, cafés and restaurants

Pavement cafés and restaurants line the long place Drouet d'Erlon: Au Bureau, the Glue Pot, the Grand Café and the Café Leffe, a beer specialist.

Other nearby establishments include the bar of the Best Western Hotel "La Paix", which serves cocktails and Champagne on its terrace overlooking a pleasant garden and, a little further away, Arrigo's Bar, an American-syle bar; Le Palais, located on place Myron-Herrick, is the traditional meeting place of intellectuals and artists.

Regional specialities

— *Jambon de Reims* (ham from Reims)
— *Coq au vin* (chicken in wine sauce)
— *Pieds de porc de Ste-Menehould* (pig's trotters from Ste-Menehould)
— *Cerises de Dormans* (cherries from Dormans)
— *Biscuits roses et croquignoles de Reims* (pink biscuits and cracknels from Reims)
— *Bouchons de champagne au chocolat* (chocolate sweets shaped like Champagne corks)
— *Sorbet au marc de champagne* (sorbet flavoured with Champagne brandy)
— *Ratafia* (a Champagne-based aperitif)

palace to the baptistery situated near the cathedral. According to legend, a dove brought a phial containing holy oil used by Remi to anoint Clovis. This phial was carefully preserved and used for the coronation of every king of France from the 11C to 1825, the most famous being that of Charles VII in 1429, at the height of the Hundred Years War, in the presence of Joan of Arc.

From the end of the 5C and during the whole medieval period, Reims was an important religious, political and artistic centre. The powerful archbishops of Reims played the role of arbiters between kings and princes who came to stay at the Abbaye de St-Remi. One of the archbishops, **Gerbert**, became pope in 999.

During the 11C, 12C and 13C, the town expanded and acquired some splendid edifices such as the abbey church of St-Remi and the cathedral. **Guillaume aux Blanches Mains**, who was archbishop from 1176 to 1202, contributed to the prosperity of the town by granting it a charter and, by the beginning of the 13C, Reims had doubled in size. Wool from the region's many sheep made Reims a bastion of the cloth industry as early as the 12C. Champagne later became the town's other main source of prosperity. Today the textile industry has practically disappeared and, although the production of Champagne is still one of the town's main activities, new industries are developing (chemicals, pharmaceutical products, domestic appliances, electronic engineering, metalwork, foodstuffs, insurance).

The city's artistic tradition is also being maintained by the famous stained-glass workshops which once employed the talents of Villon, Chagall, Braque and Da Silva.

★★★CATHÉDRALE NOTRE-DAME (BY) *allow 1hr*

Owing to its homogenous architectural style, its superb sculptures and its spiritual role over more than a 1 000 of French and European history, the Cathédrale Notre-Dame undoubtedly deserves to be considered as one of the finest cathedrals in Christendom.

In 1210, Archbishop Aubry de Humbert decided to build a Gothic cathedral (the third to be erected on this site) modelled on those which were being built at the time in Paris (1163), Soissons (1180) and Chartres (1194). The edifice was designed by Jean d'Orbais and five successive architects followed the original plans, which accounts for the extraordinary homogeneity of the cathedral. Their names were inscribed on the original paving stones which unfortunately disappeared in the 18C. Jean d'Orbais built the chancel, Jean le Loup the nave and the west front which Gaucher de Reims decorated with statues and three portals, Bernard de Soissons designed the rose-window and the gables and finished the nave vaulting. By 1285, the interior had been completed. The towers were erected in the 15C; others were planned but a severe fire, which damaged the roof structure in 1481, halted the project.

The cathedral was regrettably altered in the 18C (suppression of the roodscreen, of some stained glass and of the labyrinth), but it was not damaged during the Revolution. Unfortunately, a long restoration programme had just been completed when, in September 1914, heavy shelling set fire to the timber framework causing the bells and the lead of the stained glass to melt and the stone to split. More shell damage occurred throughout the war and a new restoration programme was launched, partly financed by the Rockefeller Foundation. The damaged timber framework was replaced by a concrete roof structure. The cathedral was finally reconsecrated in 1937.

Exterior

A wealth of statues decorate the outside of the cathedral, more than 2 300 in fact. Some of them, however, which were badly damaged by war and bad weather, are now exhibited in the Palais du Tau and have been replaced by copies.

West front – Best seen in the setting sun, the west front of Reims cathedral is reminiscent of Notre-Dame in Paris but here the vertical lines are emphasized by the pointed gables and pinnacles, the slender colonnettes and the tall statues decorating the kings' gallery.

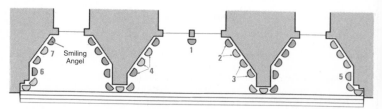

Notre-Dame Cathedral - Doorways on the façade

☟ 1st Workshop   ☟ 2nd Workshop   ☟ 3rd Workshop   ☟ 4th Workshop

The **three doorways**, in line with the three naves, are surmounted by elaborately carved gables contrasting with the openwork tympanums. The 13C statues adorning the doorways are from four workshops employed successively. Statues from the first one *(yellow on the plan)* are reminiscent of those of Chartres cathedral; statues from the second workshop *(lilac on the plan)* reveal the influence of antique art (draping of the clothes and facial expression); statues from the third *(pink on the plan)* are carved in a simpler style, similar to that used at Amiens; statues from the fourth *(green on the plan)* combine elements from the first three and assert a truly original regional style represented in particular by the famous smiling angel and characterised by an amazing liveliness and freedom of expression.

Central doorway (the Virgin's portal) – Against the upright post, the smiling Virgin (1); on the right, the Visitation (2) and the Annunciation (3); on the left, Jesus at the Temple (4); on the gable, the Coronation of the Virgin (copy).

Right doorway – On the right, Christ's forerunners, Simeon, Abraham, Isaiah, Moses (5); on the gable, the Last Judgement; on the archivolt, St John's visions of the Apocalypse.

Left doorway – The saints of Reims, including Helena (6) and Nikasius (7) and, on his left, the Smiling Angel; on the gable, a group representing the Passion.

Situated above the rose-window and the scene depicting David slaying Goliath, the kings' gallery includes 56 statues (height: 4.5m/15ft, weight: 6-7t); in the centre, Clovis' christening.

Walk along the north side of the cathedral.

The north side of the cathedral has retained its original features: the buttresses are surmounted by recesses containing a large angel with open wings.

North transept – The façade has three doorways decorated with statues which are older than those of the west front. The right doorway comes from the Romanesque cathedral: the typanum is adorned with a Virgin in glory framed by foliage beneath a rounded arch. The upright post of the middle portal is decorated with a statue of Pope Calixtus. The embrasures of the left doorway have retained their six fine statues representing the apostles and the tympanum is carved with picturesque scenes of the Last Judgement.

East end – From cours Anatole-France, there is a fine view of the east end of the cathedral with its radiating chapels surmounted by arcaded galleries and its superposed flying buttresses.

Interior ⊘

Inside, the cathedral is well lit and its proportions are remarkable (length: 138m/151yd; height: 38m/42yd); the impression of loftiness is enhanced by the narrowness of the nave in relation to its length and by the succession of very pointed transverse arches.

The three-storey elevations of the **nave** consist of the main arcading supported by round piers, a blind triforium (level with the roofing of the aisles) and tall clerestory windows, divided into lancets by mullions. Capitals are decorated with floral motifs.

The **chancel** has only two bays but the space used for services extends into the nave as there was always a large number of canons and a lot of space was needed for coronations. The chancel used to be closed off by a rood screen on which the royal throne was placed. Pillars get gradually narrower and closer together, thus increasing the impression of height. The radiating chapels are linked by a passage typical of the region's architectural style.

The **inside of the west front**★★ was the work of Gaucher from Reims. The large rose-window (diameter: 12m/40ft) is located above the triforium arcading backed by stained-glass windows of similar shape. A smaller rose decorates the doorway. On either side, a number of recesses contain statues. Floral motifs, similar to those of the nave capitals, complete the decoration. The inside of the central doorway is very well preserved: on the left the life of the Virgin is represented and on the right scenes from the life of John the Baptist.

★★**Stained glass** – The 13C stained-glass windows suffered considerable damage: some were replaced by clear glass in the 18C, others were destroyed

Chagall window

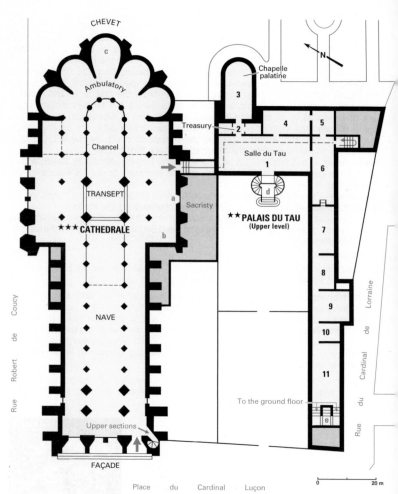

CHEVET

c

Ambulatory

Chancel

TRANSEPT

Sacristy

★★★ CATHEDRALE

a

b

NAVE

Rue Robert de Coucy

Upper sections

FAÇADE

Place du Cardinal Luçon

Chapelle palatine

Treasury

Salle du Tau
1

d

★★ PALAIS DU TAU
(Upper level)

To the ground floor

e

Rue du Cardinal de Lorraine

N

3

2

4

5

6

7

8

9

10

11

0   20 m

during the First World War. Those of the apse are still intact: in the centre is the donor with suffragan bishops on either side. The great 13C rose-window, dedicated to the Virgin, looks its best in the setting sun.

Jacques Simon, a member of the family of stained-glass makers who have been restoring the cathedral for generations, was able to restore some of the damaged ones and even to reconstruct the missing ones from drawings his ancestors made before the First World War. Note in particular the wine-growers' window (a). His daughter Brigitte Simon-Marcq made a series of abstract windows including one entitled the River Jordan to the right of the christening font (b) in the south transept.

In 1974, Marc Chagall decorated the apsidal chapel (c) with luminous blue-based stained-glass windows. They were made in the Simon workshop: in the centre, Abraham's Sacrifice and the Crucifixion; on the left, a Tree of Jesse and on the right, great events which took place in the cathedral such as Clovis' christening and St Louis' coronation.

The cathedral has retained a 15C astronomical clock. Each hour struck starts two processions: the Adoration of the Magi and the Flight to Egypt.

★★PALAIS DU TAU ⊘ (BY **S**) *1hr*

The archbishops' palace, first built on this site in 1138, owes its strange name to its T shape which resembles ancient episcopal croziers; it contains the cathedral treasury and some of the original statues. The present building, designed in 1690 by Robert de Cotte and Mansart, has retained a 13C chapel and the 15C great hall known as the Salle du Tau. Severely damaged in September 1914, at the same time as the cathedral, it was restored over a considerable number of years.

Tour – The palace is accessible from the south transept of the cathedral. Stairs lead to the Gothic **lower room** covered with ribbed vaulting, where stone fragments were stored. An exhibition shows the evolution of the cathedral site and of the canons' district which has disappeared. From there, the stone fragments (part of the rood screen) housed in the lower chapel can be seen.

Walk upstairs and through the Salle du Goliath.

The **Salle du Tau** (**1**) was used for the festivities which followed coronations. Lined with cloth bearing fleurs-de-lis, the symbol of French royalty, and decorated with two huge 15C tapestries from Arras illustrating the story of Clovis, it is covered with an elegant vault shaped like a ship's hull.

The **treasury** (**2**) is exhibited in two rooms: the left-hand one, lined with blue velvet, houses royal presents preserved during the Revolution such as Charlemagne's 9C talisman, which contains a piece of the True Cross, the coronation chalice, a 12C cup, the reliquary of the Holy Thorn, carved out of an 11C crystal, the 15C reliquary of the Resurrection, the reliquary of St Ursula, a delicate cornelian vase decorated with statuettes enamelled in 1505.

The right-hand room contains ornaments used for the coronation of Charles X: the reliquary of the Holy Phial, a large offering vase and two gold and silver loaves, the necklace of the order of the Holy Spirit worn by Louis-Philippe and a copy of Louis XV's crown.

The doorway of the **chapel** (**3**), built between 1215 and 1235, is surmounted by the Adoration of the Magi. The altar is decorated with the cross and six gilt silver candelabra made for the wedding of Napoleon and Marie-Louise.

The **Salle Charles X** (**4**) is devoted to the coronation of 1825. It contains the royal cloak as well as garments used by heralds and a painting of *Charles X in regal dress* by Gérard.

The **Antichambre des appartements du roi** (**5**), which illustrates the restoration of the cathedral sculptures, leads to the Musée de l'Œuvre de la Cathédrale.

The **Salle du Goliath** (**6**) contains monumental statues of St Paul, St James, Goliath (5.4m/18ft) wearing a coat of mail, as well as allegorical representations of the Synagogue (blindfolded) and the Church, damaged by shelling.

The **Salle des petites sculptures** (**7**) houses refined heads from the north transept and Passion doorways, the statues of Abraham and Aaron from the south doorway, two wingless angels and a 17C tapestry from Brussels depicting the story of Clovis (battle of Tolbiac).

Note, in the **Salle du Cantique des Cantiques** (**8**), four precious 17C hand-embroidered pieces of cloth made of wool and silk.

The **Salon carré** (**9**) is adorned with 17C tapestries, depicting scenes from Christ's childhood, woven in Reims. Two large statues of Magdalene and St Peter originally decorated the west front.

The **Salle du roi de Juda** (**10**) contains large statues including that of Judah (14C, kings' gallery) and three tapestries illustrating the Life of the Virgin.

Nine more sections of this tapestry are in the Galerie du couronnement de la Vierge (**11**) together with three kings from the north transept, three kings from the south transept and the statue of the Pilgrim from Emmaus which used to stand on the right of the great rose-window.

The Coronation of the Virgin (**e**) originally decorating the gable of the central doorway, overlooks the staircase.

Before leaving the courtyard, note the 15C angel (**d**) used as a weathercock.

★★BASILIQUE ET MUSÉE ST-REMI (CZ) *1hr 30min*

★★**Basilique St-Remi** – Remi was buried in 533 in a small chapel dedicated to St Christopher. Shortly afterwards, a basilica was constructed. Then the Abbaye de St-Remi was founded in the 8C by a group of Benedictine monks. Work on the present basilica began c 1007, but the project was deemed too ambitious and abandoned. The Carolingian church was demolished and the new basilica was erected during the course of the 11C. The chancel was built over the grave of St Remi. The church was consecrated by Pope Leon X in 1049.

However the building was remodelled at the end of the 12C and the Gothic basilica we see today dates from that period. A few minor changes occurred in the 16C and 17C.

Used as a barn during the Revolution, the church was restored in the 19C and again after the First World War. Many archbishops of Reims and the first kings of France were buried inside; the Holy Phial was kept in the church.

Exterior – The west front is overlooked by two square towers, 56m/184ft high: the south tower dates from the 11C whereas the north tower was built in the 19C together with the gable which separates them. The lower parts date from the 12C. Gallo-Roman columns, supporting the statues of St Remi and St Peter, frame the central doorway.

The transept dates from the 11C except for the façade of the south transept (late 15C). Note the statue of St Michael above the gable.

The buttresses surrounding the chancel are characteristic of 12C early Gothic. Admire the radiating chapels, the ambulatory and the clerestory windows in groups of three.

★★★ **Interior** – The basilica is very narrow (26m/85ft) in relation to its length (122m/400ft) and dimly lit, which makes it look even longer. The 11C nave consists of 11 bays with rounded main arcades resting on piers whose capitals are decorated with animals and foliage. Note the "crown of light" symbolising the life of St Remi, a copy of the original destroyed during the Revolution.

The four-storey Gothic chancel is closed off by a 17C Renaissance screen and lit by 12C stained-glass windows depicting the Crucifixion, the apostles, prophets and archbishops of Reims.

Behind the altar, **St Remi's grave**, rebuilt in 1847, has retained its 17C statues located in the recesses and representing St Remi, Clovis and the twelve peers who took part in the coronation.

Colonnades surrounding the chancel separate the ambulatory from the radiating chapels whose entrance is marked by two isolated columns. The polychrome motifs decorating the capitals are the original ones and the statues date from the 13C and 18C. The 45 stone slabs, inlaid with lead (biblical scenes), which can be seen in the first bay of the north aisle, come from the former Abbaye St-Nicaise.

The south transept houses an Entombment dating from 1530 and the altarpiece of the Three Christenings (1610) showing Christ between Constantine and Clovis.

★★ **Musée St-Remi** ⊘ (**M³**) – The museum is housed in the former royal abbey of St-Remi, consisting of a remarkably well-restored group of 17C and 18C buildings which have retained part of the medieval abbey such as the 13C parlour and the chapter-house.

The museum contains regional art collections from the origins until the end of the Middle Ages, with two exceptions, the military history section and the St-Remi tapestries.

Ground floor – The main courtyard leads to a building with an imposing façade in the Louis XVI style. The cloister, designed by Jean Bonhomme, dates from 1709; it leans against the basilica whose flying buttresses overlap into one of the galleries

The **chapter-house** is adorned with a series of magnificent Romanesque capitals. The former 17C refectory and kitchen contain the Gallo-Roman collections illustrating the ancient city of Durocortorum which later became Reims. Note the fine mosaics, the large relief map (1:2 000) and **Jovin's tomb★**, a splendid 3C and 4C Roman sarcophagus.

Musée St-Remi – Tapestry illustrating St Remi's life (1531)

First floor – A superb staircase, dating from 1778, leads to the gallery where the **St-Remi tapestries**★★ are exhibited; commissioned by Archbishop Robert de Lenoncourt for the basilica, they were made between 1523 and 1531. Each one consists of several scenes depicting various episodes of St Remi's life and the miracles he accomplished.

On the left of the staircase, three small rooms are devoted to the history of the site on which the abbey was built: 12C stone and bronze sculptures, 17C enamel work from the Limoges area illustrating the lives of St Timothy, Apollinarius and Maurus.

Follow the regional archeological trail round the cloister from the Paleolithic and the Neolithic periods (tools and funeral objects) through to the Protohistoric period (Bronze Age to the Roman conquest, including a wealth of objects discovered in chariot graves and in the large Gaulish necropolises) and up to Gallo-Roman times (handicraft, agriculture, clothing, jewellery, medecine, games, household items). The Merovingian period is represented by jewellery, pottery, glassware and weapons found in nearby necropolises. The exhibits displayed in the flying-buttress gallery were siezed during the Revolution: St Gibrien's crozier, the 14C Virgin's triptych, carved out of ivory.

The next gallery shows the evolution of medieval sculpture from the 11C to the 16C; note the delicately carved tympanum and the carved-wood console representing Samson and the lion.

The Gothic room contains fragments of religious or lay monuments which have disappeared: carvings from the Église St-Nicaise, reconstruction of the façade of the 13C Maison des Musiciens (House of Musicians), adorned with five statues.

A large room contains uniforms, military gear, weapons, documents etc, illustrating the main events of the city's **military history**; note in particular the glass cabinets devoted to the Champagne regiments, to the famous battles of the Revolutionary period, or to the military parade which took place on the occasion of Charles X's coronation in 1825.

★★CHAMPAGNE CELLARS

The famous Champagne firms are gathered in the Champ de Mars district (**BCX**) and along the limestone slopes of St-Nicaise hill (**CZ**), full of galleries known as *crayères*, often dating from the Gallo-Roman period. The depth and extent of the galleries makes them ideal Champagne cellars.

Pommery ⊘ (**CZ F**) – Founded in 1836 by Narcisse Gréno and Louis Alexandre Pommery, it was expanded by the latter's widow who inaugurated Brut Champagne and had the present buildings erected in the Elizabethan style in 1878. She also linked the Gallo-Roman crayères by building 18km/11mi of galleries and acquired many vineyards so that Pommery now owns 300ha/731 acres of the finest Champagne vines.

The tour enables visitors to discover the different stages of Champagne-making through galleries decorated with 19C sculptures and to see a 75 000l/16 500gal tun by Émile Gallé, dating from 1904.

Taittinger ⊘ (**CZ K**) – In 1734, the Fourneaux family of wine merchants launched into the production of sparkling wine made according to Dom Pérignon's methods. In 1932, Pierre Taittinger took over the management of the firm which was renamed after him. Today, the Taittinger vineyards extend over 250ha/618 acres and the firm owns 6 grape-harvesting centres on the Montagne de Reims, the Château de la Marquetterie in Pierry, the Hôtel des Comtes de Champagne in Reims *(see Town centre below)* and superb cellars.

Visitors can enjoy a fascinating tour of the cellars among 15 million bottles maturing in the cool Gallo-Roman galleries and in the crypts of the former 13C Abbaye St-Nicaise, destroyed during the Revolution.

Veuve Clicquot-Ponsardin ⊘ (**CZ Z**) – This firm, founded in 1772 by Philippe Clicquot, was considerably expanded by his son's widow whose maiden name was Ponsardin. In 1816, she introduced *remuage (see page 63)* into the process of Champagne-making. Today, Veuve Clicquot-Ponsardin, which owns 265ha/655 acres of vines and exports three quarters of its production, is one of the best known Champagne firms outside France.

Ruinart ⊘ (**CZ L**) – Founded in 1729, this Champagne firm prospered during the Restauration period (1814-1830) and again after 1949, having gone through years of decline during the two world wars. Today Ruinart, which belongs to the Moët-Hennessy group, specialises in top-quality Champagne. Its Gallo-Roman galleries are particularly interesting.

Piper-Heidsieck ⊘ (**CZ V**) – The firm was founded in 1785. The various stages of Champagne-making are explained by means of an audio-visual presentation and visitors can afterwards tour the cellars, extending 16km/10mi underground, in a gondola car.

Mumm ⊘ (**BX N**) – After its creation in 1827, this firm prospered throughout the 19C in Europe and in America; today, it owns 420ha/1 038 acres of vines and its cellars *(open to the public)* extend over a total distance of 25km/16mi.

TOWN CENTRE *allow 2hr*

From the square in front of the cathedral, walk along rue Rockefeller and turn right onto rue Chanzy.

★**Musée des Beaux-Arts** ⊘ (BY M¹) – The Fine Arts Museum, housed in the former 18C Abbaye St-Denis whose church was destroyed during the Revolution, covers the period from the Renaissance to the present times.

Ground floor – Exhibits include:
– 13 portraits (16C) of German princes by Cranach the Elder and Cranach the Younger; these are extremely realistic drawings enhanced by gouache and oil paint.
– 26 landscapes by Corot (1796-1875) and the portrait of a seated Italian youth, painted by Corot during his stay in Rome in 1826.
– ceramics produced by the most important French and foreign manufacturers as well as a few sculptures by René de Saint-Marceaux (1845-1915), a native of Reims.

First floor – The first room contains some strange grisaille works enhanced by colours, painted during the 15C and 16C, which include four series of picturesque scenes (the Apostles, Christ's Vengeance and Christ's Passion). They may have been used as sets for mystery plays or lined along the way from St-Remi to the cathedral on coronation days.
The following rooms are devoted to French painting from the 17C to the present day, including works by: Philippe de Champaigne *(The Habert de Monmort Children)*; the Le Nain brothers *(Venus in Vulcan's Forge* and *Peasants' Meal)*; Vouet and Poussin; Boucher *(The Odalisque)*; David *(Marat's Death)*; the Barbizon School (Daubigny, Théodore Rousseau, Harpignies, Millet); the pre-Impressionists (Lépine, Boudin, Jongkind); the Impressionists (Pissarro, Monet, Sisley and Renoir); modern painting (Dufy, Matisse).

Continue along rue Chanzy then turn left onto the lively pedestrian rue de Vesle.

Note the small doorway which used to give access to the south transept of the Église St-Jacques.

Turn right onto rue Max-Dormoy.

Église St-Jacques ⊘ (ABY) – The 13C-14C Gothic nave with a traditional triforium is prolonged by a Flamboyant Gothic chancel (early 16C) framed by two Renaissance chapels (mid-16C) with Corinthian columns. The modern stained-glass windows were designed by Vieira da Silva (side chapels) and Sima (chancel).

Place Drouet-d'Erlon (AY 38) – Reserved for pedestrians, this lively space lined with cafés, restaurants, hotels and cinemas is the heart of the city.

Walk up to the Fontaine Subé, erected in 1903, turn right onto rue de l'Étape and continue as far as rue de l'Arbalète.

★**Hôtel de la Salle** (BY E) – This Renaissance edifice, built between 1545 and 1556, is the birthplace of **Jean-Baptiste de la Salle** *(see below)*. The harmonious façade, adorned with Doric pilasters at ground-floor level and Ionic ones at first-floor level, is flanked by a pavilion whose carriage entrance is decorated by statues of Adam and Eve on either side.
An elaborately carved frieze runs across the façade.
A picturesque openwork stair turret rises in a corner of the courtyard.

Turn left onto rue du Dr-Jacquin.

Jean-Baptiste de la Salle and schooling for the poor

Small schools intended for children of poor families began to open in Reims from 1674 onwards, at the instigation of Canon Roland. His work was continued by Jean-Baptiste de la Salle.
Born in Reims in 1651, Jean-Baptiste de la Salle belonged to a rich aristocratic family who intended him to pursue a brillant career within the Church. However, the young canon decided instead to devote his energies and his wealth to educating the poor. He began by founding the Communauté des Sœurs du Saint Enfant Jésus, which spread throughout the countryside. The nuns ran schools, and catechism classes but they also taught adults. A few years later, Jean-Baptiste de la Salle founded the Communauté des Frères des Écoles chrétiennes, which expanded considerably.
In 1695, he published a work entitled *The Running of Schools*, in which he explained his theories about teaching: he was in favour of collective teaching and wanted French to replace Latin. However, his ideas, which were revolutionary at the time, only triumphed long after his death (Rouen 1719).

Hôtel de ville (BX **H**) – The imposing 17C façade was saved from the fire which destroyed the building in 1917. The pediment is decorated with an equestrian low-relief sculpture representing Louis XIII.

Continue along rue du Tambour.

"Hôtel des Comtes de Champagne" (BX **D**) – This Gothic mansion belongs to the Taittinger Champagne firm.
The Maison des Musiciens, whose first storey has been reconstructed and exhibited in the Musée St-Remi, was located next door.

The street leads to place du Forum, formerly place des Marchés.

Cryptoportique gallo-romain ☉ (BY **R**) – This large half-buried Gallo-Roman monument, dating from the 2C AD, stands on the site of the ancient city's forum.

★**Musée-hôtel Le Vergeur** ☉ (BX **M²**) – This mansion, dating from the 13C, 15C and 16C, offers a picturesque façade with a timber-framed upper part over a stone base and overlapping gables. A Renaissance wing, built at right angles and over-looking the garden, has an interesting frieze carved with warring scenes.
The 13C great hall and the floor above it contain paintings, engravings and plans concerning the history of Reims and the splendour of coronation ceremonies.
The living quarters, decorated with woodwork and antique furniture, recall the daily life of Baron Hugues Krafft, a patron of the arts who lived in the mansion until his death in 1935 and bequeathed it together with all his possessions to the Friends of Old Reims.
One of the drawing rooms contains an exceptional collection of engravings by Dürer including the Apocalypse and the Great Passion.

Walk along rue Colbert to place Royale.

★**Place Royale** (BY) – The square, designed by Legendre in 1760, is characteristic of the Louis XVI style: arcades, roofs edged by balusters. The former Hôtel des Fermes, on the south side, houses administrative offices. The statue of Louis XV by Pigalle, which used to stand in the centre of the square, was destroyed during the Revolution and the holy coronation phial was smashed on the pedestal; another statue by Cartellier replaced the original during the Restauration (1814-1830).

Follow rue Carnot on the right.

Porte du Chapitre (BY **B**) – This 16C gate, flanked by two corbelled turrets, formed the main entrance of the chapter-house.

Walk through the gateway to return to the cathedral.

ADDITIONAL SIGHTS

★**Chapelle Foujita** ☉ (BX) – Designed and decorated by **Léonard Foujita** (1886-1968) and donated by the Champagne firm Mumm, the chapel was inaugurated in 1966. It celebrates the mystical inspiration felt by the Japanese painter in the Basilique St-Remi. Foujita, who belonged to the early-20C school of art known as the École de Paris, converted to the Christian faith and was baptized in Reims cathedral.
The interior of the chapel is decorated with stained glass and frescoes depicting scenes of the Old and New Testaments.

Salle de Reddition ☉ (AX) – *12 rue Franklin-Roosevelt.* General Eisenhower established his headquarters in this technical college towards the end of the Second World War and this is also where the German capitulation act was signed on 7 May 1945. The Salle de la Signature (Signing Room) has remained as it was at the time with its maps etc.

★**Porte Mars** (ABX) – This triumphal arch (height: 13.5m/44ft) of the Corinthian order was erected in honour of the Roman Emperor Augustus sometimes after the 3C AD. During the Middle Ages, it was included in the ramparts and used as a town gate. It consists of three arches decorated inside with low-relief sculptures depicting Jupiter and Leda, as well as the founders of Rome, Romulus and Remus.

Promenades (AXY) – These vast shaded areas were designed in the 18C to replace the moat and glacis of the old fortifications. They provide a useful parking area close to the town centre. A fun fair invades the Hautes Promenades at Christmas and Easter. A remarkable wrought-iron **railing**, made in 1774 for the coronation of Louis XVI, stands at the end of the Basses Promenades.
Not far from there, along boulevard du Général-Leclerc, stand two 19C buildings, the **Cirque** (1 100 seats) and the **Manège** (600 seats) where various events are held.

Centre des Congrès (AY) – The congress centre designed by Claude Vasconi and inaugurated in 1994, looks like "a ship moored along the canal". The glass-and-aluminium edifice, incorporating the latest technological equipment, includes two amphitheatres, 10 conference rooms, a large exhibition hall...

Comédie de Reims (AY) – This former general cultural centre completed in 1970 now specialises in drama; it is a good example of functional contemporary architecture with several auditoriums on different levels.

Centre historique de l'automobile française ⊘ (**CY M**) – This French car centre houses a collection of vintage cars and prototypes in excellent condition including some of the first cars ever made (De Dion-Bouton), several Hispano-Suiza (1929-1935), the strange Scarab used by General de Gaulle in 1943, as well as racing cars of various periods.

Ancien collège des Jésuites ⊘ (**CZ W**) – In 1606, the Jesuits were allowed by King Henri IV to found a college in Reims; they then erected the chapel (1617-1678) which now stands on place Museaux and the buildings surrounding the courtyard. Clinging to one of the walls and still giving grapes is a 300-year-old vine, brought back from Palestine by the Jesuits. The college prospered until the Jesuits were expelled from France in 1764; it was then turned into a general hospital.

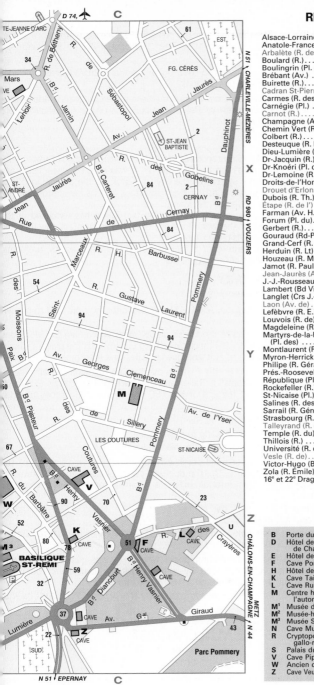

REIMS

Alsace-Lorraine (R. d') ..... CX 2
Anatole-France (Cours) .... BY 3
Arbalète (R. de l') .... BY 4
Boulard (R.). .... BY 6
Boulingrin (Pl. de). .... BX 7
Brébant (Av.) .... AY 8
Buirette (R.). .... AY 12
Cadran St-Pierre (R.). ...... BY 13
Carmes (R. des) .... BZ 16
Carnégie (Pl.) .... BY 17
Carnot (R.). .... BY 19
Champagne (Av. de) ...... CZ 22
Chemin Vert (R. du). .... CZ 23
Colbert (R.). .... BXY 26
Desteuque (R. E.). .... BY 31
Dieu-Lumière (R.). .... CZ 32
Dr-Jacquin (R.) .... BXY 33
Dr-Knoëri (Pl. du). .... CX 34
Dr-Lemoine (R.). .... BX 35
Droits-de-l'Homme (Pl. des) CZ 37
Drouet d'Erlon (Pl.). .... AY 38
Dubois (R. Th.) .... AY 39
Étape (R. de l') .... AY 40
Farman (Av. H.) .... CZ 43
Forum (Pl. du). .... BY 47
Gerbert (R.). .... BCY 50
Gouraud (Rd-Pt Gén.) ..... CZ 51
Grand-Cerf (R. du) .... CZ 52
Herduin (R. Lt) .... BY 53
Houzeau (R. Muiron). ...... CY 54
Jamot (R. Paul). .... BY 56
Jean-Jaurès (Av.) .... BCX
J.-J.-Rousseau (R.) .... BX 57
Lambert (Bd Victor). ...... CZ 59
Langlet (Crs J.-B.) .... BY 60
Laon (Av. de) .... ABX
Lefèbvre (R. E.). .... CX 61
Louvois (R. de) .... BZ 62
Magdeleine (R.) .... AY 63
Martyrs-de-la-Résistance
 (Pl. des) .... BY 65
Montlaurent (R.). .... CY 67
Myron-Herrick (Pl.) .... BY 68
Philipe (R. Gérard) .... CZ 70
Prés.-Roosevelt (R.) ...... AX 72
République (Pl. de la) ..... BX 73
Rockefeller (R.). .... BY 75
St-Nicaise (Pl.) .... CZ 78
Salines (R. des). .... CZ 80
Sarrail (R. Gén.). .... BX 82
Strasbourg (R. de). .... CX 84
Talleyrand (R. de) .... ABY
Temple (R. du) .... BX 85
Thillois (R.) .... AY 86
Université (R. de l') .... BY 88
Vesle (R. de) .... ABY
Victor-Hugo (Bd) .... CZ 90
Zola (R. Émile). .... AX 92
16ᵉ et 22ᵉ Dragons (R. des) . CY 94

B   Porte du Chapitre
D   Hôtel des Comtes
    de Champagne
E   Hôtel de la Salle
F   Cave Pommery
H   Hôtel de Ville
K   Cave Taittinger
L   Cave Ruinart
M   Centre historique de
    l'automobile française
M¹ Musée des Beaux-Arts
M² Musée-hôtel le Vergeur
M³ Musée St-Rémi
N   Cave Mumm
R   Cryptoportique
    gallo-romain
S   Palais du Tau
V   Cave Piper-Heidsieck
W   Ancien collège des Jésuites
Z   Cave Veuve Clicquot-Ponsardin

The tour includes the **refectory**, decorated with 17C woodwork and paintings by Jean Helart depicting the life of St Ignatius Loyola and St Francis-Xavier. Note the magnificent table top carved out of one single piece of oak; a branch of the same tree was used to make the table of the public prosecutor's office upstairs.

A Renaissance staircase leads to the **library★**, elaborately adorned with Baroque woodwork and a coffered ceiling supported by garlands, scrolls and cherubs. It was the setting chosen by Patrice Chéreau for his film *La Reine Margot* with Isabelle Adjani and Daniel Auteuil, in which Margot, the wife of the future Henri IV, condemns the St Bartholomew massacre initiated in 1572 by her mother, Catherine de Medicis. Note the small reading cubicles and the table with hoof-shaped feet. The tour of the underground galleries (refreshing in summer) includes a 17C cellar, a 12C gallery and a Gallo-Roman gallery.

Planétarium et Horloge astronomique ⊙ – The former Jesuit college houses a plane
tarium and an astronomical clock made between 1930 and 1952 by Jean Legros, a
native from Reims.

Parc Pommery ⊙ (CZ) – This park, covering an area of 22ha/54 acres, includes
sports grounds and children's playgrounds.

Faculté des Lettres – *Access from avenue du Général-de-Gaulle (AZ) and avenue
du Général-Eisenhower, southwest of Reims*. The buildings of the Arts faculty were
designed by Dubard de Gaillarbois.

EXCURSIONS

Fort de la Pompelle – *9km/5.6mi southeast; leave Reims along avenue H Farman (CZ)*.
The fort sits on top of a hill rising to 120m/394ft. It was built between 1880 and
1883 as part of the defence system of the city of Reims. At the beginning of the
First World War, it was under constant German attack but its resistance contributed to the victory of the Battle of the Marne.
From the lower parking area, a path leads to the fort which has remained in the
state it was in at the end of the war. Guns are displayed in front of the fort and
trenches and casemates are visible on the south side.
The **museum** ⊙ houses mementoes of the First World War (decorations, uniforms,
weapons and a rare **collection of German helmets★**).

MASSIF DE ST-THIERRY

50km/31mi round tour – allow 1hr 30min

*Leave Reims along avenue de Laon, N 44 (AX) and turn onto the first road to the left
(D 26) after La Neuvillette.*
The road rises along the slopes of the Massif de St-Tierry, which, like the Montagne
de Reims, is a section of the Ile-de-France cliff jutting out towards the plain of Champagne. The area has a wealth of Romanesque churches preceded by a porch.

St-Thierry – This village lying on the foothills overlooking the plain of Reims has a
12C **church** with a porch. Archbishop Talleyrand, the uncle of the famous early-19C
minister, had a castle built at the end of the 18C on the site of an abbey founded
in the 6C by St Thierry.

Chenay – Views of the Montagne de Reims.
In Trigny, turn right onto D 530 leading to Hermonville.
Asparagus and strawberries are grown in this sandy area.

Hermonville – An imposing arcaded porch extends across the whole width of the
west front of the church (late 12C). The doorway recess shelters an 18C statue of
the Virgin. The early-Gothic interior offers a striking contrast with the 18C
baldaquined altar.
*Drive west along D 30 across the highest point of the Massif de St-Thierry. In
Bouvancourt, turn left onto D 375.*
Just before reaching Pévy, enjoy the charming bird's-eye view of the village nestling
inside the valley with the Vesle Valley beyond.

Pévy – This village has an interesting **church** whose Romanesque nave contrasts
with the Gothic chancel surmounted by a belfry with a saddleback roof. The
interior houses a Romanesque font and a 16C stone altarpiece.
*Follow D 75 down to the River Vesle and cross over at Jonchery; N 31 leads back to
Reims.*

REMIREMONT

Population 9068
Michelin map 62 fold 16 or 242 fold 34

The small town of Remiremont, situated in the deep and densely forested upper valley
of the River Moselle, was once the seat of a famous abbey.

The chapter of the "Ladies from Remiremont" – In 620, a nobleman named
Romaric founded a convent on a height overlooking the confluence of the Moselle and
the Moselotte. However, the convent soon settled in the valley below and acquired a
rich and powerful chapter under the direct control of the Pope and the Holy Roman
Emperor. The canonesses, who were all aristocrats of ancient lineage, lived in mansions
surrounding the convent. The mother superior, who had the title of "princess of the
Holy Empire", and her two assistants were the only ones to take their vows; the other
nuns were free but had to attend services.
This chapter was, for centuries, one of the most important in the western world. The
Revolution ended its prosperity. Some of the 60 abbesses were famous personalities:
Catherine of Lorraine who, in 1638, drove away Turenne when he besieged the town;
Marie-Christine of Saxe, who was the aunt of three French kings (Louis XVI, Louis XVII
and Charles X); Louise-Adélaïde of Bourbon, the Prince de Condé's daughter.

ABBATIALE ST-PIERRE *allow 15min*

The former abbey church, surmounted by an onion-shaped belfry, is, for the most part, Gothic but the west front and the belfry were rebuilt in the 18C. Note the beautiful 17C marble ornamentation of the chancel which includes a monumental altarpiece intended for the display of reliquaries. The statue of Notre-Dame-du-Trésor, located in the right-hand chapel, dates from the 11C.

Beneath the chancel, there is an 11C **crypt★** with groined vaulting resting on monoliths.

The former 18C abbatial palace, adjacent to the church, has a beautiful façade. A few of the 17C and 18C mansions inhabited by the canonesses still surround the church and the palace.

ADDITIONAL SIGHTS

★Rue Charles-de-Gaulle – This picturesque arcaded street with flower-decked pillars is a fine example of 18C town planning.

Musée municipal, Fondation Ch.-de-Bruyère ⊙ – *70 rue Ch.-de-Gaulle.*
The town museum is housed in two different buildings. The collections of the Fondation Ch.-de-Bruyère are displayed on two floors. The ground floor is devoted to local history and handicraft from Lorraine and the ornithological collection is housed in an outside gallery. On the first floor, precious manuscripts and tapestries from the former abbey are displayed together with Gothic sculpture from the Lorraine region, 18C ceramics and paintings. One room contains 17C paintings from northern countries (Rembrandt's School). The great gallery offers a panorama of painting from the 19C and early 20C.

Musée municipal, Fondation Charles-Friry ⊙ – *12 rue Général-Humbert.*
This section of the town museum, housed in one of the former canonesses' mansion (18C and 19C), contains collections of documents, statues, objets d'art etc, connected with the "Ladies from Remiremont" or with local and regional history, as well as numerous 17C-18C paintings, including *Le Veilleur à la sacoche* ("The Hurdy-gurdy Player") by Georges de La Tour, prints by Goya and Callot and furniture from various periods.

The garden, which partly recreates the "Grand Jardin" of the abbey, is decorated with two ornamental fountains and a few other features from the abbey.

Promenade du Calvaire – This promenade area offers an overall view of the town and of the Moselle Valley to the north.

The nearby **Forêt de Fossard** across the river, bears traces of ancient religious settlements going back to the 7C. It is crisscrossed by marked footpaths ideal for hiking *(starting-point: St-Étienne).*

RETHEL

Population 7 923
Michelin map 56 fold 7 or 241 fold 13

Rethel lies on the banks of the River Aisne and of the Canal des Ardennes. The town had to be almost completely rebuilt after being destroyed during May and June 1940. The French poet, **Paul Verlaine**, spent several quiet years in Rethel during the 1870s teaching literature, history, geography and English.

Église St-Nicolas ⊙ – The church, which stands on top of a hill, was carefully restored at the end of the Second World War. This unusual Gothic edifice in fact consists of two churches built side by side and an imposing tower.

The left-hand church (12C-13C) acquired new vaulting in the 16C; it was used by monks from a Benedictine monastery.

The right-hand church (15C-16C) was the parish church. Characteristic features include a wide aisle lit by Flamboyant Gothic windows and a richly decorated doorway completed in 1511, a fine example of Flamboyant Gothic ornamentation: note the statue of St Nicholas bonded to the upright post and the Assumption decorating the gable, reminiscent of the Coronation of the Virgin on the central doorway of Reims cathedral.

The early-17C tower illustrates the characteristic superposition of the classical orders.

Musée du Rethelois et du Porcien ⊙ – The museum is devoted to archeology, folklore, former colonial territories, regional prints and religious art.

Admission times and charges for the sights described are listed at the end of the guide. Every sight for which there are times and charges is identified by the symbol ⊙ in the Sights section of the guide.

RIBEAUVILLÉ ★

Population 4 774
Michelin map 87 fold 17 or 242 fold 31 – Local map see Route des VINS

Ribeauvillé lies in a picturesque site at the foot of the Vosges mountains crowned with old castles. The small town is renowned for Riesling, a famous Alsatian white wine made in the area.

Pfifferdaj – The "day of the fifes" is one of the last traditional festivals in Alsace whose origin goes back to ancient times. It takes place on the first Sunday in September. Travelling musicians used to gather in the town to pay homage to their suzerain. The statutes of their powerful corporation were recorded by Colmar's Council. Today, the Pfifferdaj is a folk festival with a historic procession and free wine-tasting at the "Fontaine du Vin", place de l'Hôtel-de-ville.

★★GRAND'RUE

Start from the tourist office housed in the former guard-house (1829).
The street is lined with picturesque timber-framed flower-decked houses.

Pfifferhüs (Restaurant des Ménétriers) (B) – *No 14.* Two statues standing on a loggia above the door illustrate the Annunciation.

Ribeauvillé

"Halle au Blé" (B F) – *Place de la 1ʳᵉ-Armée.* Once the site of a weekly granary exchange, the old covered market sits atop a secret passageway.

Fontaine Renaissance (A E) – Built in 1536, the red-and-yellow-sandstone fountain is surmounted by a heraldic lion.

Hôtel de ville (A H) – The town hall houses a small **museum** ⊙ containing 17C gold plate and vermeil goblets.

★**Tour des Bouchers (A)** – This former belfry used to mark the separation between the upper and the middle town. The base dates from the 13C.

Maison ancienne (A B) – *No 78.* Beautiful 17C timber-framed house.

Place de la Sinne – This is a charming little square, lined with timber-framed houses, with a fountain (1860) in its centre.

ADDITIONAL SIGHTS

Église St-Grégoire-le-Grand (A) – The church dates from the 13C-15C. Note the tympanum of the west doorway and the fine ironwork of the door. In the nave, strong and weak pillars alternate in characteristic Rhineland fashion. The capitals are particularly beautiful. In the south aisle, there is a 15C carved-wood Virgin and Child, gilt and painted, wearing the local headdress; the north aisle contains a carved group illustrating the Mount of Olives; the Baroque organ was made by Rinck.

Nids de cigognes (B D) – Two old towers, standing at the town's southern and eastern entrances, are surmounted by stork nests.

Maisons anciennes – 16C and 17C houses can be seen along rue des Juifs, rue Klobb, rue Flesch and rue des Tanneurs (note the openings in the roof of no 12, which helped to dry skins).

★CHÂTEAU DE ST-ULRICH

Leave Ribeauvillé by ⑤ on the town plan.
The Grand'Rue offers a fine vista of the castle ruins.
Leave the car in the parking area situated on the roadside (D 416), about 800m/875yd out of town. Walk up along the Chemin des stations (20min) or the Chemin "Sarazin" (40min).

RIBEAUVILLÉ

Abbé-Kemp (R. de l')	A 2	Gaulle (Av. du Gén.-de)	B 9	Rempart-	
Bergheim (Rte de)	B	Gouraud (Pl.)	B 10	de-la-Streng (R. du)	AB
Château (R. du)	A 3	Grand'Rue	AB	République (Pl. de la)	A
Flesch (R.)	B 5	Halles-aux-Blés (R.)	B 12	Ste-Marie-	
Fontaine (R. de la)	A 6	Juifs (R. des)	B	aux-Mines (Rte)	A 15
Frères-Mertian		Klée (R.)	B	Sinne (Pl. de la)	A 16
(R. des)	A 7	Klobb (R.)	A	Tanneurs (R. des)	B 18
		Lutzelbach (R. du)	A	Vignoble (R. du)	A
		Mairie (Pl. de la)	A 13	Ire-Armée (Pl. de la)	B
		Marne (R. de la)	A	3-Décembre (R. du)	AB

Pedestrian zone in tourist season

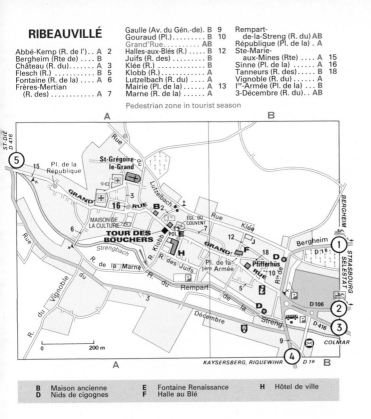

B Maison ancienne	**E** Fontaine Renaissance	**H** Hôtel de ville
D Nids de cigognes	**F** Halle au Blé	

Notre-Dame-de-Dusenbach – This place of pilgrimage includes the Virgin's Chapel, a convent, a neo-Gothic church (1903) and a pilgrims' shelter (1913). The **Chapelle de la Vierge** has been destroyed three times since it was founded in 1221. It was rebuilt for the last time in 1894 in neo-Gothic style on the edge of a promontory towering above the narrow Dusenbach Valley. The chapel contains murals by Talenti (1938) and, above the altar, a 15C Pietà in polychrome wood, said to perform miracles.

Follow the Chemin Sarazin then the path leading to the castles.

Stop by the **Rocher Kahl**, at the halfway mark. From this granite scree, there is a fine bird's-eye view of the Strengbach Valley and its forested slopes.

The path leads to a major intersection of forest lanes: continue straight on along the narrow path signposted "Ribeauvillé par les châteaux".

Château du Haut-Ribeaupierre – It is possible to walk through the ruins of this 12C castle but the keep is closed to the public.

Retrace your steps (avoiding the direct path linking Haut-Ribeaupierre and St-Ulrich) back to the intersection and follow the marked path leading down to St-Ulrich.

★**Château de St-Ulrich** – The stairs leading to the castle start from the foot of the keep, on the left (1).The **castle** was not only a fortress, like most castles in the Vosges region, but also the luxury residence of the Comtes de Ribeaupierre, one of the oldest aristocratic families in Alsace. The stairs lead through the castle gate (2) to a small

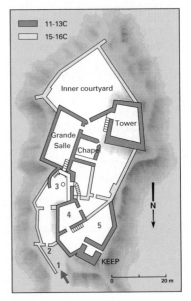

courtyard which offers a fine view of the ruins of Girsberg castle and of the Plaine d'Alsace. A door at the end of the courtyard, beyond the water tank (3), gives access to the Romanesque Great Hall, lit by nine twinned rounded windows, which was once covered by a timber ceiling.

Return to the small courtyard and walk up the stairs to the chapel, leaving the entrance of the 12C tower on your right. West of the chapel stands an enormous square tower accessible via outside stairs. Retrace your steps to visit the oldest part of the castle including Romanesque living quarters (4), whose windows are decorated with fleurs-de-lis, another courtyard (5) and the keep. The red-sandstone square keep, built on a granite base, towers over the rest of the castle and makes a remarkable viewpoint. From the top, reached by walking up 64 steps, the **panorama**★★ extends over the Strengbach Valley, the ruins of the **Château de Girsberg** (dating from the 12C and abandoned in the 17C), Ribeauvillé and the Plaine d'Alsace.

COL DE FRÉLAND *47km/29mi – allow 5hr*

Leave Ribeauvillé by ⑤ on the town plan.

The road *(D 416)* follows the River Strengbach which flows rapidly through the beautiful Ribeauvillé Forest. After driving 7km/4.3mi, turn left towards Aubure along a picturesque cliff road offering glimpses of the valley on the left.

Aubure – The resort is pleasantly situated on a sunny plateau and surrounded by fine pine and fir forests.

Turn left onto D 11^{III}.

On the way down from the Col de Fréland, 1.5km/0.9mi from the pass, turn left onto a narrow road, which runs through a beautiful **pine forest**★, one of the finest to be seen in France. The tall straight trees (60cm/2ft in diameter and 30m/98ft high) are quite impressive.

After coming out of the forest, drive on for another 1km/0.6mi and turn back to return to D 11^{III}.

There is a clear view of the Weiss Valley and part of the Val d'Orbey.

Continue past Fréland and, 1.5km/0.9mi beyond the intersection with D 11^{IV} to Orbey, turn left onto N 415.

★★**Kaysersberg** – *See KAYSERSBERG.*

The road joins the Route des Vins which takes you back to Ribeauvillé, through villages camped on the hillside among famous vineyards.

Kientzheim, Sigolsheim, Bennwihr, Mittelwihr, Beblenheim – *See Route des VINS.*

★★★**Riquewihr** – *See RIQUEWIHR.*

Hunawihr – *See Route des VINS.*

Drive back to Ribeauvillé.

★★CASTLES OVERLOOKING THE PLAINE D'ALSACE

46km/29mi round tour – allow 2hr

Leave Ribeauvillé by ① on the town plan, D 1^B.

This round tour offers views of the castles built along the line of the Vosges mountains.

Bergheim – *See Route des VINS.*

St-Hippolyte – *See Route des VINS.*

Turn right 4km/2.5mi beyond St-Hippolyte then left 1km/0.6mi further on to take the one-way road which goes round the castle.

★★**Haut-Kœnigsbourg** – *See HAUT-KŒNIGSBOURG.*

Return to D 1^{B1} and turn right then right again onto D 48^I.

★**From Schaentzel to Lièpvre** – The picturesque road, lined with imposing fir trees, runs rapidly downhill, offering superb views of the Liepvrette Valley and the ruined castles towering above it to the north.

Return to D 1^{B1} and turn right onto D 42.

Thannenkirch – This charming village lies in restful surroundings, amid dense forests.

The road follows the deep Bergenbach Valley down to the Plaine d'Alsace.

At Bergheim, turn right towards Ribeauvillé.

The ruins of St-Ulrich, Girsberg and Haut-Ribeaupierre castles stand out on the right.

The main car parks are indicated on the town plans

RIQUEWIHR ★★★

Population 1 075
Michelin map 87 fold 17 or 242 fold 31 – Local map see Route des VINS

Riquewihr is an attractive little Alsatian town lying at the heart of a wine-growing area, which has been actively engaged in the production of the famous Riesling for generations, the liveliest period being grape-harvest time. Having been spared by the many wars which ravaged the region, the town looks today just as it did in the 16C. Yet life in Riquewihr was not always as peaceful; it was sold in 1324 to the duke of Wurtemberg, who remained its suzerain until the Revolution but the town suffered frequent incursions from the troops of rival feudal lords such as the bishop of Strasbourg and the duke of Lorraine. Its marvellous wine, however, consistently enabled Riquewihr to overcome the worst situations throughout its troubled past.

Riquewihr and its vineyards

TOUR OF THE TOWN *2hr*

Leave the car outside of town *(parking fee)*. Walk through the archway of the town hall and follow rue du Général-de-Gaulle straight ahead. On the left is the Cour du Château at the end of which stands the castle.

Château (B) – Completed in 1540, the castle has retained its mullioned windows, its gable decorated with antlers and its stair turret. A small open-air archeological museum and the Altar of Freedom erected in 1790 can be seen on the east side.

Musée d'histoire des PTT d'Alsace ⊙ – A stagecoach with three compartments (1835 model) is parked at the entrance. Three rooms on the ground floor (temporary exhibitions) and six rooms on the first floor of the castle follow the evolution of means of communication in Alsace from the Gallo-Roman period to the 20C. Models (the *Great Eastern*, a liner turned into a cable ship in 1865), documents, photos, stamps, some of the first postcards, costumes, telegraphs and telephones etc, illustrate the history of foot messengers, ordinary mail, airmail, the telegraph and the telephone.

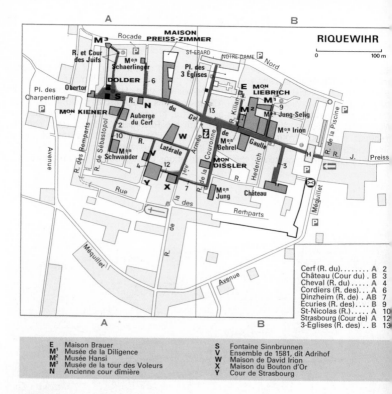

RIQUEWIHR

0   100 m

Cerf (R. du)........ A 2
Château (Cour du) . B 3
Cheval (R. du) ..... A 4
Cordiers (R. des)... A 6
Dinzheim (R. de) . AB 7
Écuries (R. des).... B 9
St-Nicolas (R.)..... A 10
Strasbourg (Cour de) A 12
3-Églises (R. des) .. B 13

E	Maison Brauer	S	Fontaine Sinnbrunnen
M¹	Musée de la Diligence	V	Ensemble de 1581, dit Adrihof
M²	Musée Hansi	W	Maison de David Irion
M³	Musée de la tour des Voleurs	X	Maison du Bouton d'Or
N	Ancienne cour dîmière	Y	Cour de Strasbourg

There is also a model of Chappe's telegraph station which has been reconstructed in its original location in Saverne.

Follow rue du Général-de-Gaulle.

No 12, known as the **Maison Irion**, dating from 1606, has a corner oriel; opposite, there is an old 16C well. Next door, the **Maison Jung-Selig** (1561) has a carved timber frame.

Musée de la Diligence ⊙ (B **M¹**) – Housed in the former seigneurial stables (16C), the museum displays various stagecoaches from the 18C (first wicker mail coach dating from 1793) to the beginning of the 20C, together with postilions' uniforms and boots, mail record-books and signs. There is a model of the Trois-Maisons posting-house in the Haut-Rhin *département*, along the road from Belfort to Basle. During the course of your visit, you will hear an aria from the light opera *The Postilion from Longjumeau* composed by Adolphe Adam in 1836. The last room illustrates the period during which craftsmen such as blacksmiths, saddlers and cartwrights were actively employed repairing mail coaches.

Musée Hansi ⊙ (B **M²**) – This museum contains watercolours, lithographs, etchings, decorated ceramics and posters by the talented artist and cartoonist from Colmar, JJ Waltz, known as Hansi *(see COLMAR)* whose brother was a chemist in Riquewihr.

★**Maison Liebrich** (B) – A well dating from 1603 and a huge winepress from 1817 stand in the picturesque courtyard of this 16C house, surrounded by balustraded wooden galleries (added in the 17C).
Opposite stands the **Maison Behrel** adorned with a lovely oriel (1514) surmounted by openwork added in 1709.

Take the second turn on the right and follow rue Kilian.

Maison Brauer (B **E**) – This house, situated at the end of the street, has a fine doorway dating from 1618.

Continue along rue des Trois-Églises.

Place des Trois-Églises (AB) – The square is framed by two former churches, St-Érard and Notre-Dame, converted into dwellings, and a 19C Protestant church.

Return to rue du Général-de-Gaulle.

★**Maison Preiss-Zimmer** (A) – This former hostel dates from 1686. The window-frames are decorated with cables, vines and fruit; several successive courtyards form a picturesque ensemble. The house which belonged to the wine-growers' guild stands in the last-but-one courtyard.
The nail-maker's house *(no 45)* was built in 1600.

Turn right onto rue des Cordiers.

Maison Schaerlinger (**A**) – *No 7.* Beautifully carved beams distinguish this attractive house (1672).

Return to rue du Général-de-Gaulle.

Opposite stands the former tithe court (**N**) of the lords of Ribeaupierre.

Rue et cour des Juifs (**A**) – The narrow rue des Juifs gives access to the picturesque Cour des Juifs, a former ghetto, from which a narrow passageway and wooden stairs lead to the ramparts and the **Musée de la tour des Voleurs** ⊘ (**M³**). The tour includes the torture chamber, the oubliette, the guard-room and the caretaker's lodgings of this former prison.

On place de la Sinn, which marks the end of rue du Général-de-Gaulle, stands an imposing gate, the Porte Haute or Dolder. Note the lovely **Fontaine Sinnbrunnen** (**S**) on the right, which dates from 1580.

★**Dolder** (**A**) – Erected in 1291, this gate was reinforced during the 15C and 16C. The upper parts are quite picturesque.

Musée ⊘ – The museum occupies the four floors of Dolder *(walk up the stairs on the left of the door)*. It houses mementoes, prints, weapons and objects connected with local history (tools, furniture, locks...).

An annual sound and light show, inspired by the vicissitudes of the town's long history, beginning with the construction of the tower in 1291, takes place at the foot of the city wall.

Walk through the gate to reach Obertor.

Obertor (**A**) – Note the portcullis and the place where the former drawbridge (1600) was fixed. On the left, you can see a section of the ramparts and a defence tower.

Turn back, walk through Dolder and along rue du Général-de-Gaulle then turn right onto rue du Cerf.

★**Maison Kiener** (**A**) – *No 2.* The house built in 1574 is surmounted by a pediment with an inscription and a low-relief carving depicting Death getting hold of the founder of the house. The rounded doorway is built at an angle to make it easier for vehicles to enter. The courtyard is very picturesque with its spiral staircase, corbelled storeys and its old well (1576). The old inn opposite, Auberge du Cerf, dates from 1566.

Continue along rue du Cerf prolonged by rue St-Nicolas.

Maison Schwander (**A**) – *No 6.* It was built in 1605 with a spiral staircase, beautiful wooden galleries and an old well in the courtyard.

Retrace your steps back to rue Latérale, turn right and right again onto rue du Cheval.

At no 5 is a fine court, called Adrihof (**A V**), dating from 1581 (the well was added in 1786), which once belonged to Autrey abbey.

Return to rue Latérale.

Rue Latérale (**A**) – The street is lined with lovely houses including the Maison David Irion (**W**) at no 6, which has retained its oriel dating from 1551 and a lovely Renaissance doorway in the courtyard.

Turn right onto rue de la 1ʳᵉ-Armée.

The **Maison du Bouton d'Or** (**X**) at no 16, goes back to 1566. An alleyway, starting just round the corner, leads to another court known as the **Cour de Strasbourg** (**Y**) dating from 1597.

Retrace your steps once more then carry straight on past the Maison du Bouton d'Or along rue Dinzheim, which leads to rue de la Couronne.

The **Maison Jung** (**B**) at no 18 was built in 1683 opposite an old well, **Kuhlebrunnen**. The Maison Dissler stands further along on the left.

★**Maison Dissler** (**B**) – *No 6.* With its scrolled gables and loggia, this stone-built house (1610) is an interesting example of Renaissance style in the Rhine region.

Continue along rue de la Couronne to rue du Général-de-Gaulle and turn right towards the town hall.

The chapter on Practical Information at the end of the guide lists:
– local or national organisations providing additional information,
– recreational sports,
– thematic tours,
– suggested reading,
– events of interest to the tourist,
– admission times and charges.

ROCROI★

Population 2 566
Michelin map 53 fold 18 or 241 fold 6

Vauban, Louis XIV's military engineer, redesigned the fortifications of this 16C strong-hold, situated on the Ardennes plateau, round a vast parade ground.
Rocroi, whose name means "king's rock", changed its name to Roc Libre (free rock) during the Révolution!

Remparts – The ramparts form a bastioned wall characteristic of military architec-ture at the time of Vauban, who was appointed *Commissaire général des fortifica-tions* in 1678. Starting from the Porte de France to the southwest, follow the tourist trail running along the east front, which gives a good idea of the complexity of the defence system.

Musée ⊙ – Housed in the former guard-house, the museum presents an inter-active audio-visual show illustrating the sequence of manœuvres which led the young duke of Enghien, the future Grand Condé, to victory over the Spanish army at the battle of Rocroi (1643). There is also a reconstruction of the battle with tiny lead soldiers and several documents relating to the history of the stronghold.

EXCURSIONS

Bois des Potées – *Drive southwest along D 877 to la Patte d'Oie then turn left onto a narrow road signposted Censes-Gallois. Leave the car and continue on foot to the main crossroads in the forest.*
A very old **oak tree**, surrounded by firs, stands about 100m/110yd from the intersection.

Vallée de Misère – *Drive east along D 1.*
The road follows the winding Vallée de Misère lined with forested slopes. This used to be a remote area deprived of any resources (hence its name) until the dam of the Revin power station was built.

ROSHEIM★

Population 4 016
Michelin map 87 fold 15 or 242 fold 23 – Local map see Route des VINS

Rosheim is a small wine-growing town which has retained, within its ruined ramparts, some of the oldest buildings in Alsace.

SIGHTS

★**Église St-Pierre-et-St-Paul** – The church is an interesting specimen of 12C architecture in the Rhine region.
Considerably restored during the 19C, it fortunately regained its original aspect in 1968. The yellow-sandstone edifice has a massive 16C octagonal belfry surmount-ing the crossing. Note the flat strips decorating the west front and the walls, known as Lombardy banding because this kind of ornamentation was introduced by the Lombards (Italian bankers who shared with the Jews the monopoly of money transactions). Arcading runs along the top of the nave and the aisles and links up with the Lombardy banding. Lions devouring humans adorn the gable of the west front (another Lombardy feature). The symbols of the evangelists are represented at the four corners of the apsidal window.
Inside, strong piers alternate with weak piers surmounted by carved capitals (note in particular the ring of small heads, all different). The restored organ by Silber-mann dates from 1733.

Porte du Lion, Porte Basse and Porte de l'École – These gates formed part of the town's fortifications.

Puits à chaîne and Zittglœckel – A well dating from 1605 and a clock tower stand on the town hall square.

Maisons anciennes – Numerous old houses line rue du Général-de-Gaulle and the narrow adjacent streets.

Maison païenne – Situated between no 21 and no 23 rue du Général-de-Gaulle, this house is the oldest edifice built of Alsatian stone (second half of the 12C). It has two storeys pierced by small openings.

*The annual Michelin Red Guide France gives the addresses and telephone numbers of main car dealers, tyre specialists,
and garages which do general repairs and offer a 24-hour breakdown service.
It is well worth buying the current edition*

ROUFFACH ★

Population 4 303
Michelin map 87 fold 18 or 242 fold 35 – Local map see Route des VINS

Rouffach is a prosperous agricultural centre nestling at the foot of vine-covered hills. The Holy Roman Emperor once owned a castle here (now in ruins) and the town has retained several interesting buildings from its rich medieval past: two churches, some old houses and a machicolated tower.

Rouffach was the birthplace of François-Joseph Lefebvre (1755-1820), one of Napoleon's colourful marshals, who distinguished himself during the Napoleonic wars and became duke of Danzig, but remained unaffected by his social position and often returned to his humble origins in Rouffach.

SIGHTS

Église Notre-Dame-de-l'Assomption – This church was mostly built in the 12C-13C although the transept is older (11C-12C). The nave and the chancel date from the 13C, the west front and the first bay of the nave from the 14C. The north and south towers were added in the 19C; the latter was never completed owing to the Franco-Prussian war of 1870.

Inside, the main arcades comprise strong piers alternating with weak ones as is the custom in 12C architecture from the Rhine region. All the columns are surmounted by crocket capitals.

Note the octagonal christening font (1492) in the south transept. An elegant staircase, leaning against the piers of the crossing, is all that remains of the 14C rood screen. On the left of the high altar, there is a lovely 15C tabernacle. A Virgin and Child surmounted by a canopy, carved c 1500, is bonded to one of the pillars of the nave on the north side.

Tour des Sorcières – The machicolated tower covered with a four-sided roof crowned by a stork's nest dates from the 13C and 15C and was used as a prison until the 18C.

Maisons anciennes – The old covered market (late 15C- early 16C) stands on place de la République; nearby, to the left of the Tour des Sorcières, is the Gothic Maison de l'Œuvre Notre-Dame and the former town hall with its beautiful Renaissance façade surmounted by a twin gable. There are three other interesting houses at nos 11, 17 and 23 rue Poincaré.

Église des Récollets ⊘ – The church was built between 1280 and 1300 but the aisles were remodelled in the 15C. A pulpit with an openwork balustrade is bonded to one of the butresses. A stork's nest sits on the top.

EXCURSION

Pfaffenheim – *3km/1.9mi north along N 83.*
This wine-growing village, whose origins go back to the end of the 9C, has retained a church with a 13C apse, adorned with floral friezes and a blind gallery with slender colonnettes. Notches which can be seen in the lower part might have been made by wine-growers sharpening their pruning knives.

ST-DIÉ ★

Population 22 635
Michelin map 87 fold 16 or 242 fold 27

Situated in a fertile basin overlooked by red-sandstone ridges covered with firs, St-Dié owes its name to a monastery founded in the 7C by St Déodat shortened to St Dié.

The town was partly destroyed by fire on four occasions, the last one being in November 1944, towards the end of the Second World War.

Textile and wood industries are the town's main economic activities.

The continent discovered by Christopher Columbus was first named "America", in honour of the explorer Amerigo Vespucci, in a work entitled *Cosmographiæ Introductio*, published in St-Dié in 1507 by a team of scientists who called themselves the "Gymnase vosgien". In October, the town hosts an international event devoted to the science of geography.

SIGHTS

★**Cathédrale St-Dié** – The former collegiate church became a cathedral in 1777. Its imposing classical west front dating from the early 18C is flanked by two square towers. There is a fine Romanesque doorway on the south side. The greatest part of the edifice was blown up in November 1944. The vaulting and the east end were rebuilt as they were before the explosion and the building was consecrated in 1974.

Interior ⊙ – The transept, the chancel and the apse (decorated with a large funeral recess) have regained their 14C look. In the Romanesque nave, strong piers alternate with weak ones surmounted with carved **capitals★** having miraculously been spared by the explosion (Melusine appears on the last pillar before the chancel on the right). Note how the arches of the aisles are narrower at the entrance of the transept. The transverse arches and ribbed vaulting of the nave date from the 13C. There is a 14C Virgin and Child against the column situated on the right of the crossing. In 1987, the cathedral acquired some fine abstract **stained-glass windows★** made by a group of 10 artists (Alfred Manessier, Jean Le Moal, Geneviève Asse...) headed by Jean Bazaine. A subtle blend of warm and cold colours and the mingling of serene and distorted shapes lead to the climax of the symbolic progression from darkness to light, the Easter blaze of glory being represented by the three stained-glass windows of the chancel.

Some 13C windows in the second chapel on the north side, illustrate episodes from the life of St Déodat.

★**Cloître gothique** – This former canon cloister, linking the cathedral and the Église Notre-Dame-de-Galilée, is remarkable; built in the 15C and 16C, it was never completed.

Note the Flamboyant openings on the side of the courtyard and the ribbed vaulting resting on engaged colonnettes and pilasters. A 15C outdoor pulpit leans against a buttress of the east gallery.

Église Notre-Dame-de-Galilée ⊙ – Used as a parish church during the reconstruction of the cathedral, Notre-Dame is characteristic of Romanesque architecture in southern Lorraine. The plain west front is preceded by a belfry-porch with simple capitals. The originality of the nave lies in its groined vaulting, an unusual feature in such a large nave. Strong and weak piers alternate as is the tradition in the Rhine and southern Lorraine regions.

Musée Pierre-Noël – Musée de la vie dans les Hautes Vosges ⊙ – The museum, which was rebuilt on the site of the former episcopal palace (the monumental entrance alone has survived), includes an archeological section (finds from the site of La Bure), an ornithological section (350 stuffed birds) and other sections devoted to the Vosges Forest, wood and textile crafts, agriculture and stock farming, ceramics from eastern regions and glassware.

A large room is devoted to Jules Ferry, a native of St-Dié.

There is also a Franco-German military exhibition including an important display about the pilot René Fonck, an ace of the 1914-1918 war, born near St-Dié.

In addition, the museum houses the Goll collection of modern art.

Bibliothèque ⊙ – The library has a stock of 230 000 works including 600 manuscripts and 140 incunabula (early printed books). The treasury room contains a copy of the extremely rare *Cosmographiæ Introductio* and an illuminated gradual – a kind of missile – from the early 16C, with miniatures illustrating work in the mines during the Middle Ages.

Tour de la Liberté ⊙ – This entirely white edifice, made of steel, canvas and cables, rises 36m/118ft above ground and weighs more than 1 440t. Erected in Paris for the Bicentenary of the Revolution in 1989, the Tower of Liberty was moved to its present location a year later. On the second floor, there is an unusual display of **jewellery** created by Heger de Lœwenfeld after paintings by Georges Braque.

From the viewpoint, there is a stunning view of the town and the blue line of the Vosges mountains.

St-Dié – Tour de la Liberté

A.de Val Roger/MICHELIN

ST-DIÉ

EXCURSIONS

Camp celtique de la Bure – *7.5km/4.6mi then 45min on foot there and back. Drive out of St-Dié along N 59 and, 4km/2.5mi further on, turn right towards La Pêcherie then right again onto the forest road to La Bure and finally left onto the forest road to La Crenée.*
Leave the car at the Col de la Crenée and take the path running along the ridge (starting behind a forest shelter) and leading to the main entrance of the camp (large explanatory panel).
This archeological site has revealed traces of constant human occupation beginning roughly in 2000 BC and ending in the 4C AD.
Occupying the western extremity (alt 582m/1 909ft) of a ridge known as the Crête de la Bure, the camp is elliptical and measures 340m/372yd by 110m/120yd diagonally. The outer wall consisted of an earth base (2.25m/7.5ft thick) and a wooden palisade interrupted by two gates and two posterns. The eastern approach of the camp was barred as early as the 1C BC by a wall (*murus gallicus*, 7m/23ft thick) preceded by a ditch and from AD 300 onwards by a second Roman-type rampart. There were several pools in the camp (two of them were dedicated to Gaulish goddesses) and important ironworks (two anvils weighing 11kg/24lb and 23.5kg/52lb were discovered together with 450kg/992lb of iron slag). Among the reproductions displayed on the ramparts, note the stela bearing the effigy of a horse-fish and, in the middle of the camp, the stela of a 3C blacksmith. The archeological finds are exhibited in the St-Dié Museum.
From the camp, there are fine **views★** *(viewing table)* of the Meurthe Valley to the west and of the St-Dié Basin to the south.

From St-Dié to the Donon pass – *43km/27mi – allow 2hr 30min. Drive out of St-Dié along N 59.*
Étival-Clairefontaine – This small town, lies on the banks of the Valdange, a tributary of the River Meurthe. The ruins of a paper-mill dating from 1512 can still be seen on the riverside. The modern mill has been set up in Clairefontaine on the banks of the Meurthe. The former **church★** of a Premonstratensian abbey, built of sandstone from the Vosges region, has retained its nave and aisles in transitional style (Romanesque to Gothic) but the west front and the north side date from the 18C. Traces of the stairs and doorways leading to the monastery can clearly be seen in the north transept.
Moyenmoutier – The place owes its name to a monastery founded in the 7C halfway between the abbey of Senones and that of Étival (literally: "the monastery in the middle"). The vast abbey church, rebuilt in the 18C, is one of the finest religious buildings of that period in the whole Vosges region. The oak stalls (early 18C), which occupy the front part of the chancel, are beautifully carved and inlaid. The organ case is a copy of the old one which is now in St-Dié cathedral; note also the 16C statue of the Virgin on the south side of the nave.
Senones – See SENONES.
The **itinerary★** from Senones to the Donon pass is described under Senones.

ST-DIZIER
Population 33 552
Michelin map 61 fold 9 or 241 fold 30

This modern industrial town with a concentration of smelting works, ironworks and steelworks was once a mighty stronghold with a garrison of some 2 500 soldiers. In 1544 it successfully withstood an attack by the Holy Emperor, Charles V, and his army of 100 000 men. It was here that, in 1814, Napoleon won his last victory before being exiled to the island of Elba.
Besides its military activities, the town has been involved in the floating of logs down the River Marne since the 16C and in 1900, **Hector Guimard**, one of the initiators of Art Nouveau in France, used the St-Dizier ironworks for his ornamental creations. His initiative was at the origin of a now established activity.
Many houses were decorated by Guimard, outside and inside, in Art Nouveau style: balconies, window sills, palmettes, door leaves, banisters...
Four itineraries will lead you through the town in search of these various ornamental features *(apply at the tourist office)*.

EXCURSIONS

Vallée de la Blaise – *See WASSY.*
★Lac du Der-Chantecoq – *See Lac du DER-CHANTECOQ.*

Abbaye de Trois-Fontaines – *11km/6.8mi north. Drive out of St-Dizier along D 157 and continue along D 16.*
The remains of the former Cistercian abbey, founded in 1118 by monks from Clairvaux *(see Abbaye de CLAIRVAUX)*, rebuilt in the 18C and partly destroyed during the Revolution, stand at the heart of the forest. A monumental 18C doorway leads to the main courtyard and, beyond, to the park (3ha/7.5 acres) dotted with statues. The former conventual buildings and the ruins of the 12C abbey church can also be seen.

Marais de ST-GOND

Michelin maps 56 folds 15, 16 and 61 folds 5, 6 or 241 fold 29

This marshland, situated below the Ile-de-France cliff and covering more than 3 000ha/7 413 acres over an area 15km/9mi long and 4km/2.5mi wide, owes its name to a 7C coenobite. Water from the marsh is drained by the Petit Morin.

In September 1914, the area and the surrounding heights were the scene of fierce fighting between von Bülow's second German army and **General Foch**'s 9th French army. Foch eventually succeeded in driving the Germans back to the River Marne.

MARSHLAND AND VINEYARDS

36km/22mi round tour starting from Mondement – allow 1hr 30min

This drive goes through the solitary expanses of the marshland area which has been partly drained and turned into pastures or agricultural land (maize). The south-facing slopes of the limestone hills surrounding the marsh are covered with vineyards producing a fine white wine.

Mondement – The Mondement hill (alt 223m/732ft), overlooking the marsh and commanding the way to the River Seine, was at the centre of the fighting in September 1914. The German troops eventually withdrew after suffering heavy losses. A monument commemorates these events.

The view extends over the St-Gond marsh to Mont Aimé and the Champagne hills.

Allemant – This tiny village clinging to the hillside has a surprisingly large Flamboyant Gothic church with a double transept and a high tower surmounting the crossing. From the adjacent cemetery, the view extends towards the Ile-de-France cliff on the left, the St-Gond marsh and Fère-Champenoise plain on the right.

Coizard – Charming Romanesque village church.

Villevenard – Wine-growing village. One's attention is immediately drawn to the tastefully restored 12C **church**, its harmonious proportions, its Romanesque nave with small rounded openings and its fine octagonal tower surmounting the crossing.

ST-JEAN-SAVERNE

Population 559
Michelin map 87 fold 14 or 242 fold 19
Local map see Parc Naturel Régional des VOSGES DU NORD

The village church is all that remains of an abbey for Benedictine nuns founded at the beginning of the 12C and subsequently ransacked by the Armagnacs and the Swedes.

SIGHTS

Église – The church is surmounted by an 18C belfry built over an interesting Romanesque doorway. Inside, the unity of style is remarkable, with strong piers alternating with weak ones in typical Rhineland fashion. The early-Gothic pointed vaulting is said to be the oldest in Alsace.

At the chancel end of the south aisle, on the right, note the primitive style of the tympanum situated over the sacristy door, which depicts the Lamb carrying the Cross under palmette motifs. At the entrance of the chancel, there are fine cubic-shaped capitals decorated with foliage. The organ dates from the 18C. The sacristy contains nine 16C tapestries originally in the Benedictine abbey.

Chapelle St-Michel ⊙ – *2km/1.2mi then 30min on foot there and back starting from the Église St-Jean. Follow the road going through the forest to Mont-St Michel and turn sharply left 1.5km/0.9mi further on.*

Chapelle – The chapel dates from the same period as the abbey, but it was remodelled in the 17C and restored in 1984.

École des Sorcières – Follow a path on the right of the chapel to the extremity of the rocky spur forming a platform *(viewing table)* from which the view extends over the hills of Alsace and the Black Forest in the distance. The platform forms a circular hollow known as the witches' school because, according to legend, witches used to gather there at night.

Trou des Sorcières – *Return to the chapel.* Walk down the 57 steps starting on the south side then follow a path on the left which skirts the foot of the cliff and leads to a cave; at the end of this cave, there is a narrow opening known as the witches' hole.

ST-MIHIEL ★

Population 5 367
Michelin map 57 folds 11 and 12 or 241 fold 27

St-Mihiel has had close links with the famous Benedictine abbey of the same name since it was founded in 709 near the present town and relocated in 815 along the banks of the Meuse by one of Charlemagne's counsellors. In 1301, St-Mihiel became the main town of the Barrois region lying east of the River Meuse.

The city then prospered both economically and culturally, the 16C being a particularly brilliant period: renowned drapers and goldsmiths settled in St-Mihiel and the fame of **Ligier Richier** and his school of sculpture spread throughout eastern France. Born in St-Mihiel in 1500, Richier surrounded himself with talented sculptors and apprentices. In 1559, he was asked to "decorate" the town for the arrival of Duke Charles III and his wife. In later life, however, he was converted to the Protestant faith and went to live in Geneva where he died in 1567. Fine examples of his considerable output can be seen in Bar-le-Duc, Hattonchâtel, Étain and Briey.

In September 1914, the German army launched a thrust in that area in order to skirt round the powerful stronghold of Verdun. They succeeded in establishing a bridgehead on the west bank of the Meuse, known as the **St-Mihiel Bulge**, which prevented supplies and reinforcements from reaching Verdun via the Meuse Valley through the duration of the war.

SIGHTS

Église St-Michel – The abbey church was almost entirely rebuilt in the 17C, nevertheless retaining its 12C square belfry and Romanesque porch. The large nave, comprising five bays, is flanked by aisles of equal height and shallow side chapels as is usual in hall-churches. The Gothic vaulting rests on massive fluted columns crowned by Doric capitals. The deep chancel is decorated with 80 beautifully carved stalls.

The first side chapel along the south aisle houses one of Ligier Richier's masterpieces, the **Fainting Virgin supported by St John ★**. This group was carved in walnut in 1531.

The baptismal chapel on the same side contains the *Child with Skulls*, carved in 1608 by Jean Richier, Ligier Richier's grandson. The magnificent organ case dates from 1679-1681.

Bâtiments abbatiaux – The vast conventual buildings, adjacent to the church, which were rebuilt in the 17C with a façade in the Louis XIV style, are still almost intact.

Bibliothèque ⊙ – The library has, since 1775, been housed in a large hall decorated with woodwork and ceilings in the Louis XIV style. It contains 8 000 works including 70 manuscripts (beautiful 15C gradual), 80 incunabula (the first book printed in Lorraine) and part of the Cardinal de Retz's library.

Église St-Étienne – The nave of this original hall-church was built between 1500 and 1545. Note the modern stained-glass windows and the Renaissance altarpiece in the apse. But the church is above all famous for the **Sepulchre ★★** or Entombment sculpted by Ligier Richier from 1554 to 1564, situated in the middle bay of the south aisle. It consists of 13 life-size figures depicting the preparations for Christ's Entombment *(light switch on the right)*.

Maison du Roi – *2 rue Notre-Dame*. This 14C Gothic house belonged in the 15C to King René of Anjou, who also had the title of Duc de Bar.

Falaises – The cliffs consist of seven limestone rocks, over 20m/66ft high, overlooking the east bank of the river. In 1772, Mangeot, a native of St-Mihiel, carved a representation of the Holy Sepulchre in the first rock. From the top of the "cliffs", there is a fine view of the town and the Meuse Valley.

EXCURSIONS

Bois d'Ailly – *7km/4.3mi southeast along D 907 and a signposted forest road*.
There are several reminders of the heavy fighting which took place in this wood in September 1914: a row of trenches (complete with shelters and communication trenches) starting from the memorial leads to the Tranchée de la Soif (the "thirst trench") where a few soldiers held on for three days against a strong unit of the German Imperial Guard.

Sampigny, Musée Raymond-Poincaré ⊙ – *9km/5.6mi south along D 964*.
The former summer residence of Raymond Poincaré, one of the outstanding personalities of France's Third Republic, houses mementoes, objects and documents connected with the life of this exceptional politician. The opulent villa was built for Poincaré in 1906 by Bourgon, an architect from Nancy.

Raymond Poincaré (1860-1934) was a liberal republican at heart, as well as a brilliant barrister and a writer (he entered the French Academy in 1909). Re-elected without interruption for 48 years, he became in turn a regional councillor, a member of parliament, a minister, a senator, the prime minister and the president of the Republic. As president during the First World War, he chose Clemenceau as his prime minister in 1917 at a turning point in the war.

★**Hattonchâtel** – *19km/12mi northeast along D 901 to Vigneulles then left to Hattonchâtel.*
This once fortified village, built on a promontory, owes its name to a 9C castle belonging to a bishop of Verdun named Hatton. The collegiate chapter rebuilt the **church** and erected the chapel and the cloister (1328-1360).
Walk through the courtyard of the cloister to the chapel which contains a magnificent **altarpiece** in polychrome stone dating from 1523, believed to be by Ligier Richier, which depicts three biblical scenes separated by Renaissance pilasters: the Bearing of the cross and St Veronica on the left, the Crucifixion and the Fainting Virgin in the centre and the Entombment on the right. There is an earlier altarpiece (14C) over the high altar of the church as well as a fine 16C statue of the Virgin Mary near the right-hand altar and modern stained glass by Gruber.
The neo-Romanesque town hall houses the **Musée Louise-Cottin** ⊙ containing about 100 paintings by this artist (1907-1974) who excelled at portrait, still-life and genre painting.
Situated at the end of a promontory, the former **castle** ⊙, dismantled in 1634 by order of Richelieu, was restored in 15C style between 1924 and 1928. The view extends as far as Nancy.

Lac de Madine – *9km/5.6mi south of Hattonchâtel along D 179 to Nonsard.*
This large lake covering an area of 1 100ha/2 718 acres and its surroundings form a vast outdoor leisure park offering many nautical activities (boating, swimming, sailing, pedalo rides) and other sporting activities (tennis, golf, riding...) as well as the possibility of relaxing in a pleasant country setting (catering, accommodation and camping).
It is also possible to take a 20km/12.4mi walk or bike ride round the lake.

★★**Butte de Montsec** – *19km/12mi east of St-Mihiel along D 119.*
The **monument**★ standing at the top of an isolated hill (alt 275m/902ft) was erected by the Americans to commemorate the offensive of September 1918 which enabled the American First Army to break through the St-Mihiel bulge and take 15 000 prisoners. From the memorial, the **view**★★ embraces the Woëvre Valley and Côtes de Meuse to the west and Lake Madine to the north.

▶**Vallée du Rupt de Mad** – Continuing along D 119 for another 4km/2.5mi, one comes to the village of Richecourt in the picturesque Rupt de Mad Valley.

ST-NICOLAS-DE-PORT ★★

Population 7 702
Michelin map 62 fold 5 or 242 fold 22

The splendid Flamboyant basilica of St-Nicolas-de-Port, which looks as impressive as a cathedral, stands in the centre of a small industrial town. It has been a popular place of pilgrimage since the 11C. Pilgrims flocked to the city which became the most prosperous economic centre in Lorraine and the venue of international fairs.
It was here that, in 1477, the troops of the duke of Lorraine, René II, fought the army of the duke of Burgundy, Charles the Bold, who died in the battle. In 1635, during the Thirty Years War, the town was ransacked by the Swedes and only the church, dedicated to the patron saint of Lorraine, was spared.
The road skirting the north bank of the River Meurthe offers a fine view of the town.

★★BASILIQUE ST-NICOLAS ⊙ 45min

The present edifice is a splendid shrine containing part of one of St Nicholas' fingers.
Knights from Lorraine brought the precious relic back from Bari in Italy and placed it in a chapel dedicated to Our Lady. There followed a series of miracles and a church had to be built to accommodate the growing number of pilgrims. Joan of Arc came to pray in the church in 1429 before embarking on her mission. The huge church dating from the late 15C and early 16C suffered fire and war damage and the roof was only repaired in 1735. It became a basilica in 1950.
Having been damaged again in 1940, this time by bombing, the church needed extensive restoration to recover its past splendour. A bequest from Madame Camille Croue-Friedman, a native of St-Nicolas-de-Port, who died in the United States in 1980, provided the answer and, since 1983, the basilica has looked like a building site once again.

Exterior – The present edifice, built over a period of only 50 years (1495-1544) with funds from the dukes of Lorraine, is a superb specimen of Flamboyant Gothic architecture.

The west front can be favourably compared to that of Toul cathedral, both having similar proportions and high towers. It features three doorways surmounted by Flamboyant gables.

The central doorway has retained the statue representing St Nicholas' miracle (in the recess of the central pillar), believed to be the work of Claude Richier, the brother of the famous sculptor, Ligier Richier.

The towers rise to 85m/279ft and 87m/285ft. Note on the north side, level with the transept and the chancel, a row of six basket-handled recesses in which traders used to set up shop when a pilgrimage was on.

There is a good view of the east end from rue Anatole-France.

Interior – The lofty nave is well lit and covered with lierne and tierceron vaulting whose highest point reaches 32m/105ft above ground level, as in Strasbourg cathedral; its diagonal arches rest on tall plain columns. The aisles are similarly constructed; the transept vaulting, supported by very tall pillars (28m/92ft high, the highest in France), rises to the same height as that of the central nave. This was often the case in the Champagne region and records show that a stonemason from Troyes cathedral took part in the construction of St-Nicolas in 1505.

The stained-glass windows of the apse, dating from 1507-1510, are particularly remarkable; they were made by Nicole Droguet whereas those of the aisle and chapels on the north side are the work of Valentin Bousch from Strasbourg; both date from the same period. Note that the Renaissance influence can already be felt in the decorative motifs used.

The sanctuary which received St Nicholas' relic in the 11C was probably located where the **baptismal chapel** (accessible from behind the Virgin's altar) now stands. It contains interesting 16C fonts and a beautiful early-Renaissance altarpiece surmounted by openwork pinnacles. Several 16C painted wood panels illustrate scenes from the life of St Nicholas. The **treasury** includes a silver gilt reliquary-arm of St Nicholas (19C), the cardinal of Lorraine's ship (16C), two 18C enamels and a silver reliquary of the True Cross (15C).

ADDITIONAL SIGHT

Musée français de la Brasserie ⊙ – The museum is housed in the brewery which closed down in 1985.

The visit begins with an audio-visual presentation which explains the brewing process. Two stained-glass panels by Jacques Gruber light up the Salle Moreau.

The Art Deco brewing tower, lit by wide windows, houses various installations: the laboratory, the malt loft, the hops storeroom, the brewing room with its fine copper vats, the room containing the refrigerating equipment and the cold room with the fermentation vats.

The visit ends with beer-tasting in the basement.

EXCURSIONS

Varangéville – *North of the town, between the River Meurthe and the Marne-Rhine canal.*
Dating from the early 15C, the Flamboyant Gothic church contains a superb "forest" of ribbed pillars with palm motifs and interesting statues, including a Virgin and Child dating from the early 14C and a 16C Entombment.

Dombasle-sur-Meurthe – *5km/3mi west.*
Lying between the River Meurthe and the Marne-Rhine canal, the town is an industrial centre specialising in chemicals (**Solvay** group from Belgium), mainly sodium carbonate, salt and by-products. The plant is situated on both sides of D 400; its lime kilns are among the largest in the world.

Salt, which is the raw material of this industry, has been mined from the **Haraucourt** plateau since 1904 (1 400 000t per year). The process consists in injecting fresh water into the soil in order to dissolve the salt and extract it that way. This intensive mining concerns an area of 200ha/494 acres. Huge craters are visible from D 80 and D 81.

Rosières-aux-Salines – *6km southeast along N 4 then right onto D 116.*
A stud farm took over the buildings of the former salt plant which closed down in 1760. The farm houses some 30 thoroughbred stallions.

Michelin Green Guides cover the world's great cities:
New York, London, Paris, Rome, Brussels,
Barcelona, Berlin, Vienna, Washington DC,
San Francisco, Chicago, Venice

Ste-MENEHOULD

Population 5 178
Michelin map 56 fold 19 or 241 fold 22

Situated in the Aisne Valley, on the edge of the Argonne Forest, Ste-Menehould occupies a strategic position at the entrance of the Islettes pass. The town, which was the birthplace of Dom Pérignon *(see ÉPERNAY: Excursions)*, is overlooked by a hillock known as "Le château".
In June 1791, during the Revolution, Louis XVI secretly fled Paris with his family, intending to return at the head of an army and restore his authority. However, the king was recognised at the Ste-Menehould posting-house by a young boy who gave the alarm and the party was stopped at Varennes *(see ARGONNE)*. Today, the *gendarmerie* (police station) stands on the site of the former posting-house.

SIGHTS *allow 1hr*

Place du Général-Leclerc – Split into two by the main road *(N 3)*, the square is lined by a fine group of pink-brick buildings – including the **town hall** (1730) – with stone ties and bluish-slate roofs, designed by Philippe de la Force who rebuilt the city after the fire of 1719.

Musée ⊙ – Housed in an 18C mansion, the museum contains various regional collections: history, religious art, geology. Note the model (more than 2 000 pieces) of the battle of Montfaucon which took place in 888 between King Eudes' army and Vikings sailing up the River Meuse.

"Le château" – *Accessible by car up a ramp or on foot along a path and up some steps.*
This is the upper town, looking like a Champagne village with its low timber-framed, flower-decked houses. From the top, there is a fine **view★** of the lower town, its roofs covered with curved tiles and the 19C Église St-Charles.
The 13C-15C **Église Notre Dame** (also called Église du Château) is surrounded by its cemetery. The walls, rebuilt in the 18C, are decorated with brick and white-stone ties.

EXCURSIONS

★Château de Braux-Ste-Cohière – *5.5km/3.4mi west. See Château de BRAUX-STE COHIÈRE.*

Valmy – *12km/7.5mi west.*
A decisive battle took place near this village in September 1792 between French and Prussian troops. Although there were relatively few casualties, the psychological consequences were enormous. French soldiers were ill-equipped patriotic volunteers and the fact that they withstood the attack of the Prussian army and forced it to retreat boosted the morale of the whole French nation; two days later the Republic was proclaimed.
The **Moulin de Valmy**, reconstructed in 1947, is identical to the windmill next to which stood François-Christophe **Kellermann**, the French commanding officer, at the time of the Prussian attack. Four viewing tables show the position of the two armies. The view extends over the Champagne region and the Argonne Forest.

Mont STE-ODILE★★

Michelin map 87 fold 15 or 242 fold 23
Local map see Région du HOHWALD

Mont Ste-Odile is undoubtedly one of the most popular sights in Alsace: tourists are attracted by the site and the panorama, whereas the devout are inspired by the holiness of the place.

HISTORICAL NOTES

The so-called "pagan wall" *(Mur Païen)* which winds its way on the top of Mont-Ste-Odile testifies to human presence in the area probably dating back to prehistoric times or in any case to the Celtic or Gaulish period.
In the 7C, Hohenburg castle was the summer residence of Duke Étichon, **St Odile**'s father. According to legend *(see p 53)*, the blind baby girl was rejected by her father and subsequently saved and raised by her nurse. She recovered her sight miraculously and later escaped her father's determination to marry her to a knight. Her vocation became clear and her father eventually made her a present of Hohenburg where she founded her convent.
She also founded Niedermunster abbey c 700. It was destroyed in the 16C but its ruins can still be seen east of the convent.

After St Odile's death, the convent became an important place of pilgrimage. The most famous abbess was **Herrade de Landsberg** who, in the 12C, wrote and illuminated a shortened history of the world since the Creation for the benefit of her nuns. The book, entitled *Hortus Deliciarum* ("Garden of Delights"), kept in Strasbourg, was destroyed by Prussian shells in 1870.

In 1546, a terrible fire devastated the monastery; the Chapelle Ste-Odile alone was spared. During the Revolution, the convent became state property. In 1853, it was bought back by the bishop of Strasbourg and became a monastery once more.

COUVENT *30min*

The forested escarpments of Mont Ste-Odile (alt 764m/2 507ft) tower over the Plaine d'Alsace. The convent is situated at the northern end of the promontory. Pilgrims flock here all year round and particularly for the feast of St Odile.

The porch, located beneath the former hostel, gives access to the main courtyard shaded by lime trees and framed by the present hostel on the left, the church on the right and the south wing of the convent at the end.

Église conventuelle –
Destroyed by fire, the monastery church was rebuilt in 1692. The three-naved building is adorned with fine woodwork (chancel) and confessionals richly carved in the 18C. Note also the inlaid panels of the Stations of the Cross.

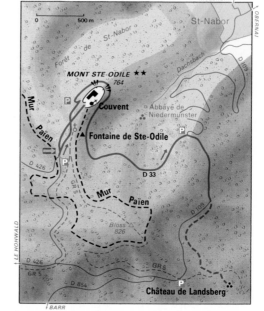

★Chapelle de la Croix –
Access from inside the monastery church, through a door situated on the left. This is the oldest part of the convent, going back to the 11C. The four groined vaults are supported by a single Romanesque pillar with carved capital. A sarcophagus housed the remains of Duke Étichon, Odile's father.

On the left, a low doorway decorated with Carolingian carvings leads to the small Chapelle Ste-Odile.

Chapelle Ste-Odile – An 8C sarcophagus contains St Odile's relics. This 12C chapel is presumed to have been built on the site of the previous chapel where St Odile died.

The nave is Romanesque and the chancel is Gothic. Two 17C low-relief carvings depict the christening of St Odile, and Étichon spared the sufferings of Purgatory by the grave of his daughter's prayers.

Terrasse – The terrace has two excellent viewpoints *(viewing tables)*, one in the northwest corner offering a view of the Champ du Feu and Bruche Valley, the other at the northeast extremity, affording a splendid **panorama★★** of the Plaine d'Alsace and the Black Forest. The spire of Strasbourg cathedral is visible when the weather is clear.

Chapelle des Larmes – This is the first of the chapels standing in the northeast corner of the terrace. It was built on the site of the Merovingian cemetery (several graves have been preserved).

A stone slab behind a railing is said to have been worn by St Odile kneeling on it daily as she prayed for her father's salvation.

Chapelle des Anges – This chapel houses a fine mosaic dating from 1947, illustrating a theme from the *Hortus Deliciarum (see Historical notes above)*.

Fontaine de Ste-Odile – The road leading down to St-Nabor *(D 33)* runs past the spring *(protected by a railing)* which is said to have gushed forth from the rock at St Odile's request to quench the thirst of an exhausted blind man. It is now a place of pilgrimage for people with eye complaints.

MUR PAÏEN *30min on foot there and back*

As you come out of the convent, walk down 33 steps on the left then follow the path starting at the foot of the stairs.

It would take four or five hours to walk round the remains of this mysterious wall running through forests and screes over a distance of more than 10km/6mi. Its average thickness is 1.7m/5.5ft and it reaches a height of 3m/10ft in the best-preserved parts. However, seeing even a part of this monumental work is already an awe-inspiring experience; note the cavities carved in the huge blocks to insert the tenons used to join them together.

Return to the convent along the same path.

A path *(starting from the southern parking area)* offers a fine walk along the pagan wall

EXCURSION

Château de Landsberg – *4km/2.5mi southeast along D 109, then 1hr on foot there and back down the signposted path.*

The itinerary offers a pleasant walk through the forest, past the former Landsberg inn to a platform beneath the castle which can be seen through the trees.

This is the birthplace of the famous abbess, Herrade de Landsberg, author of the *Hortus Deliciarum (see Historical notes above).* The 13C castle is now in ruins.

SARREBOURG

Population 13 311
Michelin map 87 fold 14 or 242 fold 19

This city of Roman origin belonged to the bishops of Metz during the Middle Ages and then to the duchy of Lorraine before becoming part of the kingdom of France in the late 17C.

SIGHTS

Chapelle des Cordeliers ⊙ – This deconsecrated Franciscan chapel houses the Syndicat d'initiative (tourist office). Erected in the 13C, the edifice was rebuilt in the 17C and its west front is lit by a huge stained-glass window by Marc Chagall illustrating "peace" (12m/39ft high and 7.5m/25ft wide). It consists of 13 000 pieces of glass weighing 900kg/1 985lb. In the centre, vivid blues, reds and green symbolize the Tree of Life in Genesis with Adam and Eve surrounded by the Serpent, Christ's cross, the prophet Isaiah, the Lamb, the Candelabra, angel accompanying Abraham, Jesus entering Jerusalem... At the foot of the Tree, Birth, Work, Suffering and Death illustrate mankind.

Musée du Pays de Sarrebourg ⊙ – *13 avenue de France.* The museum contains regional archeological collections: finds from the Gallo-Roman villa in St-Ulrich and from necropolises and sanctuaries of the Vosges mountains, 14C statuettes and low relief ceramics from Sarrebourg, medieval sculpture (beautiful 15C Crucifix) as well as a remarkable collection of 18C ceramics and procelain from nearby Niderviller.

Cimetière national des Prisonniers – The cemetery is situated on the outskirts of town, on the right of rue de Verdun (D 27). It contains some 13 000 graves of soldiers of the First World War. The monument facing the gate, entitled *Giant in Chains*, was sculpted by Stoll while he was a prisoner of war.

EXCURSIONS

Réding – *2km/1.2mi northeast along N 4 then left in Petit-Eich.*

In 1977, during the restoration of the Chapelle Ste-Agathe, 13C frescoes illustrating the emblems of the Evangelists were discovered on the chancel vaulting.

St-Ulrich, Villa gallo-romaine ⊙ – *4km/2.5mi northwest.* The villa was the residence of a rich landowner and stood at the heart of a vast estate probably covering 2 000ha/4 942 acres. Built in the 1C AD, it was extended during the 2C to include more than 100 rooms, courtyards, galleries, cellars and even baths. Important restoration work is in progress.

Hartzviller, Cristallerie – *10km south. Drive out of Sarrebourg along D 44.*

Hesse – The small abbey **church**, partly Romanesque and partly Gothic, has several interesting capitals in the transept and ancient funeral slabs along the north aisle.

As you leave Hesse, turn left onto D 96° leading to Hartzviller.

Cristallerie ⊙ – During the tour of the crystalworks, visitors can see some 80 glass-blowers at work.

Fénétrange – *15km/9mi north along D 43.*

This small town has retained several beautiful medieval houses and an elegant castle with a curved façade overlooking a circular courtyard. The **collegiate church of St-Remi** is a fine edifice rebuilt in the 15C with a short lofty nave covered with ribbed vaulting and a vast polygonal apse lit by stained-glass windows partially dating from the 15C. The choir stalls, the pulpit and the organ date from the 18C.

SARREGUEMINES

Population 23 117
Michelin map 57 fold 16 and 17 or 242 fold 11

This border town, situated at the confluence of the Sarre and the Blies, offers pleasant walks along the river banks. Sarreguemines used to be the seat of a feudal domain guarding the borders of the duchy of Lorraine.

Pottery – The Sarreguemines manufacture was founded in 1790 by three merchants from Strasbourg but it soon encountered financial difficulties and, in 1799, Paul Utzschneider solved the problem by diversifying the factory's output: fine earthenware with printed motifs, fine stoneware... His son-in-law, Alexandre de Geiger extended the workshops and developed new techniques including majolica (earthenware with embossed motifs covered with coloured enamel). His son took over in 1870 and, after the annexation of Lorraine in 1871, subsidiary companies were founded in Digoin in 1877 and Vitry-le-Francois in 1881. Production reached its peak at the turn of the century: more than 3 000 workers produced majolica, porcelain, dinner sets and panels. Bought by the Lunéville-St-Clément group in 1979, the pottery now essentially produces floor tiles. In 1982, it was renamed Sarreguemines-Bâtiment.

SIGHTS

Musée ⊘ – *17 rue Poincaré*. Housed in the former residence of the manager of the earthenware manufacture, the museum illustrates local history in attractive fashion. The **ceramics collection★** retraces the history and main production of Sarreguemines pottery over the past 200 years. The **winter garden★★**, designed by Paul de Geiger in 1882 is particularly remarkable. Note, on the wall facing the entrance, the monumental majolica fountain with Renaissance-style decoration offering a shimmering display of yellows, greens, ochres and browns. On either side, there are panels depicting the small pavilion (left) and the factory buildings (right). Dinner services and decorative objects placed in the centre of the room illustrate changing techniques linked to the evolution of fashion and society.

Circuit de la faïence ⊘ – A tourist trail links the main sites connected with the manufacture of earthenware in Sarreguemines *(brochure available from the tourist office or the museum).*

"The Earth"

Ville de Sarreguemines A Mertz

In his house, now turned into a **museum**, Paul de Geiger set up a magnificent winter garden decorated with ceramic tiles.

Behind the town hall, visitors can see the former **oven** of one of the workshops. Around 1860, there were about 30 similar conical brick-built ovens.

On the east bank of the Sarre, standing in a vast park, the **casino** (1890), once reserved for the personnel of the manufacture, has been refurbished as a concert hall and congress centre. The façade is decorated with an allegorical panel by Sandier representing ceramics. Next door stands the small pavilion erected for Paul de Geiger.

Further away, behind the factory, lies the **garden-city** built in 1926. The houses, which are all identical and surrounded by a small garden, are lined along parallel avenues.

The **Wackenmühle** is the only remaining mill; situated on the south bank of the Blies, it was used by the manufacture. It contains an exhibition about the life of the workers and manufacturing process of industrial ceramics.

PARC ARCHÉOLOGIQUE EUROPÉEN DE BLIESBRUCK-REINHEIM ⊘ *9.5km/5.9mi east via Bliesbruck*

On either side of the border separating Saarland from the Moselle region, lies the site of an antique city which has been the object of Franco-German excavations since 1978.

The settlement, which apparently goes back to the Neolithic period, became important after the arrival of the Celts. The grave of the "princess from Reinheim" (c 400 BC) dates from that period; gold jewellery and a wine service found in it will be displayed in a reconstructed **tumulus** near the remains of a large 2C villa.

The small city, whose name remains a mystery, reached its heyday during the Gallo-Roman period (from the 1C to the 4C AD). At that time, it extended over some 20ha/50 acres and had a population of around 5 000 inhabitants. This "vicus" was a handicraft centre, a market town and probably a religious and administrative centre as well.

The **public baths**★, located in Bliesbruck, have been reconstructed in Siberian pine and the site is now protected by a huge glass structure. A marked itinerary dotted with explanations enables visitors to get a better appreciation of what they see.

Two areas once inhabited by craftsmen lie on either side of the main Roman way; one is open to the public, but excavations are still going on in the other.

At certain times of the year, there are demonstrations of the techniques used by Gallo-Roman craftsmen.

In Reinheim, one can see the remains of a vast villa dating from the same period as the "vicus".

SAVERNE★

Population 10 278
Michelin map 87 fold 14 or 242 fold 19

Saverne is a pleasant town situated along the Zorn Valley, at the point where the river flows into the Plaine d'Alsace. The Marne-Rhine canal also runs through Saverne and a lock (A F) operates in the lively town centre. The marina, facing the castle, can accommodate 70 boats.

The 16C peasant rebellion ended tragically in Saverne when the duke of Lorraine besieged the town; he promised to spare the lives of the 20 000 peasants if they came out of the town unarmed, but when they did, they were massacred to the last one by the duke's soldiers in spite of his efforts to stop them.

From the 13C to the Revolution, Saverne belonged to the bishops of Strasbourg. These princes stayed in the castle and sometimes welcomed royal visitors (Louis XIV in 1681, Louis XV in 1744). One of them, **Louis de Rohan**, the famous cardinal who was mixed up in the necklace scandal involving Queen Marie-Antoinette, rebuilt the edifice destroyed by fire and led a life of luxury.

In November 1944, Saverne was liberated by General Leclerc's division.

SIGHTS

★**Château** (B) – Acquired by the town in 1814, the castle of the House of Rohan became State property in 1852 and, until 1870 it was used as a home for the widows of civil servants who had died in fulfilling their duties. Between 1870 and 1944 it was turned into barracks. The fine red-sandstone building in the Louis XV style stands in a beautiful park bound by the Marne-Rhine canal.

The south façade is visible from the square but, in order to see the north façade which is the most attractive, you will have to walk through the gate and along the right side of the castle. This **façade**★★, which is over 140m/153yd long is very impressive with its fluted pilasters and its peristyle supported by eight columns of the Corinthian order.

Musée ⊙ – The museum is housed in part of the central building and in the right wing. The basement contains archeological collections dating mainly from the Gallo-Roman period. The second floor is devoted to the fine arts and to the town's history: medieval sculpture, archeological finds from the nearby castles (Haut-Barr, Geroldseck, Wangenbourg), mementoes of the House of Rohan, Louise Weiss's bequest (this politician, who died in 1983, defended feminism and Europe).

★**Maisons anciennes** (B E) – The two finest old houses (17C) including the **Maison Katz** *(see Introduction: Architecture and art)* stand on either side of the town hall. Others can be seen at no 96 Grand'Rue, on the corner of rue des Églises and rue des Pères and on the corner of rue des Pères and rue Poincaré.

Église paroissiale (B B) – Rebuilt in the 14C and 15C, the parish church has retained a Romanesque belfry-porch dating from the 12C. On the right of the doorway, there is a fine outside staircase. The 15C nave houses a pulpit (1495) by Hans Hammer and a 16C high-relief marble sculpture representing Mary and John mourning Christ. The chapel of the Holy Sacrament in the north aisle is adorned with a 16C Pietà and a large low-relief woodcarving, painted and gilt, also dating from the 16C, depicting the Assumption. The stained-glass windows of the chapel made in the 14C, 15C and 16C, illustrate the Adoration of the Magi and scenes from the Passion.

Gallo-Roman and Frankish gravestones can be seen in the garden adjacent to the church.

Ancien cloître des Récollets (A D) – The cloister, built in 1303, has lovely red-sandstone pointed arcades and nine murals (added in the 17C, now restored) in the first gallery on the right of the entrance, which depict (from west to east) the Assumption, the Adoration of the Magi, the Annunciation, the Stigmatisation of St Francis, a Christian's Fight for the Good Cause, the Choice of True Goodness and the Last Judgement.

SAVERNE

Bouxwiller (R. de) ..... B 2	Dettwiller (R. de) ...... B 6	Joffre (R. Mar.)......... B 16
Clés (R. des) .... B 3	Églises (R. des) .... B 8	Pères (R. des) .... B 17
Côte (R. de la)......... A 5	Foch (R. Mar.) .... A 12	Poincaré (R.).......... A 20
	Gare (R. de la) .... A 13	Poste (R. de la)....... B 22
	Gaulle (Pl. Gén. de).... B 14	19-Novembre
	Grand'Rue .... AB	(R. du) .... A 23

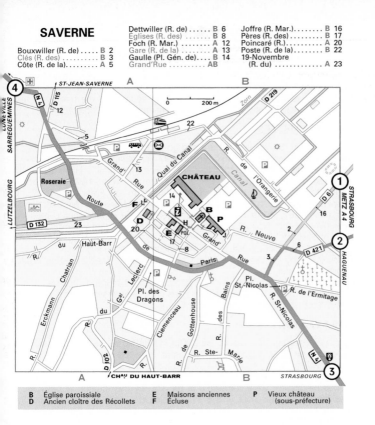

B	Église paroissiale	**E**	Maisons anciennes	**P**	Vieux château
D	Ancien cloître des Récollets	**F**	Écluse		(sous-préfecture)

Vieux château (B P) – The old castle, which was the former residence of the bishops, is now an administrative building. Note the beautiful Renaissance doorway of the stair tower.

Roseraie ⊙ (A) – Seven thousand rose bushes representing 450 varieties grow in this splendid park situated on the bank of the River Zorn.
Saverne's annual rose festival includes an international competition of new varieties and a flower show. Rose-flavoured chocolate sweets and shortbread biscuits topped with rose petals have been specially created to celebrate the town's dedication to roses.

EXCURSIONS

Jardin botanique du col de Saverne ⊙ – *3km/1.9mi then 15min on foot there and back. Leave Saverne by ④ on the town plan (N 4). Drive for 2.5km/1.5mi to the parking area on the right-hand side of the road. Cross the road and follow the signpost.*
Situated at an altitude of 335m/1 099ft, inside a loop of the road, this botanical garden (2.3ha/5.7 acres) includes an arboretum, an Alpine garden, a small bog and numerous species of fern. Sixteen varieties of orchids flower during the months of May and June.

Saut du Prince Charles (Prince Charles's jump) – *From the botanical garden, walk through the forest along a forest track.*
According to legend, a prince named Charles jumped over the red-sandstone cliff with his horse. There is a fine view of the foothills of the Vosges mountains and the Plaine d'Alsace.
On the way back, follow a path to the left leading down to the bottom of the cliff.
The overhang bears an inscription dated 1524, which mentions the building of the road beneath the cliff.

★**Château du Haut-Barr** – *5km/3mi; 30min tour of the castle. See Château du HAUT-BARR.*

St-Jean-Saverne – *5km/3mi north. See ST-JEAN-SAVERNE.*

The key on page 4 explains the abbreviations and symbols used in the text or on the maps.

267

SEDAN

Population 21 667
Michelin map 53 fold 19 or 241 fold 10

The town, which was rebuilt after the Second World War, lies on the banks of the River Meuse, beneath the castle and the old town. South of the town, a 13ha/32-acre artificial lake is convenient for bathing and sailing. In addition to the traditional textile industry, industrial activities include metalworks, chemicals and foodstuffs.

HISTORICAL NOTES

According to tradition, the origins of the town go back to Gaulish times but in fact the name Sedan is mentioned for the first time in 997 as belonging to Mouzon abbey. In 1594, it became the property of the La Tour d'Auvergne family. Henri de La Tour d'Auvergne, Viscount of **Turenne** and Marshal of France (1611-1675) was born in Sedan before the town was reunited to the kingdom of France in 1642. This illustrious soldier faithfully served Louis XIII and his son Louis XIV, fighting the Spaniards during the Thirty Years War and later defeating the Fronde thus consolidating young Louis XIV's throne. He had just won back the Alsace region when he was killed at the battle of Sasbach.

The Revocation of the Edict of Nantes was detrimental to Sedan's cloth industry, which had been developed by Protestants, it likewise put an end to the flourishing Academy of the Reformed Religion.

The capitulation of Sedan on 2 September 1870, during the Franco-Prussian war, led to the proclamation of the Third Republic in Paris on 4 September. Seventy years later, in May 1940, another defeat at Sedan tolled the end of the Third Republic.

★CHÂTEAU FORT ⊙ (BY)

This fortress covering an area of 35 000m²/41 860sq yd on seven levels is the largest in Europe. It was built on a rock spur in several stages on the site of a former monastery dating from the 11C and 13C. Work began in 1424; the twin towers and the ramparts date from that period. The latter (30m/98ft high), surrounded by ditches, were completed in the 16C by the addition of bastions. The **Palais des Princes (BY)** was built in the 17C outside the walls and the original living quarters which used to stand within the ramparts were partly demolished in the 18C. Between 1642 and 1962, the stronghold was army property. The town then acquired it and undertook its restoration. From the towers and the ramparts, there are fine views of the town with its slate roofs.

Tour – *Audio-guided tours, explanatory panels.* The tour of the castle, known as the "**historium**" includes a number of reconstructed scenes illustrating the lifestyle of princes, soldiers and servants in the past.

The **museum** houses archeological collections (gathered during excavations beneath the castle: medieval pottery, ceramics), ethnographic exhibits and documents relating to the town's history. One room is devoted to the Franco-Prussian war of 1870 and to the First World War. The 15C framework of the **Grosse tour** (large tower) is remarkable. An audio-visual presentation completes the panorama of the castle's history.

It is possible to drive round the fortress or to walk along boulevard du Grand Jardin (benches) to the Résidence des Ardennes overlooking the town. From the esplanade, there is a superb **view**★ of the Meuse Valley.

Sedan – The town and the castle

SEDAN

Alsace-Lorraine (Pl. d') **BZ** 2
Armes (Pl. d') .... **BY** 3
Bayle (R. de) .... **BY** 4
Berchet (R.) .... **BY** 5
Blanpain (R.) .... **BY** 6
Capucins (Rampe).... **BY** 7
Carnot (R.) .... **BY** 8
Crussy (Pl.) .... **BY** 9
Fleuranges (R. de).... **AY** 10
Francs-Bourgeois
    (R. des)............ **BY** 12

Gambetta (R.) .... **BY** 13
Goulden (Pl.)......... **BY** 14
Halle (Pl. de la) ...... **BY** 15
Horloge (R. de l') ..... **BY** 17
Jardin (Bd du Gd) .... **BY** 18
La Rochefoucauld (R. de) **BY** 20
Lattre-de-Tassigny
    (Bd Mar.-de) .... **AZ** 21
Leclerc (Av. du Mar.) . **BY** 24
Margueritte
    (Av. du G.) .... **ABY** 26
Martyrs-de-la-
    Résistance (Av. des) **AY** 27

Mesnil (R. du) .... **BY**
Nassau (Pl.)........... **BZ** 31
Promenoir-des-Prêtres **BY** 33
Rivage (R. du)......... **BY** 34
Rochette (Bd de la) ... **BY** 35
Rovigo (R.)........... **BY** 36
Strasbourg (R. de).... **BZ** 39
Turenne (Pl.).......... **BY** 41
Vesseron-Lejay (R.)... **AY** 42
Wuidet-Bizot (R.) ..... **BZ** 44

B   Ancien Hôtel de ville

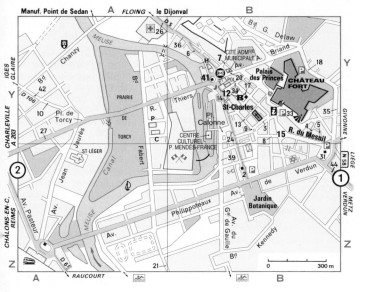

ADDITIONAL SIGHTS

Old town (BY) – Sedan flourished as a cloth-manufacturing centre during the second half of the 17C and above all during the 18C. The manufactures usually consisted of a large house along the street, workshops in the wings and a building closing off the courtyard at the back. The technical evolution which took place in the 19C meant that these buildings were turned into dwellings. Some of them can still be seen today.

– **no 33 place de la Halle** (**15**). This 18C mansion facing the square and backing onto the Promenoir des Prêtres, was probably used as a private house and a warehouse. The main building is prolonged by curved wings which straighten out as in the case of the Dijonval. Note the wrought-iron banisters.

– **no 1 place Turenne** (**41**). The gate giving access to the courtyard is more elaborately decorated than that which opens onto the street. Note in the courtyard the system used to lift heavy bundles.

– **no 1 rue du Mesnil**. Built as a private mansion in 1626, the Hôtel de Lambermont became a royal manufacture and was granted privileges in 1726. Note the heads surmounting the windows in the first courtyard: they are believed to represent Elizabeth of Nassau, her family and friends.
Opposite stands another draper's house dating from 1747.

– **no 3 rue Berchet** (**5**). This former dyer's workshop was acquired in 1823 by the owner of the royal manufacture.

– **no 8 rue de Bayle** (**4**). Private mansion and cloth manufacture, whose façade is decorated at each end by a colossal order pilaster and a projecting cornice.

– **no 1 rue des Francs-Bourgeois** (**12**). This 18C building, which was probably a draper's workshop, has openings with arched lintels, curved balconies and a staircase with wrought-iron banisters.

– **no 1 rampe des Capucins** (**7**). Former manufacture of fine cloth. At the back of the courtyard, on the right, there is an interesting staircase with wooden banisters.

Dijonval ⊘ (ABY 26) – *Avenue du Général-Margueritte.* This royal cloth manufacture founded in 1646 continued to operate until 1958. Its imposing 18C façade extends on either side of a central pavilion adorned with a pediment and surmounted by a campanile. On the courtyard side, the central building is flanked by curved wings prolonged by long straight ones. The windows are decorated with ovoli carved with geometric motifs. It now houses the **Musée des anciennes Industries du Sedanais** (Traditional Industries Museum).

Manufacture du Point de Sedan ⊘ (AY) – In this traditional manufacture, weavers can be seen working on looms dating from 1878; they make carpets with New Zealand wool on linen base. The motif is drawn on graduated paper and transcribed onto a piece of cardboard (each perforation represents one stitch in the chosen colour). Several thousand spools of coloured wool are used and it takes over a month to make a carpet.

Cloth-manufacturing in Sedan

Sedan's textile tradition goes back to the Middle Ages but the manufacture of cloth and lace really flourished from the end of the 16C, following the Wars of Religion and a sudden influx of Protestants. The lace stitch, imported by the Calvinist community, was called Point de Sedan by foreign buyers. When the town was returned to France in 1642, Sedan became the capital of fine woolens with the creation of the Dijonval manufacture. The industry began to decline in the 18C. However, in 1878, an industrialist and an engineer from the Ardennes region invented a device which made it possible to tie the wool "stitch" onto a linen warp and weft. Lacemaking is no longer one of the town's activities and the last cloth manufacture has closed down but the carpet industry carries on for prestigious clients including sovereigns and embassies.

Église St-Charles (BY) – This edifice dating from 1593 was a Calvinist church until the Revocation of the Edict of Nantes. In 1688 Robert de Cotte added a vast rotunda-shaped chancel.

Ancien hôtel de ville (BY B) – The former town hall, designed by Salomon de Brosse, was built in 1613. Note the embossed façade decorated with vermicular motifs.

Jardin botanique (BZ) – This small heaven of peace in the town centre is very pleasant.

Follow avenue du Maréchal-Leclerc to place Calonne. From the bridge spanning an arm of the River Meuse, there is a **view** of the grass-covered river banks and of the two arches of the old mill.

EXCURSION

Aérodrome de Sedan-Douzy: Musée des débuts de l'aviation ⊘ – *10km/6mi east by* ① *on the town plan.* The museum of early flying is devoted to the pioneer Roger Sommer (1877-1965), who not only piloted aircraft but also built them. A replica of the 1910 biplane, used for India's first air link in 1911, is exhibited together with numerous documents dating from the early 20C. In addition, there is an important collection of postcards recalling famous pilots such as Blériot and Farman. Modern aviation is illustrated by about 100 models of aircrafts.

To best enjoy the major tourist attractions, which draw big crowds, try to avoid visiting at the peak periods of the day or year.

SÉLESTAT ★

Population 15 538
Michelin map 87 folds 6 and 16 or 242 fold 27 – Local map see Route des VINS

This ancient city, lying on the west bank of the river Ill, between Strasbourg and Colmar, has two fine churches and some interesting houses. A modern town involved in various industrial activities (textiles, leather goods, non-ferrous metals etc) has developed around the old one. Sélestat was an important Humanist centre in the 15C and 16C.

Martin Bucer – Born in Sélestat in 1491, Martin Bucer entered a Dominican monastery after completing his studies. His meeting with Luther in Heidelberg in 1518 changed the course of his life.
He left his monastery converted the town of Wissembourg to the ideas of the Reformation and settled in Strasbourg as pastor of Sainte-Aurélie. Influenced by Humanism, this open-minded thinker tried, through his writings and his actions, to restore a common doctrine among all Protestants. His spiritual influence spread throughout southern Germany and the state of Hesse.
After the defeat of the Schmalkalden League opposed to the Hapsburgs, Bucer was forced by Emperor Charles V to go into exile in 1549. He settled in Cambridge where he died in 1551.

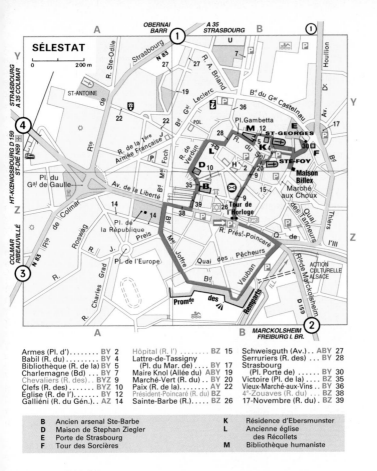

SÉLESTAT

0   200 m

Armes (Pl. d')	BY 2	Hôpital (R. l')	BZ 15
Babil (R. du)	BY 4	Lattre-de-Tassigny	
Bibliothèque (R. de la)	BY 5	(Pl. du Mar. de)	AY 17
Charlemagne (Bd)	BY 7	Maire Knol (Allée du)	ABY 19
Chevaliers (R. des)	BYZ 9	Marché-Vert (R. du)	BY 20
Clefs (R. des)	BYZ 10	Paix (R. de la)	AY 22
Église (R. de l')	BY 12	Président-Poincaré (R. du)	BZ
Galliéni (R. du Gén.)	AZ 14	Sainte-Barbe (R.)	BZ 26

Schweisguth (Av.)	ABY 27
Serruriers (R. des)	BY 28
Strasbourg	
(Pl. Porte de)	BY 30
Victoire (Pl. de la)	BZ 35
Vieux-Marché-aux-Vins	BY 36
4e-Zouaves (R. du)	BZ 38
17-Novembre (R. du)	BZ 39

B	Ancien arsenal Ste-Barbe		**K**	Résidence d'Ebersmunster
D	Maison de Stephan Ziegler		**L**	Ancienne église
E	Porte de Strasbourg			des Récollets
F	Tour des Sorcières		**M**	Bibliothèque humaniste

★OLD TOWN (BYZ) allow 2hr

Start at the beginning of rue du Président-Poincaré.

Tour de l'Horloge – The clock tower dates from the 14C except for the upper parts which were restored in 1614.

Walk beneath the clock tower, then follow rue des Chevaliers straight ahead which leads to place du Marché-Vert and the Église Ste-Foy.

★**Église Ste-Foy** – This fine Romanesque church (12C) built of red sandstone and granite from the Vosges, stands on the site of a Benedictine priory church. The west front, extensively remodelled, has two towers surmounted by modern Rhenish-style spires. The porch is decorated with arcading, cornices and historiated capitals. A third octagonal tower surmounting the transept rises 43m/141ft above ground level.

The three-naved edifice is built over a crypt which formed part of the previous church. The capitals of the nave are beautifully decorated with floral motifs modelled on churches from the Lorraine region.

Come out of the church through the small door situated behind the pulpit and follow the narrow lane on the right leading to place du Marché-aux-Choux.

Maison Billex – Note the fine two-storey Renaissance oriel. In 1681, the city of Strasbourg signed its surrender to Louis XIV in this house.

Walk to the Église St-Georges.

On the way, you will get a glimpse of the **Tour des Sorcières (F)** on the right: part of the fortifications demolished by Louis XIV, and of the **Porte de Strasbourg (E)**, designed by Vauban in 1679.

Walking round the east end of the church, one skirts the 18C building of the canonesses from Andlau.

★**Église St-Georges** – This imposing Gothic church built between the 13C and 15C was considerably remodelled, particularly in the 19C. Three doorways have retained their original door leaves with their strap-hinges.

The nave is preceded by a wide narthex which covers the whole width of the west front and opens on the south side *(place St-Georges)* through an elegant doorway.

The interior is a mixture of several styles. The vaulting dates mainly from the 14C. The musician angels on the stained-glass windows of the west front date from the late 14C or early 15C; the rose-window (14C) of the south doorway of the narthex illustrates the Ten Commandments; three stained-glass windows in the chancel, dating from the 15C, depict scenes from the lives of St Catherine, St Agnes and St Helena; the new stained-glass windows of the east end and the chancel were made by Max Ingrand. The stone pulpit was carved and gilt at the time of the Renaissance.

Walk along rue de l'Église.

Résidence d'Ebersmunster (K) – *no 8.* This house, built in 1541, is the urban residence of the Benedictine monks. The Renaissance doorway, surmounted by ovoli, is decorated with Italian motifs.

A few yards further on, turn left onto the narrow rue de la Bibliothèque.

★**Bibliothèque humaniste** ⊙ **(M)** – Towards the middle of the 15C, Sélestat's Latin school flourished into a great Humanist school which explains the extent of its splendid library housed on the first floor of the former Halle aux Blés (granary exchange) dating from 1843.

The library consists of two separate collections: that of the Latin library founded in 1452 and the private collection bequeathed in 1547 by Beatus Rhenanus, a Humanist and close friend of Erasmus.

Sélestat – 13C Bible in the Humanist library

The great hall houses precious manuscripts including the Merovingian Lectionary (late 7C), the oldest work still kept in Alsace, the Book of the Miracles of St Foy (12C), the Cosmographiæ Introductio printed in St-Dié *(see ST-DIÉ).* The library of Beatus Rhenanus which comprises more than 2 000 works is the only Humanist collection not to have been dispersed.

Note also the fine carved-wood head of Christ (late 15C), two early-16C altarpieces and a relief plan of the town as it was in the 16C.

The reading room contains two showcases displaying jewellery, vases and weapons from prehistoric times to the Merovingian period as well as medieval wood carvings and Alsatian earthenware and porcelain. Another interesting exhibit *(in a small showcase)* is the plaster cast of the funeral mask of a woman buried in the Église Ste-Foy in the 12C.

Walk to the end of place Gambetta and turn left onto rue des Serruriers.

The **Ancienne Église des Récollets (L)**, formerly part of a Franciscan monastery, is now a Protestant church. The chancel is all that is left of the monastery.

Turn left onto rue de Verdun.

Maison de Stephan Ziegler (D) – This Renaissance house was built in the 16C by one of the town's master builders.

Rue de Verdun leads to place de la Victoire where the former arsenal stands.

Arsenal Ste-Barbe (B) – The former arsenal is an attractive 14C building; its lovely façade is adorned with a double-flight staircase leading to a small canopy preceding the entrance. The gable is crenellated and the roof is crowned by two stork nests.

Continue straight on along rue du 17-Novembre and turn right onto rue du 4e-Zouaves then left again along boulevard du Maréchal-Joffre which leads to the ramparts.

Promenade des Remparts – From these fortifications erected by Vauban, there is a fine view of the foothills of the Vosges and of Haut-Kœnigsbourg.

Turn left onto rue du Président-Poincaré to return to your starting point.

EXCURSIONS

Château de Ramstein and Château d'Ortenbourg – *7km/4.3mi then 15min on foot. Leave Sélestat by ④ on the town plan (N 59); drive for 4.5km/2.8mi then turn right onto D 35 towards Scherwiller; 2km/1.2mi further on, turn left onto an unsurfaced path. Leave the car in Huhnelmuhl, near the inn and follow the path leading to the two castles 300m/328yd apart.*
The ruins are interesting and there is a lovely view of the Val de Villé and Plaine de Sélestat.

Château de Frankenbourg – *11km/6.8mi then 1hr 45min on foot. Leave Sélestat by ④ on the town plan (N 59) and drive to Hurst then turn right onto D 167 to la Vancelle. Leave the car 2km/1.2mi further on and follow the path on the right.*
From the ruins of the castle (alt 703m/2 306ft), there are fine views of the Liepvrette Valley and Val de Villé.

Parc d'animaux de Kintzheim – *8.5km/5.3mi. Leave Sélestat by ④ on the town plan (D 159).* This excursion will be of particular interest to animal lovers who will be able to visit two experimental centres for the acclimatization of very different species such as birds of prey and monkeys.

Château de Kintzheim, Volerie des Aigles ⊙ – *30min on foot there and back.*
The courtyard of the ruined castle is home to about 80 diurnal and nocturnal birds of prey. Some of them take part in spectacular **training demonstrations★** organised during the visit *(except in bad weather).*

Return to you car and continue along the forest road then D 159; 2km/1.2mi further on, turn right onto a path leading to the electrified fence surrounding the Montagne des Singes.

Montagne des Singes ⊙ – In this large park, planted with pine trees and laid out on top of a hill, 300 barbary apes, well-adapted to the Alsatian climate, live in total freedom. View of Haut-Kœnigsbourg castle to the southwest.

Marckolsheim: Mémorial Musée de la Ligne Maginot du Rhin – *15km/9.3mi southeast. Leave Sélestat by ② on the town plan (D 424); 1.5km/0.9mi beyond Marckolsheim, the pillbox of the Memorial can be seen on the right-hand side of N 424. See Ligne MAGINOT.*

Benfeld – *20km/12.4mi northeast. Leave Sélestat by ① on the town plan (N 83).*

Ebersmunster – *See EBERSMUNSTER.*

Benfeld – This small town has an elegant 16C **town hall** with a lovely carved doorway giving access to the polygonal turret dating from 1617, decorated with a shield bearing the town's coat of arms. The clock has three jacks striking the hours: Death, a Knight in armour and "Stubenhansel", a Traitor who, in 1331, sold the city to its enemies for a purse full of gold, which he holds in his hand.

Vallée de la SEMOY ★

Michelin map 53 folds 18 and 19 or 241 fold 6
Local map see Vallée de la MEUSE

From the Belgian border to the Meuse, the River Semoy (called Semois in Belgium) meanders across pastureland between steep slopes covered with forests of oak, fir and birch trees and inhabited by roe-deer and wild boars. The green secluded valley is the paradise of anglers fishing for trout and of anyone yearning for solitude.

FROM MONTHERMÉ TO LINCHAMPS *19km/11.8mi – 1hr 30min*

★Monthermé – *See MONTHERMÉ.*

Leave Monthermé along D 31.

The road runs below the Roc de la Tour then rises to the top of the cliff offering bird's-eye **views★** of Tournavaux nestling in a slightly widened part of the valley.

Turn right onto D 31^D towards Tournavaux then continue along this road to the camp site at Haulmé.

Sentier des Rapides – *1hr on foot there and back.* The path starts at the end of the parking area and follows the tumultuous river flowing through wild scenery.

Return to D 31.

The road runs down to Thilay then crosses the Semoy. Beyond Naux lying inside a deep meander of the river, the itinerary crosses the Semoy once more.

Les Hautes-Rivières – This is the largest village along the French section of the River Semoy. It extends over 2km/1.2mi to Sorendal.

Drive south along D 13 towards Nouzonville, climbing 1.5km/0.9mi to the beginning of the path leading to the Croix d'Enfer.

Croix d'Enfer – *30min on foot there and back.* View of the valley, of the village of Les Hautes-Rivières and of the Vallon de Linchamps.

★**Vallon de Linchamps** – *North of Hautes-Rivières along D 13.* Beautiful remote area.

The rural, isolated village of **Linchamps** is the starting point of walks through the **Ravin de l'Ours** and **Bois des Haies**, across a hilly area reaching altitudes in excess of 500m/1 640ft.

SENONES

Population 3 157
Michelin map 87 fold 16 or 242 fold 27

This small town, surrounded by forested heights, developed near a Benedictine abbey and became in 1751 the capital of the principality of Salm-Salm, a sovereign state whose inhabitants asked to become French in 1793. Senones has retained a few princely residences and 18C mansions.

Every year in July and August, a historic display staging the Prince of Salm's Guard takes place on Sunday mornings.

Ancienne abbaye – The former abbey has a fine 18C stone staircase with wrought-iron banisters, which used to lead to the apartments of **Dom Calmet**, one of the last erudite abbots, and to those of Voltaire who stayed with him in 1754.

Église – The church, built in the 19C, incorporates a 12C octagonal tower. It contains Dom Calmet's grave by Falguière.

EXCURSION

★**From Senones to Col du Donon** – *20km/12.4mi northeast. From Senones, drive north along D 424 to La Petite-Raon (2km/1.2mi) then turn left onto D 49.*

The road enters the Val de Senones and Rabodeau Valley, going through **Moussey**. The forest road, which prolongs D 49 beyond Moussey, runs along the narrow and remote valley of the River Rabodeau. The **Col de Prayé** marked the former border between France and Germany. The road reaches the **Col du Donon** (alt 727m/2 385ft; *see Massif du DONON*).

SESSENHEIM

Population 1 542
Michelin map 87 fold 3 or 242 fold 16

This charming Alsatian village, frequented by the German poet and dramatist Goethe, lies between the Haguenau Forest and the Rhine.

Goethe and Friederike – In October 1770, Goethe who was studying law in Strasbourg, accompanied one of his friends to the house of the pastor of Sessenheim. He fell in love with the clergyman's younger daughter and, over the next few months, the two young lovers took long walks through the countryside and spent idyllic hours under the bower of the presbytery. In August 1771, however, Goethe went back to Frankfurt leaving Friederike shattered. Eight years later, the now famous poet stopped in Sessenheim on his way to Switzerland but the past idyll was not rekindled by this meeting. Later on, Goethe immortalized Friederike in his Memoirs.

SIGHTS

Auberge "Au bœuf" ⊙ – The old inn stands on the left of the Protestant church. Inside this typically Alsatian establishment prints, letters and portraits relating to Goethe and Friederike are displayed.

Église protestante – Note the pastor's stall *(Pfarrstuhl)* where Goethe and Friederike used to sit side by side to listen to her father preaching. The tombstones of Friederike's parents are set into the south wall. The barn of the presbytery, which has been restored, is the only remaining building from the days of Goethe's visits.

Mémorial Goethe – Situated next to the presbytery, the memorial was inaugurated in 1962.

SÉZANNE

Population 5 833
Michelin map 61 fold 5 or 237 folds 22 and 34

Sézanne is a small provincial town, peacefully settled on a hillside riddled with underground galleries and cellars. A ring of wide avenues, replacing the former fortifications, surrounds the old town.
Trade fairs were frequently held in the town from medieval times onwards and today Sézanne is a lively agricultural (cereal silos) and industrial centre: spectacles, pharmaceutical products, detergents and heat-resistant products. The hillside vineyards produce still white wine.
From the Épernay road to the north *(RD 951)* there is a picturesque view of the town.

Église St-Denis – This Flamboyant Gothic church flanked by a Renaissance tower, stands in the town centre, on the edge of place de la République. Two small dwellings are bonded to the foot of the massive square tower (42m/138ft high). Note the clock framed by two carved friezes.
A double-flight staircase leads to a small doorway with Renaissance carved leaves which gives access to the church. The Flamboyant Gothic interior is very homogenous and the star vaulting noteworthy. A chapel situated along the north aisle contains a 16C *Ecce Homo*; another chapel on the south side houses a statuette of St Vincent which used to decorate the top of a brotherhood staff.
As you leave the church, have a look at the **Doré well** facing the west front.

Mail des Cordeliers – Chestnut trees line the walkway along the former ramparts; the flattened remains of two round towers recall the castle that once stood here.
View of the hillside covered with orchards and vineyards.

EXCURSIONS

Corroy – *18km/11mi east along N 4 to Connantre, then right onto D 305.*
This village boasts a remarkable church with a 13C Champagne-style porch on the west front. The porch has twinned arcades and is covered with a 15C timber frame shaped like a ship's hull. The long nave covered with a 12C timber frame is prolonged by the chancel, the apse and two chapels built in the late 16C.

FORÊT DE TRACONNE *54km/34mi round tour – allow 2hr*

The dense Traconne Forest, covering almost 3 000ha/7 413 acres, mainly consists of hornbeam thickets beneath tall oak trees.
Drive west out of Sézanne along D 239.
In Launat, turn left towards Le Meix-St-Époing and, 500m/0.3mi further on, right towards Bricot-la-Ville.

Bricot-la-Ville – This tiny village hidden at the heart of the forest has a charming little church, a manor house and a lovely pond covered with water lilies; an abbey of Benedictine nuns stood here from the 12C to the 16C.
Continue to Châtillon-sur-Morin (fortified church).
The road follows the Grand Morin Valley: clearings alternate with copses as in an English-style garden.
In Châtillon-sur-Morin, turn left onto D 86 which joins D 48. In Essarts-le-Vicomte, turn left onto D 49.

L'Étoile – On the edge of this grass-covered roundabout, which has a column surmounted by an 18C iron cross in its centre, stands a twisted stunted birch from the Bois des Faux de Verzy *(see Parc naturel régional de la Montagne de REIMS).*
Follow D 49 to Barbonne-Fayel then turn right onto D 50.

Fontaine-Denis-Nuisy – A 13C fresco of the Last Judgement, located in the north transept of the church, depicts damned souls roasting in a vast cauldron.
Drive along D 350 towards St-Quentin-le-Verger.
Shortly after Nuisy, you will see a dolmen on the right.
In St-Quentin-le-Verger, turn left onto D 351 then right onto the Villeneuve-St-Vistre road. RD 373 will lead you back to Sézanne.

The Michelin on-line route planning service is available on a pay-per-route basis, or you may opt for a subscription package. This option affords you multiple route plans at considerable savings. Plan your next trip in minutes with Michelin on Internet: www.michelin-travel.com.
Bon voyage!

SIERCK-LES-BAINS

Population 1 825
Michelin map 57 fold 4 or 242 fold 6

Sierck lies in a picturesque setting on the banks of the River Moselle, close to the German border. The old village spreads up the hill crowned by a fortress. In the 12C, the duke of Lorraine and the archbishop of Trier fought over its ownership; it was ransacked and burned down by the Swedes during the Thirty Years War and by Turenne's army in 1661. It was again severely damaged at the beginning of the Second World War.

CHÂTEAU ⊘

Built on a rocky promontory, the castle has retained most of its 11C fortifications: walls, casemates, massive towers pierced with loopholes (Tour de l'Artillerie, Tour du Guet, Tour de la Redoute, Tour des Pères Récollets).
From the castle, there is a lovely **view**★ of the Moselle Valley overlooked by the Stromberg whose slopes are covered with vineyards.
The nearby **Chapelle de Marienfloss**, which is all that remains of a once flourishing Carthusian monastery and important place of pilgrimage, has been restored and extended.

EXCURSIONS

Rustroff – *1km/0.6mi northeast*. The village **church** stands at the end of the steep high street. Rebuilt in the 19C, it contains a beautiful 15C altarpiece in painted wood and a small Pietà dating from the beginning of the 16C.

Château de Mensberg – *8km/5mi northeast along N 153 then right along D 64. As you come to the village of Manderen, drive up the steep lane on the left.*
The imposing ruins of the fortress, rebuilt in the 17C on the site of the 13C castle, spread over the summit of the wooded hill. In 1705, during the War of the Spanish Succession, John Churchill, **Duke of Marlborough**, used it as his head-quarters.

SIGNY-L'ABBAYE

Population 1 404
Michelin maps 53 folds 17, 18 and 56 fold 7 or 241 folds 9 and 10

The village developed in the Vaux Valley, near a famous Cistercian abbey founded in 1134 by Bernard de Clairvaux and destroyed in 1793. The Gibergeon chasm located in the centre of the village supplies the River Vaux.
Signy-l'Abbaye is a pleasant resort for walking enthusiasts.

FORÊT DE SIGNY *32km/20mi round tour – allow 2hr 30min*

Signy Forest, which extends over an area of 3 535ha/8 735 acres, comprises two massifs separated by the **Vaux Valley**: the "small forest" (oaks and beeches) to the southeast and the damper "large forest" (oaks, ashes and maples) to the north-west. The forest yields quality timber.
Drive northwest out of Signy along the Liart road (D 27) which follows the Vaux Valley; 5km/3mi from Signy, turn left onto the forest road (Route forestière de la Grande Terre).
The road runs past the **Fontaine Rouge** *(100m/110yd on the right)*, a ferrous spring marking the start of a 4km/2.5mi footpath, then goes through the oak forest and reaches the path *(parking area)* leading down to the **Gros Frêne**. A stump and a slice of the trunk nearby are all that remains of this imposing ash tree, fallen in 1989 *(about 45min there and back)*. Two marked footpaths, 5km/3mi and 6km/3.7mi long, start from the parking area.
Continue to the Vaux Valley and turn right onto D 2 to Lalobbe, then left onto D 102 to Wasigny.

Wasigny – The castle (16C-17C), is situated at the entrance of the village, in pleasant surroundings, by the riverside. A fine 15C covered market stands in the village centre.
Turn left onto D 11. It joins up with D 985 which leads back to Signy-l'Abbaye.
The road then runs through the beech forest. On the way down, there are fine **views** of Signy and the surrounding area.

Le SIMSERHOF★

Access – *4km/2.5mi west of Bitche along D 35 then along the military road starting opposite the former barracks at Le Légeret.*

A tour of this structural work *(gros ouvrage)*, which was one of the most important along the Maginot Line *(see Ligne MAGINOT)*, leads visitors to the discovery of a very specific type of fortification whose role in 1940 remains largely unknown. Completed in 1935, the fort was designed for a mixed garrison (infantry, artillery, engineers) of 1 200 men with supplies, munitions and fuel for a full three months.

TOUR ⊙

The only parts visible from the outside are the south-facing entrance block, with its 7t armoured door and its flankers, and the firing or observation cupolas surmounting the combat blocks scattered over several kilometres so as to overlook the plain below (a few can be seen from D 35A, Hottwiller road, 1km/0.6mi from D 35). Trees and thickets have replaced the barbed wire fencing and rails sticking out of the ground to bar access to the fort.

The underground part of the work is in two sections: the service section at the back and the combat section in front, both on the same level and linked by a 5km/3mi gallery fitted with a railway line. The total length of the Simserhof galleries is 10km/6mi. The tour takes in the back section first, with its living quarters, common rooms, kitchens, offices, supply stores etc; the power station installations are kept in working order. The munitions store has been turned into a museum (periscopes, diascopes, episcopes, photographs).

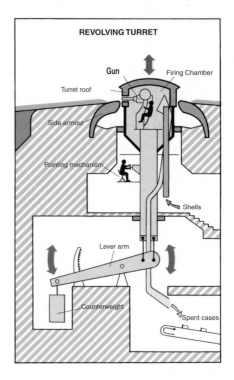

REVOLVING TURRET

Gun
Firing Chamber
Turret roof
Side armour
Pointing mechanism
Shells
Lever arm
Counterweight
Spent cases

The front section (combat headquarters, shell bunker etc) is linked to the firing blocks by vertical wells equipped with elevators and stairs. The tour ends with a combat block: the lower level is occupied by the base of the revolving turret; the upper level contains two twinned 75mm/3in guns which can be seen rotating and aiming.

Colline de SION-VAUDÉMONT★★

The horseshoe-shaped hill of Sion-Vaudémont stands isolated in front of the Côtes de Meuse. It is one of the most famous viewpoints overlooking the Lorraine region as well as a historic site called the "Colline inspirée" by Maurice Barrès, a native of the area, who celebrated it in one of his novels.

Maurice Barrès (1862-1923), born in the nearby town of Charmes, became a famous writer and a politician but he spent several months a year in his grandparents' house which he modernised. During his stay, he loved to climb the hill of Sion. His deep attachment to his native Lorraine can be felt throughout his works, particularly *La Colline inspirée*.

For 2 000 years, the hill has been a kind of mystical place for pagan worshippers and later for Christians. After the Franco-Prussian War of 1870, and after each of the two world wars, pilgrims came to pray on top of the hill. In 1973, the unveiling of the Peace monument was celebrated.

★**Sion** – *30min. Leave the car in the parking area and walk up to the Hôtel Notre-Dame then take the path on the left, alongside the cemetery, to reach the esplanade shaded by lime trees.*

Basilique – The basilica dates mainly from the 18C; a monumental belfry (1860) towers over the porch. The restored apse (early 14C) contains the statue of Notre-Dame-de-Sion (Our lady of Sion), a 15C crowned Virgin in gilt stone.
A small **museum** ⊙ of local history is housed across the inner courtyard.

★Panorama – *As you come out of the church, walk to the right along the courtyard and turn right on the corner of the convent wall.* From the calvary, a vast panorama unfolds (*viewing table* – alt 497m/1 631ft). There is another viewpoint on the west side of the plateau; it can be reached along a lane starting on the left, at the entrance of the parking area.
Nearby, lower down, is the village of Saxon-Sion.

★★Signal de Vaudémont – *30min. 2.5km/1.5mi south of Sion. As you leave Sion, ignore the path on the right leading to Saxon-Sion and, near a calvary, continue straight on along D 53, a ridge road running right across the hill.*
The **Barrès Monument** stands at the top of the Signal de Vaudémont (alt 541m/1 775ft); it is 22m/72ft high and was erected in 1928 to celebrate the memory of Maurice Barrès. There is a superb **panorama★★** of the Lorraine plateau. It is possible to continue to the village of Vaudémont on the opposite side of the hill.
Vaudémont – The ruins of Vaudémont castle, birthplace of the House of the dukes of Lorraine, stand near the church (Tour Brunehaut). The village has retained its original aspect. The Grand'Rue is lined with semi-detached houses or farms with a round-arched gateway giving access to the barn. Houses have only one storey although there is a loft under the roof and a cellar accessible from the street. Built of rubble stone, they have very little ornamentation (stone frame round doors and windows), except for a few inscriptions, statues and relief sculpture.

★Château de Haroué ⊘ – *10.5km/6.5mi from Sion. Drive along D 913 to Tantonville then east for 3.5km/2.2mi along D 9 to Haroué.*
The imposing residence of the princes of Beauvau-Craon lies on the banks of the Madon; it was built from 1720 onwards by Boffrand, the architect of Duke Leopold of Lorraine. Surrounded by a moat, the edifice is preceded by a main courtyard enclosed by railings made by Jean Lamour. The statues decorating the park are the work of Guibal who, like Lamour, worked on place Stanislas in Nancy. The **tour** of the castle includes the chapel, the main staircase with banisters by Lamour and the apartments. The furniture by Bellanger dating from the Restauration (1814-1830) was a present from King Louis XVIII; the **tapestries★** depicting the story of Alexander the Great (17C) were woven at La Malgrange near Nancy. Portraits by François Pourbus, Rigaud and Gérard and landscapes by Hubert Robert can also be seen. The **Chinese drawing room** owes its name to its decoration including Chinese-style paintings by Pillement, dating from 1747. The **Hébert drawing room** is named after the painter Hébert who decorated it in 1858-59 for Napoleon III's visit. The reception room, in which King Stanislas was received several times, contains a 17C bed which once belonged to the Medicis.

SOULTZ-HAUT-RHIN
Population 5 867
Michelin map 87 fold 18 or 242 fold 35

This ancient town grew up around a rock salt vein which still exists today. Many old houses dating from the 16C, 17C and 18C, are adorned with oriels, stair turrets, porches bearing the construction date and inner courtyards which passersby may glimpse through open doors. The Promenade de la citadelle (citadel walk), on the west side, follows a section of the ramparts, including the Tour des Sorcières (witches' tower).

SIGHTS

Église St-Maurice – The church, which shows great unity of style, was built between 1270 and 1489. The tympanum of the south doorway bears a 14C representation of St Maurice on horseback, above the Adoration of the Magi. Inside, there is a fine early-17C pulpit, a large organ by Silbermann dating from 1750, a late-15C relief sculpture in polychrome wood, with St George slaying the dragon in the foreground, and a huge mural depicting St Christopher.

Musée du Bucheneck ⊘ – The museum is housed in a former 11C fortress, which was the seat of the episcopal bailiff from 1289 to the Revolution. Remodelled several times, the building now contains various collections concerning the town's history, in particular a model of the city as it looked in 1838, and portraits of members of the town's leading families.

La Nef des jouets ⊘ – This rich toy collection is displayed in the former headquarters of the Order of the Knights of the Hospital of St John at Jerusalem, the present Order of the Knights of Malta, dating from the end of the 12C. The varied collection includes toys made of clay, cardboard, wood and plastic, both popular and sophisticated.

Maisons anciennes – Note in particular:
– Maison Litty, the former Hôtel St-Michel (1622) at no 15 rue des Sœurs;
– a wine-grower's house (1656) at no 5 rue du Temple;
– Maison Horn (1588) at no 42 rue de Lattre-de-Tassigny;
– Maison Hubschwerlin (16C) with its lovely inner courtyard, its oriel and stair turret.
In rue Jean-Jaurès stands the family mansion (1605) of the Heeckeren d'Anthès, a powerful Alsatian industrial dynasty; one of its members, Georges-Charles de Heeckeren, killed the Russian writer Pouchkine in a dual near St-Petersbourg in 1837.

STRASBOURG★★★

Conurbation 388 483
Michelin map 87 folds 4 and 5 or 242 folds 20 and 24

This important modern city lying on the banks of the River Ill, with its busy river port and renowned university is the intellectual and economic capital of Alsace. Built round its famous cathedral, Strasbourg is also a town rich in art treasures, which has been the "capital" of Europe since 1949, for it is here that the European Council is located. An important music festival takes place every year in June followed by the European Fair in early September.

EUROPEAN BY TRADITION

Famous oath – Argentoratum, which was but a small fishing and hunting village at the time of Julius Caesar, soon became a prosperous city and a major cross-roads between eastern and western Europe: Strateburgum, the city of roads... This geographical position meant that Strasbourg found itself on the path of all invasions from across the Rhine and was destroyed, burnt down, ransacked and rebuilt many times throughout its history. In 842, it was chosen as a place of reconciliation by two of Charlemagne's grandsons. This oath of fidelity is the first official text written both in a Romance and a Germanic language.

Gutenberg in Strasbourg – Born in Mainz in 1395, Gutenberg had to flee his native town for political reasons and came to settle in Strasbourg in 1434. He formed an association with three Alsatians to perfect a secret process which he had invented. But their association ended in a law suit in 1439 and this is how we know that the invention in question was the printing press. Gutenberg went back to Mainz in 1448 and, with his partner Johann Fust, he perfected the invention which deeply changed our society.

IEAN GVTTEMBERG

D'après une estampe/EXPLORER

The pot of steaming porridge – The wars which followed the Reformation divided Alsace into two camps and in 1576, the municipality of Strasbourg decided to organise a large shooting competition as a means of getting the two sides together and calming things down. People from neighbouring Swabia and Bavaria and from the free Swiss cities were also invited. The shooting ground was located on the site of the present Parc Contades. The team from Zurich won the competition and 48 burghers from the town decided to go to Strasbourg to celebrate the town's victory. It was a long journey in rowing boats along the Limmat, the Aar and the Rhine. The burghers thus decided to set a record: the idea was to cover the distance in less time than it took for a huge pot of steaming porridge, laid down in the centre of the boat, to cool right down. The journey lasted only 17 hours and the porridge was still warm on arrival. "If you are ever in danger, said the leader of the Swiss party to his hosts, you will know that we can fly to your rescue in less time than it takes for porridge to cool down". Three centuries later, in 1870, loyal descendants of these famous burghers from Zurich came to help Strasbourg, being shelled by the Prussians, thus fulfilling their ancestors' promise.

Goethe's student days – In 1770, Strasbourg University was not aware that it would benefit greatly from the fame of one of its former students, the writer Johann Wolfgang von Goethe. He had lodgings in rue du Vieux-Marché-aux-Poissons, in a boarding house run by two unmarried ladies, where a group of jovial fellows used to meet and drink a quantity of Alsace wine which astounded the young Goethe. In order to test his will-power, Goethe, who suffered from vertigo, would go up to the top of the cathedral and hang on to the balustrade. One of his favourite occupations was to go to Sessenheim to see Friederike Brion *(see SESSENHEIM)*. He was also anxious to find the grave of Erwin of Steinbach who designed the west front of the cathedral. However, having become a doctor of the faculty in August 1771, Goethe returned to Frankfurt, abandoning Friederike and his investigations. Forty-five years later, one of his former fellow students discovered Erwin's grave under a pile of coal in the small cemetery close to the cathedral.

Rouget de Lisle's Marseillaise – By the time the Revolution began, Strasbourg had been French for more than 100 years, since in 1681 the city had acknowledged Louis XIV, who already ruled over the rest of Alsace, as its "sovereign and protector".

STRABOURG AGGLOMÉRATION

BISCHEIM

Marais (R. du)	CS	121
Périgueux (Av. de)	BS	159
Robertsau (R. de la)	BS	179
Triage (R. du)	BS	219

ECKBOLSHEIM

Gaulle (Av. du Gén.-de)	BS	67
Wasselonne (Route de)	BS	237

HOENHEIM

Fontaine (R. de la)	BR	55
République (R. de la)	BR	174

ILLKIRCH-GRAFFENSTTADEN

Bürkell (Route)	BT	24
Ceinture (R. de la)	BT	27
Faisanderie (R. de la)	BT	48
Industrie (R. de l')	BT	97
Kastler (R. Alfred)	BT	99
Lixenbühl (R.)	BT	115
Messmer (Av.)	BT	138

(Neuhof etc.)

Neuhof (Route de)	BT	144
Strasbourg (Rte de)	BT	207
Vignes (R. des)	BT	233

LINGOLSHEIM

Eckbolsheim (R. d')	BS	44
Ostwald (R. d')	BT	152
Prés (R. des)	BS	168

OBERHAUSBERGEN

Mittelhausbergen (Rte de)	BS	139
Oberhausbergen (Rte de)	BS	149

OSTWALD

Foch (R. du Maréchal)	BT	54
Gelspolsheim (R. de)	BT	73
Leclerc (R. du Gén.)	BT	112
Vosges (R. des)	BT	232
23-Novembre (R. du)	BT	246

SCHILTIGHEIM

Bischwiller (Route de)	BS	18
Gaulle (Rte du Gén.-de)	BS	70
Hausbergen (Route de)	BS	81
Mendès-France (Av. P.)	BS	132
Pompiers (R. des)	BS	164
St-Junien (R. de)	BS	184

STRASBOURG

Atenheim (Route d')	CT	9
Bauerngrund (R. de)	CT	15
Forêt Noire (Av. de la)	CS	56
Ganzau (R. de la)	BT	66
Holtzheim (R. de)	AS	88
Ill (R. de l')	CS	96
Jacoutot (Quai)	CS	97
Neuhof (Route de)	CT	144
Plaine des Bouchers (R. de la)	BS	163
Polygone (Route du)	BS	165
Pont (R. du)	BT	166
Ribeauvillé (R. de)	CS	177
Romains (Route des)	BS	180
Schirmeck (Route de)	BS	198

BREWERY 🍺

DOCKS:

AUGUSTE-DETŒUF	CT	Ⓐ
GASTON-HŒLLING	CT	Ⓑ
ADRIEN-WEIRICH	CT	Ⓒ
DARSE IV	CT	Ⓓ
VAUBAN	CS	Ⓔ
DUSUZEAU	CS	Ⓕ
REMPARTS	CS	Ⓛ
ALBERT-AUBERGER	CS	Ⓛ
COMMERCE	CS	Ⓝ
INDUSTRIE	CS	Ⓡ

D — Maison de la Télévision FR3 Alsace

M⁵ — Musée zoologique de l'université et de la ville

On 24 April 1792, the mayor of Strasbourg, Frédéric de Dietrich, offered a farewell dinner to a group of volunteers from the Rhine army. The men talked about the necessity for the troops to have a song which would rouse their enthusiasm and the mayor light-heartedly asked one of the young officers named Rouget de Lisle, if he would write such a song. The young man went home and worked all night. The next morning, he went to a friend's house and sang for him his *Chant de guerre pour l'Armée du Rhin* (War Song for the Rhine Army). They then went to Dietrich's home where the mayor's niece accompanied Rouget de Lisle at the piano. The orchestral score was completed the next day and the work was sent to a publisher. Shortly afterwards, volunteers from Marseille on their way north adopted the song which became known as the "Marseillaise". It was designated the French national anthem in 1795 and again in 1879. A plaque on the Banque de France building, at no 4 rue Broglie, recalls the memory of Rouget de Lisle.

A great "chef" – The Maréchal de Contades, who became the military governor of Alsace in 1762, was a distinguished gourmet who loved to regale his guests. Among them was Jean-Jacques Rousseau who said in a letter to a friend that he was getting tired of these frequent dinners. In 1778, Contades engaged a new cook, **Jean-Pierre Clause**, a native of Dieuze, then 21 years old. Alsatian geese were to bring him fame. Being asked to surpass himself on an important occasion, he decided to use the birds' liver; he surrounded the liver with finely chopped veal and lard and wrapped it in pastry then cooked it slowly until golden. The marshal's guests were enthusiastic and

VISITING TIPS

Theatre performances, concerts, conferences, exhibitions, sporting events, and other entertainment are listed in the monthly brochure "Strasbourg actualités" or the weekly "Hebdoscope" (7 F).

Getting around

The efficient public transport network includes 25 bus lines and one tramway line (operating from 4.30am to half past midnight) stopping at 18 stations. It is possible to buy one, five or ten tickets at a time; each one being valid for 1hr on any journey throughout the network. Day passes called "Tourpass" (19F) are valid for 24hr and for any number of journeys. Three car parks (Rotonde, Étoile and Baggersee) provide direct access to the tramway. It is possible to travel with a bike (except during rush hours ie 7-9am), loading being done through the rear door of the tram.

Sightseeing

The "Strasbourg Pass" (50F), available from the tourist office and at hotels, includes several free admissions and half-price admissions and is valid for three days.
Themed guided tours of the town on foot are organised every Saturday at 2.30pm from April to June and September to November; for the months of July, August and December, obtain the relevant brochure or apply at the tourist office.
Guided tours of Old Strasbourg aboard a mini-train (50min) take place from the end of March to early November; departure from place de la Cathédrale every half hour.
The association known as "Taxi 13" organises a guided round tour (about 1hr). For information ☎ 03 88 75 19 19.

Markets

Markets are generally on from 7am to 1pm. Traditional markets are held on Wednesdays and Fridays place Broglie and quai de Turckheim, on Tuesdays and Saturdays boulevard de la Marne, on Wednesdays rue de Zurich; a market is held by local producers on Saturdays place du Marché-aux-Poissons; a flea-market takes place on Wednesdays and Saturdays (9am to 6pm) rue du Vieil-Hôpital and place de la Grande-Boucherie; the book market is on Wednesdays and Saturdays (9am to 6pm) place and rue de Gutenberg; the Christmas market is held in December.

Events

Folk shows in the courtyard of the Rohan palace from early June to late August, every Sunday at 10.30am and on certain evenings (details in local newspapers); music festival (June), jazz festival (July), Musica, festival of current music (end of September to beginning of October).

"Winstubs"

Typical Alsatian establishments serving regional dishes and wines in suitable surroundings:
Zum Strissel, 5 place de la Grande-Boucherie; S'burjerstuewel (chez Yvonne), 10 rue Sanglier; le Clou, 3 rue Chaudron; la Petite Marie, 8 rue Brûlée; Muensterstuebel, 8 place du Marché-aux-Cochons-de-Lait.

Virtual Visit

An excellent Web site in English, loaded with useful information for tourists, business travellers, ongoing events, history, shopping, sports etc , can help you fine-tune the details of a trip to Strasbourg: www.strasbourg.com (Strasbourg On-Line).

begged in vain to obtain the recipe from the young chef. In 1784, Clause left Contades to marry a pastry cook's widow and, until his death in 1827, he made and sold his goose-liver pâté which became famous the world over.

1870-1918 – On 27 September 1870, Strasbourg capitulated after being besieged and shelled by the Germans for 50 days (the garrison lost 600 men and 1 500 civilians were killed).

According to the terms of the Treaty of Frankfurt (10 May 1871), Strasbourg was to become a German city, which it remained until 11 November 1918. A few days later, on 22 November, General Gouraud officially entered the old city and on 25 November, French troops paraded in front of the imperial palace.

Second World War – From 1940 to 1944, the Germans occupied Strasbourg once more. In November 1944, a French unit, the second armoured division led by **General Leclerc**, had the honour of liberating the town. The whole operation lasted three days. On 25 November General Vaterrodt surrendered and 6 000 German soldiers were made prisoners.

In January 1945, the town was once again threatened by the German counter-offensive. It was saved thanks to General de Gaulle's personal appeal to the Allies and to the decision of General de Lattre de Tassigny to send an Algerian division to support the troops defending the town.

European crossroads – Even before the end of the Second World War, major politicians of that period (Winston Churchill, Robert Schuman, Konrad Adenauer, Charles de Gaulle...) agreed that Strasbourg should officially assume the role it had played throughout its history and become a European crossroads. Reconciliation between former enemies would have its roots in a city that had become a symbol, Strasbourg, lying alongside a mighty river once dotted with defensive works and now acting as a major link between neighbouring countries at the heart of Europe.

The **European Council** was created on 5 May 1949; all the countries of western Europe are members. Eastern European countries can attend as guests. The Council, which has a purely consultative role, sends recommendations to governments and establishes conventions which commit the states signing the agreements, with the object of harmonising legislation in various fields of common interest. The most famous is the European Convention for the Safeguard of Human Rights (1950).

the European Council created the **European flag** (12 gold stars arranged in a circle on a sky-blue background). It shares its chamber with the **European Parliament**, an important institution of the European Union; its members have been elected by universal suffrage since 1979; its role is consultative, financial and restraining.

Strasbourg shares with Brussels and Luxembourg the privilege of housing the main institutions of the European Union. Luxembourg houses the **Court of Justice** and the general secretariat of the European Parliament, whereas the **Council**, which has executive and legislative powers, and the **Commission**, which administers and controls, are both based in Brussels.

★★★CATHÉDRALE NOTRE-DAME ⊘ (KZ) *1hr 30min*

Notre-Dame is one of the finest and most original Gothic cathedrals. Enjoy the best **view★** of it from rue Mercière (**KZ 135**).

The edifice owes a great deal of its charm to the pink sandstone from the Vosges with which it was built.

Foundation and construction – Work began in 1015 on a Romanesque edifice on the site of a temple dedicated to Hercules. Bernard of Clairvaux celebrated mass in the church in 1145 but it was destroyed by fire and rebuilding did not start until 1176. By that time, the cathedral architects were influenced by Gothic art newly introduced in Alsace. In 1284, **Erwin of Steinbach** began the construction of the splendid west front in pure Gothic style. Unfortunately, he died in 1318 before he had time to complete his work.

In 1365, the recently built towers were joined together up to the level of the platform and then the north tower was raised. Finally, in 1439, Johann Hültz from Cologne surmounted the tower with the famous spire which confers to the cathedral its amazing outline.

"Œuvre Notre-Dame" – This unique institution was founded to collect donations for the building work, upkeep and improvement of the cathedral. The first recorded donation dates from 1205.

Erwin himself set an example: being poor, he bequeathed only a small sum to which he nevertheless added his horse.

The Reformation – The Reformation whose main spokesman was **Martin Bucer** (1491-1551), established in Strasbourg in 1523 *(see Sélestat)*, was well received in Alsace. The groundwork had been done by a preacher who is still well-known in Strasbourg, **Geiler of Kaysersberg**; in his sermons, he continually condemned the loose morals of the times and the Church's lack of firmness.

The Foolish Virgins – right-hand doorway of the cathedral

For many years, the old and the new religions fought for supremacy in the cathedral, Luther's proposals being posted on the main door. The intercession of Emperor Charles V from Augsburg in the mid 16C led to concessions on both sides but the Protestant faith finally triumphed and the cathedral only returned to Catholicism in 1681, during the reign of Louis XIV.

Glorious days – During the 200 years preceding the Revolution of 1789, the history of Strasbourg did not differ from that of its cathedral. When Louis XIV entered the town, the bishop welcomed him in front of the cathedral. In 1725, Louis XV married Marie Leszczynska in the cathedral and in 1744, having recovered from a serious illness, the king was welcomed in the cathedral by a wildly enthusiastic crowd. Finally, in 1770, on her way to marry the future Louis XVI, Marie-Antoinette was greeted in the cathedral by Louis de Rohan *(see p 287)*.

Hard times – No fewer than 230 statues were destroyed during the Revolution. Fortunately, 67 others decorating the west front were saved. Then there was talk of doing away with the spire until someone had the brilliant idea of dressing it with a huge bright-red Phrygian cap. Hültz's masterpiece was saved.
In August and September 1870, Prussian shells set fire to the roof and the spire was hit by 13 of them.
In 1944, allied bombing damaged the transept tower and the north aisle.

Exterior

★★**West front** – *(Illustration p 37)*. Erwin of Steinbach was the architect in charge of building to slightly above the Apostles' Gallery surmounting the rose-window. It has been superbly restored and now looks as splendid as when it was first built, with its wealth of colonnettes, stone needles and sculptures.
The **central doorway** is the most richly decorated. Statues and low-relief sculptures were made at different periods. The tympanum is made of four historiated bands: the first three, dating from the 13C, are remarkably realistic; the fourth is modern.
1) From left to right: Jesus entering Jerusalem, the Last Supper, Judas embracing Jesus; Peter severing the ear of a soldier named Malchus; Jesus brought before Pilate; the Flagellation.
2) Jesus wearing the Crown of Thorns, then bearing his Cross; Jesus crucified positioned above Adam's coffin, between the Synagogue and the Church collecting his blood; the Deposition; the Resurrection (soldiers sleeping beneath the tomb).

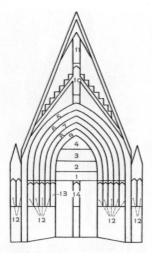

3) Judas being hanged; monsters coming out of Hell; Adam and Eve freed by Christ; Magdalene at Jesus' feet; Thomas, surrounded by the Apostles, touches Christ's wounds.

4) The Ascension. Carvings decorating the recessed arches, remade after the Revolution are to be looked at from the outside.

5) The Creation; the story of Eve, Adam, Cain and Abel.

6) The story of Abraham, Noah, Moses, Jacob, Joshua, Jonas and Samson.

7) Martyrdom of the Apostles, of St Stephen and St Laurence.

8) The four Evangelists and the Doctors of the Church.

9) Jesus healing the sick and bringing the dead back to life. A double gable surmounts the doorway.

10) Statue of Solomon on his throne.

11) The Virgin and Child. Fine 13C and 14C statues decorate the sides of the doorway.

12) Prophets.

13) A sibyl.

14) Modern statue of the Virgin and Child.

The magnificent rose-window above the central doorway has a 15m/49ft diameter. The decoration of the **right-hand doorway**, illustrating the parable of the Wise Virgins and the Foolish Virgins, includes several famous statues; some of them have been replaced by copies (the original ones are in the Musée de l'Œuvre Notre-Dame).

On the left, the amiable, attractive Seducer, dressed in contemporary fashion, offers the apple to the most daring of the Foolish Virgins who is about to unbutton her dress. Behind the back of this evil spirit, hideous animals symbolise Vice, but the Foolish Virgins are deceived by appearances; they have thrown their lamps away and are ready to sin.

On the right, on the contrary, the divine Spouse meets the Wise Virgins who have kept their lamps and are ready to welcome him. The base of these statues are carved with a calendar bearing the signs of the Zodiac and the months of the year. The 14C statues of the **left-hand doorway** represent the Virtues. Slim and full of majesty in their long flowing gowns, they strike the Vices down.

★★★**Tower** ⊙ – The west-front platform is 66m/217ft high (328 steps; *30min*). The tower rises another 40m/131ft above the platform and is surmounted by a spire whose point is 142m/466ft above ground level (only 9m/30ft lower than the cast-iron spire of Rouen cathedral).

Johann Hültz's spire, octagonal at the base, consists of six tiers of openwork turrets housing the stairs and is topped by a double cross. It is a light and graceful masterpiece.

From the platform there is a fine **view**★ of Strasbourg, in particular the old town with its picturesque superposed dormer-windows, of the suburbs and the Rhine Valley framed by the Black Forest and the Vosges.

South side – The beautiful 13C **Clock doorway**, the cathedral's oldest doorway, opens on the south side. It consists of two adjacent Romanesque doors separated by a statue of Solomon on a pedestal which recalls his famous Judgement. This part had to be remade. On either side of the doorway are copies of the statues of the Church and the Synagogue (the originals are in the Musée de l'Œuvre Notre-Dame).

On the left, the Church, wearing a crown and looking strong and proud, holds the Cross in one hand and the Chalice in the other. On the right, the Synagogue, looking tired and sad, bends over in an effort to catch the fragments of her lance and the Tables of the Law which are dropping out of her hands. The band which covers her eyes is the symbol of error. These graceful and expressive statues are among the most attractive specimens of 13C French sculpture. The tympanum of the left-hand door depicts the **Death of the Virgin**★★. As he was dying, Delacroix loved to look at a reproduction of this carving. The figurine which Jesus is holding in his left hand represents Mary's soul.

The outside dial of the astronomical clock can be seen above the two doors.

Transept – The present tower surmounting the crossing was erected between 1874 and 1878.

North side – The restored **St-Laurence doorway**, dating from the late 15C, illustrates the martyrdom of St Laurence (the carved group was remade in the 19C). On the left of the doorway are the statues of the Virgin, of the three kings and of a shepherd; on the right are five statues including that of St Laurence (the originals are in the Musée de l'Œuvre Notre-Dame).

Interior

The cathedral is 103m/113yd long (Amiens 145m/159yd, Notre-Dame de Paris 130m/142yd, St-Denis 108m/118yd). The nave is 32m/105ft high (Amiens 42m/138ft, Notre-Dame de Paris 35m/115ft, St-Denis 29m/95ft). The **stained-glass windows★★★**, dating from the 12C, 13C and 14C, are remarkable (500 000 pieces make up the 4 600 panels) but have been damaged over the centuries.

When the sun is shining, a strange phenomenon occurs: a white ray (at the winter solstice) or a green ray (at the two equinoxes) shines on the stone canopy surmounting Christ on the pulpit; the canopy is in fact used as a marker for the astonomical clock.

Nave and south aisle – Work on the nave, which consists of seven bays, began in the 13C. The stained glass of the clerestory windows and that of the aisles date from the 13C and 14C. Note the 50 or so statuettes decorating the hexagonal **pulpit★★ (1)**, in true Flamboyant Gothic style, designed by Hans Hammer for the Reformation preacher Geiler of Kaysersberg.

The **organ★★ (8)** hanging over the nave beneath the triforium, displays its magnificent polychrome organ case (14C and 15C) across the full width of a bay. The corbelled loft is carved with a representation of Samson with, on either side, a town herald and a pretzel seller in period costume. These articulated characters would sometimes come to life during sermons to entertain the congregation as testifies a complaint lodged by a preacher in 1501. The present instrument is modern (1981).

St Catherine's chapel spreads across the two bays of the south aisle adjacent to the transept; it contains an epitaph of the Death of Mary **(2)**, dating from 1480 and 14C stained-glass windows.

South transept – The **Angels** or **Last Judgement★★ pier (3)**, erected in the 13C, stands in the centre. It is adorned with statues on three tiers, which make an extremely harmonious group, revealing the delicate perfection of Gothic art.

The **Astronomical Clock★** ⊙ **(4)** is the cathedral's most popular feature. It was restored by Schwilgué, a native of Strasbourg, in 1838.

The seven days of the week are represented by chariots led by gods, who appear through an opening beneath the dial: Diana on Mondays, then Mars, Mercury, Jupiter, Venus, Saturn and Apollo. A series of automata strikes twice every quarter hour. The first stroke is made by one of the two angels surrounding the "average time" dial, at the centre of the Lions Gallery. The second stroke is made by one of the four characters representing the "four ages"

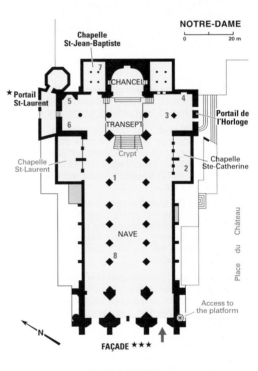

NOTRE-DAME

0   20 m

Chapelle St-Jean-Baptiste

7

CHANCEL

★Portail St-Laurent

5

4

6

TRANSEPT

3

Portail de l'Horloge

Crypt

Chapelle St-Laurent

Chapelle Ste-Catherine

2

1

Place du Château

NAVE

8

Access to the platform

N

FAÇADE ★★★

Place de la Cathédrale

of man who pass in front of Death in the upper part of the clock (the Child strikes the first quarter, the Adolescent the second, the Man the third and the Old Man the last). The hours are struck by Death. On the last stroke, the second angel of the Lions Gallery reverses his hourglass.

The astronomical clock is half an hour behind normal time. The midday chiming occurs at 12.30pm. As soon as it happens, a great parade takes place in the recess at the top of the clock. The Apostles pass in front of Christ and bow to him; Jesus blesses them as the cock, perched on the left-hand tower, flaps his wings and crows three times. The central mechanism of the clock is wound once a week. The astronomical indications are calculated for an indeterminate period.

On the left of the clock, a 13C stained-glass window depicts a huge St Christopher, 8m/26ft tall.

Time and Time Again

The cathedral's unique timepiece comes complete with its own legend. Around 1350, when the interior of the cathedral was finally finished, mathematician Jehan Boernave offered to create an astronomical clock which would be the most extraordinary on earth. In exchange, he asked only that his name be engraved on a plaque above the cathedral door. For five years he laboured on the 12m/39ft timepiece, embellished with allegorical sculptures. Boernave called it "The Three Kings", in reference to the wise men paying homage to the Virgin and Child occupying the centre of the work, as though the mother and babe commanded the very march of time.

At the inauguration, the rooster beat its wings and crowed out midday. It was a triumphant moment for the clocksmith, acclaimed throughout the town and honoured by a banquet sponsored by the city guilds. But the cock's crow, a reminder of Peter's denial of Christ, also spelled treason for Boernave. A powerful jealousy took hold of the guild members, who feared that the craftsman would take his experience elsewhere and perhaps create an even greater clock. The same night, they lay in wait for Boernave and brutally blinded him.

The next day, the sightless man found his way to the cathedral and indicated that he needed to adjust a secret mechanism. He penetrated the works, feeling his way, and when he emerged, the clock had been stilled. Unmoved by pleas and threats, he refused to set it in motion again.

In 1547, another astronomer tried to repair the clock, but not until 1571 did Conrad Dasypodius manage to give the cathedral a working astronomical clock, which was, in turn, restored by Jean-Baptiste Schwilgué in 1838, and still marks time today.

Chancel – The arcading, paintings and stained-glass windows are modern. The stained glass of the axial window, depicting the Virgin and Child, is the work of Max Ingrand. It was offered to the cathedral by the European Council in 1956.

North transept – It contains splendid Flamboyant Gothic christening fonts (5). On the opposite wall, an unusual stone group represents Christ on the Mount of Olives (6). Carved in 1498 for the cemetery of St Thomas' church, it was transferred to the cathedral in the 17C.
The 13C and 14C stained-glass windows depict several emperors of the Holy Roman Empire.

Chapelle St-Jean-Baptiste and crypt – The 13C chapel contains the tomb of Bishop Conrad of Lichtenberg (7) who began the construction of the west front. It is believed to be the work of Erwin. Opposite, one can see an epitaph of Canon Busang with the Virgin and Child by Van Leyden. On the left of the steps leading up to the chancel, a staircase leads down to the Romanesque crypt (fine capitals).

★★**Tapestries** – The cathedral owns 14 very large and splendid 17C tapestries which are hung between the pillars of the nave on special occasions (certain religious holidays or for exceptional municipal or European events). Commissioned by the chapter of Notre-Dame in Paris, they were bought by the canons of Strasbourg in 1739 for the sum of 10 000 *livres* (French unit of money before the Revolution). Visitors who are lucky enough to see them all on display will be reminded that through the period known as the *Ancien Régime* (prior to 1789), French churches were liberally decorated with such hangings. The remarkable collection in Strasbourg depicts scenes from the life of the Virgin, designed by Philippe de Champaigne, Charles Poerson and Jacques Stella.

★★★**OLD TOWN** *allow one day*

The old town nestles round the cathedral, on the island formed by the two arms of the River Ill.

★**Place de la Cathédrale** (KZ 26) – It is situated along the west front and north side of the cathedral. The **Pharmacie du Cerf** (F) on the corner of rue Mercière, which dates from 1268, is believed to be the oldest chemist's in France.
On the north side of the cathedral, the **Maison Kammerzell**★ (1589) (Q), restored in 1954, is decorated with frescoes and splendid woodcarvings. The door dates from 1467. It is now occupied by a restaurant.

Place du Château – It is lined with the Musée de l'Œuvre Notre-Dame, the Museum of Modern Art *(see Museums)* and the Palais Rohan.

★**Palais Rohan** (KZ) – The palace was built in 1704 for Cardinal Armand de Rohan-Soubise, but the most famous representative of the House of Rohan was undoubtedly the Flamboyant Louis de Rohan implicated in the "necklace affair" which contributed to discredit Marie-Antoinette just before the Revolution of 1789.

The "necklace affair" – **Louis de Rohan** was a handsome socialite and a spendthrift. Having welcomed Marie-Antoinette in Strasbourg when she arrived from her native Austria, he was sent as ambassador to her mother, Empress Maria-Theresa whom he shocked by his immodest behaviour. Back in France he tried to win Queen Marie-Antoinette's favour by offering her an outrageously expensive necklace which the king had refused her. He borrowed large sums of money and entrusted a certain Madame de la Motte with the deal. But the adventuress stole the necklace and Rohan could not pay the jewellers. The ensuing scandal considerably tarnished the queen's reputation and contributed to the mistrust the French people felt for her. Madame de la Motte was caught, whipped and branded in public. As for Rohan, he was arrested but later acquitted and exiled. He returned to Strasbourg and crossed the Rhine at the start of the Revolution. He died in Ettenheim in 1803.

The palace – Designed in the 18C by Robert de Cotte, the king's first architect, the palace has a beautiful Classical façade with a central pediment. The imposing **façade**, overlooking the terrace on the river side, is also Classical and decorated with columns of the Corinthian order.

The edifice houses the rich museums of the Palais Rohan *(see Museums)*.

Follow rue de Rohan then turn right onto rue des Cordiers leading to the charming **place du Marché-aux-Cochons-de-Lait**★ (KZ 124) lined with old houses including a 16C house with wooden galleries. The adjacent place de la Grande-Boucherie looks typically Alsatian.

Turn left onto rue du Vieux-Marché-aux-Poissons. The **Ancienne Douane** (KZ) stands on the right; this former custom house, rebuilt in 1965, was originally a warehouse used by the town's river traffic. It houses temporary exhibitions.

Opposite, the Grande Boucherie buildings, dating from 1586, contain the Musée historique *(see Museums)*.

Pont du Corbeau (KZ) – This is the former "execution" bridge from which infanticides and parricides, tied up in sacks, were plunged into the water until they died; those condemned for lesser crimes were put inside iron cages and dipped into the river at the spot where waste water from the Boucherie flowed in.

A carriage entrance at no 1 quai des Bateliers, gives access to the Cour du Corbeau.

★**Cour du Corbeau** (KZ) – This picturesque courtyard goes back to the 14C. Note the old well on the right dating from 1560. This former fashionable inn welcomed some illustrious guests: Turenne, King Johann-Casimir of Poland, Frederick the Great, Emperor Joseph II.

Quai St-Nicolas (KZ) – The embankment is lined with some fine old houses; three of them have been turned into a museum *(Musée alsacien: see Museums)*.

Louis Pasteur lived at no 18 (Y). A little further along is St Nicholas' church, dating from the 15C, where Albert Schweitzer preached from 1899 to 1913.

Retrace your steps across the bridge and turn left onto rue de la Douane and continue along quai St-Thomas.

Église St-Thomas ⊘ (JZ) – This five-naved church, rebuilt at the end of the 12C, became a Lutheran cathedral in 1529. It contains the famous **mausoleum of the Maréchal de Saxe**★★ (Moritz von Sachsen, Marshal of France), one of Pigalle's masterpieces (18C). The allegorical sculpture represents France weeping and holding the marshal's hand while trying to push Death aside. Strength, symbolised by Hercules, gives way to grief and Love can be seen crying as he puts out his torch. On the left, a lion (Holland), a leopard (England) and an eagle (Austria), are represented vanquished, next to crumpled flags.

The 12C tomb of **Bishop Adeloch** is located in a small chapel. The organ is by Silbermann (18C).

Walk along rue de la Monnaie to the Pont St-Martin.

The bridge offers a fine **view**★ of the "Bain-aux-Plantes district" *(see below)*.

The river divides into four arms (watermills, dams and locks can still be seen).

As you walk along rue des Dentelles, note the 18C house at no 12 and an older one at no 10 dating from the 16C.

The street leads to place Benjamin-Zix and the beginning of rue du Bain-aux-Plantes.

★★**La Petite France** (HZ) – This is one of the most interesting and best preserved areas of the old town, with its houses reflecting in the canal. At dusk the whole district is fascinating. It was once the fishermen's, tanners' and millers' district.

La Petite France

For centuries, **rue du Bain-aux-Plantes**★★ was the district of the tanners' guild. The street is lined with old buildings dating from the Alsatian Renaissance (16C-17C); these timber-framed corbelled houses are adorned with galleries and gables. Note, along the canal on the left, the tanners' house (Gerwerstub, no 42), dating from 1572, and on the right, no 33 on the corner of rue du fossé-des-Tanneurs and the extremely narrow rue des Cheveux; nos 31, 27 and 25 (1651) are also noteworthy.

★**Ponts Couverts** (HZ) – This is the name given to three successive bridges spanning the River Ill; each bridge is guarded by a massive square tower, once part of the 14C fortifications. The three towers used to be linked by covered wooden bridges. The fourth tower, known as the Tour du Boureau, at the end of quai Turckheim, also formed part of the city's fortifications.

Turn right just before the last tower and walk along quai de l'Ill, the only way to reach the terrace of the Vauban dam.

Barrage Vauban ⊘ (HZ) – From the panoramic terrace *(viewing table, telescope)*, covering the whole length of the casemate bridge, known as the "Barrage Vauban" (part of Vauban's fortifications), built right across the Ill, there is a striking **view**★★ of the Ponts Couverts and their four towers in the foreground, of the Petite France district and its canals in the background, and of the cathedral on the right. The ground floor of the dam houses an archeological display: statues and stone fragments from the town' churches.

Go back over the Pont Couverts. Follow quai de la Petite France running alongside the canal and admire the romantic **view**★ of the old houses reflecting in the water. *Walk across the Pont du Faisan. Turn right onto rue du Bain-aux-Plantes, then left onto rue du Fossé-des-Tanneurs.*

Turn right onto Grand'Rue lined with 16C-18C houses and continue along rue Gutenberg to the square of the same name.

On **place Gutenberg** stand the **Hôtel de la Chambre de Commerce** (Chamber of Commerce building) (**KZ C**), a fine Renaissance edifice, and Gutenberg's statue by David d'Angers. No 52 rue du Vieux-Marché-aux-Poissons *(going south)* is the birthplace of Jean Arp (1887-1966), a sculptor, painter, poet and major protagonist of modern art.

Rue Mercière takes you back to place de la Cathédrale.

MUSEUMS

Musées du Palais Rohan ⊘ – *Go to the end of the courtyard on the left.*
The fine restored museums exhibit, in the official apartments of the cardinals of Rohan, an important part of their furniture and collections.

★★**Musée des Arts décoratifs** – The Museum of Decorative Arts is housed on the ground floor and in the right-hand part of the edifice *(stables wing and Hans-Hang pavilions)*. The **Grands Appartements** (official apartments) rank among the finest 18C

French interiors. They were the official residence of the bishops of Strasbourg; several distinguished guests stayed in these rooms: Louis XV in 1744, Marie-Antoinette in 1770 and Napoleon in 1805 and 1806.

The synod room, the king's bedroom, the assembly room, the cardinals' library, the morning room and the emperor's bedroom are particularly remarkable for their decoration, their ceremonial furniture, their tapestries (tapestry by Constantin after Rubens, c 1625) and their 18C pictures.

The museum, which is devoted to the **arts and crafts of Strasbourg and eastern France**, from the end of the 17C to the mid 19C, contains the famous **ceramics collection★★**, one of the most important of its kind in France. The collection includes earthenware and porcelain from the Strasbourg and Haguenau manufacture, founded and run by the **Hannong** family from 1721 to 1781, and from the Niderviller manufacture, founded in 1748 by the Baron de Beyerlé, the director of Strasbourg's royal mint. These two factories rank among the most prestigious French manufactures of earthenware and porcelain.

Particularly remarkable are the "blue" period pieces, polychrome ones which marked the transition, terrines shaped like animals or vegetables and above all magnificent crimson-based floral decorations which were a source of inspiration for many European manufactures after 1750.

The museum also contains beautiful pieces of gold plate, pewter pottery, wrought iron, clock parts (decorative elements of the cathedral's astronomical clock, including the 14C mechanical cock), wardrobes, cabinets and seats made by local cabinetmakers and Alsatian painting and sculpture.

Musée des Arts Décoratifs

Dish from the Hannong manufacture

★ **Musée des Beaux-Arts** – *The Fine Arts Museum is housed on the 1st and 2nd floors of the main building.* It contains an interesting collection of paintings mainly from the Middle Ages to the 18C.

Italian painting (primitive and Renaissance works) is very well represented; note in particular the *Annunciation Angel* by Filippino Lippi, the *Virgin and Child with St John the Baptist* by Piero di Cosimo, a juvenile *Virgin and Child* by Botticelli, a magnificent *St Sebastian* by Cima da Conegliano and *Judith and the Servant*, one of Correggio's earliest paintings.

The Spanish School is represented by a few pictures, including works by Zurbarán, Murillo, Goya and above all a *Mater Dolorosa* by El Greco.

The collection of paintings from the 15C-17C **Dutch School** is particularly rich: fine *Christ of Mercy* by Simon Marmion, *Engaged Couple* by Lucas of Leyden, several works by Rubens *(Christ in Glory* and *Visitation)*, *St John* (portrait of the artist) and portrait of a woman by Van Dyck, *Going for a Walk* by Pieter de Hooch.

The French and Alsatian schools of the 17C-19C are illustrated by several works including *The Beautiful Woman from Strasbourg* by N de Largillière (1703).

The museum also houses an important collection of **still-life paintings** from the 16C to the 18C, among them the famous ***Bunch of Flowers*** by "Velvet" Brueghel.

The *Portrait of Cardinal Richelieu* by Philippe de Champaigne is one of the museum's recent acquisitions.

★★ **Musée archéologique** – *Located in the basement.* The museum houses regional archeological collections concerning the prehistory and early history of Alsace from 600 000 BC to AD 800.

The prehistory section contains Paleolithic finds from Achenheim and Neolithic collections offering an insight into the life of the first farmers who settled in Alsace as early as 5500 BC.

There are also numerous objects illustrating the Bronze-Age and Iron-Age civilizations: ceramics, weapons and tools, jewellery, ceremonial plates and dishes imported from Greece or Italy, and the Ohnenheim funeral chariot.

The Roman section includes remarkable collections of stone carvings and inscriptions (votive and funeral sculpture) as well as fine glassware and numerous objects of daily life in Gallo-Roman times. Fragments from the Donon sanctuary.

The Merovingian period is represented by collections of weapons and jewellery and a few outstanding items such as the Baldenheim helmet or the military decorations from Ittenheim.

Musée alsacien – Traditional dresser

★★ **Musée alsacien** ⊘ (**KZ M³**) – This museum of popular art, located in three 16C-17C houses including an aristocratic house, gives a good insight into the history, customs and traditions of the Alsace region. The tour of the museum through the maze of stairs and wooden galleries overlooking inner courtyards, enables visitors to discover a wealth of quaint little rooms. The displays include costumes, prints, ancient toys, "flour-spitting" masks that used to decorate old mills, and reconstructions of interiors such as the apothecary's laboratory and wood-panelled bedrooms furnished with box beds, painted furniture and monumental stoves. Some of the rooms are specifically devoted to wine-growing, agriculture, rope-making, religious prints (Protestant and Catholic), Judaism and to the memory of Jean-Frédéric Oberlin *(see Vallée de la BRUCHE).*

★★ **Musée de l'Œuvre Notre-Dame** ⊘ (**KZ M¹**) – *A tour of this museum is a must after a visit of the cathedral.*
The museum is devoted to medieval and Renaissance Alsatian art; the collections are displayed in the wings of the Maison de l'Œuvre, dating from 1347 and 1578-1585, in the former Hôtellerie du Cerf (14C) and in a small 17C house, surrounding four small courtyards: Cour de l'Œuvre, Cour de la Boulangerie, Cour des Maréchaux and Cour du Cerf (looking like a medieval garden).

The Maison de l'Œuvre played an important role in the history of the cathedral *(see p 282)*. The bombing which occurred on 11 August 1944 partly destroyed the oldest of the two wings.

The hall which contains pre-Romanesque sculpture gives access to the Romanesque sculpture rooms and to the room displaying 12C and 13C stained glass, some of it originally decorating the Romanesque cathedral; note the cloister of the Benedictine nuns of Eschau (12C) and the famous **Christ's Head**★★ from Wissembourg, the oldest representational stained glass known (c 1070).

From there, one goes through the Cour de l'Œuvre, with a partly Flamboyant and partly Renaissance decoration, and enters the former meeting hall of the builders and stonemasons' guild, whose woodwork and ceiling date from 1582 and which contains the statues of the cathedral's St Laurence doorway. Next comes the main room of the Hôtellerie du Cerf where 13C works originally decorating the cathedral are exhibited: statues from the south doorway and from the doorways of the west front including the Church and the Synagogue, the Wise Virgins, the Foolish Virgins and the Seducer.

The small garden of the Cour du Cerf is planted with vegetables, medicinal and ornamental plants in order to recreate the *Paradisgärtlein* depicted by medieval Alsatian paintings and prints.

The fine oak staircase, dating from the 18C, leads to small rooms containing 17C prints showing the cathedral at different periods and famous drawings on parchment which reveal the original intentions of the architects who built the west front and the spire between the 13C and 15C. From the landing, there is a fine view of the carved-wood galleries of the Cour des Maréchaux. The first floor houses an important collection of 15C-17C gold plate from Strasbourg.

The second floor is devoted to the evolution of Alsatian art in the 15C; stained glass on the left and on the right, in rooms with period woodwork and ceilings, sculpture and **paintings**★★ of the Alsatian School: Conrad Witz and Alsatian primitives, Nicolas of Leyden.

Visitors go back to the first floor by means of the fine spiral staircase dating from 1580 which leads to the 16C and 17C rooms.

In the Renaissance wing, a room is devoted to **Hans Baldung Grien** (1484-1545), a student of Dürer, who was the main representative of the Renaissance in Strasbourg. The archive room is also housed in this wing.

The east wing contains displays of Alsatian and Rhenish furniture as well as 16C and 17C sculpture, a collection of 17C still-life paintings, some of them by **Sébastien Stoskopff** (1597-1657); miniatures, interiors and costumes from Strasbourg dating from the 17C, glassware.

★★**Musée d'Art Moderne et Contemporain** ⊘ (**HZ M⁴**) – Standing on the bank of the River Ill, this modern building clad with pink granite and white concrete panels was designed by Adrien Fainsilber, the architect of the Cité des Sciences et de l'Industrie at La Villette in Paris.

A central glass nave, more than 100m/110yd long and 25m/82ft high, leads to the exhibition rooms presenting a vast panorama of modern and contemporary art. The exhibition area covers almost 5 000m²/5 980sq yd and the atmosphere is conducive to contemplation.

The museum, which is intended to be a meeting place, has an auditorium, a library, an educational department, a bookseller's, a gift shop, a restaurant and cafeteria upstairs.

Modern art from 1870 to 1950 – *Located on the ground floor.* The works exhibited illustrate the various artistic expressions which have left their stamp on the history of modern art, from the academic works of William Bouguereau *(The Consoling Virgin)* to the abstract works of Kandinsky, Baumeister and Poliakoff of Magneli.

Renoir, Sisley and Monet illustrate Impressionism. Paintings by Signac and a few Nabis such as Gauguin, Vuillard and Maurice Denis show that the post-Impressionists were looking for something different. Art at the turn of the century is represented by a group of Symbolist works headed by Gustav Klimt's *Plenitude*.

Several rooms are devoted to **Jean Arp** and his wife Sophie Taeuber-Arp, who made, in collaboration with Theo Van Doesburg, a series of stained-glass panels recreating the constructivist interiors (1926-1928) of l'Aubette, an 18C building situated on place Kléber. The desk designed by Arp and Sophie Taeuber's carpet are next to items connected with the Bauhaus, the De Stijl movement and the modern approach (furniture by Eileen Gray and Marcel Breuer, dining room designed by Kandinsky). One room is entirely devoted to Arp's sculpture.

Artists such as Marinot, Dufy, Vlaminck, Campendonk, connected with Fauvism and Expressionism, are adepts of pure bright colours. In striking contrast, *Still Life* (1911) by George Braque is a typical Cubist work.

As a reaction against the first World War, the Dadaists signed derisory even absurd works (Janco, Schwitters). Following in their footsteps, the Surrealists with Victor Brauner, Max Ernst and Arp tried to introduce the world of dreams into their works. Arp and others such as Magnelli, Domela, Marcelle Cahn and Luc Peire, adopt an abstract mode of expression.

Furniture and inlaid items by **Charles Spindler**, sculpture by François-Rupert Carabin, Ringel d'Illzach and Bugatti, and early 20C stained-glass panels made in Strasbourg testify to the renewal of art and decorative arts in Alsace around 1900.

The **Salle Doré** was specifically designed for the display of the huge painting by Gustave Doré (1869), depicting *Christ leaving the Prætorium*. A cabinet shows Doré's talents as a sculptor and above all as an illustrator *(Dante's Inferno)*. A balcony situated at the entrance of the restaurant makes it possible to look down into this room.

The **graphic arts** room contains rotating displays of prints and drawings from 1870 to the present day, posters from the 1880s to the 1920s and a collection of photographs.

From 1950 onwards – *Upstairs.* In the first room, works by Picasso, Richier, Pinot-Gallizio, Kudo and Baselitz reflect the uncertain times. The next room illustrates the Fluxus movement with Filliou and Brecht, and the so-called "Poor Art" *(Arte povera)* movement with Kounellis, Penone and Merz who strive to show the energy of the simplest objects. The 1960s and 1970s are represented by the experiments of Buren, Parmentier, Toroni, Rutault, Morellet and Lavier, which blossom in the 1980s and 1990s with Toni Grand, Miroslav Balka, Christian Boltanski, Philippe Ramette, Maurice Blaussyld and Javier Pérez. The last room exhibits the most contemporary works in quick rotation; Nam June Paik, Collin-Thiébaut *(Clandestine Museum in Strasbourg)*, Gerhard Mertz *(Dove sta Memoria)* and Sarkis are some of the artists represented, the last three having lived or worked in Strasbourg.

Between these rooms, magazines, photographs, ordinary objects show the link between art and daily life.

The panoramic terrace offers views of the Vauban dam and Ponts Couverts.

STRASBOURG

Abreuvoir (R. de l')	LZ	3
Arc-en-Ciel (R. de l')	KLY	7
Austerlitz (R. d')	KZ	10
Auvergne (Pont d')	LY	12
Bateliers (R. des)	LZ	14
Bonnes-Gens (R. des)	JY	19
Boudier (R. du)	JZ	20
Castelnau (R. Gén. de)	KY	25
Cathédrale (Pl. de la)	KZ	26
Chaudron (R. du)	KY	28
Cheveux (R. des)	JZ	29
Corbeau (Pl. du)	KZ	31
Cordiers (R. des)	KZ	32
Courtine (R. de la)	LY	34
Dentelles (R. des)	JZ	36
Division-Leclerc (R. de la)	JKZ	
Écarlate (R. de l')	JZ	43
Escarpée (R.)	JZ	45
Étudiants (R. et Pl. des)	KY	46
Faisan (Pont du)	JZ	47
Fossé-des-Tanneurs (R. du)	JZ	57
Fossé-des-Treize (R. du)	KY	58
Francs-Bourgeois R. des)	JZ	60
Frey (Quai Ch.)	JZ	63
Gdes-Arcades (R. des)	JKY	
Grande-Boucherie (Pl. de la)	KZ	76
Gutenberg (R.)	JKZ	78
Haute-Montée (R.)	JY	
Homme-de-Fer (Pl. de l')	JY	
Hôpital-Militaire (R. de l')	LZ	
Humann (Rue)	HZ	
III (Quai de l')	HZ	
Kellemann (Quai)	JY	
Kléber (Place)	JY	
Krutenau (R. de la)	LZ	
Kuss (Pont)	HY	
Lamey (R. Auguste)	LY	
Lezay-Marnésia (Quai)	LY	
Luther (Rue Martin)	JZ	
Maire-Kuss (R. du)	HY	
Marché-aux-Cochons-de-Lait (Pl. du)	KZ	
Marché-aux-Poissons (Pl. du)	KZ	

★**Musée historique** ⊙ (**KZ M²**) – The history museum is housed in the 15C Grande
Boucherie building. The military art section is one of the foremost public collections
of weapons and uniforms in France, behind that of the Musée de l'Armée in Les
Invalides (Paris).

Guns from the 17C to the 19C, made in the royal foundry, armours, 200 uniforms
with the service records of the soldiers who wore them, all of them from the
Alsace region and 17C weapons are all worth noting, not forgetting the collection
of toy soldiers made of painted cardboard, a speciality of Strasbourg since before
the Revolution.

The town-planning section displays models, drawings, prints etc, illustrating Old
Strasbourg, a relief plan (1727) from the royal collections founded by Vauban and
Louvois.

The historic section contains documents and objects connected with the town's
history.

arché-Gayot (Pl. du) . KYZ 126
arché-Neuf (Pl. du) .. KYZ 127
arquin (R. du) ...... KZ 129
ésange (R. de la) .... JKY 135
ercière (Rue) .... KZ 135
onnaie (R. de la) .... JZ 141
unch (Rue) .... LZ 142
oyer (Rue du) .... JY 147
ée-Bleue (R. de la) .. KY
bernai (Rue d') .... HZ 150
tre (R. de l') .... KY 153
ix (Av. de la) .... KLY 154
rchemin (R. du) ...... KY 156
rre (R. Fg-de) .... KZ
ntonniers (R. des) ... LY 169
collets (R. des) ...... KLY 172
-Étienne (Quai) ...... LY 183
-Michel (R.) .... HZ 187
-Nicolas (Pont) .... KZ 189

St-Pierre-le-Jeune (Pl.). JKY 190
Ste-Madeleine
  (Pont et R.) .... KLZ 192
Salzmann (R.) .... JZ 193
Sanglier (R. du) .... KY 194
Saverne (Pont de) ..... HY 195
Sébastopol (R. de) ..... JY 202
Serruriers (R. des) .... JKZ 205
Temple Neuf (Pl. du) ... KY 213
Temple Neuf (R. du) .. KY 214
Théâtre (Pont du) ...... KY 216
Thomann (Rue) .... KY 217
Tonneliers (R. des) .... KZ 220
Turckheim (Quai) ..... KY 225
Vieil-Hôpital (R. du) .... KZ 228
Vieux-Marché-aux-
  Poissons (R.) .... KZ 229
Vieux-Marché-aux-Vins
  (R. et Pl. du) .... JY 230

Vieux-Seigle (R. du)..... JZ 231
Wasselonne (R. de)..... HZ 238
22-Novembre
  (R. du)............. HJY

C   Hôtel de la Chambre
       de Commerce
F   Pharmacie du Cerf
H   Hôtel de Ville
M¹ Musée de l'Œuvre
       Notre-Dame
M² Musée historique
M³ Musée alsacien
M⁴ Musée d'Art moderne
       et contemporain
Q   Maison Kammerzell
Y   Maison de Pasteur

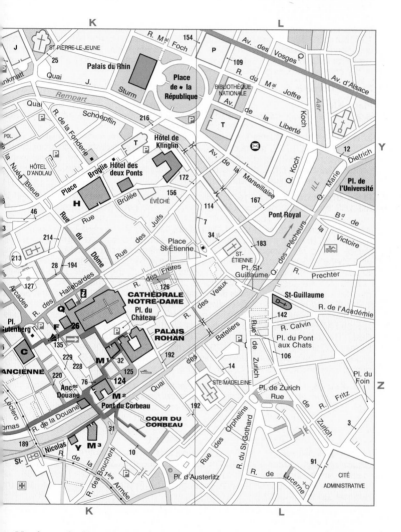

Musée zoologique de l'université et de la ville ⊘ (**CS M⁵**) – Housed on two partly renovated floors, this museum presents regional and world fauna in its natural environment: cold regions, the Andes, the savannah, Alsace... Rich collections of insects and stuffed birds are exhibited.

Permanent and temporary (two per year) exhibitions deal with biology and ecology.

ADDITIONAL SIGHTS

Église St-Guillaume ⊘ (**LZ**) – The church was built between 1300 and 1307. The nave is lit by beautiful stained-glass windows (1465) by Pierre d'Andlau. However, the main attraction is the 14C two-storey tomb of the Werd brothers; Philippe, in canon's clothes, occupies the lower slab and above it, Ulrich, dressed as a knight, rests on two lions.

Église St-Pierre-le-Vieux (HYZ) – This church consists in fact of two adjacent churches; one is Catholic and the other Protestant. The north transept of the Catholic church (rebuilt in 1866) contains 16C carved-wood panels by Veit Wagner, depicting scenes from the life of St Peter and St Valerus. The **scenes★** from the Passion (late 15C-early 16C), which can be seen at the end of the chancel, are believed to be the work of Henri Lutzelmann, a native of Strasbourg. The south transept contains **painted panels★** by members of the Schongauer School (15C) illustrating the Resurrection and Christ's apparitions. *In order to see these works in better lighting conditions, press the switch on the left.*

Église St-Pierre-le-Jeune ⊙ (JY) – Three successive churches were built on this site. All that remains of the first church is a tomb with five funeral recesses, recently estimated to date from the end of the Roman occupation (4C AD); the lovely restored cloister belonged to the church built in 1031 (except for the east gallery which dates from the 14C). The present Protestant church, dating from the 13C but considerably restored around 1900, contains a fine Gothic **rood screen** decorated with paintings from 1620. The organ was made in 1780. The christening fonts located in the Trinity chapel are by Hans Hammer (1491). The woodwork in the chancel and the pulpit date from the 18C.

Rue du Dôme (KY) – The street is lined with beautiful 18C mansions.

Place Kléber (JY) – This is the most famous square in the city. On the north side is an 18C building called "l'Aubette" because the different units of the garrison came here at dawn *(aube)* to fetch their orders.
In the centre stands Kléber's statue, erected in 1840; he is buried beneath it. Born in Strasbourg in 1753, murdered in Cairo in 1800, **Jean-Baptiste Kléber** is one of the most illustrious natives of Strasbourg, a brilliant general of the Revolutionary period. The base of the statue is decorated with two low-relief carvings depicting his victories at Altenkirchen and Heliopolis.

Place Broglie (KY) – This rectangular open space planted with trees, was laid in the 18C by Marshal de Broglie, who was then the governor of Alsace. The south side is lined with the 18C **town hall★** built by Massol, the former residence of the counts of Hanau-Lichtenberg and then of the Landgraves of Hess-Darmstadt.
Standing at the eastern end, the municipal theatre is decorated with columns and muses carved by Ohmacht (1820). The monument dedicated to Marshal Leclerc who liberated Strasbourg in 1944, was erected in front of the theatre *(see p 282)*. To the right of the theatre, the imposing façade of the former **Hôtel de Klinglin** (1736) can be seen on the waterside; the edifice also opens onto rue Brûlée (no 19: lovely doorway). **Charles de Foucauld**, the missionary murdered in the Sahara in 1916, was born at no 4 place Broglie in 1858.
The district adjoining place Broglie (rue des Pucelles, rue du Dôme, rue des Juifs, rue de l'Arc-en-Ciel) used to be inhabited by the aristocracy and the upper middle class. The area has retained several 18C mansions, particularly rue Brûlée: the former Hôtel des Deux-Ponts (1754) at no 13, the bishop's residence at no 16 and at no 9 the town hall's side entrance; no 25 rue de la Nuée-Bleue, on the other side of place Broglie, is the former Hôtel d'Andlau dating from 1732.

19C district – *The tour of this area requires the use of a car. Leave from place Broglie and cross the bridge over the Fossé du Faux-Rempart.*
After 1870, the Germans erected a great number of monumental public buildings in neo-Gothic Renaissance style. They intended to transfer the town centre to the northeast, and include the orangery and the university. This district with its broad avenues is a rare example of Prussian architecture.

Place de la République (KY) – The central part of this vast square is occupied by a circular garden shaded by trees; in its centre stands a war memorial by Drivier (1936); on the left is the **Palais du Rhin**, the former imperial palace (1883-1888); on the right is the National Theatre, housed in the former Landtag palace, and the National Library.

Follow avenue de la Marseillaise on the right. Drive across the Pont-Royal. Turn left onto quai du Maire-Dietrich.

On the left, at the confluence of the Aar and Ill, St Paul's Protestant church stands in lovely surroundings; it was built in the 19C in neo-Gothic style.

Place de l'Université (LY) – This fine square is adorned with flower-beds and fountains. Goethe's statue stands at the entrance of the gardens *(see p 279)*. The Palais de l'Université was erected in 1885 in the Italian Renaissance style. Allée de la Robertsau leads to the **Orangery** *(see below)*.

Contades (BS) – This park situated north of place de la République, was named after the military governor of Alsace who had it laid in the late 18C. On the edge of the park stands the **Synagogue de la Paix**, built in 1955 to replace the synagogue destroyed in 1940.

★Palais de l'Europe ⊙ **and Palais des Droits de l'Homme** (CS) – *Leave the town centre along quai des Pêcheurs* (LY). *Entrance in allée Spach.* The palace houses the **European Council**, including the council of ministers, the parliamentary assembly and the international secretariat. The new buildings, inaugurated in 1977 were designed by the French architect Henri Bernard. The palace contains 1350 offices, meeting rooms for the various commissions and committees, a library and the largest parliamentary amphitheatre in Europe. The ceiling is supported by a 12-ribbed wooden fan, a symbol which is repeated in the palace's entrance hall.

Nearby, on the banks of the River Ill, stands the new **Palais des Droits de l'Homme**, designed by Richard Rogers, which houses the European Court of Human Rights dependent on the European Council.

★**Orangery** (CS) – *Leave the town centre along quai des Pêcheurs.*
The splendid park was designed by Le Nôtre in 1692 and remodelled in 1804 for Empress Josephine's stay. The Josephine pavilion, rebuilt following a fire in 1968, is used for temporary exhibitions, theatrical performances and concerts.
The **Buerehiesel Restaurant** overlooking the lake is an old Alsatian farmhouse with carved timbers. (1607).

Maison de la Télévision FR3-Alsace (BS D) – Television house was built in 1961; a monumental (30 x 6m/98 x 20ft) ceramic by Lurçat, symbolising the Creation, decorates the concave façade of the auditorium.

Haras national ⊘ – The stud is located near the Petite France district, in a pink-sandstone building dating from the 17C and 18C: a medieval hospital for travellers (1360), remodelled and extended into a private mansion and converted into a royal stud by Louis XV in 1763. The stables house some 30 stallions of various breeds: Arabs, English thoroughbreds, Anglo-Arabs, French saddle horses, French saddle ponies, Connemara ponies, draught horses. From mid-March to mid-July, the stallions are sent to various establishments for breeding purposes.

★**Boat trips on the River Ill** ⊘ (KZ) – Departure from the Palais Rohan pier: tour of the Petite France then along the Fossé du Faux-Rempart to the Palais de l'Europe.

Strasbourg from above ⊘– A variety of short flights over the city and surroundings are available from the Aéro-Club d'Alsace *(see Admission times and charges)*.

PORT AUTONOME

Situated at one of the main intersections of major European routes, Strasbourg is the second largest river port in France, after Paris, and one of the most important ports along the River Rhine. Its impact on eastern France's economy equals that of a major maritime port because of the exceptionally good navigable conditions of the Rhine (now canalised between Basle and Iffezheim), comparable to an international sound, 800km/497mi long. The advantages of Strasbourg's geographical situation are enhanced by the network of waterways, railway lines and roads linking the whole region with western and central Europe.

Harbour installations – The harbour consists of a vast expanse of water covering a total area of 205ha/507 acres lined by banks extending over 37km/23mi and including 15 docks and two outer harbours. The land area comprises 552ha/1 364 acres set aside for commercial and industrial use and 5ha/12 acres for coal stocking; there are numerous warehouses and important installations for stocking cereals and fuel oils. The main areas of activity are fuel, timber, foodstuffs, chemicals, metals, mechanical engineering, building and civil engineering, transport and distribution.
The harbour's communications network includes 154km/96mi of railway lines and 34km/21mi of roads. Handling equipment consists of a hundred traditional vehicles and specialised equipment for heavy loads up to 350t and for loading and unloading containers. Strasbourg is France's first river port for container traffic, owing to regular links with North Sea ports in less than 48hr. Other main activities are concerned with cereal, foodstuff/fodder (700 000t per year) and oil-product traffic; the fuel dock can accommodate the whole production of the Alsatian refinery (Cie Rhénane de raffinage), which gets its supply of crude oil through the south European pipeline.
Finally, the Eurofret-Strasbourg installations (155 000m^2/185 380sq yd of warehouses), a vast terminal with efficient water, rail and road services, presently covers an area of 50ha/124 acres with the possibility of extending it to 110ha/272 acres.

Activities – As eastern France's main centre of import-export, stocking and transit of goods, Strasbourg harbour welcomes an international fleet of barges of various sizes from 280t to over 2000t, sometimes linked in groups of two to four barges of 1500t to 3000t each (2 to 6 barges on the lower Rhine).
The harbour's average worldwide yearly traffic reaching 10 million tonnes is shared between traditional goods traffic and packaged goods or container traffic.

Overall view and excursion along the Rhine – *25km/16mi round tour – allow 1hr 15min.*
This tour offers the most interesting views of the Rhine and the harbour installations.

From the Pont d'Austerlitz, follow N 4.

Shortly before reaching the Pont Vauban, turn right onto rue du Havre which is parallel to the René-Graff dock; rue de la Rochelle, which prolongs it, leads to the southern and most modern part of the harbour, with its three main docks: Auguste-Detœuf (cereals), Gaston-Hælling and Adrien-Weirich (containers and heavy goods) as well as basin IV. The Eurofret-Strasbourg centre is located between the last two docks *(access via rue de Rheinfeld and rue de Bayonne).*

Turn back along rue de la Rochelle and rue du Havre. At the end of the latter, turn right and drive across the Pont Vauban which spans the Vauban dock.

Avenue du Pont de l'Europe leads to the Rhine. The river, which at this point is 250m/273yd wide, is spanned by the **Pont de l'Europe** (CS) (1960) consisting of two metal arches and linking Strasbourg with Kehl on the German side. This bridge replaces the famous Kehl bridge (1861), destroyed during the war.

Turn back once more and bear right to follow rue Coulaux, then rue du Port-du-Rhin (view of the Bassin du Commerce).

From the **Pont d'Anvers** (CS), the view embraces several docks: on the left, the entrance of the large Bassin Vauban and Bassin Dusuzeau (harbour station); on the right, the Bassin des Remparts. Drive over the bridge and turn right onto rue du Général-Picquart skirting the Bassin des Remparts where the *Naviscope* is moored. This former barge-driver has been turned into a **Musée du Rhin et de la Navigation** ⊙ (Rhine Museum).

Drive along rue Boussingault then cross the Marne-Rhine canal and turn right along quai Jacoutot which follows the canal.

From the **Pont Jean-Millot** (CS), at the entrance of the Albert-Auberger dock, the view takes in the Rhine on the left and the north entrance of the harbour. The Marne-Rhine canal and three docks (Bassin Louis-Armand, Bassin du Commerce and Bassin de l'Industrie) open into the northern outer harbour.

* **Harbour tour** ⊙ – Tours of the harbour installations and boat trip on the Rhine including negotiating a lock, are organised by the port authorities.

Le STRUTHOF

Michelin map 87 fold 15 or 242 fold 23 – Local map see Region du HOHWALD

During the Second World War, the Nazis built a "death camp" on this site. The platforms on which the huts stood were built by the prisoners who brought the building materials up from the bottom of the valley on their backs; around 10 000 of them died fulfilling this task. The camp received various convoys of prisoners from occupied countries. These convoys, marked with the letters "NN" *(Nacht und Nebel,* Night and Fog), which included many French citizens, were intended to be sent to the gas chambers.
The last three miles of the road between Rothau and the camp were also built by the prisoners.

Ancien camp de concentration ⊙ – Parts of the former concentration camp still stand, such as the double fence of barbed wire, the main gate, the crematorium, the prisoners' cells and two huts (a dormitory and the old kitchen) now turned into museums.

Cimetière et mémorial – *Alongside D 130.*
The necropolis situated above the camp contains the remains of 1120 prisoners. In front stands the commemorative monument, a kind of huge truncated column hollowed out and engraved on the inside with the tall silhouette of a prisoner. The base is the tomb of an unknown French prisoner.

SUNDGAU ★

Michelin map 87 folds 9, 10, 19 and 20 or 242 folds 39, 43 and 44

The Sundgau or southernmost area of Alsace, adjacent to the foothills of the Jura mountains, stretches from north to south between Mulhouse and the Swiss border and from east to west between the Rhine and the Largue Valley. The altitude rises gently in a northwest-southeast direction to more than 800m/2 625ft in the limestone hills prolonging the Swiss Jura. The area has been deeply carved by the tributaries of the upper Ill; the resulting hills and limestone cliffs are crowned by forests of beeches and firs and the valleys are dotted with numerous lakes – full of carps, a local gastronomic speciality – pastures and rich crops. Flower-decked farmhouses often have timber-framed walls roughcast in an ochre colour or clad with wooden planks and are covered with long sloping roofs.
Altkirch is the only town of some importance, but many prosperous villages are scattered along the rivers or across sunny hillsides.

ROUND TOUR STARTING FROM ALTKIRCH

117km/73mi — allow half a day

Pleasant walks can be added to this itinerary, particularly in the southern part of the area, known as the "Alsatian Jura".

Altkirch *— See ALTKIRCH.*

Drive east out of Altkirch along D 419 which follows the south bank of the Ill.

St-Morand — This village is a place of pilgrimage. The **church** contains the beautiful 12C sarcophagus of the area's patron saint, Morand, who converted the Sungdau to Christianity.
The road continues along the Thalbach Valley before reaching the plateau. It then runs down towards the Rhine offering views of the northern part of the Jura mountains, the Basle depression and the Black Forest.

As you enter Ranspach-le-Bas, turn off D 419 to the right. On leaving Ranspach-le-Haut, turn left towards Folgensbourg.

Revolving turrets from the Maginot Line can be seen on both sides of the road *(see Ligne MAGINOT).*

In Folgensbourg, turn south onto D 473 then left onto D 21bis towards St-Blaise.

The itinerary offers a fine view of the Basle depression, of the town and of the Rhine flowing into the Plaine d'Alsace.

In St-Blaise, follow D 9bis to Leymen.

Château du Landskron — *30min on foot there and back.*
This castle, believed to date from the 11C, is in ruins. Reinforced by Vauban in the 17C, it was besieged and destroyed in 1814. From its privileged position on a height overlooking the border, the view embraces the small town of Leymen below and, further north, the forested Sundgau and Basle region.

Return to St-Blaise.

In Oltingue, the road joins the upper Ill Valley, overlooked in the south by the ridge of the Alsatian Jura.

Oltingue — A folk museum, the **Maison du Sundgau** ⊘, stands in the centre of this charming village. It surveys the different architectural styles of the region and contains a selection of furniture, crockery and kitchen utensils illustrating rural life in the past. Note the large bread oven in the bakery, the steps of an old staircase, each cut out of a tree trunk, cob walls, a collection of *kougelhopf* tins appropriately shaped for each feast day and a series of ceramic tiles used to decorate stoves.

In Rædersdorf, continue along D 21^B towards Kiffis.

Beyond the crossroads, one can see on the left a new set of pillboxes of the Maginot Line *(the one closest to the road, about 100m/110yd away, is open to the public).*

Hippoltskirch — The **chapel** ⊘ has several remarkable features includiing a painted coffered ceiling, a painted-wood balustrade along the gallery and ex-votos on the walls, some of them showing a naive style of painting. On the left of the nave, there is a miracle-working statue of Our Lady, once the object of a pilgrimage, to whom the ex-votos are dedicated.
Leave Kiffis on your left and follow the "international road" (D 21B^{III}) which skirts the Swiss border (and even crosses it beyond Moulin-Neuf over a very short distance) along the bottom of a wooded coomb.

Lucelle — This lakeside village at the southern-most end of the Alsace region, once stood next to a wealthy Cistercian abbey.

Drive north along D 432.

★**Ferrette** — The former capital of the Sundgau was, from the 10C onwards, the residence of independent counts whose authority extended over a large part of Alsace. This region became the property of the House of Austria in the 14C and was ceded to France in 1648 by the Treaty of Westphalia. The prince of Monaco is still entitled to be called "count of Ferrette".
The small ancient town, lying in a picturesque **site**★, is overlooked by the ruins of two castles built on an impressive rockspur rising to an altitude of 612m/2008ft. Marked footpaths lead to the foot of the castles. From the platform, there is a fine **view**★ of the Vosges mountains, of the Rhine and Ill valleys, of the Black Forest and of the foothills of the Jura mountains. The surrounding wooded hills offer a choice of interesting walks.

Drive to Bouxwiller along D 473.

Bouxwiller – This pretty village adorned with many fountains is built across one of the slopes of the valley. The **Église** St-Jacques contains a lovely 18C gilt-wood pulpit, originally in the Luppach monastery, and an elaborate Baroque altarpiece, decorated with columns and richly painted and gilt.

D 9bis, which follows the upper Ill Valley, leads to Grentzingen.

★**Grentzingen** – The characteristic timber-framed houses of this flower-decked village are lined up at right angles to the road. A few of them have retained their original ochre colour and their awning. Note the roofs with their canted gables.

Turn left in Grentzingen.

The road runs through **Riespach**, a village with typical regional houses.

Feldbach – The restored 12C Romanesque church is in two parts, one for the nuns and one for the congregation. The nave, which has successively round and square pillars, ends with an oven-vaulted apse.

D 432 runs through the green valleys of the Feldbach and the Ill back to Altkirch.

Now on the Web! Visit our site at www.michelin-travel.com.
Route planning service complete with tourist information and maps which you can print.
Have a good trip!

THANN ★

Population 7 751
Michelin map 87 fold 18 or 242 fold 35
Local map see Route des CRÊTES and Route des VINS

This small southern town, situated west of Mulhouse, is renowned for having the most richly decorated Gothic church in the whole of Alsace. The local wine, known as Rangen wine, has been famous since the 16C as a potent wine "to be consumed in moderation and at home"!

From legend to history – The foundation of Thann, like that of many Alsatian towns and villages, is steeped in legend. When Bishop Thiébaut (Theobald) of Gubbio in Umbria died in 1160, he bequeathed his episcopal ring to his most trusted servant who took it, together with the bishop's thumb, hid it inside his staff and arrived in Alsace the following year. One night, he went to sleep in a fir forest after having driven his staff into the ground. As he was about to leave in the morning, he was unable to lift his staff out of the ground. At the same time, three bright lights appeared above three fir trees; the lord of the nearby castle of Engelbourg saw the lights and having arrived promptly, he decided to build a chapel on the very site where the miracle had occurred. The chapel soon became a popular place of pilgrimage and a town grew all around. It was named Thann, which means fir tree.

Every year in June, three fir trees are burnt in front of the church to commemorate this event.

During the First World War, Thann was liberated as early as 7 August 1914 but was thereafter shelled for four years by the Germans. On 10 December 1944, Thann was occupied by French troops coming down from the Hundsrück pass. But the frontline settled just a few hundred yards from the town and for two months Thann was shelled by German forces desperately holding on to Vieux-Thann. It was finally freed on 29 January 1945.

★★COLLÉGIALE ST-THIÉBAUT ⊘ 30min

The Gothic architecture of the collegiate church (14C-early 16C) shows a continuous progression towards the Flamboyant Gothic style.

Exterior – There is a remarkable **doorway**★★ on the west front. It is 15m/49ft high and has an elegant tympanum surmounting two doors, each having its own smaller tympanum. The right-hand one depicts The Adoration of the Magi, the left-hand one the Crucifixion; above them, the larger tympanum illustrating the Life of the Virgin is framed by five recessed arches carved with musician angels, the kings of Judea, Genesis, martyrs and prophets. Over 450 characters in all decorate the doorway.

Walk round the north side of the church to admire the Flamboyant doorway adorned with fine 15C statues: St John the Baptist and St Theobald on either side of the upright post to which is bonded a statue of the Virgin and Child.

Continue towards the town hall to get an overall view of the lofty chancel with its high roof covered with glazed tiles and the belfry (76m/249ft high) surmounted by an openwork stone spire.

Interior – The height of the nave and chancel is remarkable. A polychrome wooden statue of the wine-growers' Virgin, carved c 1510, is bonded to the central buttress pier of the pentagonal chapel *(accessible from the south aisle)*. The Virgin is holding Jesus, who is mischievously hiding a bunch of grapes behind his back. At the end of the aisle, in the St-Thiébaut chapel, a polychrome carved-wood statue of the saint dating from 1520 stands on the altar.

Chancel – The deep chancel is adorned with the 15C statues of the twelve Apostles in polychrome stone. A large crucifix (1894) in polychrome wood by Klem from Comar hangs in the entrance. However, the outstanding feature is undoubtedly a superb group of 51 15C oak **stalls**★★ (partly restored at the beginning of the 20C), which express all the fantasy of the Middle Ages. There is a profusion of foliage, gnomes and comics characters carved with great precision *(see Introduction: Architecture and art)*. The chancel is flooded with light pouring in through eight superb 15C **stained-glass windows**★.

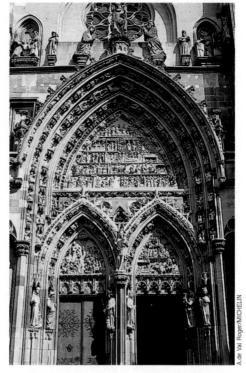

Thann – Doorway of the Collégiale St-Thiébaut

ADDITIONAL SIGHTS

Musée des Amis de Thann ⊘ (**M**) – Housed in the former corn exchange dating from 1519, the museum's collections spread on four levels illustrate the town's history and provide additional information about the collegiate church. The main themes dealt with are: vineyards (series of panels from the former vineyard-keepers' hut), the castle and fortifications, the collegiate church and the cult of St Theobald, furniture and popular art, mementoes of two World Wars, the beginnings of the textile industry.

Tour des Sorcières (**D**) – This 15C tower surmounted by an onion-shaped roof is all that remains of the old fortifications. The most picturesque view of the tower is from the bridge across the Thur. Inside, the **Cave Charles-Hippler** illustrates the wine-grower's work and presents the various types of wine-growing soils.

THANN

Aspach (R. d')	2
Clemenceau (R.)	4
Gaulle (R. Gén.-de)	6
Jacquot (R. A.)	7
Lattre-de-Tassigny (Pl. de)	8
Lebert (R. H.)	10
Paix (R. de la)	11
Poincaré (Av.)	12
St-Jacques (R.)	13
1ʳᵉ Armée (R. de la)	14
7-Août (R. du)	15

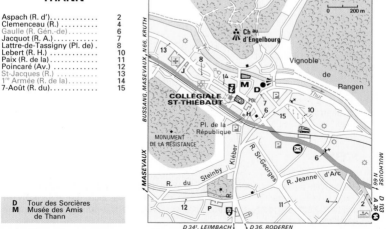

D   Tour des Sorcières
M   Musée des Amis
     de Thann

Œil de la Sorcière – *30min on foot there and back.* Engelbourg castle (the angels' castle), built by the counts of Ferrette, became the property of the Hapsburgs and, in 1648, of the king of France who, 10 years later, gave it to Mazarin whose heirs kept it until the Revolution.

In 1673, Louis XIV gave the order for it to be dismantled. During the demolition

> **"Bangards" or Vineyard-keepers**
>
> Vineyard-keepers' names have been recorded in the Twchamser Chronicle since 1483. The vineyard-keepers' hut, dating from the 16C, was the home of four keepers elected by the guilds for a year. This institution survived until 1832. At the end of their service, some keepers would leave a memento in the form of low-relief stone carvings or painted wooden panels.

process, the lower part of the keep remained intact and the centre appeared to be overlooking the plain. Popular imagination promptly found a name for this unusual ruin, the "witch's eye".

From the ruin, there is a view of Thann, the Plaine d'Alsace and the Black Forest in the distance. A monument to the Alsatian Resistance stands on top of the Staufen, across the valley.

ROUTE JOFFRE *18km/11mi from Thann to Masevaux*

Drive northwest along N 66 to Bitschwiller and turn left onto D 14^BIV.

This road was built by the army during the First World War to establish vital communications between the valleys of the Doller and the Thur.

Its military role was revived during the winter of 1944-45, when French troops used it to attack Thann from the north.

On the way up to Col du Hundsrück, the road affords a magnificent **view★★** of the Thur Valley overlooked to the north by the Grand Ballon (alt 1 424m/4 672ft). The road then winds its way up to the pass through the forest.

Col du Hundsrück – Alt 748m/2 454ft. View of the Sundgau (*see SUNDGAU)* and the Jura mountains to the south and of the Plaine d'Alsace to the east.

Beyond the Col du Schirm, the road runs down towards the Doller Valley and goes through the hamlet of **Houppach**; a pilgrimage takes place in Notre-Dame d'Houppach, the village chapel also known as Klein Einsiedeln.

Masevaux – This small industrial and commercial town developed round an abbey founded by Mason, St Odile's nephew, in memory of his son who had drowned in the Doller. There are some lovely squares adorned with 18C fountains and surrounded by 16C and 17C houses.

THIONVILLE

Conurbation 132 413
Michelin map 57 folds 3 and 4 or 242 fold 5

This former stronghold is the metropolis of the iron industry, the nerve centre of the whole industrial area which extends along the west bank of the River Moselle, 100m/328ft wide at that point. The town centre has retained a few houses with lovely old façades. The former convent of the Poor Clares' order (1629), facing the river, has beautiful arcades and now houses the town hall.

HISTORICAL NOTES

A castle built in Merovingian times and called "Theodonis villa" was one of Charlemagne's favourite residences. In the 13C, Thionville was a stronghold belonging to the counts of Luxemburg who built a mighty castle. The fortified town successively belonged to the House of Burgundy, the Hapsburgs, and the Low Countries then in Spanish hands. The Spaniards commissioned a Flemish engineer to rebuild the fortifications between 1590 and 1600. Finally, Thionville became French in 1659 by the Treaty of the Pyrenees.

The city was besieged many times. During the German occupation (1870-1914), three powerful forts were built in the vicinity.

Upstream of Thionville, major works undertaken along the River Moselle included the extension of the Thionville-Illange harbour.

SIGHTS

Tour aux Puces – This mighty 11C-12C medieval keep, also known as the Tour au Puits (Well Tower), is the most important remaining part of the feudal castle of the counts of Luxemburg. It has no fewer than 14 sides and the complexity of its interior confers a certain architectural originality to the edifice which houses the municipal museum.

Musée municipal ⊙ – The museum retraces the history of Thionville and the surrounding area from Neolithic times to the siege of 1870. There is a rich Gallo-Roman section and an important collection of stone fragments from the late Middle Ages and 16C and 18C cast-iron firebacks.

The different occasions on which the town was besieged are illustrated by maps, prints, objects...

Part of the town walls (retaining wall) can be seen along the Moselle. Public gardens and walks (Parc Napoléon) have been laid on top.

Église St-Maximin – This vast sturdy Classical church houses an 18C organ; the organ case is decorated with a profusion of bright motifs.

★**Château de la Grange** ⊙ – *North of the town, left of N 53.*

Designed in 1731 by Robert de Cotte, the castle was erected over the base of a fortress used until the 17C as an outer defence work guarding the town's citadel. It was bought in 1672 by the Marquis de Fouquet and still belongs to his descendants. The large kitchen contains traditional Lorraine furniture; note the fireplace surmounted by a lovely basket-handled arch. In the dining room, there is a white and gold earthenware stove, almost 5m/16ft high, built for the marquis; facing the windows are two glass cases containing collections of Boch and Chantilly porcelain.

Flemish tapestries from the early 17C illustrating the theme of the Trojan War hang in the entrance hall. At the bottom of the main staircase, with its fine 18C wrought-iron banisters, there are two remarkable Chinese vases in cloisonné enamel, and two low-relief sculptures from the school of Jean Goujon. Opposite the sedan chair, an Alsatian stove from Rouffach, dating from 1804, is decorated with religious scenes.

An old Persian carpet covers the white and black chequered floor of the red drawing room.

The Empire-style bathroom contains a bath cut out of a single block of white marble, which belonged to Pauline Bonaparte (Napoleon's sister).

The large blue drawing room contains fine Louis XV furniture; note the floor inlaid with star-

Château de la Grange – The dining room

Prune Création, Metz

shaped designs. The library, located in the former chapel, houses a remarkable collection of celadon ceramics from the Far East (between the two windows).

The original French-style gardens were replaced in the 19C by an English-style park.

IRON COUNTRY

67km/42mi round tour – allow 2hr 30min.

Drive southwest out of Thionville along N 53.

Economic development – In the 19C, Lorraine became France's main steel-producing region; its output, which still represented two thirds of the total French production in 1965, has now dropped to barely 25%.

Mining difficulties led to the closure of all the region's mines except that of Audun-le-Tiche, worked by the ARBED concern from Luxemburg.

Major restructuring has meant a reduction in the number of employees from 95 000 in 1964 to 78 000 in 1975, 30 000 in 1985 and around 14 000 in 1994. Having diversified its production and invested heavily in new technology, the steel industry has now regained a certain competitiveness. Thus the Usinor-Sacilor group ranks third in the world.

The area has turned to other industries such as the car industry and nuclear energy.

The long string of factories starts immediately south of Thionville, past the Daspich level crossing: the industrial site of Sollac-Florange, one of the Sollac factories (Société Lorraine de Laminage continu) and a branch of the Usinor-Sacilor group, the European leader in its field.

In Serémange-Erzange, turn left onto D 17 towards St-Nicolas-en-Forêt.

The road rises offering extended views of the **Industrial Fensch Valley** (Unimetal-Sollac Florange, Lorfonte blast furnace, Ebange ciment factory).

In St-Nicolas-en-Forêt, from the Bout-des-Terres roundabout to the end of boule-vard des Vosges, there is a panoramic view of the Moselle Valley.

Continue beyond Hayange – where the Sogérail factory producing rails for the TGV is situated – towards Neufchef.

Musées des Mines de Fer de Lorraine – The iron-ore deposits, located in the upper reaches of the Moselle, extend over a distance of 120km/75mi from the Haye Forest to Luxemburg. In just over 100 years, three billion tonnes of "minette", a type of ore with a relatively low iron content (about 33%) have been extracted; peak production was reached in 1962 with 62 million tonnes. There was a subsequent decline owing to competition from imported ore, richer in iron content, and to a drop in traditional outlets. The mines closed down one after the other; the closure of the Roncourt mine in August 1993 put an end to the mining activity in the area, with the exception of the Bure-Tressange site *(4km/2.5mi east of Aumetz)*, which exports its ore to Luxemburg via an underground route.

Although all mining activity has stopped, the museums at Aumetz and Neufchef, which can both be visited on the same day *(catering available on location in Neufchef)*, recall the history of mining in the area.

Aumetz is situated halfway between Longwy and Thionville.

Musée des Mines de Fer d'Aumetz ⊙ – The former Bassompierre mine was accessible by a shaft 240m/787ft deep, which had to be filled in together with all the galleries when the mine was abandoned. Above ground, the pithead frame was retained as were various buildings housing the compressor room, the forge, the huge extracting machine etc. Below ground, visitors can see a lung-examination centre for the control of siderosis.

Drive to Neufchef along N 52 then D 17.

★**Musée des Mines de Fer de Neufchef** ⊙ – This hillside mine did not require the drilling of a shaft, which means that it is now more easily accessible to the public. Extracting processes of different periods, showing the evolution of mining techniques, have been recreated along a 1.5km/0.9mi-long stretch: 1820, introduction of crank-drills; 1860, tip-trucks are put into use; early 20C, the use of compressors and pneumatic drills becomes generalised; 1930s, ore-extracting machines are introduced... After the Second World War, new scraping machines appeared together with the electric detonator, used in a different context in the film *The Bridge on the River Kwai*. Improvements introduced during the 1970s could be seen as attempts to reverse the course of history.

The 1868 pump exhibited is a reminder that water infiltration was the main source of danger in this type of shallow mine; the stables underline the fact that draught horses from the Ardennes were used until 1950 to pull tip-trucks.

Above ground, a large building provides information about the formation of iron ore, deposits, a miner's job and social environment.

Beyond Neufchef, the road runs through the dense Moyeuvre Forest, split into two by the picturesque Conroy Valley.

Briey – Situated at the heart of a prosperous industrial area, Briey expanded in a remarkable way during the 1950s and, in 1960, Le Corbusier built his third "**Cité Radieuse**" including 339 homes on a forested site northwest of the town. Today, Briey is a peaceful but lively administrative town.

The **Église St-Gengoult**, a Romanesque church extended during the Gothic period, has a main nave flanked by double aisles on either side. At the top of the north aisle there is a 16C stone carving representing Christ in bonds and a late-15C Pietà in polychrome wood in the last side chapel off the south aisle; note how the Virgin is represented taking her veil to wipe her son's wounds. The chancel contains a moving **calvary★** (behind the high altar) comprising six wooden life-size figures carved c 1530 by artists from the school of Ligier Richier, possibly by the master himself.

From the small garden located on the north side of the church, there is a panoramic view of the **Sangsue**, a vast water expanse created by the Woigot dam which offers water sports activities and walks through the surrounding forested area.

Beyond Homécourt, the road *(D 41 then D 11)*, running through the **Orne Valley**, is lined with housing estates and factories.

From Rombas, drive towards D 953 in Hagondange.

Hagondange – On the right-hand side of D 47 stands an interesting modern church with an isolated campanile consisting of two concrete slabs.

Driving north from Hagondange to Uckange, you will notice, on the right of D 953, the Richemont steelworks established here in 1960.

The metalworks of the Uckange industrial centre mark the beginning of the Thionville suburbs.

THE MAGINOT LINE AROUND THIONVILLE

Fort de Guentrange – *Northwest. Drive out of Thionville along allée de la Libération, then turn right towards Guentrange. See Ligne MAGINOT.*

★**Hackenberg** – *20km/12mi east. Drive out of Thionville along D 918 for 12km/7.5mi then turn left onto D 60. Beyond Helling, follow the signposts.*
The largest structural work along the Maginot Line is situated near the village of Vecking, in 160ha/395 acres of forest. *See Le HACKENBERG and Ligne MAGINOT.*

Zeiterholz and Immerhof – *14km/8.7mi north. Leave Thionville by rue du Général-Mangin then pick up the A 31 motorway to Luxemburg; 8km/5mi further on, take the Hettange-Volmerange exit. Follow D 15 towards Hettange for a third of a mile then D 57 towards Entrange via Entrange-Cité, which leads to the Zeiterholz (see Ligne MAGINOT).*

Drive to Hettange-Grande via Entrange-Cité.

Turn left onto D 15 (signpost) to reach the Immerhof (see Ligne MAGINOT).

Vallée de la THUR ★
Michelin map 87 folds 18 and 19 or 242 fold 35

This large furrow carved out by ancient glaciers is a very busy industrial area.
The upper Thur Valley and the Urbès Vale have retained a charming rural character along slopes covered with forests and pastures. The lower Thur Valley is dotted with small towns which have a long-standing tradition in the textile industry.
Famous local personalities are all industrialists, connected with the metal, textile and chemical industries: Risler, Kœchlin, Kestner, Stehelin.

LOWER VALLEY

From Thann to Husseren-Wesserling

12km/7.5mi – about 30min – local map see Parc Naturel Régional des BALLONS DES VOSGES.

★**Thann** – *See THANN.*

Drive northwest out of Thann along N 66.

The vineyards soon give way to factories. The Thur Valley narrows and widens successively. In spite of their factories, the villages are charming, set amid an undulating landscape of pastures and orchards, crisscrossed by streams and torrents.

Willer-sur-Thur – A road *(D 13^{BVI})* branches off to the right, joins up with the scenic Route des Crêtes and leads to the Grand Ballon (alt 1424m/4 672ft), the highest summit of the Vosges mountains *(see Route des CRÊTES)*.

Moosch – A cemetery situated on the east slope of the valley contains the graves of almost 1 000 French soldiers killed during the First World War.

St-Amarin – The little town has given its name to this part of the Thur Valley situated between Moosch and Wildenstein. The **Musée Serret et de la vallée de St-Amarin** ⊙ is devoted to local history: old prints and pictures of the area, Alsatian headdresses, weapons, wrought-iron work, emblems of brotherhoods.

Ranspach – A botanic trail *(2.5km/1.5mi)*, marked by a holly leaf, starts from the top of the village, beyond a factory. Panels explain the characteristics of all the trees and bushes along the path. It is an easy and pleasant walk.

Husseren-Wesserling – An important printed-fabric manufacture is located in this small town, situated on the former hunting grounds of the prince abbots of Murbach. The factory and houses are built round morainic deposits left behind by ancient glaciers, through which the River Thur has dug its way.
The **Musée du Textile et des Costumes** ⊙ is housed in a former industrial building at the heart of a vast park planted with rare trees. The museum deals with three main themes: from raw material (cotton) to fabric, the history of the great industrial families from the 18C to today, and costumes (the evolution of feminine fashion, crafts and occupations connected with fashion such as florist, embroiderer, glovemaker). Reconstructed scenes illustrate 19C fashion at different times of the day.

★UPPER VALLEY

From Husseren-Wesserling to Grand Ventron

46km/29mi – about 2hr – local map see Parc Naturel Régional des BALLONS DES VOSGES.

Husseren-Wesserling – *See above.*

The upper valley of the River Thur is dotted with granite knolls spared by the eroding action of ancient glaciers. Three of these knolls overlook Oderen. A fourth, the forested Schlossberg, situated upstream, is crowned by the **ruins of Wildenstein castle**.

Oderen – From the southern approach to the village, there is a fine view, ahead and slighty to the left, of the picturesque escarpments of the Fellering woods.

In Kruth, turn left onto D 13⁸¹.

★**Cascade St-Nicolas** – The waterfall, which consists of several charming smaller ones, drops to the bottom of a lovely deep vale with densely forested slopes.

Return to Kruth.

Between Kruth and Wildenstein, the road runs to the right of the Schlossberg through a narrow passage where the Thur once flowed.

Another road runs along the other side of the Schlossberg and the **Kruth-Wildenstein dam**, an earth dike with a waterproof central core of clay, which is one of the major works of the Thur Valley's harnessing project *(the road can only be followed in the Wildenstein-Kruth direction; it is closed in winter).*

Beyond Wildenstein, the road starts rising towards the Col de Bramont, offering a beautiful vista of the Thur Valley followed by a picturesque run through the forest.

Col de Bramont – Alt 956m/3 136ft. The pass is situated on the main ridge of the Vosges mountains.

★★**Grand Ventron** – *The access road branches off from the pass. Turn left onto the forest road (8km/5mi) which goes through the Col de la Vierge on its way to la Chaume du Grand Ventron.*

From the summit (alt 1 202m/3 944ft), there is a vast **panorama**★★ of the Thur Valley and the Vosges summits, including the Hohneck, Grand Ballon and Ballon d'Alsace.

URBÈS VALE

From Husseren-Wesserling to the Col de Bussang.

11km/7mi – about 30min – local map see Parc Naturel Régional des BALLONS DES VOSGES.

Husseren-Wesserling – *See Lower valley above.*

The road *(N 66)* starts along the Thur Valley then enters the Urbès Vale blocked by morainic deposits.

See d'Urbès – The depression in which the lake (or see) is situated, was scooped out during the Quarternary Era by the glacier which carved the Thur Valley. The lake lies behind a moraine left by the glacier. A bog-type vegetation covers the area, progressively filling up the depression.

A marked **path** *(1hr 30min)*, dotted with explanatory panels about local flora, fauna and traditional activities, makes it easier to explore this remarkable place.

The road then rises gently towards the Col de Bussang, affording lovely views of the Thur Valley and the surrounding heights.

Col de Bussang – From the pass, it is possible to drive down the upper Moselle Valley *(see La MOSELLE: Upper valley of the Moselle).*

TOUL★

Population 17 311
Michelin map 62 fold 4 or 242 fold 17

Situated on the banks of the River Moselle, Toul occupies a strategic position at the intersection of several main roads and waterways.

The town lies at the point where the Moselle changed its course during the Quarternary Era, suddenly veering northeast to join the Meurthe just north of Nancy.

The antique city of Tullum, which was already a bishopric by the 4C AD, soon became so prosperous that it was granted its independence in 928 under the terms of the Mainz Charter. Throughout the Middle Ages, the burghers of Toul strived to free themselves from the bishop's authority; they finally succeeded in taking control of the city's administration which consisted of an alderman assisted by 10 dispensers of justice and a town council of 30 members.

However, Toul, which was surrounded by powerful neighbours, often asked for the protection of the king of France, which prompted Henri II, in 1552, to leave a permanent garrison in the town. Less than 100 years later, Toul finally became French by the Treaty of Westphalia (1648). At the end of the 18C, the seat of the bishopric was transferred to Nancy.

In 1700, Vauban, Louis XIV's military engineer, built new ramparts round the city (the Porte de Metz is all that remains today) whose fortifications were subsequently improved at regular intervals so that on the eve of the First World War, Toul was acknowledged as one of the best defended strongholds in Europe.

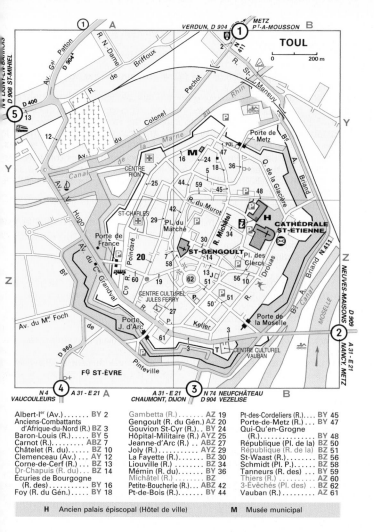

Albert-Ier (Av.) . . . . **BY** 2	Gambetta (R.) . . . . **AZ** 19	Pt-des-Cordeliers (R.) . . . . **BY** 45
Anciens-Combattants	Gengoult (R. du Gén.) **AZ** 20	Porte-de-Metz (R.) . . . **BY** 47
d'Afrique-du-Nord (R.) **BZ** 3	Gouvion St-Cyr (R.) . . **BY** 24	Qui-Qu'en-Grogne
Baron-Louis (R.) . . . . . **BY** 5	Hôpital-Militaire (R.) **AYZ** 25	(R.) . . . . **BY** 48
Carnot (R.) . . . . **ABZ** 7	Jeanne-d'Arc (R.) . . **ABZ** 27	République (Pl. de la) **BZ** 50
Châtelet (R. du) . . . . . . **ABZ** 10	Joly (R.) . . . . **AYZ** 29	République (R. de la) **BZ** 51
Clemenceau (Av.) . . . . **AY** 12	La Fayette (R.) . . . . . . **BZ** 30	St-Waast (R.) . . . . **BZ** 56
Corne-de-Cerf (R.) . . . **BZ** 13	Liouville (R.) . . . . **BZ** 34	Schmidt (Pl. P.) . . . . . . **BZ** 58
Dr-Chapuis (R. du) . . . **BY** 14	Mémin (R. du) . . . . . . **BY** 36	Tanneurs (R. des) . . . **BY** 59
Écuries de Bourgogne	Michâtel (R.) . . . . **BZ**	Thiers (R.) . . . . **BZ** 60
(R. des) . . . . **BY** 16	Petite-Boucherie (R.) . . **ABZ** 42	3-Evêchés (Pl. des) . . **BZ** 62
Foy (R. du Gén.) . . . . . **BY** 18	Pt-de-Bois (R.) . . . . . . **BY** 44	Vauban (R.) . . . . **AZ** 61

H   Ancien palais épiscopal (Hôtel de ville)   **M**   Musée municipal

★★CATHÉDRALE ST-ÉTIENNE ◷ (BZ) *1hr*

Work began on the chancel at the beginning of the 13C but the edifice was only completed in the 16C.

The cathedral's magnificent **west front★★**, built between 1460 and 1496, is a superb example of the Flamboyant style. It is framed by two octagonal towers (65m/213ft high), intended to be surmounted by openwork spires.

A large crucifix set inside a gable stands above the doorway whose statues were destroyed during the Revolution.

The interior shows characteristic features of the Champagne Gothic style: high and low galleries over the main arcades and the aisles, extremely pointed arcades, absence of triforium. The nave (30m/98ft high) is the most attractive part of the edifice.

Note, on the right, the fine **Renaissance chapel** surmounted by a coffered cupola.

Between the third and fourth bays, only half the piers are topped by capitals. This detail marks the place where the 14C part ends and the 15C part begins.

Many **tombstones** dating from the 14C to the 18C pave the floor of the cathedral, particularly in the transept. Before leaving, have a look at the elegant Louis XV-style loft supporting the monumental organ (1963) placed beneath the great rose-window.

Access to the cloister is through the small doorway opening onto place des Clercs.

★**Cloître** – The cloister, one of the largest in France, was built in the 13C and 14C. It only consists of three galleries with large openings forming equilateral arches; note the beautiful capitals decorated with foliage. The walls are adorned with trefoil arcading (in typical Champagne style) and interesting gargoyles. The **former chapter hall** houses an annual summer exhibition about the "birth of a cathedral".

Ancien palais épiscopal (**BZ H**) – This edifice, built between 1735 and 1743, was restored and is now the town hall. The imposing **façade★**, adorned with colossal-order pilasters, is in striking contrast with the graceful elegance of the cathedral's west front.

ADDITIONAL SIGHTS

Église St-Gengoult ⊘ (**BZ**) – This former collegiate church, erected in the 13C and 15C, is a fine sample of Champagne Gothic architecture. The west front has an elegant doorway dating from the 15C.

Inside, unusual features include the short but elegant nave and the very wide transept. Note the missing triforium and the style difference between the last two bays and of the first two which have to support the weight of the towers. The apsidal chapels open onto the chancel and the transept, a frequent occurrence in typical Champagne architecture. The chapels are lit by fine 13C **stained-glass windows**.

★★**Cloître** – The cloister dates from the 16C. The Flamboyant openings confer considerable elegance to the ensemble. The outside decoration of the galleries is in Renaissance style (capitals, medallions) and gables underline the elevation of the arcades. The star vaulting has ornately worked keystones.

Walk round the cloister and come out onto place du Marché.

Maisons anciennes – There are Renaissance houses along **rue du Général-Gengoult** (**AZ 10**) at nos 30, 28 and 26; one 14C house at no 8; the 17C is represented by nos 6 and 6bis (former Pimodan mansion) and no 4; **rue Michâtel** (**BZ**) is also lined with a fine Renaissance house decorated with gargoyles.

★**Musée municipal** ⊘ (**BY M**)– *25 rue Gouvion-St-Cyr.* Housed on two floors in the former 18C Maison-Dieu (almshouse), the town museum contains various collections: painting, sculpture, Flemish tapestries, ceramics (Toul-Bellevue manufacture), religious art, antique and medieval archeology (graves and Merovingian jewellery), popular art and traditions. A reconstructed drawing room in the Louis XVI style is decorated with a painting by F Boucher, *The Enjoyable Lesson*. The two world wars are illustrated by weapons, uniforms, mementoes of the main opponents' daily life. The **sick room**★ is a Gothic building of the early 13C, remodelled many times, used as a sanctuary and as a hospital ward for all kinds of sick people. The pointed vaulting is supported by six strong pillars. Today it contains a collection of stone fragments.

EXCURSIONS

Église Notre-Dame-d'Écrouves – *4km/2.5mi west. Leave Toul by ⑤ on the town plan.*

Built on a south-facing hillside once covered with vineyards, overlooking Toul's industrial depression, the former Église d'Écrouves, dedicated to Our Lady of the Nativity, has retained its 12C massive square belfry pierced with openings decorated with three colonnettes. The high 13C nave has had a double row of windows opening onto the roof space of the aisles since the edifice was reinforced in the 14C.

Villey-le-Sec – *7km/4.3mi east along N 4 then D 909.*

This village, lying on top of a ridge overlooking the east bank of the Moselle, is the only example in France of a village combined with a fortified work of the late 19C. Rebuilt in 1955, the **church** is decorated with modern stained-glass windows and a 14C stone statue of the Virgin.

Ensemble fortifié ⊘ – *Leave the car at the exit of the village, on the way to Toul.* Built in the space of five years, this fortified work did not play any defensive role during the First World War and was abandoned. It was restored and partly rearmed by private means. The north battery with its special armour-plating, its ditch, its caponiers, its observation cupolas, its armour-plated revolving turret equipped with a 75mm/3in gun, whose firing chamber can be visited, appears like a forerunner of the later structural works of the Maginot Line.

Visitors are brought to the fort by narrow-gauge railway.

View of the south battery and southwest curtain wall.

The fort houses the ammunition stores and barracks, a museum **(Musée Séré de Rivières)** and a memorial crypt. There is also a military railway, an armour-plated turret equipped with a 155mm/6in gun in working order and an 1879 model of a Hotchkiss machine-gun.

Liverdun – *18.5km/11.5mi northeast. Drive out of Toul along N 4 to Gondreville and continue along D 90 which follows the east bank of the Moselle.*

Liverdun nestles in a pleasant setting, inside a meander of the Moselle. Access to the small town on its south side is through a 16C towngate. The 13C church contains St Eucharius' tomb consisting of a 13C statue in a 16C frame. Note the broken-barrel-vaulted aisles set at right angles to the nave like the transept.

Place de la Fontaine behind the church is lined with 16C arcading.

Guided tours of the town ⊘ are available.

Michelin maps and town plans are oriented with north at the top of the page.

Conurbation 122 763
Michelin map 61 folds 16 and 17 or 241 fold 37

The former capital of Champagne became a prosperous commercial city through its famous annual fairs as well as an artistic centre with a wealth of churches, museums, old houses and mansions.

The town has now expanded outside the ring of boulevards surrounding the centre, whose shape suggests a Champagne cork; it is surrounded by suburbs and industrial zones. Troyes, which has been the main French hosiery centre since the 16C, has extended its industrial activities to other industries such as mechanical engineering, tyres, printing and wrapping-packaging.

HISTORICAL NOTES

St Loup and Attila – Built on the site of a Gaulish fortress, Troyes was Christianised in the 3C AD. In 451, the Huns led by Attila invaded Gaul, ransacking and destroying everything on their way. Reims was burnt down. The bishop of Troyes, St Loup, went to meet Attila in his camp and offered himself in exhange for the safety of his town. Attila was impressed and agreed to spare Troyes.

The counts of Champagne – In the 10C, the city came under the authority of the counts of Champagne. Some of them embellished it and made it prosperous. One of them, Henri I founded 13 churches, 13 hospitals – including the Hôtel-Dieu – extended the town and fully deserved his nickname ,"the liberal".

His grandson, Thibaud IV, a knight-poet, founded the Champagne fairs and brought fame to the town.

When the last heiress of the counts of Champagne, Jeanne, married the king of France, Philippe le Bel, in 1284, her dowry included the Champagne region.

The shameful Treaty of Troyes – During the strife between Burgundians and Armagnacs at the height of the Hundred Years War, **Isabeau of Bavaria**, the wife of the mad French king, Charles VI, signed the shameful Treaty of Troyes disowning the dauphin (heir to the French throne) and sealing the marriage of Catherine of France with Henry V of England who was proclaimed regent pending his accession to the French throne on the death of Charles VI. Burgundian and English troops then occupied Troyes which was liberated by Joan of Arc in 1429.

Major artistic centre – The city's artistic activities multiplied from the Renaissance onwards. Ignoring the Italian influence which pervaded French artistic expression, artists continued to work along the lines of the great medieval tradition. The school of architecture was famous throughout Champagne and even in neighbouring Burgundy. Sculptors such as Jean Gailde and Jacques Julyot created a wealth of charming works. Stained-glass-makers, such as Jehan Soudain and **Linard Gontier**, were also well established and, between the 14C and 17C, their workshops produced all the fine stained glass decorating the town's churches. This artistic tradition continued into the 17C with painters like **Pierre Mignard** and **François Girardon**, both native of Troyes.

"Capital" of hosiery – This long-standing tradition began at the beginning of the 16C, with a handful of manufacturers of hand-knitted bonnets and stockings.

In 1745, the Trinity Hospital (Hôtel de Mauroy) introduced special looms so that poor children in its care could learn to make stockings. The experiment was successful and in 1774, the hosiers' guild counted no fewer than 30 members. The industry further developed in the 19C and today it includes 250 firms employing 15 000 people.

★★OLD TOWN *allow 2hr*

In medieval times, Troyes consisted of two separate districts: the Cité, the aristocratic and ecclesiastical centre surrounding the cathedral, and the Bourg, the commercial middle-class area, where the Champagne fairs took place. In 1524, a fire swept through the town. The prosperous inhabitants took this opportunity to build the more opulent houses which you can see today as you stroll through the old town.

The timber-framed houses had cob walls and corbelled upper floors often supported by carved consoles and surmounted by pointed gables and tiled roofs. More opulent houses had walls of limestone rubble and brick in the traditional Champagne style.

The most elegant mansions were built of stone, an expensive building material in that region owing to the absence of hard-stone quarries.

Place Alexandre-Israël (CZ) – The square is overlooked by the Louis XIII-style façade of the town hall.

Start walking along rue Champeaux.

Rue Champeaux (CZ 12) – This unusually wide 16C street was the district's main artery.

VISITING TIPS

The main tourist office is located at 16 boulevard Carnot, ☎ 03 25 73 00 36; there is another information centre in rue Mignard (opposite the Église St-Jean).

Strolls through the town

A **tourist itinerary** (about 1hr 30min on foot; brochure available from the tourist office) offers visitors a chance to discover the most outstanding sights; this itinerary is easily followed thanks to the special markings in the town and on monuments.

Guided tours of the old town lasting about two hours are organised daily in summer (early July to early September): traditional tours, themed tours and night tours; apply at the tourist office.

The show entitled "Chemin des Bâtisseurs de Cathédrales" is an itinerary which takes you through the old town by night, linking four churches with Son et lumière displays (15min; every weekend from 21 June to the end of August).

Concerts take place in the evening, every weekend from 21 June to the end of August. Several sights are brought to life by free concerts (Jazz, rock, classical music, choral music...).

Technical visits: from July to October, several businesses welcome tourists by appointment (apply at the tourist office).

The **cathedral** and **churches** of St-Jean, St-Urbain, Ste-Madeleine and St-Pantaléon are open daily (except Sunday morning) all year round from 10am to noon and 2pm to 4pm, with information stands for visitors.

In summer, opening hours are longer and two more churches are open: St-Remy and St-Nizier.

Markets

A market takes place daily in Les Halles (covered market), place St-Remy. The most important is the Saturday market.

Market days in the Chartreux district are Wednesdays and Sundays (mornings only).

A local-speciality market is held on the third Wednesday of every month along the alleyways of boulevard Jules-Guesde.

Shopping

Numerous commercial activities liven up the town centre all year round. Factory shops are situated on the outskirts of town (St-Julien-les-Villas and Pont-Ste-Marie).

Local specialities include andouillettes de Troyes (sausages made with chitterling), Chaource cheese, sauerkraut cooked in cider or Champagne, rosé wine from Les Riceys and Cacibel (an aperitive made with cider, blackcurrant juice and honey).

Evenings out

Rue Champeaux and place Alexandre-Israël: numerous pavement cafés and restaurants with small orchestras on summer evenings.

Rue Paillot-de-Montabert: the Montabert and the Tricasse are two music bars popular with the local youth.

Rue de la République: La Choppe offers a wide choice of beers, whiskies and cocktails.

Ruelle des Chats: La Gouttière is a convivial bar serving non-alcoholic drinks and offering themed evenings (concerts, exhibitions, discussions...).

Rue de la Cité: the Café du Musée is the favourite haunt of beer lovers (more than 300 different beers).

The Théâtre de Champagne (boulevard Gambetta) and the Théâtre de la Madeleine (rue Jules-Lebocey) stage many performances. Apply for the brochure entitled "Théâtres de Troyes" published every season.

On the corner of rue Paillot-de-Montabert stands the **Maison du Boulanger (N)** which houses the Thibaud-de-Champagne cultural centre; opposite, you can see the **Tourelle de l'Orfèvre (V)** which owes its name to its first owner, a goldsmith. Partly clad with slates forming a chequered pattern, it is supported by caryatids and a telamon with goat's feet.

Turn round as you walk towards the Église St-Jean *(see p 311)* to admire this picturesque 16C architectural ensemble.

Walk alongside the church then follow rue Mignard which leads you back to rue Champeaux.

Across the street stands the **Hôtel Juvénal-des-Ursins** (**B**) dating from 1526. The white-stone façade is pierced by a doorway surmounted by a triangular pediment and a charming Renaissance oratory.

Ruelle des Chats – A medieval atmosphere pervades this narrow lane lined with houses whose gables are so close that a cat can jump from one roof to the other. The bollards marking the entrance of the alleyway were placed there to prevent carriage wheels from hitting the walls of the houses. The street was closed by a portcullis at night.

The road widens and becomes rue des Chats.

On the left, a passageway leads to the **Cour du Mortier d'or**, a fine courtyard reconstructed with various ancient elements: note (on the rue des Chats side) the wooden lintel carved with a charming Annunciation and, opposite, near rue des Quinze-Vingts, a corbel carved with the head of a warrior wearing a helmet.

Continue along the lane, then take rue de la Madeleine leading to the church of the same name.

Walk past the Flamboyant doorway of the former charnel house (1525) decorated with a salamander, the emblem of King Francis I, and his initial "F".

Retrace your steps to rue Charbonnet and turn right.

Hôtel de Marisy – Erected in 1531, this beautiful stone mansion is adorned with a charming Renaissance corner turret, decorated with figures and emblems.

Turn left onto rue des Quinze-Vingts then right towards place Audiffred.

Note the 18C mansion now housing the Chamber of Commerce and Industry.

Continue to place Jean-Jaurès.

On the corner of place Jean-Jaurès and rue Turenne, an old house has been erected over a modern one-storey building (note the main doorway situated on the first floor).

Walk along place Jean-Jaurès, where the Corn Exchange once stood, to rue de Vauluisant.

Rue de Vauluisant (**CZ 74**) – The house on the corner of this street and place Jean-Jaurès is a fine example of Champagne bond (brick and limestone rubble). The corbelled upper part rests on consoles decorated with carved heads; on the corner stands a fine Virgin of the Apocalypse.

Continue along rue de Vauluisant past the Hôtel de Vauluisant to rue Turenne.

Hôtel de Chapelaines – *55 rue Turenne.* Beautiful Renaissance façade.

Follow rue Général-Saussier, then turn left onto rue de la Trinité.

★**Hôtel de Mauroy** (**CZ M³**) – This mansion is an interesting example of 16C local architecture. The façade overlooking the street shows a chequered bond typical of the Champagne region, whereas on the courtyard side (accessible during the tour of the museum), the building features a polygonal turret surrounded by timber-framing, bricks, a chequered slate-cladding and string-courses. Note also the Corinthian columns supporting the wooden gallery. The building was erected in 1550 by wealthy merchants and was turned into the Hôpital de la Trinité through the generosity of Jean de Mauroy. It was a home for poor children who were taught a trade during their stay. In 1745 special looms for making stockings were brought in and this marked the beginning of machine-made hosiery in Troyes. In 1966, the building was restored and turned into a museum.

Next door, on the corner of rue de la Trinité and rue Thérèse-Bordet, stands the Maison des Allemands.

Maison des Allemands (**CZ K**) – Built in the 16C and decorated in the 18C, this timber-framed house used to welcome German merchants in town for the fairs, hence its name. It is now the library of an ancient guild of craftsmen, the Compagnons du Devoir et du Tour de France.

Turn right onto rue Thérèse-Bordet, then right again onto rue Larivey leading to rue Général-Saussier.

Rue Général-Saussier – The street is lined with fine old houses; no 26: Hôtel des Angoiselles with a pinnacled tower; a passageway leads to the picturesque inner courtyard surrounded by a gallery; no 11: 18C stone mansion where Napoleon stayed; no 13: fine stone-and-brick house roofed with glazed ceramic tiles, built during the first half of the 17C.

Retrace your steps and turn right onto rue de la Montée-des-Changes, which becomes a passageway beyond rue Émile-Zola and leads to place du Marché-au-Pain.

Place du Marché-au-Pain (**CZ 42**) – During the Champagne fairs, the square was occupied by money changers. Note the fine view of the clock tower of the Église St-Jean.

Rue Urbain-IV takes you back to place Alexandre-Israël.

CHURCHES

★★Cathédrale St-Pierre-et-St-Paul (DEY) – The cathedral, built between the 13C and 17C, has remarkable proportions, an exceptionally rich decoration and a beautiful nave. Martin Chambiges, who built the transept of Beauvais cathedral and also worked on Sens cathedral, contributed to the ornate west front (early 16C) adorned with a splendid Flamboyant rose-window. The three doorways are surmounted with richly carved gables. Sculptures and statues were destroyed during the Revolution. The cathedral was intended to have two towers, but the north tower alone (restoration work in progress) was completed in the 17C (height: 66m/217ft). A plaque on the base of the tower reminds visitors that Joan of Arc stayed in Troyes on 10 July 1429.

Walk along the north side of the cathedral in order to admire the north-transept doorway (13C) surmounted by a huge rose-window.

Interior – This vast sanctuary conveys an impression of power and lightness, of elegance and harmonious proportions.

The **stained-glass windows★★** date from different periods. Those of the chancel and ambulatory go back to the 13C. Note the warmth and intensity of the colours; they mainly depict isolated characters (popes and emperors) and scenes from the life of the Virgin Mary. The windows of the nave, dating from the 16C, are completely different: they are more like real paintings on glass with red as the dominant colour. The most remarkable are, on the north side, the Story of the True Cross, the Legend of St Sebastian, the Story of Job and that of Toby; on the south side, the Story of Daniel and that of Joseph, the Parable of the Prodigal Son and a magnificent Tree of Jesse.

The rose-window of the west front by Martin Chambiges, was completed in 1546 and decorated with stained glass by Jehan Soudain: the Patriarchs surrounding God the Father. The rose is partially concealed behind the 18C organ case from Clairvaux abbey. The fourth chapel along the north aisle is lit by the famous stained glass made in 1625 by Linard Gontier and known as the **"mystical winepress"**: Christ is seen lying beneath the winepress with blood coming out of the wound in his side and filling a chalice. Out of his chest grows a vine whose branches support the twelve apostles.

★Treasury ⊘ – The cathedral treasury, exhibited in a 13C vaulted room, includes an 11C ivory box, four 11C cloisonné enamels representing the symbols of the four Evangelists, a 9C manuscript psalter with gold lettering, two missal covers inlaid with precious gems, the 12C reliquary of St Bernard, late 12C regional enamels, a 14C red cope embroidered with medallions and religious gold plate from the 16C to 19C.

★Basilique St-Urbain (DY) – This is a perfect example of 13C Gothic architecture from the Champagne region. It was built between 1262 and 1286, by order of Pope Urban V, a native of Troyes, on the site of his father's workshop.

Exterior – The west front dates from the 19C but the doorway beneath the porch goes back to the 13C; the tympanum is decorated with the Last Judgement. Walk alongside the edifice to the east end to admire the graceful flying buttresses, the elegant windows, the delicate pinnacles, the gargoyles and the profusion of decorative features. The side doorways are protected by 14C porches.

LAUROS-GIRAUDON

St-Urbain-de-Troyes – The Virgin with the Grapes

Interior – One's attention is immediately drawn to the chancel, built in one go. Stained-glass windows are spread over a considerable area, a rare occurrence in early-Gothic architecture. The medallions of the low windows, the clerestory windows and high chancel windows, and the medallions of the Chapelle St-Joseph on the left of the chancel (Annunciation, Visitation, Holy Innocents) are all decorated with **13C stained-glass panels**.

The chapel on the right of the chancel contains the smiling **"Virgin with the Grapes"**, a fine example of 16C local sculpture; on the left, note the group surrounding St Roch, dressed in late-15C fashion.

In the chancel, on the left-hand side, there is a polychrome low-relief sculpture over the tomb of Pope Urbain IV (1185-1264).

★**Église Ste-Madeleine** (CZ) – This is the town's oldest church. The original late-12C building was remodelled in the 16C; a new apse was erected between 1498 and 1501 and a Renaissance tower added to the west front.
The nave contains a remarkable stone rood screen.

★★**Roodscreen** – The Flamboyant rood screen was carved between 1508 and 1517 by Jean Gailde, a local sculptor and architect. It consists of three pointed arches underlined by delicate festoons and is decorated with a profusion of foliage and carved figurines dressed in Renaissance fashion.
The work is surmounted by a balustrade with fleur-de-lis motifs; on the chancel side, a staircase, lined with grotesques, leads to the gallery. Note, on the side overlooking the north aisle, a graceful 16C Flemish sculpture in painted and gilt wood.

★**Stained-glass windows** – The east end is decorated with brightly coloured Renaissance windows: from left to right the life of St Louis (1507), the Creation (1500), the legend of St Eloi (1506), the Tree of Jesse (1510), the Passion (1494), the life of Mary Magdalene (1506) and the triumph of the Cross.

In the south aisle, against a pillar of the nave, stands a statue of **Martha**★, by the Master of Chaource, one of the main exponents of 16C sculpture in Troyes *(see p 315)*.
Opposite, in the north aisle, there is a wooden statue of Robert de Molesme (early 15C), who founded the Cistercian order.

Église Ste-Madeleine – Rood screen

★**Église St-Pantaléon** (CZ) – This 16C church, covered with a wooden vault in the 17C and lit by tall Renaissance windows with *grisaille* stained glass, contains an important collection of statues mostly standing against the pillars of the nave; these statues come from churches which were destroyed during the Revolution. Note, against the first pillar on the right, the statue of St James by **Dominique Florentin**, which is a self-portrait and, opposite, the pulpit, a Gothic Mater Dolorosa; the pillars of the chancel are adorned with Charity and Faith by Dominique Florentin, which denote an Italian influence. The second chapel on the south side houses a group in polychrome wood depicting St Crépin's and St Crépinien's arrest; two Jewish priests can be seen in the south transept.

Église St-Jean (CZ) – It was in this church that the marriage of Catherine de France (daughter of Charles VI and Isabeau of Bavaria) and Henry V of England was celebrated in 1420. The clock tower dates from the 14C. The Gothic nave is relatively low whereas the chancel, rebuilt at the beginning of the 16C, is quite high. The altar is surmounted by two paintings by Mignard: *God the Father* and

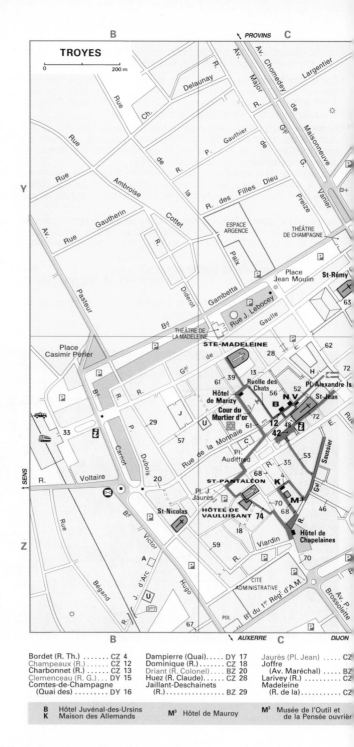

TROYES

0   200 m

Bordet (R. Th.)	CZ 4	Dampierre (Quai)	DY 17	Jaurès (Pl. Jean) .... CZ
Champeaux (R.)	CZ 12	Dominique (R.)	CZ 18	Joffre
Charbonnet (R.)	CZ 13	Driant (R. Colonel)	BZ 20	(Av. Maréchal) ..... BZ
Clemenceau (R. G.)	DY 15	Huez (R. Claude)	CZ 28	Larivey (R.) .... CZ
Comtes-de-Champagne		Jaillant-Deschainets		Madeleine
(Quai des)	DY 16	(R.)	BZ 29	(R. de la) .... CZ

B	Hôtel Juvénal-des-Ursins		**M³**	Hôtel de Mauroy	**M³** Musée de l'Outil et
K	Maison des Allemands				de la Pensée ouvrièr

Christ's Baptism. The marble-and-bronze tabernacle was made in 1692 after draw ings by Girardon. Note, in the south ambulatory (second chapel) the 16C ston group representing the Virgin visiting Elisabeth.

Église St-Nicolas ⊘ (**BZ**) – Rebuilt after the fire of 1524, this church has a sout doorway flanked by pilasters and decorated with statues by François Gentil. Inside the gallery is markedly ornate. Take the staircase in the aisle to admire th keystone pendentives of the Flamboyant vaulting. Among the statues housed in thi chapel, the most remarkable are those depicting Christ falling under the weight o his cross, Christ in bonds and St Agnes smiling to a lamb. The low-relief carving beneath the gallery date from the 16C.

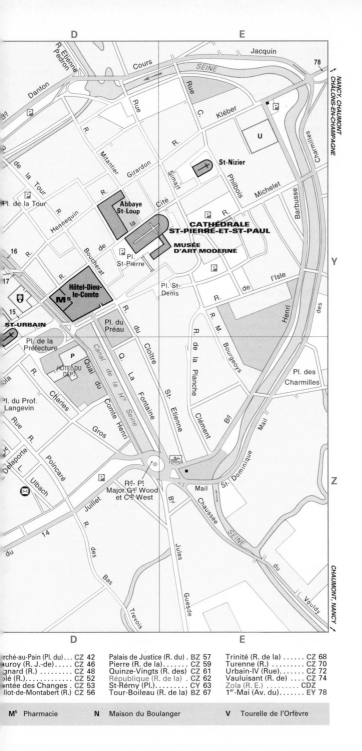

...rché-au-Pain (Pl. du)... CZ 42
...uroy (R. J.-de)..... CZ 46
...gnard (R.) .... CZ 48
...lé (R.)............. CZ 52
...ntée des Changes . CZ 53
...llot-de-Montabert (R.) CZ 56

Palais de Justice (R. du) . BZ 57
Pierre (R. de la)....... CZ 59
Quinze-Vingts (R. des) CZ 61
République (R. de la) . CZ 62
St-Rémy (Pl.)......... CY 63
Tour-Boileau (R. de la) BZ 67

Trinité (R. de la) ...... CZ 68
Turenne (R.) .... CZ 70
Urbain-IV (Rue)....... CZ 72
Vauluisant (R. de) .... CZ 74
Zola (R. E.) .... CDZ
1er-Mai (Av. du)....... EY 78

M⁵	Pharmacie	N	Maison du Boulanger	V	Tourelle de l'Orfèvre

Église St-Remy ⊘ (CY) – Originally built in the 14C and 16C, the now-restored church has a delicate spiral steeple covered with slates and flanked by pointed pinnacles.

The interior is adorned with numerous 16C wooden panels painted in grisaille, as well as low-relief medallions (Death praying, Jesus and the Virgin) and a bronze crucifix by Girardon, who was one of St-Remy's parishioners.

Église St-Nizier ⊘ (EY) – This 16C church covered with brightly coloured glazed tiles can be seen from afar. It contains a beautiful Entombment and a 16C Pietà.

313

MUSEUMS

★★Musée d'Art moderne ⊘ (EY) – In 1976, two local industrialists, Pierre and Denise Levy, donated to the state the numerous works of art they had been collecting since 1939. The town then decided to house the collection in the buildings of the former bishop's palace.

There are 388 paintings from the 19C and the early 20C, 1 277 drawings, 104 sculptures, glassware and works of African and Oceanian art.

Fauvism★★ is particularly well represented. The fauves ("wild beasts") were co-called for their pure, brilliant colours applied straight from the tube in what was qualified as an "agressive" style. The Levy collection includes works by Derain *(Hyde Park, Big Ben)*, Vlaminck *(Landscape in Chatou)*, Braque *(Landscape at l'Estaque)* and Van Dongen.

The first few rooms contain earlier paintings by Courbet, Degas, Seurat *(The Anglers*, a study which he used for his painting *The Grande Jatte)*, Vallotton *(Woman Sewing Indoors)* and Vuillard.

More recent works include paintings by Robert Delaunay before his abstract period, works by Roger de la Fresnaye, Modigliani, Soutine, Buffet, Nicolas de Staël, Balthus and numerous post-fauvist paintings by **Derain**.

There are also a number of works by Maurice Marinot, a painter who became a stained-glass maker; note his unusual Art Deco creations.

★★Maison de l'Outil et de la Pensée ouvrière ⊘ (CZ **M³**) – This museum is housed in the Hôtel de Mauroy *(see p 309)* restored by the Compagnons du Devoir.

An itinerary *(detailed notice available)* enables visitors to admire a great number of 18C tools used for various crafts, exhibited in large glass cases. Some of these tools were carved or engraved by the craftsman who used them.

A large room, in the courtyard on the left, contains works by master craftsmen.

The **library**, adjacent to the museum, is devoted to literature concerning the working class and includes many technical works, encyclopaedias and history books.

★Hôtel de Vauluisant ⊘ (CZ) – This 16C mansion has a fine Renaissance turreted façade and 17C side buildings. Note the large reception room with its French-style ceiling and its magnificent stone fireplace. The mansion contains two museums.

★Musée historique de Troyes et de Champagne – The museum is in two sections.

The first section illustrates regional art from the Romanesque period to the end of the 16C with works by members of the famous School of Troyes: sculpture, including a Christ on the cross believed to be by the Master of Chaource, paintings and a few objets d'art.

The second section, Troyes through the Ages, shows the evolution of the town by means of drawings, paintings, prints, photographs and various objects.

Musée de la Bonneterie – This museum is devoted to hosiery, which has been the town's main activity since the 16C. Several rooms illustrate the history of hosiery and the different manufacturing processes; there is a fine collection of embroidered stockings as well as several machines and looms, the oldest dating from the 18C. The reconstruction of a 19C workshop shows the evolution of techniques.

Abbaye St-Loup ⊘ (DY) – The buildings of the former abbey, dating from the 17C and 18C and extended later, now house two museums and the library.

Musée d'Histoire naturelle – The Natural History Museum, occupying part of the ground floor, contains a collection of mammals and birds from all over the world. Skeletons, rocks and meteorites are exhibited in the cloister.

★Musée des Beaux-Arts et d'Archéologie – **Regional archeological collections★** from prehistory to the Merovingian period are displayed in the former cellars of the abbey. Main exhibits include the Apollo from Vaupoisson, a Gallo-Roman bronze statue, and the Pouan treasury, an exceptional collection of weapons and jewellery found in a 5C Merovingian grave.

The gallery of **medieval sculpture** testifies to the creative activity of the Champagne region from the 13C to the 15C: capitals, gargoyles, 13C Christ on the Cross.

The mezzanine houses the collection of **drawings and miniatures** from the 16C to the 18C, shown in rotation.

The gallery of **painting** displays works of all the major schools from the 15C to the 19C. The 17C is particularly well represented with paintings by Rubens, Van Dyck, Philippe de Champaigne, Jacques de Létrin, Le Brun, Mignard... There is also a rich collection of 18C works by Watteau *(The Enchanter* and *The Adventurer)*, Natoire, Boucher, Fragonard, Lépicié, Greuze *(Portrait of a Child with a Cat)*, David and Elisabeth Vigée-Lebrun *(The Countess of Bossancourt)*.

These rooms also contain sculpture (works by Girardon), 16C enamels and furniture.

Bibliothèque – Founded in 1651, the library owns more than 340 000 works, including 8 000 manuscripts and 700 incunabula from the 7C onwards. The **great hall**, which can be seen through a glass panel on the first floor of the museum, used to be the canons' dormitory.

Hôtel-Dieu-le-Comte (DY) – This 18C edifice houses a branch of Reims University. The fine wrought-iron gate opening onto rue de la Cité was made in 1760 by Pierre Delphin. The **pharmacy★** ⊙ (**M⁵**) contains a rich collection of 18C earthenware jars, 320 painted wooden boxes decorated with plant motifs and 16C and 17C bronze mortars. The former laboratory has been turned into a museum: 16C reliquary busts, pewter jugs... Chapel dating from the 18C.

EXCURSIONS

★★**Parc naturel régional de la Forêt d'Orient** – *21km/13mi east along avenue du 1ᵉʳ-Mai* (EY 78), *then leave N 19 and follow the route de Mesnil-St-Père on the left. See Parc naturel régional de la FORÊT D'ORIENT.*

St-Parres-aux-Tertres – *5km/3mi east along avenue du 1ᵉʳ-Mai* (EY 78) *and N 19.* The 16C church stands on the spot where St Parres, a 3C local martyr, is believed to be burried. The south doorway has retained its Renaissance ornamentation. Inside, note the lovely 16C stained-glass windows and many works of art: statue of St Parres in the north chapel, Virgin and Child in the south chapel. A building, known as the **Nécropole paléochrétienne**, has been purposely erected to display Gallo-Roman sarcophagi and various objects found in graves discovered near the church.

Bouilly; Chaource – *34km/21mi. Leave Troyes along boulevard Victor-Hugo* (BZ), *boulevard de Belgique and N 77.*

Bouilly – The 16C **Église St-Laurent** ⊙, restored in the 18C has a remarkable Renaissance stone altarpiece over the high altar, representing scenes from the Passion; beneath the altarpiece, note the delicate low-relief carving depicting the legend of St Laurence; among the 16C statues, there is an interesting St Sebastian and a fine St Margaret.

★**Chaource** – This village, which has given its name to a famous creamy cheese, has retained a few 15C timber-framed houses. In the **Église St-Jean-Baptiste★**, the semi-basement chapel on the left of the 13C chancel contains an **Entombment★★** carved in 1515 by the Master of Chaource; the facial expression of the Holy Women is extremely moving. The third chapel on the left houses a 16C **gilt-wood crib** in the shape of a polyptych. Note also the statue of **St Barbe** of the same period in the first chapel on the left.

Isle-Aumont; Rumilly-lès-Vaudes; Bar-sur-Seine – *41km/25.5mi. Leave Troyes along avenue Pierre-Brossolette and drive 8.5km/5mi then turn right onto D 444.*

Isle-Aumont – There have been settlements on the Isle-Aumont promontory since Neolithic times: pagan and Christian sanctuaries, Viking camp, necropolis, monasteries and castles succeeded one another and the site still bears traces of all of them. Several edifices preceded the present **church** ⊙ which has retained the 10C semi-circular apse beneath the present chancel. A Gothic nave was added, in the 15C to 16C, to the 12C Romanesque nave which now contains sarcophagi, capitals and a statue of Martha. In the Gothic nave on the right, note the fine 13C wooden crucifix.

Return to N 71 and drive southeast to St-Parres-lès-Vaudes then turn right onto D 28.

Rumilly-lès-Vaudes – Fine 16C church with a richly carved doorway, containing a splendid polychrome-stone **altarpiece★** dating from 1533 and a few 16C stained-glass windows, some of them by Linard Gontier.
The elegant castle, flanked by turrets, also dates from the 16C.

Return to N 71, turn right and continue to Bar-sur-Seine.

Bar-sur-Seine – From its prosperous past (16C-17C), this small town has retained a fine ensemble of old houses. The Église St-Étienne is a mixture of Gothic and Renaissance styles. The **interior★** offers an interesting set of grisaille stained-glass windows typical of the local 16C school. Four low-relief sculptures in the south transept are believed to be the work of Dominique Florentin. The alabaster panels of the north transept, illustrating the life of the Virgin, together with the statues of St Anne and St Joseph are by François Gentil.

Pont-Ste-Marie; Ste-Maure; Fontaine-lès-Grès – *46km/29mi. Drive east out of Troyes along avenue du 1ᵉʳ-Mai* (EY 78).

Pont-Ste-Marie – The 16C **church** ⊙ has a fine west front adorned with three monumental doorways; the central doorway is Flamboyant whereas the other two are fine examples of the Renaissance style. Beautiful stained-glass window by Linard Gontier.

Follow D 78 northwest to Ste-Maure.

Ste-Maure – 15C church with Renaissance chancel containing the tomb of St Maure (9C sarcophagus).

Continue along D 78 to Rilly -Ste-Syre and turn left to Fontaine-lès-Grès.

Fontaine-lès-Grès – The **Église St-Agnès★** was erected in 1956 by the architect Michel Marot. This triangular church is surmounted by a slender steeple. Inside, light filters through an opening concealed in the steeple and falls onto the high altar, lighting a 13C wooden crucifix of the Spanish School.

Follow N 19 back to Troyes.

TURCKHEIM ★

Population 3 567
Michelin map 87 fold 17 or 242 fold 31 – Local map see Route des VINS

This ancient little town lying just outside Colmar, on the north bank of the River Flecht, has retained its fortifications and its long-standing traditions: every evening at 10pm *(from May to October)*, Alsace's last night watchman walks through the streets, wrapped in his great coat and carrying his halberd, his lamp and his horn. He stops and sings at every street corner.

It was here that **Turenne**, France's 17C military genius, won one of his most famous battles against a far-superior imperial army from across the Rhine, during the Alsatian campaign of 1674-75 which cost him his life.

Today, Turckheim is one of the main centres of the paper industry in eastern France.

SIGHTS

Portes de la ville – The town, shaped like a triangle, had three main gates. The **Porte de France**, facing the river embankment consists of a massive 14C quadrangular tower crowned by a stork nest. The Porte du Brand (named after a famous local wine) and the Porte de Munster (named after the nearby town and a famous local cheese) are situated on the other two angles.

Place Turenne – The square is surrounded by ancient houses: on the right is the former guard-house with a fountain in front. Across the square is the brightly painted town hall surmounted by a Renaissance gable; behind it stands the old church with its partly Romanesque tower.

Hôtel des Deux-Clefs – This is the former town hostel, renovated in 1620, a charming Alsatian house adorned with an elegant loggia and carved beams.

Grand'Rue – The street is lined with numerous late-16C and early-17C houses. Note the timber-framed house *(on the right as you walk away from place Turenne)* with its oriel resting on a wooden pillar.

Sentier viticole – *2km/1.2mi, about 1hr on foot. The wine trail starts beyond the Porte du Brand, near a small oratory.* The path, which goes through the vineyards, is lined with explanatory panels.

Circuit historique – The historic itinerary *(50min; booklet available from the tourist office)* offers visitors the opportunity of discovering the architectural heritage of this ancient imperial city.

VAUCOULEURS

Population 2 401
Michelin map 62 fold 3 or 242 fold 21

Pleasantly situated opposite the hills stretched along the east bank of the River Meuse, Vaucouleurs has retained part of its 13C fortifications.

In May 1428, a young shepherdess from Domrémy *(19km/12mi south)* arrived in Vaucouleurs to see the governor and told him that God had sent her to save France. Robert de Baudricourt's first reaction was to send her back to her village but Joan of Arc persisted and after several months, urged by public enthusiasm, Baudricourt gave in and agreed to help. In February 1429, Joan left Vaucouleurs with a small escort by the Porte de France on her way to meet the king of France and her destiny which would eventually lead her to Rouen where she died on 30 May 1431.

SIGHTS

Chapelle castrale ⊙ – The chapel was built over the 13C crypt of the former castle chapel consisting of three separate chapels. The central chapel contains the statue of Notre-Dame-des-Voûtes before which Joan used to pray during her stay in Vaucouleurs.

Porte de France – Joan of Arc and her escort left Vaucouleurs through this gate. Very little remains of the original gate.

Château – Excavations were undertaken to expose the ruins of the castle where Joan was received by Baudricourt in 1428. All that is left is the upper part of the Porte de France rebuilt in the 17C and an arch of the main doorway. A neo-Gothic church was built on the site. A huge lime tree is believed to date back to Joan of Arc's time.

Église – The vaulting of the 18C church is decorated with frescoes. The churchwardens' pew and the pulpit (1717) are elaborately carved.

Musée Jeanne d'Arc ⊙ – Housed in the right wing of the town hall, this museum is devoted to local history and archeology.

The most remarkable exhibit is the **Christ de Septfonds**, a magnificent oak crucifix from a nearby chapel where Joan of Arc went to pray for guidance when, at first, Baudricourt refused to take her seriously.

On place de l'Hôtel de ville (place A. François) stands a statue of Joan of Arc brought back from Algiers.

EXCURSION

★**Domrémy-la-Pucelle** – 19km/12mi south along D 964 then D 164.
This humble village is the birthplace of Joan of Arc (1412-1431), the pious peasant girl who heard voices ordering her to deliver France and the king from the English. An important annual pilgrimage takes place on the second Sunday in May, Joan of Arc's feast day, in the Bois-Chenu basilica (see below).

The **church** which Joan of Arc knew was remodelled in the 15C and extended in 1825. The entrance is now situated where the former chancel stood. However, it has retained of few objects which were familiar to the young girl: a stoop on the right as you go in, a statue of St Margaret (14C) against the first pillar on the right, the font over which she was christened in the transept.

★**Maison natale de Jeanne d'Arc** ⊙ – The house in which Joan of Arc was born is that of a comfortable peasant family; the walls are thick and the door is surmounted by the emblem of the family next to the arms of the kingdom of France. A recess houses a copy of a 16C statue of Joan kneeling (the original is in the museum).

On the left-hand side of the house, a small museum contains maps, documents, prints concerning the history of the region and Joan of Arc's youth and mission.

Basilique du Bois-Chenu – 1.5km/0.9mi along D 53 towards Coussey.
Consecrated in 1926, the basilica stands on the site where Joan heard the voices of St Catherine, St Margaret and St Michael telling her about her mission. Start with the crypt (entrance on the left); statue of Notre-Dame-de-Bermont before which Joan prayed every Saturday. Walk up the fine staircase decorated with the emblems of the towns where Joan stayed. The basilica contains frescoes illustrating Joan's life.

Leave by the side door. The Stations of the Cross lead to the adjacent wood.

VERDUN★★

Population 20 753
Michelin map 57 fold 11 or 241 fold 23

This ancient stronghold occupies a strategic positon on the west bank of the Meuse, which flows between well-defined hills. The upper town – cathedral and citadel – is camped on an outcrop overlooking the river.

HISTORICAL NOTES

Verdun started out as a Gaulish fortress, then became a Roman fort under the name of Virodunum Castrum. In 843, the treaty splitting the Carolingian Empire into three kingdoms was signed in the city which was ceded to the kingdom of Lorraine. In 552, Verdun was siezed by Henri II and became part of the French kingdom.

Occupied briefly by the Prussians in 1792, it was liberated following the French victory at Valmy in the Argonne (see STE-MENEHOULD: Excursions).

In 1870, the town was again besieged by the Prussians and was forced to capitulate. The occupation lasted three years.

At the start of the First World War, Verdun was, together with Toul, the most powerful stronghold in eastern France. The famous and extremely bloody Battle of Verdun, took place all round the town between February 1916 and August 1917 (see p 320).

★CITADELLE SOUTERRAINE ⊙ 30min

The citadel was built on the site of the famous Abbaye de St-Vanne, founded in 952. One of the abbey's 12C towers was retained by Vauban when he rebuilt the citadel.

In 1916-17, the citadel was used as a rest area for troops taking part in the Battle of Verdun. The 7km/4.3mi of galleries were equipped to fulfill the needs of a whole army: arsenal, telephone exchange, hospital with operating theatre, kitchens, bakery (nine ovens could turn out 28 000 rations of bread in 24 hours), butcher's and cooperative.

Tour – A self-guided vehicle takes visitors on a **round tour**★★ of the citadel where the soldiers' daily life during the Battle of Verdun is recreated through sound effects, lively scenes, virtual pictures (HQ, bakery) and reconstructed scenes, in particular "life in the trenches".

On 10 November 1920, during a ceremony staged in the Salle des Fêtes (meeting hall), in the presence of the French war minister, André Maginot, the youngest volunteer, a soldier in the 132nd infantry regiment, named Auguste Thin, was asked to choose among eight coffins, that of the unknown soldier, who would be laid to rest beneath the Arc de Triomphe. He added the figures of his regiment and chose the sixth coffin.

VERDUN

Alsace-Lorraine (Av.)	CZ	2
Beaurepaire (R.)	CZ	3
Chevert (Pl.)	CZ	4
Douaumont (Av. de)	CY	6
Foch (Pl. Mar.)	CY	7
Fort-de-Vaux (R. du)	CZ	8
Lattre-de-Tassigny (Av. Mar. de)	CY	10
Mautroté (R.)	BY	13
Mgr-Ginisty (Pl.)	BY	16
Mazel (R.)	CY	17
Prés.-Poincaré (R.)	CZ	17
République (Q. de la)	CY	18
Rû (R. de)	BZ	19
St-Paul (R.)	CY	20
St-Pierre (R.)	BY	21
Soupirs (Allée des)	BY	24

Large statues of marshals and generals of the French Empire, of the war of 1870 and of the First World War stand inside the fortification ditches, some 0.8km/0.5mi from the citadel.

★VILLE HAUTE *1hr 30min*

★**Cathédrale Notre-Dame** – Standing at the highest point of the town, the Romanesque cathedral was built between 990 and 1024 in characteristic Rhenish style, with two chancels and two transepts. The west chancel is typically Rhenish, the east chancel (1130-1140), denotes the Burgundian influence. The nave was covered with pointed vaulting in the 14C.

After the fire of 1755 which destroyed the Romanesque towers, it was decided to introduce the Baroque style when doing repair work. On the west side, two balustraded square towers were erected on the base of the former belfries; in the nave, the existing Gothic vaulting was replaced by rounded vaulting and the pillars were decorated with mouldings; the high altar was surmounted by an imposing baldaquin with twisted columns; the crypt was filled in and the Romanesque doorways concealed. The Romanesque part of the edifice was fortunately restored following the shelling of 1916. The 12C crypt was excavated and the **Portail du Lion** (Lion's doorway) brought to light, with its fine tympanum illustrating Christ in glory inside a mandorla, surrounded by the symbols of the four Evangelists. All the stained glass destroyed in 1916 has been replaced.

Crypt – Note the beautiful capitals decorated with acanthus leaves along the aisles. The new capitals are carved with scenes illustrating Life in the trenches, Suffering and Death.

★**Cloître** (BZ **B**) – The cloister, built on the south side of the cathedral, consists of three galleries: one of these, on the east side has retained three 14C arched openings which once led to the chapter-house; the other two galleries were built in the Flamboyant style between 1509 and 1517 and covered with network vaulting; however, the Romanesque doorway leading inside the church was retained, as were several 12C sculptures decorating the buttresses of the apse (Adam and Ève, Annunciation).

★**Palais épiscopal** – The bishop's palace was built in the 18C by Robert de Cotte on a rock spur overlooking the Meuse. The courtyard, shaped like an elongated semicircle precedes the main building. The town's library is located in the west wing. The other part of the palace houses the Centre mondial de la Paix.

Centre mondial de la Paix ⊘ – The permanent exhibition of the World Peace Centre is divided into seven sections: war, the earth and its frontiers, from war to peace, Europe, the United Nations for peace, human rights, peace concepts.
The centre, which has a specialised information department, welcomes groups of school children.

Porte Châtel – The 13C gate is crowned by 15C machicolations.

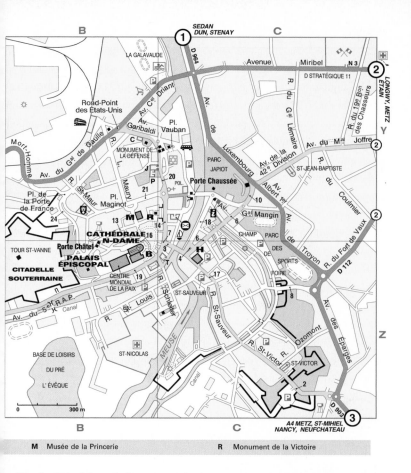

M Musée de la Princerie	R Monument de la Victoire

Musée de la Princerie ⊙ (**BY M**) – The museum is housed in the former residence of the "Princier" or "Primicier" who was the most important ecclesiastical dignitary after the bishop. The edifice is an elegant mansion with a 16C arcaded courtyard. The rooms are devoted to prehistory, to the Gallo-Roman and Merovingian periods, to the Middle Ages and to the Renaissance. Note the 12C carved-ivory comb *(first room)*, several medieval statues, ancient earthenware from the Argonne region and paintings by local artists such as Jules Bastien Lepage and Louis Hector Leroux.

ADDITIONAL SIGHTS

Monument de la Victoire ⊙ (**BY R**) – Seventy-three steps lead to a terrace on which stands a high pyramid surmounted by the statue of a warrior wearing a helmet and leaning on his sword, as a symbol of Verdun's defence.
The **crypt** beneath the monument bears the list of all the ex-servicemen who were awarded the medal of Verdun.

Hôtel de ville (**CZ H**) – Former private mansion dating from 1623. The first-floor rooms house decorations, flags, various objects offered to the town at the end of the First World War as well as the list of all those who took part in the Battle of Verdun.

Porte Chaussée (**CY**) – This 14C building used to guard the entrance of the town and served as a prison; it is flanked by two round towers with crenellations and machicolations; the protruding front part was added in the 17C.

EXCURSION

Étain – *20km/12.4mi northeast along N 3.* This large village was entirely rebuilt after the First World War. The church, dating from the 14C and 15C, has been restored. Note the carved arch leading to the Flamboyant chancel, lit by modern stained-glass windows by Gruber, and the carved keystones of the chancel.
Along the south aisle, the chapel of the Sacred Heart contains a group depicting Mary gazing at her dead Son, believed to be by Ligier Richier.
Senon – *9.5km/6mi north along N 18 then left onto D 14 via Amel-sur-l'Étang.*
The **church** ⊙ was built during the transition period from the Gothic to the Renaissance (1526-1536) styles. It consists of three naves of equal height and has retained some beautiful Renaissance capitals.

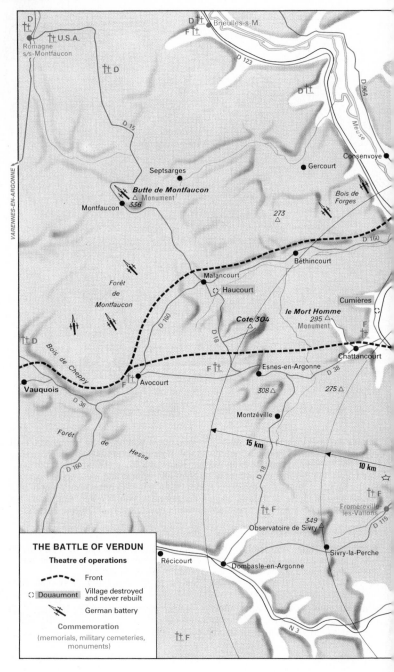

THE BATTLE OF VERDUN

Theatre of operations

- - - - - Front

◇ Douaumont   Village destroyed and never rebuilt

German battery

Commemoration

(memorials, military cemeteries, monuments)

★★★THE BATTLEFIELDS

Thousands of visitors come every year and wander through the battlefields where fierce fighting took place from 21 February 1916 to 20 August 1917 in what is now known as the **Battle of Verdun**.

The Battle of Verdun

German troops had, since 1914, been trying in vain to skirt round Verdun and then to take it. They had, however succeeded in hampering communications between Verdun and the rear by holding on to what came to be known as the St-Mihiel bulge *(see ST-MIHIEL)*.

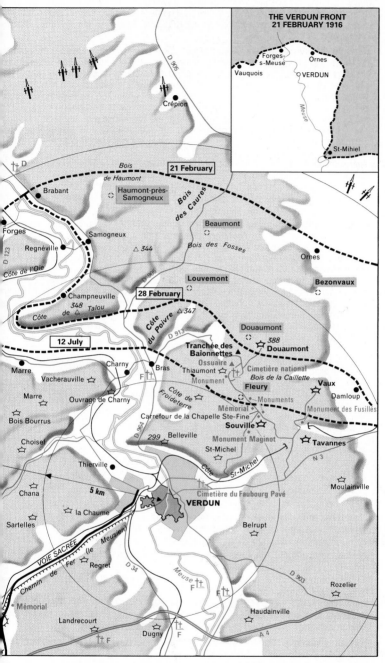

THE VERDUN FRONT 21 FEBRUARY 1916

Forges-s-Meuse
Ornes
Vauquois
VERDUN
Meuse
St-Mihiel

21 February

Bois de Haumont
Brabant
Haumont-près-Samogneux
Bois des Caures
Forges
Samogneux
Beaumont
Regnéville
△ 344
Bois des Fosses
Côte de l'Oie
Ornes

Louvemont
Bezonvaux

28 February

Champneuville
348 Talou
Côte de △ 347
Douaumont
Côte du Poivre
388
Douaumont

12 July

Marre
Charny
Bras
Ossuaire
Cimetière national
Vaux
Vacherauville
Thiaumont
Bois de la Caillette
Damloup
Monument
Fleury
Marre
Côte de Froideterre
Monuments
Monument des Fusillés
Ouvrage de Charny
Bois Bourrus
Carrefour de la Chapelle Ste-Fine
Mémorial
Choisel
299
Belleville
Souville
Monument Maginot
Tavannes
Thierville
St-Michel
Chana
5 km
Côte St-Michel
Moulainville
Sartelles
la Chaume
Cimetière du Faubourg Pavé
VERDUN
Belrupt
VOIE SACRÉE
Chemin de Fer (le Meusien)
Regret
Meuse
Rozelier
Mémorial
Haudainville
Landrecourt
Dugny

Verdun nevertheless remained a formidable obstacle with its powerful citadel, its ring of forts and its gullied wooded plateaux. Yet this is where the German army, led by General von Falkenhayn, decided to strike a heavy blow in February 1916 in the hope of weakening the French army, lifting their own morale and thwarting the offensive which they suspected the Allies to be preparing (it actually came in July on the Somme). The Kronprinz, Emperor William II's own son, was entrusted with the operation.

There were in fact two battles of Verdun: the first amounted to the German offensive, masterfully orchestrated, which began with a surprise attack and met with dogged French resistance; this situation led to a stalemate in which the role of the infantry was capital and soldiers on both sides fought with equal bravery, French determination making the difference in the end.

The second battle began with the French counter-offensive, just as fierce but less static, since the war had started to move again (Battle of the Somme, Russian offensive).

German offensive (February-August 1916) – It began on 21 February, 13km/8mi north of Verdun, with the heaviest concentratration of shelling ever experienced. The resistance was stronger than expected but the Germans progressed slowly and the Fort de Douaumont soon fell, thus becoming a threat to the city. General Pétain, who was made commander in chief of the Verdun forces, began to organise the defence of the city. Reinforcements and supplies were brought in via the only available route, Bar-le-Duc to Verdun, nicknamed the "**sacred way**".

The frontal attack was finally stopped on 26 February and, in March and April, German troops widened the front on both banks of the Meuse but failed to take several key positions.

There followed a savage war of attrition: forts, ruined villages or woods were taken over and over again at a terrible cost in human lives.

On 11 July, German troops finally received the order to remain on the defensive.

The Russian offensive and the Franco-British offensive on the Somme put an end to any hope the Germans may have had of taking the advantage at Verdun.

French counter-offensive (October 1916-October 1917) – Three brilliant but costly offensives enabled French troops to take back all lost ground:

– the **Bataille de Douaumont-Vaux** (24 October-2 November 1916) on the east bank,
– the **Bataille de Louvemont-Bezonvaux** (15-18 December 1916), also on the east bank which cleared the Vaux and Douaumont sectors once and for all.
– the **Bataille de la Cote 304 et du Mort-Homme** (20-24 August 1917) on the west bank; German troops were forced back to the positions they held on 22 February 1916 and tried in vain to counter-attack until well into October. The pressure on Verdun was released but it was only in September-October 1918, following the Franco-American offensive, that the front line was pushed back beyond its position of February 1916.

Because of its military and moral consequences, the Battle of Verdun marked the turning point of the war. The fierceness and atrocity of the fighting justified the name given to it: "l'enfer de Verdun" (Verdun's hell).

In less than two years, this battle involved several million soldiers and caused the death of 400 000 Frenchmen and almost as many Germans as well as several thousand American soldiers.

Several decades later, a huge area covering some 200km²/72sq mi on both banks of the Meuse still bears the marks of the fighting.

East bank of the Meuse
21km/13mi – about 3hr. Michelin map 241 folds 19 and 23

This was the main sector of the Battle, where the decisive turning point occurred.

Drive east along avenue de la 42e-Division then avenue du Maréchal-Joffre and leave Verdun by ② on the town plan, N 3 towards Étain.

Cimetière militaire du Faubourg-Pavé – Drive through le Faubourg-Pavé; on the left, there is a cemetery containing the gaves of 5 000 soldiers.

Turn left past the cemetery onto D 112 towards Mogeville.

On the right, 6km/3.7mi further on, stand the **Monument Maginot** and the Souville fort.

At the intersection of D 112 and D 913, turn right onto D 913 towards Verdun then left onto D 913ᴬ towards the Fort de Vaux.

The terrain is in a complete upheaval. On the right, slightly off the road, stands the **Monument des Fusillés de Tavannes**, a reminder of an episode of the Second World War *(it is possible to drive along the path to the monument).*

Fort de Vaux ⊘ – Thirst drove the garrison to surrender on 7 June 1916 after two months' heroic resistance; the fort was reoccupied by the French five months later. The tour enables visitors to see a number of galleries. From the top, there is a good view of the ossuary, cemetery and fort of Douaumont, the Côtes de la Meuse and Plaine de la Woëvre.

Return to D 913 and turn right towards Fleury and Douaumont.

On the left, the Souville fort, the last bastion guarding Verdun, can barely be seen. At the Chapelle Ste-Fine crossroads, the Monument du Lion marks the most forward position reached by the Germans.

Mémorial de Verdun ⊘ – Video films, an illustrated map and slide shows explain the various stages of the battle and a collection of uniforms, weapons, pieces of equipment and documents illustrate the fierce fighting which took place.

From the memorial, the Douaumont ossuary, cemetery and fort can be seen through a telescope.

A little further on, a stela marks the site of the former village of **Fleury-devant-Douaumont**, which was taken 16 times.

Turn right onto D 913[8] leading to Douaumont.

Fort de Douaumont ⊙ – The fort was stone-built on a height in 1885, (388m/1 273ft) which accounted for its strategic importance. Reinforced several times, it was covered with a layer of concrete 1m/3ft thick resting over a layer of sand also 1m/3ft thick. Taken by surprise at the beginning of the German offensive, it was recaptured by the French at the end of October.

The tour takes visitors through galleries, casemates and arsenals which show the importance of this fortress. A chapel marks the site of the walled-up gallery where 679 German soldiers, killed in the accidental explosion of an ammunition dump, were buried on 8 May 1916.

From the top of the fort, there is an overall view of the 1916 battlefield and of the ossuary.

Slightly further on, to the right, a chapel stands on the site of the village church of Douaumont completely destroyed during the initial German attack.

Return to D 913 and turn right.

Ossuaire de Douaumont ⊙ – The ossuary, which was erected to receive the unidentified remains of some 130 000 French and German soldiers killed during the battle, is the most important French monument of the 1914-1918 war. It consists of a long gallery (137m/150yd) comprising 18 bays, each housing two granite sarcophagi. The Catholic chapel is located beneath the main vault. At the centre of the monument stands the *Tour des morts* ("Tower of the dead"), 46m/151ft high, shaped like a shell and carved with four crosses. The first floor of the tower houses a small war museum. The tower is crowned by the light of the dead and a bell weighing 2.3t. At the top *(204 steps)*, viewing tables enable visitors to spot the different sectors of the battlefield through the windows.

Another room presents audio-visual programmes about heroism.

The 15 000 crosses of the **national cemetery** are lined up in front of the ossuary.

A small path starting on the left of the parking area, leads to the Fort de Thiaumont, taken many times during the battle.

Tranchée des Baïonnettes – A massive door leads to the monument built over the trench where, on 10 June 1916, two companies of the 137 infantry regiment were buried following intense shelling. The tip end of their rifles showing above ground was the only sign of their presence.

West bank of the Meuse

50km/31mi – about 2hr 30min. Michelin map 241 folds 19, 22 and 23

The fighting was just as fierce on the west bank. In September 1918, American troops led by General Pershing played a key role in this sector.

Drive out of Verdun northwest along D 38 to Chattancourt and turn right towards le Mort-Homme.

Le Mort-Homme – This wooded height was the site of fierce fighting. All the German attacks of March 1916 were halted on this ridge.

Return to Chattancourt, turn right onto D 38 and right again onto D 18 shortly after Esnes-en-Argonne; 2km/1.2mi further on, a path on the right leads to the Cote 304.

La Cote 304 – For nearly 14 months the Germans met unflinching resistance from the French who knew the considerable strategic importance of this site.

Butte de Montfaucon – This is the highest point of the area (336m/1 102ft); the village which stood at the top was fortified and used by the Germans as an observation point.

A **monument** ⊙ was erected by the American government to commemorate the victory of the 1st American army during the offensive of September-November 1918. A monumental staircase leads to a column (57m/187ft high, 235 steps) surmounted by a Statue of Liberty. From the top, there is an overall **view★** of the battlefield northwest of Verdun, including the Butte de Vauquois and Cote 304 with the Douaumont beacon in the distance. The ruins of the village of Montfaucon can be seen near the monument; the village was totally destroyed and rebuilt 100m/110yd further west.

Cimetière américain de Romagne-sous-Montfaucon – The American cemetery extending over 52ha/128 acres contains more than 14 000 graves in strict alignment in a setting of shaded lawns, a pond and flower beds. In the centre stands the chapel and the side galleries bear the names of the missing soldiers (954); in the right-hand gallery, a map showing the area of the battlefield has been engraved in the stone.

The road runs through the cemetery.

In Romagne, turn left onto D 998, left again onto D 946 to Varennes-en-Argonne and continue along D 38 for 5km/3mi then turn right.

Butte de Vauquois – *As you leave Vauquois, follow the surfaced path on the right which leads to the knoll. Park the car and walk up to the summit.*

VIGNORY★

Population 335
Michelin map 61 fold 20 or 241 fold 39

The village nestles inside a vale overlooked by the ruins of a 13C keep and 15C castle.

★**Église St-Étienne** – Built c 1000 by the lord of Vignory, this church is a rare example of mid-11C Romanesque architecture.

The square belfry is adorned with a storey of blind arcading surmounted by two storeys of twinned openings and topped by a stone cone covered with an octagonal roof.

Vignory – Nave of the Église St-Étienne

★ Interior – Although re-modelled, the church has retained its original aspect with a nave extending over nine bays and separated from the aisles by three-storey elevations: main arcading at ground level resting on rectangular piers, triforium above consisting of twinned openings separated by columns with carved capitals, and clerestory at the top.
The chancel, linked to the nave by a high triumphal arch, is divided into two parts: a forward area with two-storey elevations and an oven-vaulted apse separated from the ambulatory by seven columns; some of these are surmounted by capitals elaborately carved with lions, gazelles etc.

Between the 14C and 16C, five chapels were added to the south aisle.

The church contains a wealth of sculpture from the 14C, 15C and 16C. Note the 14C monumental statue of the Virgin carrying Jesus who is holding a bird in his hand. However, the most remarkable sculpture is to be seen in the first chapel of the south aisle: it consists of an altar front featuring the Coronation of the Virgin between St Peter and St Paul and an altarpiece illustrating scenes from the Passion. The same regional workshop (late 14C, 15C) produced a series of small Nativity scenes to be found in the fourth chapel.

Route des VINS★★★

Michelin map 87 folds 14 to 19 or 242 folds 19, 23, 27, 31 and 35

The itinerary, known as the Route des Vins (the Wine Road), winds its way from Marlenheim to Thann, the northern and southern gateways to Alsace where there are information centres about Alsatian vineyards and wines. The well-signposted road runs along the foothills of the Vosges crowned by old towers and ruined castles, through many famous villages and small towns scattered about the vineyards: Barr, Mittelbergheim, Andlau, Dambach-la-Ville, Bergheim, Ribeauvillé, Riquewihr, Turckheim, Eguisheim etc.

A tour of the vineyards at harvest time is a fascinating experience. The animation is at its height and tourists can fully appreciate the lifestyle of the local people deeply committed to their wine-growing activities.

Alsatian vineyards – Wine-growing in Alsace goes back to the 3C AD; since then, the region has been concerned with looking after its vineyards to the exclusion of any other form of agriculture. The landscape is characterised by terrace cultivation, with high stakes and low walls climbing the foothills of the Vosges. In the region entitled to the *appellation contrôlée* (label of origin), vineyards cover an area of 14 500ha/35 83 acres at an altitude varying from 200-400m/656-1 312ft.

The extremely variable annual production averages some 160 million bottles. Local life is centred on wine-growing, the work it involves and the festivities which punctuate the calendar of this activity involving 6 000 families. Alsatian vineyards produce a quality wine acknowledged by the area's three *appellations d'origine contrôlée*, Alsace, Alsace Grand Cru and Crémant d'Alsace. Great vintage years usually produce two prestigious specialities: *Vendanges tardives* ("late harvest") and *Sélections de grains nobles* ("selected grapes"), powerful wines with a deep aroma, made from over-ripe grapes.

Vines require a lot of care as wine-growers are constantly looking for the perfect harmony between the different types of vines and the soil. The numerous flower-decked villages dotted along the Wine Road, nestling round their church and town hall, are one of the most charming aspects of the Alsace region, no doubt enhanced as far as visitors are concerned by convivial wine-tasting opportunities.
St Stephen's Brotherhood, based in Kientzheim castle (see drive ② below) near Kaysersberg, awards high-quality seals to the best wines every year.

THE BAS-RHIN REGION

① From Marlenheim to Châtenois
68km/42mi – allow 4hr

Between Marlenheim and Rosheim, the road stays clear of the foothills of the Vosges.

Marlenheim – Renowned wine-growing centre.

Wangen – Wangen is a typical wine-growing village with twisting lanes lined with old houses and arched gates. Until 1830 the villagers had to pay St Stephen's abbey in Strasbourg an annual tax calculated in litres of wine. The *Fête de la Fontaine* ("Fountain Festival") is a reminder of this ancient custom: on the Sunday following 3 July, wine flows freely from Wangen's fountain.

Westhoffen – Typical wine-growing village.

Avolsheim – This village has retained an old baptistery and, 500m/547yd south, a famous church believed to be the oldest sanctuary in Alsace.
The **Chapelle St-Ulrich** is a former baptistery built c 1000 in the shape of a clover leaf, containing fine 13C frescoes depicting the Trinity, the four Evangelists and scenes from the Old Testament.
The Église St-Pierre, known also as Dompeter (ad Dominum Petrum), stands in rural surroundings, at the centre of a small cemetery. Although partly rebuilt in the 18C and 19C, the church, surmounted by an octagonal belfry, is a moving example of early-Romanesque architecture (the edifice was consecrated by Pope Léon IX in 1049). Original features include the base of the belfry-porch with the interesting narthex and doorway, the side doorways with carved lintels and, inside, the massive square piers supporting heavy rounded arcades.

★**Molsheim** – *See MOLSHEIM.*

★**Rosheim** – *See ROSHEIM.*

Driving out of Rosheim, note (ahead and slightly to the left) the ruins of Landsberg castle crowning the first foothills of the Vosges. The road runs through hilly terrain offering numerous viewpoints across the Plaine d'Alsace, with castles perched on promontories (Ottrott, Ortenbourg, Ramstein).

Boersch – This typical Alsatian village has retained three ancient gates and a picturesque **square**★ lined with old houses, the most remarkable being the town hall dating from the 16C. A Renaissance well marks the entrance of the square.

Ottrott – *See Région du HOHWALD: Drive ②.*

★★**Obernai** – *See OBERNAI.*

Barr – Barr is an industrial town (famous tanneries) and an important wine-growing centre producing quality wines: Sylvaner, Riesling and above all Gewürz-traminer. The annual wine fair is held in the town hall, a fine 17C building decorated with a loggia and a carved balcony; go into the courtyard to admire the rear part.
A former partly seigneurial and partly middle-class residence known as the **Folie Marco** ⊙, houses a **museum** containing 17C-19C furniture, porcelain, pewter and mementoes of local history; a section is devoted to *la schlitte (see Vallée de MUNSTER: Muhlbach).*

Mittelbergheim – See Région du HOHWALD: Drive ②.

★**Andlau** – *See ANDLAU.*

Itterswiller – The flower-decked houses of this charming wine-growing village climbing up the hillside are lined along the high street. A footpath leads visitors on a tour of the vineyards (about 1hr, viewpoint).

Dambach-la-Ville – This renowned wine-growing centre (Frankstein vintages) lies in a picturesque setting overlooked by wooded heights. The attractive town centre with its flower-decked timber-framed houses was once surrounded by ramparts, of which three town gates are still standing.
Turn left 400m/437yd beyond the Porte Haute (upper gate).
At the top of the road, turn right onto a path which rises to the **Chapelle St-Sébastien**. Extended view of the Plaine d'Alsace and the vineyards. Inside, the late-17C Baroque altar in carved wood illustrates the Holy Family; the Holy Spirit and the Heavenly Father can be seen above, with St Sebastian further up. Outside, on the east gable end, note the 16C ossuary.

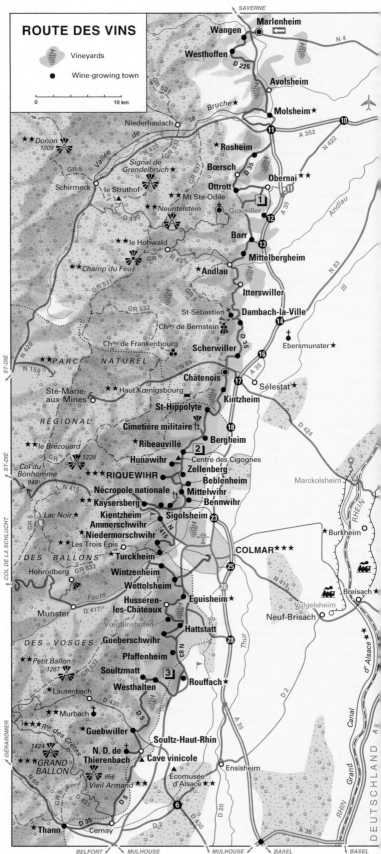

ROUTE DES VINS

Vineyards

Wine-growing town

0   10 km

SAVERNE

Marlenheim
Wangen
Westhoffen
D 225
Avolsheim
N 4
GR 531
la Bruche ★
Molsheim ★
Niederhaslach
A 352
10
N 422
11
Vallée
de
N 420
GR 532
GR 537
★★ Donon
1009
Rosheim ★
Bœrsch
D 35
Ottrott
Obernai ★★
N 422
Andlau
Signal de
Grendelbruch ★
GR 5
Schirmeck
le Struthof
1
A 35
12
Goxwiller
★ Mt Ste-Odile
★★ Neuntelstein
D 130
Barr
13
Mittelbergheim
★★ le Hohwald
GR 5   D 425
N 83
★ Champ du Feu
★ Andlau
Itterswiller
GR 531
GR 532
St-Sébastien
Dambach-la-Ville
14
Ch⁰ᵘ de Bernstein
Ebersmunster ★
N 420
Ch⁰ᵘ de Frankenbourg
Scherwiller
N 159
★★ PARC   NATUREL
D 35
16
M 59
D 424
★★ Haut Kœnigsbourg
Châtenois
17
Sélestat ★
Ste-Marie-
aux-Mines
RÉGIONAL
Kintzheim
A 35
ST-DIÉ
St-Hippolyte
Cimetière militaire ††
18
★★ le Brézouard
★ Ribeauvillé
Bergheim
ST-DIÉ
1228
Hunawihr
2
Centre des Cigognes
Col du
Bonhomme
949
★★★ RIQUEWIHR
Zellenberg
Marckolsheim
N 415
Nécropole nationale ††
Beblenheim
RHIN
★ Kaysersberg
Mittelwihr
Bennwihr
D 424
Lac Noir
Kientzheim
Sigolsheim
23
Burkheim ★
Ammerschwihr
Niedermorschwihr
N 415
DES   BALLONS
Les Trois Épis
COLMAR ★★★
Breisach
Hohrodberg
GR 532
Turckheim
25
Wintzenheim
Völgelsheim
Fecht
26
Wettolsheim
N 415
Neuf-Brisach
Munster
D 417
Husseren-
les-Châteaux
Eguisheim ★
DES   VOSGES
Vœgtlinshofen
Hattstatt
d' Alsace ★★
Gueberschwihr
N 83
28
Thur
★★ Petit Ballon
1267
Pfaffenheim
3
GR 532
Soultzmatt
Rouffach ★
★ Lautenbach
Westhalten
D 430
D 5
★★ Murbach †
A 35
D 2
★★★ Rte des Crêtes
1424
★ Guebwiller
GÉRARDMER
★★ GRAND
BALLON
N. D. de †
Thierenbach
Soultz-Haut-Rhin
956
▲ Cave vinicole
Vieil Armand ★★
Écomusée
d'Alsace ★★
Ensisheim
N 66
GR 5
D 431
D 5
6
D 20
D 2
D 430
A 36
Canal   Grand   RHIN
Canal   A 5
★ Thann
Cernay
DEUTSCHLAND
BELFORT   MULHOUSE   MULHOUSE   BASEL   BASEL

Itterswiller

The path continues (2hr on foot there and back) to the ruined **Château de Bernstein** (12C-13C), built on a granite ridge (residential building, pentagonal keep). There is a fine view of the Plaine d'Alsace.

Scherwiller – This is the place where, in 1525, Duke Antoine of Lorraine won a battle against rebellious peasants, which put an end to their uprisal.

Châtenois – Note the unusual Romanesque belfry, surmounted by a spire and four timber bartizans, and the picturesque 15C gatehouse known as the *Tour des Sorcières* ("witches' tower") crowned by a stork's nest.

THE HAUT-RHIN REGION

2 From Châtenois to Colmar

54km/34mi – allow 5hr

Châtenois – *See above.*

As far south as Ribeauvillé, the road is overlooked by numerous castles: the imposing mass of Haut-Kœnigsbourg, the ruins of Kintzheim, Frankenbourg, St-Ulrich, Girsberg and Haut-Ribeaupierre.

Kintzheim – *See SÉLESTAT: Excursions.*

St-Hippolyte – This village is most attractive with its numerous flower-decked fountains and its lovely Gothic church dating from the 14C and 15C.

Bergheim – The Porte Haute, a 14C fortified gate, leads inside this wine-growiing village shaded by an old lime tree believed to date back to 1300. The northern section of the medieval wall, which protected Bergheim from the Burgundians in 1470, is still standing with three of its original round towers. The village has many old houses and a picturesque market square adorned with a lovely fountain and decorated with flowers in summer.
The red-sandstone **church** ⊙ has retained 14C features (apse, chancel and lower part of the belfry); the rest dates from the 18C as does the town hall.

Cimetière militaire allemand – *1.2km/0.7mi north of Bergheim along a road branching off D 1B on the left.* Built on a hillside, the cemetery contains the graves (facing the fatherland) of German soldiers killed during the Second World War. From the cross standing at the top, the fine **view**★ extends westwards to the heights of the Vosges, northwards to Haut-Kœnigsbourg castle and eastwards to Sélestat and the Plaine d'Alsace.

★**Ribeauvillé** – *See RIBEAUVILLÉ.*

Beyond Ribeauvillé, the road rises halfway up the hillsides offering a wider panorama of the Plaine d'Alsace. The heart of the Alsatian wine-growing centre is situated here, between Ribeauvillé and Colmar. Charming villages and famous wine-growing centres are scattered across the rolling hills lying on the edge of the Vosges.

Hunawihr – The square belfry of the church is as massive as a keep. The church is surrounded by a 14C wall which had only one entrance defended by a tower. The six bastions flanking the wall can still be seen. From the church, there is a good view of the conical Taennchel summit, of the three castles of Ribeauvillé and of the Plaine d'Alsace.

The church is used for Catholic and Protestant church services, which explains the way the nave looks. The chancel has been reserved for Catholic parishioners since the reign of Louis XIV. The chapel situated on the left of the chancel contains 15C-16C frescoes depicting the life of St Nicholas, the miracles he accomplished and the canonization of St Huna.

A centre devoted to the return of storks (**Centre de réintroduction des cigognes** ⊘) has been trying to encourage storks to remain in Alsace throughout the winter and to nest at the centre or in nearby villages. More than 200 storks are fed and looked after in the centre. Every afternoon, there is a show involving various animals who are particularly clever at fishing: cormorants, penguins, sea-lions and otters. In 1991, a centre for the safeguard and reproduction of otters was created.

The **Jardin des Papillons exotiques vivants** ⊘ includes more than 150 species of exotic butterflies of all sizes and colours, flying about freely inside a hothouse full of luxuriant vegetation (orchids, passion flowers).

A short distance from Hunawihr, at the top of a hill, stands the small village of **Zellenberg** overlooking Riqhewihr and the vineyards. A **historic trail** *(40min, booklet available from the town hall or the tourist offices of Ribeauvillé and Riquewihr)* leads visitors round the most interesting old buildings.

★★★**Riquewihr** – *See RIQUEWIHR.*

Beblenheim – The village lies close to the Sonnenglantz ("Sunshine"), a famous hillside producing high-quality wines on its 35ha/86 acres of vineyards (Alsatian Tokay, Muscatel and Gewürztraminer).

Mittelwihr – At the southern end of the village stands the "Mur des Fleurs Martyres", a wall which, throughout the German occupation was decked with blue, white and red flowers as a token of Alsatian loyalty.

The hillsides all around enjoy a micro-climate which causes almond trees to flower and yield ripe fruit. The reputation of the Riesling and Gewürztraminer made in this area is steadily growing.

Benwihr – This is another famous wine-growing village, whose modern **church** is brightly lit by a colourful stained-glass window stretching right across the south side. Note the soft tones of the stained glass decorating the chapel on the left.

Sigolsheim – This is supposed to be the place where, in 833, the sons of Louis the Meek, Charlemagne's son, met before capturing their father to have him imprisoned.

The Église St-Pierre-et-St-Paul dates from the 12C. The Romanesque doorway is adorned with a tympanum carved in a style similar to those of Kaysersberg and Andlau.

Follow rue de la 1re-Armée (the main street) leading, beyond the Couvent des Capucins, to the national necropolis.

Nécropole nationale de Sigolsheim – *5min on foot there and back from the parking area; 124 steps.*
The necropolis, standing on top of a hill and surrounded by vineyards, contains the graves of 1 684 French soldiers killed in 1944. From the central platform, there is a splendid **panorama★** of the nearby summits and castles, as well as of Colmar and the Plaine d'Alsace.

Kientzheim – This wine-growing village has retained several interesting medieval buildings, fortifications, old houses, squares, wells and sundials.

The **Porte Basse** is a fortified gate surmounted by a grinning head which was placed there as a warning to attackers that they did not stand a chance to get past this mighty tower. The medieval **castle**, remodelled in the 16C, is the headquarters of St Stephen's Brotherhood, the official body controlling the quality of Alsatian wines. Housed in an outbuilding, the **Musée du Vignoble et des Vins d'Alsace** ⊘ is devoted to all aspects of wine-growing from vineyards to wines. Note the monumental winepress and some rare tools, no longer in use.

Inside the church, next to a 14C statue of the Virgin (north-side altar), are the **tombstones★** of Lazarus von Schwendi (d 1583), who brought Tokay vines back from Hungary, and of his son *(see KAYSERSBERG).*

The **Chapelle Sts-Felix-et-Régule** contains naive paintings on canvas and on wood, dating from 1667 to 1865.

★★**Kaysersberg** – *See KAYSERSBERG.*

Ammerschwihr – Situated at the foot of vine-covered hills, Ammerschwihr was destroyed by fire following the bombings of December 1944 and January 1945. The town was rebuilt in traditional Alsatian style but it has nevertheless retained one or two interesting old buildings. The Gothic **Église St-Martin** contains some fine sculptures, Christ between the Virgin and St John at the beginning of the Chancel and Christ with palm branches (15C-16C) in the chapel along the north aisle. A beautiful Renaissance staircase leads from the south aisle up to the gallery. The chancel is lit by modern stained glass.

The **Porte Haute** on the western edge of the town, has a square tower decorated with the arms of the town and a painted sundial and crowned by a stork's nest.

★**Niedermorschwihr** – This lovely village set among vineyards has a modern church with a 13C spiral belfry. The high street is lined with old houses adorned with oriels and wooden balconies.

Between Niedermorschwihr and Turckheim, the road winds its way across a hill covered with vineyards and offers a wide view of the plain.

★**Turckheim** – See TURCKHEIM.

Wintzenheim – This famous wine-growing centre (Hengst vintage) is a pleasant city, fortified in 1275, which has retained a few old houses (rue des Laboureurs) and the ancient manor of the Knights of St John, now the town hall.

★★**Colmar** – See COLMAR.

③ From Colmar to Thann
59km/37mi – allow 3hr

★★**Colmar** – See COLMAR.
Leave Colmar by ⑤ on the town plan, along D 417.

Wettolsheim – This village claims the honour of being the birthplace of Alsatian wine-growing, which was introduced here during the Roman occupation and later spread to the rest of the country.

★**Eguisheim** – See EGUISHEIM.
The picturesque road is overlooked by the ruins of the "three castles" of Eguisheim and the view extends over a wide area of the Plaine d'Alsace.

Husseren-les-Châteaux – This is the highest point of the Alsatian vineyards (alt 380m/1 247ft). Husseren is the starting point of a tour of the three castles of Eguisheim *(see EGUISHEIM: Route des Cinq Châteaux)* towering above the village.

Hattstatt – This once-fortified old village has an early-11C church with a 15C chancel containing a stone altar of the same period. The baptistery also dates from the 15C. Note the fine Renaissance calvary on the left-hand side of the nave. The pulpit and the altarpiece are Baroque.

Gueberschwihr – A magnificent Romanesque belfry (all that remains of an early-12C church) overlooks this peaceful village, camped on a hillside and surrounded by vineyards.

Pfaffenheim – See ROUFFACH: Excursion.

★**Rouffach** – See ROUFFACH.
Shortly beyond Rouffach, the Grand Ballon *(see Route des CRÊTES: Drive ②)* comes into view.

Westhalten – Picturesque village surrounded by vineyards and orchards, with two fountains and several old houses.

Soultzmatt – Charming city lying along the banks of the Ohmbach. The local Sylvaner, Riesling and Gewürztraminer are highly rated as are the mineral springs. The **Château de Wagenbourg** stands nearby.

★**Guebwiller** – See GUEBWILLER.

Soultz-Haut-Rhin – See SOULTZ-HAUT-RHIN.
Turn right onto D 5¹.

Basilique Notre-Dame de Thierenbach – The onion-shaped belfry can be seen from afar. The basilica was built in 1723 in the Austrian Baroque style by the architect Peter Thumb. An important pilgrimage, going back to the 8C and dedicated to Notre-Dame-de-l'Espérance takes place in the church. Major events include Christmas celebrations for children every Sunday in January and feast days dedicated to Mary, in particular the 15 August. The basilica contains two Pietà: the miracle-working Virgin dating from 1350 and the Mater Dolorosa dating from 1510 situated in the Reconciliation chapel.
Return to Soultz-Haut-Rhin and follow D 5 towards Cernay.

Cave vinicole du Vieil-Armand – This cooperative, situated on the outskirts of Soultz, groups 130 wine-growers looking after 150ha/371 acres of vineyards.
Two great wines are produced: Rangen, the most southern of Alsatian wines and Ollwiller, grown just beneath Vieil Armand. The cooperative organises tastings of regional wines. In the basement, the wine-grower's museum contains equipment used in the old days in vineyards and cellars.
Continue along D 5 then turn right onto D 35.

★**Thann** – See THANN.

VITRY-LE-FRANÇOIS

Population 17 032
Michelin map 61 fold 8 or 241 fold 30

Vitry-le-François is the capital of the **Perthois** area, a fertile plain extending from the River Marne to the Trois-Fontaines Forest. The town occupies a strategic position on the east bank of the Marne, at the foot of the Champagne limestone cliff and at the intersection of the Marne-Rhine and Marne-Saône canals.

Vitry was built by King Francis I who gave it his name. He commissioned an engineer from Bologna who designed the grid plan, the fortifications reinforced by bastions and a citadel destroyed in the 17C.

In 1940, the city was bombed and pounded by artillery fire to the point that 90% of it was destroyed. After the war, it was rebuilt along the lines of the original plan.

SIGHTS

Église Notre-Dame ⊘ – The 17C-18C church overlooking the place d'Armes is an interesting example of the Classical style with a harmonious and well-proportioned west front flanked by twinned towers adorned with scrolls and surmounted by flame vases. Inside, note the imposing nave and transept prolonged by a late-19C apse. The furniture includes a baldaquined altar, an organ case originally in the Abbaye de Trois-Fontaines and an 18C pulpit and churchwardens' pew in carved wood. The Crucifixion, painted in 1737 by Jean Restout is worth seeing in the last chapel along the north aisle.

Hôtel de ville – The town hall is housed in the 17C buildings of a former convent.

Porte du Pont – Fine triumpal arch (1748) erected in honour of Louis XIV. Taken down in 1938, it was only re-erected in 1984.

EXCURSIONS

★**St-Amand-sur-Fion** – *10km/6mi north along the Route de Châlons (N 44) then D 260.* Lying on the banks of the River Fion, the village has retained timber-framed houses, six mills and a wash-house. The **church**★ is a successful mixture of Romanesque (central doorway, part of the nave) and Gothic (chancel and nave) styles. The grace of the lofty interior is enhanced by the pink colour of the stone. The apse is pierced by windows on three storeys, the middle storey being a triforium which continues along the transept showing characteristics of the Flamboyant style. The beautiful arcaded porch dates from the 15C. Note the carved capitals and the 17C rood beam.

Vitry-en-Perthois – *4km/2.5mi along D 982.*
This village was rebuilt on the site of a medieval city destroyed by fire in 1544. From the bridge spanning the River Saulx, there is a pastoral view of the river with a mill.

Ponthion – *10km/6mi northeast along D 982 then D 995.*
Situated between the Marne-Rhine canal and the River Saulx, Ponthion has a church dating from the 11C and 15C, preceded by a lovely 12C porch. In 754, a meeting between Pope Stephen II and Pepin the Short, the first Carolingian king, led to the creation of the Papal States.

VITTEL‡‡

Population 6 296
Michelin map 62 fold 14 or 242 fold 29 – Local map see p 332

This sought-after spa resort owes its fame to the therapeutic qualities of its water and its situation at the heart of a picturesque wooded area. The spa establishment lies outside the town; Vittel water is used mainly for the treatment of arthritis, gout, migraine and allergies, as well as kidney and liver disorders.

Institut de l'eau Perrier Vittel – An exhibition entitled "Water and Life" is housed in the former baths built by Charles Garnier in 1884; it illustrates the scientific, technical and industrial aspects of water.

★**Parc** (BY) – This landscaped park, covering an area of 25ha/62 acres, is adorned with a bandstand where numerous concerts take place during the season. It is adjacent to vast sportsgrounds (horse racing, polo, golf, tennis etc). The new Palais des Congrès (Congress Hall) was inaugurated in 1970.
Situated on the western edge of town, the **Usine d'embouteillage** ⊘ (bottling factory) (AZ) of Vittel SA, open to the public, shows the production of plastic and glass bottles and the bottling and packaging process with a turnover of 5.4 million bottles of different sizes per day.

HIKE

Croix de mission de Norroy and Chapelle Ste-Anne – *3hr on foot there and back. Leave Vittel northwards along avenue A.-Bouloumié (AY 3).*
With the riding centre on your right, follow a surfaced path on the left which runs across pastures then rises through woods. The itinerary crosses D 18 before reaching the Croix de mission de Norroy after a steep climb.

Croix de mission de Norroy – The view extends northwest to the Vair and Mouzon valleys, south to a ridge known as the Crête des Faucilles and southeast to the Vosges summits.

Turn left and walk through a small wood.

Chapelle Ste-Anne – The chapel stands on the edge of the Châtillon Forest, beside a fine oak tree. The unassuming building contains a 16C altarpiece of the twelve apostles (the heads are broken). Fine view northwest of the Vair Valley.

Continue straight on.

Walk through the Châtillon Forest. As you come out of the woods, there is another view of Vittel. *Return to the town.*

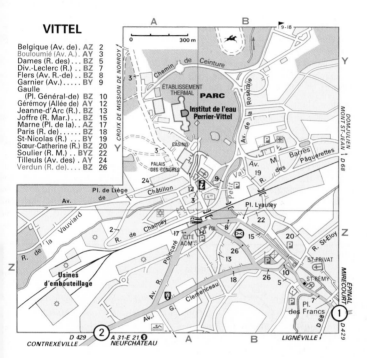

VITTEL

Belgique (Av. de). **AZ** 2
Bouloumié (Av. A.). **AY** 3
Dames (R. des) ... **BZ** 5
Div.-Leclerc (R.) .. **BZ** 7
Flers (Av. R.-de) .. **BZ** 8
Garnier (Av.) ..... **BY** 9
Gaulle
  (Pl. Général-de) **BZ** 10
Gérémoy (Allée de) **AY** 12
Jeanne-d'Arc (R.). **BZ** 13
Joffre (R. Mar.) ... **BZ** 15
Marne (Pl. de la).. **AZ** 17
Paris (R. de)...... **BZ** 18
St-Nicolas (R.) ... **BY** 19
Sœur-Catherine (R.) **BZ** 20
Soulier (R. M.) .. **BYZ** 22
Tilleuls (Av. des) . **AY** 24
Verdun (R. de).... **BZ** 26

EXCURSIONS

Domjulien – *8km/5mi northeast along D 68.*
The 15C-16C church, although considerably remodelled, contains some remarkable sculptures mainly situated in the north aisle: an altarpiece (1541) representing the Crucifixion and the twelve apostles; an early-16C Entombment with angels carrying the instruments of Christ's Passion; statues of St George (16C) and St Julian.
A fine 15C statue of the Virgin and Child playing with an angel stands on the right-hand side altar.

FORÊT DOMANIALE DE DARNEY

80km/50mi round tour – about 3hr

Leave Vittel by ① on the town plan and drive 3.5km/2.2mi along D 429 then turn right.

The forested massif covers an area of 15 000ha/37 067 acres of which 8 000ha/19 768 acres form the state-owned Darney Forest. Although beeches are the dominant species, the forest still yields oak timber of exceptional quality.

Thuillières – The **castle** ⊙ was built by the architect Germain Boffrand (1667-1754) for his own use when he was working in the area.
Just beyond Thuillières on the left, the chapel of a former hermitage can be seen nestling inside the picturesque vale of Chèvre-Roche.

Darney – It was here that, in June 1918, President Poincaré of France, speaking in the name of the Allies, declared the independence of Czechoslovakia. A small **Czechoslovak museum** 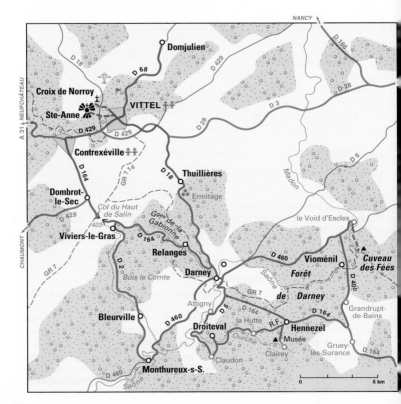 is housed in the former town hall, known as the "castle".

The church was consecrated in 1789; it contains some fine woodwork, particularly in the chancel.

On the way out of town, note, on the left, an 18C monumental stone calvary.

Continue along D 164 then turn right onto D 5.

The road goes through Attigny then winds its way along the wooded valley of the River Saône.

In Claudon, turn left onto D 5^E leading to Droiteval.

Droiteval – The village has retained the church of the former Cistercian abbey founded in 1128.

In Droiteval, turn right by a flower-decked property situated at the end of a small lake and continue along a narrow scenic road which follows the River Ourche.

Beyond the Senennes forest lodge, the path turns left then right and carries on past La Hutte and Thiétry before reaching Hennezel.

Hennezel – This village situated at the heart of the forest once had 19 glassworks founded in the 15C by glass-blowers from Bohemia.

South of Hennezel *(1.5km/0.9mi)*, just before Clairey, the small **Musée de la Résidence** illustrates various crafts connected with forestry as well as local resistance during the Second World War.

Drive east along D 164 to Gruey-lès-Surance and turn left.

The monument, standing across the road from Grandrupt-de-Bains, is dedicated to the memory of 117 members of the Resistance who died in concentration camps.

Vioménil – The source of the River Saône is situated nearby.

From Vioménil, drive along D 40 to rejoin D 460 and turn right; continue beyond the D 3 intersection to the bend preceding the village of Void-d'Escles. In that bend, a forest road branches off and follows the Madon Valley to the Cuveau des Fées (2km/1.2mi).

Cuveau des Fées – *1hr 30min on foot there and back.* Leave the car at the beginning of the path climbing to the new Chapelle St-Martin and the cave of the same name (it is dangerous to venture into the cave), both situated at the entrance of the secluded vale where the Madon takes its source, a place which has had religious meaning since time immemorial. From there, another path climbs the left-hand slope of the vale to the Cuveau des Fées, a strange flat rock carved by human hands to form an octagonal basin over 2m/6ft in diameter, whose base might have been used by druids for their sacrifices;

Return the same way to D 460 and follow it the Darney. From there it is easy to return to Vittel.

LA VÔGE

62km/38mi round tour – about 1hr 30min

Leave Vittel by ② on the town plan along D 429 which runs through the wooded area of the Grand Ban.

This sandstone region, known as la Vôge, marking the transition between the Vosges mountains and the Lorraine plateau, has retained part of its thick mantle of forest which, in the past, contributed to its isolation.

Contrexéville – *(see Introduction: Architecture and art)*. Known since the 18C, this popular spa town lying in wooded surroundings has five mineral springs used in the treatment of kidney and liver diseases, excess of cholesterol and obesity. In addition, the thermal establishment proposes slimming and fitness formulae.
The resort is also the ideal starting point of excursions through the region. The **Lac de la Folie** (1.5km/0.9mi northwest) is a large expanse of water (12ha/30 acres) surrounded by woods, with fishing facilities *(see Practical information)*.

Dombrot-le-Sec – Inside the **church** ⊙, note the massive piers, some with carved capitals, the fine gallery, the 18C wrought-iron work (rood beam and chancel balustrade), the 14C Virgin and Child and the 16C statue of St Anne.
The road goes across the Col du Haut de Salin (spot height: 403m/1 322ft).

Viviers-le-Gras – Beautiful 18C fountains.

Turn right onto D 2.

Bleurville – The Romans built baths here.

In Bleurville, take rue St-Pierre leading up to the church then follow rue Bézout on the left and leave the village towards Monthureux-sur-Saône.

Monthureux-sur-Saône – This village, built on a rock spur, has retained some of its old houses. The parish **church**, rebuilt in the 16C, contains an **Entombment★** (Rhenish School) with life-size characters in polychrome wood round the central figure of Christ lying down.

Darney – *See Forêt domaniale de Darney above.*

Relanges – Interesting **church**. The porch columns and west-front gable date from the 11C; the transept, apses and tower from the 12C; the nave and aisles were rebuilt in the 16C. The east end and the square belfry towering over the crossing are particularly noteworthy.
The road goes through the forested massif of Bois le Comte and follows a narrow valley known as the **Gorges de la Gabionne**.

Drive along D 164 back to Contrexéville then along D 429 to Vittel.

Parc Naturel Régional des
VOSGES DU NORD ★★

Michelin map 87 folds 2, 3 and 14 or 242 folds 11, 12, 15, 16 and 19

Vosges du Nord – The northern Vosges are relatively low yet often steep mountains which differ considerably from the rest of the massif. Their sandstone cover has been torn open by deep valleys and shaped into horizontal plateaux or rolling hills generally less than 500m/1 640ft high.
Erosion has carved the sandstone crust forming isolated jagged rocks with strange shapes reminiscent of towers, giant mushrooms or huge arches.
Apart from these rocks, real fortresses still stand on the densely forested heights. One of them, Fleckenstein castle *(see drive 2 below)* makes an excellent viewpoint from which to survey the Vosges du Nord.
A detour south of Wissembourg via Seebach, Hunspach and Hoffen will acquaint visitors with charming Alsatian villages where they may see some lovely costumes or take part in local merrymaking *(messti)*.

The nature park – Created in 1976, the nature park includes the northern part of the Vosges massif. Covering an area of more than 120 000ha/296 532 acres, it extends from the north of the Lorraine plateau to the Plaine d'Alsace and from the German border in the north to the A4 Metz-Strasbourg motorway in the south.

Parc Naturel Régional des VOSGES DU NORD

Forests covering more than 60% of the whole area consist of beeches, oaks, pines and spruces. Valleys are dotted with lakes and meadows. The purpose of the park is to safeguard the natural heritage, preserve the quality of life and enable the public to enjoy it.

Various activities (hikes, riding tours, bike tours, courses in nature discovery, themed excursions, lying in wait for game...) enable visitors to discover local flora and fauna in their natural environment and to get an insight into the lifestyle and economic activities of the region.

The park comprises 101 municipalities, some 30 ruined castles and fortresses, some of the works of the Maginot Line, technical museums (the Meisenthal Glass and Crystal Museum, the oil museum in Merkwiller) and museums of popular art (painted pictures in Pfaffenhoffen, cake tins in La Petite-Pierre).

These itineraries across the forested sandstone Vosges are meant to enable visitors to see a few monuments and admire some of the most typical landscapes in the region.

The Parc naturel régional des Vosges du Nord has been designated by UNESCO as one of the biosphere's world reserves.

THE HANAU REGION

① From Saverne to Niederbronn

141km/88mi – allow 4hr 30min

★**Saverne** – *See SAVERNE.*

Soon after leaving Saverne via Ottersthal, D 115 crosses the green Muhlbach Vale then passes beneath the motorway.

St-Jean-Saverne – *See ST-JEAN-SAVERNE.*

Just beyond St-Jean-de-Saverne, the ruins of Haut-Barr castle can be seen overlooking Saverne from a wooded height; more to the right are the equally impressive ruins of Griffon castle.

Bear left towards Dossenheim-sur-Zinsel.

★**Neuwiller-lès-Saverne** – *See NEUWILLER-LÈS-SAVERNE.*

Bouxwiller – This small town was, until 1791, the capital of the county of Hanau-Lichtenberg, extending across the Rhine. The princes' castle did not survive the Revolution, but the picturesque streets are lined with houses of the German Renaissance. Part of the ramparts have also been restored.

The **Musée du pays de Hanau** ☉ houses collections of painted furniture, glassware from Bouxwiller, reconstructions of interiors...

The **church** ☉, dating from the 17C contains a fine **pulpit**★ (c 1600) carved in stone and painted, an organ by Silbermann with an ornate organ case, a seigneurial box decorated with stuccowork and woodwork.

A **geological trail**, 6km/3.7mi long, extremely rich in fossils, leads to the summit of Bastberg offering views of the town (viewing tables). The summit is also accessible by car from Imbsheim *(from Bouxwiller, follow D 6 then turn right just before Imbsheim).*

Festivities in Bouxwiller: in December, "Christmas in the Hanau region" (Christmas market, see Calendar of events).

From Bouxwiller, D 6 and D 7 lead to Weiterswiller.

Beyond Weiterswiller, the picturesque road runs through the forest.

A detour via la Petite-Pierre and Imsthal Lake is recommended.

★**La Petite-Pierre** – *See la PETITE-PIERRE.*

Étang d'Imsthal – *The path leading to the lake branches off D 178 2.5km/1.5mi from la Petite-Pierre.*

The lake, lying at the bottom of a basin in the middle of pastureland ringed by forests, offers a charming outing *(parking reserved for hotel clients).*

Return to D 178, turn left then right onto D 122.

Graufthal – In this hamlet of the Zinsel Valley, you can see troglodyte houses dug into the red-sandstone cliffs (70m/230ft high). They were inhabited until 1958.

Return to La Petite-Pierre and follow the Ingwiller road leading down into the Mittelbach Valley. Beyond Sparsbach, the forest gives way to cultivated areas.

Beyond Ingwiller, D 919 follows the Moder Valley. Drive 3.5km/2.2mi northwest then turn right onto D 181.

Château de Lichtenberg ⊙ – Follow the Lichtenberg high street prolonged by D 257 to the path leading to the castle and leave the car.

The castle, which has retained its 13C keep, was restored following damage caused by shelling during the 1870 Franco-Prussian War.

Reipertswiller – The old **Église St-Jacques** overlooking the village has a 12C square belfry and a Gothic chancel built c 1480 by the last member of the Lichtenberg family.

Rejoin D 919 in Wimmenau.

It is in the area of **Wingen-sur-Moder** that the Lalique crystal and glassworks are situated.

Just before leaving Wingen, turn right onto D 256.

The picturesque cliffroad overlooks densely forested slopes furrowed by small green valleys.

Pierre des 12 apôtres – This standing stone is very old but it was only carved in the 18C following a vow. Under the cross, one can see the twelve Apostles in groups of three.

From the **Colonne de Wingen**, there is a very fine view of the Meisenthal Valley.

Turn left onto D 83 towards Meisentha.

Meisenthal – In the centre of the village, the former glassworks (closed in 1970) house the **Maison du verre et du cristal** ⊙, a glass and crystal museum presenting a reconstruction of the manufacturing process (ovens, documentary film) and glassware produced by the works since the 18C.

In Soucht, 2km/1.2mi beyond Meisenthal, a former workshop houses a **Musée du Sabotier** ⊙, a clog-makers' museum.

Goetzenbruck – The glass industry is the main activity of this community; important factory producing glasses for spectacles.

Turn left onto D 37^B.

St-Louis-lès-Bitche – The former **cristalleries de St-Louis**, ⊙ founded in 1767, produce a variety of ornaments and objects used at the table.

Return to Goetzenbruck. As you leave the village, note the view of the wooded heights surrounding Baerenthal.

Baerenthal – This charming village is situated on the north bank of the River Zinsel. It is possible to go round the Baerenthal Lake, a nature reserve with an exceptionally rich flora. An observation tower makes it possible to look at birdlife, particularly in spring and autumn (migrating birds).

In Lemberg, turn right onto D 36.

The road is narrow and winding. After Mouterhouse, it follows the **Zinsel du Nord**, a charming valley once dotted with numerous metalworks belonging to the De Dietrich family, now almost all gone.

Leave the valley at Zinswiller and turn left onto D 28.

Oberbronn – Picturesque village set against wooded slopes.

Beyond Oberbronn, you will see, on the left, the ruins of Wasenbourg castle.

‡‡ **Niederbronn-les-Bains** – *See NIEDERBRONN-LES-BAINS.*

CASTLE COUNTRY

Situated on the borders of the German palatinate, of Lorraine and of Alsace, this area is dotted with ruined castles built during the 12C and early 13C by the powerful dukes of Alsace, the Hohenstaufens, or by noble landowners who contested their authority. The castles were destroyed or abandoned even before the 18C. Today, their scattered ruins are full of romantic atmosphere.

PRACTICAL INFORMATION

A wide range of information concerning the Parc naturel régional des Vosges du Nord is available from the Association pour le développement des Vosges du Nord, maison du Parc, 67290 la Petite-Pierre, ☎ 03 88 70 46 55.

The information includes in particular: a brochure entitled *Séjours Découverte* (staying in the nature park), topoguides *Les oiseaux* (birds), *Cerfs et chevreuils* (deer and roe-deer), or *Châteaux forts* (castles).

The association also provides details about hiking without luggage (on foot or by bicycle) from hotel to hotel within the park (3 to 12-day themed stays).

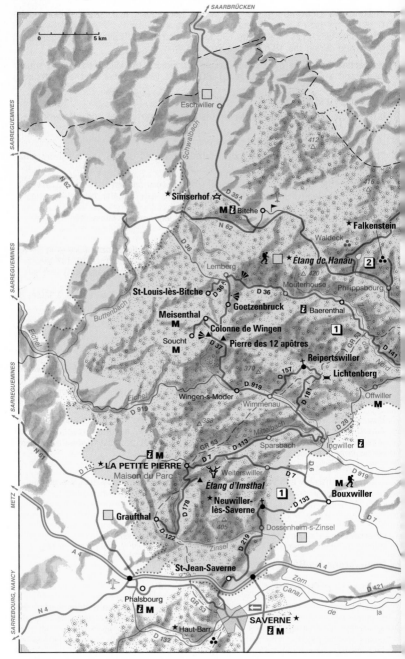

② The mountain road from Niederbronn to Wissembourg
67km/42mi – allow 2hr

Niederbronn-les-Bains – *See NIEDERBRONN-LES-BAINS.*
Leave Niederbronn along the pleasant Flakensteinbach Valley.

★Château de Falkenstein – *See Château de FALKENSTEIN.*
Turn right 3km/1.9mi beyond Philippsbourg; leave a small lake on the left and continue to Hanau Lake.

★Étang de Hanau – The lake is situated at the heart of a bog area, in pleasant wooded surroundings crisscrossed by marked footpaths. Nature lovers have a choice between two hikes:

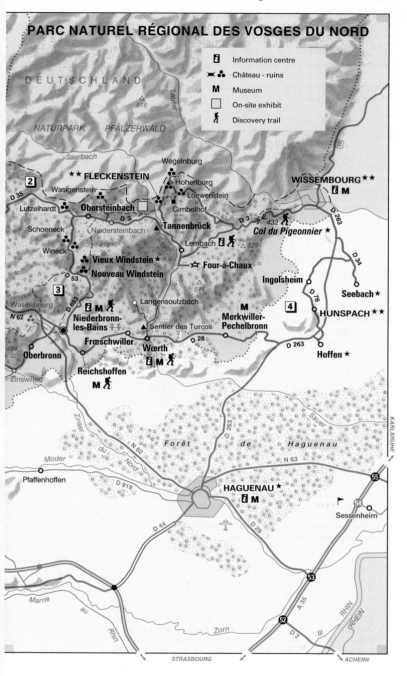

PARC NATUREL RÉGIONAL DES VOSGES DU NORD

- the **Sentier botanique de la tourbière** *(access: 300m/328yd left of the restaurant parking area along D 162; start from the picnic area situated beyond the tennis courts, allow 45min).* The trail offers the opportunity of discovering an exceptional natural environment requiring strict safeguard regulations: bogs. These humid areas retain priceless information about successive ice ages. Along the way, explanatory panels provide information about the flora.

- **Promenade de l'arche naturelle de Erbsenfelsen** *(access: from the restaurant parking area, follow the no 3 blue markings, going via the back of the tennis courts, allow 1hr 30min).* After the botanic trail, the path crosses a forest road then turns right and leads in 20min to the foot of the ruined Waldeck castle. Follow no 3 markings which take you round the mound. At the end of the road, a path *(1.5km/0.9mi)* leads through an oak and beech forest to an impressive natural sandstone arch. A little further on, take a path going down on the right and follow the yellow-ring markings to get back to the lake.

Turn right 1km/0.6mi further on.

The road runs along what used to be the eastern border of Lorraine in the 17C. On the left you can see the hamlet of Waldeck and, perched on a wooded height, the tall square keep of its castle. The road then runs through a forested area dotted with sandstone formations.

The former "royal way", created in the 18C, then runs past more ruins: the **Château de Lutzelhardt**, erected in the 12C by the dukes of Lorraine *(access: path on the left, just beyond the forest lodge of Lutzelhardt)*; **Grand**- and **Petit-Wasigenstein** *(access along the Niedersteinbach-Wengelsbach road)*. The castles stand on the site of the fierce battle which took place between the king of the Burgonds, Gunther, and the king of Aquitaine, Walthari, celebrated in the epic poem *Waltharilied*, written in the 10C by the monk Eckhardt de St-Gall.

Obersteinbach – Picturesque village with timber-framed houses on red-sandstone bases.

Beyond Niedersteinbach, the tree-lined road crosses the River Sauer.

Tannenbrück – The Moselle army commanded by Hoche distinguished itself here in 1793.

The nearby Fleckenstein Lake offers swimming and relaxation.

★★**Château de Fleckenstein** – The castle was built in the 12C as part of the defence system of the northern border of the duchy of Alsace. In the 13C, it probably became an imperial possession and was one of the most powerful Alsatian baronies at the end of the 15C, including 35 villages. The castle was destroyed in 1680 and the Fleckenstein family became extinct shortly afterwards.

The ruins occupy a remarkable position near the German border, on a rock spur standing more than 20m/66ft high in wooded surroundings.

Tour ⊙ – The lower courtyard surrounded by a wall is accessible through a fortified gate. Note the impressive square tower which was built against the main rock during the Gothic period.

Inside, stairs lead to several rooms hewn out of the rock, including the amazing *Salle des chevaliers* ("Knights' hall") with its central monolithic pillar, and then onto the platform (8m/26ft wide) where the seigneurial residence stood; there is a fine **view** of the upper Sauer Valley and of the confluence of the Sauer and Steinbach.

One of the rooms of the castle contains a collection of objects found on the site.

"Tour des quatre châteaux forts" (tour of the four castles) – *4km/2.5mi. Allow 2hr.* Start from the parking area at the foot of **Fleckenstein** castle *(see above)*. Walk along the path marked by a red rectangle then, a few yards further on, follow the picturesque *Sentier des rochers* (red triangle) leading to the Maiden's fountain, which, according to legend, witnessed an unhappy love affair. Turn left (blue rectangle); across the German border stands **Wegelnburg**, another Imperial fortress taken over by brigands and largely destroyed at the end of the 13C. It offers a remarkable view of the border area. Retrace your steps to the Maiden's fountain and continue straight ahead (red rectangle) towards **Hohenburg**, another Fleckenstein possession destroyed in 1680; the lower Renaissance part has retained a powerful artillery bastion and the seigneurial residence. Continue southwards to **Loewenstein castle**, destroyed in 1386 after serving as the headquarters of a group of robber-barons, including the cunning Lindenschmidt; the same path marked with a red rectangle runs past a typical red-sandstone crag (Krappenfels) on its way to the Gimbel farmhouse *(a farm-inn serving meals during the season)*. Superb **view** of Fleckenstein castle. The path on the right (red-white-red rectangle) leads back to the Fleckenstein parking area.

Retrace your steps and follow the forest road on the left towards Gimbelhof.

On the way up you will see a disused red-sandstone quarry and then, on the right, a very densely forested area. **Hohenbourg** castle stands opposite *(see above)*.

When you reach a clearing at the Litschhof pass, you will have to make a choice: if you have not done the tour of the four castles on foot, then bear left towards the inn and follow the "Grimbelhof" markings (see above), then turn back towards Wingen; if you have been on the tour of the four castles, go straight to Wingen (right). Turn left in Petit Wingen then left again in Climbach.

★**Col du Pigeonnier** – *Access on the left of the road coming from Climbach; 30min walk there and back.* Follow the Sentier de la Scherhol (marked with red circles) through the forest above the Club Vosgien refuge. After walking for about 15min, you will see a viewpoint offering a superb **view**★ of the Plaine d'Alsace and Black Forest. *Return along the same path or walk round the Scherhol through the forest and back to the pass (allow another 15min).*

On the way down, as the path comes out of the forest, there is a fine view of the village of Weiler on the left and of the green Lauter Valley. Beyond the crossroads, the view extends ahead towards Wissembourg; the German border area can be seen in the distance.

Drive along D 3 and D 77 to Wissembourg.

★★**Wissembourg** – *See WISSEMBOURG.*

③ From Wissembourg to Niederbronn via Windstein
42km/26mi – allow half a day

Leave Wissembourg by ④ on the town plan along D 77 then follow D 3 to Lembach.

Lembach – This charming small town has retained several **old buildings**: large houses, wash-houses, inns *(1hr round tour starting from the town hall)*.
A panoramic tour *(departure from the town hall; 1hr)* offers the possibility of fully appreciating the surroundings from viewpoints situated all round the village. On each site, explanations are centred on specific themes such as urban development, relief and vegetation, geology and biological environments such as orchards and hedges.
Along the road to Woerth on the left, 1km/0.6mi from the village, you will see the entrance of the **Ouvrage du Four à Chaux** *(see Ligne MAGINOT)*.

Obersteinbach – *See drive ② above.*

On the way out, D 53 follows the winding route of one of the main medieval roads. It is overlooked by several ruins which probably formed part of a line of defence guarding Haguenau's imperial castle at the end of the 12C *(see HAGUENAU)*.

Schœneck castle, standing on a rocky ridge, belonged to a member of the Lichtenberg family who also owned **Wineck** castle facing it.

Châteaux de Windstein – *Turn left towards Windstein. Parking area at the end of the left-hand branch of the road, in front of the restaurant-hotel "Aux châteaux".*
The two Windstein castles, standing 500m/547yd apart, are believed to date from the end of the 12C (Old Windstein) and from 1340 (New Windstein). They were both destroyed in 1676 by French troops under the Baron of Montclar's command.

★**Vieux Windstein** (Old Windstein) – *45min on foot there and back.* The dilapidated ruins stand at the top of a wooded knoll (alt 340m/1 115ft). The troglodyte part of the castle (stairs, bedrooms, cells, well 41m/135ft deep), is in a better condition. Admire the fine **panorama**★ of the surrounding summits and the Nagelsthal below.

Nouveau Windstein (New Windstein) – *30min on foot there and back.* Standing on its own mound, the new castle is less picturesque but its ruins are nevertheless elegant: note the lovely pointed windows.

Continue along D 653 to Niederbronn.

VILLAGES OF NORTHERN ALSACE

④ From Niederbronn to Wissembourg across the plain
60km/37mi – allow 3hr

Niederbronn-les-Bains – *See NIEDERBRONN-LES-BAINS.*

The road goes through villages which were caught up in the 1870 Franco-Prussian War. Numerous monuments erected on the roadside commemorate the sacrifice of soldiers killed in the fighting.

Reichshoffen – The village witnessed the heroic cavalry charge which ended in a massacre in Morsbronn-les-Bains nearby. The **Musée du Fer** ⊙ illustrates the history of local mines and ironworks since the 14C.

Froeschwiller – Charming, typically Alsatian village.

Morsbronn-les-Bains – Small spa resort; the hot-water (41.5°C/106.7°F) springs contain sodium chloride.

Woerth – The castle houses the **Musée de la Bataille du 6 août 1870** ⊙: uniforms, weapons, equipment, documents and pictures concerning the two armies facing each other. Note the large diorama of the battle.
The **Sentier des Turcos** *(starting a few yards beyond the Alko France factory, on the left, on the way out of Woerth towards Lembach)* is a historic trail *(2km/1.2mi)* illustrating the main stages of the battle with the help of explanatory panels.
A **nature trail** *(2.5km/1.5mi)* also starts from Woerth towards **Langensoultzbach**; a set of panels provides information on trees along the way.

Merkwiller-Pechelbronn – This was the main centre of the oil-fields of northern Alsace. All extracting operations stopped in 1970 but a small museum, the **Musée du Pétrole** ⊙, illustrates the main aspects of this former activity. Merkwiller-Pechelbronn is now a spa resort with a hot spring (Source des Hélions, 65°C/149°F) used for the treatment of rheumatism. The spa establishment is closed for renovation.

★**Hoffen** – This traditional village nestles round its church and its strange town hall supported by three wooden pillars. A lime tree planted during the Revolution stands next to the old public well.

★★**Hunspach** – White timber-framed houses line their canopied façades along the streets of this typical Alsatian village with a long-standing rural tradition (farmyards, orchards, fountains).

Ingolsheim – This large agricultural village is surrounded by orchards and dotted with gardens and farmyards.

★**Seebach** – This flower-decked village is typically Alsatian with its canopied timber-framed houses surrounded by gardens. The area has also retained its traditional costumes quite different from those of nearby villages.
Shortly before reaching Wissembourg, you will catch sight of two monuments, a French one and a German one, commemorating the battle which took place just outside Wissembourg in August 1870, during the Franco-Prussian War.

★★**Wissembourg** – *See WISSEMBOURG.*

VOUZIERS

Population 4 807
Michelin map 56 fold 8 or 241 fold 18

From a simple medieval village, Vouziers became an important trading centre following the creation in 1516 by King Francis I of one of the fairs which brought fame and prosperity to the Champagne region. The town was seriously damaged during the two world wars.
Roland Garros, the pilot who flew across the Mediterranean in 1913, is buried in the cemetery.

Église St-Maurille – The west front is adorned with an interesting triple **doorway**★ in Renaissance style. Dating from the 16C, the richly decorated portals were the first part of a new church whose construction was interrupted by the Wars of Religion. For more than 200 years, the doorway stood isolated in front of the church. In 1769, it was joined to the existing edifice by means of two additional

Vouziers – Central doorway of the Église St-Maurille

bays. The statues of the four Evangelists are placed in recesses separating the three portals. The tympanum of the left-hand one represents a skeleton, whereas the right-hand one shows the risen Christ. A series of pendants representing the Good Shepherd and six Apostles hang from the first of the recessed arches of the central doorway. The tympanum depicts the Annunciation.
The church contains a lovely Renaissance Virgin.

EXCURSIONS

St-Morel – *8km/5mi south. From Vouziers, drive along D 982 and, after 7km/4.3mi, turn right onto D 21.* The 15C church has three naves of equal height. It is in this area that the famous pilot, Roland Garros, was shot down in October 1918.

LE MONT DIEU *26km/16mi northeast*

This excursion to a remote Carthusian monastery takes in the Canal des Ardennes and the Lac de Bairon on the way.

Drive northeast out of Vouziers along D 977, turn left after 1km/0.6mi onto D 14 to Semuy then right onto D 25 which follows the Canal des Ardennes as far as Le Chesne.

Canal des Ardennes – The canal which was dug during the reign of Louis-Philippe (1830-1848), links the River Meuse to the River Aisne and to the waterways of the Seine Basin. There are 27 locks between Semuy and Le Chesne, over a distance of just 9km/5.6mi; the most interesting is in Montgon. Northeast of Le Chesne, the canal follows the green valley of the River Bar.

Leave Le Chesne north along D 991 and turn immediately right onto a narrow road leading to the Lac de Bairon.

Lac de Bairon – This lake (4km/2.5mi wide), set in hilly surroundings, is used as a reservoir of the Canal des Ardennes. It is divided into two by a causeway. There is a fine view of it from D 991. A section has been set aside as a bird sanctuary. The lake offers various activities including fishing, canoeing, walking...

From the lake, drive to D 12 which leads to D 977 and turn left.

The road runs through the Forêt du Mont Dieu. The former Carthusian monastery is signalled on the right.

★**Ancienne chartreuse du Mont Dieu** – Founded in 1132 by Odon, an abbot of St Remi in Reims, the monastery covered more than 12ha/30 acres surrounded by a triple wall. Damaged in the 16C, during the Wars of Religion, it was used as a prison at the time of the Revolution and was subsequently partly demolished.
Little remains of the former monastery *(private property)* except some 17C buildings, built of pink brick with stone surrounds, set in a remote vale framed by dark woods.

WASSY

Population 3 291
Michelin map 61 fold 9 or 241 fold 34

This quiet little town, lying along the River Blaise at the heart of "humid Champagne", has retained the traditional ironworks which brought prosperity at a time when, before the First World War, Wassy was one of the main centres of iron-ore mining and metalwork in France.

The Wassy massacre – In 1562, François de Guise returned to Wassy one Sunday when the protestant community was assembled in a vast barn. The duke's men began quarrelling with some of the Protestants and, having entered the barn, they massacred all those they could lay their hands on. The duke later disavowed the massacre although he had done nothing to stop it. This event deeply stirred the growing Protestant population of France and was one of the causes of the Wars of Religion which tore the country apart until 1598 when the Edict of Nantes was signed, granting religious freedom to all French subjects.

SIGHTS

Place Notre-Dame – The square lies in the town centre.
The **Église Notre-Dame**, dating from the late 12C has both Romanesque and Gothic features such as a Romanesque belfry and Gothic doorway, Romanesque capitals and Gothic vaulting.
The **Hôtel de ville** ⟡, built in 1775 contains an interesting astronomical clock (early 19C) by François Pernot.

From place Notre-Dame, walk to rue du Temple.

Temple ⊙ – The Protestant church was built on the site of the barn where the massacre took place. It houses a Protestant museum illustrating the history of the reformed church of Wassy in the 15C and 17C.

Paul and Camille Claudel lived opposite with their parents. Paul later became a poet and playwright and his sister Camille a talented sculptor and close friend of Rodin.

Lac-réservoir des Leschères – *1km/0.6mi south; signposted "La Digue" from Wassy*. This reservoir supplies the Canal de la Blaise, where swimming and fishing are possible.

VALLÉE DE LA BLAISE

Between Juzennecourt and St-Dizier, the Blaise Valley is a nature lovers' paradise. The river, abounding in trout, meanders through pastures between forested slopes. Hillside villages such as Lamothe-en-Blaisy or riverside ones like Daillancourt, are most attractive with their white-stone houses.

Metalwork is a long-standing tradition in the valley: as early as 1157, monks from Clairvaux founded the first industrial forge in Wassy and smelting works and workshops gradually settled along the river, burning wood from the nearby forests, using water power and iron ore mined locally.

In 1840, **Osne-le-Val** was the birthplace of ornamental cast-iron. In 1900, Hector Guimard chose **St-Dizier** for his Art Nouveau creations. Today, the area produces urban furniture for many towns throughout the world: statues, fountains, benches...

In addition, some 100 highly specialised metalworks supply the aeronautical industry, the car industry, the chemical industry....

An unmarked road, known as the **Route du Fer** ⊙, links the main sites which testify to this ancient metalworking tradition.

St-Dizier – *See ST-DIZIER*.

Wassy – *See above*.

Dommartin-le-Franc – The former **smelting works** ⊙ built in 1834 have been restored and are now used for exhibitions about metalwork in the past and ornamental cast-iron.

Doulevant-le-Château – This village, surrounded by beautiful forests, is well known for its wrought-iron and cast-iron workshops. The 13C-16C church has a fine Renaissance doorway.

Cirey-sur-Blaise – Between 1733 and 1749, Voltaire stayed for long periods in the **castle** ⊙ of his friend the Marquise du Châtelet, whom he called the "divine Émilie". He wrote several of his works here, including two tragedies: *Alzire* and *Mahomet*.

The castle consists of a pavilion in the Louis XIII style and an 18C wing built by Madame du Châtelet and Voltaire. Note the **doorway** in the Rocaille style designed by Voltaire. The tour takes in the library, the chapel, the kitchens, reception rooms adorned with tapestries and Voltaire's small theatre.

Sommevoire – This village, nestling in a vale where the River Voire takes its source, became a centre of the metalwork industry during the 19C, specialising in the production of ornamental cast-iron (fountains, lamps, vases, religious statues) initiated by Antoine Durenne. The **Paradis** ⊙ houses a collection of his models, monumental plaster casts, some of them by eminent artists such as Bartholdi. The **Église St-Pierre** ⊙, deconsecrated, is used as an exhibition hall for cast-iron creations.

Osne-le-Val – This was the birthplace of ornamental cast-iron in France in the 19C. A building of the **Usine du Val d'Osne** ⊙, which closed down in 1986 houses an annual exhibition about ornamental cast-iron (prints, photos, bronze-casting demonstration).

Consult the Places to Stay map at the beginning of this guide to select the a stopover or holiday destination. The map offers the following categories:
- *Short holidays*
- *Weekend breaks*
- *Overnight stops*
- *Resorts*

Depending on the region, this map also shows marinas, ski areas, spas, centres for mountain expeditions, etc.

WISSEMBOURG★★

Population 7 443
Michelin map 87 fold 2 or 242 fold 12

A village developed beside a prosperous Benedictine abbey and, by the 12C Wissembourg was already mentioned under it own name; the city became a member of Decapolis *(see MULHOUSE)* in 1354. Today, it still retains a considerable part of its fortifications and most of its ancient urban features. The River Lauter which flows here, splits into several arms, giving character to the town and creating a peaceful atmosphere. The annual fair which takes place on Whit Monday offers visitors the opportunity to see many Alsatian costumes.

Royal engagement – Stanislas Leszczynski, the deposed king of Poland *(see NANCY)*, having lost his fortune, settled in Wissembourg with his daughter Maria and a few royal friends and led a simple life until, in 1725, the Duc d'Antin arrived from Paris and announced that King Louis XV had decided to marry his daughter. The royal couple was married by proxy in Strasbourg cathedral; Louis XV was 15 years old, Maria 22.

★OLD TOWN *45min*

From place du Marché-aux-Choux, follow rue de la République to place de la République, in the lively town centre; the **Hôtel de ville** (B H), built of pink sandstone with pediment, small tower and clock (1741-1752), stands on the square.
Turn left onto rue du Marché-aux-Poissons leading to the river; lovely vista of the east end of St-Pierre-et-St-Paul at the other extremity of the street.
Walk across the small bridge over the Lauter and take a look at the houses, with their single-slope roofs and dormer windows, lining the banks of the river; note, in particular, the **Maison du Sel** (AB K) with its balconied dormer windows protected by canopies; the house dates from 1450.

Follow avenue de la Sous-Préfecture.

On the left is the abbey's former **tithe barn** (A N).

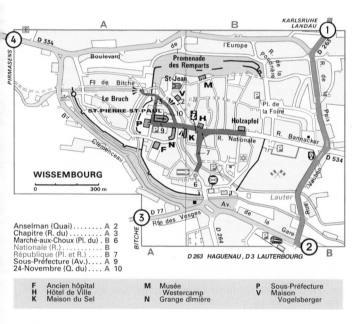

Anselman (Quai) . . . . A 2
Chapitre (R. du) . . . . A 3
Marché-aux-Choux (Pl. du) . B 6
Nationale (R.) . . . . B
République (Pl. et R.) . . . . B 7
Sous-Préfecture (Av.) . . . . A 9
24-Novembre (Q. du) . . . . A 10

F	Ancien hôpital	M	Musée	P	Sous-Préfecture
H	Hôtel de Ville		Westercamp	V	Maison
K	Maison du Sel	N	Grange dîmière		Vogelsberger

★**Église St-Pierre-et-St-Paul** (A)– The church, built of sandstone, is the former church of the Benedictine monastery, dating from the 13C.
The square belfry on the right side of the church is all that remains of the previous Romanesque edifice. The statues were beheaded during the Revolution and the paintings disappeared.
The ancient Head of Christ from Wissembourg, decorating the medallion of the 11C stained-glass kept in Strasbourg, comes from the abbey church.
Inside, the Gothic style is predominant; note, in the south aisle, a red-sandstone Holy Sepulchre mutilated, which dates from the 15C; in the south transept there are traces of frescoes: the Apostles, Christ's Passion, the Resurrection, Whitsun, the Last Judgement. A 15C fresco, depicting St Christopher holding Jesus in his arms welcomes visitors who enter the church through the south door. It is the largest painted character known in France (11m/36ft).

The chancel is lit by 13C stained-glass windows, restored in the 19C. The oldest stained glass is the little rose on the gable of the north transept, which depicts the Virgin and Child (second half of the 12C).

On the north side of the church, a whole gallery and two bays are all that remains of a splendid **cloister** which was never completed, one of the finest cloisters in the whole Rhine Valley.

The **Sous-Préfecture** (**A P**), situated at the end of the avenue is an elegant late-18C pavilion.

Turn right onto rue du Chapitre.

Beyond the church, the street skirts the cloister and the 11C chapel.

At the end of rue du Chapitre, turn left towards the bridge spanning the Lauter.

Quartier du Bruch (**A**) – From the bridge, there is a picturesque view of this old district. The canted corner of the first house, dating from 1550, is decorated with a small loggia or oriel.

Walk back along quai du 24-Novembre.

Across the Lauter, standing along quai Anselman, is the **Maison Vogelsberger** (**A V**) with its richly decorated Renaissance doorway and painted coat of arms, dating from 1540.

Return to avenue de la Sous-Préfecture and carry straight on along rue Nationale.

The Gothic house flanked by corner turrets and known as **Holzapfel** (**B**), was a posting-house from 1793 to 1854; Napoleon stayed there in 1806.

ADDITIONAL SIGHTS

Musée Westercamp ⊙ (**B M**) – Housed in a 16C building, the museum contains antique furniture (superb wardrobes), peasant costumes and mementoes from the 1870 battlefield as well as prehistoric and Roman exhibits.

Promenade des Remparts (**AB**) – This picturesque itinerary which follows the bank of the former ramparts offers a good view of the old district and of the impressive towers of the Église St-Pierre-et-St-Paul, with, in the background, the undulating outline of the Vosges.

Église St-Jean (**A**) – The Protestant church dates from the 15C except for its belfry which is Romanesque. Inside, note the network vaulting of the north aisle. In the courtyard, on the north side of the church, there are ancient gravestones carved out of red sandstone.

Ancien Hôpital (**A F**) – This was the residence of Stanislas Leszczinski and his daughter.

EXCURSIONS

Vignoble de Cleebourg – The northern section of the Wine Road runs along the foothills of the northern Vosges, through vineyards specialising in two types of vines: Tokay pinot gris and Pinot blanc Auxerrois.

There are wine-tasting opportunities in the Cleebourg cellars.

Return to Wissembourg via Rott and D 3.

Altenstadt – *2km/1.2mi east by ② on the town plan.*

The village has retained an interesting Romanesque **church** dating from the 11C and 12C. The nave and the aisles have ceilings. The chancel was raised in the 19C. As you enter, note the unusual porch (7m/23ft deep). The 11C belfry, decorated with Lombardy banding, was given a third storey in the 12C.

Ouvrage d'artillerie de Schoenenbourg – *12km7.5mi south along D 264 the D 65; signposting. See Ligne MAGINOT.*

World Heritage List

In 1972, The United Nations Educational, Scientific and Cultural Organization (UNESCO) adopted a Convention for the preservation of cultural and natural sites. To date, more than 150 States Parties have signed this international agreement, which has listed over 500 sites "of outstanding universal value" on the World Heritage List. Each year, a committee of representatives from 21 countries, assisted by technical organizations (ICOMOS - International Council on Monuments and Sites; IUCN- International Union for Conservation of Nature and Natural Resources; ICCROM -International Centre for the Study of the Preservation and Restoration of Cultural Property, the Rome Centre), evaluates the proposals for new sites to be included on the list, which grows longer as new nominations are accepted and more countries sign the Convention. To be considered, a site must be nominated by the country in which it is located.

The protected **cultural heritage** sites may be monuments (buildings, sculptures, archaeological structures, etc.) with unique historical, artistic or scientific features; groups of buildings (such as religious communities, ancient cities); or sites (human settlements, examples of exceptional landscapes, cultural landscapes) which are the combined works of man and nature of exceptional beauty. **Natural heritage** sites may be a testimony to the stages of the earth's geological history or to the development of human cultures and creative genius or represent significant ongoing ecological processes, contain superlative natural phenomena or provide a habitat for threatened species.

Signatories of the Convention pledge to co-operate to preserve and protect these sites around the world as a common heritage to be shared by all humanity, and contribute to the **World Heritage Fund**. The Fund serves to carry out studies, plan conservation measures, train local specialists, supply equipment for the protection of a park or the restoration of a monument, etc.

Some of the most well-known places which the World Heritage Committee has inscribed include: Australia's Great Barrier Reef (1981), the Canadian Rocky Mountain Parks (1984), The Great Wall of China (1987), the Statue of Liberty (1984), the Kremlin (1990), Mont-Saint-Michel and its Bay (France - 1979), Durham Castle and Cathedral (1986).

UNESCO World Heritage sites included in this guide are:

Place Stanislas, Place de la Carrière and Place d'Alliance in Nancy

The temporary residence of a king without a kingdom – Stanislas Leszcynski – is an example of an enlightened monarchy responding to the needs of the public. Constructed between 1752 and 1756 by a brilliant team under the direction of the architect Héré, this project illustrates a perfect coherence between the desire for prestige and a concern for functionality.

Strasbourg, Grande île

The historic centre of the Alsatian capital lies between two arms of the River III. The district occupied by the Cathedral, four ancient churches and the Palais Rohan recalls the typical medieval city plan, and shows the evolution of the city from the 15C to the 18C.

Cathedral of Notre-Dame, former Abbey of Saint-Remi and Palace of Tau, Reims

The Cathedral, with the sculpted decorations embellishing the Gothic architecture, is a masterpiece. The former abbey has conserved its beautiful 9C nave where the holy anointing of the kings of France was first carried out by Saint Remi. The Tau Palace was almost entirely reconstructed in the 17C.

Krug Champagne cellars

Practical
information

Planning your trip

Climate and seasons

The variety of landscape in the regions of Alsace and Champagne is also reflected in the weather. The Ardennes uplands are known for heavy precipitation, low clouds, fog and frost; a bleak climate which may be the reason why this area has one of the lowest population densities in Europe. The lower plains of Champagne are part of the Paris basin and share its milder climate; temperatures occasionally drop below freezing between November and March, the hottest days are in July and August.

In Alsace, comparable variations can be observed between the plain and the Vosges mountains. The average annual temperature in Colmar, for example, is 10.3°C/50.5°F while the Grand Ballon (the highest summit) averages just 3°C/37.4°F. Prevailing winds arrive from the West or Southwest, carrying rain and snow. When these weather systems run up against the Vosges, the precipitation falls, leaving the eastern plain fairly dry. Colmar holds the record for the lowest yearly rainfall in France.

While the uplands are generally wetter and cooler throughout the area, visitors travelling mountain roads may experience a curious phenomenon of temperature inversion, which occurs when the atmospheric pressure is high. At such times, while a thick mist swathes the plain, the mountains bask in bright sunlight; temperatures may be 10°C/50°F higher than in the valley below. The luminosity and extensive view are uniquely magnificent.

Visitors will enjoy the summer months for holidays, but other seasons have their own charms. In the autumn, the vineyards and forests are rich with colour and harvest time livens up the villages, as the cool evening air brings red to your cheeks. Hunting season in the Ardennes forest opens in November. Winter resorts in the Vosges are especially attractive to cross-country skiers and snow-shoers, who appreciate the largely unspoiled beauty of the forest, and the traditional mountain villages (many areas have satisfactory downhill runs as well, and are equipped with snow-makers). The main resorts are Le Bonhomme (700m), La Bresse-Hohneck (650m), Gerardmer (750m), Saint-Maurice-sur-Moselle (560m) and Ventron (630m).

Mulhouse – Hôtel de ville

French Tourist Offices

For information, brochures, maps and assistance in planning a trip to France travellers should apply to the official tourist office in their own country:

Australia - New Zealand
Sydney – BNP Building, 12 Castlereagh Street
Sydney, New South Wales 2000
☎ (61) 2 231 52 44 – Fax: (61) 2 221 86 82.

Canada
Montreal – College Suite 490
Montreal PQ H3A 2W9
☎ (514) 288-4264 – Fax: (514) 845 48 68.

Eire
Dublin – 38 Lower Abbey St, Dublin 1.
☎ (1) 703 40 46 – Fax: (1) 874 73 24.

United Kingdom
London – 179 Piccadilly, London WI
☎ (0891) 244 123 – Fax: (0171) 493 6594.

United States
East Coast: New York – 444 Madison Avenue, NY 10022
☎ 212-838-7800 – Fax: (212) 838 7855.
Mid West: Chicago – 676 North Michigan Avenue, Suite 3360
Chicago, IL 60611
☎ (312) 751 7800 – Fax: (312) 337 6339.
West Coast: Los Angeles – 9454 Wilshire Boulevard, Suite 715
Beverly Hills, CA 90212.
☎ (310) 271 2693 – Fax: (310) 276 2835.

Cyberspace
www.info.france-usa.org
The French Embassy's Web site provides basic information (geography, demographics, history), a news digest and business-related information. It offers special pages for children, and pages devoted to culture, language study and travel, and you can reach other selected French sites (regions, cities, ministries) with a hypertext link.

www.fr-holidaystore.co.uk
The new French Travel Centre in London has gone on-line with this service, providing information on all of the regions of France, including updated special travel offers and details on available accommodation.

www.visiteurope.com
The European Travel Commission provides useful information on travelling to and around 27 European countries, and includes links to some commercial booking services (ie, vehicle hire), rail schedules, weather reports and more.

Local tourist offices

In addition to the French tourist offices abroad listed above, visitors may wish to contact local offices for more precise information, to receive brochures and maps. Below, the addresses are given for each local tourist office by département. The index lists the département after each town; the *Introduction* at the beginning of this guide also gives information on the administrative divisions of France.

For **regional** information, address inquires to the
Comité régional de tourisme (CRT):

Alsace: 6, avenue de la Marseillaise, B.P. 219, 67005 Strasbourg cedex
☎ 03 88 25 01 66.

Lorraine: 1, place Gabriel-Hocquard, B.P. 1004, 57036 Metz cedex 1
☎ 03 87 37 02 16.

Champagne-Ardenne: 5, rue de Jericho, 51037 Châlons-sur-Marne, cedex
☎ 03 26 70 31 28.

For information on each **département**, address enquires to the
Comité départemental de tourisme (CDT):

Ardennes: 24, place Ducale,
08000 Charleville-Mézières
☎ 03 24 55 06 08.
Aube: Hôtel du Départment,
B.P. 394, 10026 Troyes cedex
☎ 03 25 42 50 91.
Bas-Rhin: Office départemental,
9, rue du Dôme
B.P. 53, 67061 Strasbourg cedex
☎ 03 88 15 45 80.
Haut-Rhin: Maison du tourisme de Haute-Alsace, 1, rue Schlumberger
68006 Colmar cedex
☎ 03 89 20 10 68.

Haute-Marne: 40 bis, avenue Foch, 52000 Chamont
☎ 03 25 30 39 00.
Marne: 13 bis, rue Carnot, B.P. 74, 51000 Châlons-en-Champagne
☎ 03 26 68 37 52.
Meurthe-et-Moselle: Comité départmental, 48, rue du Sergent-Blandan, B.P. 65, 54035 Nancy cedex
☎ 03 83 94 52 90.
Vosges: Comité départemental, 7, rue Gilbert, B.P. 332, 88008 Épinal cedex
☎ 03 29 82 49 93.
The guide Bonjour les Vosges is available on request.

Further information can be obtained from the *Syndicats d'Initiative*, as the tourist offices in most large towns are called. The addresses and telephone numbers are listed after the symbol 🖪, in the Admission times and charges following.

Travellers with special needs –The sights described in this guide which are easily accessible to people of reduced mobility are indicated in the Admission times and charges by the symbol &.

Useful information on transportation, holidaymaking and sports associations for the disabled is available from the *Comité National Français de Liaison pour la Réadaptation des Handicapés* (CNRH), 236bis, rue de Tolbiac, 75013 Paris. Call their international information number ☎ 01 53 80 66 44, or write to request a catalogue of publications. Web-surfers can find information for slow walkers, mature travellers and others with special needs at www.access-able.com. If you are a member of a sports club and would like to practice your sport in France, or meet others who do, ask the CNRH for information on clubs in the *Fedération Française du Sport Adapté* (FFSA Paris, ☎ 01 48 72 80 72). For information on museum access for the disabled contact La Direction, *Les Musées de France, Service Accueil des Publics Spécifiques*, 6 rue des Pyramides, 75041 Paris Cedex 1, ☎ 01 40 15 35 88.

The **Michelin Red Guide France** and the **Michelin Camping Caravaning France** indicate hotels and camp sites with facilities suitable for physically handicapped people.

Formalities

Passport – Visitors entering France must be in possession of a valid national passport (or in the case of British nationals, a Visitor's Passport). In case of loss or theft report to the embassy or consulate and the local police.

Visa – No entry visa is required for Canadian and US citizens staying less than three months; it is required of Australian citizens in accordance with French security measures. If you need a visa, apply to the French Consulate (visa issued the same day longer if submitted by mail).

US citizens should obtain the booklet *Safe Trip Abroad* ($1.25) which provides useful information on obtaining a passport, visa requirements, customs regulations, medical care etc for international travellers. It is published by the Government Printing Office and may be ordered by phone (1-202-512-1800), consulted or ordered via Internet (www.access.gpo.gov). General passport information is available by phone toll-free from the Federal Information Center (item 5 on the automated menu) ☎ 800-688-9889. US passport application forms can be downloaded from http://travel.state.gov.

Customs – Apply to the Customs Office (UK) for a leaflet on customs regulations and the full range of duty-free allowances. The US Customs Service offers a publication *Know Before You Go* for US citizens. For the office nearest you, look in the Federal Government section of your phone book, under US Department of the Treasury (or consult www.customs.ustreas.gov). There are no customs formalities for holiday-makers bringing their caravans into France for a stay of less than six months. No customs document is necessary for pleasure boats and outboard motors for a stay of less than six months but the registration certificate should be kept on board.

Americans can bring home, tax-free, up to US$400 worth of goods; Canadians up to CND$300; Australians up to AUS$400 and New Zealanders up to NZ$700.

Persons living in a Member State of the European Union are not restricted in regard to purchasing goods for private use, but the recommended allowances for alcoholic beverages and tobacco are as follows:

Spirits (whisky, gin, vodka etc.)	10 litres	Cigarettes	800
Fortified wines (vermouth, ports etc.)	20 litres	Cigarillos	400
Wine (not more than 60 sparkling)	90 litres	Cigars	200
Beer	110 litres	Smoking tobacco	1 kg

Embassies and consulates in France

Australia	Embassy	4 avenue Jean-Rey, 75015 Paris ☎ 01 40 59 33 00 – Fax: 01 40 59 33 10.
Canada	Embassy	35 avenue Montaigne, 75008 Paris ☎ 01 44 43 29 00 – Fax: 01 44 43 29 99.
Eire	Embassy	4 rue Rude, 75016 Paris ☎ 01 44 17 67 00 – Fax: 01 45 00 84 17.
New Zealand	Embassy	7 ter rue Léonard-de-Vinci, 75016 Paris ☎ 01 45 00 24 11 – Fax: 01 45 26 39.
UK	Embassy	35 rue du Faubourg St-Honoré, 75008 Paris ☎ 01 42 66 91 42 – Fax: 01 42 66 95 90.
	Consulate	16 rue d'Anjou, 75008 Paris ☎ 01 42 66 06 68 (visas).

USA	Embassy	2 avenue Gabriel, 75008 Paris
		☎ 01 43 12 22 22 – Fax: 01 42 66 97 83.
	Consulate	2 rue St-Florentin, 75001 Paris
		☎ 01 42 96 14 88.
	Consulate	15 avenue d'Alsace, 67082 Strasbourg
		☎ 03 88 35 31 04.

Public holidays

Museums and other monuments may be closed or may vary their hours of admission on the following public holidays:

1	January	New Year's Day *(Jour de l'An)*
	Easter Day and Easter Monday *(Pâques)*	
1	May	May Day
8	May	VE Day
	Whit Sunday and Monday *(Pentecôte)*	
	Ascension Day *(Ascension)*	
14	July	France's National Day (Bastille Day)
15	August	Assumption *(Assomption)*
1	November	All Saint's Day *(Toussaint)*
11	November	Armistice Day
25	December	Christmas Day *(Noël)*

National museums and art galleries are closed on Tuesdays; municipal museums are generally closed on Mondays. In addition to the usual school holidays at Christmas and in the spring and summer, there are long mid-term breaks (10 days to a fortnight) in February and early November.

Getting there

By air – Choose between scheduled flights on national airlines or commercial and package-tour flights with rail or coach link-ups or Fly-Drive schemes. Contact airlines and travel agents for information. There are daily flights from Paris and other European cities to **Strasbourg International Airport**; shuttles run passengers into town every half-hour, Mon-Fri, and as planes arrive on weekends. The 30min trip costs 35F. **EuroAirport**, serving Basel and Mulhouse, also provides a shuttle service to the Mulhouse train station (30min, 35F).

By rail – French Railways (SNCF) and British companies operate a daily service via the Channel Tunnel on Eurostar (3hr) between London (Waterloo International Station, ☎ 0345 881 881) and Paris (Gare du Nord).

The French National Railway (SNCF) operates an extensive network of lines including many high speed passenger trains (TGV) and rail services throughout France. The main connecting stations from Paris (Gare de l'Est) to the region are Colmar, Mulhouse, Nancy, Reims, Strasbourg and Troyes.

Rail passes offering unlimited travel, and group travel tickets offering savings for parties are available under certain conditions. **Eurailpass, Flexipass** and **Saver Pass** are options available in the US for travel in Europe and must be purchased in the US – ☎ 1 800 4 EURAIL or www.raileurope.com.us; Eurporail provides timetables and information on special fares via internet www.eurail.on.ca (☎ 1-888-667-9731, Fax 1-519-645-0682); or consult your travel agent.

In the UK, information and bookings can be obtained from French Railways, 179 Piccadilly, London W1V 0BA, ☎ 0891 515 477, in mainline stations, or from travel agencies.

The SNCF operates a telephone information, reservation and pre-payment service in English, from 7am to 10pm (French time). In France, ☎ 08 36 35 35 39. From abroad, ☎ 00 33 8 36 35 35 39. Internet: www.sncf.fr. Ask about discount rates if you are over 60, a student, or travelling with your family.

A rail ticket used within France must be validated *(composter)* by using the orange automatic date-stamping machines at the platform entrance.

Baggage trolleys (10F coin required – refundable) are available at mainline stations.

By coach (bus) – Regular coach services are operated from London to Paris. For further information, contact **Eurolines**:

London: 52 Grosvenor Gardens, Victoria, London SW1W 0AU. ☎ 0171 730 8235.
Paris: 28, avenue du Général de Gaulle, 93541 Bagnolet. ☎ 01 49 72 51 51.

By sea – There are numerous **cross-Channel services** (passenger and car ferries, hover-craft, SeaCat) from the United Kingdom and Eire. For details contact travel agencies or:

P&O Stena Lines, Channel House, Channel View Road, Dover CT17 9TJ. Reservations: ☎ 0990 980 980.

Portsmouth Commercial Port, George Byng Way, Portsmouth, Hampshire PO2 8SP. ☎ 01705 297 391.

Hoverspeed, International Hoverport, Marine Parade, Dover, Kent CT17 9TG. ☎ 01304 240 241.

Brittany Ferries, Millbay Docks, Plymouth, Devon PLI 3EW. ☎ 0990 360360.

The Brittany Centre, Wharf Road, Portsmouth, Hampshire PO2 8RU. ☎ 01705 827 701.

Sally Direct, Ferry Terminal, Ramsgate, Kent CT 11 8RP ☎ 0845 600 2626, **Fax 01843 853 536.**

Motoring in France

Planning your route – The area covered in this guide is easily reached by main motorways and national routes. **Michelin map 911** indicates the main itineraries as well as alternate routes for avoiding heavy traffic during busy holiday periods, and gives estimated travel times. **Michelin map 914** is a detailed atlas of French motorways, indicating tolls, rest areas and services along the route; it includes a table for calculating distances and times. In France, use the Minitel service **3615 MICHELIN** to plan an itinerary. The newest Michelin route-planning service is available on Internet, **www.michelin-travel.com**. Travellers can calculate a precise route using such options as shortest route, route avoiding toll roads, Michelin-recommended route, and gain access to tourist information (hotels, restaurants, attractions). The service is available on a pay-per-route basis or by subscription.

Documents – Travellers from other European Union countries and North America can drive in France with a valid national or home-state **driving licence**. An **international driving licence** is useful because the information on it appears in nine languages (traffic officers are empowered to fine motorists). A permit is available (US$10) from the National Auto Club, Touring Department, 188 The Embarcadero, Suite 300, San Francisco CA 94105; or contact your local branch of the American Automobile Association. For the vehicle it is necessary to have the registration papers (logbook) and a nationality plate of the approved size.

Insurance – Certain motoring organisations (AAA, AA, RAC) offer accident insurance and breakdown service schemes for members. Check with your current insurance company in regard to coverage while abroad. If you plan to hire a car using your credit card, check with the company, which may provide liability insurance automatically (and thus save you having to pay the optional fee for optimum coverage).

Highway Code – The minimum driving age is 18. Traffic drives on the right. It is compulsory for the front-seat passengers to wear **seat belts** and it is also compulsory for the back-seat passengers when the car is fitted with them. Children under the age of 10 must travel on the back seat of the vehicle. Full or dipped headlights must be switched on in poor visibility and at night; use side-lights only when the vehicle is stationary.

In the case of a **breakdown** a red warning triangle or hazard warning lights are obligatory. In the absence of stop signs at intersections, cars must **yield to the right**. Traffic on main roads outside built-up areas (priority indicated by a yellow diamond sign) and on roundabouts has right of way. Vehicles must stop when the lights turn red at road junctions and may filter to the right only when indicated by an amber arrow.

The regulations on **drinking and driving** (limited to 0.50 g/litre) and **speeding** are strictly enforced – usually by an on-the-spot fine and/or confiscation of the vehicle.

Speed limits – Although liable to modification, these are as follows:

– toll motorways *(péage)* 130kph-80mph (110kph-68mph when raining);

– dual carriageways and motorways without tolls 110kph-68mph (100kph-62mph when raining);

– other roads 90kph-56mph (80kph-50mph when raining) and in towns 50kph-31mph;

– outside lane on motorways during daylight, on level ground and with good visibility – minimum speed limit of 80kph (50mph).

Parking Regulations – In town there are zones where parking is either restricted or subject to a fee; tickets should be obtained from the ticket machines (*horodateurs* - small change necessary) and displayed inside the windscreen on the driver's side; failure to display may result in a fine, or towing and impoundment. In some towns you may find blue parking zones *(zone bleue)* marked by a blue line on the pavement or road and a blue signpost with a P and a small square underneath. In this case you have to display a cardboard disc with various times indicated on it. This will enable you to stay for 1hr30min (2hr30min over lunch time) free. Discs are available in super markets or petrol stations (ask for a *disque de stationnement*); they are sometimes given away free.

Tolls – In France, most motorway sections are subject to a toll *(péage)*. This can be expensive, especially if you drive south (eg Calais to Tours, around 190F for a car). You can pay in cash or with a credit card (Visa, Mastercard).

Car Rental – There are car rental agencies at airports, railway stations and in all large towns throughout France. European cars have manual transmission; automatic cars are available in larger cities only if an advance reservation is made. Drivers must be over 21; between ages 21-25, drivers are required to pay an extra daily fee of 50-100F; some companies allow drivers under 23 only if the reservation has been made through a travel agent. It is relatively expensive to hire a car in France; Americans in particular will notice the difference and should make arrangements before leaving, take advantage of Fly-Drive offers, or seek advice from a travel agent, specifying requirements.

Central Reservation in France:

Avis: 01 46 10 60 60   **Europcar:** 01 30 43 82 82
Budget: 01 46 86 65 65   **Hertz:** 01 47 88 51 51
Baron's Limousine and Driver: 01 45 30 21 21

Global Motorhome rents fully-equipped recreational vehicles in a range of sizes; Paris pick-up. The toll-free US number is 800-468-3876 (order a video *Europe by RV* ☏ 800-406-3348).

Petrol (US: gas) – French service stations dispense: *sans plomb 98* (super unleaded 98), *sans plomb 95* (super unleaded 95) and *diesel/gazole* (diesel). Petrol is considerably more expensive in France than in the USA, and also more expensive than in the UK.

General information

Medical treatment – First aid, medical advice and chemists' night service rota are available from chemists/drugstores *(pharmacie)* identified by the green cross sign.

It is advisable to take out comprehensive insurance cover as the recipient of medical treatment in French hospitals or clinics must pay the bill. Nationals of non-EU countries should check with their insurance companies about policy limitations. Reimbursement can then be negotiated with the insurance company according to the policy held.

All prescription drugs should be clearly labelled; it is recommended that you carry a copy of the prescription. American Express offers its members a service, "Global Assist", for any medical, legal or personal emergency – call collect from anywhere in France ☏ 01 47 16 25 29.

British and Irish citizens should apply to the Department of Health and Social Security for form E 111, which entitles the holder to urgent treatment for accident or unexpected illness in EU countries. A refund of part of the costs of treatment can be obtained on application in person or by post to the local Social Security Offices *(Caisse Primaire d'Assurance Maladie)*.

The American Hospital of Paris is open 24hr for emergencies as well as consultations, with English-speaking staff, at 63, boulevard. Victor Hugo, 92200 Neuilly sur Seine, ☏ 01 46 41 25 25. Accredited by major insurance companies.

The British Hospital is just outside Paris in Levallois-Perret, 3, rue Barbès, ☏ 01 46 39 22 22

Currency – There are no restrictions on the amount of currency visitors can take into France. Visitors carrying a lot of cash are advised to complete a currency declaration form on arrival, because there are restrictions on currency export.

Notes and coins– *See illustration following.* The unit of currency in France is the French franc subdivided into 100 centimes. European currency units known as **euros** are being printed, and as of 1999 the banking and finance industries will begin making the changeover. Banknotes are scheduled to go into circulation in January 2002, with national instruments phased out by July of that year. In the meantime, both euro and franc values (1 euro is about 6.50F) are given in more and more instances (store and restaurant receipts, bank documents etc).

Banks – Banks are open from 9am to noon and 2pm to 4pm and branches are closed either on Monday or Saturday. Banks close early on the day before a bank holiday. A passport is necessary as identification when cashing travellers or ordinary cheques in banks. Commission charges vary and hotels usually charge more than banks for cashing cheques for non-residents. Most banks and many larger post offices have **cash dispensers** (ATM) which accept international credit cards (have your PIN number handy). These machines *(distributeurs)* are located outside many different banks, and easily identified by the luminous sign showing a hand holding notes. Visa and Mastercard are accepted almost everywhere; American Express cards can only be used in dispensers in Paris at 11, rue Scribe (Amex office), and inside the Gare de Lyon and the Gare Montparnasse train stations.

Credit Cards – American Express, Visa, Mastercard-Eurocard and Diners Club are widely accepted in shops, hotels and restaurants and petrol stations. If your card is lost or stolen, call the following 24-hour hotlines:

American Express	01 47 77 72 00	Visa	01 42 77 11 90
Mastercard/Eurocard	01 45 67 84 84	Diners Club	01 47 62 75 00

You must report any loss or theft of credit cards or travellers' cheques to the local police who will issue you with a certificate (useful proof to show the issuing company).

Post – Main post offices open Monday to Friday 8am to 7pm, Saturday 8am to noon. Smaller branch post offices generally close at lunch time between noon and 2pm and at 4pm.

Postage via air mail:

> UK: letter (20g) 3.00 F
>
> North America: letter (20g) 4.40 F
>
> Australia and NZ: letter (20g) 5.20F

Stamps are also available from newsagents and bureaux de tabac. Stamp collectors should ask for timbres de collection in any post office.

Time – France is 1hr ahead of Greenwich Mean Time (GMT).

R. Corbel

When it is **noon in France**, it is

3 am	in Los Angeles
6 am	in New York
11 am	in Dublin
11 am	in London
7 pm	in Perth
9 pm	in Sydney
11 pm	in Auckland

In France "am" and "pm" are not used but the 24-hour clock is widely applied.

Tipping – Since a service charge is automatically included in the price of meals and accommodation in France, it is not necessary to tip in restaurants and hotels. However taxi drivers, bellboys, doormen, petrol station attendants or anybody who has been of assistance are usually tipped at the customer's discretion. Most French people give an extra tip in restaurants and cafés (at least 50 centimes for a drink and several francs for a meal).

Electricity – The electric current is 220 volts. Circular two-pin plugs are the rule. Adapters should be bought before your leave home; they are on sale in most airports.

Telephoning

Public Telephones – Most public phones in France use pre-paid phone cards (télé carte). Some telephone booths accept credit cards (Visa, Mastercard/Eurocard: minimum monthly charge 20F). Télécartes (50 or 120 units) can be bought in post offices, branches of France Télécom, bureaux de tabac (cafés that sell cigarettes) and news agents and can be used to make calls in France and abroad. Calls can be received at phone boxes where the blue bell sign is shown; the phone will not ring, so keep your eye on the little message screen.

National calls – French telephone numbers have 10 digits. Paris and Paris region numbers begin with 01; 02 in northwest France; 03 in northeast France; 04 in southeast France and Corsica; 05 in southwest France.

International calls – To call France from abroad, dial the country code (33) + 9-digit number (omit the initial 0). When calling abroad from France dial 00, then dial the country code followed by the area code and number of your correspondent.
International dialling codes (00 + code):

Australia	61	New Zealand	64
Canada	1	United Kingdom	44
Eire	353	United States	1

To use your **personal calling card** dial:

AT&T	0-800 99 00 11	Sprint	0-800 99 00 87
MCI	0-800 99 00 19	Canada Direct . . .	0-800 99 00 16

International Information, US/Canada: 00 33 12 11
International operator: 00 33 12 + country code
Local directory assistance: 12
Toll-free numbers in France begin with 0 800.

Emergency numbers:
Police: 17 **"SAMU"** (Paramedics): 15 Fire *(Pompiers)*: 18

Minitel – France Télécom operates a system offering directory enquiries (free of charge up to 3min), travel and entertainment reservations, and other services (cost varies between 0.37F - 5.57F/min). These small computer-like terminals can be found in some post offices, hotels and France Télécom agencies and in many French homes. 3614 PAGES E is the code for **Directory assistance in English** (turn on the unit, dial 3614, hit the "connexion" button when you get the tone, type in "PAGES E", and follow the instructions on the screen). For route planning, use Michelin services **3615 MICHELIN** (tourist and route information) and **3617 MICHELIN** (information sent by fax).

Cellular phones in France have numbers which begin with 06. Two-watt (lighter, shorter reach) and eight-watt models are on the market, using the Itinéris (France Télécom) or SFR network. "Mobicartes" are pre-paid phone cards that fit into mobile units. Cell phone rentals (delivery or airport pickup provided):

Ellinas Phone Rental	01 47 20 70 00
Euro Exaphone	01 44 09 77 78
Rent a Cell Express	01 53 93 78 00

Accommodation

The Places to Stay map in the *Introduction* indicates recommended places for overnight stops, spas, and winter resorts; it can be used in conjunction with the **Michelin Red Guide France** which lists a selection of hotels and restaurants.

Loisirs-Accueil is a booking service which has offices in most French *départements*. For information contact Réservation Loisirs Accueil, 280, boulevard St-Germain, 75007 Paris; ☎ 01 44 11 10 44.

Accueil de France tourist offices which are open all year make hotel bookings for a small fee, for personal (non-business) callers only. The head office is in Paris (127, avenue des Champs-Élysée, ☎ 01 49 52 53 54 for information only) and there are offices in many large towns and resorts.

Logis et Auberges de France publishes a brochure (a selection of inns) which is available from the French Government Tourist Office.

Relais et Châteaux, 9, avenue Marceau, 75016 Paris, ☎ 01 47 42 20 92, lists hotel accommodation in châteaux and manor houses around France.

Maison des Gîtes de France has a list of self-catering (often rural) accommodation where you can stay in this region (and all over France). Generally, the service lists cottages or apartments decorated in the local style where you will be able to make yourself at home. Gîtes de France have offices in Paris: 59, rue St-Lazare 75009 Paris, ☎ 01 49 70 75 75.
You must purchase the list (a small guide book with details and ratings) for the area that interests you and make reservations directly through the proprietor.

Bed and Breakfast – **Gîtes de France** *(see above)* publishes a booklet on bed and breakfast accommodation *(chambres d'hôte)* which include a room and breakfast at a reasonable price.

Notes and coins

500 Francs featuring scientists Pierre and Marie Curie (1858-1906), (1867-1934)

200 Francs featuring engineer Gustave Eiffel (1832-1923)

100 Francs featuring painter Paul Cézanne (1839-1906)

50 Francs featuring pilot and writer Antoine de Saint-Exupéry (1900-1944)

20 Francs

10 Francs

5 Francs

2 Francs

1 Franc

50 Centimes

20 Centimes

10 Centimes

5 Centime

You can also contact **Bed & Breakfast (UK and France)**, 94-96 Bell St, Henley-on-Thames, Oxon RG9 1XS, ☎ 01491 578 803, Fax: 01491 410 806; e-mail: bookings@bedbreak.demon.co.uk.

Youth Hostels – There are two main youth hostel associations *(auberges de jeunesse)* in France: **Ligue Française pour les Auberges de Jeunesse**, 38, boulevard Raspail, 75007 Paris, ☎ 01 45 48 69 84, Fax: 01 45 44 57 47 and **Fédération Unie des Auberges de Jeunesse (FUAJ)** 27, rue Pajol, 75018 Paris, ☎ 01 44 89 87 27, Fax: 01 44 89 87 10.

The **International Youth Hostel Federation** (www.iyhf.org) is establishing a computerised booking network (IBN), which allows hostellers to view bed availability and to reserve as much as six months in advance. The annual guide *Hostelling International Europe* is on sale in book shops and can be ordered from your national association. US: American Hostels Inc, 733 15th Street NW, Suite 840, Washington DC 20005. UK: Youth Hostels Association, Trevelyan House, 8 St Stephen's Hill, St Albans, Hertfordshire AL1 2DY.

Obernai – Place de l'Étoile

FUAJ publishes booklets in French and English for hostellers and adventurers. Order from the address listed above or via the Internet (www.fuaj.org).

Camping – There are numerous officially graded sites with varying standards of facilities along the coast, inland, and in the mountains. The **Michelin Guide Camping Caravaning France** lists a selection of camp sites. An International Camping Carnet for caravans is useful but not compulsory; it may be obtained from motoring organisations or from the Camping and Caravaning Club (Greenfields House, Westwook Way, Coventry CV4 8JH, ☎ 01203 694 995).

The **Fédération française des Stations Vertes de Vacances** publishes an annual list of **rural localities**, selected for their tranquillity, and the outdoor activities available. Information from the Federation, 16, rue Nodot, 21000 Dijon, ☎ 03 80 43 49 47. The guide **Bienvenue à la ferme** (Editions Solar) includes the addresses of farmers providing guest facilities who have signed a charter drawn up by the Chambers of Agriculture. *Bienvenue à la ferme* farms, vetted for quality and meeting official standards, can be identified by the yellow flower which serves as their logo. For the Vosges, write to the Chambre d'Agriculture des Vosges, Relais Agriculture et Tourisme, 17, rue André-Vitu, La Colombière, 88025 Épinal cedex, ☎ 03 29 33 00 33, Fax: 03 29 29 23 60. For Champagne-Ardenne, contact the Chambre Régionale d'Agriculture, complexe agricole du Mont Bernard, 51000 Châlons-sur-Marne, ☎ 03 26 65 18 52, Fax: 03 26 66 87 15.

Ramblers can consult the guide entitled *Gîtes et refuges France* et Frontières by A and S Mouraret (Editions La Cadole, 74, rue Albert-Perdreaux, 78140 Vélizy, ☎ 01 34 65 10 40). The guide has been written mainly for those who enjoy rambling, riding and cycling holidays.

Gourmets…
The introductory chapter of this guide describes the region's gastronomic specialities and best local wines. The annual Michelin Red Guide France offers an up-to-date selection of good restaurants

Regional specialities and wines

The Michelin **Red Guide France** provides a very wide selection of restaurants, for all tastes and pocketbooks, serving the finest specialities in the regions of Alsace-Lorraine and Champagne-Ardenne as well as the rest of France.

When the word *repas* ("meal") is printed in red, it refers to a high-quality but reasonably-priced meal. Pictograms indicate places with charming decor, a beautiful view, or a quiet setting. This is a gourmet guide you can trust.

Fermes-auberges (Farm-inns) may or may not offer overnight accommodation, but they do serve farm produce and local speciality dishes.

The tradition of serving farm-style meals to travellers is a century old in the Hautes-Vosges, where dairy farmers were known as *marcaires*. The **repas marcaire** proposed by many farms usually includes a **tourte de la vallée de Munster** (deep-dish pie with smoked pork, onions, garlic), followed by a blueberry tart. The *Guide des Fermes-Auberges* in the Hautes-Vosges is available (40F) from the Association des fermes-auberges du Haut-Rhin et départements limitrophes, BP 371, 68007 Colmar cedex. Write to the Comité régional du tourisme *(address above)* for a catologue of farms in Lorraine Fermes-auberges, les saveurs du terroir lorrain.

Alsace-Lorraine

Choucroute is synonymous with Alsatian cuisine. The basic ingredient is white cabbage prepared in brine. The word is related phonetically to its German origin, *sauerkraut*. Typically, it is served with potatoes and a daunting portion of sausages, bacon, chops and other smoked or boiled pork. Modern tastes for lighter dishes have inspired many variations, in particular preparations using several varieties of fish or wildfowl; juniper berries add a burst of flavour. The choice of **game** is very wide, and partridge takes pride of place in seasonal choucroute. **Baeckeoffe** is a stew made of layers of different meats (usually mutton, pork and beef), potatoes and onions.

Yet pork remains the meat of choice, as evidenced by the many *charcuterie* shops selling salted and smoked hams, knuckles, trotters and bacon, Strasbourg sausage (pork and beef in a plump frankfurter), spicy *cervelas*, salamis, blood puddings and pork pies.

There is a long tradition of Jewish cuisine in Alsace too, and its influence is felt in the use of geese and goose fat in the place of pork, as well as the celebrated **carpe à la juiv** (gefilte fish), a dish which is made ahead of time and served cold. Another popular freshwater fish dish is **matelote**, a stew made from a variety of species which may include pike, tench, perch, trout and eel. **Frog soup** has been a tradition in Alsace since at least the 13C.

The well-known **quiche lorraine** joins other savoury pies, **tarte à l'oignon (ziewelküeche)** and **tarte flambée (flammeküeche)**, along with the delicious but unpronounceable **roïgabrageln** (potato and onion hash) on menus in many popular establishments. Of course, while you are waiting, you may ask for a salty **bretzel** to go with your beer.

Munster is the only cheese which is special to the region. The tasty, strong-flavoured cheese is named after the valley town in the Vosges mountains. Semi-soft, with distinctive orange crust, a small portion of munster is served at the end of a meal with a little dish of cumin or caraway seeds, and a glass of Gewürztraminer.

D. Hée/Michelin

Baked goods entice the visitor passing by the innumerable shops selling all sort of breads, cakes and pastries. Among the specialities is the familiar **Kugelhopf** (the name derives from the German *Kuge* "ball"), a light tube cake with raisins and almonds baked in a distinctive fluted and twisted mould. There are many seasonal treats, especially around Christmas time starting early December with the S Nicholas **bonshommes**, in festive shapes going on through New Year with **neujoh weke** brioche, and up until St Agatha feast day (5 February), when the patro saint of bakers is celebrated. **Bredeles** are also associated with Christmas, although they can be bought all year round nowadays and come in a variety of shapes; these buttery biscuits are flavoured with vanill lemon, aniseed or almonds. **Pain d'épice** (spice cake or gingerbread) also comes in every shape and size.

la mirabelle *(Prunus syriaca)* is found in orchards all over Lorraine. The golden-rose fruit weighs no more than 15g (about half an ounce), stone included. It is used to make ice cream, tarts and jams, or served in syrup. **Mirabelle de Lorraine** is the official name of the distilled liqueur which is commonly served after a meal. Every year, the **fête de la mirabelle** is held in Metz from the last weekend in August through to the first weekend in September.

Vineyards near Kaysersberg

Alsatian wines are predominantly white, and are identified by the grape types (rather than by the château or domain). The varieties are **Sylvaner, Muscat, Riesling, Pinot Gris, Gewürztraminer, Pinot Blanc** and **Pinot Noir** *(see the Introduction for information on their distinctive qualities)*. There is also a wine called **Edelzwicker**, made from a blend, and this is often served by the carafe in restaurants. Wines labelled **Crémant d'Alsace** are sparkling (but without the finesse of Champagne). There is a single *Appellation contrôlée* for the wines of Alsace (granted in 1962), and one superior *appellation*, **Alsace Grand Cru** (authorised in 1975). Yet restaurants distinguish wines by the names of the individual vineyards and by such designations as *Réserve Particulière, Réserve Personnelle, Cuvée Spéciale* or *Cuvée Exceptionnelle* which, while they may help buyers keep track of vintages, are meaningless to the ordinary customer. The indication **Vendanges Tardives** signifies that the grapes were harvested late in the autumn, and this extra ripening time produces a subtler, sweeter, more complex wine, generally on the expensive side, and requiring a few years to develop fully in the bottle.

Champagne-Ardenne

Not surprisingly, cuisine in the region of Champagne production relies on sauces made from the sparkling wine, ladled generously over plump pullet hens, wild thrush, kidneys, stuffed trout, grilled pike, crayfish or snails. A delicious palate-freshener served between courses is a **sorbet** made from *marc de Champagne*.

Cabbage dishes are nearly as popular as in Alsace, served with smoked ham and sausage. Pig's feet are a speciality of Ste-Menehould, served in a white wine sauce flavoured with onions, mustard and pickles. Every French gourmet is familiar with **la véritable andouillette de Troyes**, a traditional pure pork sausage seasoned with onions.

The once impenetrable Ardennes Forest is home to a great variety of game, and hunting is a popular pastime. Traditional recipes seem to have been handed down unchanged from the Dark Ages, robust restorative cookery for cold winter nights. **Sanglier** (wild boar) is emblematic of the region, and served in *pâtés* and *terrines*, or as a main course in a rich red wine sauce flavoured with spices and herbs, accompanied by potatoes and onions. **Marcassin** (young boar) is preferred for its subtler flavour and greater tenderness. A typical country inn menu may include: **Civet de lièvre** (hare), **bécasse au champagne** (woodcock), **grives** (thrush), served up with sage leaves and juniper berries. **Jambon cru des Ardennes** is ham cured with green juniper or broomwood for a distinctive flavour; **boudin blanc** is a speciality sausage made from white pork, bacon, ham, fresh eggs and milk, especially in Rethel (a celebratory fair is held the last weekend of April) and Haybes-sur-Meuse (where the recipe includes onions).

Freshwater fish including **truite** and **brochet** (trout and pike) are served stuffed, grilled, in sauce, in **matelote** (stew) or as **quenelles** (seasoned dumplings).

Conversion tables

Weights and measures

1 kilogram (kg)	2.2 pounds (lb)	2.2 pounds
1 metric ton (tn)	1.1 tons	1.1 tons

to convert kilograms to pounds, multiply by 2.2

1 litre (l)	2.1 pints (pt)	1.8 pints
1 litre	0.3 gallon (gal)	0.2 gallon

to convert litres to gallons, multiply by 0.26 (US) or 0.22 (UK)

1 hectare (ha)	2.5 acres	2.5 acres
1 square kilometre (km²)	0.4 square miles (sq mi)	0.4 square miles

to convert hectares to acres, multiply by 2.4

1 centimetre (cm)	0.4 inches (in)	0.4 inches
1 metre (m)	3.3 feet (ft) - 39.4 inches - 1.1 yards (yd)	
1 kilometre (km)	0.6 miles (mi)	0.6 miles

to convert metres to feet, multiply by 3.28 . kilometres to miles, multiply by 0.6

Clothing

Women	EU	US	UK	EU	US	UK	Men
	35	4	2½	40	7½	7	
	36	5	3½	41	8½	8	
	37	6	4½	42	9½	9	
Shoes	38	7	5½	43	10½	10	Shoes
	39	8	6½	44	11½	11	
	40	9	7½	45	12½	12	
	41	10	8½	46	13½	13	
	36	4	8	46	36	36	
	38	6	10	48	38	38	
Dresses &	40	8	12	50	40	40	Suits
Suits	42	12	14	52	42	42	
	44	14	16	54	44	44	
	46	16	18	56	46	48	
	36	08	30	37	14½	14,5	
	38	10	32	38	15	15	
Blouses &	40	12	14	39	15½	15½	Shirts
sweaters	42	14	36	40	15¾	15¾	
	44	16	38	41	16	16	
	46	18	40	42	16½	16½	

Sizes often vary depending on the designer. These equivalents are given for guidance only.

Speed

kph	10	30	50	70	80	90	100	110	120	130
mph	6	19	31	43	50	56	62	68	75	81

Temperature

Celsius (°C)	0°	5°	10°	15°	20°	25°	30°	40°	60°	80°	100
Fahrenheit (°F)	32°	41°	50°	59°	68°	77°	86°	104°	140°	176°	212

To convert Celsius into Fahrenheit, multiply °C by 9, divide by 5, and add 32
To convert Fahrenheit into Celsius, subtract 32 from °F, multiply by 5, and divide by 9

A few other local specialities are **Rocroi** cheese, apple and pear **cider**, sweet **galette au sucre** pastries and blue **ardoises**, nougat covered with white chocolate, shaped to resemble slate roof tiles.

Champagne is not only the name of a geographical region, but is, of course, the exclusive home of the world's best-loved sparkling wine. The *Introduction* to this guide gives an explanation of how it is made. Here is some information for travellers wishing to buy Champagne; there is no dearth of opportunites to do so.

Most Champagne is marketed by the *maison* (house) that blends and bottles it. Big companies with well-known brand names, **Grandes Marques**, open their cellars to tourists, and have a corner on the export market as well: **Moët et Chandon, Canard Duchêne, Heidsieck, Henriot, Krug, Lanson, Mercier, Mumm, Pommery et Greno, Roederer, Taittinger** and **Veuve Clicquot-Ponsardin**, to name a few.

Other companies act as a **Marque Acheteur** (buyer's own brand), and produce wines which are labelled for distribution under a specific trade name for supermarkets, department stores, restaurants etc. These companies may be subsidiaries of the Grandes Marques, but rarely sell Champagne under their own company name.

Finally, there are **Récoltant-manipulants**, small growers who produce unblended wines for sale to domestic markets, and **Négociant-manipulants**, small firms which blend local products, and may even provide some superior first-pressing juice to more prestigious houses. While the Grandes Marques generally offer better quality (at a higher price), some growers also produce exceptionally good sparkling wine.

Vintage Champagne is made with grapes harvested in a single year, although an admixture of 10% from another year is permitted, and the grapes do not all come from the same vineyard. To bear the vintage label, Champagne must be aged at least three years.

Champagne is a fairly sweet wine, and while aficionados claim that it can accompany any part of a meal, whatever that meal's constituents, it is most often enjoyed as an *apéritif* before dinner, or with dessert. The sweetness of the wine comes from the final stage when sugar is added to stimulate the fermentation that creates its delightful, delicate bubbles. Truly "dry" Champagne is **Brut Zero** or **Brut Sauvage**, no sugar added, and rather astringent. With sugar percentages between 1 and over 6%, the order of sweetness is as follows: **Brut, Extra Sec** or **Extra Dry, Sec, Demi-Sec, Doux** or **Rich**.

Before the discovery of the *méthode champenoise*, a number of respectable still wines were made in the area, the most northerly wine-producing region in France. Red, white and rosé wines benefit from the *appellation contrôlée* **Coteaux Champenois. Bouzy Rouge** comes in an elegant bottle, like Champagne, and **Ratafia** is a popular fortified sweet wine served as an *apéritif*. A little-known wine which is hard to find outside the region is **Rosé des Riceys**, from a pretty village on the wine route – well-worth a detour for those seeking something special!

Shopping

Opening hours – Department stores are open Monday to Saturday, 9am to 6.30 or 7.30pm. Smaller shops may close during the lunch hour. Grocers, wine merchants, bakeries and other food shops are open from 7am to 6.30 or 7.30pm. Some open on Sunday mornings, and may close on Mondays. Bakery and pastry shops sometimes close on Wednesdays.

VAT refunds – The French Value Added Tax *(TVA)* of 20.6% is included in the price of most of the goods (clothing, luxury items) you purchase. Travellers from outside the European Union can seek a refund. In practice, the system works when you buy more than 2 000F of goods in the same shop at the same time and pay with a credit card. The paperwork is time-consuming, and only the main department stores or luxury stores catering to tourists, are actually able to provide the service without hassle. Enquire before you pay.

Christmas every day

The year-end holiday season is lively and popular in Alsace, but even travellers who visit at other seasons will find the spirit of Noël. The pretty towns on the wine route re always festive with red geraniums, bright against the lush green vineyards or the deeper green on the hillsides. **Kaysersberg**, for example, is known for its Christmas market, but many of the shops are decked out year round with cookie cutters, recipe and craft books, holiday tableware, stockings to stuff, party linens, gift boxes, sweets, candles, decorations for your tree ...

A souvenir both typical and useful would be a **Kugelhopf mould**; they are everywhere in shop windows, some too lovely to think of putting in the oven! Any friend at home would be pleased to receive a gift from **Baccarat**, the famous crystal manufacturers who make useful and unique objects, including resolutely modern jewellery. Visitors to

Strasbourg – Christmas market

Mulhouse can enjoy the fine shop in the **Musée de l'Impression sur étoffes**; wonderfu fabrics have been finely made into ties, scarves and linens and there are some item that will go straight to any designer's heart, including books and stationery.

Celebrations and markets – Since the time of the Holy Roman Empire, the feast o St Nicholas has been the occasion to offer toys and treats to young children. Cele brations take place on the night before and the day of 6 December, or on the firs Saturday or Sunday of December. Many towns and villages in Lorraine hold publi events, including St-Nicolas-de-Port (torchlight procession), Nancy (parade with float and fireworks), Metz (marching bands) and Épinal (parade).

In Alsace, about 50 different **Christkendelsmarkts** are held during the month of Decem ber, all week long in the larger towns, and weekends in smaller places.

Active tours

Touring the region on foot

There is an extensive network of well-marked footpaths in France which mak rambling *(la randonnée)* a breeze. Several **Grande Randonnée (GR)** trails, recognisable fo the red and white horizontal marks on trees, rocks and in town on walls, signpost etc, go through the region. Along with the GR exist the **Petite Randonnée (PR)** paths which are usually blazed with blue (2hr walk), yellow (2hr15min-3hr45min) or gree (4-6hr) marks. Of course, with appropriate maps, you can combine walks to suit you desires.

To use these trails, obtain the "Topo-Guide" for the area published by the *Fédératio Française de la Randonnée Pédestre*, 9, rue Geoffroy-Marie, 75009 Paris, ☎ 01 4 01 80 80. Some English-language editions are available. An annual guide ("Rand Guide") which includes ideas for overnight itineraries and places to stay as well a information on the difficulty and accessibility of trails, is published by the *Comit national des sentiers de Grande Randonnée*, 64, rue de Gergovie, 75014 Paris, ☎ 0 45 45 31 02. Another source of maps and guides for excursions on foot is the *Institu National Géographique (IGN)*, which has a boutique in Paris at 107, rue de la Boéti (off the Champs-Élysées); to order from abroad, contact IGN-Sologne, Administratio des Ventes, 41200 Romorantin-Lanthenay, ☎ (33) 2 54 96 54 42, Fax (33) 2 54 8 14 66, or visit the Web site (www.ign.fr) for addresses of wholesalers in you country. Among their publications, France 903 is a map showing all of the GR and P in France (29F); the "Série Bleue" and "Top 25" maps, at a scale of 1:25 00 (1cm=250m), show all paths, whether waymarked or not, as well as refuges, cam sites, beaches etc (46-58F) for a precise area. In the region, you can find many of the publications cited above in bookstores, at sports centres or equipment shops, and in some of the country inns and hotels which cater to the sporting crowd. Some guides can be ordered from McCarta (*Footpaths of Europe* series), 15 Highbury Place, London N5 1QP, ☎ 017 354 16 16.

Le Club Vosgien – Founded in 1872, this is the oldest ramblers' association in France, and also the largest, with 33 000 members. They have joined forces to protect natural and historic sites, and maintain the marks on 16 000km – nearly 10 000 miles – of trails. The club sponsors a quarterly publication, *Les Vosges*, and publishes detailed maps and guides to paths on the Lorraine plateau, in the Jura mountains of Alsace, the Vosges and the Alsatian plain. Check with local tourist

Waymarked footpaths

offices for the dates of scheduled group rambles. The club's emblem is a holly leaf. As early as 1897, they began marking out a trail across the Vosges with a red rectangle, still seen on hiking trails in the region.

The Grande Randonnée trails in the regions are:

GR 2   Across the Pays d'Othe, through a hilly landscape and along the River Seine.
GR 5   From the border of Luxembourg to the Ballon d'Alsace, through the Lorraine regional nature park.
GR 7   Across the Vosges from the Ballon d'Alsace to Bourbonne-les-Bains, and continuing into the region of Burgundy.
GR 12   A section of European footpath no 3 (Atlantic-Bohemia), cutting across the French and Belgian Ardennes.

Stepping smart

Choosing the right equipment for a rambling expedition is essential: flexible hiking shoes with non-slip soles, a rain jacket or poncho, an extra sweater, sun protection (hat, glasses, lotion), drinking water (1-2l per person), high energy snacks (chocolate, cereal bars, banana ...), and a first aid kit. Of course, you'll need a good map (and a compass if you plan to leave the main trails). Plan your itinerary well, keeping in mind that while the average walking speed for an adult is 4kph/2.5mph, you will need time to eat and rest, and children will not keep up the same pace. Leave your itinerary with someone before setting out (innkeeper or fellow camper).

Respect for nature is a cardinal rule and includes the following precautions: don't smoke or light fires in the forest, which are particularly susceptible in the dry summer months; always carry your rubbish out; leave wild flowers as they are; walk around, not through, farmers' fields; close gates behind you.

If you are caught in an electrical storm, avoid high ground, and do not move along a ridge top; do not seek shelter under overhanging rocks, isolated trees in otherwise open areas, at the entrance to caves or other openings in the rocks, or in the proximity of metal fences or gates. Do not use a metallic survival blanket. If possible, position yourself at least 15m/15yd from the highest point around you (rock or tree); crouch with your knees up and without touching the rock face with your hands or any exposed part of your body. An automobile is a good refuge as its rubber tires ground it and provide protection for those inside.

GR 14	Follows the Montagne de Reims through vineyard and forest, then contin ues across the chalk hills of Champagne to Bar-le-Duc before turning towards the Ardennes.
GR 24	The loop starts at Bar-sur-Seine, goes through the Forêt d'Orient regional nature park, vineyards and farmland.
GR 53	From Sarrebourg to the Ballon d'Alsace.
GR 714	From Bar-le-Duc to Vittel, linking GR 14 and GR 7.

Touring the region by cycle

For general information concerning France, write or call the **Fédération Française de Cyclotourisme** (8, rue Jean-Marie-Jégo, 75013 Paris, ☎ 01 44 16 88 88). Off-road and mountain bike (*VTT*, in French) enthusiasts, contact the **Fédération Française de Cyclisme** (5, rue de Rome, 93561 Rosny-sous-Bois) and request the "Guide des centres VTT". The IGN *(see address above, under touring on foot)* offers Map 906, "Mountain bike and cycle touring in France" (29F).

Local tourist offices have a list of cycle hire firms. Regional associations and mountain bike centres include:

Association Vosges VTT
Comité départemental du tourisme
7, rue Gilbert
88000 Épinal ☎ 03 29 82 49 93.
Comité de Lorraine de la FFC
Maison des Sports
13, rue Jena Moulin
54510 Tomblaine ☎ 03 83 21 35 12.
Centre VTT de la forêt d'Argonne
Argonne Passions
La-Grange-aux-Bois
51800 Ste-Menehould ☎ 03 26 60 81 16.

Lac du Der-Chantecoq
Maison du Lac
51290 Giffaumont-Champaubert
☎ 03 26 72 62 80.
Office du tourisme des Crêtes préardennaises
rue Roger-Ponsard
08430 Launois-sur-Vence
Ligue d'Alsace de cyclotourisme
☎ 03 88 30 43 76.

Touring the region on horseback

The **Délégation Nationale du Tourisme Équestre** (30, avenue d'Iéna, 75116 Paris, ☎ 01 53 67 44 44) publishes an annual review called *Tourisme et Loisirs Équestres en France*. It lists all the possibilities for riding by region and *département*. It is also possible to contact regional associations directly, by writing to the following *Associations Régionales du Tourisme Équestre:*

Alsace	Maison des Associations, bureau 212, 6, route d'Ingersheim 68000 Colmar ☎ 03 89 24 43 18.
Lorraine	M. Baret, 32, rue Géricote, 55160 Mont-Villers ☎ 03 29 87 39 91.
Meurthe-et-Moselle	Mme Dossier, 46 bis, avenue du Maréchal-Foch 54200 Dommartin-lès-Toul
Meuse	M. Sepulchre, Centre de tourisme équestre 55290 Biencourt-sur-Orge ☎ 03 29 75 94 26.
Moselle	M. Collignon, 53, rue Principale 57940 Volstroff ☎ 03 82 56 85 12.

Riding the plains of Champagne

Vosges
                                M. Flieller, 32, chemin du Rupt-du-Moulin
                                88310 Ventron ☎ 03 29 24 18 20.

In **Champagne-Ardenne**, information is available from the Association de Champagne-Ardenne pour le tourisme équestre (ACATE), 51170 Arcis-le-Ponsart, ☎ 03 26 48 86 39. A topographical map, *Les Ardennes à cheval*, shows 330km/205mi of bridle paths; it is available from the Hôtel du département, 08011 Charleville-Mézières, ☎ 03 24 59 60 60.

Laifour – La Meuse

Touring the region on board a boat

Houseboats provide a slow and easy view of the countryside. In the region covered in this guide, you can travel on several **canals**: canal de l'Est, canal des Ardennes, canal de l'Aisne à la Marne, canal latéral de la Marne, canal de la Marne à la Saône, canal de la Marne au Rhin, canal des Houillères de la Sarre. Contact the regional tourist office for information *(see Planning your trip, above)*, or contact rental agencies:

Locaboat Plaisance	Port-au-Bois
	89300 Joigny ☎ 03 86 91 72 72.
	Port-Amont, Chemin de Halage, BP 11
	57820 Lutzelbourg ☎ 03 87 25 70 15.
Nicols	route du Puy-St-Bonnet
	49300 Cholet ☎ 02 41 56 46 56.
	11, rue de l'Orangerie
	Saverne 67700 ☎ 03 88 91 34 80.
Ardennes Nautisme	16, rue du Château BP 78
	08202 Sedan ☎ 03 24 27 05 15.
Ardennes Plaisance	75, rue des Forges-St-Charles
	08000 Charleville-Mézières ☎ 03 24 56 47 61.

Cruises may last a few hours or two weeks. In the region, you can travel on the Rhine, Moselle, Sarre, Neckar, Main, Danube, Meuse, Marne and Seine rivers. **Alsace-Croisières** offers many trips out of Strasbourg (information and reservations: 12, rue de la Division-Leclerc, 67000 Strasbourg, ☎ 03 88 76 44 44). You can tour the city while enjoying lunch or dinner on boats leaving from the quai Finkwiller (Société rhenane de Restauration, 15 bis, rue de Nantes, 67100, Strasbourg ☎ 03 88 84 10 01). To sail the Marne, go to Cumières (Croisi-Champagne, BP 22 51480 Cumières, ☎ 03 26 54 49 51), for the Seine, the rendezvous is at Bray-sur-Seine (Association Loisirs nautiques et équestres, 8, rue de la Ruelle-de-Mars, 77480 Montigny-le-Guesdier, ☎ 01 60 67 23 52). Local travel agents also advertise and book cruises.

Touring the region from above

For a unique view and memorable experience, consider a **hot air balloon** tour.

Aérovision	4, rue de Hohrod, 68140 Munster ☎ 03 89 77 22 81.
Pilâtre de Rozier	6, place du Temple, 57530 Courcelles-Chaussy
	☎ 03 87 64 08 08.
Champagne air show	15 bis, place St-Nicaise, 51100 Reims, ☎ 03 26 82 59 60.

Sports and Recreation

Water sports

The entire region covered by this guide is favoured by lakes, canals and rivers, providing many opportunities for recreational activities.

Lake	Nearest	Swimming	Boating	Fishing
Alfeld	Kirchberg	–	–	🎣
Armance	Troyes	🏊	–	🎣
Bairon	Le Chesne	🏊	⛵	–
Blanc	Orbey	–	–	🎣
Blanchemer	La Bresse	–	–	🎣
Charmes	Langres	🏊	–	–
Corbeaux	La Bresse	–	–	🎣
Der-Chantecoq	Vitry-le-François	🏊	⛵	🎣
Folie	Contrexéville	🏊	⛵	🎣
Gérardmer	Gérardmer	🏊	⛵	🎣
Hanau	Falkenstein-	🏊	⛵	🎣
Lauch	Le Markstein	–	–	🎣
Liez	Langres	🏊	⛵	🎣
Longemer	Gérardmer	🏊	⛵	🎣
Madine	Hattonchâtel	🏊	⛵	🎣
Mouche	Langres	–	–	–
Noir	Orbey	–	–	–
Orient	Troyes	🏊	⛵	–
Pierre-Percée	Badonviller	–	⛵	🎣
Retournemer	Gérardmer	–	–	–
Temple	Troyes	–	–	–
Vielles-Forges	Revin	🏊	⛵	–
Vert	Hohrodberg	–	–	–
Vingeanne	Langres	🏊	⛵	–

Fishing in France is regulated by the *Conseil supérieur de la pêche* (134, avenue de Malakoff, 75116, Paris ☎ 01 45 02 20 20), which publishes a map, *La Pêche er. France*. When fishing in France, you will need to buy a permit *(carte de pêche)*, and familiarise yourself with local limits. Permits and information are available at tourist offices and in many cafés and bars located near the popular fishing spots.

Skiing

The Vosges mountains are perfect for easy-going skiers. In the pine forests, gentle landscapes unfold between 600m and 1 400m altitude (1 968-4 600ft). Resorts offer downhill and cross-country trails, snowboarding, biathlon, jumping, snowshoeing, dog-sledding, and every other form of gliding on the snow, or peaceful walks through the wintry countryside.
The mountains are equipped with 170 lifts for downhill skiing; different ski areas have snow-making machines and lights for night skiing. The larger resorts are Gérardmer, la Bresse, le Markstein and Lac Blanc. Le Schnepfenried is appreciated for the panoramic view of the crests forming "the blue line of the Vosges". Cross-country skiers can enjoy more than 1 000km/621mi of marked and groomed trails.
For information and reservations, contact local tourist offices, or log in to www.ski-france.fr on the Internet, for the latest update on snow conditions (some sites also list available accommodation).

Hunting

The Ardennes Forest, thick and sparsely populated, is a good place to pursue deer and wild boar. Some addresses to contact for complete information: Fédération départementale des chasseurs des Ardennes, ☎ 03 24 56 07 35; Saint-Hubert Club de France, 10, rue Lisbonne, 75008 Paris, ☎ 01 45 22 38 90; L'Union nationale des fédérations départementales des chasseurs, 48, rue d'Alésia, 75014 Paris, ☎ 01 43 27 85 76.

The domaine de la Maison forestière de Garmaine (Hameau de Vauremont, 5, rue de la Croix-Verte, 51160 Germaine, ☎ 03 26 51 08 27) organises one-day and weekend parties, including hunting from an observation tower, in a 400ha/988-acre park, or in a 1 200ha/2 970-acre wooded perimeter.

And more ...

Golf is growing more popular in France, and the region of Lorraine offers numerous courses, for regular players and novices. The Comité régional du tourisme *(see address under Planning your trip, Local tourist offices)* publishes a brochure-map with all of the addresses and services available, including nearby lodging.

Canoeing-Kayaking is practised on the rivers of Champagne and Ardennes. The more challenging courses are on the Blaise, Saulx, Rognon and Aire rivers. Gentler waters are the Meuse (at Sedan), the Aube and the Marne. The IGN *(address above, under Active tours, Touring on foot)* publishes map 905, "Water Sports in France", with sites classified by level of difficulty.

Bases de Loisirs are recreational areas where travellers are likely to find various facilities for sports and recreation, such as beaches, camping and picnic areas, bike and hiking trails. When it is time to stretch your legs, keep an eye out for signs, or look for the green diamond on your Michelin map.

Spas and hydrotherapy

The Vosges mountains on the Lorraine side and the region of Lorraine itself are especially blessed with thermal springs which have given rise to spa resorts. The Alsatian side of the range also has its share of resorts.
None of the waters are sulphurous, but all other types of spring water are found and used in treating various chronic affections.

Mineral springs and hot springs – Natural springs result when water filters through permeable layers of the earth's surface until it meets resistance in the form of an impermeable layer of rock. The water flows along this impenetrable layer until it breaks through to the open air, and the water surges forth.
A mineral spring can be water surging forth in this way, or water rising from deep within the earth, which has collected mineral substances and gases as it flows towards the surface.
Hot springs produce water which hits the air at a temperature of at least 35°C/95°F.
Springs are found in zones where the earth's crust is fairly thin, where boulders have been thrown into place by eruptions or cracking. Many are found along the Lorraine plateau fault line or near crystalline mountain ranges and peaks.

Water, water everywhere – Water from mineral or hot springs is usually unstable, and contact with the air changes its properties. This is why its therapeutic virtues are best enjoyed at the source. Spa therapy is based on this principle.
The two geographic zones in the Vosges, the "plain" to the west and the "mountain" to the east and southeast, have different types of springs, each with its own specificity.
The plain is dominated by cold springs, water which has filtered through the earth's crust and re-emerges enriched with calcium and magnesium and, in some cases, lithium and sodium.
The best-known resort in the area is certainly **Vittel**; the waters were reputed in Roman times, then forgotten, only to be rediscovered in 1845. In 1854, the Bouloumié family began actively promoting and marketing the spring water.
Vittel and the neighbouring spa at **Contrexéville** treat kidney and liver afflictions. In conjunction with therapeutic activities at the spa, the water is bottled for sale, and many tourists visit the plants each year (with Évian, among the world's largest bottling operations).
The springs found in the mountainous region are quite different. Of volcanic origin, their properties depend less on mineral content than on temperature and radioactivity.
Also known to the Romans, who appreciated warm springs, as did the Celts and the Gauls, these waters have a long-standing reputation.
Plombières, with 27 hot springs, some of which reach 80°C/176°F, is reputed for the treatment of rheumatism and enteronitis.

Poster by Jean d'Yien (1931)

Bain-les-Bains is a spa specialising in the treatment of heart and artery troubles. **Luxeuil-les-Bains** treats gynecological ailments.

The most recent arrival on the scene is **Amnéville**, where *curistes* come to relieve the symptoms of rheumatism and respiratory problems, using the therapeutic waters of the St-Éloy source, which emerge at 41°C/106°F.

Bourbonne-les-Bains, located on the border of Lorraine and Champagne, boasts warm radioactive water with a slight chlorine content. Louis XV created a military hospital on the site, for the treatment of soldiers wounded by crossbows. Today, the spa is prescribed for the purposes of healing bones.

In Alsace, **Niederbronn-les-Bains** is recognised for the treatment of digestive and kidney afflictions and arterial sclerosis. **Morsbronn-les-Bains** is a small spa specialising in rheumatic disorders.

Hydrotherapy and tourism – The benefits of spa treatments were rediscovered in the 18C-19C. At that time, "taking the waters" was reserved for wealthy clients with time to spare. Today, the French national health system recognises the therapeutic value of many cures, and patients' stays are provided for, all or in part, by the social security.

Treatment occupies only part of the day, so the spas offer their guests many other activities to pass the time pleasantly: sports and recreation, various forms of entertainment. The beautiful natural settings provide the opportunity for outdoor excursions.

In addition to traditional treatment courses, which usually last three weeks, many resorts offer shorter stays for clients with a specific goal in mind: stress relief and relaxation, fitness and shaping up, giving up smoking, losing weight etc.

The Association des stations thermales vosgiennes publishes a brochure, *Vosges thermales*, with information on Bains-les-Bains, Contrexéville, Plombières and Vittel. To obtain a copy write to BP 332, 88008 Épinal.

You can also get information by contacting the Fédération thermale et climatique française, 16, rue de l'Estrapade, 75005 Paris, ☎ 01 43 25 11 85.

Via Internet, connect to www.tourisme.fr and search the category "Spas and Fitness" for precise information (in French in most cases) on accommodation, short-stay treatments, entertainment etc.

Or contact the spas directly:

Amnéville: rheumatic disorders, post-traumatic injury treatment, respiratory affliction. **Open**: February to December.

– Centre thermal St-Éloy, BP 83, 57360 Amnéville, ☎ 03 87 70 19 09.
– Office de tourisme, Centre thermal et touristique, 57360 Amnéville, ☎ 03 87 70 10 40.

Bain-les-Bains – Roman bath

Bains-les-Bains: cardio-vascular ailments, rheumatic disorders, post-traumatic injury treatment.
Open: April to October.
– Thermes de Bains-les-Bains, 1, avenue du Docteur-Mathieu, 88240 Bains-les-Bains, ☎ 03 29 36 32 04.
– Office de tourisme, place du Bain-Romain, BP 4, 88240 Bains-les-Bains, ☎ 03 29 36 31 75.

Bourbonne-les-Bains: rheumatic disorders, respiratory ailments.
Open: March to November.
– Établissement thermal, BP 15, 52400 Bourbonne-les-Bains, ☎ 03 25 90 07 20.
– Office de tourisme, place des Bains, BP 34, 52400 Bourbonne-les-Bains, ☎ 03 25 90 01 71.

Contrexéville: kidney problems, excess weight.
Open: April to October.
– Établissement thermal, 88140 Contrexéville, ☎ 03 29 08 03 24.
– Office de tourisme, 116, rue du Shah-de-Perse, BP 42, 88142 Contrexéville cedex, ☎ 03 29 08 08 68.

Luxeuil-les-Bains: phlebology, gynecology.
Open: year round.
– Établissement thermal, avenue des Thermes, BP 51, 70302 Luxeuil-les-Bains, ☎ 03 84 40 44 22.
– Office de tourisme, 1, avenue des Thermes, BP 71, 70302 Luxeuil-les-Bains, ☎ 03 84 40 06 41.

Morsbronn-les-Bains: rheumatic disorders, post-traumatic injury treatment.
Open: year round.
– Établissement thermal, 12, route Haguenau, 67360 Morsbronn-les-Bains, ☎ 03 88 09 83 00.
– Syndicat d'initiative, rue Principale, 67360 Morsbronn-les-Bains, ☎ 03 88 09 30 18.

Niederbronn-les-Bains: rheumatic disorders, post-traumatic injury treatment, physical therapy
Open: April to December.
– Établissement thermal, 16-18, rue du Maréchal-Leclerc, 67110 Niederbronn-les-Bains, ☎ 03 88 80 88 80 (year round).
– Établissement thermal saisonnier, place des Thermes, ☎ 03 88 80 30 70 (in season).
– Office de tourisme, 2, place de l'Hôtel-de-Ville, 67110 Niederbronn-les-Bains, ☎ 03 88 80 89 70.

Plombières-les-Bains: Digestive ailments, rheumatic disorders.
Open: April to October.
– Société thermale SEML, place Maurice-Janot, 88370 Plombières, ☎ 03 29 66 02 17.
– Office de tourisme, "sous les Arcades", 16, rue Stanislas, BP 15, 88370 Plombières, ☎ 03 29 66 01 30.

Vittel: Liver and kidney ailments, rheumatic disorders, post-traumatic injury treatment, nutritional problems.
Open: year round (except January).
– Thermes de Vittel, Parc thermal, BP 43, 88805 Vittel cedex, ☎ 03 29 08 76 54.
– Maison du tourisme, 136, avenue Bouloumié, 88800 Vittel, ☎ 03 29 08 08 88.

Discovering the region

Excursion Trains

Steam and diesel locomotives offer tourists a charming ride through the countryside. In Alsace, discover the **vallée de la Canner** on a train leaving from Vigy; the **vallée de la Doller** from **Cernay** to Sentheim, or take the **Chemin de fer forestier** from Abreschviller to Grand Soldat. A line runs along the Rhine between the port of **Neuf-Brisach** and Baltzenheim, and connects to a boat trip.
For details, see Admission times and charges, following.

Draisines – In the past, pedal cars, hand cars and trolleys were propelled by railroad workers maintaining or inspecting the track. Today, this mode of locomotion can be used to explore the vallée de la Mortagne. Energetic travellers can pedal along 20km/12mi of otherwise unused railways, starting from Magnières. Rental is for an hour or a half day, from 9am to 7pm. Information and reservations: ☎ 03 83 72 34 73.

Self-propulsion

The **Chemin de fer touristique du Sud des Ardennes** steams down part of the Aisne Valley from Attigny to Challerange, passing through Vouzier (31km/19mi); or from Attigny to Amagne-Lucquy (9.5km/6mi). Another line follows the Meuse Valley from Mouzon to Stenay (24km/15mi). These trains run from June to September. Information is available from the association Les Amis de la traction vapeur en Ardenne, cour de la Gare, 08130 Attigny, ☎ 03 24 42 26 14.
A steam locomotive travels the **Chemin de fer à vapeur des 3 vallées**; one of the three lines runs from Givet to Dinant, Belgium. *See Admission times and charges for Givet.*

In the holiday season, **mini-trains** carry tourists around the historic districts of some towns, including Strasbourg, Colmar, Nancy, Riquewihr and Guebwiller in Alsace; Châlons-en-Champagne, Épernay, Langres, Reims, Troyes and around the Der-Chantecoq Lake in Champagne-Ardenne. Information at the local tourist office.

Thematic Routes

In the regions covered in this guide, there are numerous **routes touristiques**, itineraries plotted out for motorists who wish to explore a particular aspect of the area. The best-known routes in Alsace are the **Route des Crêts** (along the top of the Vosges crest from Thann to the Col du Bonhomme) and the **Route des Vins**, or wine road, both described in this guide. Motorists will notice many other routes signposted in the region: Route du Rhin, Route de l'Amitié, Route du Cristal (Alsace-Lorraine); Route des Légendes, Route des Fortifications, Route Rimbaud-Verlaine (Champagne-Ardenne), to name a few. Other routes *(gastronomiques)* are dedicated to regional culinary specialities, cheeses, beers, trout, choucroute... **Routes historiques** guide motorists to towns, villages, châteaux, manors, abbeys, parks and gardens.

The CNMHS (national agency for historic monuments) offers a pass for access to more than 100 monuments managed by this organisation in France, including access to exhibits held within them. The pass (280F) is valid for one year, in all of France, beginning on the date of purchase. It is on sale at the monuments and in some tourist offices.

Discovering animal life

Bird-watchers will find that the many lakes in Champagne-Ardenne attract a sizeable feathered population. A part of the **Lac de Bairon** has been set aside as a bird refuge, as has part of the **Lac d'Orient** in the Forêt d'Orient nature park. The **Lac du Der-Chantecoq** and nearby ponds have observatories and discovery trails. The Ferme aux Grues is devoted to the largest wading birds in Europe: cranes, their migratory habits, how to observe them, conservation measures. The Maison de l'Oiseau et du Poisson has exhibits and displays concerning the lake's ecosystem; birds and fish.

There are many **animal parks** in the region, some offering entertainment in the form of shows and demonstrations, many keeping their animals in semi-captivity.

– Parc de vision de Belval (tour in your car)

– Parc de St-Laurent near Charleville-Mézières (several tours possible)

– Parc de la Bannie near Bourbonne-les-Bains

– Game park in the Forêt d'Orient park, near the Maison du Parc

– Parc ornithologique de Madine in Heudicourt-sous-les-Côtes.

– Centre de réintroduction des cigognes (storks) et centre de reproduction de la loutre (otter) in Hunawihr.

– Serre à papillons (butterfly conservatory) in Hunawihr.

– Montagne des singes (monkey mountain) in Kintzheim.

– Volerie des aigles (eagle aviary) in Kintzheim.

– Zoo and botanical gardens in Mulhouse.

– Zoo and tropical aquarium in Nancy.

– "Les Naïades" aquarium in Ottrott.

– Zoo de l'Orangerie in Strasbourg.

– Arche de Haye in Velaine-en-Haye.

There are many communities of storks in Alsace, in particular in Eguisheim, Ensisheim, Kaysersberg, Kintzheim, Molsheim, Rouffach, Soultz, Turckheim, Ungersheim and La Wantzenau.

Roaming the vineyards

In Alsace, the **Route des Vins** carries travellers from Marlenheim to Thann, linking up the charming little wine-growing villages of the region. In Champagne, take the **Route touristique du Champagne**, where many sign posts point the way to vineyards, Champagne houses and cooperatives.

Visiting wine cellars – Many producers in both regions open their *caves* to visitors, and often offer tasting sessions in the bargain. Here are just a few addresses among many, many others:

Wine cellars in Alsace

Dambach-la Ville
39, rue de la Gare – ☎ 03 88 92 40 03.

Eguisheim
Charles Baur, 6, Grand'Rue – ☎ 03 89 41 32 49.

Kaysersberg
Caveau des viticulteurs
20, rue du Général-de-Gaulle – ☎ 03 89 47 17 87.

Obernai
30, rue du Général-Leclerc – ☎ 03 88 95 61 18.

Ribeauvillé
Domaine du moulin de Dusenbach – 25, route de Ste-Marie-aux-Mines – ☎ 03 89 73 72 18.

Rouffach
Domaine du lycée viticole – 8, Aux-Remparts – ☎ 03 89 49 60 17.

Other useful addresses:

CIVA, Centre interprofessionnel des vins d'Alsace, Maison des vins d'Alsace, 12, avenue de la Foire-aux-Vins, BP 1217, 68012 Colmar Cedex, ☎ 03 89 20 16 20.

L'**Espace Alsace Coopération** (☎ 03 89 47 91 33), in **Beblenheim**, on the wine route, has a good selection of regional wines produced by cooperatives, along with other local products.

Cave Boeckel, Mittelbergheim

Alsatian wine pitcher

Wine festivals – Harvest festivals are held in October throughout Alsace, other celebrations take place from April to October:

April	**Ammerschwihr**	1st half of August	**Colmar**
1 May	**Molsheim**	1st weekend of August	**Turckheim**
Ascension	**Guebwiller**	last weekend of August	**Eguisheim**
mid-July	**Barr**	September	**Riquewihr**
4th weekend in July	**Ribeauvillé**		

Wine cellars in Champagne

Ambonnay	Serge Pierlot, 10, rue St-Vincent, ☎ 03 26 57 01 11.
Ambonnay-Grand-Cru	Soutiran-Pelletier, ☎ 03 26 57 80 80.
Ay	Maison du vin d'Ay, Pierre Laurain, 2, rue Roger-Sondag, ☎ 03 26 55 18 90.
Celles-sur-Ource	Marcel Vezien, ☎ 03 25 38 50 22.
Cogny	Breton Fils, 12, rue Courte-Pilate, ☎ 03 26 59 31 03.
Château-Thierry	Pannier, 23, rue Roger-Catillon, ☎ 03 23 69 13 10.
Fossoy	Dehu Père et Fils, 3, rue St-Georges, ☎ 03 23 71 90 47.
Gyé-sur-Seine	Cheurlin et Fils, 13, rue de la Gare, ☎ 03 25 38 20 27.
Hautvillers	J-M Gobillard et Fils, 38, rue de lÉglise, ☎ 03 26 51 00 24.
Loches-sur-Ource	Jean-Paul Richardot, rue Renée-Guinton, ☎ 03 25 29 71 20.
Ludes	Forget-Chemin, 15, rue Victor-Hugo, ☎ 03 26 61 12 17.
Mardeuil	Beaumont de Crayères, 64, rue de la Liberté, ☎ 03 26 55 29 40.
Le Mesnil-sur-Oger	Launois Père et Fils, 3, avenue de la République, ☎ 03 26 57 50 15.
Oger	Jean Milan, 6, route d'Avize, ☎ 03 26 57 50 09.
Les Riceys	Morize Père et Fils, 122, rue du Général-de-Gaulle, ☎ 03 25 29 30 02.
Trélou-sur-Marne	Veuve Olivier et Fils, 10, route de Dormans, ☎ 03 23 70 24 01.
Verzy	Étienne Lefevre, 30, rue de Villers, ☎ 03 26 97 96 99.
Verzy	Fresnet-Juillet, 10, rue Beaumont, ☎ 03 26 97 93 40.
Vincelles	H. Blin et Co., 5, rue de Verdun, ☎ 03 23 83 68 60.

Breweries

– **Heineken**, 4, rue St-Charles, 67300 Schiltigheim, ☎ 03 88 19 59 53.
– **Kanterbrau**, 2, rue Gabriel-Bour, 54250 Champigneulles, ☎ 03 83 39 50 37.
– **Kronenbourg**, 68, route d'Oberhausbergen, 67000 Strasbourg, ☎ 03 88 27 41 59.
– **Météor**, rue du Général-Lebocq, 67270 Hochfelden, ☎ 03 88 71 73 73.
The tour is completed by a visit to the Stenay Beer Museum and the Musée français de la Brasserie in St-Nicolas-de-Port.

Sized to fit

Magnum: 2 bottles	Mathusalem: 8 bottles
Jéroboam: 4 bottles	Salmanazar: 12 bottles
Réhoboam: 6 bottles	Balthazar: 16 bottles
	Nabuchodonosor: 20 bottles

M. Rodvc. CEPHAS TOP

Other local crafts and industries

Here are a few more suggestions for discovering the people and trades of the region:
– **Papeteries de Clairefontaine**, Paper and stationery manufacturers, 19, rue de l'Abbaye, BP 1, 88480 Étival-Clairefontaine, ☎ 03 29 52 22 11.
– **Émaux St-Jean-l'Aigle**, Enamels, château de la Faïencerie, 54400 Longwy, ☎ 03 82 24 58 20.
– **Manufacture de Niderviller**, Ceramics, 2, rue de la Faïencerie, 57116 Niderviller, ☎ 03 87 23 80 04.
– **Seita**, Cigar production, 7A, rue de la Krutenau, 67070 Strasbourg cedex, ☎ 03 88 35 29 00.
– **Confiserie, chocolaterie Roger Lalonde**, Chocolates and confections, 2, avenue Milton, 54000 Nancy, ☎ 03 83 40 23 63.
– **Centre européen de recherche et de formation aux arts verriers**, Glass crafts, rue de la Liberté, 54112 Vannes-le-Châtel, ☎ 03 83 25 49 90.

Beer fermenting in a cellar

– **Daum, Compagnie Française du Cristal**, Crystal manufactory, 54112 Vannes-le-Châtel, ☎ 03 83 25 41 01.
– **Portieux**, Crystal manufactory, 35, rue des Arts, 88330 Portieux, ☎ 03 87 23 80 04.
– **Fromagerie Jean Pire**, Cheese makers, rue de la Grande-Chaudière, Tailette 08230 Rocroi, ☎ 03 24 54 10 84.
– **Bio-Plantes**, Medicinal and savoury herbs, 10210 Pargues, ☎ 03 25 40 12 53.
– **Cristalleries royales de Champagne**, Crystal manufactory and "ecomuseum", 13, rue Gustave-Marquot, 10310 Bayel, ☎ 03 25 92 37 60.
– **Automobiles Citroën**, BP 1, 08001 Charleville-Mézières, ☎ 03 24 56 65 65.

Excursions to neighbouring countries

The region is bordered by Germany to the north and east, Switzerland to the south, Belgium and Luxembourg to the north.

Visitors to Alsace will naturally be drawn to the other side of the Rhine and such lovely towns as Freiberg, Belchen and Baden-Baden in the Black Forest. Consult the **Michelin Green Guide Germany** for tourist information, and the **Red Guide Deutschland** for hotels and restaurants.
Basel, in Switzerland, is also a popular tourist destination, especially at carnival time. The three days before the beginning of Lent mark the only Catholic ceremony to have survived the Reformation, a festival of parades and costumed revelry. The Green Guide Switzerland is useful for visiting Basel and the surrounding region. The **Red Guide Switzerland** makes it easy to choose where to spend the night and to find a special restaurant.
The Ardennes Forest covers most of the Belgian provinces of Luxembourg, Namur and Liège and part of the Grand Duchy as well as the French *département*. The valley of the Meuse River meanders to the North Sea by way of **Dinant**. This picturesque town is just 60km/37mi from Charleville-Mézières. Travellers will enjoy local honey cakes known as *coques*, baked in decorative wooden molds, and may take advantage of boat trips on the river *(board in front of the town hall)*. Carry on to **Bouillon**, nestled in a river bend, and renown for its medieval fortress. **Chimay** is a familiar name to beer-lovers as the home of the Trappist monks at Notre-Dame-de-Scourmount abbey. Round off the excursion with a stop at the **Orval abbey**, in the Gaume Forest. The tour includes a short film on monastery life, and a visit to the ruins dating from the Middle Ages to the 18C. From Dinant to Orval, the distance is 99km/61mi.

For further information, see the Green Guide Belgium and the Red Guide Benelux.

Monks on the Web! If you love Trappist beer and would like to know more about how it is made, take a virtual tour of the abbey where Chimay is brewed: www.chimay.be.

Suggested reading

Héloïse and Abélard

Latinists may regale themselves with the beautiful **Letters** written by these medieval lovers. Although their authenticity has sometimes been called into question (they may have been "improved" by scribes who came after), there is no denying the beauty and profound humanity of sentiment which rings true in all ages. If your Latin is rusty, there are various modern translations available.

Peter Abélard, by Helen Waddell, was first published in 1933 and has had over 30 reprints (London, Constable and Co Ltd, 1968). This slim volume is a novel but reads like a true account, moving in its simplicity.

Stealing Heaven: the Love Story of Héloïse and Abélard, by Marion Meade (NY, Soho Press, 1979), tells the story from a woman's perspective. This sensuous historical novel of epic proportions is an immersion in 12C France.

Poets for every purpose

The Complete Fables of La Fontaine, edited and with rhymed verse translation by Norman B Spector (Evanston, Ill., Northwestern University Press, 1988). No verse is unturned in this collection which presents the French text opposite its translation, keen wit intact.

Verlaine, a seminal Symbolist and critical author, left an extensive body of work. Readily available in translation (ie by Jacques LeClerque, Westport Conn., Greenwood Press, 1977) are such famous books as *Songs Without Words*, *Yesteryear and Yesterday*, *The Accursed Poets*, *Confessions of a Poet*.

Rimbaud got quite a few stanzas out before putting down his pen at age 20. His best-known works available in translation include *A Season in Hell and The Drunken Boat*. **Rimbaud and Jim Morrison: the Rebel as Poet**, by Wallace Fowlie (Durham NC, Duke University Press, 1994), was inspired by a letter written to the author by the Doors' founder and lead singer, thanking him for publishing his translations of Rimbaud. The illustrated volume is a twinned tale exploring the symmetry of two lives and the parallels between European literary tradition and American rock music.

The ravages of war

The Debacle, by Emile Zola (translated by LW Tancock, Penguin, 1972) takes place during the Franco-Prussian war of 1870, describes the tragic events of the defeat at Sedan as well as the uprising of the Paris Commune. The author carried out extensive research (arms, strategy, tactics) to produce this remarkably factual novel depicting the battle and its aftermath.

The Pity of War, Niall Ferguson (London, Allen Lane, 1998). This radical, readable reassessment of the powers driving nations and individuals into the terrible conflict of the First World War focuses on life in the trenches.

A Balcony in the Forest, by Julien Gracq (translated by Richard Howard, London, Harper Collins, 1992), is set in the Ardennes Forest in the winter of 1939-40, during the "phony war". Following a winter of solitude and contemplation of nature, a young officer on the Maginot Line must face attacking Panzer divisions.

A Time for Trumpets: The Untold Story of the Battle of the Bulge, Charles B MacDonald (NY, Morrow, 1984). The author was one of the 600 000 American soldiers who fought against Hitler's vanguard troops in the mists and snow of the Ardennes Forest on 16 December, 1944 – Germany's last desperate gamble and the turning point of the war.

Memoirs of Hope: Renewal and Endeavour, Charles de Gaulle (NY, Simon and Schuster, 1971). Written in Colombey-les-Deux-Églises, the General's memoirs also include descriptions of the landscape of Champagne beyond the windows of his study.

Words on wine

Among the many books on wines of the region: *The Wines of Alsace* (Tom Stevenson, London, Faber and Faber, 1993); *Alsace Wines* (Pamela V Price, London, Sotheby Publications, 1984); *The Wine Lover's Guide to Champagne and North East France* (Michael Busselle, NY, Viking, 1989); *The Glory of Champagne* (Don Hewitson, London, MacMillan, 1989).

A few films

La Grande Illusion (J Renoir, 1937), prisoners of war in the castle of Haut-Koenigsbourg; *Tess* (R Polanski, 1978), filmed around Verdun; *Au revoir les enfants* (L Malle, 1987), filmed in Provins; *Camille Claudel* (B Nuytten, 1988), filmed in Villeneuve-sur-Fère; *Total Eclipse* (A Holland, 1995), the story of Verlaine and Rimbaud.

Calendar of events

Music

Vandœuvre-lès-Nancy . . . . . "Musique Action", ☎ 03 83 57 52 24.

Late May to mid-June
Mulhouse . . . . Bach Festival.

June
Strasbourg . . . . Music Festival.
Vittel . . . . Guitar Festival.

July
Colmar . . . . International Music Festival, ☎ 03 89 20 68 94.

July and August
Reims . . . . Summer music festival.
Sound and light show on the cathedral façade.
Joinville . . . . "L'été du Grand Jardin" (concerts).

July to September, Saturdays
Reims . . . . Music and Lights, St-Remi Basilica.

1st half of September
Cons-la-Grandville 57 2 *(1)* "Rencontres musicales", ☎ 03 82 44 97 66.

Late September to early October
Strasbourg . . . . Musica, international contemporary music festival, ☎ 03 88 21 02 02.

Mid-October
Nancy . . . . Nancy Jazz Pulsations, ☎ 03 83 37 83 79.

Mid-November
Metz and in Lorraine . . . . . "Musiques Volantes", ☎ 03 87 32 43 98.

Late January to late March
Joinville . . . . "Les claviers d'hiver" (in the château).

Pilgrimages

Around 8 May
Notre-Dame de l'Épine . . . . Pilgrimage.

16 July
Avioth . . . . Notre-Dame d'Avioth.

15 August
N.-D.-de-Thierenbach . . . . . Dedicated to the Virgin Mary, torch-lit procession the night before.
Notre-Dame de l'Épine . . . . Pilgrimage.

15 August and 8 September
Oderen . . . . To Notre-Dame-du-Bon-Secours.

1st Sunday after 8 September
Bar-sur-Seine . . . . To Notre-Dame-du-Chêne.

13 December
Ste-Odile . . . . Feast day of St Odile: the biggest pilgrimage in Alsace.

Culinary festivities

Late April
Rethel . . . . "Boudin blanc" festival.

Around the feast of the Ascension
Ungersheim . . . . Pork festival.

Pentecost
Fumay . . . . "Boudin blanc" festival.

Revin	Bread festival.

1st half of July

Ribeauvillé	Kugelhopf festival.

July and August
Pierre-Percée 62 7 *(1)*	Local produce festival.

1st half of August
Munchhouse	Fried carp festival.

Last weekend of August
Erstein 87 5 *(1)*	Sugar festival.

Late August, early September
Metz	Mirabelle festival: Flower-decorated floats, parade and hot-air balloons.
Colmar	Choucroute festival.
Bar-sur-Aube	Champagne wines fair.

September
Geispolsheim 62 10 *(1)* . . .	Choucroute festival.
Baccarat	"Pâté lorrain" festival.
Fumay	St Michael's day "Boudin noir" festival.
Renwez	"Fête de la gastronomie".

2nd Sunday in September
Pays d'Othe	Cider festival.

3rd weekend in September
Brienne-le-Château	"Choucroute de Champagne" festival.

Late September
Montigny-le-Roi	Bassigny growers fair.
Chaource	Gourmet forum.

11 November
Givet	Onion Fair.

Other events

Saturday or Sunday following the 22 January
In all wine-growing towns	St Vincent Festival, honouring the patron saint of wine-growers.

February
Gérardmer	"Fantastica": Fantasy film festival.

Last Saturday in March
Châlons-en-Champagne . . .	Carnival.

Wednesday before Easter
Épinal	"Champs Golots" festival: Children float illuminated boats on the pool near the town hall.

Thursday before Easter
Les Riceys	"Grand Jeudi" Fair.

Late March, early April
Givet	"Fête de l'eau vive" (water sports).

The day before Ascension through to the following Sunday
St-André-les-Vergers	Local festivities.

April
Gérardmer	Daffodil Festival: Parade floats decorated with daffodils.

1 May
Neuf-Brisach, Chaource	May Day: Lily-of-the-valley festival.

May
Azannes-et-Soumazannes 57 1 *(1)*	Festival of traditional trades and crafts.
La Bresse	International Festival of wood sculpture.

Wissembourg . . . . Opening of the annual fun fair (until the following Sunday). Folk dancing, parade of traditional costumes, horse races.

Chaumont . . . . Graphic Arts forums.

Châlons-en-Champagne . . . "Furies" street theatre and circus festival,
☎ 03 26 65 90 06.

Reims . . . . "Fêtes Johanniques" and folklore festival.

Château-Thierry . . . . Jean de la Fontaine festival.

Troyes . . . . Champagne Fair.

Monthermé, Nouzouville . . Three valleys festival (story tellers, exhibits).

Braux-Ste-Cohière . . . . Summer festival.

Riquewihr . . . . Sound and light show (Dolder).

Saverne . . . . Rose festival.

Vallée de St-Amarin . . . . . . Midsummer night festival: Bonfires light up the valley.

Thann . . . . "Crémation des Trois Sapins": ceremonial fire, burning three pine trees in front of the church.

Épinal . . . . International festival of imagery.

Verdun . . . . Seasonal events and show.

Langres . . . . Theatre festival with the Compagnie Humbert.

Seebach . . . . "Streisselhochzeit".

**Vendeuvre-sur-Barse
(weekends)** . . . . "Vindovera" historical drama, ☎ 03 25 41 44 76.

Renwez . . . . Lumberjack competitions.

Bussang . . . . "Théâtre du Peuple": dramatic arts interpreted by companies uniting professionals and amateurs.

Troyes . . . . "In the footsteps of the cathedral builders".

Vendresse 56 8 *(1)* . . . . Sound and light show at the Cassine château, ☎ 03 24 26 02 68.

Charleville-Mézières . . . . . . Marionette show.

Langres . . . . "La ronde des hallebardiers", historical drama.

Sélestat . . . . Flower-decorated floats on parade.

Gérardmer . . . . Light show and fireworks over the lake.

Ribeauvillé – Fête des Ménétriers

15 August
Marlenheim . . . . "L'Ami Fritz" marriage celebration. Regional costumes.

Last weekend in August
Haguenau . . . . Hops festival, world folklore festival.

1st Sunday in September
Ribeauvillé . . . . "Fête des Ménétriers" or "Pfifferdaj": Historical parade, wine flows freely.

1st half of September
Strasbourg . . . . European fair.

September, even-numbered years
Troyes . . . . 48-hour vintage car rally

October
St-Dié-des-Vosges . . . . International geography festival.

December
Throughout Alsace and Lorraine . . . . St-Nicolas Feast
Christmas markets.
Braux-Ste-Cohière . . . . Shepherd's Christmas.

(1) For places not described in the guide, the Michelin map number and fold are given.

St Nicholas

The legend of St Nicholas – Saint Nicolas, bishop of Myra in Asia Minor in the 4C, is known for offering a dowry to three impoverished girls. He is also said to have prevented the execution of three officers unjustly accused. Perhaps because of images relating to the number three, he has also been associated, since the 12C in France, with the miraculous resurrection of three young children whom had been cut up and set to cure by a butcher.

These various legends have created a popular figure who, the night of 5 December, distributed gifts to good children in the countries of northern Europe (Lorraine, Germany, Belgium, the Netherlands, Switzerland).

Feast of St-Nicolas – The Feast is celebrated either on the eve of 6 December or the 6 December, or sometimes the first Saturday or Sunday following. Many towns in Lorraine have celebrations, especially St-Nicolas-de-Port (torch-lit procession in the basilica), Nancy (parade and fireworks), Metz (musical parade), and Épinal (floats in a parade).

Useful French words and phrases

ARCHITECTURAL TERMS

See Introduction: Architecture and art

SIGHTS

beffroi	belfry	monastère	monastery
cimetière	cemetery	moulin	windmill
cloître	cloisters	musée	museum
cour	courtyard	place	square
couvent	convent	pont	bridge
écluse	lock (canal)	port	port/harbour
halle	covered market	porte	gateway
jardin	garden	quai	quay
mairie	town hall	remparts	ramparts
maison	house	rue	street
marché	market		

NATURAL SITES

abîme	chasm	grotte	cave
barrage	dam	plage	beach
belvédère	viewpoint	rivière	river
col	pass	ruisseau	stream
côte	coast, hillside	signal	beacon
forêt	forest	source	spring

ON THE ROAD

car park	parking	petrol/gas station	station essence
driving licence	permis de conduire	right	droite
east	Est	south	Sud
garage (for repairs)	garage	toll	péage
left	gauche	traffic lights	feu tricolore
motorway/highway	autoroute	tyre	pneu
north	Nord	west	Ouest
parking meter	horodateur	wheel clamp	sabot
petrol/gas	essence	zebra crossing	passage clouté

TIME

today	aujourd'hui	week	semaine
tomorrow	demain	Monday	lundi
yesterday	hier	Tuesday	mardi
winter	hiver	Wednesday	mercredi
spring	printemps	Thursday	jeudi
summer	été	Friday	vendredi
autumn/fall	automne	Saturday	samedi
		Sunday	dimanche

NUMBERS

0	zéro	8	huit	16	seize	60	soixante
1	un	9	neuf	17	dix-sept	70	soixante-dix
2	deux	10	dix	18	dix-huit	80	quatre-vingt
3	trois	11	onze	19	dix-neuf	90	quatre-vingt-dix
4	quatre	12	douze	20	vingt	100	cent
5	cinq	13	treize	30	trente	1000	mille
6	six	14	quatorze	40	quarante		
7	sept	15	quinze	50	cinquante		

SHOPPING

bank	banque	grocer's	épicerie
baker's	boulangerie	newsagent, bookshop	librairie
big	grand		
butcher's	boucherie	open	ouvert
chemist's/drugstore	pharmacie	post office	poste
closed	fermé	push	pousser
cough mixture	sirop pour la toux	pull	tirer
entrance	entrée	shop	magasin
exit	sortie	small	petit
fishmonger's	poissonnerie	stamps	timbres

FOOD AND DRINK

beef	bœuf	lamb	agneau
beer	bière	lunch	déjeuner
butter	beurre	green salad	salade
bread	pain	meat	viande
breakfast	petit-déjeuner	mineral water	eau minérale
cheese	fromage	mixed salad	salade composée
chicken	poulet	orange juice	jus d'orange
dessert	dessert	plate	assiette
dinner	dîner	pork	porc
fish	poisson	red wine	vin rouge
fork	fourchette	salt	sel
fruit	fruits	spoon	cuillère
sugar	sucre	vegetables	légumes
glass	verre	water	de l'eau
ice cream	glace	white wine	vin blanc
ice cubes	glaçons	yoghurt	yaourt
ham	jambon		
knife	couteau		

PERSONAL DOCUMENTS AND TRAVEL

airport	aéroport	shuttle	navette
credit card	carte de crédit	suitcase	valise
customs	douane	train/	billet de train/
passport	passeport	plane ticket	d'avion
platform	voie	wallet	portefeuille
railway station	gare		

CLOTHING

coat	manteau	socks	chaussettes
jumper	pull	stockings	bas
raincoat	imperméable	suit	costume/tailleur
shirt	chemise	tights	collant
shoes	chaussures	trousers	pantalon

USEFUL PHRASES

goodbye	au revoir
hello/good morning	bonjour
how	comment
excuse me	excusez-moi
thank you	merci
yes/no	oui/non
I am sorry	pardon
why	pourquoi
when	quand
please	s'il vous plaît
Do you speak English?	Parlez-vous anglais?
I don't understand.	Je ne comprends pas.
Talk slowly.	Parlez lentement.
Where's...?	Où est...?
When does the ... leave?	A quelle heure part...?
When does the ... arrive?	A quelle heure arrive...?
When does the museum open?	A quelle heure ouvre le musée?
When is the show?	A quelle heure est la représentation?
When is breakfast served?	A quelle heure sert-on le petit-déjeuner?
What does it cost?	Combien cela coûte?
Where can I buy a newspaper in English?	Où puis-je acheter un journal en anglais?
Where is the nearest petrol/gas station?	Où se trouve la station essence la plus proche?
Where can I change traveller's cheques?	Où puis-je échanger des traveller's chèques?
Where are the toilets?	Où sont les toilettes?
Do you accept credit cards?	Acceptez-vous les cartes de crédit?
I need a receipt.	Je voudrais un reçu.

Admission times and charges

TAKE NOTE...

Every sight for which the times and charges are listed is indicated by the symbol ⌚ in the text in the main part of this guide.
The admission charges quoted here are full price for one adult. Most places offer reduced rates or free admission for children.
Many sights are closed on public holidays (listed in Practical information).
The symbol ♿ indicates places which are accessible to persons of reduced mobility.

The information is listed in the same order as the entries in the alphabetical section of the guide. Admission times and charges are liable to alteration without prior notice; the information printed here was, as far as possible, correct at the time of going to press. Dates given are inclusive. Special rates may be offered for family groups, students or senior citizens; proof of age or student status required. In some cases admission is free on certain days (Wednesdays, Sundays or public holidays). Ticket offices often close 30-45min before the actual closing time.

When guided tours are indicated, the departure time of the last tour of the morning or afternoon will be up to an hour before closing time. Most guided tours are conducted by French-speaking guides but in some cases the term may refer to recorded tours loaned out to visitors. A number of popular sights can provide guided tours, notes or pamphlets in other languages, although their availability may not be clearly posted. It is best to ask at the ticket office or book stall if any information in English is available. The symbol 🅰 *indicates that a tour is given by a lecturer from the Historic Monuments Association. The indication "guided tours" at the beginning of an entry means that only accompanied visits are allowed.*

Churches and chapels are usually closed during the lunch period from noon-2pm and do not admit visitors during services, except for worship; tourists should refrain from visits when services are being held. Visitors to chapels are often accompanied by the person who keeps the key; a donation is welcome.

Enquire at the local tourist office or Tourist Information Centre (Office de Tourisme, Maison de Tourisme or Syndicat d'Initiative) – the address of which is shown following the symbol ℹ *– for information on local happenings (fairs, festivals, sports events, market days etc).*

A

ALTKIRCH

ℹ Place Xavier-Jourdain – 68130 – ☎ 03 89 40 02 90

Musée sundgauvien – Open July and Aug, daily (except Mon), 2.30-5pm; the rest of the year, Sun and holidays only, 2.30-5pm. 15F. ☎ 03 89 40 21 80.

Excursion

Luemschwiller, church – Open Sun only, 10am-6pm. During the week, contact the presbytery.

AMNÉVILLE

Parc zoologique du bois de Coulange – ♿ Open Apr to Sept, daily, 10am-7.30pm (Sun and holidays 8pm); Oct to Mar, 10am-dusk. 65F (adult), 45F (child). ☎ 03 87 70 25 60.

ARGONNE

Clermont en Argonne ℹ 5, place de la République – 55120 – ☎ 03 29 88 42 22

Église St-Didier – Enquire at the tourist office.

Chapelle Ste-Anne – Closed for renovation. Enquire at the tourist office.

Varennes-en-Argonne, Musée d'Argonne – Open July and Aug, daily, 10.30am-noon and 2.30-6pm; May, June and 1-15 Sept, daily, 3-6pm; 15-30 Apr and mid-Sept to mid-Oct, Sat, Sun and holidays, 3-6pm. Closed mid-Oct to Easter. 20F. ☎ 03 29 80 71 01.

Beaulieu-en-Argonne, Pressoir – Open Mar to Nov, daily, 9am-6pm.

Rarécourt, Musée de la Faïence – Open July and Aug, daily, 10.30am-noon and 2-6.30pm. 25F.

B

BACCARAT

Musée du Cristal – Open Apr to - Oct, daily, 9.30am-12.30pm and 2-6.30pm; the rest of the year, 10am-noon and 2-6pm. Closed 1 Jan and 25 Dec. 15F. ☎ 03 83 76 60 06.

Parc Naturel Régional des BALLONS DES VOSGES

Sentheim, Maison de la Géologie – Open May to Sept, Wed, Sat and Sun, 2-6pm. 10F. ☎ 03 89 82 55 55.

Baccarat – Ewer in Charles-X-style

Ste-Marie-aux-Mines ⓘ Place du Prensureux – 68160 – ☎ 03 89 58 80 50

Guided tours of the town – Contact the tourist office.

Maison de Pays – Open June to Sept, daily, 10am-noon and 2-5pm; the rest of the year by appointment, minimum 10 persons. Closed 1 Jan, 1 May, 1 and 11 Nov and 25 Dec. 25F. ☎ 03 89 58 56 67.

Mine St-Barthélemy – Guided tours (45min) July and Aug, daily, 9.30am-noon and 2-6pm; also open Whitsun weekend and the last two Sun in June, 9.30am-noon and 2-6pm. 30F. ☎ 03 89 58 72 28.

Mine d'argent St-Louis-Eisenthur — Guided tours (3hr) by appointment, apply to ASEPAM, centre du patrimoine minier, 4, rue Weisgerber, 68160 Ste-Marie-aux-Mines, ☎ 03 89 58 62 11 or contact the tourist office.

BAR LE DUC ⓘ 5, rue Jeanne d'Arc – 55805 – ☎ 03 29 79 11 13

Église St-Étienne – Open July and Aug, daily, 10am-7pm; the rest of the year, enquire at the tourist office.

Musée Barrois – Open daily (except Tues), 2 (Sat and Sun, 3pm) to 6pm. Closed 1 Jan, 1 May, 14 July, 15 Aug, 1 Nov and 25 Dec. 12F. ☎ 03 29 76 14 67.

BAR-SUR-AUBE ⓘ 33, rue d'Aube – 10200 – ☎ 03 25 27 24 25

Église St-Pierre – Open Mon-Sat, 9am-7pm.

Cellier aux moines – Open daily, 9am-4pm. Closed Jan and Feb. ☎ 03 25 27 08 01.

Excursions:

Nigloland – ♿ Open beginning of Apr to early Sept, daily, 9.30, 10 or 10.30am, according to the season, to 4.30, 5 or 6pm, according to the season. Closed the rest of the year. 75F (adult), 65 F (under-twelve), free admission (child less than 1m/3.28ft tall). ☎ 03 25 27 94 52.

Bayel ⓘ rue Belle-Verrière – 10310 – ☎ 03 25 92 42 68

Crystalworks – ♿ Guided tours (1hr) Mon-Fri, 9.30 and 11am; enquire about Sat. Closed Sun and holidays, 1 Jan, 1 May, mid-July to mid-Aug. 25F (combined ticket with Écomusée 40F). ☎ 03 25 92 42 68.

Écomusée – Open daily, 9.30am-1pm and 2-6pm. Closed Sun mornings, 1 Jan, 1 May, end of Dec to early Jan. 25 F. ☎ 03 25 92 42 68.

Colombé-le-Sec, Ferme du Cellier – Guided tours (30min) May to Oct, Sat, 2-6pm, by prior appointment with the Association Renaissance de l'abbaye de Clairvaux, 11, rue Nationale, 10200 Bar-sur-Aube, ☎ 03 25 27 88 17.

BITCHE ⓘ Hôtel de ville - porte de Strasbourg – 57230 – ☎ 03 87 06 16 16

Citadel – Audio-guided tours (2hr) Mar to mid-Nov, daily, 10am-5pm (July and Aug 6pm). 38F (adult), 23F (child). ☎ 03 87 96 18 82.

BOURBONNE-LES-BAINS

Museum – Open mid-Apr to early Oct, Tues, Thur, Fri, 2-6pm. Closed 2 Sun out of every three, 1 May and 14 July. 10F. Enquire at the town hall. ☎ 03 25 90 14 80.

Parc animalier de la Bannie – Open early Mar to mid-Sept, daily (except Fri), 2-5pm, Sun, 11.30am-5.30pm, holidays, 2-5.30pm; the rest of the year, Wed and Sat, 2-5pm. Closed 15 Sept to 31 Oct. Free admission.

Château de BRAUX-STE-COHIÈRE

Open mid-June to early Sept, daily (except Tues), 10am-noon and 2-6pm (Sun 8pm). 35F. ☎ 03 26 60 83 51.

BRIENNE-LE-CHÂTEAU

Musée Napoléon – Open daily (except Tues), 9am-noon and 2-5.30pm. Closed holidays and Dec to Feb. 20F. ☏ 03 25 92 82 41.

Excursion

Brienne-la-Vallée, Écomusée de la Forêt d'Orient – Open May to mid-Sept, Mon-Fri, 10am-6pm, Sat and Sun, 2-6pm; the rest of the year, 2-5pm. Closed mid-Nov to end of Mar. 25F. ☏ 03 25 92 95 84.

Rosnay-l'Hôpital, Église Notre-Dame – Enquire at the town hall, Tues and Fri, 5-7pm.

Vallée de la BRUCHE

Waldersbach, Musée Oberlin – Open July and Aug, daily (except Tues), 2-6pm; Apr to June and Sept to Oct, Wed, Thur, Sat and Sun, 2-6pm. 15F. ☏ 03 88 97 30 27.

Mutzig, Musée régional des armes — Open early May to mid-Oct, daily (except Mon and Tues), 2-5.30pm (Sun and holidays, 6pm). 13F. ☏ 03 88 38 73 43.

C

CHÂLONS-EN-CHAMPAGNE   🖪 3, quai des Arts – 51000 – ☏ 03 26 65 17 89

Guided tours of the town 🅰 – Contact the tourist office.

Cathédrale St-Étienne – To visit the cathedral, enquire at the tourist office.

Cathedral Treasury – Guided tours (15min), enquire at the tourist office.

Église Notre-Dame-en-Vaux – Open Mon-Sat, 10am-noon and 2-6pm.

Musée du cloître de Notre-Dame-en-Vaux – Open daily (except Tues), 10am-noon and 2-6pm (Oct to Mar, Mon-Fri, 5pm). Closed 1 Jan, 1 May, 1 and 11 Nov, 25 Dec. 25F. ☏ 03 26 64 03 87.

Bibliothèque – Guided tours (1hr), 9am-noon and 2-5.30pm. Closed Thur mornings, Mon, Sun and holidays. Apply one week in advance to Mlle Husson. ☏ 03 26 69 38 51.

Musée municipal – Open daily (except Tues), 2-6pm; Sun, 2.30-6.30pm. Closed holidays. 15F. ☏ 03 26 69 38 01 (town hall).

Église St-Alpin – Guided tours, enquire at the tourist office.

Musée Garinet – Open daily (except Tues), 2-6pm. Closed holidays. 10F. ☏ 03 26 69 38 53.

Couvent Ste-Marie – To visit the convent, apply at the tourist office.

Église St-Loup — Enquire at the presbytery, 5, place Notre-Dame or at the tourist office.

Musée Schiller et Goethe – Open July and Aug, daily (except Tues), 2-6pm, Sun, 2.30-6.30pm; the rest of the year, Sat, 2-6pm, Sun, 2.30-6.30pm. Closed holidays. 10F. ☏ 03 26 69 38 01.

CHARLEVILLE-MÉZIÈRES   🖪 4, place Ducale – 08109 – ☏ 03 24 33 00 17

Musée de l'Ardenne – ♿ Open daily (except Mon), 10am-noon and 2-6pm. Closed 1 Jan, 1 May and 25 Dec. 25F. ☏ 03 24 32 44 60.

Musée Rimbaud – Open daily (except Mon), 10am-noon and 2-6pm. Closed 1 Jan, 1 May and 25 Dec. 20F. ☏ 03 24 32 44 65.

Excursions:

Mohon, Église St-Lié – Open 8am-noon; afternoon, apply at the presbytery, 21, place de Mohon, ☏ 03 24 57 13 15.

Warcq, church – Guided tours daily, 2-6pm. Tourist office, ☏ 03 24 59 48 20.

St-Laurent, zoological park – Open Apr to Sept, Mon-Fri (except Thur), 2-6pm, Sat, Sun and holidays, 1.30-7pm; the rest of the year, daily (except Thur), 1.30-5.30pm. Free admission. ☏ 03 24 32 44 80.

CHÂTEAU-THIERRY   🖪 12, place de l'Hôtel-de-Ville – 02400 – ☏ 03 23 83 10 14

Maison natale de La Fontaine – Open daily (except Tues), 10am-noon and 2-6pm. 17F. Free admission on Wed. ☏ 03 23 83 51 14.

Caves de champagne Pannier – Enquire beforehand. ☏ 03 23 69 51 30.

CHÂTEAU-THIERRY

Excursions:

Condé-en-Brie, castle – Guided tours (1hr) June to Aug, daily, 2.30, 3.30 and sometimes 4.30pm; May and Sept, Sun and holidays, 2.30, 3.30 and sometimes 4.30pm. 32F. ☎ 03 23 82 42 25.

Essômes-sur-Marne, church – Guided tours May to Sept, Thur, Fri, Sat and Sun mornings; otherwise, apply at the town hall.

CHAUMONT 🅳 place Général-de-Gaulle – 52000 – ☎ 03 25 03 80 80

Donjon – Open June to Sept, daily (except Tues), 2.30-6.30pm (Sat, Sun and holidays 7pm). 5F. ☎ 03 25 03 80 80.

Les silos, Maison du livre et de l'affiche – &. Open Tues, Thur and Fri, 2-7pm, Wed and Sat, 10am-6pm, Sun, 2-6pm (large exhibition hall only). Free admission. ☎ 03 25 03 86 82.

Musée – Open July to mid-Sept, daily (except Tues), 2.30-6.30pm; the rest of the year, 2-6pm. Closed 1 Jan, 1 May and 25 Dec. 5F. ☎ 03 25 03 01 99.

Condé-en-Brie Castle – Fresco decorating the Grand Salon

Chapelle des Jésuites – Open for exhibitions, daily (except Tues), 3.30-7pm. Free admission. ☎ 03 25 30 60 57.

Excursion:

Prez-sous-Lafauche, Zoo de bois – &. Open June to mid-Sept, daily (except Tues), 2-6.30pm. 15F. ☎ 03 25 31 57 76.

Abbaye de CLAIRVAUX

Tour of the abbey – Guided tours (1hr30min) of historic buildings, May to Oct, Sat, 1.45, 3.15 and 4.45pm. 30F. ☎ 03 25 27 88 17. Identification papers necessary. The Information Centre and permanent exhibition in the Hostellerie des Dames are open Mon-Fri, 2-6pm.

COLMAR 🅳 4, rue Unterlinden – 68000 – ☎ 03 89 20 68 92

Guided tours of the town – Contact the tourist office.

Musée d'Unterlinden – Open Apr to Oct, daily, 9am-6pm; Nov to Mar, daily (except Tues), 9am-noon and 2-5pm. Closed 1 Jan, 1 May, 1 Nov and 25 Dec. 32F. ☎ 03 89 41 89 23.

Église St-Matthieu – Open spring school holidays, May holidays, 15 June to 15 Oct, daily, 10am-noon and 3-5pm. ☎ 03 89 41 44 96.

Musée Bartholdi – Open daily (except Tues), 10am-noon and 2-6pm. Closed 1 May, 1 Nov, 25 Dec, Jan and Feb. 20F. ☎ 03 89 41 90 60.

Église des Dominicains – Open daily, 10am-1pm and 3-6pm; possibly without break from 10am-6pm. 8F.

Muséum d'Histoire naturelle – Open daily (except Tues), 10am-noon and 2-5pm, Sun, 2-6pm. Closed 1 May, 1 Nov, 25 Dec, Jan and Feb. 20F. ☎ 03 89 23 84 15.

Boat trips – Boarding beneath the Pont St-Pierre, Apr to Sept, daily, 10am-7pm; Apr and May, Sat-Sun, holidays and school holidays, 10am-6pm. Time: 30min. 30F (adult), free for under-tens. ☎ 03 89 41 01 94.

Musée animé du Jouet et des Petits Trains – Open daily (except Tues), 10am-noon and 2-6pm; July and Aug without lunch break. Closed 1 Jan, 1 May, 1 Nov and 25 Dec. 25F. ☎ 03 89 41 93 10.

Maison des vins d'Alsace – Open Mon-Fri, 8am-noon and 2-5pm. ☎ 03 89 20 16 20.

Excursions:

Neuf-Brisach

Musée Vauban – &. Open Apr to Oct, daily (except Tues), 10am-noon and 2-5pm. 15F. ☎ 03 89 72 56 66.

Association CFTR (steam-train trips) – Departure from Vogelsheim station, near Neuf-Brisach, from Whitsun to last Sun in Sept, Sat, Sun and holidays, 3pm, return 6.15pm. Combined train and boat trip: 90F (adult), 45F (child). Information: ☎ 03 89 71 51 42.

COLOMBEY-LES-DEUX-ÉGLISES

La Boisserie – Open daily (except Tues), 10am-noon and 2-5.30pm (Oct to Apr, 5pm). Hours are liable to be shorter in winter. Closed 25 Dec and Jan. 18F. ☎ 03 25 01 52 52.

Mémorial – Open Apr to Oct, daily, 9am-6pm; the rest of the year, 10am-noon and 2-4pm. 10F.

CÔTE DES BLANCS

Le Mesnil-sur-Oger, Musée de la Vigne et du Vin – Guided tours (2hr), Mon-Sat, 10am and 3pm, Sun, 10.30am; it is preferable to apply the day before. Closed 1 Jan, Easter and 25 Dec. 35F (wine-tasting included). ☎ 03 26 57 50 15.

Route des CRÊTES

Haut-Chitelet, Jardin d'Altitude – Open July and Aug, daily, 10am-6pm; June, 10am-noon and 2-6pm; Sept, 10am-noon and 2-5.30pm. 15F. ☎ 03 29 63 31 46.

Vieil-Armand, Monument national du Vieil-Armand – Open Apr to Oct, daily, 8.30am-noon and 2-6.30pm. 12F. ☎ 03 89 23 12 03.

Cernay

Museum – Enquire at the tourist office, ☎ 03 89 75 50 35.

Tour of the Doller Valley – Steam trains: June to Sept, Sun and holidays; departure from Cernay St-André at 11am and 3.30pm, return to Cernay St-André at 3 and 6.30pm. 55F return. Diesel trains: July and Aug, daily (except Mon and Tues); departure from Cernay St-André at 3pm, return to Cernay St-André at 5.30pm. 45F return. Information: ☎ 03 89 82 88 48.

D

Région de DABO-WANGENBOURG

Plan incliné de St-Louis-Arzviller – Guided tours including going down the inclined plane in a boat (1hr30min), mid-Mar to mid-Nov; hours vary according to the season; July and Aug, 10.15 and 11.30am, 1.35, 2.50, 4.05 and 5.20pm. 38F. ☎ 03 87 25 30 69.

Rocher de Dabo – Open June to 15 Sept, daily, 9am-7pm; 16 Sept to 31 Oct, 9am-6pm; 15 Mar to 31 May, 9am-6pm (Sat, 6.30pm, Sun, 7pm). 10F. ☎ 03 87 07 40 12 (town hall).

Wasselonne, Protestant church – Open in summer, Sun, 2-5pm.

Lac du DER-CHANTECOQ

Information available from the tourist office, Maison du Lac, 51290 Giffaumont-Champaubert. ☎ 03 26 72 62 80.

Boat trips on the lake – From Giffaumont harbour, 1 May to 15 Sept, every afternoon (except Mon), hourly, 2-6pm; Easter to end of Apr, Sun afternoon, only. 31F (adult), 19F (child). For more information, contact the tourist office.

Giffaumont, Grange aux abeilles – Open May to Sept, daily, afternoons only; Mar, Apr, Oct and Nov, Sat, Sun and holidays. Free admission. ☎ 03 26 72 61 97.

Ferme de Berzillières – Open July and Aug, daily, afternoons only; May, June and Sept, Sat, Sun and holidays, afternoons. 20F. ☎ 03 25 04 22 52.

Maison de l'Oiseau et du Poisson – Open July and Aug, daily, 10.30am-7pm; the rest of the year, contact ☎ 03 26 74 00 00. 35F.

Ferme aux Grues – Open end of Oct to end of Mar, daily, 9am-5.30pm. Free admission. ☎ 03 26 72 54 10.

Village-musée de Ste-Marie-du-Lac-Nuisement – Open July and Aug, daily, 2.30-7pm; Easter to Sept, Sat, Sun and holidays, 2.30-7pm. 15F. ☎ 03 26 72 63 25.

Château d'eau panoramique de Ste-Marie-du-Lac-Nuisement – Open daily, 10am-6pm (Oct to Apr, 4.30pm). 2F.

Château d'eau panoramique along D 55 – Open daily, 10am-6pm (Oct to Apr, 4.30pm). 2F. ☎ 03 26 72 62 80.

Massif du DONON

Abreschviller, Forest train – Trips available in May and June, Sat, 3pm, Sun and holidays, 10.30am, 2.30, 3.15, 4 and 4.50pm; July and Aug, Mon-Sat, 2.45 and 4.15pm, Sun and holidays, 10.30am, 2.30, 3.15, 4 and 4.50pm; Sept to early Oct, Sat, 3pm, Sun and holidays, 2.45 and 4.15pm. 49F (adult), 34F (child). Information: ☎ 03 87 03 79 12.

Massif du DONON

Scierie de la Hallière – Open July to Sept, daily (except Mon), 2.30-6.30pm; May to June, Sun and holidays, 2.30-6.30pm. 15F. ☎ 03 83 74 49 71.

Pierre-Percée, Exhibition – Open end of June to end of Aug, daily, 2-6.30pm. Free admission. ☎ 03 83 73 56 86.

Lac de Pierre-Percée, Vedette "Cristal" – Departures: early Apr to end of Sept, Sun and holidays, 2, 3, 4 and 5pm; 26 June to 2 Sept, daily, 2, 3, 4 and 5pm. 40F (adult), 15F (child). Information: ☎ 03 83 73 04 45.

E

ÉCOMUSÉE D'ALSACE

Museum open July and Aug, daily, 9am-7pm; Apr to June and Sept, daily, 9.30am-6pm; Mar and Oct, daily, 10am-5pm; the rest of the year, daily, 10.30am-4.30pm. 76F (adult), 46F (child 6 to 16). ☎ 03 89 74 44 74.

EGUISHEIM
🚪 18, rue des 3 Châteaux – 68420 – ☎ 03 89 23 40 33

Guided tours of the town – Contact the tourist office.

ENSISHEIM

Musée de la Régence – Open daily (except Tues), 2-5.30pm. Closed every other weekend and holidays. 11F. ☎ 03 89 26 49 54.

ÉPERNAY
🚪 7, avenue Champagne – 51202 – ☎ 03 26 55 33 00

Moët et Chandon – Guided tours (45min) year-round, Mon-Fri, 9.30-11.45am and 2-4.45pm; Apr to 15 Nov, Sat, Sun and holidays as well, 9.30-11.45am and 2-4.45pm. 35F. ☎ 03 26 51 20 20.

Mercier – ♿ Guided tours (1hr), daily, 9.30-11.30am and 2-4.30pm. Closed Dec to Feb, Tues and Wed and 20 Dec to 5 Jan. Mon-Fri 25F, Sat and Sun 30F. ☎ 03 26 51 22 22.

De Castellane – Guided tours (30min) Apr to Oct, daily, 10-11.15am and 2-5.15pm. 20F. ☎ 03 26 51 19 11.

Musée Municipal – Closed for refurbishing.

Jardin des papillons – ♿ Open June to 16 Aug, daily (except Mon), 10am-noon and 2-6pm. 22F. ☎ 03 26 51 19 11.

Excursion:

Parc du Sourdon – Open Apr to 31 Oct, 9am-7pm. 10F. ☎ 03 26 59 95 00.

ÉPINAL
🚪 13, rue de la Comédie – 88000 – ☎ 03 29 82 53 32

Guided tours of the town – Contact the tourist office.

Parc du Château – Open Mar to Oct, daily, 7.30am-6pm (7 or 8pm according to the season); the rest of the year, daily, 8am-5pm.

Musée départemental d'Art ancien et contemporain – Open daily (except Tues), 10am-noon and 2-6pm. Closed 1 Jan, 1 May, 1 Nov and 25 Dec. 30F. ☎ 03 29 82 20 33.

Imagerie d'Épinal (Exhibition gallery and Écomusée) – Open daily (except Sun mornings), 8.30am-noon and 2-6.30pm. Closed 1 Jan and 25 Dec. Audio-visual programme (20min). 30F. ☎ 03 29 31 28 88.

Église Notre-Dame – Closed Sun afternoons.

Excursion:

Fort d'Uxegney – Open mid-June to mid-Sept, Sat, guided tours, 2 and 4pm, Sun, 1.30-5.20pm. 20F.

F

FISMES

Excursion:

Courville, church – Apply to Mme Ronseaux, 5, rue Saucelle, Courville, ☎ 03 26 48 15 38.

Parc Naturel Régional de la FORÊT D'ORIENT

Maison du Parc – Open year-round, Mon-Fri, 9am-noon and 2-6pm, Sat, Sun and holidays, 9.30am-12.30pm and 2.30-6.30pm (mid-Feb to 30 Apr, 6pm; Oct to mid-Feb, 5.30pm). ☎ 03 25 43 81 90.

Boat trips:

Le Winger – Departures from Mesnil-St-Père harbour, mid-Mar to mid-Sept, daily. Time: 45min. 25F (adult), 15F (child). ☏ 03 25 41 21 64.

Le Bateau lvre – Guided trip (1hr), 15 Apr to 15 Sept, daily, 9am-5pm; cruise with meal at 11.30am and 7pm on request (apply 8 days in advance). Boat trip: 25F (adult), 15F (child); meal: 150F (adult), 80F (child). ☏ 03 25 41 20 72.

Parc de vision animalier – Open July and Aug, daily (except Thur and Fri), 5pm-dusk; Apr to June and Sept, Sat and Sun, 5pm-dusk; the rest of the year, Sun and holidays, 2pm-dusk. Closed 1 Jan and 25 Dec. 20F. ☏ 03 25 43 81 90.

G

Région de GÉRARDMER

Textile factories – Open mid-June to mid-Sept only (except Aug). Enquire at the tourist office, ☏ 03 29 27 27 27.

Boat trips – Guided tour of the lake (20min). 20F. Electric-canoe hire: 75F for 30min.

Domaine de la Moineaudière – ♿ Open daily, 9.30am-noon and 2-6.30pm. Closed for 10 days in Jan, 15 days in Mar and mid-Oct to mid-Dec. 26F. ☏ 03 29 63 37 11.

GIVET   🛈 Place de la Tour – 08600 – ☏ 03 24 42 03 54

Tour Victoire – Open July and Aug, daily (except Sun and Mon mornings), 10am-noon and 2-6pm. 10F.

Centre européen des métiers d'art – Open daily (except Sun and Mon mornings), 10am-noon and 2.30-6pm. Closed 1 Jan and 25 Dec. ☏ 03 24 42 73 36.

Fort de Charlemont – Open July and Aug, daily, 10am-noon and 2-5.15pm. 15F. ☏ 03 24 42 03 54.

Chemin de fer des Trois Vallées – Steam and diesel trains run from May to mid-Sept, Sat, Sun and holidays. Enquire at the tourist office, in Givet station ☏ 03 24 41 36 04 or in Mariembourg, Belgium, ☏ 00 32 60 31 24 40.

Excursion:

Grottes de Nichet – Guided tours (1hr) Apr to May and Sept, daily, 2-5pm; June to Aug, daily, 10am-noon and 1.30-6.30pm. 30F. ☏ 03 24 42 00 14.

GRAND CANAL D'ALSACE

Fessenheim

Centrale nucléaire – Information Centre: open Mon-Sat, 9am-noon and 2-6pm. Power station: guided tours (3hr) of installations (lecture, film, exhibition, simulator, engine room), Mon-Sat, 9am-noon and 2-5pm by appointment made 2 weeks in advance (minimum age 10 if accompanied by parents, identification papers necessary). For information and reservations, contact EDF - Centre Nucléaire de production d'électricité, BP 15, 68740 Fessenheim, ☏ 03 89 83 51 23.

Maison de l'Hydraulique – Open July and Aug, daily, 2-6pm, guided tour, 3pm; the rest of the year, guided tours on request made 2 weeks in advance to EDF - Energie Est, 54, avenue Robert-Schumann, 68050 Mulhouse cedex.

GUEBWILLER   🛈 73, rue de la République – 68500 – ☏ 03 89 76 10 63

Guided tours of the town – Contact the tourist office.

Ancien couvent des Dominicains: centre polymusical – Open June to Sept, Tues-Fri, 10am-noon and 2-6.30pm, Sat and Sun, 2-6.30pm; the rest of the year, Mon-Fri, 10am-noon and 2-5.30pm. Jazz venue Fri-Sat, 9pm except during school holidays. Concerts in the church in summer. Closed 24 Dec to 2 Jan. ☏ 03 89 74 19 96.

Musée du Florival – Open Mon-Fri (except Tues), 2-6pm, Sat and Sun and holidays, 10am-noon and 2-6pm. Closed 1 Jan, 1 May and 25 Dec. 15F. ☏ 03 89 74 22 89.

H

HACKENBERG

Guided tours (2hr) Apr to Oct, Sat, Sun and holidays, 2.30-3.30pm; July and Aug, Wed as well, 2-3pm. 25F. ☏ 03 82 82 30 08.

HAGUENAU   🛈 Place de la gare – 67500 – ☏ 03 88 93 70 00

Guided tours of the town – Contact the tourist office.

Musée historique – Open Mon-Fri, 10am-noon and 2-6pm, Sat and Sun and holidays, 3-5.30pm (July and Aug, 2-6pm). Closed Tues mornings in July and Aug, all day Tues the rest of the year, 1 Jan, Easter, 1 May, 1 Nov and 25 Dec. 20F. ☏ 03 88 93 79 22.

Soufflenheim – Ceramics with flower motifs

Musée alsacien – Open Mon-Fri (except Tues mornings), 9am-noon and 2-6pm, Sat, Sun and holidays, 2-5pm. Closed 1 Jan, Easter, 1 May, 1 Nov and 25 Dec. 15F. ☎ 03 88 73 30 41.

Excursions:

Soufflenheim, Ceramics workshops – Open Mon-Fri, 9am-noon and 2-5pm. Closed Sat, Sun, holidays and July and Aug. Hours vary according to the workshop. Ask the tourist office for a list of the various workshops which can be visited.

Betschdorf, Museum – Open Easter to 1 Nov, daily, 10am-noon and 1-5pm. 15F. ☎ 03 88 54 48 07.

HAUT-BARR

Tower of Claude Chappe's telegraph – Open June to end of Sept, daily (except Mon), noon-6pm. 10F. ☎ 03 88 52 98 99.

Château du HAUT-KOENIGSBOURG

Open July and Aug, daily, 9am-6.30pm; May to June and Sept, daily, 9am-6pm; Mar to Apr and Oct, daily, 9am-noon and 1-5.30pm; Jan to Feb and Nov to Dec, daily, 9.30am-noon and 1-4.30pm. Closed 1 Jan, 1 May and 25 Dec. 40F (adult), 25F (child). The ticket office closes 30min before the castle at the end of the day. ☎ 03 88 82 50 60.

Région du HOHWALD

Ottrott, Les Naïades – ♿ Open daily, 9.30am-6pm. 42F. ☎ 03 88 95 90 32.

J

JOINVILLE
🔖 Place Saunoise – 52300 – ☎ 03 25 94 17 90

Château du Grand Jardin – Open Apr to Sept, daily (except Tues), 10am-noon and 2-7pm; the rest of the year, Mon-Fri (except Tues), 2-6pm, Sat and Sun, 10am-noon and 2-6pm. Closed during the Christmas holidays. 20F. ☎ 03 25 94 17 54.

Auditoire – Guided tours (1hr30min) July and Aug, Sat, 5-9pm, Sun, 3-6.30pm; 15 May to 30 June, Sun, 3-6.30pm; Sept to Oct, Sun, 2.30-5.30pm; May to Oct, Mon-Fri, by appointment, apply at the tourist office, preferably the day before. 20F. ☎ 03 25 94 17 90.

Église Notre-Dame – For guided tours apply at the tourist office.

Chapelle Ste-Anne – Open Wed-Fri; enquire at the tourist office.

K

KAYSERSBERG

Musée communal – Open July and Aug, daily, 10am-noon and 2-6pm; June and Sept, Sat and Sun only, 10am-noon and 2-6pm. 10F.

Centre culturel Albert Schweitzer – Open Easter and May-Oct, daily, 9am-noon and 2-6pm. Closed 1 May. 10F. ☎ 03 89 78 22 78.

L

LANGRES
🔖 Place Bel-Air – 52200 – ☎ 03 25 87 67 67

Guided tours of the town 🅰 – Contact the tourist office.

Cloître de la cathédrale – Open at the same time as the library, Tues and Thur, 3-6pm, Wed and Sat, 9.30-11.30am and 1.30-6pm, Fri, 4-7pm.

Cathédrale St-Mammès:
Trésor – Open July and Aug, daily (except Tues), 2.30-6pm.
Tour – Open July and Aug, daily (except Tues), 2.30-6pm. 10F (Tour and Trésor). ☎ 03 25 87 67 67.

Musée d'Art et d'Histoire – Open daily (except Tues), 10am-noon and 2-6pm (5pm in winter). Closed 1 Jan, 1 May, 1 Nov and 25 Dec. 20F. ☎ 03 25 87 08 05.

Tours de Navarre et d'Orval – Open July and Aug, daily, 10am-12.30pm and 2.30-7pm; May to June and Sept, Sat, Sun and holidays only, 2.30-5.30pm. 10F. ☎ 03 25 87 67 67.

Excursions:

Faverolles, Atelier archéologique – Open July and Aug, daily (except Tues), 3-7pm; mid-Apr to 1 Nov, Sat, Sun and holidays only, 3-6pm. 15F. ☎ 03 25 87 67 67.

Langres – Glazed earthenware from Aprey (18C)

Fort du Cognelot – Guided tours (1hr) July and Aug, Sun, 3.30 and 5pm. 20F. Enquire at the tourist office in Langres.

Château du Pailly – Audio-guided tours of the exterior, of the park and of the great hall of the keep, July and Aug, daily (except Tues), 3-6pm. 15F. Enquire at the tourist office in Langres.

Andilly-en-Bassigny, Gallo-Roman excavations – Closed, work in progress.

Fayl-Billot, Exhibition rooms of the national school of wickerwork – Open daily (except Tues), 10am-noon and 2-6pm. Closed 1 Jan and 25 Dec. 15F. ☎ 03 25 88 63 02.

St-Géosmes, church – Recently reopened, enquire at the tourist office.

LUNÉVILLE

Castle:

Chapel – Closed for renovation.

Musée – Open daily (except Tues), 10am-noon and 2-6pm (Oct to Mar, 5pm). Closed 1 Jan, Mon before Shrove Tues and 25 Dec. 10F. ☎ 03 83 76 23 57.

Musée de la Moto et du Vélo – Open daily (exept Mon), 9am-noon and 2-6pm. 20F. ☎ 03 83 74 10 56.

LUXEUIL-LES-BAINS
🖸 1, avenue des Thermes – 70302 – ☎ 03 84 40 06 41

Guided tours of the town – Contact the tourist office.

Musée de la tour des Échevins – Open Apr to Oct, Wed-Sat, 10am-noon and 2-6.30pm, Sun, 2-6pm; the rest of the year, Wed-Sat, 10am-noon and 2-5.30pm, Sun, 2-5pm. Closed Nov. 12F.

Ancienne abbaye St-Colomban – Guided tours (2hr) provided on the third Thur of every month at 3pm. Enquire at the tourist office. 25F. ☎ 03 84 40 06 41.

Musée Maurice Baumont – Open June to July, 15 Feb to 15 Mar and 15 Oct to 15 Nov, daily, 10am-noon and 2-6pm. 12F. ☎ 03 84 40 46 60.

M

Ligne MAGINOT

Petit ouvrage de Villy-la-Ferté – Guided tours (1hr30min) July and Aug, daily, 2-4.30pm (beginning of last tour); Palm Sun to All Saints Day, Sun and holidays, 2-4.30pm. 15F. ☎ 03 24 27 50 80 (it is recommended to telephone in advance).

Gros ouvrage de Fermont – Guided tours (2hr30min) July and Aug, daily, 2-5pm; May to June, daily, around 2 and 3.30pm; Apr, Sat, Sun and holidays around 2 and 3.30pm; Sept, Sat and Sun around 2 and 3.30pm. Warm clothing and walking shoes recommended. 30F. ☎ 03 82 39 35 34.

Ligne MAGINOT

Fort de Guentrange – Guided tours (1hr30min) May to Sept, first and third Sun of every month, 3pm. 15F. ☎ 03 82 88 12 15.

Abri du Zeiterholz – Guided tours (1hr30min) May to Sept, on the first and third Sun of every month, 2-4pm. 10F. ☎ 03 82 55 11 43.

Petit ouvrage de l'Immerhof – Guided tours (1hr30min) Apr to Sept, second and fourth Sun of every month and holidays, 2pm. 18F. ☎ 03 82 53 09 61.

Gros ouvrage du Michelsberg – Guided tours (1hr30min) Apr to Sept, Sun, 2-6pm. 15F. ☎ 03 82 34 66 67.

Petit ouvrage du Bambesch – Guided tours (1hr30min) Apr to Sept, second and fourth Sun of every month, Easter Mon, Whit Monday and 15 Aug, 2-6pm. 20F. ☎ 03 87 90 31 95.

Rohrbach-lès-Bitche, Fort Casso – Guided tours (1hr30min) Apr to Oct, Sat, Sun and holidays, 3pm; Nov to Mar, first Sat and Sun of every month, 3pm. Closed 1 Nov, 25 and 26 Dec. 20F. ☎ 03 87 02 77 99.

Casemate de Dambach-Neunhoffen – Open mid-June to mid-Sept, Sun, 2-5pm. 5F. ☎ 03 88 09 22 25.

Lembach, Four à Chaux – Guided tours (1hr30min) mid-Mar to end of Apr and Oct to mid-Nov, daily, 10am, 2 and 3pm; May to June, daily, 10am, 2, 3 and 4pm; July to Sept, daily, 10 and 11am, 2, 3, 4 and 5pm. 20F. ☎ 03 88 94 43 16.

Ouvrage d'artillerie de Schœnenbourg – Open May to Sept, Mon-Sat, 2-4pm, Sun, 9.30-10.30am and 2-4pm; Apr and Oct, Sun and holidays only, 9.30-10.30am and 2-4pm. 25F. ☎ 03 88 80 59 39 (tourist office in Hunspach).

Hatten

Musée de l'Abri – Open Mar to 11 Nov, Thur-Sat, 10am-noon and 2-5pm, Sun, 10am-6pm; mid-June to mid-Sept, daily. Closed 12 Nov to end of Feb. 20F. ☎ 03 88 80 14 90.

Casemate d'infanterie Esch – Open May to Sept, Sun, 10am-noon and 1.30-6pm. 10F. ☎ 03 88 80 05 07.

Marcholsheim, Mémorial-musée de la Ligne Maginot du Rhin – ♿ Open 15 June to 14 Sept, daily, 9am-noon and 2-6pm; mid-Mar to mid-June and mid-Sept to mid-Nov, Sun and holidays only, 9am-noon and 2-6pm. 8F. ☎ 03 88 58 52 20 (town hall).

MARMOUTIER

Musée d'Arts et Traditions populaires – Guided tours (1hr30min) May to Oct, Sun and holidays, 10am-noon and 2-6pm. 20F. ☎ 03 88 71 46 84.

MARSAL

Maison du Sel – Open 1 Feb to 14 June and 16 Sept to 31 Dec, Mon-Sat, 2-6pm, Sun and holidays, 10am-noon and 2-6pm; 15 June to 15 Sept, Mon-Wed, 2-6pm, Thur-Sun, 10am-noon and 2-6pm. Closed Jan. 18F. ☎ 03 87 01 16 75.

METZ
🛈 Place d'Armes – 57000 – ☎ 03 87 55 53 76

Guided tours of the town 🄰 – Contact the tourist office. In July and Aug, guided walking tours by night are also provided.

Cathédrale St-Étienne – Guided tours provided daily (except Sun mornings). 15F or 25F (crypt and treasury included). Enquire at the Association de l'Oeuvre de la cathédrale, 2, place de Chambre, ☎ 03 87 75 54 61.

Crypt and Treasury – Open May to Oct, daily (except Sun mornings), 9.30am-6.15pm; the rest of the year, 9.30am-noon and 2-6pm. Closed 1 May and 15 Aug. 12F. ☎ 03 87 75 54 61.

Musées de la Cour d'Or – Open daily, 10am-noon and 2-6pm. Closed 1 Jan, Good Friday, 1 May, 1 and 11 Nov and 25 Dec. 30F, free admission Wed and Sun mornings. ☎ 03 87 75 10 18.

Église St-Pierre-aux-Nonnains – Open Apr to Sept, daily (except Mon), 2-6pm; the rest of the year, Sat and Sun, 2-6pm. Closed 1 May, Easter and 25 Dec. ☎ 03 87 39 92 00.

Chapelle des Templiers – Open mid-June to mid-Sept, daily (except Mon), 2-6pm. ☎ 03 87 39 92 00.

Ancien couvent des Récollets – Open Mon-Fri, 9am-noon and 2-5pm. Closed Sat, Sun and holidays.

Église St-Vincent – Closed for restoration.

Excursions:

Walibi-Schtroumpf – Open mid-Apr to end of Oct, daily, 10am-6pm (July to Aug 7pm). Enquire in advance about days when closed. 115F (adult), free admission (under-threes). ☎ 03 87 51 90 52.

Scy-Chazelles, Maison de Robert-Schuman – To visit Schumann's house, apply to M. Nicolas, ☎ 03 87 66 54 01 or contact the tourist office in Metz. 25F.

Château de Pange – ♿ Open June to Sept, daily, 10am-6pm. Free admission.

Vallée de la Canner – Train (steam or diesel) excursion end of Apr to early Oct, Sun and holidays, departure from Vigy, 3 and 5pm. 50F (adult) and 35F (child) return. For information, apply at Vigy station, ☎ 03 87 77 97 50.

Groupe fortifié l'Aisne – Guided tours (2hr15min) May to Oct, first Sun of every month, 2, 3 and 4pm. 20F. Warm clothing and walking shoes are recommended. ☎ 03 87 52 76 91.

Gorze, Maison de l'Histoire de la terre de Gorze – Open 15 June to 30 Sept, daily (except Mon), 2-6pm; Apr to 14 June and Oct, Sat, Sun and holidays, 2-6pm. Closed Nov-Mar. 10F. ☎ 03 87 52 04 57.

Vallée de la MEUSE

Commercy, Château Stanislas – Open July and Aug, daily (except Tues), 2-6pm; May to June and Sept, Sat, Sun and holidays only, 2-6pm. 15F. ☎ 03 29 91 02 18.

Parc de vision de Belval – Open May to Aug, daily (except Tues and Wed), 12.30pm (Sun, 10.30am) -6pm. 30F. ☎ 03 24 30 01 86.

Stenay, Musée de la Bière – Open Mar to Nov, daily, 10am-noon and 2-6pm. 30F. ☎ 03 29 80 68 78.

Bazeilles

Maison de la dernière cartouche – Open daily (except Mon), 9am-noon and 1.30-5pm. Closed 15 Dec to 5 Jan. 10F. ☎ 03 24 27 15 86.

Castle – Exterior only. ☎ 03 24 27 09 68.

Bogny-sur-Meuse

Musée de la Métallurgie – ♿ Open July and Aug, daily, 10am-noon and 2-6pm; June and Sept, daily, 2-6pm. 15F. ☎ 03 24 32 11 99.

Centre d'exposition des minéraux – Open mid-June to end of Aug, daily (except Mon), 2-6pm; Sept, Sat and Sun only, 2-6pm. 10F. ☎ 03 24 32 05 02.

Revin

Maison espagnole – Open mid-May to end of Sept, Mon-Fri, 2-6pm, Sat and Sun, 10am-noon and 1.30-6pm. 10F. ☎ 03 24 40 34 91.

Parc Maurice-Rocheteau – Open year-round, daily, 10am-8pm. Closed Sun from Nov to Mar.

Galerie d'art contemporain – Open Wed, Sat, Sun and holidays, 2-6pm. 4F. ☎ 03 24 40 10 72.

Fumay, Musée de l'Ardoise – Open Apr to Oct, daily 10am-6pm; the rest of the year, daily, 1-5pm. 15F. ☎ 03 24 41 10 25.

Site nucléaire de Chooz – Exhibition in the Information Centre at the entrance of the site, Mon-Sat, 8am-noon and 1.30-5.30pm. Guided tours (2hr30min) year-round, Mon-Fri, 9am and 2pm. No children under ten. Identification papers necessary. Foreigners are requested to apply in writing (include photocopy of passport) two weeks in advance. Book at least two weeks in advance by contacting the public relations office, ☎ 03 24 42 88 88.

MOLSHEIM

Musée de la Chartreuse – Open 15 June to 15 Sept, Mon-Fri (except Tues), 10am-noon and 2-6pm, Sat, Sun and holidays, 2-5pm; 2 May to 14 June and 16 Sept to 15 Oct, daily (except Tues), 2-5pm. 16F. ☎ 03 88 38 25 10.

Parc Naturel Régional de la MONTAGNE DE REIMS

Olizy, Musée de l'Escargot de Champagne – ♿ Guided tours (1hr) on the first Sat and Sun of every month, 2.30-5pm. Closed holidays, Nov to Mar and 1 to 15 July. 17F. ☎ 03 26 58 10 77.

Mailly-Champagne, Carrière géologique – The geological trail is open year-round. Free access. Guided tours (3hr) Apr to Nov, third Sun of every month. 20F.

Faux de Verzy – Guided tours available May to Oct, once a month. 35F. Enquire at the Maison du parc naturel régional de la Montagne de Reims in Pourcy. Guide (45F) available at the Maison du Parc.

Germaine, Maison du bûcheron – Open Easter to 1 Nov, Sat, Sun and holidays, 2.30-6.30pm. 12F. ☎ 03 26 59 44 44.

Avenay-Val-d'Or, Église St-Trésain – Contact the town hall, ☎ 03 26 52 31 33.

Fleury-la-Rivière, Coopérative vinicole – Guided tours (45min) daily (except Tues), 10.30am-12.30pm and 2-6pm, Sun and holidays, 3-7pm. Closed 1 Jan and 25 Dec. 20F. ☎ 03 26 58 42 53.

Pourcy, Maison du Parc — ♻ For information about the nature park, apply at the Maison du Parc, 51480 Pourcy. ☎ 03 26 59 44 44. The Information Centre is open Easter to 1 Nov, daily, 2.30-6.30pm; the rest of the year, Mon-Fri, 9am-noon and 2-5pm.

MONTHERMÉ
⚑ 50, rue Étienne-Dolet – 08800 – ☎ 03 24 53 06 50

Église St-Léger — Open July and Aug, Mon, Wed and Fri, 3-5pm; at other times, apply at the presbytery in Monthermé, 83, rue Doumer. ☎ 03 24 53 01 17.

MONTIER-EN-DER

Haras — Open daily, 2.30-5.30pm. Show of stallions and teams from early Sept to mid-Nov, every Thur, 3pm. Free admission. ☎ 03 25 04 22 17.

MONTMÉDY

Citadelle — Open July and Aug, daily, 9.30am-7pm; Apr to June and Sept to Oct, daily, 10am-noon and 1.30-6.30pm; 16 Feb to 31 Mar, 1 to 15 Nov and Christmas holidays, daily, 10am-noon and 1.30-5pm; 1 to 14 Feb and 15 to 30 Nov, daily, 2-5pm. Closed Dec to Jan (except Christmas holidays). 25F. ☎ 03 29 80 15 90.

Musées de la Fortification et Jules-Bastien-Lepage — Same admission times and charges as the citadel.

Excursions:

Marville, Cimetière de la chapelle St-Hilaire — To visit the chapel, apply at the town hall. ☎ 03 29 88 15 15.

Louppy-sur-Loison, Castle — Guided tours of the exterior only (45min) 15 July to 31 Aug, daily (except Mon), 2-6pm (Mon-Fri, 5pm). 9F. ☎ 03 29 88 11 16.

MONTMIRAIL

Excursion:

Verdelot, Church — To visit the church, apply at the Augustine convent.

Abbaye du Reclus — Guided tours (30min) July and Aug, daily (except Mon), 3-6pm. 15F. ☎ 03 26 80 36 11.

MONTMORT-LUCY

Château — Guided tours (1hr) 15 July to 15 Sept, Tues-Fri, 2.30 and 4.30pm; Sun, 15 Aug, Whit Sunday and Monday, 2.30, 3.30, 5 and 5.30pm. 30F. ☎ 03 26 59 10 04.

Excursions:

Étoges, Church — Open Easter to 1 Nov, daily, 10am-7pm; the rest of the year, apply at the presbytery in Congy, ☎ 03 26 59 31 17 or contact M. Roger Scieur, 47, Grande-Rue, ☎ 03 26 59 30 28.

Orbais-l'Abbaye, Church — Open Palm Sunday to 1 Nov, daily, 2-6pm.

La MOSELLE

Cattenom, Centre nucléaire de production d'électricité — Tour of the power station by appointment only: ☎ 03 82 51 70 41 or write to CNPE de Cattenom, Mission Communication, BP 41, 57570 Cattenom.

MOUZON

Musée du Feutre — Open June to Aug, daily, 2-7pm; May and Sept, daily, 2-6pm; Apr and Oct, Sat and Sun, 2-6pm. Closed Nov to Mar. 20F. ☎ 03 24 26 10 63.

Musée de la Tour de la Porte de Bourgogne — Open mid-May to mid-Sept, daily, 3-6pm. 5F. ☎ 03 24 26 10 63 (town hall).

MULHOUSE
⚑ 9, avenue Maréchal Foch – 68100 – ☎ 03 89 35 48 41

Guided tours of the town — Contact the tourist office.

Musée historique — Open daily (except Tues), 10am-noon and 2-6pm (Nov to Apr, 5pm). Closed 1 Jan, Good Friday, Easter and Whit Mondays, 1 May, 14 July, 1 and 11 Nov, 25 and 26 Dec. 20F, free admission on the first Sun of every month. ☎ 03 89 45 43 20.

Temple St-Étienne — Open 1 May to 30 Sept, daily, 10am-noon and 2-6pm (Sat, 5pm). Closed Sun mornings, Tues, and Sat afternoons when concerts are programmed. Free admission. ☎ 03 89 46 58 25.

Musée des Beaux-Arts — Open daily (except Tues), 10am-noon and 2-6pm (Nov to Apr, 5pm). Closed 1 Jan, 1 May, Good Friday, Easter and Whit Mondays, 14 July, 1 and 11 Nov, 25 and 26 Dec. 20F. ☎ 03 89 45 43 20.

Musée national de l'Automobile - collection Schlumpf – ♿ Open daily (except Tues), 10am-5.30pm. Closed 1 Jan and 25 Dec. 57F (adult), 27F (Child 6-18). ☎ 03 89 33 23 23.

Musée français du Chemin de fer – Open daily, 9am-6pm (Oct to Mar, 5pm). Closed Jan, 25 and 26 Dec. 44F (adult), 20F (child). ☎ 03 89 42 25 67.

Parc zoologique et botanique – ♿ Open May to Aug, daily, 9am-7pm; Apr and Sept, daily, 9am-6pm; Mar and Oct to Nov, daily, 9am-5pm; Jan to Feb and Dec, daily, 10am-4pm. 45F (adult; Nov to spring, 20F), 20F (child). Ticket office closes 30min before closing time. ☎ 03 89 31 85 10.

Electropolis: Musée de l'énergie électrique – Open daily, 10am-6pm. Closed Mon (except in July and Aug, Easter and Whit Mondays), 1 Jan, 25 and 26 Dec. 48F. ☎ 03 89 32 48 60.

Musée de l'Impression sur étoffes – ♿ Open daily, 9am (Oct to Apr, 10am) -6pm. Closed 1 Jan, 1 May and 25 Dec. 36F. ☎ 03 89 46 83 00.

Excursion:

Rixheim, Musée du Papier peint – Open June to Sept, daily, 9am (Sat and Sun, 10am) -noon and 2-6pm; the rest of the year, daily (except Tues), 10am-noon and 2-6pm. Closed 1 Jan, Good Friday, 1 May, 25 Dec. 30F. ☎ 03 89 64 24 56.

Vallée du MUNSTER

Munster   🚩 Place du Marché – 68140 – ☎ 03 89 77 31 80

Soultzbach-les-Bains, Church – To visit the church, contact the town hall or the presbytery.

Gunsbach, Musée Albert-Schweitzer – ♿ Guided tours (45min), daily (except Mon), 9-11.30am and 2-4.30pm. ☎ 03 89 77 31 42.

Muhlbach-sur-Munster, Musée de la Schlitte – Guided tours (40min) July and Aug, daily, 10am-noon and 3-6pm. 9F. ☎ 03 89 77 61 08 (town hall).

N

NANCY   🚩 14, place Stanislas – 54000 – ☎ 03 83 35 22 41

Guided tours of the town ▣ – Contact the tourist office.

Musée des Beaux-Arts – Open daily (except Tues), 10.30am-6pm. Closed 1 Jan, 1 May, 14 July, 1 Nov and 25 Dec. 25F, free admission on the first Sun of every month, 10.30am-1.30pm. ☎ 03 83 85 30 72.

Hôtel de ville – Guided tours of the reception rooms end of June to end of Aug, every evening, 10.20pm. 15F; Fri and Sat, guides in period costumes, 20F. Enquire at the tourist office.

Palais ducal: Musée historique lorrain – Open early May to end of Sept, daily (except Tues), 10am-6pm; the rest of the year, daily (except Tues), 10am-noon and 2-5pm (Sun and holidays, 6pm). Closed 1 Jan, Easter Sunday, 1 May, 14 July, 1 Nov and 25 Dec. 20F. ☎ 03 83 32 18 74.

Eglise et couvent des Cordeliers: musée d'Arts et Traditions populaires – Open May to end of Sept, daily (except Tues), 10am-6pm; the rest of the year, daily, 10am-noon and 2-5pm (Sun and holidays, 6pm). Closed 1 Jan, Easter Sunday, 1 May, 14 July, 1 Nov and 25 Dec. 20F. ☎ 03 83 32 18 74.

Musée de l'école de Nancy – Open daily (except Mon mornings and Tues), 10.30am-6pm. Closed 1 Jan, 1 May, 14 July, 1 Nov and 25 Dec. 20F. ☎ 03 83 40 14 86.

Musée de zoologie – Open daily, 10am-noon and 2-6pm. 30F (adult), 20F (child). ☎ 03 83 32 99 97.

Jardin botanique du Montet – ♿ Open Mon-Fri, 10am-noon and 2-5pm, Sat, Sun and holidays, 2-5pm (Apr to Sept, 6pm). Closed 1 Jan and 25 Dec. Hothouses are open daily (except on the first Tues of every month), 2-5pm. 15F. ☎ 03 83 41 47 47.

Maison de la Communication – Open year-round, Wed-Fri, 10am-noon and 2-6pm. Closed holidays. 15F. ☎ 03 83 34 85 89.

Cathedral treasury – Guided tours (30min), daily (except Wed and Sun), 10am-noon. Free admission. ☎ 03 83 35 36 76.

Excursions:

Musée de l'Aéronautique – ♿ Nancy-Essey Airport. Open daily (except Mon mornings), 10am-noon and 2-6pm (Mon-Fri and Sun during Oct and Nov, 5pm). Closed 1 Dec to 28 Feb. 30F (adult), 15F (child). ☎ 03 83 21 70 22.

Jarville-la-Malgrange, Musée de l'Histoire du Fer – Open Mon-Fri (except Tues), 2-5pm (July to Sept, 6pm), Sat, Sun and holidays, 10am-noon and 2-6pm. Closed 1 jan, Easter Sun, 1 Nov and 25 Dec. ☎ 03 83 15 27 70.

Château de Fléville – Guided tours (40min) July and Aug, daily; 2-7pm; Apr to June and Sept to 15 Nov, Sat, Sun and holidays, 2-7pm. 35F. ☎ 03 83 25 64 71.

Parc de loisirs de la forêt de Haye, Musée de l'Automobile – ♿ Open Apr to Sept, daily, 2-6pm; the rest of the year, Wed, Sat-Sun and holidays, 2-6pm. Closed between Christmas and New Year. 30F. ☎ 03 83 23 28 38.

NEUFCHÂTEAU
🏛 3, parking des Grandes Écuries – 88300 – ☎ 03 29 94 10 95

Église St-Nicolas – Open July and Aug, daily, 2-5pm. ☎ 03 29 94 10 95 (tourist office)

Église St-Christophe – Open Mon-Sat, 10am-noon.

Excursions:

St-Élophe

Church – Guided tours, daily, 10am-noon and 2-7pm. Apply to the association "Conservation du patrimoine", ☎ 03 29 06 97 94.

Museum – Open mid-Apr to 30 Sept, daily, 10am-noon and 2-6pm; the rest of the year, daily, 2-5pm. ☎ 03 29 06 97 94.

Grand

Section of piping – Guided tours (20min) July and Aug, Sun and holidays, every hour, 2-6pm; Apr to 30 Sept for groups (10 persons minimum) by appointment two weeks in advance. ☎ 03 29 06 77 37. No child under 10, not recommended to people suffering from claustrophobia. It is advisable to wear wellington boots and a windcheater. 10F.

Amphithéatre – Open Apr to 30 Sept, daily, 9am-noon and 2-7pm; the rest of the year, daily (except Tues), 10am-noon and 2-5pm. Closed 15 Dec to 15 Jan. 15F. Combined ticket including the mosaic: 20F. ☎ 03 29 06 77 37.

Mosaic – Same admission times and charges as the amphitheatre.

NEUWILLER-LES-SAVERNE

Église St-Pierre et St-Paul – Visit of the tapestries on request; apply at the Catholic presbytery, 5, cour du Chapitre, 67330, Neuwiller-lès-Saverne, ☎ 03 88 70 00 51.

Église St-Adelphe – Open Apr to Nov, daily, 8am-6pm.

NIEDERBRONN-LES-BAINS

Maison de l'Archéologie – ♿ Open Mar to Oct, daily (except Tues), 2-6pm; the rest of the year, Sun and holidays, 2-5pm. Closed 1 and 11 Nov (except if these dates fall on a Sun) and between Christmas and New Year. 15F. ☎ 03 88 80 36 37.

NOGENT-SUR-SEINE

Centre nucléaire de production d'électricité – Guided tours (2hr30min) by appointment, apply three weeks in advance. ☎ 03 25 39 32 60. The Information Centre is open Mon-Fri, 8.30am-12.30pm and 1.30-5.30pm. Free admission. ☎ 08 00 3? 94 27.

Musée Paul-Dubois - Alfred-Boucher – Open mid-June to mid-Sept, daily (except Tues), 2-6pm; first Sat in Apr to mid-June and mid-Sept to last Sun in Nov, Sat, Sun and holidays, 2-6pm. Free admission. ☎ 03 25 39 71 79.

Excursions:

Château de la Motte-Tilly – Guided tours (1h), Apr to Sept, daily (except Mon) 10-11.45am and 2-6pm; Oct, Sat and Sun, 2-6pm; Nov, Sat and Sun, 2-5pm. 32F. ☎ 03 25 39 99 67.

Ancienne abbaye du Paraclet – Tour of the exterior from 15 July to 31 Aug, 10am-noon and 2-6pm. Closed Sun and holidays. 10F.

OBERNAI
🏛 Chapelle du Beffroi – 67210 – ☎ 03 88 95 64 1?

Guided tours of the town – Contact the tourist office.

Val d'ORBEY

Lapoutroie, Musée des eaux de vie – Open daily, 9am-noon and 2-6pm. Free admission. ☎ 03 89 47 50 26.

Fréland, Maison du Pays Welche – Guided tours (1hr) June to Sept, daily (except Wed), 10am, 3 and 4.30pm; the rest of the year, 3pm. Closed mid-Feb to mid-Mar. 15F. ☎ 03 89 71 90 52.

OTTMARSHEIM

Centrale hydro-électrique – Guided tours (2hr), Mon-Thur, 8am-noon and 2-4.30pm, Fri, 8am-noon; groups of 10 persons and more (minimum age: 12) by appointment made three weeks in advance, apply to E.D.F., Énergie Est, 54, avenue Robert-Schuman, BP 1007, 68050 Mulhouse cedex. ☎ 03 89 35 20 00. Individual visitors may join a scheduled visit.

P

La PETITE PIERRE

Chapelle St-Louis: musée du Sceau alsacien – ♿ Open July to Sept and 25 Dec to 1 Jan, daily (except Mon), 10am-noon and 2-6pm; the rest of the year, Sat, Sun and holidays, 10am-noon and 2-6pm. Closed Jan. Free admission. ☎ 03 88 70 48 65.

Maison du parc – Open daily, 10am-noon and 2-6pm. Closed 24, 25 Dec and 31 Dec to 31 Jan. 25F. ☎ 03 88 01 49 59.

"Magazin" – ♿ Open July to Sept and 25 Dec to 1 Jan, daily (except Mon), 10am-noon and 2-6pm; the rest of the year, Sat, Sun and holidays only, 10am-noon and 2-6pm. Closed Jan. Free admission. ☎ 03 88 70 48 65.

PFAFFENHOFEN

Musée de l'Imagerie peinte et populaire alsacienne – Open Wed, Sat and Sun, 2-5pm. Closed holidays. 5F. The museum is due to move in spring 1999. ☎ 03 88 72 27 27.

PLOMBIÈRES-LES-BAINS
🚇 16, rue Stanislas – 88370 – ☎ 03 29 66 01 30

Guided tours of the town – Contact the tourist office.

Étuve romaine, Bain romain and Thermes Napoléon – Guided tours (1hr30min) May to Sept, Wed and Sat, 3pm; the tour starts from the tourist office. 20F. ☎ 03 29 66 01 30.

Musée Louis-Français – Open mid-Apr to mid-Oct, daily (except Tues), 2-5pm. 20F.

Pavillon des Princes – Open Apr to Oct, daily (except Mon), 2.30-6.30pm. 20F. ☎ 03 29 66 01 30.

PONT-À-MOUSSON
🚇 52, place Duroc – 54700 – ☎ 03 83 81 06 90

Ancienne abbaye des Prémontrés – Open daily, 9am-7pm. 25F. ☎ 03 83 81 10 82.

Hôtel de ville – To visit the reception rooms, enquire two to three days in advance at the Secrétariat général. ☎ 03 83 81 10 68.

PROVINS
🚇 Chemin de Villecran - BP 44 – 77160 – ☎ 01 64 60 26 26

Guided tours of the town – Contact the tourist office.

Pépinières et Roseraies – ♿ Open year-round, all day. Closed end of Dec to early Jan. ☎ 01 64 00 02 42.

Musée de Provins et du Provinois – Open Apr to 1 Nov, daily, 2-6pm; Sat, Sun, holidays and some school holidays, 2-5pm. Closed 25 Dec. 22F. ☎ 01 64 60 26 26.

Tour César – Restoration work in progress, enquire at the tourist office.

Grange aux Dîmes – Open Apr to 1 Nov, daily, 10am (Sept to Oct, Mon-Fri, 2pm) 6pm; the rest of the year, Sat, Sun, holidays and some school holidays, 2-5pm. Closed 25 Dec. 22F.

Église Ste-Croix – Closed for restoration.

Souterrains – Guided tours (45min) early Apr to 1 Nov, Mon-Fri, 3 and 4pm, Sat, Sun and holidays, 11am-6pm; the rest of the year, Sat, Sun, holidays and some school holidays, 3 and 4pm. Closed 25 Dec. 22F.

Excursion:

Beton-Bazoches, Cider press – Guided tours (30min) daily, 10am-8pm. It is recommended to phone the day before. ☎ 01 64 01 06 96 (after 5pm).

R

⊠ 2, rue Guillaume-de-Machault – 51100 – ☎ 03 26 77 45 25

Guided tours of the town 🅰 – Contact the tourist office.

Cathédrale Notre-Dame – In summer, guided tours (1hr30min) given by lecturers from the Historic Monuments Association take place daily except Sun mornings at 10.30am, 2.30 and 4pm. 35F. For additional information, apply at the tourist office. Upper parts: open mid-June to mid-Sept, daily (except Sun mornings), 10-11.30am and 2-5.30pm. 20F. Apply at the Palais du Tau.

Palais du Tau – Open mid-Mar to mid-June and early Sept to mid-Nov, daily, 9.30am-12.30pm and 2-6pm; July and Aug, daily, 9.30am-6.30pm; mid-Nov to mid-Mar, daily, 10am-noon and 2-5pm (Sat and Sun, 6pm). Closed 1 Jan, 1 May, 1 and 11 Nov and 25 Dec. 32F. ☎ 03 26 47 81 79.

Musée St-Remi – Open daily, 2-6.30pm (Sat and Sun, 7pm). Closed 1 Jan, 1 May, 14 July, 1 and 11 Nov and 25 Dec. 10F. ☎ 03 26 85 23 36.

Pommery – Guided tours (1hr) Easter to Oct, daily, 10am-5pm, preferably by appointment; the rest of the year, Mon-Fri by appointment. Closed 1 Nov and end of Dec to early Jan. 40F. ☎ 03 26 61 62 56.

Taittinger – Guided tours (about 45min) year-round, Mon-Fri, 9.30am-noon and 2-4.30pm; Mar-Nov, Sat, Sun and holidays 9-11am and 2-5pm. Closed 1Jan and 25 Dec. l20F. ☎ 03 26 85 84 33.

Veuve Clicquot-Ponsardin – Guided tours (1hr) daily by appointment; apply a few days in advance. Closed Sun year-round and holidays from Nov to Mar. Free admission. Contact Mme Danielle Brissaud. ☎ 03 26 89 54 41.

Ruinart – Guided tours (1hr30min) Mon-Fri by appointment; apply 10 days in advance to Service visites et réceptions, 4, rue des Crayères, 51053 Reims. ☎ 03 26 77 51 53.

Piper Heidsieck – Open daily, 9-11.45am and 2-5.15pm. Closed Tues and Wed from Dec to Feb, 1 Jan and 25 Dec. 35F including Champagne-tasting. ☎ 03 26 84 43 44.

Mumm – Guided tours (1hr) Mar to Oct, daily, 9-11am and 2-5pm; the rest of the year, Mon-Fri, 9-11am and 2-5pm, Sat, Sun and holidays, 2-5pm. Closed 1 Jan and 25 Dec. 20F including Champagne-tasting. ☎ 03 26 49 59 70.

Musée des Beaux-Arts – Open daily (except Tues), 10am-noon and 2-6pm. Closed 1 Jan, 1 May, 14 July, 1 and 11 Nov and 25 Dec. 10F. ☎ 03 26 47 28 44.

Église St-Jacques – Closed Mon.

Cryptoportique gallo-romain – Open 15 June to 15 Sept, daily (except Mon), 2-5pm. Free admission. ☎ 03 26 85 23 36.

Musée-hôtel Le Vergeur – Guided tours (1hr15min) daily (except Mon), 2-6pm. Closed 1 Jan, 1 May, 14 July, 1 Nov and 24 Dec to 2 Jan. 20F. ☎ 03 26 47 20 75.

Chapelle Foujita – Open May to Oct, daily (except Wed), 2-6pm. Closed 1 May and 14 July. 10F. ☎ 03 26 47 28 44.

Salle de Reddition – ♿ Open Apr to Nov, daily (except Tues), 10am-noon and 2-6pm. Closed 1 May, 14 July, 1 and 11 Nov. 10F. ☎ 03 26 47 28 44.

Centre historique de l'automobile française – Open daily (except Tues), 10am-noon and 2-6.30pm. 30F. ☎ 03 26 82 83 84.

Ancien collège des Jésuites – Guided tours (45min) Mon and Wed-Fri mornings, 10 and 11am, every afternoon, 2.15, 3.30 and 4.45pm. Exhibition area open daily 2-6pm. Closed 1 Jan, 1 May, 14 July, 1 and 11 Nov and 25 Dec. 10F. ☎ 03 26 85 51 50.

Planétarium et horloge astronomique – ♿ Shows year-round, Sat and Sun, 2.45, 3.30 and 4.45pm; during the regional school holidays, daily shows, same times (arrive 15min before). The show entitled "L'Étoile des rois mages" is programmed in Dec and Jan, daily at 2.15, 3.30 and 4.45pm. Closed 1 Jan, 1 May, 14 July, 1 and 11 Nov and 25 Dec. 10F. ☎ 03 26 85 51 50.

Parc Pommery – Open May to mid-Oct, daily, 8am-8pm; the rest of the year, daily, 10am-5pm. 12F (adult), 6F (under 14).

Excursion

Fort de la Pompelle, Museum – Open daily (except Tues), 10am-7pm (Nov to Mar, 5pm). Closed 1 May and 24 Dec to 6 Jan. 20F. ☎ 03 26 49 11 85.

⊠ 2, rue Charles-de-Gaulle – 88204 – ☎ 03 29 62 23 70

Guided tours of the town – Contact the tourist office.

Musée municipal (Fondation Ch.-de-Bruyère) – Open May to Sept, daily (except Tues), 10am-noon and 2-6pm (7pm in summer); Nov to Dec, daily (except Tues) 10am-noon and 2-5pm; Jan to Apr, daily (except Tues), 2-6pm. Closed 1 Jan, 1 May, Ascension Day, 25 Dec and Oct. 10F. Free admission Sun. ☎ 03 29 62 42 17.

Musée municipal (Fondation Charles-Friry) – Same admission times and charges as the Musée municipal (Fondation Ch.-de-Bruyère).

RETHEL

Église St-Nicolas – Open July and Aug, Mon-Fri, 2.30-5.30pm. At other times, apply at the presbytery, 13, rue Carnot.

RIBEAUVILLÉ

🛈 1, Grand'Rue – 68150 – ☎ 03 89 73 62 22

Guided tours of the town – Contact the tourist office.

Hôtel de Ville: Museum – Guided tours (45min) May to Oct, daily (except Mon and Sat), 10 and 11am, 1.45 and 2.30pm. Free admission. ☎ 03 89 73 20 00.

RIQUEWIHR

🛈 2, rue de la 1ʳᵉ-Armée – 68340 – ☎ 03 89 47 80 80

Guided tours of the town – Contact the tourist office.

Musée d'histoire des P.T.T. d'Alsace – Open early Apr to 11 Nov, daily (except Tues), 10am-noon and 2-6pm. 20F (adult), 12F (child); combined ticket with the Musée de la Diligence: 30F (adult), 12F (child). ☎ 03 89 47 93 80.

Musée de la Diligence – Same admission times and charges as the Musée d'Histoire des P.T.T. d'Alsace.

Maison Hansi – Open Jan, Sat to Sun, 2-6pm; Feb and Mar, daily (except Mon), 2-6pm; Apr to Dec, Tues-Sun, 10.30am-6pm; also open Mon in July and Aug, 2-6pm. Closed 1 Jan and 25 Dec. 10F. ☎ 03 89 47 97 00.

Musée de la tour des Voleurs – Open Good Friday to 1 Nov, daily, 9.15am-noon and 1.30-6pm. 10F.

Musée du Dolder – Open Easter to end of Oct, Sat, Sun and holidays, 9.15am-noon and 1.30-6pm; July and Aug, daily, 9.15am-noon and 1.30-6pm. 10F.

ROCROI

🛈 place d'Armes – 08230 – ☎ 03 24 54 20 06

Musée – Open May to Oct, daily, 10am-noon and 2-6pm; the rest of the year, daily, 2-5pm. Closed 1 Jan and 25 Dec. 25F. ☎ 03 24 54 20 06.

ROUFFACH

🛈 8, place de la République – 68250 – ☎ 03 89 78 53 15

Église des Récollets – Work in progress; contact the town hall.

S

ST-DIÉ

🛈 31, rue Thiers – 88100 – ☎ 03 29 56 17 62

Cathédrale St-Dié – Guided tours provided July to 15 Sept, daily (except Sat and Sun mornings), 10.30am and 4pm.

Église Notre-Dame-de-Galilée – Guided tours provided July to 15 Sept, daily (except Sat and Sun mornings), 10.30am and 4pm.

Musée Pierre-Noël - Musée de la vie dans les Hautes-Vosges – Open Wed, 10am-noon and 2-7pm (Oct to Apr, 5pm); Thur-Sun, 2-7pm (Oct to Apr, 5pm). Closed Mon, Tues and holidays. 22F. Free admission on Wed. ☎ 03 29 51 60 35.

Bibliothèque – Visit of the treasury during the school year, daily (except Sun and Mon), 10am-7pm (Sat, 6pm); during school holidays, daily (except Sun and Mon), 10am-noon and 2-7pm (Sat, 6pm). Closed some holidays. Free admission. ☎ 03 29 51 60 40.

Tour de la Liberté – Open daily, 10am-noon and 2-7pm (9pm in summer). Free admission.

Collection de bijoux – Open mid-Apr to mid-Oct, daily, 2-6pm; the rest of the year, Fri-Sun, 2-6pm. Closed holidays. 20F. ☎ 03 29 55 17 62.

ST-JEAN-SAVERNE

Chapelle St-Michel – Open Sun, 2-6pm. Closed Jan, Feb and Dec.

ST-MIHIEL

🛈 Palais abbatial – 55300 – ☎ 03 29 89 06 47

Bibliothèque – Open July and Aug, daily (except Tues), 2-6pm, also Sat, 10am-noon; the rest of the year, Sat, Sun and holidays, 2-6pm. Closed Oct to Mar. 25F. ☎ 03 29 89 15 11.

Excursions:

Sampigny, Musée Raymond-Poincaré – Open 1 May to 11 Nov, daily, 2-6pm (Fri, 5pm). Closed Sat except in July and Aug. 12F. ☎ 03 29 90 70 50.

Hattonchâtel

Musée Louise-Cottin – Open 15 Apr to 15 Oct, Mon, Wed, Sat, Sun and holidays, 2-6pm. 10F. ☎ 03 29 89 30 73.

Castle – Guided tours (20min) Easter to Sept, daily (except Tues), 9am-noon and 2-7pm. 15F. ☎ 03 29 89 57 44 (caretaker).

ST-NICOLAS-DE-PORT

Basilique – Guided tours provided (1hr) early July to second Sun in Sept, Sun and holidays, 2-6pm. Chapelle des Fonts, treasury and sacristy: 20F; towers: 10F. ☎ 03 83 46 81 50.

Musée français de la Brasserie – Open 15 June to 15 Sept, daily, 2.30-6.30pm; the rest of the year, daily (except Mon), 2-6pm. Closed 20 Dec to 5 Jan. 20F. ☎ 03 83 46 95 52.

STE-MENEHOULD
🛈 Place Leclerc – 51800 – ☎ 03 26 60 85 83

Musée – Open May to Oct, Sat, Sun and holidays, 3-6pm; Mon-Fri, apply at the town hall. Free admission. ☎ 03 26 60 80 21.

SARREBOURG
🛈 Chapelle des Cordeliers – 57400 – ☎ 03 87 03 11 82

Chapelle des Cordeliers – Contact the toutist office. 16F.

Musée du Pays de Sarrebourg – Open year-round, daily (except Sun and Tues), 8am (early July to early Aug, 9am) -noon and 2-6pm (Sat, 5pm); early July to end of Aug, Sun as well, 2-6pm. Closed holidays. 16F. ☎ 03 87 03 27 86.

Excursions:

St-Ulrich, Villa gallo-romaine – Open July and Aug, Mon, Thur and Sun, 2-6pm, Wed, Fri and Sat, 10am-noon and 2-6pm. Closed Tues, 14 July and 15 Aug. Free admission. ☎ 03 87 03 27 86.

Hartzviller, Cristallerie – Open Mon-Fri, 9-11am and 1-2pm. Closed Sat, Sun, holidays (except for the shop which is open from 1.30-5.30pm) and end of July to end of Aug. 10F. ☎ 03 87 25 10 55.

SARREGUEMINES
🛈 Rue du Maire-Massing – 57322 – ☎ 03 87 98 80 81

Musée – Open daily (except Tues), 2-6pm, Wed, 9am-noon as well. Closed 1 Jan, Easter Sunday, 1 May, Whitsun, 1 Nov and 25 Dec. 15F. ☎ 03 87 98 93 50.

Circuit touristique de la Faïence – Guided tours (2hr) mid-July to end of Sept, Sun, 3-5pm. 25F. Brochure available at the tourist office. ☎ 03 87 98 93 50.

Excursion:

Bliesbruck-Reinheim, Parc archéologique européen – Open Apr to Oct, daily (except Mon), 10am-6pm; Nov to Mar, daily (except Mon), 10am-noon and 2-5pm. Information from Centre archéologique départemental, 1, rue Robert Schuman, 57200 Bliesbruck, ☎ 03 87 02 25 79 or 03 87 02 22 32. For the display of objects found on the site and for the tumulus, enquire in Reinheim, ☎ 00 49/ 6843 9002.

SAVERNE
🛈 37, Grand'rue – 67700 – ☎ 03 88 91 80 47

Château: musée – Open 15 June to 15 Sept, daily (except Tues), 10am-noon and 2-6pm; Mar to 14 June and 16 Sept to 30 Nov, daily (except Tues), 2-5pm; Dec to Feb, Sun only, 2-5pm. Closed 1 Jan, 1 May, Good Friday, 1 Nov, 25 and 26 Dec. 15F. ☎ 03 88 91 06 28.

Roseraie – ♿ Open early June to end of Sept, daily, 9am-7pm. 15F. ☎ 03 88 71 83 33.

Excursion:

Jardin botanique du col de Saverne – Open May to June, daily (except Sat) 9am-5pm, Sun and holidays, 2-6pm; July and Aug, Mon-Fri, 9am-5pm, Sat, Sun and holidays, 2-7pm; 1 to 15 Sept, Mon-Fri only, 9am-5pm. 12F. ☎ 03 88 91 31 09.

SEDAN
🛈 Place du Château - BP 322– 08202 Cedex – ☎ 03 24 27 73 73

Château fort – Audio-guided tours July and Aug, daily, 10am-6pm; 15 Mar to 30 June and 1 to 15 Sept, 10am-noon and 1-5pm; the rest of the year, Tues-Fri 1.30-4.30pm, Sat and Sun, 10am-noon and 1-4.30pm. Closed 25 Dec. 45F (adult) 30F (child). Multimedia show: 20F (adult), 10F (child). ☎ 03 24 27 73 73.

Dijonval – Open June to Sept, daily (except Sun and Mon), 1-6pm. 15F. ☎ 03 24 27 73 77.

Manufacture du Point de Sedan – ♿ Open Mon-Sat, 8am-noon and 2-6pm. Closed holidays. ☎ 03 24 29 04 60.

Excursion:

Aérodrome de Sedan-Douzy: Musée des débuts de l'aviation – ♿ Open June-Aug, daily (except Mon), 10am-noon and 2-6pm; May and Sept, daily (except Mon), 2-6pm; Apr and Oct, Sat, Sun and holidays, 2-6pm. 13F. ☏ 03 24 26 38 70.

SÉLÉSTAT
🛈 Boulevard du Général-Leclerc– 67600 – ☏ 03 88 58 87 20

Guided tours of the town – Contact the tourist office.

Bibliothèque humaniste – Open Mon-Fri, 9am-noon and 2-6pm. Closed Sat afternoons and Sun all day except in July and Aug (open 2-5pm). 20F. ☏ 03 88 92 03 24.

Excursions:

Kintzheim

Volerie des aigles – Open from 2pm (14 July to 20 Aug, 10am); demonstrations Apr to mid-June and Sept to end of Oct, daily, 3 and 4pm (Sat and Sun, 5pm as well); mid-June to mid-July, daily, 2.30, 4 and 5pm; 14 July to 20 Aug, daily, 11.45am, 2.30, 3.45 and 5pm; 21 Aug to end of Aug, daily, 3, 4, and 5pm; 1 to 11 Nov, Wed, Sat and Sun, 3 and 4pm. 45F (adult), 30F (child). ☏ 03 88 92 84 33.

Montagne des singes – ♿ Open July and Aug, daily, 10am-6pm; May to June and Sept, daily, 10am-noon and 1-6pm; Apr and Oct to Nov, daily, 10am-noon and 1-5pm. 40F (adult), 25F (child). ☏ 03 88 92 11 09.

SESSENHEIM

Auberge "Au bœuf" – Closed Mon, Tues, 1 to 15 Feb and mid-July to early Aug. Postcard: 3F.

SIERCK-LES-BAINS

Château – Open May to Sept, daily, 10am-7pm (Sun, 8pm); the rest of the year, daily, 10am-4pm (Sun, 5pm). Closed Jan to Feb and Dec. 20F. ☏ 03 82 83 74 14.

Le SIMERSHOF

Guided tours (1hr30min) early June to mid-Sept, Mon-Sat, 10, 11am, 1.30 and 3.30pm, Sun every hour, 10am-4pm (except noon); the rest of the year, daily, 1.30 and 3pm. Closed mid-Nov to end of Jan. 30F (adult), 15F (child). Warm clothing recommended. ☏ 03 87 06 16 16.

Colline de SION-VAUDEMONT

Musée – Open daily, 3-5pm. Information, ☏ 03 83 25 12 22.

Château de Haroué – Guided tours (1hr) Apr to 11 Nov, daily, 2pm (July and Aug, 10am) -6pm. 35F. ☏ 03 83 52 40 14.

SOULTZ-HAUT-RHIN
🛈 14, place de la République – 68360 – ☏ 03 89 76 83 60

Guided tours of the town – Contact the tourist office.

Musée du Bucheneck – Open May to Sept, daily (except Tues), 2-6pm. 15F. ☏ 03 89 76 02 22.

La Nef des jouets – ♿ Open daily (except Tues), 2-6pm, also 10am-noon in July and Aug. Closed 1 Jan, 24, 25 and 31 Dec. 30F. ☏ 03 89 74 30 92.

STRASBOURG
🛈 17, place de la Cathédrale – 67200 – ☏ 03 88 52 28 28

Guided tours of the town 🄰 – Contact the tourist office.

Cathédrale Notre-Dame

Tower – Open July and Aug, daily, 8.30am-7pm; Apr to June and Sept, daily, 9am-6.30pm; Mar and Oct, daily, 9am-5.30pm; Nov to Feb, daily, 9am-4.30pm. 20F. Apply at the foot of the tower, place du Château. ☏ 03 88 43 60 32.

Astronomical clock – ♿ Guided tour (20min) daily, 12.30pm. Could be closed when long services or concert rehearsals in progress. 5F. ☏ 03 88 52 28 28.

Église St-Thomas – Closed in Jan and Feb.

Barrage Vauban – Open (including panoramic terrace) daily, 9am-8pm (mid-Oct to mid-Mar, 7pm). Free admission. ☎ 03 88 60 90 90.

Musées du Palais Rohan:

Musée des Arts décoratifs – ♿ Open daily (except Tues), 10am-noon and 1.30-6pm, Sun, 10am-5pm. Closed 1 Jan, Good Friday, 1 May, 1 and 11 Nov and 25 Dec. 20F. ☎ 03 88 52 50 00.

Musée des Beaux-Arts – Same admission times and charges as the Musée des Arts décoratifs.

Musée archéologique – ♿ Same admission times and charges as the Musée des Arts décoratifs.

Musée alsacien – Open daily (except Tues), 10am-noon and 1.30-6pm, Sun, 10am-5pm. Closed 1 Jan, Good Friday, 1 May, 1 and 11 Nov and 25 Dec. 20F. ☎ 03 88 52 50 00.

Musée de l'Œuvre-Notre-Dame – Open daily (except Mon), 10am-noon and 1.30-6pm, Sun, 10am-5pm. Closed 1 Jan, Good Friday, 1 May, 1 and 11 Nov and 25 Dec. 20F.

Musée d'Art moderne et contemporain – ♿ Open daily (except Mon), 11am-7pm (late opening on Thur until 10pm). Closed 1 Jan, Good Friday, 1 May, 1 and 11 Nov and 25 Dec. 30F. The restaurant is open daily except Mon, evenings as well. ☎ 03 88 23 31 31.

Musée historique – Closed for renovation; reopening scheduled for the summer of 1999.

Musée zoologique de l'université et de la ville – ♿ Open daily (except Tues), 10am-noon and 1.30-6pm, Sun, 10am-5pm. Closed 1 Jan, Good Friday, 1 May, 1 and 11 Nov and 25 Dec. 15F. ☎ 03 88 35 85 11.

Église St-Guillaume – To visit the church, apply at the Secrétariat, 1, rue Calvin, ☎ 03 88 36 01 36.

Église St-Pierre-le-Jeune – Open Apr to Oct, daily (except Mon), 10am-noon and 1-6pm.

Palais de l'Europe – ♿ Guided tours (1hr) by appointment. ☎ 03 88 17 20 07. Closed Sat, Sun, holidays and when the parliament is sitting.

Haras national – Open daily, 9-11.30am and 2pm (Sat and Sun, 3pm) -4.30pm. Closed Sun from Mar to 14 July and holidays. Free admission. ☎ 03 88 36 10 13.

Boat trips on the River Ill – Pier near the Palais Rohan. Departure May to Sept, daily, every 30min, 9.30am-10pm; Oct, daily, 9am-9pm; the rest of the year, 10.30,11.15am, 1, 1.45, 2.30, 3.15 and 4pm. 40F (adult), 20F (child). Night trip along the lit-up river, May to 29 Sept, daily, 9.30 and 10pm; Oct, between 7 and 9pm. 42F (adult), 21F (child). For information, ☎ 03 88 32 75 25.

Pleasure flights – Flights last between 15min and 1hr30min. Fees vary according to the length of the flight. Information from the Aéro-Club d'Alsace. Aérodrome du Polygone (BX), Strasbourg-Neudorf. ☎ 03 88 34 00 98.

Naviscope: Musée du Rhin et de la navigation – Open Wed-Fri, 2.15-6pm, Sat and Sun, 9.30am-12.30pm and 2.15-6pm; in summer hours are more flexible, enquire by phone. Closed 1 Jan, 1 May, 1 Nov and 25 Dec. 30F. ☎ 03 88 60 22 23.

Harbour tour – Guided tour (2hr30min) July and Aug, daily, 10.30am (harbour and boat trip along the Rhine) and 2.30pm (harbour and Naviscope). 50F (adult), 25F (child). Departure from the pier of the Promenade Dauphine. For further information, apply at the harbour Information Centre. ☎ 03 88 44 34 27.

Le STRUTHOF

Open Mar to mid-June, daily, 10am-noon and 2-5.30pm; mid-June to mid-Sept, daily, 10am-6pm; mid-Sept to end of Dec, daily, 10am-noon and 2-5pm. Closed 25 Dec to 28 Feb. 8F. Ticket office closes 30min before the camp. ☎ 03 88 97 04 49.

SUNDGAU

Oltingue, Maison du Sundgau – Open 15 June to 30 Sept, Tues, Thur and Sat 3-6pm, Sun, 11am-noon and 3-6pm; the rest of the year, Sun, 2-5pm. Closed Jan to Feb. 10F. 10 F. ☎ 03 89 40 79 24.

Hippoltskirch, Chapel – Open May to Sept, Sun, 11am-6pm.

T

THANN

🏛 6, place Joffre – 68800 – ☎ 03 89 37 96 20

Collégiale St-Thiébaut – Open June to Sept, daily, 9am-7pm; the rest of the year, daily, 9am-noon and 2-6pm (5pm in winter).

Musée des Amis de Thann – Open mid-May to mid-Oct, daily (except Mon), 10am-noon and 2.30-6.30pm. 15F. ☎ 03 89 37 02 31.

THIONVILLE

Tour aux Puces: Musée municipal – Open daily (except Mon), 2-6pm. Closed some holidays. 17F. ☎ 03 82 53 35 36.

Château de la Grange – Guided tours (45min) July and Aug, daily, 2.30, 3.30, 4.30 and 5.30pm; the rest of the year, Sat, Sun and holidays only, 2.30, 3.30, 4.30 and 5.30pm. Closed 1 Nov and 25 Dec. 28F. ☎ 03 82 53 85 03.

Excursions:

Aumetz, Musée des Mines de fer de Lorraine – Guided tours (1hr30min) May to Sept, daily (except Mon), 2-4.30pm. 25F. ☎ 03 82 85 76 55.

Neufchef, Musée des Mines de fer de Lorraine – Guided tours (1hr30min), daily (except Mon), 2-4.30pm. Closed 1 Jan, 24, 25 and 31 Dec. 35F. ☎ 03 82 85 76 55.

Vallée de la THUR

St-Amarin 🏛 60, rue Charles-de-Gaulle – 68550 – ☎ 03 89 82 60 01

Musée – Open May to Sept, daily (except Tues), 2-6pm. 20F. ☎ 03 89 38 24 66.

Husseren-Wesserling

Musée du Textile et des Costumes – ⟵ Open Apr to Sept, daily, 10am (Mon and Sat, 2pm) -6pm; Oct to Mar, daily (except Mon and Sat mornings), 10am-noon and 2-5pm. Closed holidays from Oct to Mar. 30F. ☎ 03 89 38 28 08.

TOUL

🏛 Parvis de la Cathédrale – 54203 – ☎ 03 83 64 11 69

Guided tours of the town – Contact the tourist office.

Cathédrale St-Étienne – Closed for restoration.

Église St-Gengoult – Apply at the tourist office.

Musée municipal – Open Apr to Oct, daily (except Tues), 10am-noon and 2-6pm; the rest of the year, daily, 2-6pm only. Closed 1 Jan, Easter Monday, 1 May, 1 Nov and 25 Dec. 16.50F. ☎ 03 83 64 13 38.

Excursions:

Villey-le-Sec, Ensemble fortifié – Guided tours (2hr) May to Sept, Sun and holidays, 3pm. 25F. ☎ 03 83 63 67 72.

Liverdun 🏛 Porte Haute – 54460 – ☎ 03 83 24 40 40

Guided tours of the town – Contact the tourist office.

TROYES

🏛 16, boulevard Carnot – 10014 – ☎ 03 25 82 62 70

Guided tours of the town — Contact the tourist office.

Cathedral Treasury – Open June to Sept, Tues-Sun, 10am-noon and 2-5pm. Free admission. ☎ 03 25 80 57 61.

Église St-Nicolas – Open Tues-Fri, 4-6pm. ☎ 03 25 73 02 98 (parish).

Église St-Remy – Open July and Aug, times available from the tourist office.

Église St-Nizier – Open July and Aug, times available from the tourist office.

Musée d'Art moderne – ⟵ Open daily (except Tues), 11am-6pm. Closed holidays. 30F. Free admission on Wed. ☎ 03 25 76 26 80.

Maison de l'Outil et de la Pensée ouvrière – Open Mon-Fri, 9am-1pm and 2-6.30pm; Sat, Sun and holidays, 10am-1pm and 2-6.30pm. 30F. ☎ 03 25 73 28 26.

Hôtel de Vauluisant – Open daily (except Tues), 10am-noon and 2-6pm. Closed holidays. 30F. Free admission on Wed. ☎ 03 25 42 33 33.

Abbaye St-Loup – Open daily (except Tues), 10am-noon and 2-6pm. Closed holidays. 30F. Free admission on Wed. ☎ 03 25 76 21 68.

Hôtel-Dieu-le-Comte: Pharmacy – Open daily (except Tues), 10am-noon and 2-6pm. Closed holidays. 20F. Free admission on Wed. ☎ 03 25 80 98 97.

Excursions:

Bouilly, Église St-Laurent – Apply at the presbytery or contact Mme Henneguy, 10, rue du Bois.

Isle-Aumont, Church – Guided tours by appointment; apply at the town hall, ☏ 03 25 41 81 11 or contact M. and Mme Jacotin, 4, rue de la Monnaie, ☏ 03 25 41 82 33.

Pont-Ste-Marie, Church – Apply at the town hall Mon-Fri, 9am-noon and 2-6pm (Fri, 5pm). ☏ 03 25 81 20 54.

Ste-Maure, Church – Apply at the town hall on Mon, Tues, Thur and Fri, 9am-noon and 2-6pm, Wed and Sat, 9am-noon. ☏ 03 25 76 90 93.

V

VAUCOULEURS
🛈 Place Achille François – 55140 – ☏ 03 29 89 51 82

Chapelle castrale – Guided tours July to Sept, daily, 9am-6pm; the rest of the year, apply at the tourist office.

Musée Jeanne d'Arc – Open May to Sept, Mon-Fri, 9am-noon and 2-6pm, Sat and Sun, 2-6pm; the rest of the year, Mon-Fri, 8am-noon and 2-6pm. Closed Tues (except in July and Aug), Easter, 1 and 11 Nov and end of Dec to early Jan. 20F. ☏ 03 29 89 51 63.

Excursion:

Domrémy-la-Pucelle, Maison natale de Jeanne-d'Arc – Open Apr to Sept, daily, 9am-12.30pm and 2-7pm; the rest of the year, daily (except Tues), 9am-12.30pm and 2-5pm. Closed 1 Jan and 25 Dec. 6F. ☏ 03 29 06 95 86.

VERDUN
🛈 Place de la Nation – 55016 – ☏ 03 29 86 14 18

Citadelle souterraine – Open (tour-reconstruction: 30min) July and Aug, daily, 9am-7pm; May to June, daily, 9am-6pm; Apr and Sept, daily, 9am-noon and 2-5.30pm; mid-Feb to end of Mar and Oct to 20 Dec, daily, 10am-noon and 2-5pm; the rest of the year, daily, 2-4pm. Closed some holidays. 35F. ☏ 03 29 86 14 18.

Palais épiscopal: Centre mondial de la Paix – Open daily (except Tues), 10am-1pm and 2-6pm. Closed mid-Nov to end of Jan. 35F. ☏ 03 29 86 55 00.

Musée de la Princerie – Open Apr to Oct, daily (except Tues), 9.30am-noon and 2-6pm. 10F. ☏ 03 29 86 10 62.

Monument de la Victoire – Open Easter to 11 Nov, daily, 9am-noon and 2-6pm. Free admission.

Excursion:

Senon, Church – Contact Mme Robert Caillard, near the church.

Battlefields

Fort de Vaux – Open May to Sept, daily, 9am-6.30pm; Apr, daily, 9am-6pm; mid-Feb to end of Mar, daily, 9.30am-noon and 1-4.30pm; mid-Sept to end of Dec, daily, 9am-noon and 1-5pm. Closed from Christmas to mid Feb. 15F. ☏ 03 29 86 14 18.

Mémorial de Verdun – Open Easter to Sept, daily, 9am-6pm; the rest of the year, daily, 9am-5.30pm. Closed end of Dec to end of Jan. 20F. Film lasts 20min. ☏ 03 29 84 35 34.

Fort de Douaumont – Open Apr to Sept, daily, 10.30am-6.30pm; mid-Feb to end of Mar, daily, 10.30am-1pm and 2-4.30pm; Oct to 20 Dec, daily, 10.30am-1pm and 2-5pm; 2 Jan to 15 Feb and 21 to 30 Dec, daily, 11am-4pm. Closed some holidays. 15F. ☏ 03 29 86 14 18.

Ossuaire de Douaumont – Open Mar to Nov, daily, 9am-noon and 2-5 or 6pm according to the season (all day without a break from mid-Apr to early Sept). The cloister and chapel are open year-round. Tower: 6F, films: 16F. For information, ☏ 03 29 84 54 81.

Butte de Montfaucon: Monument – Open mid-Apr to end of Sept, daily (except Mon and Tues), 8am (Sat and Sun, 9am) -noon and 1-5.30pm; the rest of the year, daily (except Sat and Sun), 8am-noon and 1-4.30pm. Closed holidays. Free admission. ☏ 03 29 86 14 18

Route des VINS

Barr, La Folie Marco – Guided tours (45min) July to Sept, daily (except Tues), 10am-noon and 2-6pm; June and Oct, Sat and Sun only, 10am-noon and 2-6pm. 20F. ☏ 03 88 08 66 65 (tourist office).

Bergheim, Church – Open July and Aug; the rest of the year, apply at the presbytery, 1, rue de l'église.

Hunawihr

Centre de réintroduction des cigognes – Open Apr to May and Sept to 11 Nov, daily, 10am-noon and 2-5.30pm; June, daily, 10am-5.30pm; July and Aug, daily, 10am-6.30pm. Shows at 3, 4pm (and 5 or 6pm in season). Enquire beforehand, ☎ 03 89 73 72 62. Mornings: 40F (adult), 25F (child); afternoons: 45F (adult), 30F (child).

Jardin des papillons exotiques vivants – ₺ Open Apr to 11 Nov, daily, 10am-5pm (Apr to June, 6pm; July and Aug, 7pm). 30F (adult), 20F (child). ☎ 03 89 73 69 58.

Kientzheim, Musée du vignoble et des vins d'Alsace – Open June to Oct, daily, 10am-noon and 2-6pm. 15F. ☎ 03 89 78 21 36.

VITTEL

Institut de l'eau Perrier Vittel – Open Apr to Sept, daily (except Tues), 10am-noon and 1.30-6.30pm. 20F. ☎ 03 29 08 70 41.

Usine d'embouteillage – ₺ Open Apr to Oct (guided tours 1hr), Mon afternoon to Fri, 9.30, 10.30am, 2 and 3.30pm; the rest of the year by appointment. Free admission. ☎ 03 29 08 72 50.

Excursions:

Thuillières, Castle – Guided tours (1hr) July and Aug, daily, 2.30-5.30pm. 15F. ☎ 03 29 08 29 29.

Darney, Czechoslovak museum – Guided tours (45min) by appointment two days in advance; apply at the town hall, ☎ 03 29 09 33 45; open July and Aug daily (except Tues), apply at the town hall. Closed Sun and holidays. Free admission.

Hennezel, Musée de la Résidence – Open May to Sept, daily, 2.30-6.30pm. 15F. ☎ 03 29 07 00 80.

Dombrot-le-Sec, Church – Contact M. Pierre Hermann, 240, rue du Château, ☎ 03 29 07 40 31.

Parc Naturel Régional des VOSGES DU NORD

Bouxwiller

Musée du Pays de Hanau – Open year-round, Mon-Fri, 9am-noon and 2-6pm; Sat from May to Sept and Sun year-round, 2-6pm. Closed 1 Jan, Good Friday, 1 May, 24-26 and 31 Dec. 15F. There are plans for the museum to move to the former corn exchange. ☎ 03 88 70 70 16.

Church – Open July and Aug, Fri, 3-6pm, Sat and Sun, 10am (Sun, 11am) -noon and 3-6pm; the rest of the year, apply at the town hall, ☎ 03 88 70 70 16.

Château de Lichtenberg – Open June to Aug, Mon, 1.30-6pm, Tues-Sat, 10am-6pm; the rest of the year, Mon-Sat, 10am-noon and 1-6pm, Sun and holidays, 10am-7pm; Nov to Feb, by appointment only. 15F. The ticket office closes 30min before closing time.

Meisenthal, Maison du verre et du cristal – Open Easter to 1 Nov, daily (except Tues), 2-6pm. 30F. ☎ 03 87 96 91 51.

Soucht, Musée du Sabotier – ₺ Guided tours (1hr), July and Aug, daily, 2-6pm; Easter to end of Oct, Sat and Sun, 2-6pm. 10F. ☎ 03 87 96 86 97.

St-Louis-lès-Bitche, Cristalleries de St-Louis – Guided tours (1hr) 15 Mar to 15 Oct, Mon-Fri, 9am-noon and 2-7pm. Closed Sat, Sun and holidays. 20F. ☎ 03 87 06 40 04.

Château de Fleckenstein – Open mid-Mar to mid-Apr, daily, 10am-5pm; mid-Apr to end of Sept, daily, 9.30am-6pm; Oct to mid-Nov, daily, 10am-6pm. Mon-Sat: 12F, Sun and holidays in July and Aug: 17F. ☎ 03 88 94 43 16.

Reichshoffen, Musée du Fer – Open June to Oct, daily (except Tues), 2-6pm; the rest of the year, Sun only, 2-6pm. 15F. ☎ 03 88 80 34 49.

Woerth, Musée de la bataille du 6 août 1870 – Open Apr to Oct, daily (except Tues), 2-5pm (June to Aug, 6pm); the rest of the year, Sat, Sun and holidays only, 2-5pm. Closed in Jan. 15F. ☎ 03 88 09 30 21.

Merkwiller-Pechelbronn, Musée du pétrole – ₺ Guided tours including film (1hr30min), Apr to Oct, Sun and holidays, 2.30-6pm. 15F. ☎ 03 88 80 91 08.

W

WASSY
🛈 Tour du Dôme – 52130 – ☎ 03 25 55 72 25

Hôtel de ville – Open Mon-Fri, 9am-noon and 2-5pm.

Temple – Open 15 June to 15 Sept, daily (except Mon), 2-6pm. Free admission.

Excursion:

Vallée de la Blaise, Route du Fer – For information about the Route du Fer in Haute-Marne, contact the "Association pour la sauvegarde du patrimoine métallurgique haut-marnais" (see address below).

Dommartin-le-Franc, Haut fourneau – Open Aug, daily (except Tues), 2.30-6.30pm; July, Sat and Sun, 2.30-6.30pm; Sept, Sun only, 2.30-6.30pm. For information, contact the "Association pour la sauvegarde et la promotion du patrimoine métallurgique haut-marnais", 3, rue Robert-Dehault, 52100 St-Dizier. ☎ 03 25 05 00 41.

Cirey-sur-Blaise, Castle – Guided tours (45min) 15 June to 15 Sept, daily, 2.30-6.30pm. 30F. ☎ 03 25 55 43 04.

Sommevoire

Paradis – Open mid-June to end of Sept, Sat, Sun and holidays, 2.30-6.30pm or by appointment. 5F. ☎ 03 25 55 60 59 or 03 25 55 71 46.

Église St-Pierre – Same opening times as Paradis. 10F.

Osne-le-Val, Usine du Val d'Osne – Guided tours (1hr) end of July to end of Sept, Sun, 3-6.30pm. 15F. ☎ 03 25 94 81 02.

WISSEMBOURG
🛈 9, place de la République – 67160 – ☎ 03 88 94 10 11

Guided tours of the town – Contact the tourist office.

Musée Westercamp – Guided tours (1hr), Mon, Wed and Thur, 2-6pm; Fri, Sat and Sun, 9am (Sun, 10am) -noon and 2-6pm. 15F. ☎ 03 88 54 28 14.

Index

Reims *Marne*. . . . .   Towns, sights and tourist regions followed by the name of the *département*

Verlaine . . . .   People, historical events and subjects

Isolated sights (caves, châteaux, dams, abbeys etc) are listed under their proper name.

A

Abélard, Pierre, 29, 218, 374
Abreschviller *Moselle*, 118
Accommodation, 355
Agriculture, 25
Ailly (Bois) *Meuse*, 259
Aimé (Mont) *Marne*, 109
Alfeld (Lac) *Haut-Rhin*, 73
Allemant *Marne*, 258
Altenstadt *Bas-Rhin*, 344
Altkirch *Haut-Rhin*, 66
Amance (Lac) *Aube*, 131
Ammerschwihr *Haut-Rhin*, 328
Amnéville *Moselle*, 66
Andilly-en-Bassigny *Haute-Marne*, 158
Andlau *Bas-Rhin*, 67
Andouillette, 359
Appert, Nicolas, 89
Arc-en-Barrois *Haute-Marne*, 158
Arches *Ardennes*, 92
Arches *Vosges*, 192
Architecture :
    Alsace, 42
    Champagne-Ardenne, 45
    Illustrations and terms, 35
    Lorraine, 44
    Rural, 55
Arcis-le-Ponsart *Marne*, 130
Ardennes (Canal) *Ardennes*, 341
Argent (Val), 76
Argonne *Meuse*, 68
Arp, Jean, 52, 291
Arrembécourt *Aube*, 189
Arrigny *Marne*, 116
Ars-sur-Moselle *Moselle*, 175
Art Nouveau, 52
Asfeld *Ardennes*, 70
Attila, 86, 307
Aube (Source) *Haute-Marne*, 158
Auberive *Haute-Marne*, 158
Aubure *Haut-Rhin*, 250
Augronne (Vallée), 226
Aumetz (Musée des Mines de Fer) *Moselle*, 302
Avenay-Val-d'Or *Marne*, 186
Avioth (Basilique) *Meuse*, 70

Avison (Tour-belvédère du mont) *Vosges*, 136
Avize *Marne*, 109
Avolsheim *Bas-Rhin*, 325
Ay *Marne*, 186
Aymon brothers, legend, 180

B

Baccarat *Meurthe-et-Moselle*, 71
Badonviller *Meurthe et Moselle*, 118
Baerenthal *Moselle*, 335
Bagenelles (Col) *Haut-Rhin*, 77
Bailly-le-Franc *Aube*, 189
Bains-les-Bains *Vosges*, 226
Bairon (Lac) *Ardennes*, 341
Ballon (Col), 73
Ballon (Lac) *Haut-Rhin*, 111
Ballon d'Alsace, 72
Ballon d'Alsace (Massif), 72
Ballons des Vosges (Parc Naturel Régional), 72
Bambesch (Petit ouvrage) *Moselle*, 164
Ban-de-la-Roche (Vallon) *Bas-Rhin*, 85
La Bannie (Parc anima- lier) *Haute-Marne*, 82
Barbarossa, 1, 142
Bar-le-Duc *Meuse*, 78
Barr *Bas-Rhin*, 325
Barrès, Maurice, 277
Bar-sur-Aube *Aube*, 80
Bar-sur-Seine *Aube*, 315
Bartholdi, Frédéric-Auguste, 104
Battles of the Marne, 31, 32
Bavière, Isabeau, 307
Bayard, the horse, 180
Baye *Marne*, 191
Bayel *Aube*, 81
Bazeilles *Ardennes*, 177
Beaulieu-en-Argonne *Meuse*, 69
Beaumarchais, 192
Beblenheim *Haut-Rhin*, 328
Beer, 59, 372
Belgium, 373
Belleau (Bois) *Aisne*, 96

Belval (Parc de vision) *Ardennes*, 177
Benwihr *Haut-Rhin*, 328
Bergères-les-Vertus *Marne*, 109
Bergheim *Haut-Rhin*, 327
Bernstein (Château) *Bas-Rhin*, 327
Berzillières (Ferme) *Haute-Marne*, 116
Beton-Bazoches *Seine-et-Marne*, 234
Betschdorf *Bas-Rhin*, 144
La Beuille *Vosges*, 193
Bitche *Moselle*, 81
Blanc (Lac) *Haut-Rhin*, 221
Blanchemer (Lac) *Vosges*, 135
Blécourt *Haute-Marne*, 150
Bleurville *Vosges*, 333
Bliesbruck-Reinheim (Parc archéologique européen), 265
Boating, 365
Boersch *Bas-Rhin*, 325
Boffrand, Germain, 206
Bogny-sur-Meuse *Ardennes*, 178
Bois-Chenu (Basilique) *Vosges*, 317
Bonaparte, Napoléon, 84
Le Bonhomme *Haut-Rhin*, 222
Bonhomme (Col) *Haut-Rhin*, 110, 222
Bosserville (Chartreuse) *Meurthe-et-Moselle*, 214
Bouilly *Aube*, 315
Bourbonne-les-Bains *Haute-Marne*, 82
Boursault (Château) *Marne*, 124
Boust *Moselle*, 193
Bouxwiller *Haut-Rhin*, 298
Bouxwiller *Bas-Rhin*, 334
Bramont (Col), 304
Braux *Ardennes*, 179
Braux-Ste-Cohière (Châ- teau) *Marne*, 83
La Bresse *Vosges*, 135
Le Brézouard *Haut-Rhin*, 77
Bricot-la-Ville *Marne*, 275
Brienne-la-Vieille *Aube*, 84
Brienne-le-Château *Aube*, 84

405

Briey *Meurthe-et-Moselle*, 302
La Bruche (Vallée) *Bas-Rhin*, 84
Brugny (Château) *Marne*, 123
Bucer, Martin, 270
Buhl *Haut-Rhin*, 205
La Bure (Camp celtique) *Vosges*, 257
Bussang *Vosges*, 193
Bussang (Col), 193
Buswiller *Bas-Rhin*, 225

C

Calendar of events, 375
Callot, Jacques, 206, 211
Calmet, Dom, 274
Canner (Vallée) *Moselle*, 175
Capetian dynasty, 28
Carnival, 54
Carolingian dynasty, 28
Cattenom (Centre nucléaire) *Moselle*, 194
Ceffonds *Haute-Marne*, 188
Celles (Vallée), 118
Celles-sur-Plaine *Vosges*, 118
Cernay *Haut-Rhin*, 112
Châlons-en-Champagne *Marne*, 86
Champagne (Route), 90
Champagne wine, 61, 361
Champ-le-Duc *Vosges*, 136
Champs Catalauniques, 86
Chaource *Aube*, 315
Chappe, Claude, 145
Charbonnière (Col) *Bas-Rhin*, 149
Charbonniers (Vallée) *Vosges*, 76
Charlemagne, 27
Charleville *Ardennes*, 92
Charleville-Mézières *Ardennes*, 92
Charmes (Lac) *Haute-Marne*, 157
La Charmoye (Forêt) *Marne*, 191
Chassepot, Antoine, 85
Château-Regnault *Ardennes*, 179
Château-Thierry *Aisne*, 95
Châtenois *Bas-Rhin*, 327
La Chatte pendue (Rocher) *Bas-Rhin*, 85
Chaumont *Haute-Marne*, 96
Chavanges *Aube*, 189
Chenay *Marne*, 246
Chooz (Site nucléaire) *Ardennes*, 181
Choucroute, 59, 358
Christmas markets, 362
Churchill, Winston, 34

Châtillon-sur-Broué *Marne*, 116
Cinq Châteaux (Route) *Haut-Rhin*, 121
Cirey-sur-Blaise *Haute-Marne*, 342
Claudel, Paul and Camille, 342
Clause, Jean-Pierre, 281
Cleebourg (Vignoble) *Bas-Rhin*, 344
Clermont-en-Argonne *Meuse*, 68
Climate, 348
Le Climont *Bas-Rhin*, 85
Clovis, 27, 235
Coal mines, Lorraine, 25
Le Cognelot (Fort) *Haute-Marne*, 157
Coizard *Marne*, 258
Colmar *Haut-Rhin*, 101
Colombé-le-Sec *Aube*, 81
Colombey-les-Deux-Églises *Haute-Marne*, 108
Commercy *Meuse*, 176
Commune de Paris, 30
Condé-en-Brie *Aisne*, 95
Contrexéville *Vosges*, 333
Corbeaux (Lac) *Vosges*, 135
Corroy *Marne*, 275
Cote 204 *Aisne*, 96
La Cote 304 *Meuse*, 323
Coulange (Parc zoologique du bois) *Moselle*, 66
Courville *Marne*, 129
Cramant *Marne*, 109
Crêtes (Route), 110
Croix de Lorraine, 54, 206
La Croix-aux-Mines (Circuit minier) *Vosges*, 77
Crouttes *Aisne*, 96
Cuesta, 21
Cuis *Marne*, 109
Cuisine, regional, 59, 358
Customs, 350
Cuveau des Fées *Vosges*, 332
Cuveaux (Tête) *Vosges*, 193
Cycling, 364

D

Dabo *Moselle*, 113
Dabo (Rocher) *Moselle*, 113
Dabo-Wangenbourg (Région), 113
Dambach-la-Ville *Bas-Rhin*, 325
Dambach-Neunhoffen (Casemate) *Bas-Rhin*, 165
Damery *Marne*, 186
Darney *Vosges*, 332
Decapolis, 195

Deck, Théodore, 141
Decorative arts, 50
Démineurs (Monument) *Vosges*, 73
Deneuvre *Meurthe-et-Moselle*, 71
Der-Chantecoq (Lac) *Marne and Haute-Marne*, 115
Diable (Roche) *Vosges*, 135
Dialect, Alsatian, 56
Diderot, Denis, 56, 153
Dienville *Aube*, 132
Doller (Vallée) *Haut-Rhin*, 73
Dombasle-sur-Meurthe *Meurthe-et-Moselle*, 261
Dombrot-le-Sec *Vosges*, 333
Domjulien *Vosges*, 331
Dommartin-le-Franc *Haute-Marne*, 342
Domrémy-la-Pucelle *Vosges*, 317
Donon *Bas-Rhin*, 117
Donon (Col) *Bas-Rhin*, 117, 274
Donon (Forêt) *Bas-Rhin*, 85
Donon (Massif), 117
Doré, Gustave, 291
Douaumont (Fort) *Meuse*, 323
Doulevant-le-Château *Haute-Marne*, 342
Droiteval *Vosges*, 332
Drosnay *Marne*, 189
Droyes *Haute-Marne*, 189
Dugny-sur-Meuse *Meuse*, 176
Dun-sur-Meuse *Meuse*, 176

E

Ebersmunster *Bas-Rhin*, 119
Écomusée d'Alsace *Haut-Rhin*, 119
Economy, 25
Écrouves (Église Notre-Dame) *Meurthe-et-Moselle*, 306
Eguisheim *Haut-Rhin*, 120
Eguisheim (Donjons) *Haut-Rhin*, 121
Élan (Forêt, Vallon) *Ardennes*, 94
Eloyes *Vosges*, 193
Encylopédie, 58
Enfer (Croix) *Ardennes*, 274
Ensisheim *Haut-Rhin*, 121
Épernay *Marne*, 122
Épernay (Montagne) *Marne*, 123
Epfig *Bas-Rhin*, 67
Épinal *Vosges*, 124

L'Épine (Notre-Dame) *Marne*, 128

Esch (Vallée) *Meurthe-et-Moselle*, 229

Essômes-sur-Marne *Aisne*, 96

Étain *Meuse*, 319

L'Étape *Aube*, 132

Étival-Clairefontaine *Vosges*, 257

Étoges *Marne*, 191

L'Étoile *Marne*, 275

Ettendorf (Cimetière juif) *Bas-Rhin*, 225

Étufs (Cascade) *Haute-Marne*, 158

European Union, 34

F

Fables of La Fontaine, 56, 374

Fairies, 54

Faubourg-Pavé (Cimetière militaire) *Meuse*, 322

Faverolles Mausolée gallo-romain *Haute-Marne*, 157

Fayl-Billot *Haute-Marne*, 158

Faymont (Cascade) *Vosges*, 227

Fecht (Vallée) *Haut-Rhin*, 202

Feldbach *Haut-Rhin*, 298

Fénétrange *Moselle*, 264

Fépin (Roc) *Ardennes*, 181

La Fère (Château) *Aisne*, 129

Fère-en-Tardenois *Aisne*, 129

Fermont (Gros ouvrage) *Meurthe-et-Moselle*, 163

Ferrette *Haut-Rhin*, 297

Fessenheim (Bief) *Haut-Rhin*, 139

La Feuillée Nouvelle *Vosges*, 227

First World War, 31

Fischbœdle (Lac) *Haut-Rhin*, 203

Fismes *Marne*, 129

Fleckenstein (Château) *Bas-Rhin*, 338

Fleury-devant-Douaumont *Meuse*, 322

Fleury-la-Rivière *Marne*, 186

Fléville (Château) *Meurthe-et-Moselle*, 214

Florentin, Dominique, 311

Foch, *General*, 258

Foch, *Marshal*, 32

La Folie (Lac) *Vosges*, 333

Folklore, 53

Fontaine-Denis-Nuisy *Marne*, 275

Fontaine-lès-Grès *Aube*, 315

Fontenoy-la-Joûte *Meurthe-et-Moselle*, 72

Food, regional specialities, 59, 358

Forests, 21

Forêt d'Orient (Parc Naturel Régional) *Aube*, 130

Fossard (Forêt) *Vosges*, 247

Foucauld, Charles, 294

Fouchy (Col) *Haut-Rhin*, 78

Fouday *Bas-Rhin*, 85

Foujita, Leonard, 243

Franco-Prussian war, 30

Frankenbourg (Château) *Bas-Rhin*, 273

Franks, 27

Frederick I, (see Barbarossa)

Fréland *Haut-Rhin*, 222

Fréland (Col) *Haut-Rhin*, 250

Froeschwiller *Bas-Rhin*, 339

Fromentières *Marne*, 192

Fumay *Ardennes*, 180

G

La Gabionne (Gorges), Vosges, 333

Gallé, Émile, 212

Gallieni, Marshal, 31

Le Galz *Haut-Rhin*, 221

Gambsheim (Power station) *Bas-Rhin*, 139

de Gaulle, *Charles*, 108

Gazon du Faing, 110

Géhard (Cascade) *Vosges*, 227

Génicourt-sur-Meuse *Meuse*, 176

Gérardmer *Vosges*, 133

Gérardmer (Région, Lac) *Vosges*, 133

Gérardmer-La Mauselaine *Vosges*, 133

Géraudot *Aube*, 132

Gerbert, 236

Germaine *Marne*, 186

Germany, 373

Gerstheim (Bief) *Bas-Rhin*, 139

Gertwiller *Bas-Rhin*, 147

Giffaumont-Champaubert *Marne*, 115

Gillot, *Claude*, 152

Girardon, François, 307

Girsberg (Château) *Haut-Rhin*, 249

Givet *Ardennes*, 136

Goethe, 56, 274, 279

Goetzenbruck *Moselle*, 335

Gontier, Linard, 307

de Gonzague, *Charles*, 92

Gorze *Moselle*, 175

Gorze (Aqueduc romain) *Moselle*, 175

Grand *Vosges*, 216

Grand Ballon *Haut-Rhin*, 111

Grand Canal d'Alsace, 137

Grand Soldat *Moselle*, 117

Grand Ventron, 304

Grande Belle-Vue *Bas-Rhin*, 148

La Grange (Château) *Moselle*, 301

Granges-sur-Vologne (Champ de roches) *Vosges*, 136

Graufthal *Bas-Rhin*, 334

Grendelbruch (Signal) *Bas-Rhin*, 148

Grentzingen *Haut-Rhin*, 298

Grien, Hans Baldung, 291

Griscourt *Meurthe-et-Moselle*, 229

Gros Chêne *Bas-Rhin*, 144

Grues (Ferme) *Marne*, 116

Grünewald, Matthias, 50, 102

Guebwiller *Haut-Rhin*, 140

Guebwiller (Valley) *Haut-Rhin*, 141

Guentrange (Fort) *Moselle*, 164

Guillaume aux Blanches Mains, 236

Guimard, Hector, 257

Guirbaden (Château fort) *Bas-Rhin*, 148

Gunsbach *Haut-Rhin*, 202

Gutenberg, 28, 279

H

Hackenberg *Moselle*, 142

Hagondange *Moselle*, 302

Haguenau *Bas-Rhin*, 142

Haguenau (Forêt) *Bas-Rhin*, 144

Haies (Bois) *Ardennes*, 274

La Hallière (Scierie) *Vosges*, 118

Hanau (Étang) *Moselle*, 336

Hansi, 101

Haroué (Château) *Meurthe-et-Moselle*, 278

Haslach (Forest) *Bas-Rhin*, 114

Hasselfurt (Étang) *Moselle*, 82

Hartzviller (Cristallerie) *Moselle*, 264

Hatten *Bas-Rhin*, 165

Hattstatt *Haut-Rhin*, 329

Haut-Andlau (Château) *Bas-Rhin*, 147

Haut-Barr (Château) *Bas-Rhin*, 144
Haut-Chitelet (Jardin d'Altitude) *Vosges*, 110
Haut de Faite (Roc) *Haut-Rhin*, 76
Haute Chevauchée *Meuse*, 69
Haute-Kontz *Moselle*, 194
Les Hautes-Rivières *Ardennes*, 274
Haut-Kœnigsbourg (Château) *Bas-Rhin*, 145
Haut-Ribeaupierre (Château) *Haut-Rhin*, 249
Hautvillers *Marne*, 123
Haybes *Ardennes*, 181
Haye (Parc de loisirs de la forêt) *Meurthe-et-Moselle*, 214
Heiligenberg *Bas-Rhin*, 85
Héloïse, 29, 219, 374
Hennezel *Vosges*, 332
Héré, Emmanuel, 206
Hermonville *Marne*, 246
Hesse *Moselle*, 264
Hierges *Ardennes*, 181
Hippoltskirch *Haut-Rhin*, 297
Historical table, 27
Hoffen *Bas-Rhin*, 340
Hohenburg (Château) *Bas-Rhin*, 338
Hohlandsbourg (Château) *Haut-Rhin*, 121
Hohneck *Vosges*, 110
Hohrodberg *Haut-Rhin*, 203
Le Hohwald *Bas-Rhin*, 147
Hohwald (Région) *Bas-Rhin*, 146
Holy Roman Empire, 27
La Horre (Étang) *Aube*, *Haute-Marne*, 188
Horseback riding, 364
Houppach *Haut-Rhin*, 300
Hunawihr *Haut-Rhin*, 328
Hundsrück (Col) *Haut-Rhin*, 300
Hunspach *Bas-Rhin*, 340
Hunting, 23
Husseren-les-Châteaux *Haut-Rhin*, 329
Husseren-Wesserling *Haut-Rhin*, 303
Hydrotherapy, 367

I

Ifferzheim (Power station) *Germany*, 139
Igny (Abbaye) *Marne*, 130
Immerhof (Petit ouvrage) *Moselle*, 164

Imsthal (Étang) *Bas-Rhin*, 334
Ingolsheim *Bas-Rhin*, 340
Isenmann, Caspar, 102
Isle-Aumont *Aube*, 315
Les Islettes *Meuse*, 69
Itterswiller *Bas-Rhin*, 325

J

Jarville-la-Malgrange *Meurthe-et-Moselle*, 214
Joffre, Marshal, 31
Joffre (Route) *Haut-Rhin*, 300
Joli (Mont) *Marne*, 184
Joncreuil *Aube*, 189
Jouy-aux-Arches *Moselle*, 175
La Jumenterie *Vosges*, 73

K

Kahl (Rocher) *Haut-Rhin*, 249
Kahler Wasen *Haut-Rhin*, 202
Kaysersberg *Haut-Rhin*, 150
Kaysersberg, Geiler, 282
Kellermann, François-Christophe, 262
Kembs (Bief) *Haut-Rhin*, 138
Kientzheim *Haut-Rhin*, 328
Kintzheim (Parc d'animaux) *Bas-Rhin*, 273
Kirchberg *Haut-Rhin*, 73
Kléber, Jean-Baptiste, 294
Kleinthal (Vallée) *Moselle*, 113
Klingenthal *Bas-Rhin*, 148
Kluck, von (General), 31
Kreuzweg (Col) *Bas-Rhin*, 148
Kronprinz (Abris) *Meuse*, 69

L

La Fontaine, Jean de, 56, 95
La Tour, Georges de, 50, 127, 167, 211
Lachalade *Meuse*, 69
Lagery *Marne*, 130
Laifour (Roches) *Ardennes*, 179
Lamour, Jean, 206

Landsberg, Herrade de, 263
Landsberg (Château) *Bas-Rhin*, 264
Landskron (Château) *Haut-Rhin*, 297
Langensoultzbach *Bas-Rhin*, 339
Langres *Haute-Marne*, 152
Lapoutroie *Haut-Rhin*, 222
La Salle, Jean-Baptiste, 242
de Lattre de Tassigny, Général, 34, 101
Lauch (Lac) *Haut-Rhin*, 141
Launois-sur-Vence *Ardennes*, 94
Lautenbach *Haut-Rhin*, 141
Lauw *Haut-Rhin*, 73
Laval-Dieu *Ardennes*, 179
Leclerc, General, 34, 282
Legends, 53
Lembach *Bas-Rhin*, 339
Lembach (Four à Chaux) *Bas-Rhin*, 165
Lentilles *Aube*, 188
Leo IX, Pope, 113
Leopold, 159
Les Leschères (Lac-réservoir) *Haute-Marne*, 342
Leszczynski, Stanislas, 29, 206
Levrézy *Ardennes*, 179
Lichtenberg (Château) *Bas-Rhin*, 334
Liepvrette (Vallée), 78
La Liez (Lac) *Haute-Marne*, 157
Linchamps *Ardennes*, 274
Le Linge *Haut-Rhin*, 203
Literature, 56
Liverdun *Meurthe-et-Moselle*, 306
Loewenstein (Château), 338
Longemer (Lac) *Vosges*, 133
Longue Roche *Ardennes*, 187
Lotharingia, 28
Louppy-sur-Loison *Meuse*, 190
Louvois *Marne*, 186
Louvois, Marquis, 190
Lucelle *Haut-Rhin*, 297
Luemschwiller *Haut-Rhin*, 66
Lunéville *Meurthe-et-Moselle*, 159
Lusigny-sur-Barse *Aube*, 132
Lutzelbourg (Château) *Moselle*, 113
Lutzelhardt (château) *Bas-Rhin*, 338
Luxeuil-les-Bains *Haute-Saône*, 160

M

Madine (Lac) *Meuse*, 260
Maginot (Ligne), 161
Maginot Line, 47
Maginot (Monument)
  Meuse, 322
Magnières *Meurthe-et-
  Moselle*, 71
Mailly-Champagne *Marne*,
  184
La Maix (Lac) *Vosges*,
  118
Malgré Tout (Mont)
  Ardennes, 180
Mance, Jeanne, 152
Manises (Mont) *Ardennes*,
  180
Marckolsheim (Bief)
  Bas-Rhin, 139
Marckolsheim (Mémorial
  Musée de la Ligne
  Maginot du Rhin)
  Bas-Rhin, 166
Mareuil-sur-Ay *Marne*,
  186
Marie-Antoinette, 89
Le Markstein *Haut-Rhin*,
  142
Marlborough, Duke, 276
Marlenheim *Bas-Rhin*,
  325
Marmoutier *Bas-Rhin*,
  166
Mézanne *Marne*, 275
La Marne (Source)
  Haute-Marne , 157
Marsal *Moselle*, 167
La Marseillaise, 279
Marville *Meuse*, 190
Masevaux *Haut-Rhin*,
  300
Mathaux *Aube*, 132
Méhul, Étienne, 136
Meisenthal *Moselle*, 335
Mélaire (Lacets) *Haute-
  Marne*, 150
Mensberg (Château)
  Moselle, 276
Merkwiller-Pechelbronn
  Bas-Rhin, 339
Merovingian dynasty, 27,
  50
Mesnil-St-Père *Aube*, 132
Le Mesnil-sur-Oger
  Marne, 109
Métezeau, Clément, 92
Metz *Moselle*, 167
Meurthe (Upper valley)
  Vosges, 134
Meuse (Dames) *Ardennes*,
  180
Meuse (Vallée), 176
Michelsberg (Gros
  ouvrage) *Moselle*, 164
Mignard, Pierre, 307
Mines de Fer de Lorraine
  (Musées), 302
Mirabelle, 359
Misère (Vallée) *Ardennes*,
  254
Mittelbergheim *Bas-Rhin*,
  147
Mittelwihr *Haut-Rhin*,
  328

Mohon *Ardennes*, 94
Molhain (Ancienne collé-
  giale) *Ardennes*, 181
Molsheim *Bas-Rhin*, 182
Moltke, Marshal, 31
Mondement *Marne*, 258
Montagne de Reims (Parc
  naturel régional)
  Marne, 183
Mont-devant-Sassey
  Meuse, 177
Mont d'Haurs (Fort)
  Ardennes, 137
Mont Dieu (Ancienne
  chartreuse) *Ardennes*,
  341
Montfaucon (Butte)
  Meuse, 323
Monthureux-sur-Saône
  Vosges, 333
Montier-en-Der *Haute-
  Marne*, 187
Montmédy *Meuse*, 189
Montmirail *Marne*, 190
Montmort-Lucy *Marne*,
  191
Montsec (Butte) *Meuse*,
  260
Moosch *Haut-Rhin*, 303
Morimond (Abbaye)
  Haute-Marne, 82
Le Mort-Homme *Meuse*,
  323
La Moselle (River), 192
Mossig (Vallée) *Bas-Rhin*,
  114
La Motte-Tilly (Château)
  Aube, 218
La Mouche (Lac) *Haute-
  Marne*, 157
Moussey *Vosges*, 274
Mousson (Butte)
  Meurthe-et-Moselle,
  229
Mouzon *Ardennes*, 194
Moyenmoutier *Vosges*,
  257
Muhlbach-sur-Munster
  Haut-Rhin, 203
Mulhouse *Haut-Rhin*, 195
Munster *Haut-Rhin*, 202
Munster cheese, 59, 358
Munster (Vallée) *Haut-
  Rhin*, 202
Murbach (Église) *Haut-
  Rhin*, 205
Mutigny *Marne*, 186
Mutzig *Bas-Rhin*, 85

N

Nancy *Meurthe-et-
  Moselle*, 206
Nancy, École, 52, 212
Nanteuil-la-Forêt *Marne*,
  186
Napoleon, 190
Napoleon III, 86
Nature parks, 13
Neuenberg (Sentier
  patrimoine) *Haut-Rhin*,
  77
Neuf-Brisach *Haut-Rhin*,
  107

Neufchâteau *Vosges*, 215
Neufchef (Musée des
  Mines de Fer) *Moselle*,
  302
Neuntelstein *Bas-Rhin*,
  148
Neuwiller-lès-Saverne
  Bas-Rhin, 216
Nichet (Grottes)
  Ardennes, 137
Nideck (Cascade) *Bas-
  Rhin*, 114
Nideck (Château) *Bas-
  Rhin*, 114
Niederbronn-les-Bains
  Bas-Rhin, 217
Niederbruck *Haut-Rhin*,
  73
Niederhaslach *Bas-Rhin*,
  114
Niedermorschwihr *Haut-
  Rhin*, 329
Nigloland *Aube*, 81
Nogent-sur-Seine *Aube*,
  218
Noir (Lac) *Haut-Rhin*,
  221
Norroy (Croix de mission)
  Vosges, 331
Notre-Dame-de-Dusen-
  bach (Chapelle) *Haut-
  Rhin*, 249
Nouzonville *Ardennes*,
  178
Nubécourt *Meuse*, 80
Nutzkopf (Rocher)
  Moselle, 113

O

Oberbronn *Bas-Rhin*, 335
Oberhaslach *Bas-Rhin*,
  114
Oberlin, Jean-Frédéric, 85
Obernai *Bas-Rhin*, 219
Obersteigen *Bas-Rhin*,
  114
Obersteinbach *Bas-Rhin*,
  338
Oderen *Haut-Rhin*, 304
Oger *Marne*, 109
Oiseau et du Poisson
  (Maison) *Marne*, 116
Olizy *Marne*, 183
Oltingue *Haut-Rhin*, 297
Orbais-l'Abbaye *Marne*,
  191
Orbey *Haut-Rhin*, 222
Orbey (Val) *Haut-Rhin*,
  221
Orient (Lac) *Aube*, 131
Orne (Valley) *Meurthe-et-
  Moselle*, *Moselle*, 302
Ortenbourg (Château)
  Bas-Rhin, 273
Osne-le-Val *Haute-Marne*,
  342
Ottmarsheim *Haut-Rhin*,
  222
Ottrott *Bas-Rhin*, 148
Ours (Ravin) *Ardennes*,
  274
Outines *Marne*, 189

P

Pailly (Château) *Haute-Marne*, 157
Painting, 50
Pairis (Abbaye) *Haut-Rhin*, 221
Pange (Château), Moselle, 175
Paraclet (Ancienne abbaye) *Aube*, 218
Pellerin, Jean Charles, 124
Pérignon, Dom, 123
Petit Ballon *Haut-Rhin*, 203
Petit Drumont *Vosges*, 193
Petit-Wasigenstein (Château) *Bas-Rhin*, 338
Petite Camargue alsacienne *Haut-Rhin*, 138
Petite Meurthe (Valley) *Vosges*, 135
La Petite-Pierre *Bas-Rhin*, 223
Petit Morin (Vallée) *Marne, Seine-et-Marne*, 190
Pévy *Marne*, 246
Pfaffenheim *Haut-Rhin*, 255
Pfaffenhoffen *Bas-Rhin*, 224
Pfifferdaj, 248
Pflixbourg (Donjon) *Haut-Rhin*, 121
Phony War, 33
Pierre des 12 apôtres *Bas-Rhin*, 335
Pierre-Percée *Meurthe et Moselle*, 118
Pierre-Percée (Lac) *Meurthe et Moselle*, 118
Pierry *Marne*, 109
Pigeonnier (Col) *Bas-Rhin*, 338
Piney *Aube*, 132
Plain du Canon *Vosges*, 73
Plaine (Lac), 118
Plaine (Vallée), 118
La Platale *Ardennes*, 181
Plombières-les-Bains *Vosges*, 225
Poincaré, Raymond, 80, 259
Poissons *Haute-Marne*, 150
La Pompelle (Fort) *Marne*, 246
Pompierre *Vosges*, 216
Pont-à-Mousson *Meurthe-et-Moselle*, 227
Ponthion *Marne*, 330
Pont-Ste-Marie *Aube*, 315
Les Potées (Bois) *Ardennes*, 254
Pourcy *Marne*, 186
Prayé (Col), 274

Prény *Meurthe-et-Moselle*, 229
Prez-sous-Lafauche *Haute-Marne*, 98
Provins *Seine-et-Marne*, 229
Prussian Empire, 30
Puellemontier *Haute-Marne*, 188

R

Rambling, 362
Ramstein (Château) *Bas-Rhin*, 273
Ranspach *Haut-Rhin*, 303
Raon-sur-Plaine *Vosges*, 118
Rapides (Sentier) *Ardennes*, 273
Rarécourt *Meuse*, 69
Le Reclus (Abbaye) *Marne*, 191
Réding *Moselle*, 264
Reichshoffen *Bas-Rhin*, 339
Reims *Marne*, 235
Reims, École, 123
Reipertswiller *Bas-Rhin*, 335
Relanges *Vosges*, 333
Rembercourt-aux-Pots *Meuse*, 80
Rembrandt, 127
Remi, 235
Remiremont *Vosges*, 246
Renaissance, 28
René II, Duke of Lorraine, 206
Rethel *Ardennes*, 247
Retournemer (Lac) *Vosges*, 133
Retz, Paul de Gondi cardinal de, 56, 190
Revin *Ardennes*, 180
Reyersviller *Moselle*, 82
Rhinau (Bief) *Bas-Rhin*, 139
Rhine (River), 137
Ribeauvillé *Haut-Rhin*, 248
Richier, Ligier, 259
Riespach *Haut-Rhin*, 298
Rilly-la-Montagne *Marne*, 184
Rimbaud, Arthur, 58, 93, 374
Riquewihr *Haut-Rhin*, 251
Roches (Vallée) *Vosges*, 227
Rocroi *Ardennes*, 254
Rodemack *Moselle*, 194
Roesselmann, 101
Rohan, Louis, 266
Rohrbach-lès-Bitche (Fort Casso) *Moselle*, 165
Roma (Roche) *Ardennes*, 187
Romagne-sous-Montfaucon (Cimetière américain) *Meuse*, 323

Roman de la Rose, 87
Rosheim *Bas-Rhin*, 254
Rosières-aux-Salines *Meurthe-et-Moselle*, 261
Rosnay-l'Hôpital *Aube*, 84
Rouffach *Haut-Rhin*, 255
Rouge Gazon (Tête) *Vosges*, 76
Rouget de Lisle, 279
Roussy-le-Village *Moselle*, 193
Routes, thematic, 370
Rumilly-lès-Vaudes *Aube*, 315
Rupt de Mad (Vallée) *Meuse, Meurthe-et-Moselle*, 260
Rustroff *Moselle*, 276

S

Saales *Bas-Rhin*, 84
Sabinus, 152
Sacy *Marne*, 186
St-Amand sur Fion *Marne*, 330
St-Amarin *Haut-Rhin*, 303
St Arbogast, 144
St Arnoult, 168
St Bernard, 98
St-Blaise-la-Roche *Bas-Rhin*, 85
St Clement, 168
St Columba, 160
St-Dié *Vosges*, 255
St-Dizier *Haute-Marne*, 257
St-Élophe *Vosges*, 215
Sts-Geosmes *Haute-Marne*, 158
St-Gond (Marais) *Marne*, 258
St-Hippolyte *Haut-Rhin*, 327
St-Jean-Saverne *Bas-Rhin*, 258
St-Laurent *Ardennes*, 94
St-Lié (Chapelle) *Marne*, 186
St Livier, 168
St-Louis-Arzviller (Plan incliné) *Moselle*, 113
St-Louis-lès-Bitche *Moselle*, 335
St Loup, 307
St-Loup-de-Naud *Seine-et-Marne*, 234
St-Martin (Château) *Marne*, 124
St-Maurice-sur-Moselle *Vosges*, 73
St-Mihiel *Meuse*, 259
St-Morand *Haut-Rhin*, 297
St-Morel *Ardennes*, 341
St-Nicolas (Cascade) *Haut-Rhin*, 304
St-Nicolas-de-Port *Meurthe-et-Moselle*, 260

St Odile, 53, 262
St-Parres-aux-Tertres
    Aube, 315
St-Pierre-sur-l'Hâte
    Haut-Rhin, 77
St-Quirin *Moselle*, 118
St-Roger (Chapelle)
    Ardennes, 94
St-Rouin (Ermitage)
    Meuse, 69
St-Thierry *Marne*, 246
St-Ulrich (Château)
    Haut-Rhin, 249
St-Ulrich (Villa gallo-
    romaine) *Moselle*, 264
Ste-Anne (Chapelle)
    Vosges, 331
Ste-Croix-aux-Mines
    (Sentier minier et
    botanique), 77
Ste-Germaine (Chapelle)
    Aube, 81
Ste-Marie (Col) *Haut-
    Rhin*, 76
Ste-Marie-aux-Mines
    Haut-Rhin, 77
Ste-Marie-du-Lac-Nuise-
    ment *Marne*, 116
Ste-Maure *Aube*, 315
Ste-Menehould *Marne*,
    262
Sampigny *Meuse*, 259
Sarre Blanche (Vallée)
    Moselle, 118
Sarrebourg *Moselle*, 264
Sarreguemines *Moselle*,
    265
Sarre Rouge (Vallée)
    Moselle, 117
Saut des Cuves *Vosges*,
    133
Saverne *Bas-Rhin*, 266
Saxon dynasty, 28
Scheppler, Louise, 85
Scherwiller *Bas-Rhin*, 327
Schiessrothried (Lac)
    Haut-Rhin, 203
Schirmeck *Bas-Rhin*, 85
Schlieffen plan, 31
La Schlucht (Col), 110
Schnepfenried *Haut-Rhin*,
    204
Schœneck (Château)
    Bas-Rhin, 339
Schœnenbourg (Ouvrage
    d'artillerie) *Bas-Rhin*,
    165
Schongauer, Martin, 50,
    102
Schorbach (Ossuaire)
    Moselle, 82
Schuman, Robert, 175
Schweitzer, Albert, 150
Schwendi, Lazarus von,
    151
Sculpture, 48
Scy-Chazelles *Moselle*,
    175
Second World War, 33
Sedan *Ardennes*, 268
Seebach *Bas-Rhin*, 340
Sélestat *Bas-Rhin*, 270
Semouse (Vallée), 226

Semoy (Vallée) *Ardennes*,
    273
Senones *Vosges*, 274
Sentheim *Haut-Rhin*, 76
Sept Fontaines (Ancienne
    abbaye) *Ardennes*, 94
Sept Heures (Roche)
    Ardennes, 187
Sept Villages (Roche)
    Ardennes, 187
Servance (Ballon), 76
Sessenheim *Bas-Rhin*,
    274
Sewen (Lac) *Haut-Rhin*,
    73
Shopping, 361
Sierck-les-Bains *Moselle*,
    276
Signy (Forêt) *Ardennes*,
    276
Signy-l'Abbaye *Ardennes*,
    276
Sigolsheim *Haut-Rhin*,
    328
Sillegny *Moselle*, 175
Le Simserhof *Moselle*,
    277
Sinaï (Mont) *Marne*, 185
Sindelsberg *Bas-Rhin*,
    166
Sion *Meurthe-et-Moselle*,
    277
Sion-Vaudémont (Colline)
    Meurthe-et-Moselle,
    277
Skiing, 366
Sommevoire *Haute-
    Marne*, 342
Soufflenheim *Bas-Rhin*,
    144
Soultzbach-les-Bains
    Haut-Rhin, 202
Soultz-Haut-Rhin *Haut-
    Rhin*, 278
Soultzmatt *Haut-Rhin*,
    329
Sourdon (Parc) *Marne*,
    124
Spas, 367
Spesbourg (Château)
    Bas-Rhin, 147
Spindler, Charles, 291
Sports and recreation,
    366
Stained glass, 48
*Stanislas, duke of Lor-
    raine*, (See Leszczynski)
Stanislas (Fontaine)
    Vosges, 226
Steel industry, 25
Steinbach, Erwin, 282
Stenay *Meuse*, 177
Storks, 22
Stoskopff, Sébastien, 291
Straiture (Glacière)
    Vosges, 135
Strasbourg *Bas-Rhin*, 279
Strasbourg (Beif) *Bas-
    Rhin*, 139
Le Struthof *Bas-Rhin*,
    296
Sundgau *Haut-Rhin*, 296
Switzerland, 373

T

Tannenbrück *Bas-Rhin*,
    338
Tavannes (Monument des
    Fusillés) *Meuse*, 322
Temple (Lac) *Aube*, 131
Tendon (Grande cascade)
    Vosges, 135
Thann *Haut-Rhin*, 298
Thannenkirch *Haut-Rhin*,
    250
Thibaud IV, 230
Thierenbach (Basilique
    Notre-Dame) *Haut-
    Rhin*, 329
Le Thillot *Vosges*, 193
Thionville *Moselle*, 300
Thirty Years War, 206
Thuillières *Vosges*, 331
Thur (Vallée) *Haut-Rhin*,
    303
Toul *Meurthe-et-Moselle*,
    304
La Tour (Roc) *Ardennes*,
    187
Tourist offices, 348
Traconne (Forêt) *Marne*,
    275
Trains, 370
Tranchée des Baïonnettes,
    323
Trench warfare, 32
Les Trois-Épis *Haut-Rhin*,
    221
Trois-Fontaines (Abbaye)
    Marne, 257
Trouée de la Sarre (Zone
    inondable), 165
Troyes *Aube*, 307
La Tuffière (Cascade)
    Haute-Marne, 158
Turckheim *Haut-Rhin*,
    316
Turcos (Sentier) *Bas-
    Rhin*, 339
Turenne, 316

U

UNESCO, World Heritage
    sites, 345
Urbès (See) *Haut-Rhin*,
    304
Usselkirch *Moselle*, 194

V

Le Val-d'Ajol *Vosges*, 227
Valmy *Marne*, 262
Varangéville *Meurthe-et-
    Moselle*, 261
Varennes-en-Argonne
    Meuse, 68
Vasperviller *Moselle*, 118
Vaucouleurs *Meuse*, 316
Vaudémont *Meurthe-et-
    Moselle*, 278
Vaudémont (Signal)
    Meurthe-et-Moselle,
    278

Vauquois (Butte) *Meuse*,
68, 323
Vaux (Fort) *Meuse*, 322
Vaux (Valley) *Ardennes*,
276
Verdelot *Seine-et-Marne*,
190
Verdun *Meuse*, 317
Verdun, Battle, 320
Verlaine, Paul, 58, 247,
374
Vert (Lac) *Haut-Rhin*,
110
Vertus *Marne*, 109
Verzenay *Marne*, 184
Verzy (Faux) *Marne*, 185
Vic-sur-Seille *Moselle*,
167
Vieil-Armand *Haut-Rhin*,
112
Vieil-Armand (Cave
vinicole) *Haut-Rhin*,
329
Vignory *Haute-Marne*,
324
Villenauxe-la-Grande
Aube, 219
Villevenard *Marne*, 258
Villey-le-Sec *Meurthe-et-
Moselle*, 306
Villy-la-Ferté (Petit
ouvrage) *Ardennes*,
163
Vineyards, 61, 371
La Vingeanne (Lac)
Haute-Marne, 157
Vins (Route) *Bas-Rhin*,
Haut-Rhin, 324
Vioménil *Vosges*, 332
Vireux-Molhain *Ardennes*,
181
Vitry-en-Perthois *Marne*,
330

Vitry-le-François *Marne*,
330
Vittel *Vosges*, 330
Viviers-le-Gras *Vosges*,
333
La Vôge *Vosges*, 333
Vogelgrün *Haut-Rhin*,
108
Vogelgrün (Bief) *Haut-
Rhin*, 139
Voltaire, 58
Vosges du Nord (Parc
Naturel Régional),
333, 223
Voulton *Seine-et-Marne*,
234
Vouziers *Ardennes*, 340

W

Wagenbourg (Château)
Haut-Rhin, 329
Walbourg *Bas-Rhin*, 144
Waldersbach *Bas-Rhin*, 85
Walibi Schtroumpf
Moselle, 174
Wangen *Bas-Rhin*, 325
Wangenbourg *Bas-Rhin*,
114
Warcq *Ardennes*, 94
Wasenbourg (Château)
Bas-Rhin, 217
Wasigny *Ardennes*, 276
Wasselonne *Bas-Rhin*,
114
Wasserbourg *Haut-Rhin*,
203
Wassy *Haute-Marne*, 341
Wassy, massacre, 341
Wegelnburg (Château),
338

Westhalten *Haut-Rhin*,
329
Westhoffen *Bas-Rhin*,
325
Wettolsheim *Haut-Rhin*,
329
Wettstein (Col) *Haut-
Rhin*, 203
Wildlife, 21
Willer-sur-Thur *Haut-
Rhin*, 303
Windstein (Châteaux)
Bas-Rhin, 339
Wine, 61, 358
Wineck (Château) *Bas-
Rhin*, 339
Wingen (Colonne), *Bas-
Rhin*, 335
Wingen-sur-Moder
Bas-Rhin, 335
Wintersberg *Bas-Rhin*,
217
Wintzenheim *Haut-Rhin*,
329
Wisches *Bas-Rhin*, 85
Wissembourg *Bas-Rhin*,
343
Woerth *Bas-Rhin*, 339

X - Z

Xon (Signal) *Meurthe-et-
Moselle*, 229
Zeiterholz (Abri) *Moselle*,
164
Zellenberg *Haut-Rhin*,
328
Zinsel du Nord *Moselle*,
Bas-Rhin, 335
La Zorn (Vallée), 113

Manufacture Française des Pneumatiques Michelin

Société en commandite par actions au capital de 2 000 000 000 de francs
Place des Carmes-Déchaux - 63000 Clermont-Ferrand (France)
R.C.S. Clermont-Fd B 855 200 507

Michelin et Cie, Propriétaires-Éditeurs, 1999

Dépôt légal mars 1999 – ISBN 2-06-130301-3 – ISSN 0763-1383
Toute reproduction, même partielle et quel qu'en soit le support,
est interdite sans autorisation préalable de l'éditeur.

Printed in the EU 02-99/1

Cover illustrations by OPUS CONCEPT

Notes

Notes

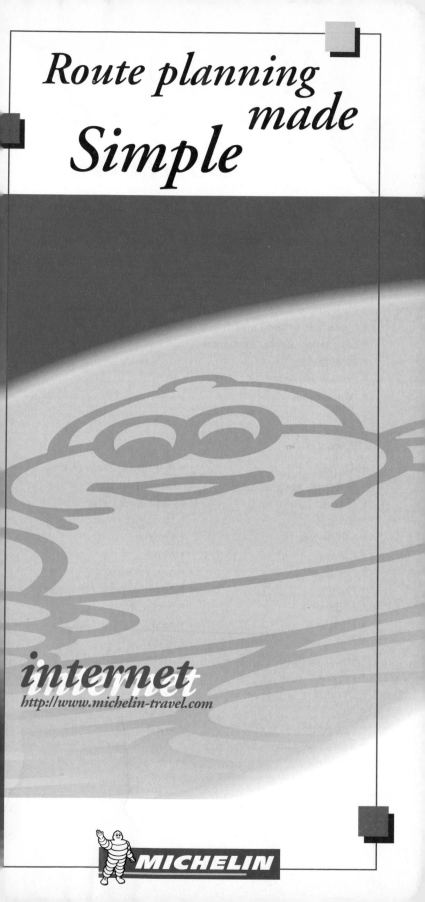

Michelin Green Guide Collection

France

- *Alsace, Lorraine, Champagne*
- *Atlantic Coast*
- *Auvergne, Rhône Valley*
- *Brittany*
- *Burgundy, Jura*
- *Châteaux of the Loire*
- *Dordogne, Berry, Limousin*
- *French Alps*
- *French Riviera*
- *Normandy*
- *Northern France and the Paris Region*
- *Paris*
- *Provence*
- *Pyrenees, Languedoc, Tarn Gorges*

World

- *Austria*
- *Belgium, Luxembourg*
- *Berlin*
- *Brussels*
- *California*
- *Canada*
- *Chicago*
- *Europe*
- *Florida*
- *France*
- *Germany*
- *Great Britain*
- *Greece*
- *Ireland*
- *Italy*
- *London*
- *Mexico, Guatemala, Belize*
- *Netherlands*
- *New England*
- *New York, New Jersey, Pennsylvania*
- *New York City*
- *Portugal*
- *Quebec*
- *Rome*
- *San Francisco*
- *Scandinavia, Finland*
- *Scotland*
- *Sicily*
- *Spain*
- *Switzerland*
- *Tuscany*
- *Venice*
- *Vienna*
- *Wales*
- *Washington DC*
- *The West Country of England*